70-299 MCSE Guide to
Implementing and Administering Security in a Microsoft® Windows® Server 2003 Network

Diane Barrett
Bill Ferguson

THOMSON
—————✦—————™
COURSE TECHNOLOGY

Australia • Canada • Mexico • Singapore • Spain • United Kingdom • United States

THOMSON

COURSE TECHNOLOGY

70-299 MCSE Guide to Implementing and
Administering Security in a Microsoft® Windows® Server 2003 Network
is published by Thomson Course Technology

Managing Editor:
Will Pitkin III

Associate Product Manager:
Sarah Santoro

Text Designer:
GEX Publishing Services

Product Manager:
Nick Lombardi

Editorial Assistant:
Jenny Smith

Compositor:
GEX Publishing Services

Production Editor:
Pam Elizian

Manufacturing Coordinator:
Melissa Hulse

Cover Design:
Steve Deschene

Technical Edit/Quality Assurance:
Christian Kunciw
Burt LaFountain

Marketing Manager:
Guy Baskaran

BRIEF
Contents

TABLE OF
Contents

CHAPTER FIVE
Planning and Deploying Patch Management   149

Introduction

Welcome to *MCSE Guide to Implementing and Administering Security in a Microsoft Windows Server 2003 Network*. This book provides in-depth coverage of the knowledge and skills required to pass Microsoft certification exam 70-299: Implementing and Administering Security in a Microsoft Windows Server 2003 Network. This course of study prepares a network professional to have the ability to securely administer a network running Windows Server 2003. These solutions include implementing, managing, maintaining, and troubleshooting security in a Windows Server 2003 network infrastructure. You will also learn how to plan and configure a Windows Server 2003 PKI.

The 70-299 exam is the cornerstone of Microsoft's security specializations for Windows Server 2003 credentials. The goal of *MCSE Guide to Implementing and Administering Security in a Microsoft Windows Server 2003 Network* is to teach strategies for securely administering a Microsoft network to individuals who desire to learn about that topic for practical purposes, as well as those who wish to pass Microsoft exam 70-299. This book provides not only the content for all the skills measured on that exam but also related information that is not directly tested.

The Intended Audience

This book was written with the network professional in mind. It provides an excellent preparation for the Microsoft exam 70-299, and also for the real-life tasks involved in securely administering today's networks, which must support and secure an ever-increasing variety of applications. The 70-299 MCSE Guide focuses on the growing trends toward Windows Server 2003 migrations and adoptions, both in the workplace and in academic computing programs. To fully benefit from the content and the projects presented here, you will need access to a classroom lab containing computers configured as listed here.

- Windows Server 2003 installed with the default settings; name the first computer Instructor, and then subsequent servers Server01, Server02, etc.

- DNS should be installed and configured on the Instructor server prior to the installation of Active Directory. Use an appropriate domain name, such as CNT1105, or a campus location. Create the zone as type Standard Primary. A reverse lookup zone based on your IP subnet should also be created. Run dcpromo.exe to upgrade the Instructor server to a domain controller in the domain. Run dcpromo.exe on subsequent servers, making them domain controllers in their own child domain, using the naming convention Domain01, Domain02, etc.

- For the Domain Users group in each domain, add the right to allow log on locally to the default domain controllers security policy.

- In each child domain, create a user account named Admin01, Admin02, etc. This name should correspond to the associated domain name, and the account should be added to the Domain Admins group. These accounts should also be added to the Enterprise Admins group in the forest root domain.

For more detailed setup instructions, see the "Set-up Instructions" section.

Chapter Descriptions

Chapter 1, "Introduction to Windows Server 2003 Security," provides an overview of the new and enhanced security features of Windows Server 2003 and gives you some background on why, as IT professionals, security should always be not only on your mind but also in your everyday network planning.

Chapter 2, "Planning and Configuring Security Policies," provides a guide for enhancing the security setting configurations of your servers and clients to help you plan a more secure environment.

Chapter 3, "Deploying and Managing Security Policies," explores and discusses the various methods that you can use to analyze the security on a machine and use security templates and polices to be sure that your network is kept in a secure state.

Chapter 4, "Troubleshooting Security Policies," discusses factors that can cause complications when managing and deploying security policies and how you should troubleshoot them to ensure the security of your network and the computers within it.

Chapter 5, "Planning and Deploying Patch Management," explains how to plan the deployment of service packs and hotfixes, evaluate the applicability of service packs and hotfixes, and implement Microsoft Software Update Services (SUS) architecture.

Chapter 6, "Managing and Troubleshooting Patch Management Infrastructure," takes a look at how to manage and troubleshooting your patch management infrastructure. This includes methods and automated processes that you can use to keep your computer software up to date and to verify that it is up to date.

Chapter 7, "Planning and Deploying Security for Network Communications," provides a detailed explanation on how to plan, deploy, implement, and maintain secure communications within your network.

Chapter 8, "Troubleshooting IPSec Policies," provides an overview of the default security policies that are installed with IPSec, the behavior of IPSec within and between networks, some tools that are used to troubleshoot issues concerning IPSec, and the use of IPSec in conjunction with certificates.

Chapter 9, "Planning and Deploying Public Key Infrastructure," outlines how to set up and operate a public key infrastructure, including various aspects of configuring and managing certification authorities, certificates, and keys. In addition it discusses backing up and restoring certification authorities.

Chapter 10, "Planning and Deploying Authentication for Remote Access Users," explains how to plan and deploy authentication for remote users, including deploying, managing, and configuring SSL certificates. It demonstrates how to configure security and authentication and troubleshoot remote access for users.

Chapter 11, "Planning and Configuring Security for Wireless Networks," gives you an understanding of the basic principles surrounding wireless networking security and explains how to use the networking services the Microsoft Windows Server 2003 operating system provides to deploy a secure and manageable WLAN infrastructure in an enterprise environment.

Chapter 12, "Troubleshooting PKI, Remote Access, and Wireless Policies," teaches you to prevent problems by being proactive in avoiding issues that can arise, shows you areas of concern that will help with troubleshooting, and exposes you to related tools and resources that are available to help make this process easier.

Chapter 13, "Advanced Problem Resolution," provides you with the knowledge to plan and configure auditing and logging properly. In addition, it will provide you with troubleshooting resource information and discuss some of the most common troubleshooting tools available.

Features and Approach

To ensure a successful learning experience, *MCSE Guide to Implementing and Administering Security in a Microsoft Windows Server 2003 Network* includes the following pedagogical features:

- **Chapter Objectives**—Each chapter begins with a detailed list of the concepts to be mastered. This list, which gives you a quick reference to the chapter's contents, is a useful study aid.

- **Activities**—Activities are incorporated throughout the text, giving you practice in setting up, managing, and troubleshooting network security. The Activities give you a strong foundation for carrying out network administration tasks in the real world. Because of this book's progressive nature, completing the Activities is essential before moving on to the end-of-chapter projects and subsequent chapters.

- **Chapter Summary**—Each chapter's text is followed by a summary of the concepts introduced in that chapter. These summaries provide a helpful way to recap and revisit the ideas covered in each chapter.

- **Key Terms**—All of the terms in the chapter that were introduced with boldfaced text are gathered together in the Key Terms list at the end of the chapter. This list provides you with a method of checking your understanding of all the terms introduced.

- **Review Questions**—The end-of-chapter assessment begins with a set of review questions that reinforces the ideas introduced in each chapter. Answering these questions will ensure that you have mastered the important concepts.

- **Case Projects**—Each chapter closes with a section that proposes certain situations. You are asked to evaluate the situations and decide on the course of action to be taken to remedy the problems described. This valuable tool will help you sharpen your decision-making and troubleshooting skills, which are important aspects of network administration.

- **On the CD ROM**—The CD-ROM includes MeasureUp® CoursePrep® test preparation software, which provides sample MCSE exam questions mirroring the look and feel of the MCSE exams.

Text and Graphic Conventions

Additional information and exercises have been added to this book to help you better understand what is being discussed in the chapter. Icons throughout the text alert you to additional materials. The icons used in this textbook are as follows:

Tips offer extra information on resources, how to attack problems, and time-saving shortcuts.

Notes present additional helpful material related to the subject being discussed.

The Caution icon identifies important information about potential mistakes or hazards.

Each Activity in this book is preceded by the Activity icon.

CASE PROJECTS

Case Project icons mark the end-of-chapter case projects, which are scenario-based assignments that ask you to independently apply what you have learned in the chapter.

Instructor's Resources

The following supplemental materials are available when this book is used in a classroom setting. All of the supplements available with this book are provided to the instructor on a single CD-ROM.

Electronic Instructor's Manual. The Instructor's Manual that accompanies this textbook includes additional instructional material to assist in class preparation, including suggestions for classroom activities, discussion topics, and additional activities.

Solutions. Solutions are provided for the end-of-chapter material, including Review Questions, and, where applicable, Activities and Case Projects.

ExamView®. This textbook is accompanied by ExamView, a powerful testing software package that allows instructors to create and administer printed, computer (LAN-based), and Internet exams. ExamView includes hundreds of questions that correspond to the topics covered in this text, enabling students to generate detailed study guides that include page references for further review. The computer-based and Internet testing components allow students to take exams at their computers and also save the instructor time by grading each exam automatically.

PowerPoint presentations. This book comes with Microsoft PowerPoint slides for each chapter. These are included as a teaching aid for classroom presentation, to make available to students on the network for chapter review, or to be printed for classroom distribution. Instructors, please feel at liberty to add your own slides for additional topics you introduce to the class.

Figure files. All of the figures and tables in the book are reproduced on the Instructor Resources CD, in bitmap format. Similar to the PowerPoint presentations, these are included as a teaching aid for classroom presentation, to make available to students for review, or to be printed for classroom distribution.

Minimum Lab Requirements

- **Hardware:**

  All hardware should be listed on Microsoft's Hardware Compatibility List for Windows Server, and Activities should meet the following hardware requirements:

Hardware Component	Windows 2003 Enterprise Server
CPU	133 MHz for x86-based computers, 733 MHz for Itanium-based computers (733 MHz recommended)
Memory	128 MB RAM (256 MB RAM recommended)
Disk Space	For setup: 1.5 GB for x86-based computers, 2.0 GB for Itanium-based computers. Ideally there should be a minimum of two 4-GB partitions (C and D), with at least 500 MB of free space left on the drive.
Drives	CD-ROM (or DVD-ROM) Floppy Disk
Networking	All lab computers should be networked. Students will work in pairs for some lab exercises. A connection to the Internet via some sort of NAT or Proxy server is also necessary.

- **Software:**

  The following software is needed for proper setup of the labs:

  - Windows Server 2003 Enterprise Edition
  - The following tool from the Microsoft Web site:
    - Microsoft Security Guidance Kit

- **Set Up Instructions:**

  To successfully complete the lab exercises, set up classroom computers as listed here:

  (1) Install Windows 2003 Enterprise Server onto drive C: of the instructor and student servers. The following specific parameters should be configured on individual servers during the installation process:

Parameter	Setting
Disk Partitioning	Create two 4-GB primary NTFS partitions during the installation process, C and D. Ensure that at least 1 GB of free space is left on the hard disk for student exercises.
Computer Names	Instructor (first server), ServerXX (subsequent student servers)
Administrator Password	Password01
Components	Default Settings

Parameter	Setting
Network Adapter	IP Address: 192.168.1.X. The instructor computer should be allocated a unique IP address on the same subnet as client computers. The suggested IP address for the Instructor machine is 192.168.1.100. Subnet Mask: 255.255.255.0 DNS: The IP address of the Instructor computer Default Gateway: The IP address for the classroom default gateway. If the Instructor computer will be used to provide Internet access via ICS or NAT, it will require a second network adapter card or modem.
Workgroup Name	Workgroup

In the previous table, *X* or *XX* should represent a unique number to be assigned to each student. For example, student "1" would be assigned a computer name of Server01 and an IP address of 192.168.1.1.

(2) Once the installation process is complete, use Device Manager to ensure that all devices are functioning correctly. In some cases, it may be necessary to download and install additional drivers for devices listed with a yellow question mark icon.

(3) Create a new folder named Source on drive D of all classroom servers. Copy the entire contents of the Windows Server 2003 CD to this folder on all servers.

(4) Create a new folder named Shared on drive D of the Instructor computer only. Share this folder using the shared folder name Shared, and ensure that the Everyone group is granted the Full Control shared folder permission. This folder will be used to store any supplemental files that may need to be made available to students during the course.

(5) Download the Microsoft Security Guidance Kit to the Shared folder on the Instructor computer. The link can be found at: *www.microsoft.com/downloads/ details.aspx?FamilyID=c3260bd0-2ebb-4496-ad07-7e9d55d0ef1f&displaylang=en*

(6) Run the Configure Your Server Wizard or dcpromo.exe on the Instructor computer to install Active Directory and DNS. Name the new domain (the first in a new forest) accordingly, such as CNT1105.net to ensure that both nonsecure and secure dynamic updates are allowed, and accept all other default options.

(7) On the Instructor server, open Active Directory Users and Computers. Right-click the CNT1105.net domain and click Raise Domain Functional Level. Change the domain functional level of only the Instructor server to Windows Server 2003.

(8)   After the previous steps are completed and the CNT1105.net domain is completely installed on the Instructor server, run dcpromo.exe on each student server to install Active Directory, making each a child domain of CNT1105.net. Name the student domains Domain*XX*, CNT1105.net, where *XX* is the student number assigned to each student. Once the process is completed on all classroom servers, all DNS zones should be configured to allow nonsecure and secure dynamic updates.

Acknowledgments

A lot goes into producing a book that readers are unaware of because they see only the end result: the collaboration and teamwork of many individuals. First, I would like to thank Course Technology for giving me the opportunity to write this book. Instrumental in making sure this work actually went to print were Will Pitkin, Nick Lombardi, and Pamela Elizian. The QA department, technical reviewers, and validation team made sure that the text was technically sound and offered practical experience. Thanks to Bill Ferguson for his contributions. Finally, special thanks to my husband, Bill, who often finds me exactly where he left me hours ago—in front of the computer.

1

INTRODUCTION TO WINDOWS SERVER 2003 SECURITY

> **After reading this chapter, you will be able to:**
> ♦ Understand the need for secure computing
> ♦ Identify the new features available in Windows Server 2003

Every day we hear about new computer security vulnerabilities, mass mailings, and worms. An article from Silicon.com reported that during the first quarter of 2003, the number of security events detected by companies jumped 84% over the preceding three months. The SQL Slammer worm infected 200,000 computers; 90% of all vulnerable servers were hit in the first 10 minutes that the worm was released on the Internet. It resulted in $1 billion in damage and cleanup costs.

As virus writers and criminal hackers become more sophisticated, the potential damage increases. Although some still rely on user vulnerability, many take advantage of vulnerabilities in software. If you want to test this theory, install Windows Server 2003 on a computer without enabling the firewall feature and connect it to the Internet. Within minutes it will automatically shut down. The majority of viruses written affect computers with Microsoft operating systems installed. As the number and variety of computer attacks increase, they put new demands on IT professionals to take preventative measures and on the technology industry to continue to innovate and develop new solutions.

This chapter gives you some background on why a test such as the 70-299 is important and why as IT professionals, security should always be not only on our minds but also in our everyday network planning.

THE NEED FOR SECURE COMPUTING

Now, more than ever, network administrators and computer users need to take proper steps to protect themselves from various types of threats, such as viruses, worms, and programs that steal confidential information. Symantec has endorsed Microsoft's new security initiatives, and they continue to support Microsoft in its efforts to help raise awareness of security risks, hacking dangers, and privacy threats. But raising awareness is only one aspect of secure computing. Blended threats are increasing rapidly and spread widely. While the response time from the discovery of a vulnerability to achieving a fix for the identified threat has become shorter, there is an increased need to write code that is more secure. Today's software programs are usually the source of computer security problems. Security holes and vulnerabilities are the result of bad software design and implementation. We need to replace our fix-and-patch approach by building software with security in mind.

We currently have laws in place that hold management responsible for data breaches. For example, California SB-1386, effective July 1, 2003, requires any organization that stores confidential information about a California resident on a computerized system to imme-diately notify those individuals upon the discovery of a breach. Confidential information includes driver's license, Social Security, account, credit card, and California identification numbers. The Health Insurance Portability and Accountability Act (HIPAA) of 1996 requires that patient health information (PHI) be kept private and secure. The Gramm-Leach-Bliley Act (GLB) establishes privacy rules for the financial industry. It requires financial institutions to ensure the security and confidentiality of the personal information that they collect. This includes information such as names, addresses, phone numbers, income, and Social Security numbers. The Sarbanes-Oxley Act, named for the two congressmen who sponsored it, was passed to restore the public's confidence in corporate governance by making chief executives of publicly traded companies personally validate financial statements and other information. Congress passed the law to avoid future accounting scandals such as those involving Enron and WorldCom.

Changing the behavior of management, progammers, and users will continue to be challenging; therefore, computing in general must become safer. Management must make secure computing a priority, operating systems and applications must be written in ways that make the user experience more secure without affecting productivity, and users must be trained to always keep security in mind. This may seem like a tall order, but many of today's vendors are already working toward making this happen.

Microsoft's Commitment to Security

In a speech in March 2004, Bill Gates spoke about Microsoft's commitment to security. He admitted that although considerable challenges lie ahead, Microsoft and the industry as a whole are making significant progress on the security front.

Microsoft has chosen to try to prevent malicious code from being able to exploit a vulnerability by isolating this code, providing more effective control over what computer processes can interact with, and making systems more capable of identifying and stopping suspicious behavior. In Windows XP Service Pack 2, a number of isolation and resiliency improvements address attacks. After you install Windows XP Service Pack 2, you might notice that some programs and devices work differently. By default, Windows Firewall is enabled and blocks unsolicited connections to your computer. After you install Windows XP SP2, client applications, such as the following, may not successfully receive data from a server:

- An FTP client
- Multimedia streaming software
- New mail notifications in some e-mail programs

Alternatively, server applications that are running on a Windows XP SP2–based computer may not respond to client requests, such as:

- A Web server like Internet Information Services (IIS)
- Remote Desktop
- File Sharing
- Back to the top
- Windows Firewall Security Alert

For additional information about configuring Windows Firewall, view the following article in the Microsoft Knowledge Base: 875357 Troubleshooting Windows Firewall settings in Windows XP Service Pack 2. For a list of programs that may require you to open ports manually go to: *http://support.microsoft.com/default.aspx?kbid=842242&product= windowsxpsp2*

Activity 1-1: Discovering Changes to Functionality in Windows XP, Service Pack 2

ACTIVITY

Time Required: 45 minutes

Objective: Learn about the changes to functionality in Windows XP with Service Pack 2.

Description: In this activity, you install and use the Microsoft Security Guidance Kit to investigate the changes to functionality to Windows XP with Service Pack 2.

1. Ask your instructor to provide a copy of the Microsoft Security Guidance Kit. If you need to download it, keep in mind that the file is more than 153 MB. The URL is *www.microsoft.com/downloads/details.aspx?FamilyID=c3260bd0-2ebb-4496-ad07-7e9d55d0ef1f&displaylang=en*. Because you will use it throughout this course, you may want to order a copy for yourself. This can be done at *www.microsoft.com/security/guidance/default.mspx*.

2. Log on with your **AdminXX** account, where *XX* is your assigned student number.

3. Install the Microsoft Security Guidance Kit. Your instructor will guide you through the installation process. Supported operating systems are Windows 2000 Service Pack 3, Windows 2000 Service Pack 4, Windows Server 2003, and Windows XP Service Pack 1. Because a large number of files will be installed, you may experience a short delay during the "preparing to install" phase. This is normal; do not think the computer is not responding or is having issues. Note: The .NET Framework will need to be installed before the Microsoft Security Guidance Kit

4. After the kit is installed, open the program (click **Start**, point to **All Programs**, point to **Microsoft Security Guidance Kit**, and then click **Microsoft Security Guidance Kit**). The Microsoft Security Guidance Kit opens.

5. On the Welcome screen, under I would like the Security Guidance Kit to display information intended for: choose An Environment with between 5 and 25 servers.

6. On the right side of the screen, find the text that reads For Information On The Security Enhancements in Microsoft Windows XP Service Pack 2, Click Here. Click the **Click Here** link. Note: You must have Internet access to perform this and the remaining steps. The Windows XP Service Pack 2: Resources for IT Professionals Web page appears.

7. Click the **Features and Functionality: What's new? What's changed?** link. Click the **Changes to Functionality in Microsoft Windows XP Service Pack 2** link.

8. Read through the article, which has eight parts.

9. Close all open windows.

Microsoft has also decided to make significant investments in the following four areas of security:

- Isolation and resiliency

- Updating

- Quality

- Access control and authentication

Isolation and Resiliency

Features included in Microsoft's isolation and resiliency area are:

- Windows Firewall, which is turned on by default.

- Internet Explorer automatically blocks unsolicited downloads and unwanted pop-ups from Web sites.

- Outlook Express and Windows Messenger instant messaging include better file attachment handling.

- Core Windows components have been recompiled with the most recent version of compiler technology to protect against stack and heap overruns.

- Exchange Edge Services, a new service, defends against e-mail server attacks and encrypts messages to optimize security.

- An integrated set of protection technologies proactively adjusts defenses on each computer based on changes in its "state."

- SmartScreen Technology, which includes a filter used in client and online e-mail programs, helps users train the filter to identify unwanted spam.

- Client Inspection technologies inspect remote devices and block network access to computers infected with a virus or worm.

- WS-Security allows for the encryption of messages and provides support for digital signatures.

Software Updates

Software updates are the primary way that customers protect against security vulnerabilities. Microsoft moved to monthly releases of updates to improve predictability and manageability. A main objective of Microsoft's commitment to updating is to have full rollback capabilities. To make updates more seamless, Microsoft has incorporated the following products:

- *System Management Server 2003*—A software management and distribution solution that allows the deployment of updates systematically

- *Microsoft Baseline Security Analyzer v1.2*—A free tool that helps you identify common security misconfigurations

- *Software Update Services*—A tool IT administrators can use for seamless updates of servers and desktop computers running Windows

Quality

Microsoft is committed to using quality standards and processes in the creation of its software, and requires its software engineers to understand and use best practices in all phases of software development. As a result, the number of critical security bulletins issued for Windows Server 2003 was approximately 25% of those for Windows 2000 Server in the first 320 days that each product was on the market. As another example, Microsoft issued three bulletins for SQL Server 2000 in the 15 months after release of Service Pack 3 compared to 13 bulletins in the 15 months prior to its release. Being developed are new internal tools that automatically check code for common errors and more thoroughly test software before its release.

Access Control and Authentication

Access control and authentication are vital aspects of maintaining an organization's security. Microsoft has made changes in these areas to improve access control and authentication:

- *Passwords*—The Windows Server 2003 family has a new feature that checks the complexity of the Administrator password during setup.

- *Smart cards*—Windows Server 2003 and Windows XP support smart cards, which are credit card–sized devices that securely store authentication and personal information.

- *Public key infrastructure (PKI)*—Windows Server 2003 includes features to help organizations implement a PKI.

- *Internet Protocol Security (IPSec)*—The Microsoft IPSec implementation is now completely standards compliant and interoperates with all other compliant IPSec implementations, including those that support Network Address Translation (NAT).

Trustworthy Computing

To secure our computing environments, we must change not only the way we write and deliver software, but also the way our society views computing in general. As previously mentioned, there are actions that individuals and companies can and should take, but often don't. **Trustworthy Computing** means helping to ensure a safe and reliable computing experience. The Trustworthy Computing Initiative is not specific to Microsoft operating systems, although the name may be not be the same; the industry as a whole now is moving toward a trusted environment. We have come to realize that computers need to be reliable enough that we can embed them in all kinds of devices, the software that operates those machines must be equally reliable, and the service components, which are also largely software-dependent, have to be dependable. Microsoft's objective of Trustworthy Computing relies on the following three dimensions to describe perspectives on trust: goals, means, and execution.

The goals set for Trustworthy Computing are designed to deliver a certain level of trust and responsibility by providing security, privacy, reliability, and business integrity. Due to the fact that network attacks have increased in frequency and sophistication, users expect that their systems will not fall prey to these attacks and that their data will remain safe. They also expect control over the use of their personal information, a consistently trouble-free computing experience, and product vendors that act responsively and responsibly.

Means are the approaches that are employed to meet goals. Basically, the goals are what are delivered, and the means are how they are delivered. Microsoft considers the following factors in regard to security, privacy, reliability, and business integrity:

- Security by design, default, and deployment
- Privacy/fair information principles

- Availability, manageability, and accuracy
- Usability, responsiveness, and transparency

The third piece of Trustworthy Computing is execution. Execution is the way that an organization carries out its operations to deliver the necessary components for a trusted environment. The three aspects of execution are intents, implementation, and evidence. Intents are the organizational and legal guidelines for the design, implementation, and support of the product. Implementation is the process whereby the intents are put into operation. Finally, the mechanism by which we verify that the implementation has delivered on the intent is the evidence.

Secure Code

In addition to training all Windows engineers to write secure code, Microsoft has trained engineers in other parts of the company. The training included specialized testing techniques and threat modeling. As a result of teaching threat modeling, half of all bugs identified during the Windows security push were found. Microsoft went so far as to train its technical writers to write documentation with security in mind, making it easier for customers to understand how to implement and maintain security on the Windows platform.

Besides fixing bugs, developers looked at other ways to improve the security design in Windows Server 2003. For example, the Universal Plug and Play (UPnP) feature was removed from Windows Server 2003. Windows developers also set out to eliminate serious, ongoing security issues that had emerged around Internet Information Services (IIS). Developers built an isolated Web application model for IIS so that every Web application running on a Web server can now be deployed in its own isolated process, thereby eliminating the risk of one application interrupting other applications or services that are running on the Web server. Windows Server 2003 was designed to take advantage of a new service account in Windows XP. Access is restricted by having everything running within IIS run in the network service account. Therefore, an application can communicate with other services over the network and within its own process, but if it's compromised it won't be able to take over the entire server.

It is now easier for developers to build secure applications. With the release of Visual Studio .NET 2003 and the .NET Framework, system administrators have more granular control in locking down Web applications and services running in their datacenters and can more readily secure deployment of Windows-based client applications over the Internet. Microsoft has also released a guide to provide developers and administrators with best security practices around .NET Framework–based solutions.

Common Language Runtime

Included in Microsoft's changes are changes to ways that developers write code. You may be asking yourself, as a network administrator, why do you need to know about these types of changes? For a variety of reasons, starting with the fact that if you don't know at least a little about programming, how do you know if you have a hardware or a software issue when you are troubleshooting? How many times have you installed an application, and then looked at what keys were in the registry? This is not to say that you need to be a master programmer, but you should know the basics. Hackers often use C++ to write virus code. More recently, a hacker wrote the Sharpei worm, which is believed to be the first virus written in C-sharp, the programming language that runs on .NET platforms.

Probably the single most important goal for the design of the common language was to Runtime simplify the development environment itself so that programmers could write less code and reuse more code. The **common language runtime** is not just a runtime at execution time, but also a runtime that is used at compile time, deployment time, and also execution time. Everything from the naming convention to the audit of arguments is done consistently across all programming models to provide a uniform programming experience.

The second major goal was to get a simpler and safer deployment. This is an effort to get rid of the concept of registry, and use zero-impact installation. In other words, if you have a new version of a program, it's copied into the computer and no registry entries are made. The program does incremental downloading of the components, so you can just load one file that tells the program component where the other pieces are. Then, as they are needed, they will be downloaded to the computer. This eliminates having to install the entire program and have it incrementally grow as new versions are released. This will improve performance.

Now that you are aware of the processes with which Microsoft has committed to make its environment more secure for users, developers, and organizations as a whole, we will delve into how this commitment has changed the way in which Microsoft has developed its newest operating system, Windows Server 2003.

NEW FEATURES THAT ENHANCE SECURITY IN WINDOWS SERVER 2003

When Windows 2000 was released, a major change from the previous generation of operating system was granularity. The concept of granularity is based on the idea that using Active Directory organizational units allows a more defined method for delegating administration. As you can tell from reading this chapter thus far, the big change in Windows Server 2003 is a push toward a more secure environment. In addition, Windows Server 2003 integrates the latest secure networking standards to enable customers to increase the productivity of their mobile workforce while maintaining the highest levels of network security.

Many exciting changes in Windows Server 2003 help make the life of a network professional a bit easier. Some of the changes we will explore include network protection via templates, secure communications, proper authentication, and new policies. Windows Server 2003 expands on the foundation established in Windows 2000 and improves the versatility, manageability, and dependability of Active Directory.

Group Policy Management Console

In previous versions of Windows, administrators were required to use several different tools to manage Group Policy, such as the Active Directory Users and Computers, Active Directory Sites and Services, and Resultant Set of Policy snap-ins. Microsoft **Group Policy Management Console (GPMC)** is a new tool for Group Policy management. It aids administrators in managing their enterprise more cost-effectively by providing a single place for managing core aspects of Group Policy. GPMC integrates the existing Group Policy functionality into a single, unified console, along with several new capabilities. It consists of a new Microsoft Management Console (MMC) snap-in and a set of scriptable interfaces for managing Group Policy. It is an improvement over the method used in Windows 2000, helps you manage both Windows 2000– and Windows Server 2003–based domains, and provides the following functionality:

- An easy-to-use user interface (UI) making Group Policy much friendlier
- The ability to back up and restore **Group Policy Objects (GPOs)**
- Effortless management of Group Policy–related security
- Scripting of policy-related tasks
- Flexibility in importing, exporting, copying, and pasting GPOs and **Windows Management Instrumentation (WMI)** filters
- HTML reporting capability of GPO settings and Resultant Set of Policy data

Figure 1-1 illustrates the Group Policy Management Console window.

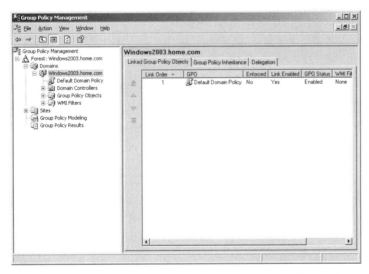

Figure 1-1   The Group Policy Management Console window

Activity 1-2: Discovering the GPMC

Time Required: 45 minutes

Objective: Discover the GPMC.

Description: In this activity, you read about the changes Microsoft has made to Group Policy management.

1. Log on with your **AdminXX** account, where *XX* is your assigned student number. Click **Start**, and then click **Internet Explorer**.

2. Go to *www.microsoft.com/windowsserver2003/techinfo/overview/gpintro.mspx*. The Introduction to Group Policy in Windows Server 2003 Web page appears.

3. Click the **gpintro.doc** link on the right side of the screen. Download the file that contains the white paper titled "Introduction to Group Policy in Windows Server 2003" and read about Group Policy in Windows Server 2003.

4. Close all open windows.

Activity 1-3: Simulating the GPMC

Time Required: 45 minutes

Objective: Discover GPMC through simulation.

Description: In this activity, you try a simulation of the changes that Microsoft has made to Group Policy management.

1. Log on with your **AdminXX** account, where *XX* is your assigned student number. Click **Start**, and then click **Internet Explorer**.

2. Go to *www.microsoft.com/windowsserver2003/evaluation/demos/sims/gpmc/viewer.htm*. The Managing Group Policy Web page appears.

3. On the left side of the screen, click the plus sign (+) next to Managing Group Policy to expand the table of contents, if necessary.

4. To start the demo, click **Launching and Configuring the GPMC**.

5. In the resulting screen in the right pane, click the **Click to Launch Exercise** link.

6. Click **Yes** to install the player(s) if necessary.

7. Follow each step in the interactive demo, as instructed.

8. When finished, start the next exercise by clicking the appropriate link in the left pane of the Managing Group Policy Web page.

9. Repeat Steps 5 through 8 for all exercises.

10. Close all open windows.

Resultant Set of Policy

Remember how hard it used to be to figure out which policies apply to whom because of the various ways in which you can apply Group Policy? The troubleshooting of security policy settings has now become easier. Windows Server 2003 introduces **Resultant Set of Policy (RSoP)**, which queries computers running Windows XP Professional or Windows Server 2003 and provides details about all policy settings that are configured for existing policies based on site, domain, domain controller, and organizational unit (OU). RSoP can also help you determine a set of applied policies and their precedence. You can run RSoP in one of two modes: planning or logging.

Figure 1-2 illustrates the Resultant Set of Policy console window.

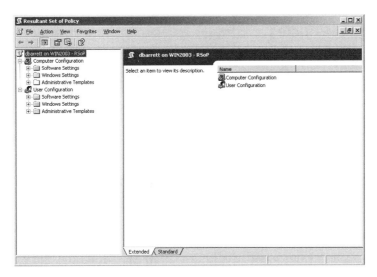

Figure 1-2   The Resultant Set of Policy console window

Cross-Forest Trusts

With the introduction of Active Directory in Microsoft Windows 2000, the forest entity was introduced, and the forest has service and data implications for all domains contained within the forest. The decision to deploy multiple forests is often associated with the need to manage directory services independently or to manage data or services without interference. When there is need to access those resources across domains, however, trusts must be created. When two organizations form a partnership or merge, and both organizations have an Active Directory forest deployed, you can use Windows Server 2003 to set up a cross-forest trust between the two forests. This allows one forest to explicitly trust certain, or all, users or groups in the other forest. You also have the capability to set permissions based on users or groups that are resident in the other forest. In essence, cross-forest trusts make it easy to conduct business with other companies using Active Directory.

NAT Traversal Support

One of the issues with deploying **Layer Two Tunneling Protocol (L2TP)** with Internet Protocol Security (IPSec) is that IPSec peers cannot be located behind a Network Address Translator (NAT). Because of the way that NAT works in Windows 2000, IPSec believes that packets sent across the NAT device have been tampered with and discards them. A new technology known as IPSec **NAT Traversal (NAT-T)** enables IPsec virtual private networks (VPNs) to work with NAT devices. Some of the leading technology companies created this solution including SSH Communications, F-Secure, Cisco Systems, Nortel Networks, and Microsoft. IPSec NAT-T is a new feature of Windows Server 2003 that allows IPSec and NAT to work together. Because Windows Server 2003 NAT devices support NAT-T, traffic can be secured by IPSec, while also being translated by a NAT device.

Software Restriction Policies

Windows Server 2003 will let a system administrator use policy or execution enforcement to prevent executable programs from running on a computer. **Software restriction policies** are used for more granular control over who receives what software. Software restriction policies specify the software that is allowed to run. Some of the features include:

- Controlling which programs can run on a computer
- Allowing users to run only specific files on multiple-user computers
- Preventing files from running on a local computer, organizational unit, site, or domain should you get a virus infection

If you do not want the software restriction policies to apply to local administrators, you can configure this as well.

Figure 1-3 illustrates the software restriction policies, with the Properties dialog box open for the Enforcement policy.

Secure Wireless and Ethernet LANs

Windows Server 2003 enables the authentication and authorization of users and computers that connect to wireless and Ethernet LANs by using Institute of Electrical and Electronics Engineers (IEEE) 802.11 specifications. It also allows for support of public certificates deployed using autoenrollment or smart cards. These security improvements enable access control to Ethernet networks in public places such as malls and airports. Because Windows Server 2003 uses the 802.1x standard for authenticating access to wired Ethernet networks and wireless 802.11 networks, it also provides support for the Extensible Authentication Protocol (EAP) used in conjunction with several different authentication methods for wireless computers:

- *EAP-Transport Layer Security (EAP-TLS)*—**EAP-Transport Layer Security (EAP-TLS)** uses certificate-based mutual authentication, negotiation of the encryption method, and encrypted key determination between the client and the authenticating server.

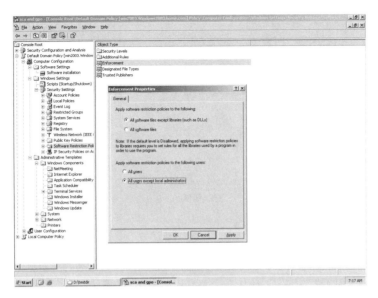

Figure 1-3   Software restriction policies

- *EAP-Microsoft Challenge Handshake Authentication Protocol version 2 (EAP-MSCHAPv2)*—**EAP-Microsoft Challenge Handshake Authentication Protocol version 2 (EAP-MSCHAPv2)** provides mutual authentication using password-based user and computer authentication. Both server and client must prove knowledge of the user's password for successful authentication.

- *Protected EAP (PEAP)*—**Protected EAP(PEAP)** provides several additional benefits within TLS including an encrypted authentication channel, dynamic keying material from TLS, fast reconnect using cached session keys, and server authentication that protects against the setting up of unauthorized access points.

New to Windows Server 2003 is the ability to create a wireless network policy in Group Policy. Windows provides the Wireless Network Policy Wizard to assist you in creating your policy.

Figure 1-4 illustrates the Wireless Network Access Policy Properties dialog box, in which you can configure wireless policy settings.

Credential Manager in Windows Server 2003 provides a secure store for user credentials. These credentials, which include passwords and X.509 certificates, provide a consistent, single sign-on experience for stationary and roaming users. In Windows Server 2003, the Secure Sockets Layer (SSL) session cache can be shared by multiple processes to reduce the number of times that a user has to perform authentication with applications. Microsoft has also developed **Rights Management Services (RMS)**, a rights management technology that helps protect data and is based on usage policies. It works with RMS-enabled

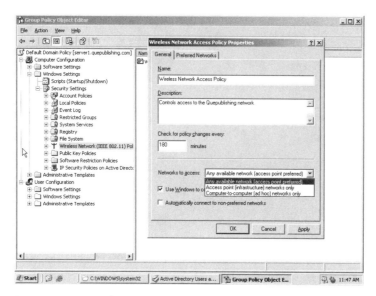

Figure 1-4   Configuring a wireless network policy

applications to help shield data from unauthorized use both online and offline and inside and outside of a firewall. A key part of Microsoft's Trustworthy Computing is the availability of technology that can reliably protect content and help keep digital information private. RMS is significant in this regard, offering a different kind of protection for sensitive information. RMS requires Windows Server 2003, a database such as Microsoft SQL Server, Windows Server Active Directory, and an RMS-enabled application or browser. RMS can also use SQL Server 2000 with Service Pack 3 for its policy and configuration information.

Internet Connection Firewall

Windows Server 2003 provides Internet security using a software-based firewall called **Internet Connection Firewall (ICF)**. ICF is firewall software that you can use to set restrictions on what information is communicated between your home or small office network and the Internet. It provides protection to computers directly connected to the Internet or to computers located behind an Internet Connection Sharing (ICS) host computer that is running ICF.

Figure 1-5 illustrates the Properties dialog box in which you enable Internet Connection Firewall.

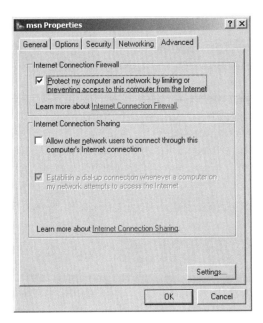

Figure 1-5   Enabling Internet Connection Firewall

Activity 1-4: Discovering Perimeter Network Security

Time Required: 45 minutes

Objective: Learn how to implement perimeter network security.

Description: In this activity, you investigate how to implement perimeter security.

1. Log on with your **AdminXX** account, where *XX* is your assigned student number. Go to **Start**, point to **All Programs**, point to **Microsoft Security Guidance Kit**, and click **Microsoft Security Guidance Kit**.

2. If the Welcome screen appears, under I would like the Security Guidance Kit to display information intended for: choose **An Environment with between 5 and 25 servers**.

3. On the left side of the screen, choose **Implement Perimeter Network Security**.

4. On the resulting screen, on the right side, scroll down to the bottom. Choose **How to Select a Perimeter Firewall and Configure Basic Security Measures**.

5. Follow the steps until you reach the end of the article.

6. Close all open windows.

Secure IAS/RADIUS Server

Internet Authentication Services (IAS) is Microsoft's implementation of **Remote Authentication Dial-In User Services (RADIUS)**. RADIUS is an industry standard offered by a number of vendors. IAS allows you to control authentication and authorization of users, who access multiple access points, via a single server. IAS also manages a variety of network connection types, such as dial-up, VPNs, and firewalls. In the role of a RADIUS proxy, IAS forwards authentication and accounting messages to other RADIUS servers. IAS can forward requests based on username, access server IP address, access server identifier, and other conditions. You can also use Group Policy to create a remote access policy using an IAS server.

Figure 1-6 illustrates remote access policies in the Internet Authentication Services console.

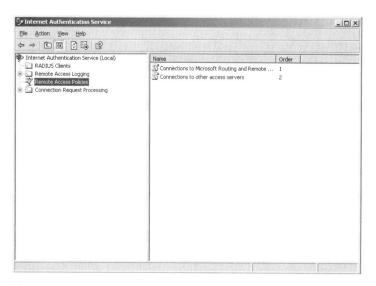

Figure 1-6   Remote access policies in IAS

IAS supports a number of authentication protocols, including the following:

- Password-based Point-to-Point Protocol (PPP) authentication protocols
- EAP

IAS supports a number of authorization methods along with allowing the addition of custom methods. The authorization methods supported are:

- Dialed Number Identification Service (DNIS)
- Automatic Number Identification/Calling Line Identification (ANI/CLI)
- Guest authorization

You can configure IAS in Windows Server 2003, Standard Edition, with a maximum of 50 RADIUS clients and a maximum of two remote RADIUS server groups. You can define a RADIUS client using a fully qualified domain name (FQDN) or an IP address, but you cannot define groups of RADIUS clients by specifying an IP address range. With IAS in Windows Server 2003, Enterprise Edition, and Windows Server 2003, Datacenter Edition, you can configure an unlimited number of RADIUS clients and remote RADIUS server groups, and you can configure RADIUS clients by specifying an IP address range.

Improved Public Key Infrastructure

Certificate Services in Windows Server 2003 have a number of new features and improvements related to **public key infrastructure (PKI)**. PKI refers to a technology that includes a series of features relating to authentication and encryption. PKI is based on a system of certificates, which are digitally signed statements that contain a public key and the name of the subject. The certificates are issued by a certification authority (CA), which can be part of your own network or operated by an external certificate issuing agency such as VeriSign.

A few new procedures are also provided to facilitate certificate template editing and certificate autoenrollment for users and computers. These features reduce the amount of resources needed to manage X.509 certificates. In Windows Server 2003, PKI services provide a simple certificate infrastructure to improve security in VPN and network communications, wireless authentication using 802.1x, smart card logon, encrypted file system, and other services.

Certificate Autoenrollment and Autorenewal

Windows Server 2003 makes it possible to automatically enroll, deploy, and renew certificates. Certificate autoenrollment and autorenewal make it easier to deploy smart cards faster and improve the security of wireless (IEEE 802.1x) connections. In Windows 2000, it was possible to autoenroll for Encrypting File System (EFS) certificates and computer certificates, but autoenrollment for users was not possible. A member of the Enterprise Admins group can now specify the types of certificates that should automatically be issued and can control autoenrollment by setting security permissions on certificate templates using the Certificate Templates snap-in. Autorenewal is a new feature similar to autoenrollment. The template is used to control who can autorenew a certificate. Every certificate in the certificate store that has a template extension can be autorenewed by the system.

Figure 1-7 illustrates the Autoenrollment Settings Properties dialog box.

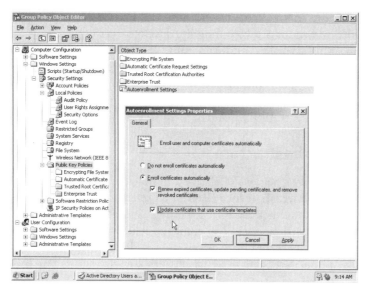

Figure 1-7   The Autoenrollment Settings Properties dialog box

Certificate Revocation List Improvements

Certificate templates were available in Windows 2000 Certificate Services, but they could not be modified or changed. A new Certificate Templates MMC snap-in enables administrators to:

- Create new certificate templates by duplicating and renaming an existing template
- Modify template properties
- Set up and apply enrollment, issuance, and application policies

Figure 1-8 illustrates the Certificate Templates window.

Delta CRLs

A Certificate Revocation List (CRL) makes the publication of revoked X.509 certificates more efficient, and makes it easier for a user to retrieve a new certificate. In addition, because you can now specify the location where a CRL will be stored, it's much easier to move it to accommodate specific business and security needs.

The certificate server included in Windows Server 2003 now supports delta CRLs. When you revoke a certificate, the revoked certificate is published in the CRL. Because CRLs can become large, Windows Server 2003 has added the concept of a **delta CRL**, which is a list of certificates that have been revoked since the last publication of a full CRL. By using delta CRLs, you can publish CRL information more frequently with less replication traffic. Delta

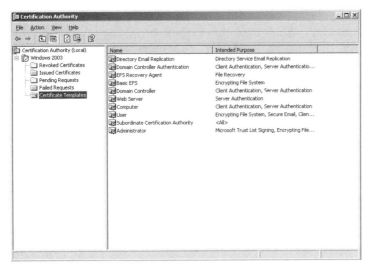

Figure 1-8 The Certificate Templates window

CRLs are published on a differential basis. In other words, each delta CRL includes all revoked certificates since the previous full CRL was published. This is similar in theory to differential backups. An application that checks CRLs therefore needs to check only the base CRL and the most recent delta CRL to obtain a complete list of revoked certificates.

CHAPTER SUMMARY

- Microsoft has decided to make significant investments in the area of security. It has committed to major investments in customer education and partnerships that will help make the computing environment safer and more secure.

- The goals set for Trustworthy Computing are designed to deliver a certain level of trust and responsibility by providing security, privacy, reliability, and business integrity.

- Microsoft GPMC is the new tool for Group Policy management. It aids administrators in managing their enterprise more cost-effectively by providing a single place for managing core aspects of Group Policy.

- Windows Server 2003 introduces RSoP, which queries computers running Windows XP Professional or Windows Server 2003 and provides details about all policy settings that are configured for existing policies based on site, domain, domain controller, and OU.

- IPSec NAT Traversal is a new feature of Windows Server 2003 and allows IPSec and NAT to work together. Because Windows Server 2003 NAT devices support NAT-T, traffic can be secured by IPSec while also being translated by a NAT device.

❑ Software restriction policies specify the software that is allowed to run. Some of the features include controlling which programs can run on your computer, permitting users to run only specific files on multiple-user computers and preventing any files from running on a local computer, an OU, a site, or a domain should you get a virus infection.

❑ ICF is firewall software that is used to set restrictions on what information is communicated from your home or small office network to and from the Internet to your network.

❑ IAS is Microsoft's implementation of RADIUS and allows you to control the authentication and authorization of users accessing multiple access points by means of a single server.

❑ By using delta CRLs, you can publish CRL information more frequently with less replication traffic.

Key Terms

common language runtime — A framework that simplifies the development environment itself so that programmers can write less code and reuse more code.

delta CRL — A list that includes all revoked certificates since the previous full CRL was published. This is similar in theory to differential backups.

EAP-Microsoft Challenge Handshake Authentication Protocol version 2 (EAP-MSCHAPv2) — A protocol that provides mutual authentication using password-based user and computer authentication. Both server and client must prove knowledge of the user's password for successful authentication.

EAP-Transport Layer Security (EAP-TLS) — A security approach that uses certificate-based mutual authentication, negotiation of the encryption method, and encrypted key determination between the client and the authenticating server.

Group Policy Management Console (GPMC) — A new tool for Group Policy management. It aids administrators in managing their enterprise more cost-effectively by providing a single place for managing core aspects of Group Policy.

Group Policy Objects (GPOs) — A collection of Group Policy settings, stored at the domain level, that affects users and computers contained in sites, domains, and organizational units.

Internet Authentication Services (IAS) — Microsoft's implementation of RADIUS, which allows you to control the authentication and authorization of users, who access multiple access points, via a single server.

Internet Connection Firewall (ICF) — Firewall software that is used to set restrictions on what information is communicated between your home or small office network and the Internet.

Layer 2 Tunneling Protocol (L2TP) — An industry-standard Internet tunneling protocol that does not require IP connectivity between the client workstation and the server.

NAT Traversal (NAT-T) — A new feature of Windows Server 2003 and allows IPSec and NAT to work together.

Protected EAP (PEAP) — A protocol that provides several additional benefits within TLS including an encrypted authentication channel, dynamic keying material from TLS, fast reconnect using cached session keys, and server authentication that protects against the setup of unauthorized access points.

public key infrastructure (PKI) — A technology that includes a series of features relating to authentication and encryption. PKI is based on a system of certificates, which are digitally signed statements that contain a public key and the name of the subject.

Remote Authentication Dial-In User Services (RADIUS) — A dial-up authentication protocol designed to bridge the gap between network access servers and an internal network infrastructure.

Resultant Set of Policy (RSoP) — A tool that queries computers running Windows XP Professional or Windows Server 2003 and provides details about all policy settings that are configured for existing policies based on site, domain, domain controller, and OU.

Rights Management Services (RMS) — A rights management technology that helps to protect data.

Software restriction policies — A method whereby you can control which programs run on your computer, permitting users to run only specific files on multiple-user computers, and can prevent any files from running on your local computer, your organizational unit, your site, or your domain should you get a virus infection.

Trustworthy Computing — Microsoft's objective of safe computing using the following three dimensions to describe perspectives on trust: goals, means, and execution.

Windows Management Instrumentation (WMI) — A management infrastructure in Windows that supports monitoring and controlling system resources through a common set of interfaces and provides a logically organized, consistent model of Windows operation, configuration, and status.

REVIEW QUESTIONS

1. Which of the following are included in Microsoft's area of security? (Choose all that apply.)
   a. Isolation and resiliency
   b. Quality
   c. Dedication
   d. Authentication and access control

2. Microsoft's objective of Trustworthy Computing incorporates which of the following? (Choose all that apply.)
   a. Goals
   b. Effort
   c. Means
   d. Execution

3. Which of the following describes RMS?

   a. A tool that queries computers running Windows XP Professional or Windows Server 2003 and provides details about all policy settings

   b. A technology that includes a series of features relating to authentication and encryption

   c. A rights management technology that helps to protect data

   d. The new tool for Group Policy management

4. Which of the following is firewall software that is used to set restrictions on what information is communicated between your home or small office network and the Internet?

   a. NAT Traversal

   b. ICF

   c. IAS

   d. RADIUS

5. Which of the following are goals set for Trustworthy Computing and are designed to deliver a certain level of trust and responsibility? (Choose all that apply.)

   a. Security

   b. Privacy

   c. Reliability

   d. Business integrity

6. Which of the following are aspects of execution? (Choose all that apply.)

   a. Evidence

   b. Intents

   c. Implementation

   d. Change

7. Which of the following describes PKI?

   a. A new tool for Group Policy management

   b. A rights management technology that helps to protect data

   c. A technology that includes a series of features relating to authentication and encryption

   d. A tool that queries computers running Windows XP Professional or Windows Server 2003 and provides details about all policy settings

8. Which of the following is Microsoft's implementation of RADIUS and allows you to control authentication and authorization of users, who access multiple access points, via a single server?

   a. PKI

   b. ICF

    c. IAS

    d. NAT-T

9. Windows Server 2003 uses the 802.1x standard for authenticating access to wired Ethernet networks and wireless 802.11 networks. It also provides support for EAP used in conjunction with which of the following authentication methods for wireless computers?

    a. EAP-TLS

    b. EAP-MSCHAPv2

    c. PEAP

    d. PAP

10. There is a new Certificate Templates MMC snap-in in Windows Server 2003 that enables administrators to do which of the following? (Choose all that apply.)

    a. Query details about all policy settings

    b. Set up and apply enrollment, issuance, and application policies

    c. Modify template properties

    d. Create new certificate templates by duplicating and renaming an existing template

11. Which of the following describes RSoP?

    a. A new tool for Group Policy management

    b. A tool that queries computers running Windows XP Professional or Windows Server 2003 and provides details about all policy settings

    c. A technology that includes a series of features relating to authentication and encryption

    d. A rights management technology that helps to protect data

12. Which of the following describes the Microsoft GPMC?

    a. A technology that includes a series of features relating to authentication and encryption

    b. A new tool for Group Policy management

    c. A tool that queries computers running Windows XP Professional or Windows Server 2003 and provides details about all policy settings

    d. A method whereby you can control which programs run on your computer

13. Windows Server 2003 has added the concept of a delta CRL, which is similar in theory to what type of backup?

    a. Incremental

    b. Differential

    c. Full

    d. Copy

14. Which of the following is a new feature of Windows Server 2003 and allows IPSec and NAT to work together?

   a. PKI

   b. NAT-T

   c. ICF

   d. RADIUS

15. Which of the following describes the Microsoft GPMC?

   a. A technology that includes a series of features relating to authentication and encryption

   b. A new tool for Group Policy management

   c. A tool that queries computers running Windows XP Professional or Windows Server 2003 and provides details about all policy settings

   d. A rights management technology that helps to protect data

CASE PROJECTS

Case Project 1-1

Evergrow, a large, multinational company, is currently running Windows XP on all client computers. Management would like to upgrade to Service Pack 2. It is your job as the network administrator to make a recommendation either for or against updating the systems with Service Pack 2. Prepare a report for management stating your case. In the report, list at least five reasons for your decision.

Case Project 1-2

You are the network administrator at Evergrow. You are currently using Windows 2000 Server and would like to upgrade to Windows Server 2003. In a previous discussion with management, the idea received a lukewarm reception. Many members were leery of Microsoft's commitment to security in light of the issues with the Slammer worm and, more recently, the scob outbreak and suggested that you look at other operating systems. You believe that for the needs of the organization Windows Server 2003 is the best operating system. Prepare a report on your findings, citing some of the ways Bill Gates stated that Microsoft is committed to security.

Case Project 1-3

Upon reading your report on Microsoft's commitment to security, management has decided that they will accept your recommendation and allow for the upgrading of the servers to Windows Server 2003. Before they do, they want to know about Trustworthy Computing. They want to know exactly what it means and how it affects the organizational environment. Prepare a short report consisting of several paragraphs to submit to management based on Microsoft's white paper entitled "Trusted Computing."

Case Project 1-4

You are the network administrator at Evergrow. You are currently using Windows 2000 Server and would like to upgrade to Windows Server 2003. In a previous discussion with management, the idea received a lukewarm reception. Many members are concerned about the cost of upgrading and have doubts that upgrading to a newer operating system will make much of a difference in the bottom line. You believe that for the needs of the organization Windows Server 2003 is the best operating system. Prepare a report on the various ways that upgrading can help the organization improve performance and provide a return on investment. Include as many features as you can to improve your chances of getting the funding to upgrade.

Case Project 1-5

You are the network administrator at Evergrow. Management has asked you to evaluate the perimeter network security because a possibility exists that the company will merge with another organization three times its size. Currently, you have 10 servers and 500 workstations. If the merger were to take place, you will have about 30 servers and 2500 users. Use the Microsoft Security Guidance Kit to evaluate both of these scenarios and then report your findings to management.

CHAPTER

2

PLANNING AND CONFIGURING SECURITY POLICIES

After reading this chapter, you will be able to:

- ♦ Define the role of servers
- ♦ Understand how security mechanisms can be used to create baseline servers
- ♦ Develop a network security structure based on server role
- ♦ Define security policies for different computer roles such as bastion hosts, IIS, and IAS
- ♦ Develop a network security structure based on client role
- ♦ Recognize and plan restriction policies based on client computer roles
- ♦ Configure client security settings
- ♦ Configure software restriction policies

The best security plans and designs in the world cannot protect an organization if the plan is made, but then forgotten about. The plan must be an essential part of standard operating procedures. Secure environments are the result of careful planning from the time you decide to deploy a new server, type of client, or application to the moment when the responsibility for that server, client, or application is passed on to those responsible for the day-to-day operation of the network. To plan a secure environment, you need a concise, consistent strategy for addressing the many aspects of today's operating systems, including security-related issues and vulnerabilities. To ensure a secure environment, security must be addressed in all possible areas of network design and planning, including areas such as server configuration, networking, and client configuration.

Because every organization has its own distinctive mix of clients, servers, and user requirements, planning a complete, secure environment has become a key challenge, especially with the mix of wireless, personal digital assistants (PDAs) and cell phones a network administrator must secure. Without a consistent approach to security, some areas of the network might be secured more tightly, while others may be overlooked or only marginally secured.

By carefully analyzing the requirements of your organization and using a concise, consistent planning process, you can establish a high-level security framework for your environment. This chapter will provide a guide for enhancing the security setting configurations of your servers and clients to help you plan a more secure environment.

DEFINING COMPUTER ROLES

Keeping the network secure and safe from attacks is an enormous undertaking especially because most computers and servers come with a wide range of services and protocols, many of which are turned on by default. But before you begin to configure the servers and clients, you must know what roles they will play and have an Active Directory design in place. Properly planning an organization's security structure will result in a much more secure Active Directory design for the organization. Then, only major changes to the environment, such as a merger or organizational restructuring, will require you to restructure the design. To achieving these results, careful planning of the following elements is needed:

- *Domains*—**Domains** are administrative units that group together various capabilities for management convenience.

- *Forests*—**Forests** are one or more Active Directory domains that share a schema and global catalog.

- *Organizational units*—**Organizational units** are Active Directory containers where users, groups, computers, and other organizational units can be placed.

The forest is the true security boundary. Microsoft recommends creating separate forests rather than domains to keep your environment secure from rogue administrators and various other threats. A domain is the management boundary of Active Directory. The domain boundary can provide independent management of services and data within each domain of the organization. Your organization may need to consider dividing the administrative control of services and data within the current Active Directory design. Active Directory design requires fully understanding your organization's requirements for services as well as data access. The way that you plan your domains, forests, and organizational units plays a critical role in defining your network's security boundaries.

After you have your security boundaries in place, you can consider the environment. In Microsoft's *Windows 2003 Security Guide*, there are specifications for the following three distinct environments, which are discussed in the next section:

- Legacy Client
- Enterprise Client
- High Security

Each of these environments can be configured using security templates. Security templates are text-based files. You can change these files using the Security Templates snap-in to the Microsoft Management Console (MMC) or by using a text editor such as Notepad. Security Templates is a standalone snap-in tool that users can use to define computer-independent security configurations. These configurations are saved as text-based .inf files. These and several predefined security templates will be discussed in the next chapter. For now, because we are taking about defining the default role for each of our servers in a particular environment, we will focus on these templates and one in particular, the Enterprise template. This template has been chosen because many organizational environments will fall into this category.

CREATING BASELINE SERVERS BASED ON ROLES

Generally the environment needs of an organization will fall into a Legacy Client, Enterprise Client, or High Security category. To help you better understand when you would use each of these environments, we will look a little closer at each one. Windows Server 2003 ships with default setting values set to a secure state. The idea behind these three environments is to provide a framework for evolving from a Legacy environment toward a High Security environment within a domain infrastructure.

Legacy Client

The **Legacy Client** is the lowest lockdown level. Organizations that want to provide a phased approach to securing their environments may choose to start at the Legacy Client environment level and then gradually move to the higher security levels as their applications and client computers are upgraded and tested with tightened security settings. The Legacy Client settings are designed to work with member servers and domain controllers running Windows Server 2003, and clients running Microsoft Windows 98, Windows NT 4.0, and later versions of Windows operating systems. The templates for this environment include:

- Domain controller
- Domain
- File server
- Internet Information Services (IIS) server

- Infrastructure server
- Print server
- Member server

Enterprise Client

The **Enterprise Client** environment is designed to provide solid security for the organization. An Enterprise Client environment is defined as only having Windows Server 2003, Windows 2000 Professional, and Windows XP Professional computers in the environment. This allows use of more restrictive security templates for added security. Using these security templates also allows the organization to introduce additional roles on top of the baseline member server template. Notice that in most of the activities you have done so far, the templates that were imported were the Enterprise Client templates. Baseline templates for this environment include:

- Domain controller
- Domain
- Certificate services
- Internet Authentication Service (IAS) server
- File server
- IIS server
- Infrastructure server
- Print server
- Member server

High Security

The **High Security** environment is the highest lockdown level. In this environment the settings are very restrictive. The High Security settings are designed to work in an Active Directory domain with member servers and domain controllers running Windows Server 2003, and clients running Windows 2000, Windows XP, and later just like the Enterprise Client settings. Because the High Security settings are so restrictive, the servers may experience some impact on performance, and managing the servers will be more challenging. In fact, many applications might not function with them. Baseline templates for this environment include:

- Domain controller
- Domain
- File server
- Bastion server

- IIS server

- Infrastructure server

- Print server

- Member server

Table 2-1 shows Microsoft's recommendations for which templates to use with the various roles. These recommendations can be found in the *Windows 2003 Security Guide*.

Table 2-1   Windows Server 2003 roles

Server Role	Description of Server Role	Security Template
Windows Server 2003 domain controllers	A group containing Active Directory domain controllers	Enterprise Client - Domain Controller.inf
Windows Server 2003 member servers	All servers that are members of the domain and reside in or below the member server OU	Enterprise Client - Member Server Baseline.inf
Windows Server 2003 file servers	A group containing locked down file servers	Enterprise Client - File Server.inf
Windows Server 2003 print servers	A group containing locked down print servers	Enterprise Client - Print Server.inf
Windows Server 2003 infrastructure servers	A group containing locked down DNS, WINS, and DHCP servers	Enterprise Client - Infrastructure Server.inf
Windows Server 2003 IAS servers	A group containing locked down IAS servers	Enterprise Client - IAS Server.inf
Windows Server 2003 Certificate Services servers	A group containing locked down Certificate Authority (CA) servers	Enterprise Client - CA Server.inf
Windows Server 2003 bastion hosts	A group containing Internet facing servers	High Security- Bastion Host.inf
Windows Server 2003 IIS servers	A group containing locked down IIS servers	Enterprise Client - IIS Server.inf

These recommendations are based on the premise that computers running Windows Server 2003 will perform specifically defined roles. If the servers in your organization have multipurpose roles, you should use the settings defined here as guidelines for creating your own security templates.

Server Roles

As mentioned previously, the first step in securing your environment is to formulate your Active Directory design plan, then determine the environment you are dealing with. From there you can move on to look at server roles and how to create a security template for the various types of servers in your environment. When determining your current environment, you should include the following:

- The role of each server along with its current configuration
- The services, protocols, and applications required to meet your business needs
- Any configuration changes that should be made to the existing servers

By identifying the role that each server plays, it is easier to determine which services and protocols are required. The structure of the domains and the organizational units (OU)s will help determine server roles. The object is to create the security requirements that will be applied in the initial server installation so that you have a baseline configuration for each type of server you will be implementing. Some of the more common server roles that you will find on a network include:

- Domain controller
- Member server
- Infrastructure server
- File server
- Print server
- Bastion host
- IIS server
- IAS server

In the next few sections, we will describe not only the purpose of each of these roles, but also guide you through establishing a baseline server for each of these particular roles.

Establishing a Baseline Domain Controller

Domain controllers store directory data for Active Directory and manage the communication between users and domains. This includes functions such as user logon processes, authentication, and directory searches. Due to the services it provides, the domain controller server role is one of the most important roles to secure in any environment with computers running Microsoft Windows Server 2003 and running Active Directory services. Any loss or compromise of a domain controller in the environment could be devastating to clients, other servers, and other devices or applications that rely on the domain controller for authentication and services.

Because they are important to the proper functioning of the network, domain controllers should always be stored in physically secure locations that are accessible only to qualified administrative staff. In fact, physical access to any server is a high security risk. Physical access by an intruder could result in unauthorized data access or modification as well as installation of hardware or software programs designed to evade security. When domain controllers must be stored in unsecured locations, branch offices for example, several security settings can be adjusted to limit the potential damage from physical threats.

The Domain Controller template requires a baseline group policy, making it similar in concept to a member server baseline policy. However, the policy is linked to the Domain Controllers OU; therefore, it takes precedence over the Default Domain Controllers policy. We will go over the member server baseline policy in detail in the next section.

Activity 2-1: Install the Group Policy Management Console

Time Required: 20 minutes

Objective: Discover the Group Policy Management Console (GPMC).

Description: In this activity, you will install the GPMC.

1. Log on with your **AdminXX** account, where *XX* is your assigned student number.

2. Open the Microsoft Security Guidance Kit; on the left side of the screen, choose **Enhance Server Security**. On the right side of the screen, scroll down until you see the section Tools.

3. Find Group Policy Management Console (GPMC) with Service Pack 1.

4. Click on the link. You will see two more links, the first one is: Click HERE for tool installation instructions and requirements. Be sure that you have Internet access, and then click on the link. Read the instructions and requirements.

5. As long as your machine meets the requirements, close the Internet requirements page and click on the link: **Click HERE to access tool installation file(s)**.

6. This will take you to the directory where the gpmc.msi file is located. Double-click the .msi file. You should see a dialog box as shown in Figure 2-1. Install the file by clicking **Next**, **I agree**, **Next**, and **Finish**.

Activity 2-2: Use Group Policy Management Console to Explore Default Domain Controller Policy

Time Required: 30 minutes

Objective: Explore the default settings installed for domain controllers by using the Group Policy Management Console.

Description: In this activity, you will look at the default settings installed for domain controllers by using the Group Policy Management Console. Note: The computer needs to have a domain set up for Activity 2-3. This can be done by running the wizard. Click **Start, Run**, type **dcpromo**, and press **Enter**.

1. Log on with your **AdminXX** account, where *XX* is your assigned student number.

2. Click **Start, Administrative Tools, Group Policy Management**.

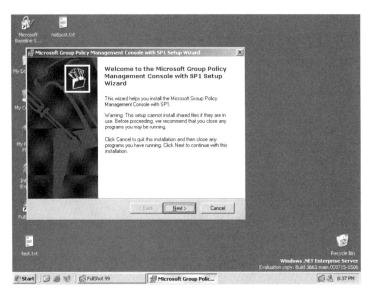

Figure 2-1   Initial install screen for the Group Policy Management Console

3. Once the console is open, expand the trees on the left side until you get to the Default Domain Controllers Policy. Click the Default Domain Controllers Policy to open the dialog box shown in Figure 2-2.

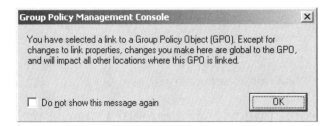

Figure 2-2   Group Policy Management Console

4. Click **OK** on the Group Policy Management Console dialog box screen.

5. Select the **Settings** tab. Depending on the security settings, you may get a warning message. To clear this click **Add**, **Add**, **Close**. Once the report is generated, click **show**, which is on the right side of the screen next to Security Settings.

6. Click **show** on each of the settings and observe the default settings.

7. Close the **MMC**.

TIP

While going through the exercise, pay special attention to the pop-up box on the console. Linking a Group Policy Object (GPO) or modifying the default GPO linked to the Domain Controllers OU will affect the entire domain. If you do not properly configure and test the GPO, linking it to Domain Controllers OU could adversely affect the operation of the domain.

Establishing a Baseline Member Server

The settings at the Member servers OU level define the common settings for all **member servers** in the domain. This is similar to creating the domain controllers policy. You create a Group Policy Object (GPO) and link it to the Member servers OU. The GPO that will be created is known as a member server baseline policy. The GPO automates the process of configuring specific security settings on each server. Server-hardening procedures are accomplished by creating a unique security template for each security environment and then importing it into a GPO linked to the parent OU for the member server to achieve the targeted level of security.

ACTIVITY

Activity 2-3: Create the Member Servers OU and Delegate Responsibility

Time Required: 20 minutes

Objective: Create the Member servers OU and delegate responsibility.

Description: In this activity, you create the Member servers OU and delegate responsibility.

1. Log on with your **AdminXX** account, where *XX* is your assigned student number.

2. Open Active Directory Users and Computers by clicking **Start**, **Administrative Tools**, **Active Directory Users and Computers**.

3. Highlight your domain. Click the **Action** menu and select **New**, then **Organizational Unit**.

4. Type **Member Servers** in the Name text box.

5. Click **OK**.

6. Highlight the **Member servers** container if necessary, click the **Action** menu, and select **All Tasks**, **Delegate Control**.

7. Click **Next** on the Welcome dialog box.

8. Click **Add**. Click **Advanced**, enter **Network Configuration Operators** in the text box after Name, and click **Find Now**. Click **OK**. The Network Configuration Operators is a group new to Windows Server 2003. This group enables you to delegate the privileges to manage certain network configuration duties such as Issue ipconfig, release, or renew commands, modify the Transmission Control Protocol/Internet Protocol (TCP/IP) properties for a local area network (LAN) connection, and modify the properties of all of the remote access connections of the users.

9. Click **OK**, then **Next**.

10. Select the **Manage Group Policy links** check box, click **Next**, then **Finish**.

11. Close the **Active Directory Users and Computers** window.

Activity 2-4: Import the Member Server Baseline Template and Link It to the Member Server OU

Time Required: 45 minutes

Objective: Learn to work with security templates by importing the Enterprise Client Member Server baseline template.

Description: In this activity, you will learn to work with security templates by importing the Enterprise Client Member Server baseline template.

1. Log on with your **AdminXX** account, where *XX* is your assigned student number.

2. Open the Group Policy Management Console by clicking **Start**, **Administrative Tools**, **Group Policy Management**.

3. Right-click the **Member servers OU**, as shown in Figure 2-3.

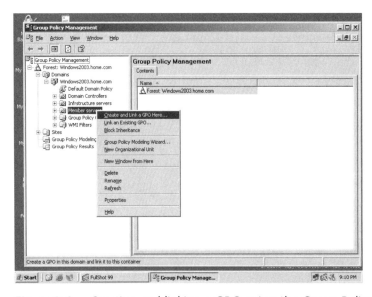

Figure 2-3   Creating and linking a GPO using the Group Policy Management Console

4. Choose **Create and Link a GPO Here…**. In the Name box, type: **Member Server Baseline Policy** and click **OK**.

5. Expand **Group Policy Objects**, right-click **Member Server Baseline Policy**, and select **Edit**.

6. Expand **Computer Configuration**, **Windows Settings**.

7. Click **Security Settings**, go to the Action menu, and choose **Import Policy**.

8. You should now see the Import Policy From window, as in Figure 2-4.

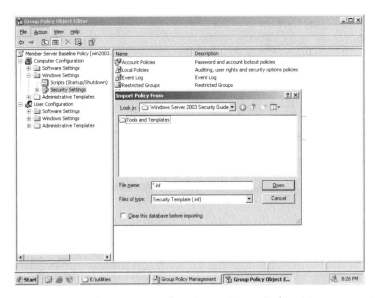

Figure 2-4   The Import Policy From Group Policy Management Console window

9. Find where you have the installed the *Windows Server 2003 Security Guide*. Open the folder, open **Tools and Templates**, then select **Security Templates**. Scroll through until you find the Enterprise Client - Member Server Baseline.inf file, as shown in Figure 2-5.

10. Highlight the template and click **Open**.

11. Expand the **Local Policies** and the **Event Log** and view the setting configuration changes that were made.

12. When finished, close the **Group Policy Object Editor** window and the **Group Policy Management** window.

Now that you know how to import the security template for the Member servers OU, you are ready to move on to explore the infrastructure server requirements and templates.

Establishing a Baseline Infrastructure Server

As network complexity grows, so does the number of enterprise users, devices, and applications. This affects your core network services and how you manage critical data services and protocols that allow users to perform functions on the network. These services connect production applications to the actual network infrastructure and store information

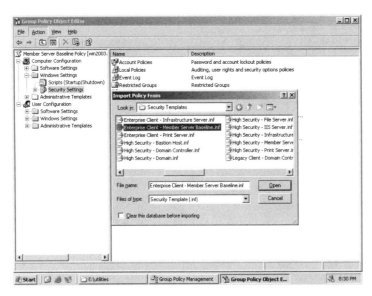

Figure 2-5   Locating a security template using Group Policy Management Console

about network components such as user access privileges and applications on the network. Services such as **Domain Name System (DNS)**, RADIUS, **Lightweight Directory Access Protocol (LDAP)**, **Dynamic Host Control Protocol (DHCP)**, and Public Key Infrastructure, are known as **network infrastructure services**. Infrastructure services are often spread across various platforms and internal departments, making them difficult to secure against risks. Having a baseline model for each type of particular infrastructure server can make this task a bit more manageable. We will be addressing the infrastructure servers that provide services such as DHCP, Windows Internet Name Service (WINS), or DNS, starting with DHCP.

Computers running the Microsoft DHCP service offer dynamic configuration of IP addresses and related information to DHCP-enabled clients on your network. This can present issues on the network. Because DHCP is an unauthenticated protocol, a user can connect to the network without providing credentials. An unauthenticated user can then obtain a lease from any available DHCP server. Any option values that the DHCP server provides with the lease, such as WINS server or DNS server IP addresses, are available to the unauthenticated user. Malicious users with physical access to the DHCP-enabled network can initiate a denial of service attack by requesting numerous leases from the server, thereby depleting the number of leases that are available to other DHCP clients.

When using DHCP, permanent addresses can be assigned to machines by reserving DHCP addresses. When you reserve a DHCP address, the client is always assigned the same IP address by the DHCP server. This can be done when you have machines that must have a constant IP address such as network printers and certain servers. DHCP reservations are used to ensure that these devices always have the same IP address, but continue to receive updated configuration information from the DHCP server. This might include servers such as:

- Windows Internet Name Service (WINS)
- DNS
- Print servers that use TCP/IP print services
- Firewalls
- Routers

To reserve an IP address, enter the following items in the New Reservation dialog box:

- Reservation name
- IP address
- MAC address
- Description of the reservation

Because using reservations requires you to input the MAC address, this is a more secure method of using DHCP, but requires more administrative overhead. Microsoft's Web site has an article on best practices for using DHCP that explains when and how to use this feature.

DHCP server authorization began with Windows Server 2000, so only Windows Server 2000 or Windows Server 2003 machines can be authorized in Active Directory. Non-Microsoft DHCP server software does not include this authorization feature. Because DHCP clients broadcast DHCP discover messages to the nearest DHCP server, if a malicious user installs a DHCP server on the organization's network, nearby DHCP clients will receive incorrect leases that might conflict with the IP addresses assigned to other DHCP clients on the network. This might reroute network traffic, causing the network to function improperly.

The following measures should be put into place for securing DHCP:

- Ensure that unauthorized persons do not have access to your network either physically or by wireless means.
- Enable audit logging for all DHCP servers on your network and check the log files on a regular basis watching carefully for an unusually high number of lease requests from clients.

In addition, there are several changes that should be made to the baseline server template for servers that will run DHCP. They are:

- For a client to obtain an IP address configuration, the DHCP service must be running. Group Policy should be used to secure and set the service to grant access solely to server administrators.
- Event Viewer entries for the DHCP service are limited to startup and shutdown events; therefore, DHCP logging should be configured so that a more detailed log is available. Limit access to these logs to server administrators.
- Use the 80/20 rule by splitting DHCP server scopes between servers so that 80% of the addresses are distributed by one DHCP server and 20% by another.

- Rename the Administrator and Guest accounts, change their passwords to be more complex, and use different names and passwords on each server. You may want to disable the Guest account instead of just renaming it, especially if there is no need to use the account.

- Enhance the level of security on servers by using IPSec filters to block unnecessary ports.

Although internal DNS servers can be less susceptible to attacks than external DNS servers, they still need to be secured. In order to stop outside intruders from accessing the internal network of your company, use separate DNS servers for internal and Internet name resolution. To provide Internet name resolution for internal hosts, you can have your internal DNS servers use a forwarder.

The following are some considerations for internal DNS servers:

- Eliminate any single point of failure by making sure that the Active Directory structure is planned properly. Analyze where the clients of each DNS zone are located and how will they resolve names if the DNS server is unavailable.

- Prevent unauthorized access to your servers by implementing Active Directory-integrated zones with secure dynamic updates. Keep the list of DNS servers that are allowed to obtain a zone transfer small.

- Monitor the server events and DNS logs. Proper monitoring of logs and server events can help prevent unauthorized access as well as diagnosis problems.

Establishing a Baseline File Server

File servers provide the most essential services for the network; therefore, they can be a challenge to secure. They often provide services for applications that require protocols such as NetBIOS, Server Message Block (SMB), and Common Internet File System (CIFS). These protocols can provide a wealth of information to unauthenticated users. Often in situations where high security is required in a Windows environment, these protocols are disabled although disabling these protocols can make accessing file servers difficult for both administrators and the users in your environment. There are additional services that are often enabled on file servers running Microsoft Windows Server 2003 that are not essential. Because each environment is different, the use and security of these services should be adjusted to the needs of your organization. Here are some considerations for securing file servers:

- Any unneeded services or executable files should be disabled or removed to prevent a potential point of attack.

- The Distributed File System (DFS) is a distributed service that integrates file shares into a single logical namespace and makes them available to users on the network. You can disable the DFS service to minimize the attack surface of the file servers, but this requires users to know the names of all the servers and shares in the environment to access them.

2

- The File Replication Service (FRS) is the automatic file replication service in Windows 2000 and Windows Server 2003. You can disable the FRS to minimize the attack surface of the file servers in your environment, but if you do so, file replication will not occur and server data will not be synchronized.

- Secure well-known accounts on file servers by renaming the Administrator and Guest accounts, and then change their passwords to long and complex values on every domain controller and server. Use different names and passwords on each server to prevent the compromising of all servers when one is compromised. Change the account descriptions to something other than the defaults to help prevent easy identification of the accounts. You can use a simple user account name for this. For example: We renamed our administrator account on one server Dolores Clayton. Be sure to record the changes in a secure location.

- Never configure a service to run under the security context of a domain account unless absolutely necessary. This will prevent domain account passwords from being obtained by utilities that dump the Local Security Authority (LSA) information.

- Internet Protocol Security (IPSec) filters can provide an effective means for enhancing the level of security required for servers. Block ports by using IPSec filters.

Establishing a Baseline Print Server

As with file servers, **print servers** provide essential services that require the protocols such as NetBIOS, SMB, and CIFS. The network administrator is faced with the same issues in securing a print as in securing a file server. These protocols can be disabled, but if you do so, accessing these servers becomes difficult for both administrators and users in the environment. Here are considerations for securing print servers:

- Under Security Options the option Microsoft network server: Digitally sign communications (always) can be enabled. This setting determines whether packet signing is required by the SMB server component. SMB packet digital signing is used to prevent man-in-the-middle attacks. It is disabled by default but it can be enabled for servers in a High Security environment. Enabling this setting allows users to print, but not view, the print queue. Users attempting to view the print queue will receive an access denied message.

- Any unneeded services or executable files should be disabled or removed to eliminate a potential point of attack. The Print Spooler service must be enabled because it manages all local and network print queues and controls all print jobs. It is the center of the Windows printing subsystem and communicates with printer drivers and I/O components.

- Secure well-known accounts on print servers by following the same procedures that are used for a file server.

- Never configure a service to run under the security context of a domain account unless absolutely necessary.

- Internet Protocol Security (IPSec) filters can provide an effective means for enhancing the level of security required for servers. Block ports by using IPSec filters.

ACTIVITY

Activity 2-5: Import the Infrastructure Server Baseline Template and Link It to the Infrastructure Server OU

Time Required: 45 minutes

Objective: Practice working with security templates by importing the Enterprise Client Infrastructure Server template.

Description: In this activity, you will practice working with security templates by importing the Enterprise Client Infrastructure Server template.

1. Log on with your **AdminXX** account, where *XX* is your assigned student number.

2. Create the Infrastructure server OU by clicking **Start**, **Administrative Tools**, **Active Directory Users and Computers**.

3. Highlight your domain. Click the **Action** menu and select **New**, then select **Organizational Unit**. Type **Infrastructure Servers** in the Name text box. Click **OK**. Close Active Directory Users and Computers.

4. Open Group Policy Management Console by clicking **Start**, **Administrative Tools**, **Group Policy Management**.

5. Right-click the **Infrastructure servers OU**.

6. Choose **Create and Link a GPO Here....** In the Name box type: **Infrastructure Server Policy**, then click **OK**.

7. Expand **Group Policy Objects**, right-click **Infrastructure Server Policy**, and select **Edit**.

8. Expand **Computer Configuration**, **Windows Settings**.

9. Click on **Security Settings**, go to the **Action** menu, choose **Import Policy**.

10. You should now see the Import Policy From window, as shown in Figure 2-6.

11. Find where you have the installed the *Windows 2003 Security Guide*. Click on the folder, select **Tools and Templates**, select **Security Guide**, then select **Security Templates**. Scroll through them until you find the Enterprise Client - Infrastructure Server.inf file.

12. Highlight the **Template** and click **Open**.

13. Expand **Local Policies** and **Event Log**, then view the setting configuration changes that were made.

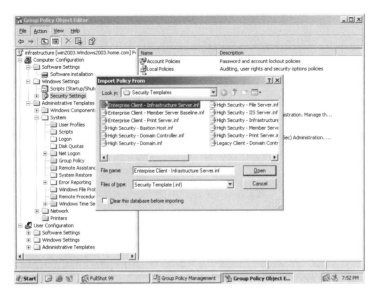

Figure 2-6   Importing a security template using the Group Policy Management Console

14. When finished, close the **Group Policy Object Editor** window and the **Group Policy Management** window.

Establishing a Baseline Bastion Host

A **bastion host** is a publicly accessible computer located on the perimeter network. You may also hear this referred to as the DMZ (demilitarized zone), or screened subnet. Although in most situations the DMZ would have some type of firewall or filtering router on each interface into the DMZ, sometimes bastion hosts are unprotected by a firewall or filtering router, leaving them highly exposed to attacks. They must be secured as much as possible to maximize their availability and yet minimize the chance of their being compromised. Because they are so vulnerable, the design and configuration of bastion hosts must be carefully thought out to reduce the chances of an attack being successful. The most secure bastion host servers limit access to only highly trusted accounts and enable the fewest services possible necessary to fully perform their functions. See Figure 2-7 for a network with a bastion host so you can better understand their placement.

Some of the most common uses for bastion hosts include:

- Web servers—**Web servers** are used for hosting externally accessible Web sites.

- *DNS servers*—**Domain Name Systems (DNS) servers** are used to resolve domain names to IP addresses.

- *File Transfer Protocol (FTP) servers*—**File Transfer Protocol (FTP) servers** are used for posting files and retrieving files.

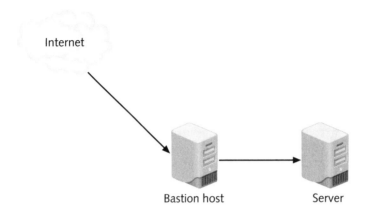

Figure 2-7   Network with a bastion host

- *Simple Mail Transport Protocol (SMTP) servers*—**Simple Mail Transport Protocol (SMTP) servers** are used to store and forward electronic mail.

- *Network News Transfer Protocol (NNTP) servers*—**Network News Transfer Protocol (NNTP) servers** are used for newsgroup postings.

It is easier to secure services when the bastion host is dedicated to performing just one role. The more roles each host has to play, the greater the likelihood that a security hole will be overlooked. When securing bastion hosts all unnecessary services, protocols, programs, and network interfaces are disabled or removed, and then each particular host is configured to fulfill a specific role. By using this method, the potential for successful attacks can be limited.

Unlike the other server roles, Group Policy cannot be applied to bastion host servers because they are configured as standalone hosts and do not belong to the domain. It is recommended by Microsoft's *Security Guide* that the High Security - Bastion Host.inf file be used to configure these servers. As in other security measures, there are tradeoffs. Applying the High Security - Bastion Host.inf security template enhances server security by reducing the attack surface of a bastion host, but makes remote management of the bastion host impossible. If you choose to increase manageability or functionality of a bastion host, the template must be modified. Make sure that the security template is configured to enable the bastion host functionality your environment requires. It is also strongly recommended that you perform a full backup of a bastion host server before applying the High Security - Bastion Host.inf security template because reverting back to the original configuration after applying the High Security – Bastion Host.inf security template is very difficult. Here are some points to evaluate as you plan the security of a bastion host:

- The Allow log on locally user right enables a user to start an interactive session on the computer. Limit the accounts that can be used to log on to a bastion host server console. This will help prevent unauthorized access to a server's file system and system services. Granting this right only to the Administrators group limits administrative access to bastion host servers and provides a better level of security.

2

■ All services not required by the operating system and those not essential to the proper operation of the bastion host's role should be disabled. This may generate numerous Event Log warnings, most of which can be ignored. Again, you are faced with a tradeoff. Enabling these services will reduce Event Log messages but increase the attack surface of the bastion host. The following is a list of the services that are not essential to the proper operation of a bastion host.

- *Automatic Updates*—Wuauserv

- *Background Intelligent Transfer Service*—BITS

- *Computer Browser*—Browser

- *DHCP Client*—Dhcp

- *Network Location Awareness (NLA)* —NLA

- *NTLM Security Support Provider*—NtLmSsp

- *Performance Logs and Alerts*—SysmonLog

- *Remote Administration Service*—SrvcSurg

- *Remote Registry Service*—RemoteRegistry

- *Server*—lanmanserver

- *TCP/IP NetBIOS Helper Service*—LMHosts

- *Terminal Services*—TermService

- *Windows Installer*—MSIServer

- *Windows Management Instrumentation Driver Extensions*—WMI

- *WMI Performance Adapter*—WmiApSrv

NOTE

Before you disable the service, be sure that you test the environment so that disabling the service will not adversely affect the operation of the applications you may be running.

■ Disabling SMB and NetBIOS over TCP/IP greatly reduces the server's attack surface. Servers operating under this configuration cannot access folders shared on the network and are more difficult to manage, but disabling these protocols protects the server from being easily compromised.

■ All services not required by the operating system and those not essential to the proper operation of the bastion host's role should be disabled.

■ Never configure a service to run under the security context of a domain account unless absolutely necessary.

- Internet Protocol Security (IPSec) filters can provide an effective means for enhancing the level of security required for servers. Block ports by using IPSec filters.

- The Error Reporting service helps Microsoft track and address errors. Error reports can potentially contain sensitive or confidential data. Because the data is transmitted in cleartext Hypertext Transfer Protocol (HTTP), it could be intercepted on the Internet and viewed by third parties. The Error Reporting setting should be set to Disabled.

Establishing a Baseline Internet Information Services Server

IIS is not installed by default on Windows Server 2003. When it is installed, it is installed in a highly secure mode. Features such as Active Server Pages (ASP), ASP.NET, server-side includes (SSIs), Web Distributed Authoring and Versioning (WebDAV) publishing, and FrontPage Server Extensions are not installed. In order to provide complete security for Web servers and applications within an organization's corporate intranet, all IIS servers, Web sites, and applications should be protected from client computers that can connect to them. In addition, each IIS server should be protected from the Web sites and applications running on the other IIS servers within a corporate intranet. There are certain measures that can be taken to enhance the security of IIS servers hosting HTML content, within a corporate intranet.

When a member server baseline policy is established, all unneeded services and executable files are disabled or removed, so to add Web server functionality the following three services must be enabled:

- The HTTP SSL service enables IIS to perform Secure Sockets Layer (SSL) functions. Disabling this service causes any services that explicitly depend on it to fail. The startup mode setting should be configured to Automatic. Group Policy should be used to secure and set the service to grant access solely to server administrators.

- The IIS Admin Service allows administration of IIS components. If this service is disabled, IIS cannot be configured, and requests for any Web services will be rejected. The startup mode setting should be configured the same way as HTTP SSL.

- The World Wide Web Publishing Service provides Web connectivity and administration of Web sites. The startup mode setting should be configured the same way as the previous two services.

IIS by default serves only static Web content. Each additional IIS feature must be individually enabled. Additional security measures that must be performed manually are:

- Installing only necessary IIS components
- Enabling only essential Web service extensions
- Placing content on a dedicated disk volume

- Securing well-known accounts

- Securing service accounts

- Blocking ports with Internet Protocol Security (IPSec) filters

- Setting NTFS permissions

- Setting IIS Web site permissions

- Configuring IIS logging

- Manually adding unique security groups to User Rights Assignments

For older versions of IIS, some of these activities may be accomplished by using the **IIS Lockdown tool**. The IIS Lockdown tool turns off unnecessary features to better protect the server from attackers. It provides templates for IIS-dependent Microsoft products such as Microsoft Exchange 5.5 and 2000. To provide multiple layers of protection against attackers, **URLScan** has been integrated into the IIS Lockdown Wizard. URLScan screens incoming requests to an IIS Web server against a ruleset. We will take a look at this tool in the next activity.

ACTIVITY

Activity 2-6: Discover IIS Lockdown Tool and URLScan

Time Required: 20 minutes

Objective: Learn about the IIS Lockdown and URLScan tools.

Description: In this activity, you investigate the IIS Lockdown and URLScan tools.

1. Log on with your **AdminXX** account, where *XX* is your assigned student number. Note: IIS and URLScan 1.0 or URLScan 2.0 must be installed for Activity 2-7 to be carried out.

2. Open a browser and go to: http://www.microsoft.com/technet/community/events/security/tnt1-87.mspx. The page should read Using Microsoft Security Tools.

3. Scroll down to Session Materials, click on the number 3 link called **Locking Down IIS**. Note: You may have to change the Internet security settings to medium from Tools, Internet Options, Security for now so that you can complete the exercise.

4. Watch the demonstration.

5. When finished, go to http://www.microsoft.com/technet/security/tools/urlscan.mspx.

6. Scroll down to the Installing UrlScan2.5 section. Click the **Download the setup .exe file** link. Click the **Download** link on the right and download the file.

7. After the download is finished, Click **Open**, click **Yes** to agree to the terms of the license, and click **OK** to complete the installation of the file.

8. Go to Start, My Computer, Windows directory -%windir%\system32\inetsrv\urlscan\logs, then open the file.

9. The file should look like Figure 2-8.

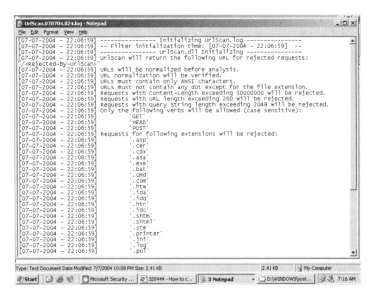

Figure 2-8   URLScan file

10. URLScan creates log files that record rejected requests. Read thorough the URLScan file. Why do you think the line "Requests with URL length exceeding 260 will be rejected" is there? Discuss this in class along with why the file extensions of .bat, .exe, .com, and .ini should be rejected requests.

Establishing a Baseline Internet Authentication Service Server

IAS is a Remote Authentication Dial-in User Service (RADIUS) server used for authentication, authorization, and accounting. It has the capability to authenticate users from Windows NT 4.0, Windows 2000, or Windows Server 2003 domains. It also supports the Routing and Remote Access Service (RRAS). Here are some recommended settings for making a template. Remember that when a member server baseline policy is established, all unneeded services and executable files are disabled or removed.

- Any unneeded services or executable files should be disabled or removed to eliminate a potential point of attack.

- Enable the IAS service. This service must be running for an IAS server to respond to client authentication requests. By using Group Policy to secure and set the startup mode, access is granted solely to server administrators, and this prevents the service from being configured or operated by unauthorized or malicious users.

- Secure well-known accounts on IAS servers by following the same procedures as for a file or print server.

- Never configure a service to run under the security context of a domain account unless absolutely necessary.

In the standard edition of Windows Server 2003, IAS can have a maximum of 50 RADIUS clients and two remote RADIUS server groups. In Enterprise and Datacenter Editions, you can configure an unlimited number of RADIUS clients and remote groups along with RADIUS clients by specifying an IP address range.

As a network administrator, it is important to understand that the job of securing the servers on your network is an ongoing process. When a new vulnerability is discovered, the environment must be reevaluated. It is imperative to stay current on security issues and how they relate to your environment.

Now that you have some experience with creating server roles, it is time to move on and look at the different roles clients may play in the environment.

CLIENT ROLES

We have discussed additional security for servers, but what about the security of the clients? Because client computers come in a variety of forms, they are a bit harder to control. In addition, client computers are often used by people who have varied levels of security awareness, or who often travel to unknown areas. User-related requirements are essential considerations in network design. There are security requirements associated with almost every user-related design decision that you make. For example, how do you verify that your users are who they say they are? Keeping in mind that the security requirements will vary for each user role, different settings should be configured for each type of client. In this section, we will look at ways to make this process a bit more manageable by separating the clients into defined roles. But what are these users' roles? How do you determine what role a user should have?

Let's start with some basic roles that organizations may have:

- Desktops

- Portable computers

- Kiosks and e-mail computers

We will discuss each of these in further detail later in the chapter. When planning for the security of each client role, one of the first security-related issues that every organization must address is what the requirements are for user access. If desired, administrators can create a single account for each user that allows the user to access the appropriate network resources. You can also meet differing security needs by varying the strength of credentials that you enforce. You can allow users to log on at different desktops, workstations, or notebooks in the domain by using the same user name and a password or smart card. Besides network resource access, there are other areas that need to be addressed where user access is concerned. Certainly you wouldn't configure access for a software developer to be the same as for a receptionist. Some additional considerations can include:

- Remote network access
- Wireless network access
- Certificates for secure e-mail and smart card logons
- Extranet access

As with server installations, Windows 2000 Professional and Windows XP Professional come with security templates. This is good place to start because many of the settings are configured based on the level of security needed. The Microsoft Security Guidance Kit comes with a wide variety of predefined templates.

Activity 2-7: Discover Microsoft Security Guidance Kit Job Aids

Time Required: 20 minutes

Objective: Discover additional security templates that can be used for configuring servers and clients.

Description: In this activity, you investigate the additional security templates that can be used for configuring servers and clients.

1. Log on with your **AdminXX** account, where *XX* is your assigned student number. Click **Start**, **All Programs**, and open the Microsoft Security Guidance Kit program.

2. On the left side of the screen, choose **Enhance Server Security**.

3. When the screen comes up, on the right side, scroll down to the Tools section, click on the last tool, called **Job Aids**. At the bottom of the screen select **click HERE to access Job Aid file(s)**.

4. Choose the **W2K Hardening Guide**, then open the **Templates** folder. Explore the different templates that are available. Do the same with the E2K Security Operations, Templates folder and the Windows XP Security Guide, Tools and Templates, Security Guide, Security Templates, and Stand Alone Clients folders.

5. How many different templates for client configurations did you see?

6. Exit the **Security Kit** and close all open windows.

Desktop

When configuring baseline security templates for desktops, the first task is to identify your users by workgroup, job function, or a combination of both. You can then identify the different types of resources that users might need access to, such as departmental or job-specific data. This step allows you to plan for different levels of access. As you

2

experienced in the last activity, there are numerous templates available for use. You may want to consider using one of these such as the Enterprise Security desktop.inf as a starting point.

Desktop computer configuration ranges can vary depending on use. Considerations include how much outside or Internet access such as e-mail and Web-based applications are needed as well as the methods of access. One word about desktop users: Watch out for alternative methods of communication that are set up, such as wireless access points and self-installed modems. You should also be cognizant of unapproved storage devices such as thumb drives and external USB drives.

Developer computer configurations on these computers will be more liberal than those of desktop computers, and the development environment should be separate from the production environment. Most development workers do not need local administrator rights, and this should be taken into consideration when building the model for this client. Again keep in mind that there are already-configured templates for desktops, and in the development area you may be able to use the standalone client template if the developers are isolated.

Portable

Companies offer flextime to employees and encourage them to telecommute in order to save on energy costs and overhead. They may also hire contractors without providing a workspace for them in company offices. Many employees travel and might have different levels of connectivity from one day to the next. Often IT professionals work from home at least part of the time. This makes for a flexible work environment. This flexibility can also mean that template considerations will need to include accessing the network remotely, encryption, and **virtual private networks (VPNs)**.

By design, mobile or laptop computers and many new types of portable devices such as portable hard drives and thumb drives have a higher risk of being stolen than a nonportable device. Often these machines hold important company data and represent a security risk if stolen or lost. Physical security should be an important consideration when building a template for these types of machines. If theft does occur, not only is there concern about the initial data loss but you must also consider the possibility of having an unauthorized person penetrate the network via remote dial-up or wireless networking. However, you can use **Encrypted File System (EFS)** to protect files. Using EFS is similar to using permissions on files and folders. An intruder who gains unauthorized physical access to your encrypted files or folders will be prevented from reading them. If the intruder tries to open or copy your encrypted file or folder he or she will receive an access denied message.

Configuring each user's computer for remote network access or relying on users to configure their own computers for remote network access may produce serious support issues. In order to reduce support issues, Connection Manager can be used to customize a self-installing service profile for mobile clients. Clients can be automatically configured to connect to your network directly or to create a VPN connection from a remote location. It allows for more gradual control over settings such as idle timeout time, maximum session time, and encryption strength. The Connection Manager Administration Kit (CMAK) will be discussed in further detail in Chapter 12.

In some types of businesses, direct wire-based connections to the network are not always practical; for example, in a warehouse setting, or where users are counting physical inventory. In these types of situations, you will use a wireless local area network (WLAN). Using a wireless local area network allows portable computers to access network connections from any point where the organization has wireless access points. However, wireless networks have significant security risks. Wireless networking signals use radio waves to send and receive information. Anyone within a certain distance of a wireless access point can access, detect, and receive data sent to and from the wireless access point. To counter this security risk, wireless access points must be secured. This can require measures such as authentication, authorization, and encryption. Securing wireless access points will be discussed in detail in Chapter 11.

Activity 2-8: Discover Microsoft Security Guidance Kit Client Checklists

Time Required: 20 minutes

Objective: Discover checklists that can be used for configuring client machines.

Description: In this activity, you investigate the checklists available in the Microsoft Security Guidance Kit for client machine configuration.

1. Log on with your **AdminXX** account, where *XX* is your assigned student number.

2. Go to **Start**, **All Programs**, then open the Microsoft Security Guidance Kit program.

3. On the left side of the screen, choose **Enhance Workstation Security**.

4. When the screen comes up, on the right side, scroll down to the How to Guides and Checklists section, click on **Checklist: Security Settings for Windows XP Clients**. Read through the checklist. When finished, on the left side of the screen, choose **Up To Recommendation**.

5. When the screen comes up, on the right side, scroll down to the How to Guides and Checklists section, click on **Checklist: Securing Standalone Windows XP Clients**. Read through the checklist. When finished, exit the Guidance Kit.

Kiosks

Kiosks and e-mail computers require the highest level of security. Because of the nature of this type of computer, it should be tightly configured and have no direct connections to internal networks. Additional considerations might include ensuring there is no device access. In fact, you should consider using the **loopback policy**. The loopback policy is used to override the user-based Group Policy with the computer-based Group Policy. This makes the desktop configuration the same regardless of who logs on. In other words, each time a user logs into the machine, no matter which user it is, the desktop is exactly the same.

PLANNING SECURITY BASED ON CLIENT ROLES

Once you have determined the client roles and the level of access that the users will need, you can begin to plan the security for the machines. In this section we will discuss three specific areas of configuration:

- Network security zones
- Security settings
- Software restriction policies

Network security zones offer a flexible way to enforce your organization's Internet security policies, based on the origin of the Web content. Security zones enable you to group sites together, place them in a zone, and then assign a security level to each zone.

Security settings can be used with administrative templates in Group Policy to restrict the settings users can change. These settings enable administrators to configure the behavior and appearance of the desktop, including the operating system, components, and applications. This helps maintain consistency across the organization.

Software restriction policies provide administrators with a means to identify software and manage its capacity to run on local computers. These policies can also be used to protect computers running Windows XP Professional in an environment against malicious viruses and Trojan horse programs. Software restriction policy integrates with Active Directory or can be used on standalone computers.

Planning Network Zones for Computer Roles

Zone security is a method that enables you to divide online Web content into groups or zones. Specific Web sites can then be assigned to each zone, depending on the degree to which the content of each site is trusted. The Web content can be anything from an HTML or graphics file to a Microsoft ActiveX control, Java applet, or executable file. Depending on the role of the computer, it may need more or less in the way of Internet security configuration. This will depend on the types of Web sites that you want to allow your users to access. You can configure the following four zones for security:

- *Internet zone*—An **Internet zone** allows access to sites that are not included in other zones. You cannot add sites to this zone. By default, it is set to the medium security level.
- *Local intranet zone*—A **local intranet zone** consists of sites with a firewall or those specified to bypass the proxy server. By default, it is set to the medium security level.

- *Trusted zone*—A **Trusted zone** is intended for sites that can be trusted to never cause harm, such as those of business partners. By default, it is assigned the low security level.

- *Restricted*—A **Restricted zone** is allowed to perform only minimal, safe operations because the content is questionable. By default, it is assigned the high security level.

After the zone is decided on, a security level is then assigned to each zone. The security level can be set at various levels from low through custom. This defines the level of browser access to Web content. In this way, security zones can control access to a site based on the zone in which the site is located and the level of trust assigned to that zone. A custom level of security can also be assigned, which enables you to assign administrator-approved control and to configure settings for ActiveX controls, downloading and installation, scripting, password authentication, cross-frame security, and Java capabilities. These settings can be configured either through Group Policy, as shown in Figure 2-9; through the Internet Explorer Customization Wizard; or through the Internet Explorer Administration Kit 6 (IEAK) Profile Manager. The security levels on each zone can be set to high, medium, medium-low, low, or custom.

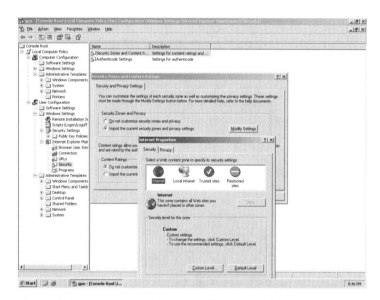

Figure 2-9 Configuration screen for network zones

The configuration of the local intranet zone requires that you have a good understanding of your existing network configuration, proxy servers, and firewalls. Because there is no method for automatically detecting your firewall, and because the zone is configured based on your specific settings, the local intranet zone cannot be guaranteed to match your network configuration. Proxy servers should be configured not to resolve an external DNS name to this zone.

PLANNING AND CONFIGURING SECURITY SETTINGS

Windows Server 2003 has more than 220 new administrative policies that were not previously available on Windows 2000. This gives you a wide range of configuration options. Group Policy administrative templates define how the policy settings appear. You can set restrictions on either a per-computer basis to apply to any user on the computer or on a per-user basis. These .adm files are text files, called **administrative templates**. They provide policy information for the items that are under the Administrative Templates folder in the console tree of the Group Policy snap-in. Figure 2-10 illustrates this concept. An .adm file has a hierarchical structure of categories and subcategories that define how the policy settings appear. It also contains the following information:

- Registry location that corresponds to the setting

- Value options or restrictions that are associated with the setting

- Setting default values

- An explanation of what the setting does

- The versions of Windows that is supported by the setting

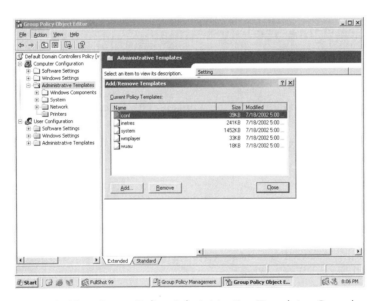

Figure 2-10   Group Policy Administrative Templates Console

These administrative template files are stored in two locations by default: inside GPOs in the Sysvol folder and in the Windows\inf directory on the local computer. Local .adm files are stored on the computer where you run Group Policy Object Editor and domain-based .adm files are stored on the Sysvol. These files have .adm extensions. The local administrative templates and their uses are:

- *System.adm*—Contains policy settings to configure the operating system. It is loaded by default in Windows Server 2000, XP, and Server 2003.

- *Wmplayer.adm*—Contains policy settings to configure Windows Media Player. It is loaded by default in Windows XP and Server 2003. Note: Wmplayer.adm is not available on 64-bit versions of Windows XP or the Server 2003 family.

- *Inetres.adm*—Contains policy settings to configure Internet Explorer. It is loaded by default in Windows 2000 Server, XP, and Server 2003.

- *Conf.adm*—Contains policy settings to configure NetMeeting. It is loaded by default in Windows 2000 Server, XP, and Server 2003. Note: Conf.adm is not available on 64-bit versions of Windows XP or the Server 2003 family.

- *Wuau.adm*—Contains policy settings to configure Windows Update. It is loaded by default in Windows 2000 Service Pack 3 (SP3), XP Service Pack 1 (SP1), and Server 2003.

The Administrative templates for Group Policy contain all registry-based policy information. Group Policy user configurations are saved in *HKEY_CURRENT_USER* and computer configurations are saved in *HKEY_LOCAL_MACHINE* either under *\Software\Policies* or *\Software\Microsoft\Windows\CurrentVersion\Policies*.

ACTIVITY

Activity 2-9: Configure Security Settings

Time Required: 45 minutes

Objective: Practice working with security settings.

Description: In this activity, you will practice working with security settings by importing a template, then evaluating the settings.

1. Log on with your **AdminXX** account, where *XX* is your assigned student number.

2. Open Group Policy Management Console by clicking **Start**, **Administrative Tools**, **Group Policy Management**.

3. Click the **Members Server Baseline Policy** so that it is highlighted.

4. Go to the top menu bar and Choose **Action**, **Edit**.

5. Highlight **Administrative Templates**. Go to the top menu bar and choose **Action**, **Add/Remove Templates**.

6. When the **Add/Remove Templates** window pops up, click **Add**.

7. Select the **office10.adm** template from the Policy Templates window. This template is one that you will find in the Microsoft Security Guidance Kit. To find it, locate the directory where you installed the kit, go to the Job Aids folder, Windows XP Security Guide, Tools and Templates folder, Security Guide, Administrative Templates. Choose the **OFFICE10.ADM** templates, then click **Open**, as shown in Figure 2-11.

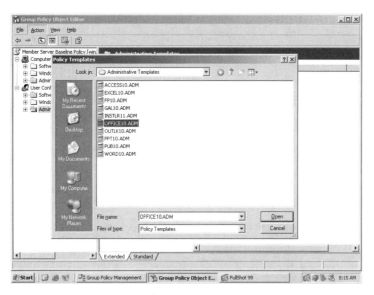

Figure 2-11   Importing the System.adm template Group Policy Management Console window

8. After the template is imported, be sure it appears in the Add/Remove Templates window. Click **Close**.

9. Expand the **Microsoft Office XP** folder.

10. Open the **Security Settings** folder and review the settings that can be enabled.

11. Discuss in class which settings you would change in the template and why you would do so.

12. When finished close the Group Policy window.

PLANNING AND CONFIGURING SOFTWARE RESTRICTION POLICIES

Software restriction policies are used to maintain more granular control over who receives what software. Software restriction policies specify the software that is allowed to run. Some of the features include controlling which programs can run on your computer, permitting users to run only specific files on multiple-user computers, and preventing any files from running on your local computer, OU, site, or domain should you get a virus infection. Software restriction policies provide a policy-based method to enforce decisions about whether the software can run, thereby forcing users to follow the parameters that are set by administrators. Keep in mind that software restriction policies are not meant to replace antivirus software. When you use software restriction policies, you can identify and specify the software that is allowed to run so that you can protect your computer environment from untrusted code. In GPO, you can define a default security level of Unrestricted or

Disallowed so that software is either allowed or not allowed to run by default. To create exceptions to this default security level, you can create rules for specific software. You can create the following types of rules:

- *Hash rules*—You can use precalculated hash values or you can create a hash rule to prevent malicious software such as viruses and Trojan horses from running.

- *Certificate rules*—Certificate rules are not turned on by default. To do so, change the Registry key HKEY_LOCAL_MACHINE\SOFTWARE\Policies\Microsoft\ Windows\Safer\CodeIdentifiers\Authenticode Enabled from 0 to 1.

- *Path rules*—Specifies a file or folder. Use caution when setting the security level to Disallowed on folders. This can adversely affect the operation of your operating system.

- *Internet zone rules*—Zone rules apply to Windows Installer packages only.

This policy can apply to all of the computers or to individual users. Software restriction policies provide a number of ways to identify software, and they provide a policy-based infrastructure to enforce decisions about whether the software can run. With software restriction policies, users must follow the guidelines that are set up by administrators when they run programs. You can also apply software restriction policies to specific users when they log on to a specific computer by using the loopback Group Policy setting. If you do not want the software restriction policies to apply to local administrators, you can configure this by selecting the All Users Except Local Administrators option under the Enforcement object of Group Policy, as shown in Figure 2-12.

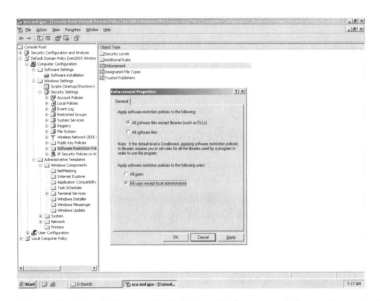

Figure 2-12 Software Restrictions Enforcement Properties window

For software restriction policies to take effect, users must update the policy settings by logging off from and then logging on to their computers.

TIP

2

ACTIVITY

Activity 2-10: Working with Software Restriction Policies

Time Required: 20 minutes

Objective: Practice working with software restriction policies.

Description: In this activity, you will enable certificates hash rules for software restriction policies.

1. Log on with your **AdminXX** account, where *XX* is your assigned student number.

2. Click **Start**, **Run**, in the Run box, type **Regedit**, then press **Enter**.

3. Expand the **Hkey_Local_Machine** key, expand the **software** key, expand the **policies** key, expand the **Microsoft** key, expand the **Windows** key, then expand the **safer** key.

4. Highlight the **codeidentifiers** key so that the keys are shown.

5. Double-click the **authenticodeenabled** key.

6. Change the number in the Value data box from **0** to **1**.

7. Click **OK** and close the Registry Editor.

CHAPTER SUMMARY

- Services such as DNS, RADIUS, LDAP, DHCP, and PKI are known as network infrastructure services. Infrastructure services are often spread across various platforms and internal departments, making them difficult to secure against risks.

- Although internal DNS servers can be less susceptible to attacks than external DNS servers, they still need to be secured. In order to stop outside intruders from accessing the internal network of your company, use separate DNS servers for internal and Internet name resolution.

- File and print servers provide the most essential services for the network; therefore, they can be a challenge to secure. They often provide services for applications that require protocols such as NetBIOS, SMB (Server Message Block), and CIFS (Common Internet File System).

- A bastion host is a publicly accessible computer located on the perimeter network. Bastion hosts must be secured as much as possible to maximize their availability and yet minimize the chance of their being compromised.

❑ In order to provide complete security for Web servers and applications within an organization's corporate intranet, all Internet Information Services (IIS) servers, Web sites, and applications should be protected from client computers that can connect to them.

❑ When configuring baseline security templates for desktops, the first task is to identify your users by workgroup, job function, or a combination of both. You can then identify the different types of resources that users might need access to, such as departmental or job-specific data. This step allows you to plan for different levels of access.

❑ The Legacy Client template is the lowest security lockdown level. The Enterprise Client environment is designed to provide solid security for the organization. The High Security environment is the highest lockdown level; in this environment the settings are very restrictive.

❑ Network security zones offer a flexible way to enforce your organization's Internet security policies, based on the origin of the Web content. Security zones enable you to group sites together, place them in a zone, and then assign a security level to each zone.

❑ Security settings can be used with administrative templates in Group Policy to restrict the settings users can change. These settings enable administrators to configure the behavior and appearance of the desktop, including the operating system, components, and applications.

❑ Software restriction policies provide administrators with a means to identify software and manage its capacity to run on local computers. These policies can also be used to protect computers running Windows XP Professional in an environment against malicious viruses and Trojan horse programs.

Key Terms

administrative templates — Templates that define how the policy settings appear. You can set restrictions on either a per-computer basis to apply to any user on the computer or on a per-user basis.

bastion host — A publicly accessible computer located on a perimeter network. You may also hear this referred to as the DMZ (demilitarized zone), or screened subnet.

domain — An administrative unit that groups together various capabilities for management convenience.

domain controller — A computer that stores directory data for Active Directory and manages communication between users and domains. This includes functions such as user logon processes, authentication, and directory searches.

Domain Name System (DNS) — A hierarchical database that contains mappings of domain names to IP addresses.

Domain Name System (DNS) servers — Network servers that resolve IP addresses to domain names so that names can be used to locate resources instead of having to know the IP addresses.

Dynamic Host Control Protocol (DHCP) — A service that offers dynamic configuration of IP addresses and related information to clients.

Encrypted File System (EFS) — A method whereby users can encrypt files and folders on an NTFS volume disk to keep them safe from access by intruders.

Enterprise Client — Template settings that are designed to work in an Active Directory domain with member servers and domain controllers running Windows Server 2003 and clients running Windows 2000.

file server — A server that provides the most essential services for the network; therefore, they can be a challenge to secure. They often provide services for applications that require protocols such as NetBIOS, SMB (Server Message Block), and CIFS (Common Internet File System).

File Transfer Protocol (FTP) servers — Servers that are used for posting files. They do not have Web pages, only a place to post and take files.

Forest — One or more Active Directory domains that share a schema and global catalog.

High Security — Template settings that are designed to work in the same environment as the enterprise client settings; however, the High Security settings are extremely restrictive and many applications may not function.

IIS lockdown tool — The IIS Lockdown tool turns off unnecessary features to better protect the server from attackers.

Internet zone — This zone allows access to sites that are not included in other zones By default, it is set to the medium security level.

kiosk — A publicly accessible computer used for e-mail or other Internet access. Because of the nature of this type of computer, it should be tightly configured and have no direct connections to internal networks.

Legacy Client — Template settings that are designed to work with member servers and domain controllers running Windows Server 2003, and clients running Microsoft Windows 98, Windows NT 4.0, and later.

Lightweight Directory Access Protocol (LDAP) — The primary access protocol for Active Directory.

local Intranet zone — This zone consists of sites with a firewall or those specified to bypass the proxy server. By default, it is set to the medium security level.

Loopback policy — A special policy used to override user-based Group Policy with computer-based Group Policy Network.

member server — A server that does not contain a configuration file. One or more servers can operate as member servers.

network infrastructure services — These services connect production applications to the actual network and store information about network components such as user access privileges and applications on the network. Services such as DNS, RADIUS, LDAP, DHCP, and PKI are known as network infrastructure services.

Network News Transfer Protocol (NNTP) servers — Servers that are used for newsgroup postings.

network security zones — A flexible way to enforce your organization's Internet security policies and Web content.

Organizational unit — Active Directory containers where you can place users, groups, computers, and other organizational units.

print server — A computer that is dedicated to managing the printers on a network. The print server can be any computer on the network.

Restricted zone — This zone is allowed to perform only minimal, safe operations because the content is questionable.

security settings — These settings enable administrators to configure the behavior and appearance of the desktop, including the operating system, components, and applications. They can be used with administrative templates in Group Policy to restrict the settings users can change.

Simple Mail Transport Protocol (SMTP) servers — Servers that are used to store and forward electronic mail.

software restriction policies — A method whereby you can control which programs run on your computer, permitting users to run only specific files on multiple-user computers, and can prevent any files from running on your local computer, your organizational unit, your site, or your domain should you get a virus infection.

Trusted zone — This zone is intended for sites that can be trusted to never cause harm, such as those of business partners.

URLScan — A tool that screens incoming requests to an IIS Web server against a ruleset.

virtual private network (VPN) — An extension of a private network that allows for traffic to be encapsulated, encrypted, and authenticated across public networks such as the Internet.

Review Questions

1. Which of the following is the lowest lockdown level of security for baseline templates?

   a. High Security

   b. Legacy Client

   c. Enterprise Client

   d. Baseline Client

2. Which of the following is the recommended template for Windows Server 2003 print servers?

   a. Enterprise Client - Member Server

   b. High Security - Bastion Host

   c. Legacy Client - Member Server

   d. Enterprise Client - Print Server

2

3. Which of the following should you adhere to when you plan the security of a bastion host? (Choose all that apply.)

   a. Limit the accounts that can be used to log on to a bastion host server console. This will help prevent unauthorized access to a server's file system and system services.

   b. All services not required by the operating system and those not essential to the proper operation of the bastion host's role should be disabled.

   c. Always configure services to run under the security context of a domain account.

   d. Internet Protocol Security (IPSec) filters can provide an effective means for enhancing the level of security required for servers. Block ports by using IPSec filters.

4. What is a publicly accessible computer located on the perimeter network that also may be referred to as the DMZ (demilitarized zone), or screened subnet?

   a. File server

   b. IAS server

   c. Bastion host

   d. Domain controller

5. Properly planning an organization's security structure will result in a much more secure Active Directory design for the organization. To achieve these results, careful planning of which of the following elements is needed? (Choose all that apply.)

   a. Domains

   b. Forests

   c. User directories

   d. Organizational units

6. Which of the following store directory data for Active Directory and manage communication between users and domains? (Choose all that apply.)

   a. Print servers

   b. Domain controllers

   c. IIS servers

   d. Bastion hosts

7. What happens if you do not properly configure and test the GPO before linking it to the Domain Controllers OU?

   a. Nothing

   b. It could adversely affect the operation of the domain.

   c. It will cause the system to crash.

   d. It could delete the whole Active Directory structure.

8. Which of the following services do domain controllers provide? (Choose three)

    a. User logon processes

    b. Web services

    c. Authentication

    d. Directory searches

9. Which of the following are network infrastructure services? (Choose all that apply.)

    a. PKI

    b. DNS

    c. RADIUS

    d. HTTP

10. Which of the following is a good reason why DHCP servers need to be secure? (Choose all that apply.)

    a. DHCP is an infrastructure server and therefore does not need to be secured.

    b. DHCP allows for anonymous connections; therefore, anyone can connect.

    c. DHCP is an unauthenticated protocol; a user can connect to the network without providing credentials.

    d. An unauthenticated user can obtain a lease from any available DHCP server.

11. Additional security measures that should be performed on an IIS server would include which of the following? (Choose three.)

    a. Installing only necessary components

    b. Enabling IAS

    c. Securing well-known accounts

    d. Placing content on a dedicated disk volume

12. The Enterprise Client environment is designed to provide solid security for the organization. Which of the following operating systems does it support ? (Choose all that apply.)

    a. Windows Server 2003

    b. Windows 2000 Professional

    c. Windows 98 SE

    d. Windows XP Professional

13. Security environment is the highest lockdown level. In this environment the settings are very restrictive. Which of the following are downsides of using this type of template? (Choose all that apply)

    a. The servers may encounter some impact on performance.

    b. The network will be more secure.

c. Managing the servers will be more challenging.

d. Many applications might not function with them.

14. Zone security is a method that enables you to divide online Web content into groups or zones. Specific Web sites can then be assigned to each zone, depending on the degree to which the content of each site is trusted. Which of the following are security zones? (Choose all that apply.)

a. Internet zone

b. Extranet zone

c. Local Intranet zone

d. Trusted zone

15. On which of the following types of client computers are you likely to find a loop-back policy?

a. Kiosks and e-mail computers

b. Developer computers

c. Mobile computers

d. Desktop computers

16. Which of the following are some of the most common uses for a bastion hosts? (Choose all that apply.)

a. File Transfer Protocol (FTP) servers

b. Domain controllers

c. Web servers

d. Domain Name System (DNS) servers

17. To which of the following types of server roles can you not apply Group Policy?

a. Domain controllers

b. Bastion hosts

c. Print servers

d. Infrastructure servers

18. Which of the following are administrative templates? (Choose all that apply)

a. Wmplayer.adm

b. Differential.adm

c. Inetres.adm

d. System.adm

19. Administrative Templates are what kind of files?

    a. Text files

    b. Zip files

    c. .pdf files

    d. .tar files

20. To create exceptions to software restriction policies, you can create rules for specific software. Which of the following are types of rules that you can create? (Choose all that apply.)

    a. Hash rules

    b. Path rules

    c. Certificate rules

    d. Internet zone rules

21. On which of the following types of client computers would you most likely use the Connection Manager Administration Kit (CMAK)?

    a. Desktops

    b. Developers computers

    c. Mobile or laptops

    d. Kiosks

22. Which of the following client computers require(s) the highest level of security?

    a. Developers computers

    b. Mobile or laptops

    c. Kiosks and e-mail computers

    d. Desktops

23. Which of the following security changes should be made to the baseline server template for servers that will run DHCP? (Choose all that apply.)

    a. Enhance the level of security on servers by using IPSec filters to block unnecessary ports.

    b. DHCP logging should be configured so that a more detailed log is available.

    c. Use the 80/20 rule by splitting DHCP server scopes between servers so that 80% of the addresses are distributed by one DHCP server and 20% by another.

    d. Do not rename the Administrator and Guest accounts or use different names and passwords on each server.

24. Which of the following are valid exceptions for software restriction policies? (Choose all that apply.)

    a. Hash

    b. Certificate

2

    c. Authentication

    d. Path

25. Which of the following would you use to control the types of software available to users?

    a. Administrative templates

    b. Network zones

    c. Security settings

    d. Software restriction policies

CASE PROJECTS

Case Project 2-1

Evergrow is a large, multinational company that is currently running an Active Directory domain with member servers and domain controllers running Windows Server 2003. All client machines are currently running Windows XP. Management would like to lock down the network now that they are growing. It is your job as the network administrator to make a recommendation for securing your environment. Choose a Microsoft model outlining the baseline templates that you would use for the servers. Your network consists of five infrastructure servers, two domain controllers, a print server, two Web servers, and two e-mail servers.

Case Project 2-2

You are the network administrator at Evergrow. You are currently using Windows 2000 Server with Windows 2000 Professional workstations and would like to upgrade to Windows 2003. You know that any loss or compromise of a domain controller in the environment could be devastating to clients, other servers, and other devices or applications that rely on the domain controller for authentication and services. Make a case for upgrading to Windows 2003 based on the settings that are configured with the Enterprise Client template. Explain how this makes the environment more secure.

Case Project 2-3

Management has decided that they will take your recommendation and allow for the upgrading of the servers to Windows 2003. Before they do though, they want to know about locking down the client computers. They want to know exactly how you can secure the mobile sales force's computers. Prepare a short report consisting of several paragraphs to submit to management based on your recommendations for a laptop and mobile lockdown plan. Include the use of the Connection Manager Administration Kit (CMAK) in your recommendation.

Case Project 2-4

You are the network administrator at Evergrow. You are currently using Windows Server 2003, and all client machines are running Windows XP. You are having some issues with the users installing their own software. You have also discovered that most of it is unlicensed, and some of the more experienced users have installed hacking tools. How will you fix this situation? Prepare a report on the various ways that you can lock down the desktops and list the tools that you would use.

Case Project 2-5

You are the network administrator at Evergrow. Management has asked you to evaluate the Perimeter Network Security, because there is the possibility that the company will merge with another organization three times its size. Currently you have 10 servers in the DMZ. If the merger were to happen, you would end up with about 30 servers in the DMZ. Formulate a plan on how to create a baseline server, then note what template you would use and what additional steps you would take to lock down the servers.

3

DEPLOYING AND MANAGING SECURITY POLICIES

After reading this chapter, you will be able to:

- Analyze current security settings by using various methods
- Use predefined security templates
- Customize security template settings
- Deploy security templates using various methods

Entering a position where a network was run by someone else, or the environment is not locked down properly, can be a daunting situation. How do you know if a machine is secure? Once you lock down a machine, how can you be sure that it stays that way? What if you need to temporarily change security levels so that you can immediately resolve an administration or network issue? Often these types of situations present issues for a network administrator because temporary changes can go unnoticed or can be forgotten about especially in a situation where you are resolving an immediate need. Changes in policy can mean that the computers on the network no longer meet the requirements for enterprise security, and you are faced with making sure that they all meet these new standards.

In order to help answer these questions and address the issues they present, Microsoft has developed some very useful tools. In this chapter we will explore and discuss the various methods that you can use not only to analyze the security on a machine but also security templates and policies that can be implemented to be sure that your network is kept in a secure state. Some of the tools you will become familiar with are Security and Configuration Analysis and Microsoft Baseline Security Analyzer. You will also learn about several command-line utilities that can be used to determine the quality of security on a machine.

ANALYZING CURRENT SECURITY CONFIGURATION

The state of an operating system and applications on a computer is dynamic, meaning that it is constantly changing. Our users tend to think of their work computer more as their own personal computer than as a tool for performing work. When this happens, our environment frequently ends up with a variety of different desktops, applications, and potential security concerns. If each computer is regularly analyzed, the network administrator can track and ensure a sufficient level of security on each computer, being sure that the computers are in compliance with company policy. By having a process in place, an administrator can also detect any security flaws that may occur in the system and fine-tune the security levels.

Security Configuration and Analysis (SCA) is a tool used to analyze security configurations and resolve security discrepancies. SCA enables you to quickly review security analysis results. In the analysis, it presents recommendations for fixing current system settings and uses colored flags to note any areas where the current settings do not match the proposed level of security. It performs the security analysis by comparing the current state of system security against an organization's defined standard for security for a given machine or class of machines or analysis database. In order to create the analysis database, SCA uses at least one security template.

 If you choose to import more than one security template, the database will merge the various templates and create a composite template. Conflicts are resolved in order of import. The last template that is imported takes precedence.

NOTE

You can use the SCA tool through the MMC. The SCA snap-in allows the analysis of current system settings against a baseline template. Performing this analysis allows you to do the following:

- Identify security holes that exist in the current configuration
- Identify the changes that a potential security policy will make to a system before actually deploying the security policy
- Identify differences between current system settings and a predefined security policy

If you create a custom security template, the SCA tools will allow you to compare your system's current settings against the settings that are defined by the security template that you created. If the custom security template defines a more secure configuration than the current settings provide, the analysis will identify the security holes that exist in the current system configuration, as well as the changes that will take place if the custom template is used to configure the system. The changes you make will not affect system security. They will affect only the analysis database because the purpose of the tool is to help you see how changes in the settings will affect the security of the computer. Table 3-1 shows the flags that are encountered when SCA is run.

Table 3-1 Security configuration and analysis flags

Flag	Flag Meaning
Red X	The entry is defined in the analysis database and on the system, but the security setting values do not match.
Green check	The entry is defined in the analysis database and on the system, and the setting values match.
Question mark	The entry is not defined in the analysis database and, therefore, was not analyzed.
Exclamation point	This item is defined in the analysis database but does not exist on the actual system.
No highlight	The item is not defined in the analysis database or on the system.

 NOTE

If an entry is not analyzed, it may be that it was not defined in the analysis database or that the user who is running the analysis may not have sufficient permission to perform analysis on a specific object or area.

You can choose to accept the current settings. Should this option be chosen, the corresponding value in the base configuration is modified to match the base configuration settings. If you change the system setting to match the base configuration, the change will be reflected when you configure the system with Security Configuration and Analysis.

 ACTIVITY

Activity 3-1: Analyze Security Settings

Time Required: 45 minutes

Objective: Practice working with Security Configuration and Analysis.

Description: In this activity, you will use the Security Configuration and Analysis MMC snap-in, then evaluate the settings on your computer.

1. Log on with your **AdminXX** account, where *XX* is your assigned student number.

2. In the Run dialog box, type: **mmc /s**.

3. On the File menu, click **Add\Remove Snap-in**, then click **Add**.

4. In Available Standalone Snap-ins, select **Security Configuration and Analysis**.

5. Click **Add**, click **Close**, and then click **OK**.

6. Right-click the **Security Configuration and Analysis** item shown on the left side of the screen.

7. Click **Open Database**. Type **test1** in the database name text box, and then click **Open**.

8. Select the **Enterprise client – Domain Controller** template to import, then click **Open**, as shown in the Figure 3-1.

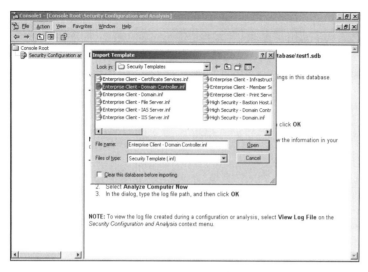

Figure 3-1   Importing a security template using the Security Configuration and Analysis Console

9. Analyze your computer security settings by right-clicking the **Security Configuration and Analysis** item on the left side of the screen.

10. Select **Analyze Computer Now**.

11. In the dialog box, type a log file path such as **D:\windows\security\logs**, then click **OK**.

12. Once the analysis is completed, expand the policies and review the settings. Your screen should look similar to the one in the Figure 3-2.

13. Close the **Security and Analysis MMC**.

14. Open the log file by going to the path where you stored the log file, such as D:\windows\security\logs. Open test1.log. Your file should look like the one in Figure 3-3.

TIP   If you are applying security settings on a single computer running Windows 2000 or Windows Server 2003, the best method to use is the SCA console. This method allows you to see the effects of the template settings before they are applied. If you require frequent analysis of a large number of computers, as with a domain-based infrastructure, use the **Secedit.exe** command prompt tool, which is discussed later in this chapter.

Here are some best practices recommended by Microsoft for using the SCA snap-in:

■ Use Security Configuration and Analysis only to configure security areas not affected by Group Policy settings. This includes areas such as security on local files

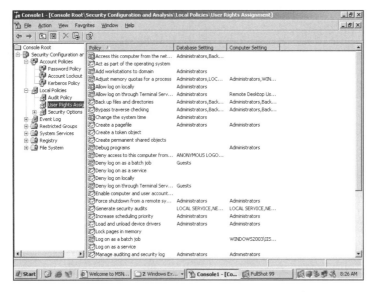

Figure 3-2   Analysis results using the Security Configuration and Analysis Console

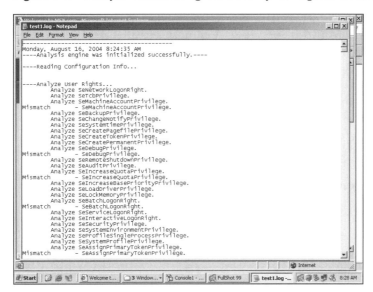

Figure 3-3   Security Configuration and Analysis log file

and folders, registry keys, and system services. Otherwise, Group Policy settings will override the local settings.

- Do not use Security Configuration and Analysis when you are configuring security for a domain or an organizational unit. Otherwise, you must configure each client individually. In that case, you can:

- Use security templates to create a template and apply it to the appropriate Group Policy Object.

- Use the Security Settings extension to Group Policy to edit individual security settings on a Group Policy Object.

You should use Configure Computer Now only to modify security areas not affected by Group Policy settings, such as security on local files and folders, registry keys, and system services. Otherwise, when the Group Policy settings are applied, The secuirty settings in the template will take precedence over local settings—such as account policies. In general, do not use Configure Computer Now when you are analyzing security for domain-based clients, because you will have to configure each client individually. In this case, you should return to the security templates, modify the template, and reapply it to the appropriate Group Policy Object.

Using Microsoft Baseline Security Analyzer

The **Microsoft Baseline Security Analyzer (MBSA)** is a tool that is used to scan one or more Windows-based computers for common security holes. The MBSA scans a Windows-based computer and checks the operating system and other installed components for security along with their current status for recommended security updates. The difference between the SCA and MBSA is that the SCA compares settings against a security template, whereas MBSA compares a computer's settings against Microsoft's released patches and listed vulnerabilities. MBSA runs on Windows 2000, Windows XP, and Windows Server 2003 systems. Several parts of the scan are optional and can be turned on or off in the interface before scanning a computer. It can also scan multiple and remote computers for common security vulnerabilities and missing security updates for the following Microsoft products:

- Windows NT 4.0

- Windows 2000

- Windows XP

- Windows Server 2003

- Internet Information Services 4.0, 5.0, and 6.0

- SQL Server 7.0 and SQL Server 2000

- Internet Explorer 5.01 and later

- Exchange 5.5 and 2000

- Windows Media Player 6.4 and later

- Office 2000 and Office XP

Table 3-2 lists the security checks that MBSA performs. The most current version is MBSA Version 1.2.1. MBSA 1.2.1 will also scan for missing security updates for these additional products:

- Microsoft Data Access Components (MDAC)
- MSXML
- Microsoft Virtual Machine
- Commerce Server
- Content Management Server
- BizTalk Server
- Host Integration Server

NOTE MBSA 1.2.1 is required for Windows XP SP2 compatibility. Users of Windows XP Service Pack 2 will need to update their MBSA to version 1.2.1 for compatibility and better integration with SP2 security improvements.

Table 3-2 MBSA security checks

Windows OS Checks	IIS Checks	SQL Checks
Missing security updates and service packs	IIS Lockdown tool (version 2.1) run	Administrators group belongs to sysadmin role
Expired account passwords	IIS sample applications installed	CmdExec role is restricted to sysadmin only
File system type on hard disks	Parent paths enabled	SQL Server running on a domain controller
Autologon feature enabled	Missing IIS security updates	sa account password exposed
Guest account enabled	IIS Admin virtual folder installed	SQL installation folders access permissions
RestrictAnonymous registry key settings	MSADC and Scripts virtual directories installed	Guest account has database access
Number of local Administrator accounts	IIS logging enabled	Everyone group has access to SQL Registry keys
Blank and/or simple local user account passwords	IIS running on a domain controller	SQL service accounts are members of the local admin
Unnecessary services running	N/A	SQL accounts have blank or simple passwords
Lists the shares present	N/A	Missing SQL security updates
Auditing enabled	N/A	SQL Server authentication mode type
Windows version running	N/A	Number of sysadmin role members

MBSA checks the following desktop application parameters:

- Internet Explorer security zone settings per local user
- Outlook security zone settings per local user
- Office products security zone settings per local user

Windows XP SP2 users who are running MBSA 1.2 should be automatically notified when they run the tool from the Start menu with an Internet connection. In order for the MBSA tool to be run on multiple machines or remotely, the Server service, Remote Registry service, and File & Print Sharing must be enabled.

ACTIVITY

Activity 3-2: Using Microsoft Baseline Security Analyzer

Time Required: 60 minutes

Objective: Practice working with the Microsoft Baseline Security Analyzer Graphical User Interface.

Description: In this activity, you will practice working with the Microsoft Baseline Security Analyzer Graphical User Interface.

1. Log on with your **AdminXX** account, where *XX* is your assigned student number.

2. Open an Internet connection.

3. You will now download Microsoft Baseline Security Analyzer V1.2. Go to *www.microsoft.com/technet/security/tools/mbsahome.mspx*.

4. The MBSA can be installed in one of four languages; choose the language appropriate for your usage and install the MBSA by double-clicking the **MSBAsetup.msi** file.

5. On the Welcome screen, click **Next**. On the License Agreement screen, select **I accept the license agreement**. Click **Next**.

6. Select the destination folder for the installation. The default location is in the root directory, program files. Click **Next**.

7. On the start installation screen, click **Install**. Once the installation is complete, click **OK**.

8. Run the MBSA program by double-clicking the shortcut on your desktop.

9. Choose the **scan a computer** option. The screen shown in Figure 3-4 appears.

10. You will now scan your own computer. Choose the **Start scan** option on the bottom of the screen.

11. Notice that the computer downloads the security update information from Microsoft before it starts the scan. When you run the analyzer, the program will connect to Microsoft's site to update the file. Once the update is complete, the scan can be run.

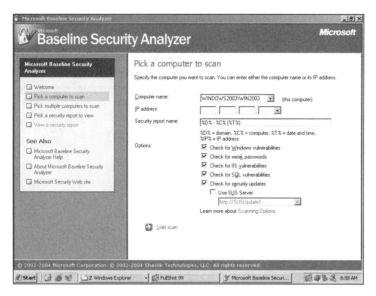

Figure 3-4   Picking a computer to scan screen of Microsoft Baseline Security Analyzer

12. After the file is updated, the program scans the computer. When finished, it will display the report, as shown in Figure 3-5.

13. Look through the report. Evaluate the issues found. How would you resolve the issues shown on the report?

14. After deciding how to resolve the issues, spend time doing so and then rescan the computer.

MBSA uses ports 138 and 139 to perform its scans and requires administrator privileges on the computer that you scan.

CAUTION   Opening ports 138 and 139 (NetBIOS) is considered a security risk, and these ports are usually closed on firewalls. If the machine you use has Internet access, the latest security XML file will be downloaded automatically, if needed. If your computer does not have Internet access, you need to download the latest XML file using the signed CAB at the following location: *http://download.microsoft. com/download/xml/security/1.0/NT5/EN-US/mssecure.cab*. The CAB file is signed to ensure that it has not been modified. You must uncompress it and store it in the same folder where MBSA is stored.

Using Command-Line Tools

The MBSA command-line interface can perform two types of scans: MBSA scans and HFNetChk scans. The MBSA scan can be run from the command line using the **mbsacli.exe command**. The HFNetChk scan will check for missing security updates and then display the results in the command-line window. The tool can be run from the

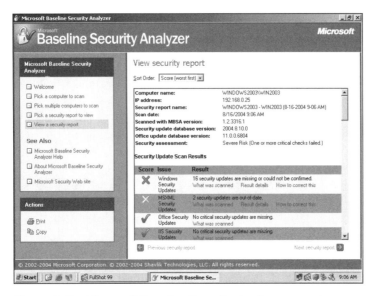

Figure 3-5 Microsoft Baseline Security Analyzer report screen

command line using the mbsacli.exe /hf command followed by any of the parameters. The default installation directory is \Program Files\Microsoft Baseline Security Analyzer\. You need to run commands from this directory because MBSA does not create an environment variable for you. The use of HFNetChk, its options, its settings, and the command-line tools used in troubleshooting will be explained in greater detail in Chapter 6. Table 3-3 shows the most common parameters that can be used with Mbsacli.exe. The user requesting a scan must be an administrator on the target machine.

Table 3-3 Commonly used Mbsacli.exe command-line parameters

Switch	Description
Msbacli.exe with no switch	Scans the local computer
/c domainname\computername	Scans the computer named
/i xxx.xxx.xxx.xxx	Scans the IP address specified
/r xxx.xxx.xxx.xxx-xxx.xxx.xxx.xxx	Scans the IP address range specified
/d domainname	Scans the domain named
/n IIS	No IIS checks
/n OS	No Windows operating system checks
/n Password	No password checks
/n SQL	No SQL checks
/n Updates	No security update checks
/sus SUS server	Checks for security updates that are approved at the specified SUS server
/s 1	Suppresses security update check notes
/s 2	Suppresses security update check notes and warnings

Table 3-3   Commonly used Mbsacli.exe command-line parameters (continued)

Switch	Description
/nosum	Will not test file checksums on security updates
/o domain - computername	Specifies the output file name template
/e	Lists errors from the last scan
/l	Lists the reports available
/ls	Lists the reports from the last scan
/lr report name	Displays an overview report
/ld report name	Displays a detailed report

When running the MBSA from a command line, the options /u (username) and /p (password) can be used to specify the username to run the scan if it is not being run under the Administrator account. Do not store usernames and passwords in text files such as command files or scripts. An individual security report is created for each computer scanned when multiple computers are scanned. Reports from a scan are stored under the *%userprofile%*\SecurityScans folder on the computer on which the MSBA tool is installed.

It is important to know the differences between the default options of the two MBSA clients: the GUI tool, Mbsa.exe, and the command-line tool, Mbsacli.exe. The MBSA GUI calls /nosum, /v, and /baseline by default. The details for these options are:

- *   /nosum*—Security update checks will not test file checksums
- *   /v*—Displays security update reason codes
- *   /baseline*—Checks only for baseline security updates

The MBSA command line calls no options and runs a default scan. In the next activity you will run a scan similar to this one so that you can better understand how this works.

ACTIVITY

Activity 3-3: Using Microsoft Baseline Security Analyzer from a Command Line

Time Required: 20 minutes

Objective: Use Microsoft Baseline Security Analyzer from a command line.

Description: In this activity, you will practice using Microsoft Baseline Security Analyzer from a command line.

1. Log on with your **AdminXX** account, where *XX* is your assigned student number.

2. Click **Start**, **Run**, then type **cmd** in the run box. Using the command line, go to the directory where the Microsoft Baseline Security Analyzer is installed. For example: D:\Program Files\ Microsoft Baseline Security Analyzer.

3. Type **mbsacli.exe**. Notice that the program connects to the Microsoft site to update the file shown in Figure 3-6.

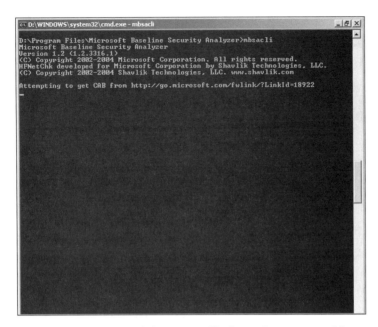

Figure 3-6   Update of the MBSA file from the command line

4. Next look at the command-line parameters that are available with Mbsacli.exe. Type mbsacli.exe /?|more. Your screen should look like the one in Figure 3-7.

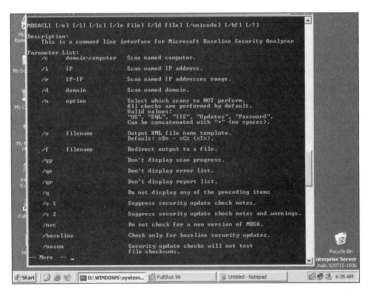

Figure 3-7   MBSA parameters available using the command line

3

5. At the end of the last line when the | more is displayed, hit **Enter** until you come to the end of the file. Using Enter displays the commands one line at a time. For a faster scroll, you can hit the spacebar, which will advance the commands a page at a time. Study the examples on how to use the parameters.

6. You will now scan your computer.

7. At the command line type **mbsacli.exe /hf -v -nosum -f d:\results.txt**, where D: is the drive in which you have installed the MBSA tool.

8. When the scan is complete, open the results.txt file and look at the results. Practice using the command with different parameters. When finished, close the command prompt window by typing **exit**.

TIP

If you're unsure of the proper command to use, you can request help with the options on the /hf switch by entering Mbsacli /hf -?

WORKING WITH SECURITY TEMPLATES

With the **Security Templates snap-in**, you can create a security policy for your network or computer by using security templates. A **security template** is a text file that represents a security configuration. You can apply a security template to the local computer, import a security template to Group Policy, or use a security template to analyze security. You can use a predefined security template that is included in Windows Server 2003, modify a predefined security template, or create a custom security template that contains the security settings that you want. All of the settings listed in this section can be configured through security templates.

Predefined Security Templates

Windows Server 2003 comes with several **predefined security templates**. These predefined security templates are provided as a starting point for creating custom security policies to meet the diverse requirements of organizations. You can customize the templates by using the Security Templates snap-in. Once you customize the security templates, they can be used to configure security on any number of computers. By default, the predefined security templates are stored in *%systemroot%*\Security\Templates. Table 3-4 lists the predefined templates.

Table 3-4 Windows Server 2003 predefined security templates

Template	Purpose
Setup security.inf	Settings that are applied during installation of the operating system for servers or client computers
DC security.inf	Domain controller default security settings installed when a server is promoted to a domain controller
Compatws.inf	The Compatible template changes the default file and registry permissions to be compatible with the requirements of most legacy applications.
Securews.inf	Defines enhanced security settings for servers and workstations. It limits the use of LAN Manager and NTLM authentication protocols.
Securedc.inf	Defines enhanced security settings for domain controllers
Hisecws.inf	Highly secure templates for clients and servers
Hisecdc.inf	Highly secure templates for domain controllers
Rootsec.inf	Used to reapply or modify the root directory permissions
Notssid.inf	Used to remove the unnecessary Terminal Server SIDs from the file system and registry locations if Terminal server will not be used

Security template settings can be viewed through the Security Templates MMC snap-in or viewed as text files. The text files are located in *%windir%*\Security\Templates.

NOTE
It is important to ensure that the templates used in a production environment are first tested then securely stored to prevent unauthorized changes to them. The folder listed in the previous paragraph is not replicated, so be sure that all templates are stored on the same domain controller to ensure version control.

ACTIVITY

Activity 3-4: Explore Predefined Security Templates

Time Required: 45 minutes

Objective: Compare the settings of the various security templates.

Description: In this activity, you will practice working with security settings by adding the Security Templates snap-in to Microsoft Management Console (MMC) and comparing the various security templates.

1. Log on with your **AdminXX** account, where *XX* is your assigned student number.

2. Click **Start**, and then click **Run**.

3. In the run box, type **mmc**, then click **OK**.

4. On the File menu, click **Add/Remove Snap-in**.

5. In the Add/Remove Snap-in dialog box, click the **Standalone** tab, and then click **Add**.

6. In the Add Standalone Snap-in dialog box, click **Security Templates**, click **Add**, click **Close**, and then click **OK**.

7. In the console tree, expand **Security Templates**, then expand **%SystemRoot%\Security\Templates**.

8. A list of predefined security templates and their descriptions appears in the right pane, as shown in Figure 3-8.

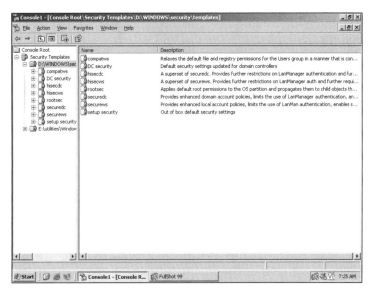

Figure 3-8 Predefined security templates

9. Expand **compatws**, **hisecws**, and the **securews.templates**.

10. Expand the **Account Policies** for each template. Click the **password policy** for each template. How do they differ?

11. Expand the **Account lockout policies** for each. How do they differ? When finished, close the MMC.

CUSTOMIZING A TEMPLATE

Besides using the predefined security templates provided, you can create a new security template with your own preferences. Before making any changes to your security settings, you should understand what the default settings of your system are and what they mean so as to avoid causing policy issues with systems, and remember to test your customization before deciding to deploy the template in a production environment. In the sections that follow, we discuss each of the settings that can be customized. These settings are listed in the order in which they appear in the exam objectives on Microsoft's site and are not necessarily the order shown in the settings configuration on the server.

Registry and File System Permissions

After you apply a template, you can change the settings to suit the needs of the organization. Registry and file permissions are changed in the Registry and File sections of the templates. After you add the file or registry key, the Database security window appears. Here you can set the permissions. The effective inheritance permissions are set through the following selections:

- *Propagate Inheritable Permissions to All Subfolders and Files*—This setting denotes that if child objects are protected or if there is a conflict, the permissions on the child object take precedence.

- *Replace All Permissions on All Subfolders and Files With Inheritable Permissions*—This setting denotes that child object permissions will be overridden.

- *Do Not Allow Permissions on This File or Folder to be Replaced*—When this setting is chosen, any settings made on a folder or registry key above this one will not be inherited.

Should you choose to remove registry settings in the templates, the settings are embedded in the templates and must be removed manually by using a registry editor. In addition, if you choose to add new settings, the Sceregvl.inf file is edited and Scecli.dll needs to be reregistered. The Sceregvl.inf file is located in the *%windir%*\inf folder.

Account Policies

Account policies are policies defined on computers that affect how user accounts can interact with the computer or domain. The effectiveness of these policies depends on how and where they are applied. The three areas that can be configured are Password, Account Lockout, and Kerberos policies. When configuring these settings, keep in mind that you can have only one domain account policy. The policy is applied at the root of the domain and becomes the policy for any system that is a member of the domain. Of course, there is always the exception, and that is when there is an account policy configured for an organizational unit (OU). These settings will affect the local policy settings on the computers contained in the OU.

Password policies control the complexity and lifetime settings for passwords so that they become more complex and secure. This reduces the likelihood of a successful password attack. Table 3-5 lists the default settings.

Table 3-5   Default password policy settings

Option	Default Setting	Possible Values and Recommended Values
Enforce password history	0 passwords remembered	0 to 24 Set to 24 to limit password reuse
Maximum password age	42 days	0 to 999 Set to either 30 or 60 days

Table 3-5 Default password policy settings (continued)

Option	Default Setting	Possible Values and Recommended Values
Minimum password age	0 days	0 to 998 Set to 2 days, this disallows immediate changes
Minimum password length	0 characters	0 to 14 Set to at least 8
Passwords must meet complexity requirements	disabled	Set to enabled
Store password using reversible encryption	disabled	Set to disabled

All of the settings in Table 3-5 should be configured per the organization's security policy. Also, setting the change frequency and password complexity too strictly can cause user frustration, leading to passwords being written down.

The Recommended values listed in column three of Table 3-5 need further discussion. The Enforce password history setting determines the number of unique new passwords that must be associated with a user account before an old password can be reused. Password reuse should be an important concern in any organization. The longer the same password is in use for a particular account, the greater the chance that an attacker will be able to determine the password through brute-force attacks. Specifying a low number for this setting will provide users the ability to utilize the same passwords repeatedly. If the Minimum password age setting is not configured as well, users can change their password as many times in a row as necessary in order to reuse their original password. By setting the Enforce password history to 24, users will have to come up with a new password every time they are required to change their old one. The risk associated with this requirement is that there is an increased risk of encountering users who write down their passwords so that they do not forget them.

The Maximum password age setting determines the number of days that a password can be used before the system requires the user to change it. Frequently changing user passwords may reduce the risk of passwords being cracked, as well as mitigate the risk of someone using an ill-acquired password. Setting the Maximum password age value too low will require users to change their passwords very often, possibly reducing security because it may increase the possibility of users writing their passwords down to avoid forgetting them. The Minimum password age setting determines the number of days that a password must be used before the user is allowed to change it. The Minimum password age value must be less than the Maximum password age value. If Enforce password history is set to 0, the user does not have to choose a new password. If password history is used, users will have to enter a new, unique password when they change their password. Set Minimum password age to a value of 2 days. Setting the number of days to 0 allows immediate password changes, which is not recommended.

The Minimum password length setting determines the least number of characters that may make up a password for a user account. In most environments, an eight-character password is recommended because it is long enough to provide adequate security and still short enough for users to more easily remember. This setting will provide adequate defense against a brute-force attack.

The Passwords must meet complexity requirements setting determines whether or not passwords must meet the following set of guidelines:

- The password does not contain all or part of the user's account name.
- The password is at least six characters long.
- The password contains characters from three of the following four categories:
  - English uppercase characters (A–Z)
  - English lowercase characters (a–z)
  - Base 10 digits (0–9)
  - Nonalphanumeric (For example: !, $, #, or %)

The Store password using reversible encryption for all users in the domain setting determines whether Microsoft Windows Server 2003, Windows 2000 Server, Windows 2000 Professional, and Windows XP Professional store passwords using reversible encryption. Never enable this setting unless business requirements outweigh the need to protect password information.

The **account lockout policy** can be used to secure the system against attacks by disabling the account after a certain number of attempts, for a certain period of time. Set Account lockout duration to 30 minutes. To specify that the account will never be locked out, the value may be set to 0. Set Account Lockout Threshold to 0, which ensures that accounts will not be locked out. This setting will prevent a DoS attack that intentionally locks out all or some accounts. In addition, this setting helps reduce help desk calls because users cannot accidentally lock themselves out of their accounts. Set the Reset Account Lockout Counter After value to 30 minutes. Not setting this value, or setting the value for too long of an interval, could allow a DoS attack.

The **Kerberos policy settings** are used for authentication services. In most environments, the default settings should be sufficient. Should they need to be changed, keep in mind that they are applied at the domain level.

Policy Files

Although Group Policy has pretty much replaced System Policy Editor since Windows 2000 operating systems came into being, there are situations in which you will still have to configure a policy file (Config.pol). These situations would include:

- *Computers that run Windows 95 and 98*—To manage these computers, you must run System Policy Editor to create config.pol files that are compatible with the local operating system.
- *Computers that run Windows NT 4.0 Workstation and Server* —To manage these computers, you must use NTConfig.pol.

■ *Windows 2000 standalone computers*—Because the only Group Policy that applies in this situation is local Group Policy, use a Registry.pol file if you want to provide settings for multiple users. Only the Windows 2000 version of System Policy Editor is compatible with Windows 2000.

The Administrative Templates extension of Group Policy saves customized registry settings in Registry.pol files. The file containing settings that are specific to the HKEY_LOCAL_MACHINE key is stored in the GPT\Machine folder. The file that contains registry settings that are specific to the HKEY_CURRENT_USER key is stored in the GPT\User subdirectory.

Audit Policies

Local policies apply to a computer. They contain an audit policy, user rights assignments, and security options. An audit log records an entry whenever users perform certain actions. The audit entry shows the action performed, the associated user account, and the date and time of the action. You can audit both successful and failed attempts at actions. An **audit policy** should be built around security goals and policies.

Security auditing is extremely important for any organization because the logs may give the only indication that a security breach has occurred. Often, failure logs are much more informative than success logs, because failures typically indicate an error. If no auditing is configured, or if the auditing is set too low, there will be either insufficient or no evidence to trace what has happened. On the other hand, if too much auditing is enabled, then the security log will fill up with meaningless entries.

 Do not monitor everything; instead, monitor what's really important. It is also important to set the proper size of the security log based on the number of audit events that you generate.

NOTE

When auditing is enabled, it generates logs in the security section of event viewer. Table 3-6 lists what can be audited under this policy and gives a description of each policy.

Table 3-6 Local audit policies

Policy	Description	Tracking Purpose and Recommendation
Audit account logon events	These events occur when a domain user account is authenticated on a domain controller.	Generates an audit entry when an account logon attempt succeeds or fails, which is useful information for accounting purposes and for post-incident forensics

Table 3-6 Local audit policies (continued)

Policy	Description	Tracking Purpose and Recommendation
Audit account management	This event includes user account or group creation, modification, or deletion; user accounts being renamed or disabled; or a password being set or changed.	Generates an audit entry when an account management event succeeds or fails, and should be enabled on all computers in your enterprise. It can track who created, changed, or deleted an account when responding to a security incident.
Audit directory service access	This shows the event of a user accessing an Active Directory object that has its own system access control list (SACL).	Enabling auditing of directory service access and configuring SACLs on directory objects generates a large volume of entries in the security logs on a domain controller. Therefore, you should enable these settings only if you actually intend to use the information created.
Audit logon events	These events are generated on domain controllers for domain account activity and on local computers for local account activity.	Generates an audit entry when an account logon attempt succeeds or fails, which is useful information for accounting purposes and for post-incident forensics
Audit object access	This tracks when a user accesses an object such as a file, folder, registry key, or printer that has its own SACL specified.	Enabling auditing of object access and configuring SACLs on objects generates a large volume of entries in the security logs on the domain controller. Therefore, you should enable these settings only if you actually intend to use the information created.
Audit privilege use	This security setting determines whether to audit each instance of a user exercising a right.	The volume of events generated by enabling these settings is very high and difficult to sort through. You should enable these settings only if you know how you will use the information that is generated.
Audit process tracking	This shows detailed tracking information on program activation, process exit, handle duplication, and indirect object access.	Enabling audit process tracking will generate a large number of events. Typically, it is set to No Auditing. These settings can provide a detailed log of the processes started and the time when they were launched for incident response.

Table 3-6 Local audit policies (continued)

Policy	Description	Tracking Purpose and Recommendation
Audit system events	This logs when an event occurs that affects either the system security or the security log, such as when a user restarts or shuts down the computer.	Because few additional events will be recorded by enabling both failure and success auditing for system events, and all of those events are very significant, it is recommended that you enable these settings on all computers.

To audit objects on a member server or a workstation, turn on the audit object access. To audit objects on a domain controller, turn on the audit directory service access.

User Rights Assignment

User rights define capacity at the local level. The **user rights assignment** is twofold: It can grant specific privileges, and it can grant logon rights to users and groups in your computing environment. Logon rights control who and how users log on to the computer, such as the right to log on to a system locally, whereas privileges are rights that allow users to perform system tasks such as backing up files and directories. Although user rights can apply to individual user accounts, they are best administered by using group accounts. Keep in mind that privileges and permissions are different and sometimes privileges can override permissions set on an object. For example, a user logged on to a domain account as a member of the Backup Operators group has the right to restore files and folders. This requires the capability to read files on which their owners may have set permissions that explicitly deny access to all users. The user right assignment allows the backup operator to bypass file and directory permissions when restoring backed-up files and directories. Figure 3-9 shows the rights assignments available and the default settings.

Windows Server 2003 has three built-in local accounts used as logon accounts for different services: Local System, Local Service, and Network Service.

These accounts are used by system processes, should never have a user assignment, and should not have the default setting changed.

You should be familiar with these as well as the Microsoft-recommended setting for each if you are going to take the 70-299 Exam. These can be found in Chapter 4 of the *Threats and Countermeasures Guide* available on the Microsoft Web site or on the *Microsoft Security Guide* CD.

Figure 3-9   User rights assignments default settings

System Services

The **System Services policies** allow an administrator to determine how services will start and who has access permissions. The startup mode can be configured using one of the three following settings:

- *Automatic*—Service automatically starts when computer is restarted
- *Manual*—Service does not start unless it is started manually
- *Disabled*—Service does not start at all

Changing the default settings for services might prevent these or other key services from running correctly, especially if the service you are stopping is a service that other services are dependent on. Verify service dependencies before starting or stopping a service. This is done by viewing the Dependencies tab of the chosen service, from the Administrative tools, Services icon.

You can start a service manually by using the Services icon in Administrative tools or by using the net start command. You can also use the sc.exe command at the command prompt to configure services. This command has parameters that can stop and start a service and show the current status of a service as well as listing any services dependencies.

The Edit Security option is the other configuration piece of System Services. This determines who can control services. To configure this, add security templates to a Microsoft Management Console, then expand the appropriate template, choose System Services, select the service you want to configure, and click the Edit Security button. Figure 3-10 shows both configuration options.

3

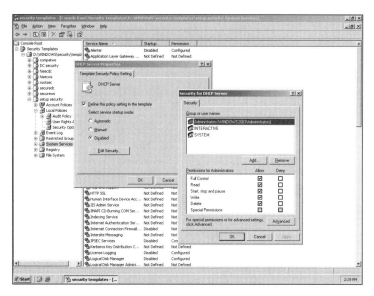

Figure 3-10   Editing System Services using Group Policy Management Console

Security Options

Security Options, which are the last of the local policies, enable or disable security settings for the computer. You use these policies to enhance security. The policies include how the Administrator and Guest account names are managed, access to the floppy drive and CD-ROM, installation of drivers, digital signing of data, and logon prompts. Many Security Options policies are available, as shown in Figure 3-11.

Microsoft expanded this category and added about 20 new settings to Windows Server 2003. Although these settings can be set in the registry, the recommended method for setting them is through a template. For a list of the recommended settings for each of these security options, see Chapter 5 of the *Threats and Countermeasures Guide*.

NOTE

The Security Options settings Network Access: Do Not Allow Anonymous Enumeration of SAM Accounts and Shares and Network Access: Do Not Allow Anonymous Enumeration of SAM Accounts replace the Windows 2000 Security Options setting Additional Restrictions for Anonymous Connections. This setting managed the registry value called Restrict Anonymous.

Restricted Groups

This security setting allows an administrator to define the following two properties for security groups: Members and Member Of. The Members list defines who belongs to the restricted group, whereas the Member Of list states which other groups the restricted group belongs to. When a **Restricted Groups policy** is defined, any user on the Members list who is not currently a member of the group is added, and any current member of the group

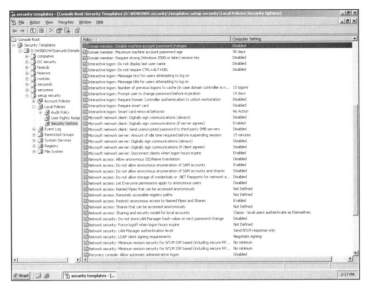

Figure 3-11 Security Options available for configuration

who is not on the members list is removed. Any members who are not specified in the policy are removed during configuration or refresh. For example, you can create a Restricted Groups policy to allow only Jim and John to be members of the Administrators group. In the meantime, Joe adds himself as a member of the Administrators group, but not via the template settings. When the Security policy is refreshed, only Jim and John will remain as members of the Administrators group, and Joe will no longer be a member of the group.

The policy can be defined either in a security template or by defining the setting on a Group Policy Object (GPO). If the Members list is empty, this means that the restricted group has no members. If the template is applied this way, any current member not on the Restricted Groups policy members list is removed. This can include default members, including administrators.

Figure 3-12 shows where the Members and Member Of members are added in the security template.

The Members list defines who belongs to the restricted group, while the Member Of list states which other groups the restricted group belongs to. Be sure that you understand the difference between the two groups. This can be a factor when doing Group Policy troubleshooting, which is explained in Chapter 4.

Activity 3-5: Work with Security Templates and Policy Settings

Time Required: 60 minutes

Objective: Add the Security Templates snap-in to a Microsoft Management Console (MMC) console, then create and define a new security template.

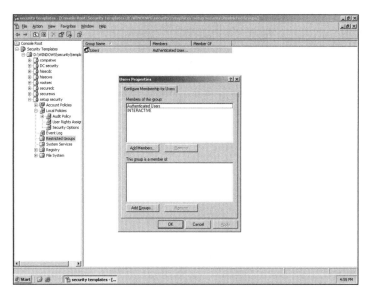

Figure 3-12   Adding Members and Member Of in the security template

Description: In this activity, you will practice working with security settings by adding the Security Templates snap-in to a Microsoft Management Console (MMC) console, then create and define a new security template.

1. Log on with your **AdminXX** account, where *XX* is your assigned student number.

2. Click **Start**, then click **Run**.

3. In the run box, type **mmc**, then click **OK**.

4. On the File menu, click **Add/Remove Snap-in**.

5. In the Add/Remove Snap-in dialog box, click the **Standalone** tab, then click **Add**.

6. In the Add Standalone Snap-in dialog box, click **Security Templates**, click **Add**, click **Close**, and then click **OK**.

7. In the console tree, expand **Security Templates**, and then select **%SystemRoot%\Security\Templates**. A list of predefined security templates and their descriptions appears in the right pane.

8. Right-click **%SystemRoot%\Security\Templates**, then click **New Template**.

9. In the Template name box, type **testtemplate** as the name for the new template. You can type a description in the Description box, such as "new template for developer workstations," then click **OK**.

10. The new security template appears in the list of security templates. Expand **testtemplate**, expand **Account Policies**, and look at the settings in each of the three Account Policies. Expand the **Local Policies**. Look at the Security Options defined. What do these settings all have in common?

11. You should have noticed that the security settings for this template are not yet defined. To set the Maximum password age policy, expand **Account Policies**, as shown in Figure 3-13.

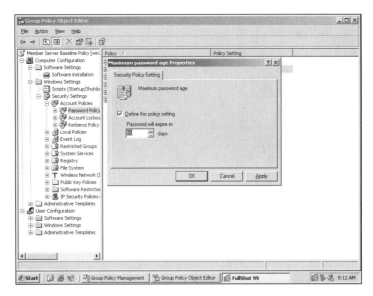

Figure 3-13   Setting the Maximum password age policy

12. Double-click **Password Policy**, if necessary, then double-click **Maximum password age**.

13. Select the **Define this policy setting** in the template check box, then set the option to **60 days**. What happens? Do you think 60 days is a good policy? Why or why not? Click **OK**. When finished, close the MMC.

Event Logs

The **Event Logs** security area defines characteristics that are related to the application, security, and system logs. Figure 3-14 shows the options that are configurable.

In addition to the settings that are configurable through the template, you can now delegate access to event logs. This is new in Windows Server 2003, and it allows you to customize the permissions on each event log on a computer by editing the value in the registry. The ACL is stored as a string in a Reg_SZ value called CustomSD for each event log. For more information on this, see the Microsoft Knowledge Base article (323076) titled "How to Set Event Log Security Locally or by Using Group Policy in Windows Server 2003" on the Microsoft Web site.

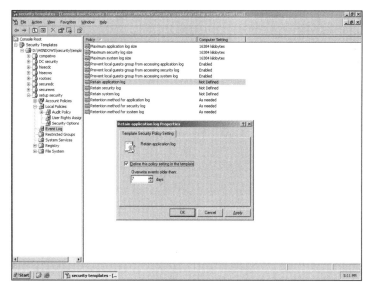

Figure 3-14   Event Log Configuration screen

Activity 3-6: Copy Settings from a Security Template into a Custom Template

Time Required: 45 minutes

Objective: Add the Security Templates snap-in to a Microsoft Management Console (MMC) console, then copy settings from an existing template to a custom template.

Description: In this activity, you will practice working with security settings by adding the Security Templates snap-in to a Microsoft Management Console (MMC) console, then copy settings from an existing template to a custom template.

1. Log on with your **AdminXX** account, where *XX* is your assigned student number.

2. Click **Start**, then click **Run**.

3. In the run box, type **mmc**, then click **OK**.

4. On the File menu, click **Add/Remove Snap-in**.

5. In the Add/Remove Snap-in dialog box, click the **Standalone** tab, then click **Add**.

6. In the Add Standalone Snap-in dialog box, click **Security Templates**, click **Add**, click **Close**, then click **OK**.

7. In the console tree, expand **Security Templates**, then expand **%SystemRoot%\Security\Templates**.

8. Use the Account Policies settings from the Hisecdc template in your testtemplate, expand **Hisecdc**, right-click **Account Policies**, and then click **Copy**.

9. Expand your **testtemplate**, right-click **Account Policies**, and then click **Paste**, as shown in Figure 3-15.

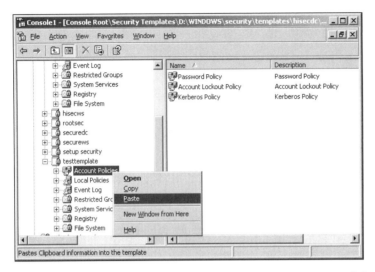

Figure 3-15   Importing security settings into a custom template

Deploying Security Templates

Security templates can be deployed in a variety of ways, depending on your needs. Before we look at the ways in which security templates can be applied, let's look at some general guidelines for dealing with templates:

- Never edit the Setup Security.inf template. This will eliminate the option to reapply the default security settings.

- Do not apply the Setup Security.inf template through Group Policy. It should be applied only to the local computer.

- Do not apply the Compatws.inf template to domain controllers. This is for workstations only.

- Instead of modifying a default template, customize it, then save the changes under a different name. This will allow you to keep the original template.

Now that some basics have been established, you can apply security templates via the SCA console, using the Group Policy Management Console, or by command-line tools and scripts. If you are applying security settings on a single computer running Windows 2000 or Windows Server 2003, the best method to use is the SCA console. This method allows you to see the effects of the template settings before they are applied. Everywhere a red X appears denotes a setting that will change.

Keep in mind that SCA is used to configure security areas that are not affected by Group Policy settings because Group Policy settings override the local settings. This tool is not to be used for configuring security for a domain or an organizational unit; it is used to directly configure local system security. Although it has limitations for applying security templates, SCA has some good features. When you import security templates and apply them, the system security is immediately changed to the levels specified in the template. Another good feature is the ability to merge templates. If you import more than one template, the database will merge them, create one template, and resolve conflicts according to the order of import.

NOTE Because you will seldom configure one machine at a time, other alternatives such as using Group Policy and scripts are also available to apply templates.

Deployment Using Active Directory–based Group Policy Objects

Security templates can also be applied to the GPO. First, we should refresh our memories on the order in which policies are applied. Remember that Group Policy can apply to computers or users. The order in which policy settings are applied is:

- Local policy
- Site-level policy
- Domain-level policy
- Domain controller policy only if it is in the domain controller container
- Organizational unit policy

This means that the local GPO is processed first, and the organizational unit to which the computer or user belongs is processed last. After going through the order in which policies apply, the precedence is determined. This is what makes working with GPOs tricky. GPOs are applied from the bottom up when multiple policies are linked to a single container object, such as a site, domain, or OU. When you have several policies, the one on the top is the last one to be applied.

Block Policy inheritance and **No Override** are also features that can be used to control which policies apply. A No Override attribute has precedence over all of the policies that are applied thereafter. GPOs cannot be linked directly to users, computers, or security groups. They can be linked only to sites, domains, and OUs. Any GPO that is linked to one of these can be set to No Override with respect to that container so that none of its policy settings can be overridden. When more than one GPO has been set to No Override, the one that is highest in the Active Directory hierarchy takes precedence.

Remember that you cannot select which policies you block when you use Block Policy inheritance. Blocking does not affect local GPOs. The Block Policy inheritance blocks all Group Policy settings that would filter down to the site, domain, or OU from a parent, no matter what GPO those settings originate from, but it will not block Group Policy settings from GPOs that are linked directly to the site, domain, or OU. If you are unsure of how Group Policy works and the review in the next chapter doesn't help, you may want to download and read "Microsoft Server 2003 Group Policy Infrastructure," available on the Microsoft Web site.

Security templates can be imported into Group Policy through Security Settings on the Group Policy tab of the domain or OU. Upon importing a security template, select the **Clear This Database Before Importing** option to clear the database of any previously stored security templates, as shown in Figure 3-16.

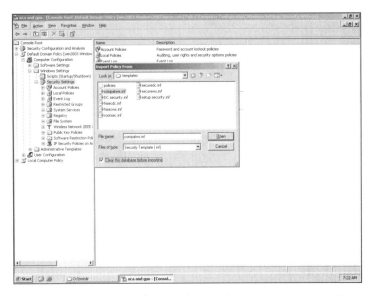

Figure 3-16   Clearing the database when importing security templates

When Group Policy security settings are changed, by default they are refreshed every 5 minutes on a domain controller and every 90 minutes on a workstation or server. The settings are also refreshed every 16 hours, even if there are no changes.

Gpupdate is a command-line utility that can be used if the policy needs to be refreshed immediately. Gpupdate replaces the Windows 2000 command secedit /refreshpolicy. The syntax is as follows:

gpupdate [/target: *computer*] [/force] [/wait:*Value*] [/logoff] [/boot]

The following is a description of the parameters:

- /target:*Computer or User*—Processes only the computer or user settings

- /force—Reapplies all settings

- /wait:*Value*—Time in seconds that policy processing waits to finish

- /logoff—Logs off after the refresh has completed

- /boot—Restarts the computer after the refresh has completed

There are some new additions to Group Policy that are part of Windows Server 2003. Resultant Set of Policy (RSoP) is a query engine that provides details about all policy settings that are configured for existing policies based on site, domain, domain controller, and OU. RSoP can also help you determine a set of applied policies and their precedence.

The Microsoft Group Policy Management Console (GPMC) is also a new feature in Windows Server 2003 for Group Policy management. It is available as a separate, downloadable component on the Microsoft Web site. GPMC allows administrators to manage Group Policy for multiple domains and sites and integrates the existing Group Policy functionality into a single console with added capabilities including backup, restore, import, copy, reporting of GPOs, RSoP, and Windows Management Instrumentation (WMI) Filters.

Deployment Using Command-Line Tools

Sometimes Group Policy can't be used to apply security templates, such as on older systems like Windows NT. To overcome these limitations, you can apply templates in several ways, including using scripts and command-line tools.

TIP

For information about a specific operating system tool, in Help and Support Center for Windows Server 2003, click **Tools**, then click **Command-line reference A-Z** or **Windows interface administrative tool reference A-Z**.

Previously, we discussed the fact that SCA can configure only one computer at a time. By using the command-line tool **Secedit.exe** in a batch file or script, you can configure security on multiple computers and do so at scheduled times. First, we will look at the commands available, then the parameters and proper syntax. The commands that can be run are secedit /analyze, secedit /configure, secedit /export, secedit /import, secedit /validate, and secedit /GenerateRollback. The parameters are as follows:

- /db *FileName*.sdb—Specifies the database filename
- /cfg *FileName*—Specifies the security template filename
- /log *FileName*—Specifies the log filename
- /quiet—States that screen output should not take place
- /overwrite—States that the database should be cleared
- /areas *Area1 Area2*—Specifies the security sections to be applied such as GROUP_ MGMT, USER_RIGHTS, and SECURITYPOLICY

TIP

Here is an example of using a secedit command: secedit /analyze /DB d:\testdir\testfile.sdb /CFG d:\testdir\securedc.inf

TIP If you are unfamiliar with command-line administration, you may want to pick up Microsoft *Windows Server 2003 Command Line Administration* (ISBN 0-619-13111-x) as a reference.

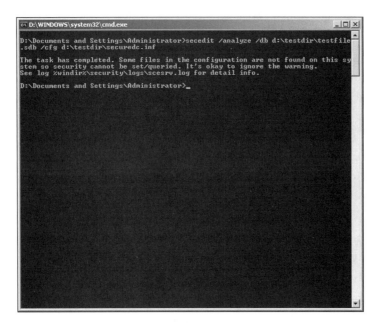

Figure 3-17   Using the secedit command

All Secedit.exe configurations and analyses are database-driven. Therefore, Secedit.exe supports switches for specifying a database (/db) as well as a configuration file (/cfg) to be imported into the database before performing the configuration. By default, the configuration file is appended to the database. To overwrite existing configuration information in the database, use the /overwrite switch. As with the Security Configuration and Analysis snap-in, you can specify a log file (/log). While the Security Configuration and Analysis snap-in always configures all security areas, Secedit.exe allows you to specify areas (/areas) to be configured.

Using the command-line tool allows you to perform security configuration and analysis in conjunction with other administrative tools, such as Microsoft Systems Management Server or the Task Scheduler built into Windows XP Professional. Secedit.exe also provides some capabilities that are not available in the graphical user interface, such as performing a batch analysis.

Deployment Using Scripting

Besides command-line tools, there are several scripting tools that can be used to deploy security templates. For example, you can write Visual Basic script files, then run them using the Cscript.exe program, or you can use the **Windows Management Instrumentation Command-Line (WMIC)** interface. If you grew up on DOS, you should be very familiar with batch files, which you can also use to apply security templates. After the script or batch files are written, you can schedule them to run through the Task Scheduler. For example, you can call the Secedit.exe command-line tool from a batch file or automatic Task Scheduler to automatically create and apply templates.

You can use the AT command to schedule or delete a task to run. The proper syntax is

AT *computername time* /Every: *date command*

For example, the command AT 2:00 Every: Monday secedit /analyze /DB c:\testdir\testfile. sdb /CFG c:\testdir\securews.inf will compare the workstation security to the securews template every Monday at 2:00. You can also use the AT command to list the tasks that are scheduled by simply typing AT at a command-line prompt.

Besides using scripting files with secedit, you can use script files with Microsoft Baseline Security Analyzer. Sample scripts can be downloaded from Microsoft's site in a file called MBSASamples.exe. A:. Because you can filter on just those checks or bulletins you are interested in, and because you can see a summary view of the whole organization, you will be able to more quickly isolate the computers in the environment that pose the greatest risk. For a given vulnerability, a quick button click will list the computers that are out of compliance. We will look at one of these scripts to get an idea of how they work.

The first sample, called Sample #1, is based upon the need to perform two phases of scanning:

- The first phase performs the scan and updates the target computers with the results.

- The next phase occurs when the user of the computer needs to check the compliance of his or her computer but does not have the local administrative rights to do so.

There are several assumptions relating to this, the first being that there could be many computers in the list of computers to be scanned. The next assumption is that each computer may have more than one user. Sample #1 does not provide a means to update more than one user profile with the scan results. Additional scripting would be needed in order for the first phase of scanning to copy the report into each user profile but should not be difficult. Before running this sample, be sure to review the command-line options being used and consult the product documentation for their specific meaning. The sample has limited the checks performed by MBSA to just the security update compliance in order to reduce the amount of time spent doing the scanning.

Demo.bat performs the first phase of scanning and copies the results back to the user profile for later viewing.

Demo.bat

set cname=%computername%

set uname=%username%

del "%userprofile%\SecurityScans\%cname%.xml"

"C:\Program Files\Microsoft Baseline Security Analyzer\mbsacli.exe" /nvc /nosum /c %cname% /n IIS+OS+SQL+Password /o %cname%

copy "%userprofile%\SecurityScans\%cname%.xml" "\\%cname%\c$\Documents and Settings\% uname%\SecurityScans\"

When viewing Demo.bat, users who are not local administrators may need to view the compliance report, so you may want to consider giving them a desktop shortcut to make this easy.

CHAPTER SUMMARY

- ❏ Security Configuration and Analysis (SCA) is a tool used to analyze security configurations and resolve security discrepancies. In the analysis, it presents recommendations for fixing current system settings and uses colored flags to note any areas where the current settings do not match the proposed level of security.

- ❏ The Microsoft Baseline Security Analyzer (MBSA) is a tool that is used to scan one or more Windows-based computers for common security holes. The MBSA will scan a Windows-based computer and check the operating system and other installed components for security along with their current status of recommended security updates.

- ❏ With the Security Templates snap-in, you can create a security policy for your network or computer by using security templates. A security template is a text file that represents a security configuration. You can apply a security template to the local computer, import a security template to Group Policy, or use a security template to analyze security.

- ❏ Windows Server 2003 comes with several predefined templates. These predefined security templates are provided as a starting point for creating custom security policies to meet the diverse requirements of organizations. You can customize the templates by using the Security Templates snap-in. Once you customize the security templates, they can be used to configure security on any number of computers.

- ❏ Besides using the predefined security templates provided, you can create a new security template with your own preferences. These settings changes include user rights assignment, security options, account policies, password policies, and restricted groups policy.

- ❏ Although Group Policy has pretty much replaced System Policy Editor since Windows 2000 operating systems came into being, there are situations in which you will still have to configure a policy file (Config.pol).

- ❏ Local policies apply to a computer and contain the audit policy, user rights assignments, and security options. Auditing should be built around security goals and policies. Do not monitor everything; instead, monitor what's really important.

❏ Security templates can be deployed in a variety of ways, depending on your needs. These include being applied via the Security and Configuration Analysis (SCA) console, using the Group Policy Management console, or by command-line tools and scripts.

❏ When Group Policy security settings are changed, by default they are refreshed every 5 minutes on a domain controller and every 90 minutes on a workstation or server. The settings are also refreshed every 16 hours, even if there are no changes.

❏ Gpupdate is a command-line utility that can be used if the policy needs to be refreshed immediately. Gpupdate replaces the Windows 2000 command secedit /refreshpolicy.

❏ Using the command-line tool Secedit.exe allows you to perform security configuration and analysis in conjunction with using other administrative tools, such as Microsoft Systems Management Server or the Task Scheduler built into Windows XP Professional. Besides command-line tools, there are several scripting tools that can be used to deploy security templates.

Key Terms

account lockout policy — The account lockout policy can be used to secure the system against attacks by disabling the account after a certain number of attempts, for a certain period of time.

account policies — Account policies are policies defined on computers that affect how user accounts can interact with the computer or domain.

audit policy — A policy that determines the security events to be reported to the network administrator.

Block Policy — Block Policy inheritance blocks all Group Policy settings that would filter down to the site, domain, or OU from a parent, no matter what GPO those settings originate from.

Event Logs — The Event Logs security area defines characteristics that are related to the application, security, and system logs.

Gpupdate — This is a command-line utility that can be used if the policy needs to be refreshed immediately.

Kerberos policy settings — The Kerberos policy settings are used for authentication services. In most environments, the default settings should be sufficient.

Microsoft Baseline Security Analyzer (MBSA) — A tool that is used to scan one or more Windows-based computers for common security holes.

mbsacli.exe command — MBSA command-line interface can perform two types of scans: MBSA scans and HFNetChk scans. The MBSA scan can be run from the command line to run the same commands as the GUI.

No Override — No Override attribute has precedence over all of the policies that are applied thereafter except the local policy.

password policies — Password policies control the complexity and lifetime settings for passwords so that they become more complex and secure.

predefined security templates — The predefined security templates are provided as a starting point for creating custom security policies to meet the diverse requirements of organizations.

Restricted Groups policy — This security setting allows an administrator to define two properties for security groups: Members and Member Of.

Secedit.exe — The command-line tool Secedit.exe can be used in a batch file or script to configure security on multiple computers and do so at scheduled times.

Security Configuration and Analysis (SCA) — A tool used to analyze security configurations and resolve security discrepancies.

Security Options — Security Options, which are the last of the local policies, enable or disable security settings for the computer. You use these policies to enhance security.

security template — A security template is a text file that represents a security configuration.

Security Templates snap-in — A method by which you can create a security policy for your network or computer by using security templates.

System Services policies — The System Services policies allow an administrator to determine how services will start and who has access permissions.

user rights assignment — The use of the user rights assignment is twofold: It can grant specific privileges, and it can grant logon rights to users and groups in your computing environment.

Windows Management Instrumentation Command-Line (WMIC) — A scripting tool that can be used to deploy security templates.

REVIEW QUESTIONS

1. You want to find out how many user accounts have blank or simple passwords such as *god* or *password*. Which of the following tools should you use?

   a. A scripting tool

   b. MBSA

   c. Gpupdate

   d. SCA

2. You notice that there are no new logon events on one of the servers for the past week. You know users are logging on, and you have verified that the audit policy is configured correctly. What can you do to correct this situation? (Choose all that apply.)

   a. Enable Audit process tracking

   b. Increase the size of the log file

   c. Change the log setting from Manual to Overwrite Events as Needed

   d. Enable the Audit account logon events

3. The help desk group is reporting that the majority of their calls are from users who have locked themselves out of their accounts. The current account lockout threshold is set to 3. What would be your first step to resolve this issue?

   a. Set the Account Lockout Duration policy to 20

   b. Set the Maximum password age policy to 60 days

   c. Set the Enforce Password History policy to 0

   d. Set the Account Lockout Threshold policy to 5

4. You have defined a Restricted Group in which Joe, Jane, and Jill are the only members of the Marketing group. Before you made this change, Bill, Bob, and Barbara were members. When the policy is refreshed who will be a member of the Marketing group?

   a. Bill, Bob, Barbara, Jill, Joe, and Jane

   b. No one; the policy conflicts with the prior policy, therefore all members are deleted.

   c. Jill, Joe, and Jane

   d. Bill, Bob, and Barbara

5. Security templates are deployed in which of the following ways? (Choose all that apply.)

   a. Group Policy

   b. SCA console

   c. MBSA

   d. Windows Management Instrumentation Command-Line (WMIC) interface

6. The network consists of a mixed Windows 2000 and Windows 2003 domain with client computers running Windows XP Professional and Windows 2000 Professional. Company policy dictates that auditing for the following be tracked:

   When an attempt is made to log on to any local computer.

   When a user account or group is created or a user account password has been changed.

   Which of the following would you enable? (Choose all that apply.)

   a. Audit account logon events, success, failure

   b. Audit account management, success

   c. Audit logon events, success, failure

   d. Audit object access, success

7. Recently, you upgraded the computers running Windows 98 machines to Windows XP. The help desk is getting a large volume of calls from the users who have been upgraded, reporting that a proprietary accounting package they are using no longer works. How do you resolve this issue?

   a. Apply the Securews.inf security template

   b. Apply the Notssid.inf security template

c. Apply the Setup security.inf security template

d. Apply the Compatws.inf security template

8. Several of your users need certain user rights on a file server. Many of these users are members of the Development group, but you don't want the entire group to have access. You create a new group called DevelopsubA, then create a new template allowing the needed user rights. How do you configure this in the restricted groups area?

a. The Members list should show DevelopsubA, and the Members Of list should show Development.

b. The Members list should show Development, and the Members Of list should show Development and DevelopsubA.

c. The Members list should show Development, and the Members Of list should show DevelopsubA.

d. The Members list should show Development and DevelopsubA, and the Members Of list should show DevelopsubA.

9. You are responsible for making sure that all computers in the domain are secure. You would like to make several adjustments but do not want the changes to affect system security. You merely want to see how changes in the settings will affect the security of the computer. Which of the following would you use?

a. HFNetChk

b. MBSA

c. Security Configuration and Analysis

d. Mbsacli.exe

10. Which of the following are predefined templates? (Choose all that apply.)

a. Setup security.inf

b. Compatws.inf

c. Hisecuritydc.inf

d. Rootsec.inf

11. All user computers are in an OU called Production. You are responsible for making sure that the domain account policies are no less secure than the account policies in the Securedc.inf template. You analyze the computers and find that there are several areas in the password policy portion that need improvement, but there are also other areas where the company policy is more restrictive than the template. The existing security level is not to be reduced. How do you increase the password policy in the areas in which it is less restrictive than the Securedc.inf template?

a. Create a new GPO and link it to the Production OU; import the Securewk.inf template into the new GPO

b. Import the Securedc.inf template into the Domain Security Policy

3

c. Create a new GPO and link it to the Production OU, make the appropriate changes, and then import this template into the new GPO

d. Create a new security template, make the appropriate changes, and then import this template into the Domain Security Policy

12. The network has client computers running various operating systems including Windows NT and Windows 98. All domain controllers must authenticate users only by using the most secure method available. Which Windows 2003 registry keys replace the Windows 2000 Restrict Anonymous value? (Choose all that apply.)

a. Network Access: Restrict anonymous accounts

b. Network Access: Restrict anonymous shares

c. Network Access: Do not allow anonymous enumeration of SAM accounts and shares

d. Network Access: Do not allow anonymous enumeration of SAM accounts

13. The information exchanged within the company is extremely sensitive. The company's written policy states that all domain controllers must accept a LAN Manager authentication level of NTLMv2 only, so that the session key is encrypted and the authentication process is more secure than NTLM. How do you configure the domain controllers in a mixed mode domain to meet these requirements?

a. Import the Securews.inf security template into the default Domain Controllers GPO for the Windows 2000 domain

b. Import the Securedc.inf security template into the default Domain Controllers GPO for the Windows 2003 domain

c. Import the Rootsec.inf security template into the default Domain Controllers GPO for the Windows 2000 domain

d. Import the Securedc.inf security template into the default Domain Controllers GPO for the Windows 2000 domain

14. You are in the process of formulating a baseline security configuration and upgrade plan for the Web servers from Windows 2000 to Windows 2003. All unnecessary services and protocols are to be uninstalled, disabled, or removed. The Web servers are in an OU called Web. How do you do this with the least administrative effort?

a. After determining the unnecessary services, create a GPO to set the unnecessary services startup type to Disabled, then link the GPO to the Web OU

b. After determining the unnecessary services, create a GPO and import the Notssid.inf security template

c. After determining the unnecessary services, create a GPO to set the unnecessary services startup type to Disabled, then link the GPO to the Domain Controllers OU

d. After determining the unnecessary services, create a GPO to set the unnecessary services startup type to Manual, then link the GPO to the Web OU

15. The majority of the company servers are hosting Web-based applications and there is a good chance that they may be compromised. To ensure that this does not happen, you want to capture changes to the security settings by generating a daily report comparing the company-required secure settings with the setting of each server. How do you do this?

    a. Create an appropriate security template. Schedule Task Scheduler to run the gpresult command daily

    b. Create an appropriate security template, write a custom script file, and then schedule Task Scheduler to run the secedit /analyze command against the template daily

    c. Create an appropriate security template, import it into Group Policy, and then set the policy to refresh daily

    d. Create an appropriate security template, create a batch file that will run secedit /analyze against the security template on start up

16. The client computers run a variety of operating systems, including Windows NT 4.0 Workstation. A logon banner displaying a warning about unauthorized use of the computer needs to be displayed on all computers. To ensure that the banner appears whenever a user logs on to the computer, which of the following should you do? (Choose all that apply.)

    a. Create a system policy file called NTConfig.pol, which includes the desired settings; place the file in a folder on the domain controller

    b. Create a GPO with the security settings configured for the interactive logon message; link the GPO to the domain

    c. Create a system policy file called Registry.pol, which includes the desired settings; place the file in a folder on the domain controller

    d. Create a system policy file called Config.pol, which includes the desired settings; place the file in a folder on the domain controller

17. It is your responsibility to analyze all security reports generated by MBSA. You run MSBA using the GUI on a domain controller. Which of the following pieces of information is not contained in the MBSA security report?

    a. Computer name

    b. IP address

    c. Security report name

    d. Administrator logon ID

18. The System Services policies allow an administrator to determine how services will start and who has access permissions. The startup mode can be configured to use which of the three following settings? (Choose all that apply.)

    a. Disabled

    b. Differential

    c. Automatic

    d. Manual

19. After you add the file or registry key, the Database security window appears. Here, you can set the permissions. The effective inheritance permissions are set by which of the following selections? (Choose all that apply.)

    a. Propagate Inheritable Permissions to All Subfolders and Files

    b. Do Not Propagate Inheritable Permissions to All Subfolders and Files

    c. Do Not Allow Permissions on This File or Folder to be Replaced

    d. Replace All Permissions on All Subfolders and Files With Inheritable Permissions

20. Security template settings can be viewed through the Security Templates MMC snap-in or viewed as text files. The text files are located in which of the following directories?

    a. %windir%\System32\logfiles

    b. %windir%\Security\Templates

    c. %windir%\temp\Temporary Internet files

    d. %windir%\Security\logfiles

21. When running the Mbsacli.exe command, which of the following switches can be used to suppresses security update check notes or warnings? (Choose two.)

    a. /sus

    b. /s 1

    c. /n Updates

    d. /s 2

22. When running the MBSA from a command line, reports from a scan are stored under which of the following folders on the computer on which the MSBA tool is installed?

    a. %userprofile%\Security logfiles

    b. %userprofile%\Temp

    c. %userprofile%\System32

    d. %userprofile%\SecurityScans

23. Gpupdate is a command-line utility that can be used if the policy needs to be refreshed immediately. Gpupdate replaces the Windows 2000 command?

    a. secedit /evaluate

    b. secedit /export

    c. secedit /refreshpolicy

    d. secedit /analyze

24. In which of the following ways can security templates be applied? (Choose all that apply.)

    a. The Security and Configuration Analysis (SCA) console

    b. Using the Group Policy Management console

     c. By command-line tools and scripts

     d. The Microsoft Baseline Security Analyzer console

25. Which of the following port does MBSA use to perform its scans?

     a. Port 110

     b. Port 138

     c. Port 139

     d. Port 153

CASE PROJECTS

Case Project 3-1

Your company's written policy states that all domain controllers must accept a LAN Manager authentication level of NTLMv2 only. The forest consists of a mixed mode Windows 2000 domain and a Windows 2003 domain with client computers running Windows 98, Windows NT Workstation, Windows 2000, and Windows XP Professional. You have enabled NTLM 2 authentication only on the clients. You need to configure the domain controllers in the mixed mode domain to meet these requirements. Management wants you to submit a written plan on how you will accomplish this. Prepare the report in a manner that nontechnical people can understand.

Case Project 3-2

You are the network administrator at Evergrow. A member of the IT team has been reading some information on Microsoft's site about Security Configuration and Analysis. Without your permission, he imported the Hisecdc.inf template into one of the file servers, and after using the SCA analysis option, he chose the Configure Computer Now and reconfigured the security on the server. Now the users are having issues using a proprietary application. Management wants you to first fix the problem, then explain to them what happened. How will you fix this problem? Prepare a plan to avoid having this happen in the future, and in it list some best practices for using the SCA snap-in.

Case Project 3-3

You are the network administrator at Evergrow. You have run the SCA. As you are viewing the results of the analysis, you notice that there are quite a few settings that have a question mark and exclamation point next to them. What does this mean? How do these flags affect the organizational environment? How would you fix the settings to eliminate the question marks and exclamation points?

Case Project 3-4

You are the network administrator at Evergrow. The domain consists of a Windows 2003 domain with computers running Windows XP Professional. Company policy states that all passwords must be complex and secure to reduce the likelihood of a successful password attack. Figure 3-18 shows your current password policy. How would you change it to meet company policy and make the system more secure?

3

Figure 3-18   Current password policy

Case Project 3-5

You are the network administrator at Evergrow. Management has asked you to analyze your current security settings to establish which workstations are not in compliance with current company policy. You are to select a predefined security template or create a new security template to use for your computers. Currently you have 10 servers and 500 workstations. The company is a software development company. In addition to the 500 workstations, there are 40 mobile laptops. Put together a plan for analyzing the current security and choose a template for the workstations and mobile computers. Explain why you chose the selected templates.

4

TROUBLESHOOTING SECURITY POLICIES

After reading this chapter, you will be able to:

♦ Troubleshoot security in a mixed operating system environment

♦ Troubleshoot security in a mixed domain level environment

♦ Troubleshoot security inheritance problems

♦ Troubleshoot security template problems

♦ Troubleshoot removal of security templates

Now that we have discussed how to plan, configure, deploy, and manage security policies, you might think that we have covered everything there is to know about them. In reality though, we have only discussed how to work with them in the best of circumstances. In this chapter we will examine what to do when situations get a bit more complicated.

Several factors can complicate managing and deploying security policies. These could include a network that has a mixture of Microsoft server and client operating systems or a network that includes multiple domains that are in different functional levels. Security policies also may not be enforced as expected because of issues regarding inheritance or a problem with the security template itself. Older policies may still be in force because their templates have yet to be removed. In this chapter, we will discuss each of these complications and how you should troubleshoot them to ensure the security of your network and the computers within it.

TROUBLESHOOTING SECURITY IN A MIXED OPERATING SYSTEM ENVIRONMENT

It stands to reason that the security of a network can only be as strong as the security of the servers and the clients within it. Because this is true, you must understand that not all servers and clients have the same capabilities in regard to security. As we discussed earlier, the latest server and client operating systems have made significant advances toward becoming more secure. Unfortunately, those advances cannot just be "rolled back" to all of the servers and clients that your organization is currently using. For this reason, you need to understand the tradeoffs and risks associated with using older server and client operating systems in your network. You should also understand the methods you can use to get the most security out of each server or client. By understanding the capabilities of servers and clients, you will be able to troubleshoot the network in regard to security issues and find the "weakest link" from a security standpoint.

Microsoft has developed and released three main server operating system families since the mid-1990s. Each family of operating systems has become more secure and has allowed more granular control than the previous operating system family. These families of server operating systems include Windows NT Server, Windows 2000 Server, and Windows Server 2003. Chances are good that your organization is using servers from more than one of these families.

In addition, Microsoft has developed and released three main client operating systems built on the Windows NT kernel. With each successive operating system they have built in additional security features and options. The clients built on the Windows NT kernel include Windows NT Workstation, Windows 2000 Professional, and Windows XP. Again, chances are very good that your organization is using more than one of these types of operating systems. In fact, your organization may also be using even older DOS-based operating systems such as Windows 95 or Windows 98.

Because each server and client operating system has its own features and limitations, it's important that you understand how they can affect your security. In the paragraphs that follow, we will discuss each of the main server operating systems and examine the security issues that they create in your network. You should understand how to troubleshoot problems related to the limitations or the configuration of each of these operating systems.

Windows NT Server

Although Windows NT offered new technology in the 1990s, it cannot compete and sometimes cannot even communicate with the newest Microsoft servers in use today. You should be aware that the highly secure templates that are often used on Windows 2000 and Windows Server 2003 servers can cause very limited communication with Windows NT servers. In addition, because the methods used to control security for files and folders were different with Windows NT, you might get unexpected results when you combine the newer access control lists (ACLs) or attempt to use Group Policies on a computer that has been migrated from Windows NT. In the following sections we will discuss each of these concepts in greater detail.

4

Communication Between Windows NT and Newer Server Operating Systems

As discussed previously, administrators have the option of using highly secure templates to strengthen their networks from attacks by intruders from the outside and from within the network itself. These templates can provide the foundation for security when only Windows 2000 and Windows Server 2003 servers are utilized. If any Windows NT servers are used, you may not be able to enforce these templates and still allow effective communication between the Windows NT servers and the newer servers. More specifically, the following will result when a highly secure template such as hisecdc.inf is used on a newer server in conjunction with servers running Windows NT:

- Domain controllers running Windows NT 4.0 or earlier cannot authenticate users logging onto a client computer unless they run Service Pack 4 or higher. Domain controllers for the domain to which the computer is joined must run Windows 2000 or later.

- Client computers cannot communicate with computers running Windows NT 4.0 unless they run Service Pack 4 or higher. (This is also true if the client computer is configured with a secure.inf template.)

- Client computers cannot communicate with a server running Windows NT 4.0 or Windows 2000 using a target server-based account if the time on the target server differs by more than 30 minutes from the time on the client computer. (This is also true if the client computer is configured with a secure.inf template.)

- If the server is a domain controller, and a hisecdc.inf template is used, then all of the other domain controllers in trusted or trusting domains must be running at least Windows 2000 Server and therefore cannot run Windows NT Server.

If any of the above conditions prevent proper communications in your network, then you have two choices. You can either upgrade all of your servers to at least Windows 2000 (preferably Windows Server 2003) or you can continue to use Windows NT 4.0 with Service Pack 4 or higher, but you will need to use a secure template (such as securedc.inf) instead of the highly secure one. Activity 4-1 will assist you in understanding security templates and their relation to Windows NT.

ACTIVITY

Activity 4-1: Understanding Security Templates and Their Relation to Windows NT

Time Required: 30 minutes

Objective: Learn about security templates used in Windows Server 2003 and how they relate to communication with Windows NT servers and clients. You should notice the differences between the security templates as they relate to the role of the computer to which they are applied.

Description: In this activity, you will investigate further the predefined templates available in Windows 2000 and Windows Server 2003. You will learn how templates started with

Windows NT 4.0 SP 4, what they do, and how they can affect communication with Windows NT servers and clients. You will then examine templates in the software on your own computer.

1. Log on with your **AdminXX** account, where *XX* is your assigned student number. Start **Internet Explorer**.

2. Go to the following Web site:

   www.microsoft.com/resources/documentation/WindowsServ/2003/ standard/proddocs/en-us/Default.asp

3. Navigate to **Security/Security Configuration Manager/Concepts/ Using Security Configuration Manager/Predefined Security Templates**.

4. Read through the article about how predefined Windows Server 2003 templates relate to the use of Windows NT.

5. Click **Start**, choose **Run**, type **mmc**, and then press **Enter**.

6. Select **File**, select **Add/Remove Snap-in**, then choose **Add**.

7. Select **Security Templates**, then choose **Add**.

8. Choose **Close**, then click **OK**.

9. Examine the security templates that you read about on the Web page. Note the differences in the security templates based on the role of the computer. Pay special attention to the Local Policies, including User Rights Assignment and Audit Policy.

10. Close the **MMC** and **Internet Explorer**.

Modified File and Folder Permissions

If you are using security templates such as DC security.inf, Rootsec.inf, and Setup security. inf on a Windows Server 2003 computer in an environment where Windows NT servers exist, the file and folder permissions on the system and boot partitions of the Windows NT computers might be affected. In addition, if you use Group Policy or directly configured security templates to control permissions on computers that were originally set through a Windows NT computer, you could get some unexpected results, including permissions that are much more relaxed than you had intended. This can occur if a server has been migrated from Windows NT 4.0.

To solve these problems you could use one of three methods. You could either carefully modify the template and test it again, provide multiple templates to apply granular file level security, or overwrite the permissions by selecting Replace permission entries on all child objects with entries shown here that apply to child objects, as shown in Figure 4-1.

Windows 2000

Because security templates in Windows 2000 function in very much the same way as those in Windows Server 2003, you are not likely to have as many issues as with Windows NT

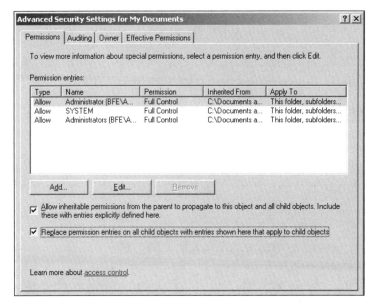

Figure 4-1   The Replace Existing Permissions setting

Server. However, you should be aware that the syntax of the default security templates for Windows 2000 differs from that of Windows Server 2003. For this reason, you should make sure that you do not import a Windows 2000 Server security template into Windows Server 2003 or vice versa. In other words, just keep the appropriate security templates on the appropriate machines, and they will communicate just fine.

Windows Server 2003

As you would expect, Windows Server 2003 templates will function as intended on Windows Server 2003 machines. You should take care to use the correct security template for the role of the server. For example, domain controllers should be assigned a hisecdc.inf, DC security.inf, or securedc.inf template. (Domain controllers will automatically be assigned a DC security.inf template when they are first promoted.) As mentioned earlier, you should not delete or change the default templates; instead, you should create new templates as needed.

Figure 4-2 illustrates the Domain Security tool on a domain controller, which can be used to import a security template. You can also import a template into a Group Policy.

Client Operating Systems

In general, the client operating systems follow the same patterns as their associated servers. In other words, Windows NT Workstation cannot authenticate to or communicate with Windows 2000 Server or Windows Server 2003 machines that are running a high-security template. If you need to use Windows NT Workstation in your network, then you will need

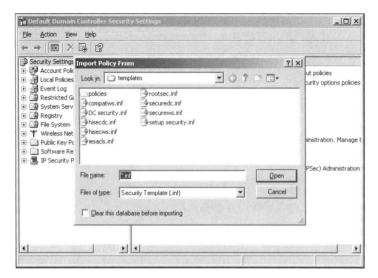

Figure 4-2   Importing a security template into a domain controller security policy

to use a template that provides less security. Windows 2000 Professional and Windows XP Professional clients can communicate with newer servers regardless of the templates that they are running. The syntax of the default templates for Windows XP Professional is different from that of Windows 2000 Professional, so you should also make sure to apply the correct type of template to the correct operating system and computer.

TROUBLESHOOTING SECURITY IN A MIXED DOMAIN LEVEL ENVIRONMENT

Another troubleshooting challenge was created by the evolution of technology and the additional security features that were added to each successive family of servers. Because each family of servers has a distinct range of capabilities, Microsoft has divided the servers into three distinct groups in regard to their functional capability. These groups are referred to as functional levels. Functional levels exist for domains as well as for an entire forest. In this discussion, we will focus on **domain functional levels**.

In Windows Server 2003, there are three possible domain functional levels, Windows 2000 mixed, Windows 2000 native, and Windows Server 2003. Each domain functional level is defined by the lowest level of server in the domain. The functional level of each domain determines the features that are available to manage the security of the users and computers within that domain. In a forest that has many domains, each domain can be individually configured with its own functional level. You should understand how a mixture of domain functional levels within the same forest can create a troubleshooting challenge for an administrator. In the following sections, we will discuss each of the domain functional levels in greater detail.

NOTE Actually one other domain functional level is possible, but it requires a registry edit. This is referred to as the Windows Server 2003 interim functional level. It is to be used when only Windows NT servers and Windows Server 2003 servers will be in the domain.

Windows 2000 Mixed

4

Windows 2000 mixed is the lowest of domain functional levels from the standpoint of security. It is also the default domain functional level when you create the first domain controller of a domain. You need to continue to use Windows 2000 mixed only when your network contains domain controllers that are running Windows NT Server as well as domain controllers that are running Windows 2000 Server. Otherwise, you can raise the domain functional level immediately. Leaving the domain at the Windows 2000 mixed functional level is roughly equivalent to leaving a Windows 2000 domain set to mixed mode; most of the old rules that governed Windows NT will still apply. To be more specific, the following limitations exist for a domain that is in Windows 2000 mixed functional level.

- You cannot create or use universal security groups.
- You cannot nest global groups within global groups or domain local groups within domain local groups.
- You cannot create or utilize cross-forest trusts.
- You cannot convert a group type from security to distribution or vice versa.
- You cannot migrate security principals (SID histories) from one domain to another, even within the same forest.

Windows 2000 Native

Native is the next highest domain functional level in Windows 2000. As you would expect, this domain functional level in Windows Server 2003 is roughly equivalent to running a Windows 2000 domain in native mode. Because each computer is upgraded individually, there will be Windows 2000 servers in the mixed Windows 2003 domain until all domain controllers have been upgraded to Windows Server 2003. The benefits and limitations that applied to domain controllers running Windows 2000 Server will also apply to domains running Windows Server 2003 at the native functional level. Some of the benefits and limitations of which you should be aware are listed here:

- You can create and use universal security type groups.
- You can nest global groups within global groups and domain local groups within domain local groups within the same domain.
- You can convert security groups to distribution groups and vice versa.
- You can use SID histories to gradually migrate security principals from one domain in a forest to another domain in the same forest.
- You cannot create cross-forest trusts.

Windows Server 2003

Windows Server 2003 domain functional level is by far the most secure and . . . well, functional of all domain functional levels. Administrators whose domains are at the Windows Server 2003 functional level can take full advantage of all of the old and new features of the Windows Server 2003 operating system. In order to raise a domain to this functional level, all domain controllers in the domain must be running Windows Server 2003. After you raise the domain to Windows Server 2003 functional level, you cannot add any Windows 2000 domain controllers.

Large organizations with many domains in multiple trees will appreciate the advantages that the Windows Server 2003 domain functional level provides. Organizations that merge with other organizations will be able to use cross-forest trusts after all of the domains and the forest itself have been raised to Windows Server 2003 domain functional level. This can dramatically decrease the number of trusts that an organization has to maintain and manage. Both of the forests involved in the cross-forest trust must be at Windows Server 2003 forest functional level. Some of the advantages of upgrading a domain to Windows Server 2003 functional level include the following:

- Cross-forest trusts are available.
- Groups can be converted from one group type and scope to another.

You can raise the forest functional level using the Active Directory Domains and Trusts tool, after all of the domains in the forest have been raised.

NOTE

Activity 4-2: Understanding Domain Functional Levels

ACTIVITY

Time Required: 30 minutes

Objective: Learn about domain functional levels and which tools can be used to change levels.

Description: In this activity, you will investigate domain functional levels, and you will examine the tools that are used to change domain functional levels on Windows Server 2003.

1. Log on with your **AdminXX** account, where *XX* is your assigned student number.
2. Click **Start**, choose **Administrative Tools**, and then choose **Active Directory Users and Computers**.
3. Right-click on the domain, then choose **Raise Domain Functional Level**.

4. Click the drop-down list arrow below Select an available domain functional level and examine the functional levels that are available.

5. Choose **Cancel**, then close **Active Directory Users and Computers**.

6. Click **Start**, select **Administrative Tools**, and then select **Active Directory Domains and Trusts**.

7. Right-click on the domain, then select **Raise Domain Functional Level**.

8. Click the drop-down list arrow below Select an available domain functional level and examine the functional levels that are available.

9. Note that the same domain functional levels are available in both tools and that you can change the domain functional level with either tool, as shown in Figures 4-3 and 4-4. Note that the domain is in the default Windows 2000 mixed functional level. Do not raise the functional level at this time.

10. Click **Cancel** to close Active Directory Domains and Trusts.

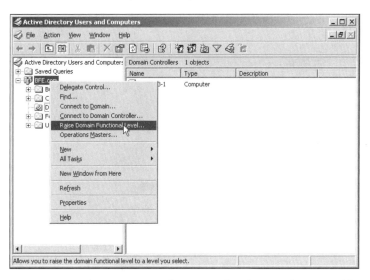

Figure 4-3 The setting used to raise the domain functional level in Active Directory Users and Computers

Figure 4-5 illustrates the drop-down list setting that is common to both Active Directory Users and Computers and Active Directory Domains and Trusts.

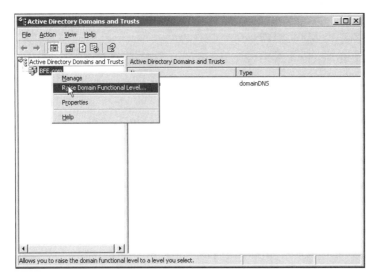

Figure 4-4   The setting used to raise the domain functional level in Active Directory
Domains and Trusts

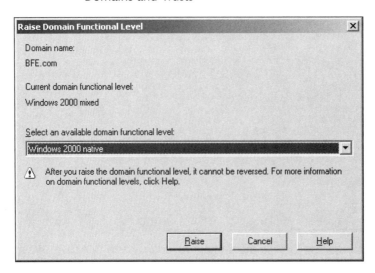

Figure 4-5   The drop-down list setting used to change the functional level of a domain

TROUBLESHOOTING SECURITY INHERITANCE PROBLEMS

One of the nicest features of Active Directory is that it is a **hierarchical database**. This
means that you can apply security settings at the higher levels and expect them to be
inherited to the lower levels of the Active Directory. This concept is collectively referred to
as **security inheritance**. For example, you can apply security templates with a Group
Policy at the domain level and expect them to be inherited by all of the OUs in the domain.

4

In most cases, your expectations will be met, but you need to understand that there are other features of Active Directory that might counteract some of your settings and cause other results.

In order to troubleshoot problems that keep normal inheritance of security settings from occurring, you need to understand all of the factors associated with security in Active Directory. Microsoft recommends that you control permissions assigned to users and computers by first placing them into a group and then controlling the permissions to the group. The basic idea is that the members of the group should inherit the permissions of the group. As mentioned before, you can also place groups into other groups to carry the inheritance even further. In addition, you can apply Group Policy to sites, domains, and OUs in the Active Directory and thereby control users and computers in a very granular fashion. In fact, Group Policies that affect the same users and computers can be applied to multiple levels in the Active Directory hierarchy.

You need to understand the types of groups that can be used in Active Directory and their effect on the permissions of users and computers and thereby on the security of your network. You should also understand Group Policy inheritance and the general order by which Group Policies are applied to the various containers of the Active Directory hierarchy. In addition, you should understand the important exceptions to these rules and how they might affect troubleshooting security. In the paragraphs that follow, we will discuss each of these concepts in greater detail.

Security Groups

Active Directory provides two different types of groups: distribution and security. **Distribution groups** are used only to create e-mail lists for distribution programs, such as Exchange, and cannot be used to control access to a resource. **Security groups** are used to control access to resources in Active Directory. We will focus the rest of this discussion on security groups.

There are three main scopes of security groups used in Active Directory: global, domain local, and universal. Each group scope is intended for a specific use and should generally contain only specific members. In the paragraphs that follow, we will discuss each type of security group and its use in detail.

Global Groups

Global groups are designed to give users access to a resource based on their membership in the global group. Global groups generally contain users who inherit permissions to use a resource from the global group's permissions. If your domain is in at least Windows 2000 native functional level, then global groups can also contain other global groups, thus extending the inheritance of permissions. The global groups themselves can be logically placed into other groups that are found within any domain in the Active Directory forest. If a user is a member of more than one global group, then his effective permissions will be a combination or accumulation of the permissions that he inherits from each of the global groups. If a global group is explicitly denied access to a resource, then the user who inherits the permissions will also be denied access to the resource. This will result even if the user is explicitly permitted access to the resource based on inherited permissions from other global groups. To avoid this type of confusion, global groups are rarely assigned permissions directly, but instead users are placed into global groups based on their role in the organization or their location. For example, a user might be a member of the Managers global group and/or a member of the Southwest global group.

Domain Local Groups

Domain local groups are designed to control access to a resource. Microsoft recommends that administrators place user accounts into global groups and then place the global groups into the domain local groups and give the domain local groups the permissions. A good way to remember this is AGDLP, which stands for "Accounts go into global groups, then global groups go into domain local groups, and finally domain local groups are assigned the permissions." Typically, only domain local groups should be directly assigned permissions to a resource; other groups, and the users within the groups, will inherit the permissions. Domain local groups generally contain global groups from their own domain as well as other domains in the forest and universal groups. If a user is a member of more than one global group, and the same global groups are members of the domain local group, then the effective permissions for the user will be the combination or accumulation of permissions from all of the relevant groups. For this reason, you should carefully check group memberships of users and groups when you are experiencing a problem with a user's permissions for a resource.

Universal Groups

Universal groups are available only when your domain is in at least Windows 2000 native functional level. Universal groups are not directly part of any domain in a multiple domain forest, but are instead shared by all of the domains in the forest. Typically, you will use a universal group when you want to give members of more than one domain in a forest access to resources that are also contained in more than one domain in the forest. This is done by placing global groups that contain members from each of the domains into the universal group and then placing the universal group into the domain local group that gives access to the resource. This expands our previous pneumonic to AGUDLP. This should be done with each resource to which the users need access. The universal groups themselves can be viewed from any domain controller, but they can be used only by domains that are in at least Windows 2000 native functional level.

Nested Groups

Technically speaking, **nesting** groups simply means putting one group into another group. According to this definition, we have had the capability to "nest" groups ever since Windows NT Server. In other words, if we consider placing a global group into a domain local group as nesting a group, then we have that capability with all of the server operating systems of which we have spoken and at all of the functional levels of each of the operating systems as well. There is, however, a narrower definition of nesting that is defined as placing a global group into another global group or a domain local group into another domain local group. It is this narrower definition that we will discuss in the paragraphs that follow.

You can nest global groups into other global groups as long as all of the global groups that will be nested are in the same domain. This is typically done to simplify the use of permission setting, while allowing the process to be selective and granular as well. For example, your organization might have an Accounts Payable global group and an Accounts Receivable global group. You could manage each of the global groups on their own and place them both into a domain local group to give the members access to a resource. Alternatively, you could create an Accounting global group and nest the Accounts Payable and Accounts Receivable global groups within it. You could then give all of the members of both groups access to a resource simply by placing the Accounting global group into the correct domain local group. In other words, when you nest the global group within the other global group, it will inherit the permissions of the group within which it is nested. In most cases, the permissions that it will inherit will be those that are directly assigned to the domain local group of which the group that it is nested within is a member.

You can also nest domain local groups in domain local groups as long as both of the domain local groups are members of the same domain. This is done for the purpose of simplifying permissions to multiple resources for the same users or global groups. For example, suppose that you have several HP LaserJet printers. You could individually assign the permissions of each printer so that the global groups that contain the appropriate users will have access to it. Alternatively, you could create a domain local group named All HP Printers and place all of the domain local groups created for each printer into the All HP Printers domain local group. You could then assign the permissions for all of the global groups, and thus the users that they contain, to the All HP Printers domain local group. Because the other domain local groups are nested within the All HP Printers group, they will inherit the permissions assigned to the All HP Printers group. The result will be that the appropriate users will be able to use all of the HP printers in your organization. Also, when you add another printer, you can just create a domain local group for it and place it in the All HP Printers group, and the permissions will already be assigned properly.

As you can see, group nesting can simplify permission assignment if you know how to use it, or it can complicate troubleshooting when you don't know what was set up or why. It makes sense if you know how you configured it, but following someone else might be a nightmare in deciphering what they configured. If you are encountering problems with user permissions, you should carefully check each of the global groups of which the users are members. The key is to make sure that those global groups are not members of another global group. Similarly, you should check each of the domain local groups used to control access to the resources in question. This is done to ensure that those domain local groups are not members of another domain local group. Carefully examining the group memberships of the users and the groups will allow you to begin to piece together the "whole story" with regard to security.

Activity 4-3: Understanding Group Scopes Available Based on Domain Functional Level

Time Required: 30 minutes

Objective: Learn about group scopes that are available at various domain functional levels.

Description: In this activity, you will investigate the group scopes that are available on Windows Server 2003 in the Windows 2000 mixed functional level versus those that are available in the Windows 2000 native functional level and above.

1. Log on with your **AdminXX** account, where *XX* is your assigned student number.

2. Click **Start**, choose **Administrative Tools**, and then select **Active Directory Users and Computers**.

3. Right-click on the domain, select **New**, and then select **Group**.

4. Ensure that the Group type selected is **Security**, then note that you can create domain local and global groups, but that security universal groups are not available. See Figure 4-6.

5. Close the **New Object – Group dialog box**.

6. Right-click on the domain, then select **Raise Domain Functional Level**.

7. Ensure that **Windows 2000 native** is selected, then select **Raise**.

8. Click **OK** on the warning that says that the operation cannot be reversed, then click **OK** once more on the dialog box that indicates that the domain functional level was raised successfully.

9. Right-click on the domain, choose **New**, and then choose **Group**.

10. Ensure that the Group type selected is **Security**, then note that you can now create security universal groups in your domain. See Figure 4-7.

11. Close the **New Object – Group** dialog box.

Figures 4-6 and 4-7 illustrate the before and after in regard to Universal group scopes when a domain is raised from Windows 2000 mixed to Windows 2000 native functional level.

Policy Application Order

Actually, you really can't understand the whole story in regard to security unless you take into account all of the security policies that might be applied to a computer and/or a user. When a computer is a member of a workgroup and the users are all local to the computer, the only security policy of which you need to be aware is the local security policy of the computer itself. It gets a bit trickier when a computer is a member of a domain and you are using domain-based user accounts. In that case, Group Policies can also be applied to the computer and/or the user. Because a group policy can be applied at multiple levels in the Active Directory, it is important that you understand **policy application order** and the effect that it can have on the resulting security policy of a computer.

4

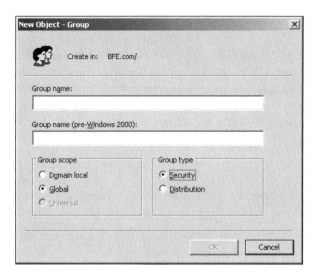

Figure 4-6 Security group scopes available at the Windows 2000 mixed domain functional level

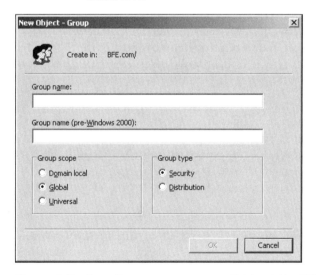

Figure 4-7 Security group scopes available at the Windows 2000 native domain functional level

In addition to the local security policies that can be applied to a computer, three levels of Group Policies can also be applied. First, Group Policies can be applied at site level for computers and/or the users in the Active Directory site. A site is a physical division of Active Directory, which generally represents a geographical location of an organization. Sites are defined and managed by an administrator using the Active Directory Sites and Services tool. In addition, a Group Policy can be applied at domain level for computers and/or users. Group Policies that are applied at domain level will affect all of the computers and/or users in the domain (depending on the configuration of the policy). Account policies such as Password Policy and Account Lockout Policy are always applied at the domain level. Finally, a Group Policy can be applied to an OU in the hierarchy, where the computer or user objects are located or to the specific OU that contains the computers and/or users. Because many types of policies can be applied to the same objects, it's important that you understand the order in which the settings in the Group Policy should be configured. It's equally important that you understand which settings are inherited by a computer, or a user, when multiple Group Policies are applied.

When multiple Group Policies are applied to the same computer or user, the application, order that determines the resultant set of policies is usually the same, with some exceptions. It's important that you understand both the usual order and the exceptions so that you can configure a server properly. We will discuss the usual order first and then the exceptions.

The usual order in which Group Policies are applied is as follows: local, site, domain, and then OU. If a computer or user object has more than one type of policy applied to it, the settings in all of the policies must be considered. Any settings that do not conflict with other settings will be applied. Settings that conflict will be applied based on the usual order of application, and the last setting that is applied will become the effective setting. In other words, if a policy at the domain level states that all computers will have the Run option in the Start menu, but a policy at the OU level states that all computers will not have the Run option in the Start menu, then the Run option will not be listed in the Start menu, because the OU policy will be applied after the domain policy. You can remember the usual order that policies are applied as LSDOU.

As we said, the usual order does have some exceptions. Any settings that relate to Account Policies, such as the Password, Account Lockout, and Kerberos policies, are set at the domain level and will apply regardless of any other settings at any other level. You should know that it is possible to set these at the OU level, but they will affect only local logons and will not override domain level settings for computers or domain user accounts.

Block Inheritance

Generally speaking, policies will be inherited by all of the objects within the Active Directory hierarchy. In most cases, this is the expected result and desired method of using policies. For example, policies that are applied at domain level will be inherited by all of the OUs in the domain. In the same manner, policies that are applied to a parent to OU will be inherited by all of the child OUs within it. This inheritance allows an administrator to manage security policies in the most efficient manner. An administrator can apply the policy to the highest level of the hierarchy that is to be managed, and it will be applied everywhere in the hierarchy.

In some cases, the administrator might want to control the application of security policies in a more granular fashion. For example, she may want to apply the policies to all of the OUs within a domain except for one or two specific OUs. In this case, she can use the **Block Inheritance** feature of Active Directory to stop the flow of inheritance and set the specific policies and settings that she desires. The Block Inheritance feature is available to any domain administrator or OU administrator.

No Override

Because OU administrators have the right to use the Block Inheritance feature, they can override the security that the domain administrators had intended for the entire domain. Likewise, an administrator who has rights to manage only a specific child OU can override the policies that the administrator for the entire hierarchy of OUs has previously set. To prevent this from occurring, these administrators can use the **No Override or Enforced** option in the security policy's settings. Setting the No Override or Enforced option at the higher level in a hierarchy prevents the other administrator, who can manage only the lower levels, from inadvertently or intentionally changing the security settings. You can use the No Override or Enforced option to ensure that a critical policy is enforced regardless of whether the OU administrator applies the Block Inheritance setting. In other words, if an OU administrator applies a Block Inheritance setting, then only those policies that do not have the No Override or Enforced setting will be blocked. No Override supersedes Block Inheritance.

No Override was the term used to refer to this option in the original Group Policy tools; however, the new Group Policy Management Console uses the term *Enforced* to refer to the same setting. After you install the Group Policy Management Console, the Enforced setting will replace the No Override setting.

You can also filter permissions within a single OU by controlling the permission settings of the members of the OU. In order for a Group Policy to actually apply to an object, that object must have Read and Apply Group Policy permission for the policy.

Activity 4-4: Understanding Block Inheritance versus No Override or Enforced for Group Policies

Time Required: 30 minutes

Objective: Learn about controlling the inheritance of Group Policies through an Active Directory hierarchy.

Description: In this activity, you will install the Group Policy Management Console from the Internet, then examine the effect of using the Block Inheritance and No Override (Enforce) features.

1. Log on with your **AdminXX** account, where *XX* is your assigned student number.

2. If you have not already installed the GPMC, open your browser, type

www.microsoft.com/downloads on the address line, and press **Enter**. If you have installed the GPMC, skip to Step 5.

3. On the Microsoft Download Center page, type **GPMC** in the box labeled Search Microsoft.com for., and then click **Go** to execute the search program.

4. Select **Download Group Policy Management Console (GPMC) with Service Pack 1**, then follow the directions and use the wizards to download and install the console.

5. Click **Start**, choose **Administrative Tools**, and then choose **Group Policy Management**.

6. Click on the plus (+) signs to expand your forest, then expand your domain.

7. Click on the plus (+) sign to expand the Group Policy Objects container.

8. Right-click on the domain, then choose **New Organizational Unit**.

9. Type the name **TestOU** for the new OU, then click **OK**.

10. Right-click the **Group Policy Objects** container, then choose **New**.

11. Type **TestGP** in the New GPO dialog box, then click **OK**.

12. Click on the **TestGP** policy within the Group Policy Objects container and drag the policy up to the domain.

13. When your domain is selected, release the policy, then click **OK** in the dialog box that asks if you want to link the policy to the domain.

14. Click on the **TestOU** container, then click the **Group Policy Inheritance** tab.

15. Note that the TestGP policy was inherited by the TestOU when you applied it to the domain.

16. Right-click on the **TestOU** container and select **Block Inheritance**.

17. Ensure that the **Group Policy Inheritance** tab is still selected and note that none of the Group Policies applied at domain level are inherited by the OU.

18. Right-click on the TestGP policy that is applied to your domain and select **Enforced**. (Be sure to right-click on the policy within the domain container, not the one within the Group Policy Objects container.)

19. Right-click on **TestOU** and select **Refresh**.

20. Note that the TestGP policy is still enforced even though Block Inheritance remains in effect for all other policies that do not have the Enforced setting applied. See Figure 4-8.

21. Close the **Group Policy Management Console**.

Figure 4-8 illustrates the fact that the Enforced setting applied higher in the Active Directory hierarchy will override the Block Inheritance setting applied at lower in the Active Directory hierarchy.

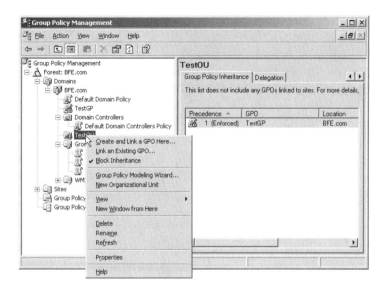

Figure 4-8   Enforced setting applied at a higher level overriding the Block Inheritance setting applied at a lower one

Troubleshooting Security Template Problems

In most cases, the fact that security templates can make many configuration changes with one quick step is a very good thing; that is, as long as nothing goes wrong in the process. When a problem does occur, it can be a challenge to determine the cause of the problem, especially when multiple templates are applied to the same objects. Windows Server 2003 includes three tools that can be used to troubleshoot these problems: **Resultant Set of Policy (RSoP)**, a suite of command-line utilities, and the Security Configuration and Analysis Microsoft Management Console (MMC). In the paragraphs that follow, we will discuss each of these tools in greater detail.

Resultant Set of Policy (RSoP)

As we discussed earlier, the settings that will actually be applied to an object will be a combination of all of the settings that can affect the object. All of the settings that do not conflict will, in effect, "snowball," and therefore settings might be applied to an object from many different policies. Settings that conflict will be subject to the rules that we discussed earlier. This being the case, we need a tool that will allow us to quickly determine which settings will apply to a user, a group of users, a computer, or a group of computers. You can use the RSoP tool to determine the effective settings on the computer that you are working from or any other computer in a Windows Server 2003 domain. You cannot use RSoP for any computers other than the one from which you are currently working if you are not on a Windows Server 2003 domain. This means that the domain must contain at least one domain controller running Windows Server 2003.

The RSoP tool has two main modes: planning mode and logging mode. The biggest difference between the two modes is their intended use. It's important that you understand the purpose of each mode. You should also know how to use RSoP in each mode. In the following sections, we will discuss each mode in greater detail.

Planning Mode

Planning mode is generally used for a "what if" scenario. You can use this mode to predict the effects of a series of policies on a specified user or computer without actually applying the policies to the object. You can use planning mode to gather information without affecting the productivity of users. Planning mode is generally initiated from the RSoP snap-in tool in a MMC.

Logging Mode

Logging mode is used to ascertain the effect of multiple policies on a user or computer. In logging mode, you are actually examining the policies that have been applied to the object. This is the mode that you are most likely to use for troubleshooting inheritance with multiple Group Policies. You can use three different methods on Windows XP Professional and Windows Server 2003 computers to gather information in logging mode, as follows:

- *The Run dialog box*—You can quickly determine the effects of all Group Policies on the current user and computer by typing rsop.msc in the Run dialog box of the computer. The analysis will begin automatically.

- *Active Directory Users and Computers*—You can specify a user/computer combination in Active Directory and analyze the effects of all of the Group Policies applied to the user and computer.

- *A custom MMC*—You can add the RSoP snap-in to an MMC and then start the Resultant Set of Policy Wizard to select the user and computer combination that you want to analyze.

ACTIVITY

Activity 4-5: Using RSoP to Determine Applied Settings with Multiple Policies

Time Required: 15 minutes

Objective: Learn about the use of RSoP to determine the effective settings of multiple policies applied to a computer and/or user.

Description: In this activity, you will use a simple version of RSoP to determine the effective settings for the computer that you are logged on to and the user account with which you are logged on.

1. Log on with your **AdminXX** account, where *XX* is your assigned student number.

2. Click **Start**, then choose **Run**.

3. On the Run line type **rsop.msc**, then choose **OK**. The system will begin to analyze the settings as shown in Figure 4-9. Wait for the system to finish the analysis.

4. Examine the Computer Configuration and User Configuration containers to determine the settings that are applied. Note that these are the effective settings for the local computer and the user who is currently logged on. See Figure 4-10.

4

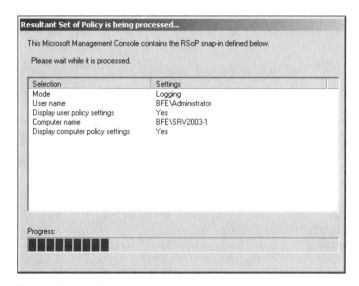

Figure 4-9   RSoP analysis

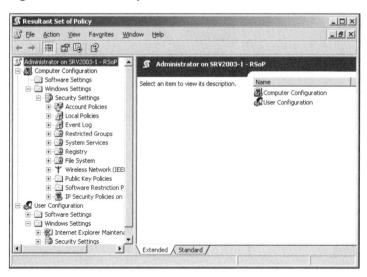

Figure 4-10   RSoP results

Using Command-Line Utilities

If you want to be able to script GPO troubleshooting of multiple computers, you might also want to use the **gpresult** tool. You can use gpresult to perform almost all of the actions that are available in RSoP logging mode (see Table 4-1), with one exception. You cannot determine policy precedence information with the gpresult tool. The gpresult command is simple to use and provides many additional switches for specific functionality. You can determine significant information about Group Policies simply by typing gpresult on a command line. The complete syntax of the command with all of the switches is as follows:

gpresult [/s *computer* [/u *domain\user* /p *password*]] [/user *target_user*] [/scope{*user*| *computer*}] [{ /v | /z}] >*filename*.txt

Table 4-1   Options Available with the gpresult Command

Option	Description
/s computer	Specifies the remote computer to be used. You can use the computer name or the IP address. If this is not specified, the local computer will be used.
/u domain\user /p password	Enables you to enter the username and password required to run the gpresult command in the context of another user. You should also specify the domain name if it is different from the domain to which you are logged on.
/usertarget_user	Specifies the user to be used. If this is not specified, the current user will be used.
/scope {computer	user}	Limits the display to a specific computer and/or user.
/v	Displays verbose policy information (much more detail).
/z	Displays all available information about Group Policy (even more than verbose).
>filename.txt	Used at the end of the command. Redirects output to a specified file. You should use this command with the /v and /z options to contain the large amounts of data that are created.

ACTIVITY

Activity 4-6: Using gpresult to Determine Applied Settings with Multiple Policies

Time Required: 15 minutes

Objective: Learn about the use of gpresult to determine the effective settings of multiple policies applied to a computer and/or user.

Description: In this activity, you will use a simple version of gpresult to determine the effective settings for the computer that you are logged onto and the user account with which you are logged on.

1. Log on with your **AdminXX** account, where *XX* is your assigned student number.

2. Click **Start**, then choose **Run**.

3. On the Run line type **cmd**, then click **OK** to access a command prompt.

4. On the command prompt type **gpresult**, then press **Enter**. The system will immediately analyze the local computer and the currently logged on user to determine the results of the settings applied, as shown in Figure 4-11.

5. Analyze the results of the output to determine which Group Policies, if any, are being applied to the computer and the currently logged on user.

6. Type **exit**, then press the **Enter** key to close the command window.

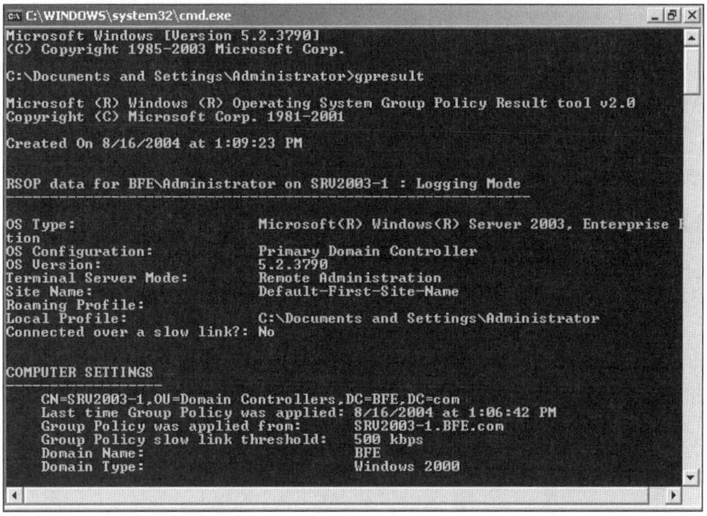

Figure 4-11 The beginning of the gpresult output

Using Security Configuration and Analysis

Security Configuration and Analysis (SCA) is a tool that you can use to ensure that the security configuration settings that you are using for multiple computers are applied as you expected and are applied the same across all computers. The SCA tool is a snap-in that you can add to an MMC. You can compare a database of settings to the current configuration of a computer to be sure that the settings that you expected to be applied are actually applied. The SCA tool provides unmistakable green check marks and red Xs to indicate whether the database setting is actually applied to the computer. You can quickly scan the settings to determine the setting that might be causing a problem. You should know how to configure and analyze a computer using the SCA tool. The following exercise will introduce you to the SCA tool and show you how to configure and analyze security settings with the tool.

Activity 4-7: Using the Security Configuration and Analysis Tool

Time Required: 30 minutes

Objective: Learn about the Security Configuration and Analysis tool.

Description: In this activity, you will take the Security Configuration and Analysis tool to the next level. You will configure a database of settings using a security template and then compare the database of settings to the current configuration of the computer. You will be able to see the changes that the tool makes and compare the database settings with the computer settings in a real configuration.

1. Log on with your **AdminXX** account, where *XX* is your assigned student number.

2. Click **Start**, select **Administrative Tools**, and then select **Domain Security Policy**.

3. Expand **Account Policies**, then select **Password Policy**.

4. In the details pane (on the right), note that the Minimum password age is 1 day and the Minimum password length is 7 characters.

5. Minimize the **Default Domain Security Settings** tool.

6. Click **Start**, choose **Run**, and then type **mmc**.

7. Choose **File**, select **Add/Remove Snap-In**, and then select **Add**.

8. Select **Security Configuration and Analysis** from the Add Standalone Snap-in menu, then select **Add**.

9. Select **Security Templates** from the Add Standalone Snap-in menu, select **Add**, and then select **Close**.

10. Choose **OK** to create the new Microsoft Management Console (MMC).

11. Expand **Security Templates**, then expand **C:\WINDOWS\security\templates**.

12. Expand the **hisecdc** template, expand **Account Policies**, and then select **Password Policy**. Note that the Minimum password age is 2 days and the Minimum password length is 8 characters.

13. In the console pane (on the left), right-click **Security Configuration and Analysis**, then choose **Open Database**.

14. In the File name box, type **passwordtest**, then select **Open**.

15. Select the **High Security - DomainController.inf** template to be used as a database to compare against the current settings on the computer, then select **Open**.

16. In the console pane, right-click **Security Configuration and Analysis**, then select **Analyze Computer Now**. Choose **OK** to use the default Error log file path. The analysis will begin as shown in Figure 4-12.

17. When the system is done with the analysis, expand **Security Configuration and Analysis** (in the console pane), expand **Account Policies**, and then select **Password Policy**.

18. Note that the details pane compares the database settings with the computer settings. Those settings that are the same are indicated with a green check mark, as shown in Figure 4-13. Note that the Minimum password age and the Minimum password length are marked with a red X to indicate that the database setting is different than the computer setting.

19. Close the console and the **Default Domain Security Settings** tool.

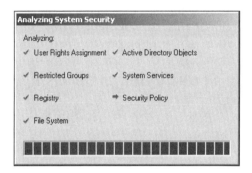

Figure 4-12   The Analyzing System Security dialog box

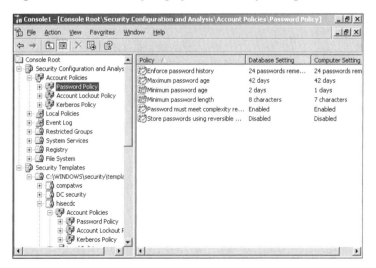

Figure 4-13   Differences between the database settings and the current computer configuration

TROUBLESHOOTING THE REMOVAL OF SECURITY TEMPLATES

Applying security templates can sometimes be easier than removing them. You should understand that the application of security template settings can sometimes cause a "domino effect" and that the resulting changes may not be reset just because you remove the security template that created them. Also, when you remove one security template from a computer, you should immediately assign another security template to replace it. Understanding how templates should be exchanged will assist you in troubleshooting a problem created when one template is exchanged for another one.

As mentioned, the process of removing a security template from a computer is generally a process of replacing it with another security template. This can be accomplished by manually editing the local security of the computer or by applying a Group Policy that enforces a different security template. You should understand how to use Group Policy to enforce the replacement of security templates within all of the computers in an OU or all of the computers within a domain. To accomplish this task, you should create a new Group Policy and then apply it to the container where you want enforce the new template.

Activity 4-8: Applying a New Security Template Using Group Policy

Time Required: 30 minutes

Objective: Learn about the application of security templates to assist in troubleshooting problems associated with replacing security templates.

Description: In this activity, you will learn how to apply a new security template to a group of computers in a domain or an OU by using Group Policy.

This example is used for illustrative purposes, you should take great care when deleting any security policy links, especially a default domain policy.

1. Log on with your **AdminXX** account, where *XX* is your assigned student number.

2. Click **Start**, select **Administrative Tools**, and then select **Group Policy Management**.

3. Expand your forest, expand your domain, and then expand the **Group Policy Objects** container.

4. Right-click the **Group Policy Objects** container, and then select **New**.

5. Type **Security Template Policy** in the New GPO dialog box, then choose **OK**.

6. In the console pane (on the left), right-click the **Security Template Policy**, then select **Edit**.

7. In the Group Policy Object Editor tool for Security Template Policy, expand **Windows Settings** under Computer Configuration, right-click **Security Settings**, then select **Import Policy**. Note that all of the templates are available to import.

8. Select the **High Security -DomainController.inf** template, then click **Open**.

9. Close the **Group Policy Object Editor** tool. The change is automatically saved to the Group Policy.

10. Click **Start**, select **Administrative Tools**, and then select **Domain Security Policy**.

11. Expand **Account Policies** and examine the Password Policy settings. Note that the Minimum password age is still 1 day and that the Minimum password length is still 7 characters.

12. Return to the Group Policy Management Console.

13. Click and hold your new **Security Template Policy**, then drag it up to the domain container. When the domain is selected, release the policy. Click **OK** to indicate that you want to link the policy to the container.

14. Right-click on the default domain policy and click **Delete**. Click **OK** in the dialog box that asks you if you want to delete this link. Also delete any other policies that are linked to the domain, such as the TestGP policy.

15. Click **Start**, select **Run**, type **cmd**, and then press **Enter** to access a command prompt.

16. At the command prompt type **gpupdate** (this will force the system to update the policy immediately instead of waiting for the refresh interval).

17. After the policy is refreshed, review the password settings in Domain Security and note that the Minimum password age and Minimum password length have been increased. (If the settings do not change, then restart your computer to make the changes take effect.)

18. Close all open windows and shut down Windows Server 2003.

NOTE As you can see, there are many factors that affect the ultimate security of your network. These include the types of servers and clients that you use, the functional level at which you run your network, the configuration of your groups for management purposes, and the configuration and management of Group Policies. Its important that you understand not just each of these factors, but also how they all relate to one another.

CHAPTER SUMMARY

- The security of a network is largely dependent upon the types of servers and clients that the network contains.

- Security has become a greater concern in the last few years, so the latest server and client operating systems incorporate significantly more security features than the earlier systems.

- Unless properly configured, Windows NT clients and servers might not even be able to communicate with the newer clients. Creating an environment that allows Windows NT clients and servers to communicate will almost certainly weaken the security of a Windows 2000 or Windows Server 2003 network.

- Another feature that was created by the evolution of security, and the resulting improved operating systems, was the development of functional levels for domains and forests. Forests can have many domains that are each configured for different functional levels. The functional level of a domain will determine which security features are available.

- Active Directory consists of a hierarchical arrangement of domains and OUs. A wise systems administrator will use the hierarchical arrangement and its inheritance properties to his or her advantage whenever possible. Users should typically not be assigned permissions directly but should instead inherit them by being a member of a group. Likewise, global groups should typically not be assigned permissions directly, but instead should inherit them from membership in a domain local or a universal group.

- The best way to remember group organization and inheritance is the acronym AGDLP, which stands for *accounts* go into *global* groups, then global groups go into *domain local* groups, and finally the *domain local* groups get the permissions. When universal groups are utilized the global groups are placed into the universal groups and the universal groups are placed into the domain local groups; in this case the acronym would be AGUDLP.

- You can nest global groups in global groups and domain local groups in domain local groups within the same domain, but only if the domain is at least at the Windows 2000 native functional level.

- Group Policies can dramatically affect the security settings of computers. Group Policies can be applied to the site, domain, or OU level of the Active Directory hierarchy. Policies that do not conflict will combine their settings. Settings in policies that do conflict will be determined based on the order in which they are assigned. The default order is site, domain, and then OU.

- The exceptions to the default order of Group Policy assignment are the settings within Account Policies. These are applied at the domain level and include, Password, Account Lockout, and Kerberos policy settings.

- For more granular control of Group Policies at the OU level, OU administrators can apply a Block Inheritance setting to their OUs. This setting will block the flow of inheritance for all Group Policies that do not specify a No Override or Enforced setting.

- The No Override or Enforced setting (the new GPMC uses the term *Enforced*) should be applied when it is essential that a Group Policy's settings be applied. It can be used by the domain administrator or the OU administrator at the top of a hierarchy of OUs. The No Override setting supercedes the Block Inheritance setting set by an OU administrator further down the hierarchy.

❑ Because security templates can make many changes very quickly, they can also be a challenge to troubleshoot. You can use three main tools to determine the effect of a security template on a user and computer: RSoP, gpresult, and Security Configuration and Analysis.

❑ You should take great care when installing security templates because they can change many settings very quickly within a computer and because they are often much easier to apply than they are to reverse.

KEY TERMS

Block Inheritance — The setting that allows an OU administrator to stop the flow of Group Policies from affecting his or her OU, provided that the policy does not have No Override or Enforce assigned by a higher-level administrator.

distribution groups — Combinations of users in Active Directory that are not used to manage security, but only as e-mail groups.

domain functional level — A setting that can be configured in Active Directory Users and Computers or Active Directory Domains and Trusts, which determines the functionality of a domain, what types of domain controllers it can have, and the security features that the domain can use.

domain local groups — Combinations of members in Active Directory that are used to manage access to a resource. Can contain users, global groups, universal groups, or other domain local groups.

global groups — Combinations of users and other global groups in Active Directory that are used to manage security. All members must come from the same domain.

gpresult — A tool that can be used to query computers running Windows 2000, Windows XP Professional, and Windows Server 2003 to determine the effect of the Group Policies on the local computer with the user currently logged on.

hierarchical database — A database that has multiple levels of authority and control such that one object is considered to be within another object.

nesting — The act of placing one group into another group; usually used to simplify permissions.

No Override or Enforced — The setting on a Group Policy that specifies that lower-level administrators cannot block the inheritance of the security settings in the policy. This is generally used by a domain administrator to ensure that policies are applied to all OUs in the domain, regardless of settings applied by OU administrators.

policy application order — The order in which Group Policies are applied to an object when the object has multiple Group Policies applied to it. The order is typically site, domain, and then OU; however, some exceptions do apply.

Resultant Set of Policy (RSoP) — A tool that queries computers running Windows XP Professional or Windows Server 2003 and provides details about all policy settings that are configured for existing policies based on site, domain, domain controller, and OU.

Security Configuration and Analysis (SCA) — An MMC snap-in tool that can be used to configure security settings onto a computer, a group of computers, or an entire domain. This tool can also be used to analyze the settings in a database against the current settings on a computer and indicate the differences.

security groups — Objects that are used to simplify permissions by combining users that share the same role in an organization and therefore need the same access to specified resources. Access to a resource can be granted by group membership rather than by assigning permission directly to a user account. Security group scopes include global, domain local, and universal.

security inheritance — The concept of the hierarchical model of Active Directory and the fact that permissions are often assigned higher in the hierarchy and inherited by the objects that are lower in the hierarchy.

universal groups — Combinations of users in Active Directory that are used to control permissions of users in multiple domains to objects that are also in multiple domains.

REVIEW QUESTIONS

1. Which is the lowest service pack that must be installed on Windows NT clients and servers so they can communicate effectively with Windows Server 2003 computers that are on their default setting?

   a. Service Pack 6

   b. Service Pack 4

   c. Service Pack 1

   d. No service packs are needed.

2. If a Windows Server 2003 computer is configured as a domain controller with a hisecdc.inf template, then which operating systems can be used as domain controllers in the domain? (Choose all that apply.)

   a. Windows Server 2003

   b. Windows 2000 Professional

   c. Windows 2000 Server

   d. Windows NT Server

3. Which types of security templates should be used on Windows Server 2003 computers? (Choose all that apply.)

   a. Windows Server 2003

   b. Windows NT Service Pack 4 or higher

   c. Windows NT Service Pack 3 or lower

   d. Windows 2000 Server

4. Which types of security templates should you use with Windows XP Professional computers?

   a. Any security template will suffice.

   b. Only Windows XP Professional

   c. Windows XP Professional and Windows 2000 Professional

   d. Windows XP Professional and Windows Server 2003

5. Which of the following are domain functional levels in Windows Server 2003? (Choose all that apply.)

   a. Windows NT mixed

   b. Windows 2000 mixed

   c. Windows Server 2003 native

   d. Windows Server 2003

6. Which of the following are true when a domain is in the Windows 2000 mixed functional level? (Choose all that apply.)

   a. You can create universal security groups.

   b. You can nest global groups within global groups in the same domain.

   c. You can nest global groups within domain local groups.

   d. You cannot use SID histories to migrate objects from one domain to another.

7. Which of the following are true when a domain is in the Windows 2000 native functional level? (Choose all that apply.)

   a. You can create universal security groups.

   b. You can convert security groups to distribution groups and vice versa.

   c. You cannot use SID histories to migrate objects from one domain to another.

   d. You can create cross-forest trusts to other forests.

8. Which of the following are true when a domain is in the Windows Server 2003 functional level? (Choose all that apply.)

   a. You can create cross-forest trusts to other forests.

   b. You cannot convert groups in regard to type or scope.

   c. You can create universal security groups.

   d. You can nest universal groups within universal groups so long as they are in the same domain.

9. Which of the following is the correct acronym for the recommended organization of security groups?

   a. ADLGP

   b. DLGAP

   c. AGDLP

   d. PADLG

10. If a password policy is set at domain level and a conflicting password policy is also set at OU level in the OU that contains the users, which policy settings will result?

   a. The settings at the domain level will override all OU settings.

   b. The result will be a combination of the settings at the domain and at the OU.

   c. The settings at the OU level will override all domain-level settings.

   d. There is not enough information given to determine the result.

11. If a software security policy is set at domain level and a conflicting software policy is also set at the OU level in the OU that contains the users, which policy settings will result?

   a. The settings at the domain level will override all OU settings.

   b. The result will be a combination of domain level and OU level settings, but OU settings will override any conflicting domain-level settings.

   c. The result will be a combination of domain-level and OU-level settings, but domain settings would override any conflicting OU-level settings.

   d. There is not enough information given to determine the result.

12. Which of the following is the correct order of application of security policies?

   a. Site, domain, OU, local

   b. Local, site, domain, OU

   c. OU, site, local, domain

   d. Domain, local, site, OU

13. If a domain administrator applies several Group Policies at the domain level and uses the No Override or Enforced option on some of them, but an OU administrator within the domain applies Block Inheritance to all Group Policies, then which of the following will result? (Choose all that apply.)

   a. The domain policies that have the No Override option will not be inherited by the OU, but all of the other policies will be inherited.

   b. The domain policies that have the No Override option will be inherited by the OU, but all of the other policies will not be inherited.

   c. The No Override option will override the Block Inheritance option.

   d. The Block Inheritance option will override the No Override option.

14. Which of the following are valid methods of using Resultant Set of Policy (RSoP) in logging mode. (Choose all that apply.)

   a. From the Run dialog box

   b. From a command prompt

   c. Within Active Directory Users and Computers

   d. Within the My Computer MMC

15. Which mode(s) of RSoP examine(s) Group Policies that are currently applied to the Active Directory?

   a. Both planning and logging mode examine Group Policies that are applied.

   b. Planning mode only

   c. Logging mode only

   d. Neither planning mode nor logging mode examine Group Policies that are applied.

4

16. Which tool can be used to create a report that contains green check marks and red Xs to compare the current security configuration of a computer with a proposed database of settings?

   a. Active Directory Users and Computers

   b. Group Policy Management Console

   c. Security Configuration and Analysis

   d. Security Templates

17. If a Windows 2003 network contains Windows NT servers and clients, which of the following are options for improving security while allowing communication between all computers? (Choose all that apply.)

   a. Remove all security templates from the Windows Server 2003 servers

   b. Upgrade all NT computers to NT Service Pack 4, then use a highly secure template

   c. Upgrade all NT computers to Windows 2000 or higher, then use a highly secure template

   d. Upgrade all NT computers to NT Service Pack 4, then use a secure template

18. Which of the following advanced security settings should you use to overwrite errant permission settings caused by migrating Windows NT computers with security templates to Windows 2000 or Windows Server 2003?

   a. Use Allow Inheritable Permissions to propagate the setting to the object and all child objects

   b. Use Replace Permissions on all child objects with entries shown that apply to the errant settings

   c. Use the Effective Permissions tab

   d. Use the Owner tab

19. Which of the following templates are valid to use on a computer that is a domain controller? (Choose all that apply.)

   a. securedc.inf

   b. hisecdc.inf

   c. securews.inf

   d. hisecws.inf

20. Which of the following types of templates are valid to use on a Windows 2000 Professional computer? (Choose all that apply.)

    a. Windows 2000 Professional

    b. Windows Server 2003

    c. Windows NT

    d. Windows 2000 Server

21. Which types of computers can be used in a Windows Server 2003 domain that is in Windows Server 2003 domain functional level? (Choose all that apply.)

    a. Windows Server 2003 domain controllers

    b. Windows XP Professional

    c. Windows 2000 Professional

    d. Windows 2000 domain controllers

22. Which types of domain controllers can be used in a Windows Server 2003 domain that is in Windows 2000 native functional level?

    a. Windows NT with SP 4 or higher

    b. Windows 2000 Server

    c. Windows Server 2003

    d. Windows NT with SP 3 or lower

23. Which type of nesting is available in a Windows Server 2003 domain that is in Windows 2000 mixed functional level?

    a. Global groups into domain local groups

    b. Global groups into global groups

    c. Domain local groups into domain local groups

    d. Global groups into universal groups

24. Which types of nesting are available in a Windows Server 2003 domain that is in Windows Server 2003 functional level? (Choose all that apply.)

    a. Global groups into global groups in any domain

    b. Global groups into global groups in the same domain

    c. Domain local groups into domain local groups in any domain

    d. Domain local groups into domain local groups in the same domain

25. Which feature is available only if a domain is in Windows Server 2003 functional level?

    a. Group nesting

    b. Universal groups

    c. SID histories

    d. Cross-forest trusts

CASE PROJECTS

Case Project 4-1

HSBC, Inc. is a large multinational company. The company is currently using Windows 2000 Advanced Server for its domain controllers and Windows NT Server for some member servers. HSBC is in the process of upgrading all servers to Windows Server 2003. Management wants to attain the highest level of security possible. What issues should they pay close attention to during and after the migration? Prepare a report for management discussing the major concerns of communication and organization as they relate to the security of the network.

Case Project 4-2

The CIO at HSBC Inc. has decided that there is no reason to upgrade all of the domain controllers from Windows 2000 Advanced Server to Windows Server 2003. His greatest concern is the huge number of trusts that he is managing now and will be managing after an upcoming merge with another company. Which feature in Windows Server 2003 will assist the CIO only if he upgrades all of the domain controllers to Windows Server 2003? Write a brief memo that explains the benefit of this feature to the CIO.

Case Project 4-3

Management at HSBC has decided that they will accept your recommendation to upgrade all domain controllers to Windows Server 2003. In fact, they have decided to buy new domain controllers to run a test environment and make the migration more seamless. They are now asking you what changes you recommend in regard to security templates. Specifically, they want to know whether the custom security templates that were developed for use with Windows 2000 Server can be imported onto the new Windows Server 2003 machines. Also they want to know how to confirm and test new security templates and how to use the new features in Windows Server 2003 to deploy them. Develop an overall strategy for either using the current templates or creating new templates and deploying them on the new servers.

Case Project 4-4

HSBC Inc. has migrated all of the Windows 2000 and Windows NT computers to Windows Server 2003. You are the only person who knows how to use troubleshooting tools to examine security templates and roll out new templates with Group Policies. You have been instructed to train three people to assist you. Write a synopsis of the key elements involved in troubleshooting security templates and the tools that you can use to implement the task.

Case Project 4-5

During the migration most security templates and security settings were not changed. After the migration, through the research of your team, you have discovered that some of the templates no longer fit the role of the server to which they are applied. You need to instruct your team in regard to removing the templates. List your key concerns and discuss the tools that you might use to remove the templates and to confirm that your new settings are in place.

5

PLANNING AND DEPLOYING PATCH MANAGEMENT

After reading this chapter and completing the exercises, you will be able to:

♦ Plan the deployment of service packs and hotfixes

♦ Evaluate the applicability of service packs and hotfixes

♦ Implement Microsoft Software Update Services (SUS) architecture

♦ Plan the batch deployment of multiple hotfixes

♦ Understand deployment considerations for various machines

♦ Post deployment review

♦ Plan a rollback strategy

Before vulnerabilities and malware became an everyday occurrence, many companies overlooked patch installation and management. Because recent worms have the capability of traveling quickly and causing large amounts of damage, being proactive in security patch management is necessary to keep your environment secure and functional. Companies should have a process in place for identifying vulnerabilities and responding as quickly as possible, especially because successful attacks often start with one vulnerable computer. With all the other various duties that a network administrator has, how can one keep up with not only the new vulnerabilities, but also the patches and updates to software and applications?

Vulnerabilities can be tracked by subscribing to Web sites such as NTBugtraq, which is located at *www.ntbugtraq.com* and CERT advisories, which can be found at *www.cert.org/advisories*. There has been a lot of publicity surrounding scenarios where bugs or vulnerabilities have been reported to software companies only to have nothing done about it. Currently, when Microsoft becomes aware of a security vulnerability, it is evaluated and verified. As necessary, a security patch is created and tested. Afterward, a security bulletin is released, and the software patch is distributed through the Microsoft Download Center or other services.

This chapter explains how to plan the deployment of service packs and hotfixes, evaluate the applicability of service packs and hotfixes, and implement Microsoft Software Update Services (SUS) architecture. It then moves on to explain the planning of batch deployment of multiple hotfixes, deployment considerations for various machines, and the postdeployment review, and it ends with planning a rollback strategy.

PLANNING THE DEPLOYMENT OF SERVICE PACKS AND HOTFIXES

Proactive patch management is necessary to keep your technology environment secure and reliable. As part of maintaining a secure environment, organizations should have a process for identifying security vulnerabilities and responding quickly. This involves having a comprehensive plan for applying software updates, configuration changes, and countermeasures to remove vulnerabilities from the environment and lessen the risk of computers being attacked. It might include using automated tools that make administrators aware of critical updates and allow them to manage and control installation.

The term **patch management** describes the method for keeping computers up to date with new software releases that are developed after an original software product is installed. **Security patch management** is a term used to describe patch management with a concentration on reducing security vulnerabilities. Security patch management is an essential element of secure IT management and operations. Each is part of an effective in-depth defense strategy that is required to reduce an organization's exposure to computer crime today.

Before we go into how to plan a patch management strategy, let's review what types of malicious threat and security vulnerabilities you may encounter. After all, you should know what it is that you are patching and why.

Types of Attacks and Vulnerabilities

There are myriad attacks that can be initiated against a network. We will go over the most common types and offer some prevention, or protection, methods. The attacks that we cover include denial of service and distributed denial of service (DoS/DDoS), backdoors, brute force, buffer overflows, man-in-the-middle, and session hijacking. We will also look at spoofing, scripting files, social engineering, viruses, worms, and Trojan horses.

Denial of Service and Distributed Denial of Service Attacks (DoS/DDoS)

Denial of service and distributed denial of service attacks (DoS/DDoS) are attacks that are focused on disrupting the resources or services that a user would expect to have access to. These types of attacks are executed by manipulating protocols and can happen without the need for the manipulated packets to be validated by the network.

In a Distributed DoS (DDoS) attack, the attacker distributes software that allows the attacker partial or full control of the infected computer system. This is also known as zombie software. Once an attacker has enough systems compromised with the installed zombie software, he can initiate an attack against a victim from a wide variety of hosts. The attacks come in the form of the standard DoS attacks, but the effects are multiplied by the total number of zombie machines under the control of the attacker.

To protect your network, you can set up filters on external routers to drop packets involved in these types of attacks. You should also set up another filter that denies traffic originating from the Internet that shows an internal network address. When you do this, the loss of ping and some services and utilities for testing network connectivity will be incurred, but this is a small price to pay for network protection. If the operating system allows, reduce the amount of time before the reset of an unfinished TCP connection. This will make it harder to keep resources unavailable for extended periods of time.

A **back door** is a program that allows access to a system without using security checks. Usually programmers put back doors in programs so they can debug and change code during test deployments of software. Because many of these back doors are undocumented, they may get left in after the final version of the software is complete, causing security risks.

Back-door programs, such as Back Orifice, NetBus, and Sub7, have two essential parts: a server and a client. The server is the infected machine, and the client is used for remotely controlling the server. These programs are known as illicit servers. Another type of back door comes in the form of a privileged user account. An existing user who already has privileges often creates the back door account. This account is set up to look like a normal user's account and is given a high-level privilege. This allows the user or an attacker to come in under an alias. To prevent this situation, you need to set proper access so that users will not have the right or privilege to alter operating system files.

ACTIVITY

Activity 5-1: Discover How a Client/Server Remote Control Program Works

Time Required: 45 minutes

Objective: Learn how a client/server remote control program is installed and used to remotely access another machine.

Description: In this activity, you install a client/server remote control program and use it to remotely access another machine. Note: For this exercise you will work with a partner or the student sitting next to you.

1. Log on with your **AdminXX** account, where *XX* is your assigned student number.

2. Open an Internet connection. Go to **www.realvnc.com/download.html**. Click **Download** under Free Edition.

3. Scroll to the bottom of the page, then select **Windows 9x/2000/NT/XP(x86)**.

4. Click the **Proceed to download** button.

5. In the download area, click the .exe file next to **full installation** and download it.

6. After the download is complete, click **Open** to start the setup.

7. On the welcome screen, click **Next**.

8. On the license screen, choose **I accept the agreement**. Click **Next**.

9. On the Select Destination Location screen, leave the default selection. Click **Next**.

10. On the Select Components screen, be sure that both the server and viewer are selected. Click **Next**.

11. On the Select Start Menu Folder screen, leave the default selection. Click **Next**.

12. On the **Select Additional Tasks** screen, leave the default selection. Click **Next**.

13. On the Ready to Install screen, click **Install**.

14. When the server installation is complete, on the server Properties screen, click **Set Password**. Choose a password and click **OK**. Click **OK** to exit the screen.

15. Next the client installation will run. On the Information screen, click **Next**.

16. Click **Finish**.

17. To run the program, right click the VNC system tray icon and choose **Add New Client**, and type in the IP address of your partner as shown in Figure 5-1. Click **OK**.

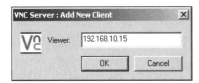

Figure 5-1   VNC add a client screen

18. In this step each student will take turns controlling his or her partner's computer. Click **Start**, **All Programs**, **RealVNC**, **VNC Viewer 4**, **Run VNC Viewer**. In the server connection details dialog box, type in the IP address of your partner. Click **OK**.

19. Type in the password your partner used when setting up the server. Click **OK**. You should now be connected to your partner's machine.

20. Once you have connected, open the **My Computer** icon and explore what you can do.

21. When finished, close **RealVNC** and **Internet Explorer**.

Brute Force Attacks

Brute force is a term used to describe a way of cracking a cryptographic key or password. It involves systematically trying every conceivable combination until a password is found or until all possible combinations have been exhausted. Brute force is a method of pure guessing. Password length and complexity play an important role when dealing with brute force programs—the more complex the password, the longer it takes to crack. Many programs exist that try to decipher password files. L0phtcrack is one such program. It's designed to crack passwords in network traffic streams or in captured password files. L0phtcrack can be found at *www.atstake.com/products/lc*. The best way to prevent brute force attacks is to enforce a strong password length and complexity policy.

Buffer Overflow Attacks

The most common attacks are **buffer overflow** attacks, which are constantly being discovered either by accident or by hackers looking to exploit unsafe code. These attacks are called buffer overflows because more data is sent to a computer's memory buffer than it is able to handle, causing it to overflow. Usually, the overflow crashes the system and leaves it in a state in which arbitrary code can be executed or an intruder can function as an administrator.

Buffer overflows are probably the most common way, currently, to cause disruption of service and lost data. This condition occurs when the data presented to an application or service exceeds the storage space allocation that has been reserved in memory for that application or service. Poor application design might allow the input of 100 characters into a field linked to a variable capable of holding only 50 characters. As a result, the application doesn't know how to handle the extra data and becomes unstable. The overflow portion of the input data must be discarded or somehow handled by the application or it could create undesirable results. Because there is no check in place to screen out bad requests, the extra data overwrites some portions of memory used by other applications and causes failures and crashes. The best way to prevent buffer overflow attacks is to improve the way that applications are programmed so that this type of vulnerability is reduced.

Man-in-the-Middle Attacks

The **man-in-the-middle attack** takes place when an attacker intercepts traffic and then tricks the parties at both ends into believing that they are communicating with each other. The attacker can also choose to alter the data or merely eavesdrop and pass it along.

NOTE

A man-in-the-middle attack can be compared to inserting an interception box between two people having a conversation.

The man-in-the-middle attack is common in Telnet and wireless technologies. It is generally difficult to implement because of physical routing issues, TCP sequence numbers, and speed. If the attack is attempted on an internal network, physical access to the network will be required.

To avoid man-in-the-middle attacks, be sure that access to wiring closets and switches is restricted; if possible, the area should be locked. Next, you should look at the services that can be exploited. DNS can be compromised and used to redirect the initial request for service, providing an opportunity to execute a man-in-the-middle attack. Domain Name System (DNS) access should be restricted to read-only for everyone except the administrator. The best way to prevent these types of attacks is to use encryption and secure protocols.

Session Hijacking

Session hijacking is a term given to an attack that takes control of a session between the server and a client. The authentication mechanism is one-way, making it easy for a hijacker to wait until the authentication cycle is completed and then generate a signal to the client. This signal causes the client to think it has been disconnected from the access point. In the meantime, the hijacker begins to transact data traffic pretending to be the original client. This starts as a man-in-the-middle attack, then adds a reset request to the client. The result is that the client is kicked off the session, while the rogue machine still communicates with the server.

Forcing a user to reauthenticate before allowing transactions to occur could help prevent this type of attack. Other protection mechanisms include the use of unique initial sequence numbers (ISNs) and Web session cookies.

Spoofing

Spoofing is making data appear to come from somewhere other than where it really originated. This is accomplished by modifying the source address of traffic or source of information. Spoofing seeks to bypass IP address filters by setting up a connection from a client and sourcing the packets with an IP address that is allowed through the filter. Services such as e-mail, Hypertext Transfer Protocol (HTTP), and File Transfer Protocol (FTP) can also be spoofed. A hacker can impersonate a valid service by sourcing traffic using the service's IP address or name. To avoid becoming a victim of spoofing, be cautious about what information you give when responding to e-mail and Web requests for information.

Scripting Files

Most Web browsers have the ability to interpret and run scripts embedded in Web pages downloaded from a Web server. These scripts can be written in a variety of scripting languages and are run by the client's browser by default. When a victim with scripts enabled in his or her browser reads a Web-based message, the malicious code may be executed unexpectedly. Users may unintentionally execute scripts written by an attacker when they follow links in Web pages, e-mail messages, or newsgroup postings.

Because the malicious scripts are executed in a context that appears to have originated from the targeted site, the attacker has full access to the document retrieved and may send data contained in the page back to their site.

To reduce the risk of being attacked through this vulnerability, scripting languages in a browser can be disabled; this provides the most protection but has the side effect of disabling functionality that is important to users. Select this option when you require the lowest possible level of risk. Another solution is being selective about how you initially visit a Web site. This will significantly reduce exposure, while still maintaining functionality.

Software Exploitation

Improperly programmed software can be exploited. **Software exploitation** is a method of searching for specific problems, weaknesses, or security holes in software code. It takes advantage of a program's flawed code. The most effective way to prevent an attacker from exploiting software bugs is to keep the latest manufacturer's patches and service packs applied as well as monitor the Web for new vulnerabilities.

Social Engineering

Sometimes the most effective way to get what we want is to just ask. **Social engineering** exploits human nature and human behavior. Social engineering is a method of obtaining sensitive information about a company through exploitation of human nature. It is an attempt to influence a person into revealing information or acting in a manner that would disclose information that normally would not have been provided and is based on the trusting side of our nature, our willingness to want to be helpful, or intimidation. Social engineering is hard to detect because we have very little influence over lack of common sense or ignorance on the part of our employees.

Odd questions or asking for forbidden information can be a dead giveaway that someone is fishing for attack information. In the situation where a corporate official needs sensitive information, the approach generally should be that this is a potential intruder and not a vice president. Having solid company policies in place for the proper request of sensitive information and user education can help prevent social engineering.

Virus

A program or piece of code that is loaded onto your computer without your knowledge is a **virus**. It is designed to attach itself to other code and replicate. It replicates when an infected file is executed or launched. At this point, it attaches to other files, adding its code to the application's code and continues to spread. Even a simple virus is dangerous because it can use all available resources and bring the system to a halt. Many viruses can replicate themselves across networks, bypassing security systems.

Activity 5-2: Learn How to Clean a Virus from an Infected Machine

Time Required: 45 minutes

Objective: Learn how to clean up a machine that is infected with a virus.

Description: In this exercise, you learn to fix a computer that is infected with a virus. You will research the virus and clean the computer. You need a desktop or laptop computer running a Windows-based operating system, TCP/IP installed, network connectivity, and Internet access.

1. Log on with your **AdminXX** account, where *XX* is your assigned student number.

2. Open an Internet connection. Go to **http://download.McAfee.com**.

3. Click the **McAfee Freescan** link on the right side of the screen.

4. Click **SCAN NOW**, click **Scan**, then log in or create an account and scan your computer. Assume that it found the Klez virus. Note: If you have issues with Active X controls in this step, change your Internet security setting to Medium.

5. Return to the downloads page in Step 2, hover over the **virus information** menu, and click **virus removal tools**.

6. Find Klez on the page and click the **Get Virus Removal Tool Now** link. Download the kremove.exe file to your desktop. Click **Open** to run the removal tool.

7. After running the program, reboot the computer and scan it again to be sure that the virus is gone.

Trojan Horses

Trojan horses are programs disguised as useful applications. Trojan horses do not replicate themselves like viruses, but they can be just as destructive. Code hidden inside the application can attack your system directly or allow the system to be compromised by the code's originator. The Trojan horse is typically hidden, so its ability to spread is dependent on the popularity of the software and a user's willingness to download and install the software.

Worms

Worms are similar in function and behavior to a virus or Trojan horse, with the exception that worms are self-replicating. A worm is built to take advantage of a security hole in an existing application or operating system, find other systems running the same software, and automatically replicate itself to the new host. This process repeats with no user intervention. After the worm is running on a system, it checks for Internet connectivity. If it exists, the worm then tries to replicate from one system to the next.

The best way to protect your environment from malware such as viruses, worms, and Trojan horses is to be sure that you have antivirus software installed on all machines and that it is updated on a regular basis.

Now that you have an idea of what types of vulnerabilities and malicious threats can infiltrate the network, it's time to move on and look at a logical and methodical plan for keeping your environment current with updates.

Applying a Four-Step Process for Updates to Your Environment

To prepare for patch management, it is essential to fully understand the business importance of patch management for your specific environment and the technologies and skills that you have (or don't have) to perform proactive patch management. Next, teams and responsibilities can be assigned to ensure that patch management is carried out effectively as part of normal operations. Successful patch management, like security and operations, is achieved through a combination of people, processes, and technology.

To determine how much effort will be needed to implement security patch management, first assess the impact of improper patch management on the business and then determine how to perform patch management effectively. The Microsoft-recommended patch management process is a four-phase approach designed to give you control over the deployment of service packs and hotfixes:

1. Assess
2. Identify
3. Evaluate and Plan
4. Deploy

Phase 1: Assess

The Assess phase is the first step in the patch management process. This is an ongoing process that you should follow to ensure that you always know what computing assets you have, how you can protect them, and how you can ensure that your software distribution architecture is able to support patch management. In order to properly assess the environment, the following steps should be taken:

1. Conduct an audit to inventory existing computing assets such as hardware types and versions, operating system types and versions, applications, and middleware.
2. Assess security threats and vulnerabilities by identifying security standards and policies, determining how security policies and standards are to be enforced, and analyzing current system vulnerabilities.
3. Determine the best source for information about software updates. Sources of information about new software updates can be e-mail notifications, Web sites, or Microsoft technical representatives.

4. Assess the existing software distribution infrastructure to determine if it can be used to distribute software updates, if it services all computers in your environment, and if it is designed to handle patching of business-critical computers. During this assessment, you may also want to consider bandwidth requirements and if the current infrastructure can properly handle software update bandwidth usage.

5. Assess operational effectiveness by determining if there are enough skilled people to perform patch management; if those responsible understand security settings, common computer vulnerabilities, software distribution techniques, remote administration, and the patch management process; if processes exist for change and release management with standard operational processes in place; and if there is an emergency deployment process.

Phase 2: Identify

The prompt for going from the Assess phase to the Identify phase of the patch management process is notification that a new software update exists. The steps in the Identify phase are to:

1. Discover new software updates in a reliable way by determining how you are notified of a new software update and how you know you can trust the source and the notification.

2. Determine whether software updates are relevant to your production environment and if the application or system the software update applies to has the vulnerability the software update is designed to address.

3. Obtain software update source files and confirm that they are safe and will install successfully by identifying and verifying the software update's owner, reviewing all accompanying documentation, and ensuring that the software update is free from viruses.

4. Determine whether the software update should be considered an emergency and submit a request for change (RFC) to deploy a new software update into production.

Phase 3: Evaluate and Plan

Submitting a request for change is the trigger for the next patch management phase, which is Evaluate and Plan. The third major step in the patch management process is evaluation of the software update and planning for its deployment into the production environment. The key steps for evaluation and planning are:

1. Determine the appropriate response by prioritizing and categorizing the request then getting authorization to deploy the software update.

2. Plan the release of the software update by determining what needs to be patched, then identifying the key issues and constraints. Finally, plan and determine the

order in which the computers within your production environment will deploy the software update.

3. Build the release by developing the scripts, tools, and procedures that administrators will use to deploy the software update into the production environment.

4. Conduct acceptance testing of the release. This allows the organization to check that the package works in an environment that closely mirrors production and that business-critical systems continue to run successfully once the software update has been deployed.

Phase 4: Deploy

Once the package is ready for deployment into production and you have approval to deploy the software update into the production environment, the Deploy phase of the patch management process can begin. The deployment of a software update should consist of the following steps:

1. Prepare for deployment by communicating the rollout schedule to the organization and staging updates on appropriate servers.

2. Deploy the software update to targeted computers by advertising the software update to client computers, monitoring and reporting on the progress of deployment, and handling failed deployments.

3. Conduct a postdeployment review by evaluating your organization's performance throughout the incident and updating the existing baseline for your environment.

Now that a systematic method for preparing an environment for patch management has been established, we will look at these phases more closely, starting with evaluating how service packs and hotfixes can affect your environment.

EVALUATING THE APPLICABILITY OF SERVICE PACKS AND HOTFIXES

Once you know what you have deployed in your production environment and have assessed security threats and vulnerabilities, you need to determine the best source of information about new software updates. Information about new software updates can be from the following sources:

- E-mail notifications
- Web sites
- Microsoft technical representatives

E-mail Notifications

To make the patching process easier, Microsoft releases its patches or hotfixes on a monthly schedule. Any system running Microsoft products in your enterprise should be evaluated for the patch requirements. Because updates are now released on a schedule, it may be easier to put a sensible plan into place. Should an attacker learn of a vulnerability and release an exploit for it before the update date, the hotfix will be posted ahead of schedule if the situation warrants.

Microsoft offers a free e-mail notification service to send information to customers about the security of Microsoft products. If you use Microsoft software, you should subscribe to the Microsoft Security Notification Service for notifications of new vulnerabilities and software updates. The security bulletins that Microsoft releases include summary information describing vulnerabilities and the products that they affect. The bulletins also include detailed technical information describing vulnerabilities and updates and workarounds, as well as deployment considerations and download instructions for any available updates. You can choose to receive either technical or nontechnical alerts.

Microsoft Security Update is a free e-mail alert service that makes it easier for small businesses to stay apprised of the latest security updates. Each time Microsoft releases an update, subscribers receive an e-mail message that explains in nontechnical terms why Microsoft has issued the update lists and which products are affected. It also provides a link to the full announcement on the Security and Privacy Web site. You can receive technical alerts by subscribing to Product Security Notification and nontechnical alerts by subscribing to Microsoft Security Update.

To register for the Microsoft Security Notification Service, go to the Microsoft Profile Center at *www.microsoft.com/technet/security/bulletin/notify.mspx*. You need only to provide an e-mail address and select a location and language preference.

ACTIVITY

Activity 5-3: Register for the Microsoft Security Notification Service

Time Required: 20 minutes

Objective: Learn how to register for the Microsoft Security Notification Service.

Description: In this exercise, register for the Microsoft Security Notification Service. To complete this exercise, you will need Internet access.

1. Log on with your **AdminXX** account, where *XX* is your assigned student number.

2. Open an Internet connection. Go to **www.microsoft.com/technet/security/bulletin/notify.mspx**.

3. Click the **Register** link for Microsoft Security Notification Service.

4. Sign in to the Subscription Center page; if you do not already have a Hotmail or MSN mail account create one, otherwise sign in using your .NET account.

5. On the My E-Mail Address page, type in your e-mail address, then click **Update**.

6. Follow the instructions on the Subscription Center Page. Open your e-mail program, open the e-mail from Microsoft, and then click on the link to verify your address.

7. This will bring you to the E-Mail Verification page. Click **Continue**. The My Information Page is displayed where you can update your personal information. Click **Subscription Center** on the left side of the page.

8. Select your country and language preference and click **Update**.

9. On the My Subscriptions page, under Available Newsletters, check **Microsoft Security Notification Service and Microsoft Security Notification Service: Comprehensive Version**. What is the difference between these two notifications?

10. Click **Update**. Click **Sign Out** on the top-right side of the screen and close the **Internet Explorer** window.

It is important to handle e-mail notifications carefully. The following guidelines are designed to help you validate each notification and ensure that it is the latest security bulletin information available:

- Immediately delete any e-mail notifications claiming to be from Microsoft that contain any attached software files. Never run or install any executable attached to an e-mail notification.

- Microsoft has a policy of never distributing software through e-mail attachments. Do not click any links directly from inside an e-mail notification. Instead, you should paste any URLs into a browser window to confirm that they direct you to a Microsoft Web site.

- Always visit the Microsoft Security Web site to read the authoritative details of a security bulletin. If you don't expect to have Internet access when receiving bulletins, familiarize yourself with Pretty Good Privacy (PGP) encryption tools and use one to verify the authenticity of the PGP signature included on each security bulletin.

Note that Microsoft digitally signs all security bulletins. This ensures that the security bulletin is indeed from Micorsoft and not a rogue bulletin that may contain information that could damage your machine. To verify the signature, download and view the certificate. The certificate's Pretty Good Privacy (PGP) key fingerprint is 5E39 0633 D6B3 9788 F776 D980 AB7A 9432. The Security Bulletin key can be downloaded from *www.microsoft.com/technet/security/bulletin/notify.mspx* and information on the digital signature is found at *www.microsoft.com/technet/security/bulletin/pgp.mspx*.

Web Sites

You can also search Microsoft security bulletins to determine whether issues exist that affect your current status, as shown in Figure 5-2. Each Microsoft security patch comes with two documents: a security bulletin and a Knowledge Base article. This allows you to do your own research on whether an update is appropriate for your environment. The downside to this method is that if you are not vigilant about checking for new updates, you could miss one that may be important to the security of your network.

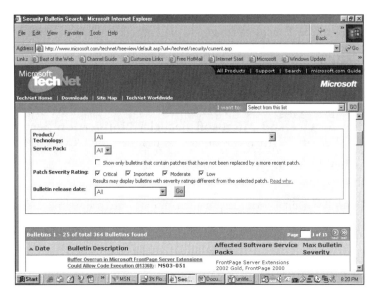

Figure 5-2   Microsoft Security Bulletin search window

Microsoft Technical Representatives

If you are the type of person who doesn't like to do your own research and don't want to be automatically notified, you can contact Microsoft directly and ask their technical representatives about the latest updates that are available and what they contain.

You can also be notified of new Knowledge Base articles through Register for the Free TechNet Flash Newsletter at *www.microsoft.com/technet/abouttn/subscriptions/flash_register. mspx*. These articles frequently contain information about software updates you should deploy to resolve issues within your production environment.

After you decide how you wish to be informed of new issues that may affect your network, it is important that you have all the information together about the layout of your network so you know whether the service pack or hotfix needs to be applied. This should include ensuring that all the computers are at a standard baseline. You can do this by creating an inventory of computers and models, operating systems, and applications as suggested in the Assess phase. Using software such as Microsoft's Systems Management Server (SMS) will make the inventory task much easier. Be sure to include software versions along with any applied updates, then use the inventory information to define standard software baselines for all computers. After the baseline is established, bring the noncompliant computers up to their required status.

After the baselines are established and you have subscribed to receive alerts, you can then determine whether you need to install a service pack or hotfix based on a combination of information. Because a large number of software updates are released regularly, all updates must be checked thoroughly for their significance to the environment. First, determine whether you are running the operating system or application. If you are, determine whether the application or system the update applies to contains the vulnerability the update is addressing. The update might be specific for only particular scenarios or configurations, so not every security update that applies to a system in your environment will be relevant.

5

To minimize the effort that is required to keep your environment current and secure, deploy only those updates that affect your environment. Software update dependencies such as features that need to be enabled or disabled or requiring a certain service pack to be installed should also be checked. Identifying dependencies is crucial because this has a direct impact on your deployment planning for the update and in case problems occur as systems are upgraded from one service pack to another.

Testing the Compatibility of Service Packs and Hotfixes for Existing Applications

After you determine that a service pack or hotfix is necessary, you should test for compatibility with existing applications. **Software Update Services (SUS)** uses the **Windows Automatic Updates service** and allows you to configure a server that contains content from a live site in your own environment to update internal servers and clients. There are two recommended ways to test update content before applying it to computers in your production environment:

1. Use two SUS servers, one for testing and one for production computers. Test the content in the test server, then approve the items on the production server.

2. Use a manually configured distribution point. Use a test server running SUS with test client computers. After the content is tested, copy the tested content and the list of approved items to a manually configured distribution point.

The next few sections will discuss these methods in finer detail, starting with using two SUS servers. Then we will move on to creating, configuring, and synchronizing a manual content distribution point.

Using Two SUS Servers

When you use two SUS servers, an Automatic Updates policy is configured for the test clients that point to the test server running SUS. Another Automatic Updates policy has the production computers pointed to the production server running SUS. The synchronization feature of SUS downloads updates from Windows Update to the test server. The updates are approved for testing, and when this has been successfully completed, the updates are approved for use on the production server.

Using a Manually Configured Distribution Point

Should you choose the second option, you can set up one server in your test lab and then publish the updates to client computers in the lab. If these clients install correctly, you can then configure your production SUS servers to publish the updates. This way, you can ensure that the changes do not have any adverse effects on your current production environment.

Creating a Content Distribution Point

A SUS server **content distribution point** is the distribution point server that will host the content that you want your servers running SUS to offer including the list of approved items. You can create a content distribution point either manually or automatically. You cannot use any port other than 80 for a content distribution point. Whether automatically or manually configured, content distribution points must always use port 80. When you install SUS, a content distribution point is automatically created on that server. The content distribution point is located in the currently running IIS Web site under a Vroot named /Content. When the server is synchronized, its content is updated from the Windows Update download servers. If you choose to maintain content from Microsoft.com, this automatic content distribution point will be empty.

You can also manually create a content distribution point on a server. The server with the manual content distribution point does not require an installation of SUS. A manually configured distribution point works by taking content that has been synchronized via SUS and copying it to the content distribution point. In other words, you are taking content from the \Content folder on a server running SUS that can connect to the Internet and copying this content to the manually created content distribution point. When doing so, it is important to copy the complete \Content directory.

Content Synchronization

During synchronization, content that is updated can be marked on the Approve updates page in one of two ways as shown in Figure 5-3:

- *Automatically approve new versions of previously approved updates*—Allows an approved item to continue to be approved if it is later updated during synchronization

- *Do not automatically approve new versions of approved updates. I will manually approve these later.*—Does not allow a previously approved item to continue to be approved if it is updated during a synchronization

In a testing environment, you should select the second option. This allows the update to be tested before being installed on your client computers. On client computers, there are no built-in features for staging content, so you can either set up a test server running SUS in a

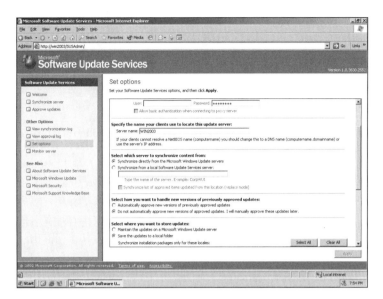

Figure 5-3   Software Update Services option window

lab and have a client computer configured to use the Automatic Updates client download to install the packages you want to test, or you can connect the test client computer to the Windows Update site and apply the packages that you want to test on that client.

Before we move on to implementing a SUS architecture, you should be aware that Microsoft intends to replace SUS with Windows Update Services (WUS). WUS is considered the successor to Microsoft Software Update Services (SUS) 2.0. It currently is in beta stage and is scheduled for release in the first half of 2005. WUS will extend the capabilities of SUS to enable updating of various versions of Office, SQL Server, Exchange, and additional Microsoft products over time, in addition to updating the versions of the Windows operating systems supported by SUS. It will also have advanced status and reporting capabilities.

Implementing Microsoft Software Update Services Architecture

There are different ways to deploy service packs and hotfixes. These methods include, SMS, SUS, Group Policy, slipstreaming, custom scripts, and implementation during a Remote Installation Services (RIS) installation. We will discuss some of these methods later in the chapter. Because SUS is a big part of the patch management and update strategy developed by Microsoft, we will start with it.

The most popular choices for software update distribution are SUS and SMS 2.0 with the SUS Feature Pack. SUS allows each software update to be approved before it is installed in the environment. In SUS environments, some Microsoft products must be updated by using other services or by manually applying software updates.

SMS does not have this limitation. It can be used to update any software product on an SMS client.

NOTE

Getting Started with Software Update Services

SUS can be used to deploy Windows-related security patches and updates to any computers running Windows 2000, Windows XP Professional, or Windows Server 2003. It is not intended to replace an enterprise software distribution solution such as SMS or Microsoft Group Policy–based distribution; it is simply a quick means to deliver critical updates. SUS has the following advantages:

- Updates can be approved individually on each SUS server. This allows the updates to be used in various testing environments as well as phased deployments.

- Clients can be configured to get updates through a SUS server instead of downloading them from Microsoft's Update site.

- SUS is a means to provide updates to computers that don't have Internet access.

- Updates can be copied from a SUS server that is connected to the Internet to an internal SUS server with no Internet access.

- The SUS server architecture is made up of parent-child relationships, and each SUS server can support up to 15,000 clients.

An SUS server requires the following:

- A server with Windows 2000 Server or Server 2003 installed

- An NTFS file system partition with at least 100 MB of available free space to install SUS SP1 and a minimum of 6 GB of storage on an NTFS partition to host the updates locally

- IIS

- Port 80 to communicate with SUS clients

The administration of SUS is completely Web based; therefore, administration can be done over a standard HTTP connection or over a secure Secure Sockets Layer (SSL)–enabled HTTPS connection.

Activity 5-4: Install Microsoft Software Update Services

ACTIVITY

Time Required: 45 minutes

Objective: Learn how to install the SUS server software.

Description: In this exercise, you learn to install the SUS server software. Note: If you still have URL Scan installed from the exercises in Chapter 2, you should uninstall it before you begin this exercise. Please be sure to install IIS prior to performing this activity if it is not already installed.

1. Log on with your **AdminXX** account, where *XX* is your assigned student number.

2. Open an Internet connection. Go to **www.microsoft.com/windowsserversystem/sus/default.mspx**.

3. Scroll to the Downloads section. Select **Download SUS with Service Pack 1 (SP1)**.

4. On the Download Center page, on the right side of the screen, click **Download** under Software Update Services 1.0 with Service Pack 1.

5. In the File Download dialog box, select **Save**. In the Save As dialog box, choose a directory to save the file to. Be sure that the file name SUS10SP1.exe is showing in the File name window. Click **Save**.

6. Once the file has completed downloading, click **Open**.

7. Server 2003 will extract files, which may take a few minutes. Then, a script will run and the Welcome to the Microsoft Software Update Services Setup Wizard screen will appear. Click **Next**.

8. On the End-User License Agreement page, select **I accept the terms in the License Agreement**. Click **Next**.

9. On the Choose setup type screen, click **Typical**.

10. On the Ready to Install page, click **install**.

11. On the Completing the Microsoft Software Update Services Setup Wizard page, click **Finish**.

12. When the SUS Web page appears, click the **Microsoft Software Update Services Overview Whitepaper** link. If the White paper ink is not there, go to *www.microsoft.com/windowsserversystem/sus/susoverview.mspx*. Download the paper and read the Server-Side: Software Update Services section on pages 16 to 22.

13. When finished, close the white paper and **Internet Explorer**.

Because the SUS server architecture is made up of parent-child relationships, a server can be configured to synchronize approved updates either manually or automatically from its parent server. SUS clients use the same Automatic Updates client that Windows Update uses, but they can also have additional configurations such as connecting to specific servers for updates, automatic update installations, or end-user prompting.

With SMS 2.0 and the SUS Feature Pack, you can easily manage security updates and distribute any type of software. The SUS Feature Pack helps condense the security patch management process by using a tool named Distribute Software Updates Wizard. The wizard compares available updates with the inventory of client computers to detect missing and previously installed updates, thereby installing only necessary updates. It offers the following features:

- Capability to update status for all clients based on new security update information
- Ability to review and authorize missing updates

5

- Allows tailor-built packages and advertisements for each update or set of updates

- Can update advertisements distributed to computers by using SMS software distribution capabilities

- Allows Windows Update–style notifications, such as not forcing applications to close when they have not been saved

- Ability to use timers that allow users to save and close applications, enabling users to postpone updates or to choose not to restart their systems

Performing Software Update Services Common Administration Tasks

When working with SUS there will be a variety of tasks to complete. The two main tasks that you will perform with SUS are synchronizing content and approving content. Before you can perform those actions, you need to configure your server. Here are some conditions in your environment that you will want to be sure to configure:

- The proxy server settings may need to be properly configured if your server running SUS needs to use a proxy server to connect to the Internet.

- The environment may require client computers to use the DNS name to locate the server running SUS. Should this be the case, you must configure a DNS name for that server.

- The server content can be synchronized from the Internet-based Windows Update servers, from another installation of SUS, or from a manually configured content distribution point.

- The administrator can customize the behavior for items that were approved by the administrator, but then have the actual content of the package updated during synchronization.

Roughly every 17 to 22 hours, your Automatic Updates client computers will poll the server running SUS for approved updates to install. If there are any new updates that need to be installed, the client computer will begin to download these new approved updates. The timing of the updates is significant enough that you should be sure to carefully plan the downloading and installation based on network available bandwidth and usage. Once an approved update has been installed, SUS does not uninstall the update if it becomes unapproved.

SUS keeps information about available updates in **metadata cache**. The metadata cache is an in-memory database that SUS uses to manage updates. The cache includes metadata that identifies and categorizes updates, as well as information on update applicability and installation. The Monitor Server page provides the administrator with a view of the current contents of the metadata cache.

SUS has two logs for tracking events, a synchronization log and an approval log. These logs are stored in XML files on the server. In addition, the logs can be accessed from the navigation pane of the administrator's SUS user interface, and a server-monitoring Web page is provided so the administrator can view the status of updates for target computers. Besides these two SUS-specific logs, events can also be recorded in the Event log.

Synchronization Log

A **synchronization log** is maintained on each server running SUS to keep track of the content synchronizations it has performed. It contains the following synchronization information:

- Time of the last synchronization
- Success and Failure notification for the synchronization operation
- Time of the next scheduled synchronization
- Update packages that have been downloaded and/or updated since the last synchronization
- Any update packages that failed synchronization
- Whether a Manual or Automatic synchronization was performed

Approval Log

The **approval log** keeps track of the content that has been approved or not approved and contains the following information:

- Documentation of any time the list of approved packages is changed
- A list of items that changed
- A new list of approved items
- Whether the server administrator or the synchronization service made this change

You can also access the synchronization and approval logs by using any text editor. The synchronization log's file name is history-Sync.xml, and the approval log's file name is History-Approve.xml. Both files are stored in the <Location of SUS Website>\AutoUpdate\Administration directory.

Event Log

In additional to the log files, events are also recorded in the Event Log. Messages are generated whenever the list of approved updates on the server changes. The synchronization service generates an Event Log message for each synchronization performed by the server including any major errors that are encountered by the synchronization service itself.

ACTIVITY

Activity 5-5: Configure Microsoft Software Update Services

Time Required: 45 minutes

Objective: Learn how to configure the SUS server software.

Description: In this exercise, you learn to configure the SUS server software.

1. Log on with your **AdminXX** account, where *XX* is your assigned student number.

2. Click **Start**, **All Programs**, **Administrative Tools**, **Microsoft Software Update Services**. When the login dialog box comes up, enter Administrator and then type the administrator password in the password box. On the left side of the screen, click **Set options**. Scroll down to the Select which server to synchronize content from: area, select **Synchronize from a local Software Update Services server**, and type in the name of your server.

3. In the Select how you want to handle new versions of previously approved updates: section, select **Do not automatically approve new versions of approved updates. I will manually approve these updates later**.

4. In the Select where you want to store updates: section, select **Save the updates to a local folder**. Under the Synchronize installation packages only for these locales: section, click **Clear All**, then check **English**. Click **Apply**.

5. When the VBScript dialog box comes up reminding you to synchronize your server, click **OK**.

6. On the left side of the screen, click on **Synchronize Now server**. Click the **Synchronization** button.

7. On the Schedule Synchronization page, choose **Synchronize using this schedule:** At this time: **21:00**, On the following day(s) **Weekly, Tuesday**. Leave the Retries attempt at **3**.

8. Click **OK.** Close the **SUS** window.

Planning a Software Update Services Deployment

No matter how much testing is done in a test environment, it doesn't always produce the effects that happen when a software update is rolled out into production. Before you can be sure that you have achieved the desired results and roll out the update in a production environment, you must determine a deployment model and perform a pilot rollout. We will discuss the pilot phase in detail shortly. During this phase, it is important to collect information about procedures, troubleshooting steps, and methods used so that you have a point of reference when you deploy the software update in production.

Determining the Deployment Model Phase

To get you started on choosing a deployment model, Table 5-1 lists the recommended methods for deploying SUS, based on an organization's size.

Table 5-1   SUS deployment models

Organization Type	Infrastructure	Connectivity Requirements
Small- to- medium business size	Single SUS server	Internet connectivity is required.
Enterprise	Multiple SUS servers	Internet connectivity is required for at least one server. Additional servers can synchronize content by connecting to SUS server or a manually configured content distribution point.
Enterprise high security	Multiple SUS servers	Internet connectivity is required for at least one server. In a high-security organization, the intranet is usually disconnected from the Internet. In this instance, clients can synchronize content from either an automatic or manual content distribution point.

When choosing a deployment model, keep in mind that in the Enterprise high-security model, the servers running SUS can be set up to synchronize content from other installations of SUS or from manually created content distribution points. This allows you to set up SUS in a network not connected to the Internet. The Automatic Updates client also does not require any access to the Internet when redirected to a local server running SUS. If you choose not to download the actual package files, the packages will remain on the Microsoft Windows Update servers. If you choose to download the packages and save the updates to a local folder, they will be stored on your server running SUS.

Pilot Phase

In order to be sure that the update patch will perform properly, administrators should consider rolling out the software update to a pilot group. This can be a group of power users or simply a small sample of computers. Some of the results you would look for include:

- After the software update is installed, the computer should restart properly.
- The software update has an uninstall program that can successfully remove the update.
- Business-critical systems and services continue to function normally after the software update has been installed.

If the update is targeted at computers connected across slow or unreliable connections or links, the recommended steps for performing a pilot rollout are as follows:

1. Approve the update on the SUS pilot server only.
2. Create a new site-level Group Policy Object (GPO) that is configured so the computers that apply this GPO point to the SUS pilot server for updates.

3. Apply Read and Apply policy settings rights to this GPO for the SUS pilot clients only.

4. Place the SUS pilot GPO at the top of the list of GPOs assigned to the site and verify that the policy cannot be overridden.

5. Delete the SUS pilot GPO upon successful deployment in production. Direct the clients back to the production SUS server for updates upon Group Policy refresh.

If pilot testing is carried out in a production environment, it poses a number of risks to the availability and integrity of systems within that environment. A release should not be piloted in production unless rollback and recovery procedures have been proven to return the simulated test environment to the state that existed prior to deployment. If a pilot test doesn't go as planned or is unsuccessful, it may be necessary to unapprove the update on the pilot SUS server and uninstall it from clients. After everything is functioning properly in the pilot test and the update can be safely installed in the rest of the environment, it's time to move into the deployment phase.

Conducting a pilot test gives the rollout team the opportunity to obtain feedback from the user population and allows them to verify that the release meets the intended requirements before full rollout begins. User feedback is also helpful in determining the likely level of support that will be needed after full implementation.

Production Phase

Software updates can be rolled out using a variety of methods, such as SMS, Group Policy, SUS, and scripts. One common configuration uses Group Policy in combination with SUS.

The goal of deployment is to successfully roll out the approved software update in your production environment. This phase includes preparing for and executing the deployment and then doing a postdeployment review. To prepare for the update, the rollout schedule should be announced to the users, and the update should be staged on the SUS server. The announcement to the users can be done through Group Policy. Figure 5-4 shows the options available.

Note the following options:

- *Notify for download and notify for install*—The user will be notified about updates and will need to select the options to download and install the updates.

- *Auto download and notify for install*—Updates are automatically downloaded, and the user will need to select the option to install the updates.

- *Auto download and schedule the install*—Users will be notified of updates and have the option to install the updates before the scheduled time or delay the restart.

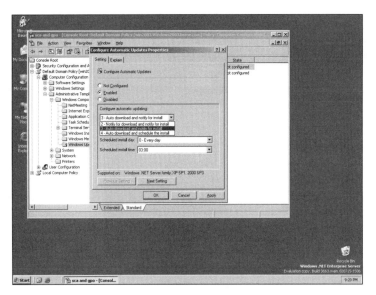

Figure 5-4   Group Policy Configure Automatic Updates window

Activity 5-6: Configure Group Policy for Software Update Services

Time Required: 30 minutes

Objective: Learn how to configure Group Policy for software updates services.

Description: In this exercise, you will learn how to configure Group policy for software update services.

1. Log on with your **AdminXX** account, where *XX* is your assigned student number.

2. Click **Start**, **Administrative Tools**, **Group Policy Management**.

3. Open the Member Server Group Policy. Expand the Computer configuration folder. Expand the **Administrative templates** folder, then expand the **Windows components** folder so that the screen looks like the Figure 5-5.

4. Expand the **Windows Update Folder**. Double-click **Configure Automatic updates**. On the Settings tab, Choose **Enabled**. Choose the option **4 – Auto download and schedule the install**.

5. Choose **7 – Every Saturday** for the Scheduled install day. Choose **22:00** for the Scheduled install time. Click **Apply**. Click **OK**.

6. Close the **Group Policy Management** window.

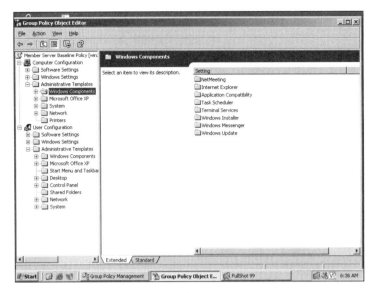

Figure 5-5   Group Policy Windows Components window

NOTE   If the Remove access to use all Windows Update features Group Policy setting in User Configuration\Administrative Templates\Windows Components\Windows Update is enabled, Automatic Updates is disabled for that logged-on user. This makes a local administrator appear as a nonadministrator, and the user will not be able to install updates.

Updates can be controlled through the Wuau.adm template, which configures Windows Update and Automatic Updates settings. Figure 5-6 shows the portion of the policy that directs the computer to a location for updates.

Use the Reschedule Automatic Updates scheduled installations GPO setting to reschedule the installation on computers that have missed a scheduled installation. This occurs when the Automatic Updates service starts.

If the No Auto-Restart for Scheduled Automatic Updates Installations policy setting has not been enabled, the Automatic Updates client will inform the user that the system will be shut down within five minutes.

Besides configuring how updates are to be received, an actual package can be used to distribute service packs by making a new software installation package (.msi file) and linking it to a GPO through the computer configuration settings, as shown in Figure 5-7.

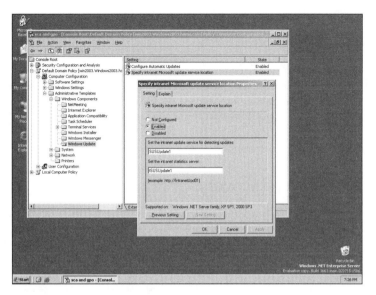

Figure 5-6   Group Policy Automatic Updates download location

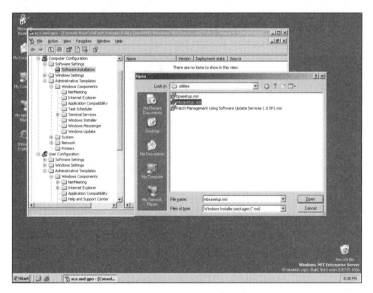

Figure 5-7   Group Policy package installation

After the users are notified, the deployment begins. Using a phased deployment minimizes the impact of any failures or undesirable effects that could happen during the initial distribution of an update. The steps necessary to deploy a software update in production include the following:

1. Advertising the update to the clients

2. Checking the deployment progress

3. Dealing with any failed deployments

A review of the deployment should be conducted afterward, typically within a few weeks. This will identify any changes or improvements that should be made to the patch management process. Once the release is deployed, users and administrative staff can monitor and evaluate performance based on real-world conditions. If this process leads to the conclusion that the release does not meet its objectives, it should be backed out and the environment restored to the state that existed before deployment began.

Server Backup and Disaster Recovery

As with any other type of server, it is a good idea to have a recovery plan in place. In order to have a fully functional server running SUS after a failure, you need to back up the Web site directory that the administration site was created in, the SUS directory that contains the content, and the IIS metabase.

You can begin the backup process by creating a backup of the **IIS metabase** using the IIS MMC snap-in, as shown in Figure 5-8. The metabase is a repository for most IIS configuration values. You will need to back up the server one file at a time. After creating the IIS metabase backup, run NTBackup to back up the data. All of this data is required for proper operation of SUS and IIS after the operating system has been restored.

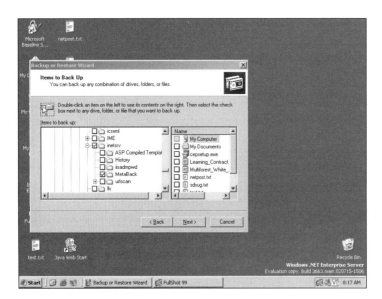

Figure 5-8   Backing up the IIS metabase

When a failure occurs and it is necessary to reinstall the operating system, here are the steps that should be taken before restoring the data back to the server. These steps are for IIS 6 servers because that is the version that comes with Windows Server 2003.

1. To ensure that the server is kept virus free, physically disconnect the server from the network.

2. Install the same operating system that the server was previously running, making sure to give the server the same computer name it previously had.

3. Install the same IIS components the server previously had installed.

4. After the operating system is installed, install the latest service pack and security fixes. Run the IIS Security Wizard before connecting the server to the network.

PLANNING THE BATCH DEPLOYMENT OF MULTIPLE HOTFIXES

What happens if, in doing your baselines, you realize that some of the computers in your environment are missing several updates, or if several hotfixes are released relatively close together and you want to apply them all? Are you stuck installing each one of them individually or can you automate the process?

This next section will discuss some of the ways in which you can install more than one update or patch in a manner that is both efficient and less time-consuming than the alternative.

Using Slipstreaming

Slipstreaming simultaneously installs service packs with an operating system. The installation includes the components that you want to install with the updates as entries in the Svcpack.inf file. In order to accomplish this, you copy the installation files for the operating system and the updates to a shared distribution folder, create the package, and then run setup to deploy the installation either from the shared distribution folder or a CD-ROM. Here are the steps in detail:

1. Create a shared folder on the network to be used as the distribution folder.

2. Restrict access for this folder to Full Access for the Administrator and Read and Execute permissions for other users.

3. Copy the contents of the operating system installation CD to the distribution folder by using xcopy.

4. Using Notepad or a similar text editor, edit the Dosnet.inf file by adding svcpack to the [OptionalSrcDirs] section to add the service pack. If this section does not exist, create it as follows:

[OptionalSrcDirs]

svcpack

5. Create a svcpack subfolder in the directory where the distribution folder is.

6. Copy the update package to the svcpack folder by using a naming format, such as WindowsServer2003-KB*xxxxx-Platform-LLL*.exe.

7. If you are deploying multiple updates, copy and rename all of the update executable files.

8. Expand the update to a unique temporary location. In other words, expand the update to somewhere other than where you are creating your distribution package. When you expand the files, two folders are created: rtmqfe and rtmgdr. From the rtmqfe folder, for each update, copy the KB*xxxxx*.cat catalog file and update binary files to the svcpack folder. Check the catalog and binary file version numbers. Copy the files to the distribution folder only if the file has a higher version number. For each binary file copied, check Dosnet.inf to determine whether each update binary file name is listed in the [Files] section. All files listed in [Files] are preceded by d1. If an update binary file name is not listed for each update under the [Files] section, add an entry as follows:

   d1, Filename

9. Delete the Svcpack.inf file.

10. Create a new Svcpack.inf file by using the procedure for deploying either a single or multiple updates.

CAUTION

Slipstreamed updates cannot be uninstalled. If an update is later determined to be the source of some problem, the OS will have to be reinstalled; you cannot just remove the update that is causing the issue.

Using Custom Scripts

To install updates you can also use custom scripts such as Windows Script Host or KixStart. Windows Script Host is ideal for both interactive and noninteractive scripting, such as logon scripting and administrative scripting. The Windows Script Host comes in two versions: a Windows-based version (Wscript.exe) and a command-line based version (Cscript.exe). You can run either of these at the command prompt. Although standard actions are sufficient to execute an installation in most cases, if you have a penchant for programming, you can add custom actions to extend the capabilities of standard installations by including executables, dynamic-link libraries, and scripts.

Using Isolated Installations

There are methods that you can use to perform a standalone installation. If you have SMS installed, it can be used to run the WindowsServer2003-KB*xxxxx-Platform-LLL*.exe program manually with a variety of installation options. In this format, KB*xxxxx* stands for the Knowledge Base article, the Platform equals ia86 or x86, and *LLL* equals the language. You can also distribute updates either by using a shared network distribution folder or by downloading the updates from the Web. Using a shared network distribution folder is the most common means of update distribution.

During a standalone installation, updates are applied to a computer that is already running Windows Server 2003. The update package automatically installs the updated system files, making the necessary registry changes. After the computer is restarted the installation is complete. You can install updates by running the update package, which extracts the update files and runs the Update.exe installation program. Update.exe will determine if you have installed a service pack. If there is no service pack, or if the service pack version was released before the updates, the Update.exe program installs the updates automatically provided the language is the same. If your service pack version was released after the updates, the installation is not completed and an error message appears, stating that the version is incorrect. If the language of the update does not match the language of the operating system, setup will not continue.

The Update.exe program registers the updates under the following registry keys:

HKEY_LOCAL_MACHINE
\Software\Microsoft\WindowsNT\CurrentVersion\Hotfix\KB*xxxxx*

HKEY_LOCAL_MACHINE\ Software\Microsoft\Updates\Windows Server 2003\SP1\ KB*xxxxx*

During the installation, information for removing the updates is stored in a hidden folder named systemroot\$NtUninstallKB*xxxxx*$.

Using QChain.exe

An **update** is a file or a collection of files that can be applied to the Windows Server 2003 family of servers to correct a specific problem. Updates are packaged in an executable file. When you install an update, files are backed up automatically so that you have the option of removing the update later if you want to. The naming conventions of the update packages are follows:

- For updates you install on 32-bit versions of the Windows Server 2003 family, the convention is WindowsServer2003-KB*xxxxx*-x86-*LLL*.exe

- For updates you install on 64-bit versions of the Windows Server 2003 family or Windows XP 64-Bit Edition Version 2003, the convention is WindowsServer2003-KB*xxxxx*-ia64-*LLL*.exe

The *xxxxx* represents the Microsoft Knowledge Base article number, and *LLL* represents the language. In addition, the platforms appear as either x86 or ia64. Fixes included in a service pack work differently from those in an update. Updates are applied only to software that is already installed when you apply the update. If you uninstall a component and later reinstall it, you must also reinstall any updates that apply to that component. After you install a service pack, fixes are applied to all components you add or reinstall without your having to reinstall the service pack.

Microsoft has released a command-line tool called **QChain.exe**. With QChain.exe, updates can be chained together so that they install without restarting the computer between each installation. Without this tool, the computer must be restarted after each update is installed. The QChain utility can be used with product updates that use Hotfix.exe or Update.exe, and is included in all Windows XP and Windows 2000 updates that have been released since May 18, 2001.

To install multiple updates with only one restart, run the update installer using the /z switch. After you install all the hotfixes, run QChain.exe and restart the computer. Table 5-2 lists the switches that the Update.exe program supports.

Table 5-2 Update.exe Switches

Switch	Description
/f	Forces closing of programs at shutdown
/n	Provides no backup files for removing hotfixes
/z	Requires no restart after installation
/q	Installs in quiet mode
/m	Uses Windows 2000 unattended Setup mode
/u	Uses Windows XP unattended Setup mode
/l	Displays a list of all installed hotfixes

When you install updates, if a file is locked or in use, it cannot be replaced. Instead, it is placed in the Pending File Rename queue and replaced after the computer restarts. If there is no restart, there is a possibility that the wrong file version may end up on the machine. All Windows NT 4.0 and Windows 2000 updates earlier than SP2 use the GetFileVersionInfo function to call the version of a file. The version number is stored in memory then written to the following registry key:

HKEY_LOCAL_MACHINE
\System\CurrentControlSet\Control\Session Manager\KnownDLLs

If you install two or more Windows NT 4.0 updates or pre-SP2 Windows 2000 updates, and the updates contain different KnownDLLs for the key, QChain does not make sure that the latest version file is installed. A post-SP2 Windows 2000 fix, GetFileVersionInfo, calls a mapped file rather than the KnownDLLs that are loaded in memory.

In March 2003, Microsoft released an updated version of QChain.exe. The updated QChain.exe tool cleans the Pending File Rename Operations key in the registry to make sure that only the latest version of a file is installed after the computer is restarted. Now you can use QChain.exe to chain post-SP2 Windows 2000 updates together and the latest version of a file is installed, regardless of the order the updates are installed. QChain.exe can be used with an optional parameter, qchain [*logfilename*], creating a file with before and after snapshots of the Pending File Rename Operations key.

After the installation is complete, verify that all the packages have installed by using the /l switch. Of course, should you choose not to use the qchain command, you can group multiple updates together in a batch file and install them as one. This will prevent you from having to restart your computer after each update is installed, just as the qchain command does. The following is an example of a QChain batch file:

@echo off

setlocal

set PATHTOFIXES=J:\Update

%PATHTOFIXES%\WindowsServer2003-KBxxxxx-Platform-LLL.exe /Z /Q

%PATHTOFIXES%\WindowsServer2003-KBxxxxx-Platform-LLL.exe /Z /Q

%PATHTOFIXES%\WindowsServer2003-KBxxxxx-Platform-LLL.exe /Z /Q

%PATHTOFIXES%\qchain.exe

DEPLOYMENT CONSIDERATIONS FOR VARIOUS MACHINES

The process you use to deploy software updates and patches in the production environment will depend on the type and nature of the release, as well as the type of machine on which you are deploying the update patch. It can also depend on whether the software update is an emergency change. Because of the urgency associated with emergency changes, there will be some differences in how you deploy them. Ideally, software updates should be released through a phased deployment. This way, you can minimize the impact of any failures or adverse effects that might be introduced by the initial distribution of a software update.

Your method of deployment will depend on whether the machines are new and are being introduced to the environment or if they are existing machines. Further considerations are if they are servers or clients. The next few sections discuss options for each of these types of machines.

New Servers and Clients

When you install operating systems on new servers or client computers, sometimes service packs or hotfixes have already been released. There is usually less administrative overhead if the machines can be installed with the proper service packs and hotfixes. Of course, this depends on your patch management policies. The options to install service packs and hotfixes with the OS include slipstreaming, custom scripts, and implementation during a **Remote Installation Services** (RIS) installation. We have already discussed slipstreaming and custom scripts earlier in the chapter.

The RIS feature simplifies the task of installing an operating system on computers in an organization. It provides a mechanism for computers to connect to a network server during the initial boot process, while the server controls a local installation of Windows. RIS can be used to automatically install client operating systems on new machines by connecting to the network via booting, obtaining a DHCP address, and then obtaining the proper image for the machine. Service packs and hotfixes can be added to the image by editing the unattended installation file. These are added in the [GuiRunOnce] section of the file by calling Update.exe for service packs or Hotfix.exe for hotfixes.

Existing Servers and Existing Clients

Previously we discussed SUS, Group Policy, and SMS. All of these methods can be used to install updates to existing servers and clients. SUS servers are the core of the update process for existing servers and clients. You should configure only one SUS parent server to automatically download software updates from the Microsoft Windows Update server. This server requires that outbound TCP port 80 be accessible through the firewall. Only updates that have gone through testing and have been approved should be approved on the parent server. The SUS parent server should download updates on a daily basis using a synchronization schedule.

With SUS, the server content is synchronized from the Windows Update server. There are two types of content that can be synchronized:

- *Update metadata*—Contains descriptions of available updates and the rules that are used to apply them to a target computer. Metadata is *always* downloaded during a synchronization process.

- *Update files*—Contains the files that are installed when an update is approved

There are two synchronization options:

- *Synchronize Now*—Manual synchronization that allows administrators to synchronize at any time

- *Synchronization Schedule*—Set to preset a day and time for synchronizing with the Windows Update service via the Internet

If a manual synchronization fails, this is logged to the synchronization log. If a scheduled synchronization fails, it will attempt to resynchronize 30 minutes later. By default it will retry three times. The number of retries can be configured differently, if needed.

All updates downloaded to your server need to be approved before the server makes them available to computers running the Automatic updates client. The approval process is done through the Approve updates page, which lists the updates available on the server. The steps to approve a package are as follows:

1. Select the check box beside the package(s) you wish to approve.

2. Click the **Approve** button located at the bottom of the page.

Files currently being downloaded are not affected by this change. The steps to not approve updates, such as for testing purposes, are as follows:

1. Clear the check box beside the package(s) you do not wish to approve.

2. Click the **Approve** button located at the bottom of the page.

If the update is to be released through a phased rollout, the synchronization of the update approvals list should be disabled from the SUS parent server. This will allow the child server(s) to have a copy of the update without it being deployed to clients.

Windows Update is used to keep Windows computers updated. It can also notify users of critical updates and security patches through the Automatic Updates client. The Automatic Updates client is available in Windows 2000 SP3 and Windows XP. Besides providing notification for updates, it also allows the configuration of automated downloads and installation preferences. It can download packages from either the Windows Update site or from a server running SUS. It also runs the cyclic redundancy check (CRC) on each package to verify that the package was not tampered with.

A Windows Installer–based setup program called WUAU22.msi is available for the Automatic Updates client. This allows you to use several methods to centrally deploy the client, which include Group Policy, SMS, and logon scripts. Beginning with Windows 2000 Service Pack 3 (SP3) and Windows XP Service Pack 1 (SP1), the Automatic Updates component has been included in the service packs, eliminating the need to download and install the client component separately. The Automatic Updates component is also included in Windows Server 2003. The WUAU22.msi file can also be used to install the Automatic Updates client on a standalone computer running Windows 2000 SP2 or higher and Windows XP.

POSTDEPLOYMENT REVIEW

To monitor the successful release of a deployed update, the MBSA tool should be run to determine whether the particular software update is no longer listed as missing in the report created by MBSA. MBSA can also identify installed updates as well as updates that have been approved on the SUS server but have yet to be installed.

Activity 5-7: Using the Microsoft Baseline Security Analyzer to Check for Missing Updates

Time Required: 30 minutes

Objective: Learn how to use the MBSA to check for missing updates.

Description: In this exercise, you will use the MBSA to check a group of machines for missing updates. Note: To perform this exercise, MBSA must be installed. This was done in Activity 3-2.

1. Log on with your **AdminXX** account, where *XX* is your assigned student number.

2. Click **Start**, **All Programs**, **Microsoft Baseline Security Analyzer**.

3. On the Welcome to the Microsoft Baseline Security Analyzer screen, select **Scan more than one computer**.

4. In the IP address range type **192.168.0.1** to **192.168.0.254**. In the Options section, uncheck all boxes except Check for security updates, as shown in Figure 5-9.

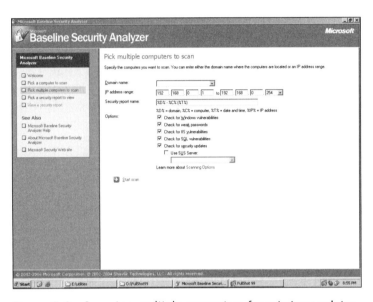

Figure 5-9   Scanning multiple computers for missing updates

5. Click **Start scan**.

6. Once the scan is complete, view the security report. Make a note of the missing updates.

7. When finished, close the **MBSA** report window.

The postimplementation review should typically be conducted within one to four weeks of a release deployment to identify improvements that should be made to the patch management process. A typical agenda for a review includes:

1. Ensure that the vulnerabilities are added to your vulnerability-scanning reports and security policy standards so the attack does not have an opportunity to recur.

2. Ensure that your build images have been updated to include the latest software updates following the deployment.

3. Discuss planned versus actual results.

4. Discuss the risks associated with the release.

5. Review your organization's performance throughout the incident. Take this opportunity to improve your response plan and include lessons learned.

6. Discuss changes to your service windows.

7. Assess the total incident damage and cost—both downtime costs and recovery costs.

8. Create another baseline or update the existing baseline for your environment.

PLANNING A ROLLBACK STRATEGY

Although testing in a simulated production environment will provide the IT team with a certain degree of confidence in the release, it does not guarantee that the release will perform flawlessly in the production environment. After a release reaches the rollout planning stage, the order of rollout as well as a rollback strategy should be determined. If serious problems are encountered during deployment, the cause of the problem must be identified and diagnosed. If an appropriate fix or workaround can be found, it should be documented, a request for change requested, and then it should be deployed in the production environment. If not, it may be necessary to use rollback procedures to remove the release from the environment. It also may be necessary to perform a number of controlled tests in the production environment to confirm that the release meets expectations.

Depending on how the update is deployed, the methods of rollback might differ. If SUS is used, it might be necessary to unapprove the update on the SUS server and uninstall it from clients. The software update should have an uninstall program that can successfully remove the update. You can do this manually using Add or Remove Programs in the Control Panel. Sometimes, updates cannot be uninstalled manually. In this case, to revert the computer back to the Last Known Good Configuration, it is possible to use the backup and restore tools for Windows 2000 and Windows Server 2003 and the System Restore utility for Windows XP.

If you install an update as part of an integrated installation, it might not appear in Add or Remove Programs. You cannot remove updates that were installed as part of an integrated installation unless you reinstall the operating system. If you install multiple updates that replace the same files, and you want to return your computer to its original state, you must remove the most recently installed update first and work your way backward.

No matter what methods you use for rollback, the most important factor is that you have a rollback strategy in place.

CHAPTER SUMMARY

❏ Proactive security patch management is necessary to keep your technology environment secure and reliable. As part of maintaining a secure environment, organizations should have a process for identifying security vulnerabilities and responding quickly. This involves having a comprehensive plan for applying software updates, configuration changes, and countermeasures to remove vulnerabilities from the environment and lessen the risk of computers being attacked.

❏ Some of the vulnerabilities and malware you will encounter include: denial of service (DoS) and distributed DoS (DDoS) attacks, back doors, brute force, buffer overflows, man-in-the-middle attacks, session hijacking, spoofing, viruses, software exploitation, Trojan horses, and worms. Besides viruses, worms, and Trojan horses, other types of malware are available including logic bombs, spyware, sniffers, and keystroke loggers that can affect the proper functioning of a system or network.

❏ The Microsoft-recommended patch management process is a four-phase approach designed to give you control over the deployment of service packs and hotfixes: Assess, Identify, Evaluate and Plan, and Deploy.

❏ Information about new software updates can be obtained from the following sources: e-mail notifications, Web sites, and Microsoft technical representatives. Microsoft has a policy of never distributing software through e-mail attachments. Do not click any links directly from inside an e-mail notification. Instead, you should paste any URLs into a browser window to confirm that they direct you to a Microsoft Web site.

❏ Software Update Services (SUS) uses the Windows Automatic Updates service and allows you to configure a server that contains content from a live site in your own environment to update internal servers and clients. SUS can be used to deploy Windows-related security patches and updates to any computers running Windows 2000, Windows XP Professional, or Windows Server 2003.

❏ There are several ways to deploy service packs and hotfixes, such as Systems Management Server (SMS), SUS, Group Policy, slipstreaming, and custom scripts and implementation during a Remote Installation Services (RIS) installation. With QChain.exe, updates can be chained together so that they install without restarting the computer between each installation. The Qchain utility can be used with product updates that use Hotfix.exe or Update.exe.

❏ If pilot testing is carried out in a production environment, it poses a number of risks to the availability and integrity of systems within that environment. A release should not be piloted in production unless rollback and recovery procedures have been proven to return the simulated test environment to the state that existed prior to deployment.

❏ To monitor successful release of a deployed update, the MBSA tool should be run to determine whether the particular software update is no longer listed as missing in the report created by MBSA. MBSA can also identify installed updates as well as updates that have been approved on the SUS server but have yet to be installed.

Key Terms

approval log — A log file that tracks the content that has been approved or not approved on a SUS server.

back door — A program that allows access to a system without using security checks. Usually programmers put back doors in programs so they can debug and change code during test deployments of software.

brute force — A term used to describe a way of cracking a cryptographic key or password. It involves systematically trying every conceivable combination until a password is found or until all possible combinations have been exhausted.

buffer overflow — An attack in which more data is sent to a computer's memory buffer than it is able to handle, causing it to overflow. Usually, the overflow crashes the system and leaves it in a state in which arbitrary code can be executed or an intruder can function as an administrator.

content distribution point — A place that will host the content that you want your SUS servers to offer.

denial of service and distributed denial of service attacks (DoS/DDoS) — Attacks that are focused on disrupting the resources or services that a user would expect to have access to. These types of attacks are executed by manipulating protocols and can happen without the need for the manipulated packets to be validated by the network.

IIS metabase — A repository for most IIS configuration values.

man-in-the-middle attack — An attack that takes place when an attacker intercepts traffic and then tricks the parties at both ends into believing that they are communicating with each other.

metadata cache — An in-memory database that SUS uses to manage updates.

patch management — A term used to describe the methods for keeping computers current with new software updates that are developed after a software product is installed.

QChain.exe — A command-line tool that allows updates to be chained together so that they install without restarting the computer between each installation.

Remote Installation Services — A service used to automatically install client operating systems on new machines by connecting to the network via booting, obtaining a DHCP address, and then obtaining the proper image for the machine.

security patch management — A term used to describe patch management with a concentration on reducing security vulnerabilities.

session hijacking — A term given to an attack that takes control of a session between the server and a client.

slipstreaming — A method used to simultaneously install service packs with an operating system.

social engineering — An attack targeted by exploiting human nature and human behavior.

software exploitation — A method of searching for specific problems, weaknesses, or security holes in software code.

Software Update Services (SUS) — A service that allows you to configure a server that contains content from a live site in your own environment to update internal servers and clients.

spoofing — Making data appear to come from somewhere other than where it really originated. This is accomplished by modifying the source address of traffic or source of information.

synchronization log — A log maintained on each SUS server to keep track of the content synchronizations it has performed.

Trojan horses — Programs disguised as useful applications. Trojan horses do not replicate themselves like viruses, but they can be just as destructive.

update — A file or a collection of files that can be applied to the Windows Server 2003 family of servers to correct a specific problem.

virus — A program or piece of code that is loaded onto your computer without your knowledge and is designed to attach itself to other code and replicate.

Windows Automatic Updates service — The service used by Software Update Services server to update internal servers and clients.

worms — A worm is built to take advantage of a security hole in an existing application or operating system, find other systems running the same software, and automatically replicate itself to the new host.

REVIEW QUESTIONS

1. You find out a Help desk technician received an e-mail from the network administrator asking him to supply his password so that he could make changes to his profile. What type of attack has been executed?

   a. Spoofing

   b. Man-in-the-middle

   c. Denial of service

   d. Virus

2. You are the security administrator for a bank. The users are complaining about the network being slow. It is not a particularly busy time of the day. You capture network packets and discover that there have been hundreds of ICMP packets being sent to the host. What type of attack is likely being executed against your network?

   a. Spoofing

   b. Man-in-the-middle

   c. Denial of service

   d. Virus

3. Which of the following accurately describes the difference between a Trojan horse and a virus?

   a. A virus needs no user intervention to replicate.

   b. A Trojan horse needs no user intervention to replicate.

   c. A virus is open source code and attacks only open source software.

   d. A Trojan horse buries itself in the operating system software and infects other systems only after a user executes the application that it is buried in.

4. Back Orifice is considered what kind of program?

   a. Virus

   b. Back door

   c. Worm

   d. Trojan horse

5. Your network is under attack. Traffic patterns indicate that an unauthorized service is relaying information to a source outside the network. What type of attack is being executed against the network?

   a. Spoofing

   b. Man-in-the-middle

   c. Trojan horse

   d. Denial of service

6. You accidentally approved an update that has adverse effects on an accounting application. After several calls from the Help desk, it has been determined that several users have already installed the update. You need to configure the Approve updates page to prevent other users from installing the application. What should you do? (Choose all that apply.)

   a. Configure the Reschedule Automatic Updates scheduled installations setting.

   b. Click the Approve button located at the bottom of the page.

   c. Clear the check box beside the package(s) you do not wish to approve.

   d. Select the check box beside the package(s) you do not wish to approve.

7. You do baselines and you realize that some of the computers in your environment are missing several updates. You want to apply them all at once and not have to restart the computer after each update. Which tool can you use to accomplish this?

   a. Qfecheck.exe

   b. HfNetChk.exe

   c. Qchain.exe

   d. Mbsacli.exe

8. You want the ability to test content in a test environment and then be able to push the content that you have tested to your production environment. You decide to use a manually configured distribution point. Which of the following steps should you include in this process? (Choose all that apply.]

   a. Create a VROOT called Content and point to the \Content\Cabs directory.

   b. Create a folder named \Content on the manually created content distribution point.

   c. Get a valid digital certificate for server authentication from your organization.

   d. Copy all the files and folders under the \Content\cabs directory from the source server running SUS to the \Content directory on the server with the manually created content distribution point.

9. To find out about fixes with the least administrative effort, you decide to subscribe to the Microsoft Security Notification Service for notifications of new vulnerabilities and software updates. How do you do this with the least amount of administrative effort?

    a. Periodically check Microsoft's Web site for updates.

    b. Do nothing. If the company owns licensed copies of Microsoft products, free security notifications and files are automatically received via e-mail.

    c. Configure all computers for Automatic Security Updates.

    d. To register for the Microsoft Security Notification Service, go to the Microsoft Profile Center.

10. Your patch management coordinator receives a security bulletin that he suspects was not actually sent by Microsoft and asks for a recommendation on what to do. What is the fastest and most secure method for finding out whether the bulletin is valid?

    a. Verify that the digital signature on the bulletin belongs to Microsoft by downloading and checking their security certificate.

    b. Call Microsoft support and verify the information.

    c. Look for a new posting on the TechNet newsgroups.

    d. Verify that the digital signature on the bulletin belongs to Microsoft by downloading their SSL key.

11. Service Pack 2 for Windows XP was just released. You want to deploy the service pack to all of your client computers with a Group Policy Object. Which file would you use?

    a. Update.xls

    b. Update.exe

    c. Update.inf

    d. Update.msi

12. Which of the following tools cannot be used to check the status of service packs or hotfixes on computers?

    a. Msbacli.exe

    b. Hfnetchk.exe

    c. Qfecheck.exe

    d. Update.exe

13. You receive a new version of a custom application with some additional security features that will benefit the company. You want to update the application with the least amount of administrative effort. Which of the following would you use?

    a. WU

    b. SUS

c. SMS 2.0 with the SUS Feature Pack

d. Group Policy

14. You are responsible for the deployment of 15 new servers. These servers will be running Windows Server 2003. The servers all have identical hardware. Which of the following do you use to automate the installation of the service pack when installing the Windows Server 2003 operating system on the new servers?

a. RIS

b. Slipstreaming

c. SUS

d. WUAU22.msi

15. You are responsible for the deployment of 15 new desktop Windows XP computers. Your planned method of distribution is from a distribution share folder. How do you automate the installation of the service pack when installing the Windows XP operating system with the least amount of administrative effort?

a. Update the distribution share by using the service pack's update/s command.

b. Install Windows XP on the computers and then configure the Automatic Updates feature to run.

c. Install Windows XP on the computers and then send an e-mail message to the users instructing them to run Windows Update.

d. Create a new WUAU22.msi file and then run it after you install Windows XP.

16. You must install several updates on various Windows 2000 Professional computers. You want to install the updates using QChain.exe and avoid having to restart the computers after each update. You also want to install the updates using unattended setup mode. Which of the following switches can you use to accomplish this?

a. /z /l

b. /z /m

c. /z /u

d. /z /f

17. Your company currently has no solution in place for making sure that the computers are kept up to date. You want to make sure that you are notified when new security updates become available so you can review them to determine whether they need to be applied. What do you need to do to receive such updates?

a. Sign up for the Microsoft Security Notification Service using the Microsoft Profile Center.

b. Select the Automatic Security Updates option in Control Panel.

c. Nothing. If the company owns licensed copies of Microsoft products, free security notifications are automatically received.

d. Periodically visit the Microsoft Web site and search for security updates.

18. You are responsible for making sure that all hotfixes and service packs are properly tested before they are applied to the computers in the production environment. You have chosen to use two SUS servers, one for testing and one for production. Which of the following would be included in this procedure? (Choose all that apply.)

    a. Set up one server in your test lab and configure an Automatic Updates policy for the client computers in the lab.

    b. Configure an Automatic Updates policy that points the test clients to the test server running SUS. Configure another Automatic Updates policy that points the production computers to the production server running SUS.

    c. Publish the updates to client computers in the lab. If these clients install correctly, you then configure your production SUS servers to publish the updates.

    d. After testing successfully, the updates are approved for use on the production server.

19. The company's corporate headquarters is located in Phoenix. The company has several other offices located throughout the United States and a total user population of approximately 2500. You want to be able to test and deploy updates and patches. Which of the following would be the best and most economical option for the company?

    a. Install SUS on a member server in the corporate headquarters and configure all client computers to perform automatic updates from this server.

    b. Install MBSA on a member server in the corporate headquarters and use Group Policy to control the distribution of updates.

    c. Configure all the client computers to download updates directly from Microsoft's Windows Update site.

    d. Install SMS using one primary server in the corporate headquarters and secondary servers in all of the other locations.

20. You are responsible for making sure that all hotfixes and service packs are properly tested before they are applied to the computers in the production environment. How should the content that is updated be marked on the Approve updates page if you intended to use a testing environment?

    a. Automatically approve new versions of previously approved updates.

    b. Notify for download and notify for installation.

    c. Do not automatically approve new versions of previously approved updates. I will manually approve these later.

    d. Automatically download and notify for installation.

21. The network has client computers running Windows XP, Windows 2000 Professional SP1, and Windows NT 4.0 Workstation. Several updates need to be installed on all computers. You use QChain to accomplish this. After you run QChain, you find that the file versions are different on some of the computers. Why is this?

    a. QChain will not work on Windows NT 4.0 or Windows 2000 earlier than SP2.

    b. All Windows NT 4.0 and Windows 2000 updates earlier than SP2 call a mapped file rather than the KnownDLLs that are loaded in memory, and the file was overwritten.

    c. All Windows NT 4.0 and Windows 2000 updates earlier than SP2 use the GetFileVersionInfo function to call the version of a file. The version of the file may have been overwritten by an older one.

    d. Qfecheck, not QChain, is the proper utility to use for installing updates on Windows NT 4.0 and Windows 2000 computers earlier than SP2.

22. Company policy dictates that all server updates must be installed within 24 hours after release by the vendor. You want to be sure that this is done with the least amount of administrative effort and intervention. How do you accomplish this?

    a. Enable Configure Automatic Updates with the Notify for Download and Notify for Install in the Default Domain Controllers Policy GPO option.

    b. Enable Configure Automatic Updates with the Auto Download and Notify for Install in the Default Domain Controllers Policy GPO option.

    c. In the System Properties for each server, on the Automatic Updates tab, under Notification Settings, select the Download Updates Automatically and Notify Me When They Are Ready to Be Installed option.

    d. Enable Configure Automatic Updates with the Auto Download and Schedule the Install in the Default Domain Controllers Policy GPO option.

23. The Microsoft-recommended patch management process is a four-phase approach designed to give you control over the deployment of service packs and hotfixes. These steps include which of the following? (Choose all that apply.)

    a. Assess

    b. Identify

    c. Notify

    d. Deploy

24. Information about new software updates can be obtained from which of the following sources? (Choose all that apply.)

    a. Microsoft technical representatives

    b. E-mail notification

    c. Web sites

    d. E-mail attachments

25. SUS can be used to deploy Windows-related security patches and updates to computers running which of the following operating systems? (Choose all that apply.)

a. Windows 98

b. Windows 2000

c. Windows XP Professional

d. Windows Server 2003

CASE PROJECTS

Case Project 5-1

Evergrow a large, multinational company is currently running Windows XP on all client machines. Management would like to upgrade to Service Pack 2. It is your job as the network administrator to formulate a plan to roll out the service pack on the existing computers. Formulate a plan to do this and submit it for review. In your plan include the method by which you would update and why.

Case Project 5-2

You are the network administrator at Evergrow. Recently a patch was applied that severely affected an accounting package used by the Finance department. Management does not want a repeat of this situation and has asked you to implement a SUS solution for patch and update testing. Currently you have 10 servers and 500 workstations. In addition to the 500 workstations, there are 40 mobile laptops. Put together a plan for deploying SUS.

Case Project 5-3

You are the network administrator at Evergrow. The current SUS solution that is in place on the network just isn't working. There isn't enough bandwidth for all the clients to download updates from Microsoft's site on a daily basis. In addition, updates to the server are done at 3:00 a.m. on Friday afternoon, slowing down the entire organization. Management has asked you to analyze your current update strategy and come up with a solution that will alleviate the issues that the users are encountering. Put together a plan to present to management.

Case Project 5-4

Evergrow is currently running Windows XP on all client machines. During a recent workstation audit, it was discovered that several updates are missing from the workstations. You want to install these updates with the least administrative effort. Formulate a plan to submit to management on how to update the workstations. In your plan include the method by which you would perform the update and why.

Case Project 5-5

You are the network administrator at Evergrow. You just received 10 new servers and 500 new workstations. Since you received your operating system software several service packs and hotfixes have been released. There is usually less administrative overhead if the machines can be installed with the proper service packs and hotfixes. Formulate a plan for installing the servers with the most current service pack and hotfixes, then formulate one for the workstations.

6

MANAGING AND TROUBLESHOOTING PATCH MANAGEMENT INFRASTRUCTURE

After reading this chapter, you will be able to:

♦ Use automated processes to verify software updates

♦ Manage software update distribution

♦ Provide a critical patching process

♦ Optimize patch management

♦ Troubleshoot patch management infrastructure

In a "perfect world," all software released by any company would have to be completely free of bugs and immune to all security attacks on the day that it is released. Unfortunately, we don't live in a perfect world. Software manufacturers typically release software to the public as soon as it has passed their tests and is performing as expected. The public, however, is the final test of the software. It is very common for bugs and security issues to be discovered after the initial release of software. When these are discovered, the software company develops and releases a software update called a patch. These patches can usually be downloaded from the company's Web site.

Some patches are less critical than others. While some patches just provide a new feature or benefit, others close a recently discovered security hole in your clients and/or servers. For this reason, it is very important that you understand the methods that you can use to keep your computer software up to date and to verify that it is up to date. Microsoft has developed special applications, services, and programs that automate the process of patch management on the clients and servers in your network. In the previous chapter, we discussed what patches are and how you should go about deploying them. In this chapter, we will discuss how to manage and troubleshoot your patch management infrastructure.

NOTE

A great reference for security vulnerabilities and the latest information in regard to security patches is the *www.cve.mitre.org* Web site. This site is kept up to date with the latest common vulnerabilities and exposures.

Using Automated Processes to Verify Software Updates

The patch management infrastructure of an organization includes all of the tools and technologies that are used to assess, test, deploy, and install software updates. This infrastructure is an essential tool for keeping the entire environment secure and reliable, and therefore it is important that it be managed and maintained properly.

When it comes to managing your infrastructure, chances are good that you may have many different types of clients in your network and that they may be at many different levels in regard to the service packs and hotfixes that are applied to them. You could go around to each client computer and examine it individually to determine which service packs and hotfixes are installed on it, but that would definitely be doing it the hard way. Instead, you could use the automated processes and products provided by Microsoft such as the **Microsoft Baseline Security Analyzer (MBSA)** and **Qfecheck.exe** to ease the complexity of checking the security status of all of the clients in your network. In this section we will discuss each of these processes in detail. You can download these products for free from the Microsoft Web site at the following links:

www.microsoft.com/technet/security/tools/mbsahome.mspx

www.microsoft.com/downloads

All organizations, whether large or small, should use automated tools that notify administrators of available updates and that provide some control over the installation of security patches. This takes a lot of the guesswork out of the patch management process. In order to do this, you must first ensure that your patch management infrastructure is properly configured and documented as explained in Chapter 5. Once the infrastructure in place, you will need to maintain it so that the infrastructure you have put in place is continually protected.

The MBSA Tool

In Chapter 3 we discussed how to use MBSA to check for security issues such as weak passwords. MBSA reports current status for recommended security updates. In Chapter 5, we discussed using the MBSA tool to determine whether a particular software update is missing as well as identifying updates that have been approved on the SUS server but have yet to be installed. Remember that the MBSA tool can be run through the graphical user interface (GUI) or it can be run from a command line.

In an ideal world, everything goes as planned and works as it is supposed to. What happens when MBSA doesn't work properly? This section will focus on how to troubleshoot MBSA when it is used as a tool to update the infrastructure.

MBSA GUI Scans

The simplest scan to perform with the MBSA tool is a GUI-based scan. As you learned in Chapter 3, you can perform a GUI scan after you install the MBSA tool by simply accessing the MBSA tool and then choosing Scan a computer. You can easily scan the local computer, select a remote computer, or even select a group of computers by their domain name or IP address range. When a scan is finished, you can review the results to determine the security vulnerabilities of the computer scanned. You can also easily access information about how to correct the problem straight from the results of the scan. The MBSA uses an Extreme Markup Language (XML)–based catalog file, MSSecure.xml, to determine the security updates that are available. The catalog file is compressed and is stored in the MSSecure.cab file. Microsoft updates and posts the catalog file to the Microsoft Download Center after a new security bulletin is released. In some circumstances, the updated catalog file may not be downloaded by SMS or by the MBSA. Perhaps the scan doesn't work properly, or doesn't even scan any computers. Table 6-1 lists some of the common issues and solutions for MBSA so that when you encounter them, you'll know how to resolve them.

Table 6-1   MBSA Issues

Issue	Cause or Solution
No permissions to access database error messages when running the SQL server check	You might not have permissions to the MASTER database.
Error reading registry when checking the Auto Logon feature	The Remote Registry service might not be enabled.
Conflicting results between MBSA and Windows Update	MBSA and WU analyze systems in different ways. Microsoft is working to resolve this so that MBSA, WU, SUS, and SMS security patch management will all use the same rules.
SQL Server security updates detected were previously shown as note messages	Microsoft has updated the Mssecure.xml file, to include detailed SQL Server security update information. Be sure that you have the most current .xml file.
Incorrect security update reports from MBSA or HfNetChk even after updates are installed	Some security updates issued by Microsoft contain workarounds for items that do not include a patch, but rather contain a tool that users can apply to modify a specific service on their systems.
Certain updates flagged as having greater file versions than expected	MBSA scans for security updates only; it cannot determine if files have been patched by other nonsecurity updates whose file versions and checksums are not included in the Mssecure.xml file.

Table 6-1   MBSA Issues (continued)

Issue	Cause or Solution
When using the Microsoft Baseline Security Analyzer (MBSA) to download the Mssecure.cab security update, you receive the following error message: No such interface supported. (0x80004002)	*This problem may occur if download managers (such as Download Express or GetRight) are installed on the computer. Download managers may affect the ability of MBSA to download the Mssecure.cab security update.*

ACTIVITY

Activity 6-1: Troubleshooting a MBSA GUI Scan

Time Required: 30 minutes

Objective: Troubleshoot MBSA.

Description: In this activity, you will troubleshoot the MBSA tool and resolve the issue so that the scan performs properly. In this exercise you will be troubleshooting a standalone machine. Note: If you wish to recreate the error in Step 1 yourself, you must remove local copies of the mssecure.xml and mssecure.cab files and disconnect from the Internet.

1. You have run a MBSA GUI scan on a machine. The report comes up as shown in Figure 6-1.

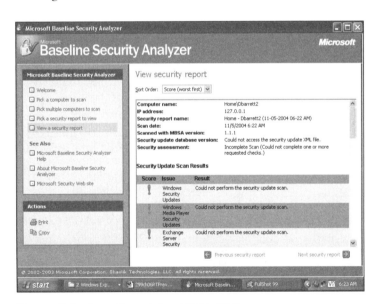

Figure 6-1   Error Report for MBSA GUI scan

2. Notice that the error says that MBSA could not perform the security update scan. This error is common when the machine cannot find the .xml file.

3. To resolve this issue, you can download the .cab file from another computer. Then, you can manually copy the .cab file to the first computer. By default, the standalone version of the MBSA stores the catalog file in the \Program Files\Microsoft Baseline Security Analyzer folder.

4. Log on with your **AdminXX** account, where *XX* is your assigned student number. Click **Internet Explorer**.

5. Go to *http://support.microsoft.com/default.aspx?scid=kb;en-us;842432*.

6. Toward to bottom of the Knowledge Base article, you will find a link to download the current English version of the mssecure.cab file, *http://go.microsoft.com/fwlink/?LinkId=23130*.

7. Download the signed mssecure.cab file to a shared directory.

8. Because you are troubleshooting a standalone machine, the downloaded file would be placed in the MBSA installation folder of the standalone machine.

9. Now, when you rerun the scan, it should run properly without the error.

MBSA Command-Line Scans

You can also perform security vulnerability checks using command-line tools. Some administrators prefer this method because they can build the commands into larger scripts that perform multiple functions.

You can perform two types of scans using the MBSA command-line interface: MBSA-style scans and HFNetChk-style scans. The MBSA-style scans will store the results in XML files that can be viewed using the MBSA interface. The Microsoft Network Security Hotfix Checker (Hfnetchk.exe)—style scans will display the scan results as text in the command-line window. The MBSA command-line parameters cannot be used with the /hf switch. Each style of scan has its own syntax for including or excluding options during the scan. Chapter 3 listed the commands that are available with the MBSA-style commands. The HfNetChk-style commands are listed in Table 6-2.

Table 6-2   HFNetChk Command-Line Parameters

Switch	Description2
-h hostname	Scans the named NetBIOS computer. To scan multiple hosts, separate the host names with a comma.
-fh filename	Scans the NetBIOS named computers specified in the named text file
-i xxx.xxx.xxx.xxx	Scans the named IP address. To scan multiple IP addresses, separate addresses with a comma.
-fip filename	Scans the IP addresses that you specified in the named text file
-r xxx.xxx.xxx.xxx - xxx.xxx.xxx.xxx	Scans a specified range of IP addresses

Table 6-2   HFNetChk Command-Line Parameters (continued)

Switch	Description2
-d domainname	Scans a specified domain
-n	Scans all the computers on the local network
-sus SUS filename or server	Specifies a text file or a URL from which to obtain the SUS file
-b	Scans a computer for updates that are marked as baseline critical by the MSRC
-fq filename	Specifies the file that contains the Qnumbers to suppress on output
-s , -s2	Suppresses note messages and/or warnings
-nosum	Will not test file checksums on security updates
-sum	Forces a checksum scan when you scan a non–English language computer
-z	Specifies to not perform registry checks
-history 1,2,3	Displays those updates that have or have not been explicitly installed
-v	Displays the reason why a test did not work in wrap mode
-o tab, wrap, -f filename	Specifies the output format that you want
-t	Displays the number of threads used to run the scan
-u username/-p password	Specifies the user/password name when scanning local or remote computer(s). Must be used together.
-x	Specifies the XML data source containing the update information
-t	Displays the number of threads that are used to run the scan
-ver	Checks if you are running the latest version of HFNetChk
-trace	Creates a debug log

Although the Microsoft Baseline Security Analyzer (MBSA) does its best to determine the installation status of a software update, there are some instances where MBSA cannot determine the installation status of the update because the detailed file and registry key information is not available for the specified security bulletin or for the update. When you run a scan on an application for which the mbsacli.exe command-line command with the /hf option is not supported, you will get a note message similar to this: Note The detection of Microsoft Office programs is not supported if you use the mbsacli.exe command-line command with the /hf option. The detection of Microsoft Office programs is supported in MBSA v1.2 if you use the Office Update Inventory Tool.

To determine whether MBSA will generate a note message or a warning message when it detects an update, Microsoft has a table of items that are checked and what type of message is output. This is available at the MBSA home page. Only programs that are supported by MBSA v1.1.1 or by MBSA v1.2 are included in this table.

Activity 6-2: Troubleshooting a MBSA Command-Line Scan

Time Required: 30 minutes

Objective: Troubleshoot an MBSA command-line scan.

Description: In this activity, you will troubleshoot a MBSA command-line scan to resolve several errors. Note: If you wish to recreate the error in Step 1 yourself, you must remove local copies of the mssecure.xml and mssecure.cab files and disconnect from the Internet.

1. You have run a MBSA command-line scan on a machine. The report comes up as shown in Figure 6-2.

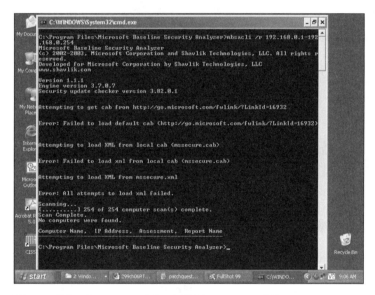

Figure 6-2   Error report for MBSA command-line scan

2. Notice that the first error is "Failed to load default cab." The line previous to that states that there was an attempt made to retrieve the file from Microsoft's Web site.

3. Log on with your **AdminXX** account, where *XX* is your assigned student number.

4. To fix this first issue, simply connect to the Internet and rerun the scan.

5. Notice that the second error is "Failed to load default cab." The line previous to that states that there was an attempt made to retrieve the file from the local directory. Assume that you cannot connect to the Internet. Note: If you wish to recreate this error yourself, you must remove local copies of the mssecure.xml and mssecure.cab files and disconnect from the Internet. You will now have to retrieve the file from

Microsoft's Web site using a different machine and copy it to the \Program Files\Microsoft Baseline Security Analyzer folder on the current machine.

6. The mssecure file should now be current.

7. Now resolve the third error. Under the Scan complete line is a statement that no computers were found.

8. Assume that the cleaning crew accidentally disconnected the network cable. To recreate this error yourself, disconnect your computer cable from the network card and run the scan.

9. Plug the cable back in. Rerun the scan. It should now look like Figure 6-3.

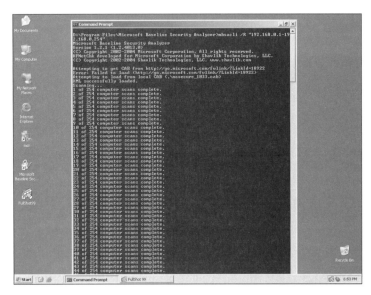

Figure 6-3   Successful scan for MBSA command-line scan

Activity 6-3: Troubleshooting an HfNetChk Command-Line Scan

Time Required: 30 minutes

Objective: Troubleshoot an HfNetChk command-line scan.

Description: In this activity, you will troubleshoot an HfNetChk command-line scan to resolve errors.

1. You have run a HfNetChk command-line scan on a machine. The report comes up as shown in Figure 6-4. To recreate this error on your own machine, first do an IPconfig so that you know what subnet you are on. Now type msbcli –hf –v –r 192.168.0.1-192.168.0.5, provided that you are not on this subnet.

2. Notice that there are several errors stating "Error 235-system not found or NetBIOS ports may be firewalled. Scan not performed."

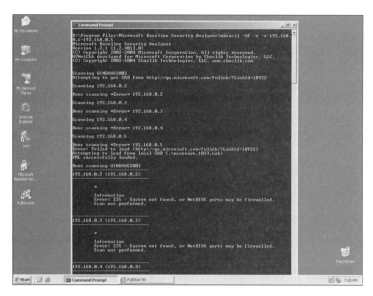

Figure 6-4   Error report for HfNetChk command-line scan

3. Log on with your **AdminXX** account, where *XX* is your assigned student number.

4. To resolve this first issue, simply connect to the Internet and go to *http://support. microsoft.com/default.aspx?scid=kb;en-us;303215.*

5. Find the link on the page labeled Error Messages. Click the link. This will take you to the error listings.

6. Scroll down to error 235. It says that you may receive this error message if no computer has the specified IP address. It also says that if there is a computer at this address, a personal firewall or port filtering device may be dropping packets that are going to TCP ports 139 and 445.

7. In this example, we will assume that you scanned the wrong subnet and that there truly are no computers with the addresses you specified in the scan. Rerunning the scan using the correct subnet will fix the error.

The Qfecheck.exe Tool

In addition to Mbsacli.exe and Hfnetchk.exe, Microsoft has released a command-line tool named Qfecheck.exe that has the ability to track and verify installed Windows 2000 and Windows XP hotfixes. It enumerates all of the installed patches by their associated Microsoft Knowledge Base article. Qfecheck.exe checks which hotfixes are installed by reading the information that is stored in the HKEY_LOCAL_MACHINE\ SOFTWARE\Microsoft\Updates registry key. It checks for:

- Files that have been hotfixed but have an outdated binary file

- The version number recorded in the registry and compares it against the current version of the installed file

- Hotfix files that are listed as current but are not recorded as valid by the installed catalogs

This tool does not tell you if any updates that you might need are missing; it simply tells you if the ones that you have installed are installed properly. After you have downloaded and installed the tool, you can run it from the command line.

ACTIVITY

Activity 6-4: Using Qfecheck Command-Line Scans

Time Required: 30 minutes

Objective: Download, install, and run the Qfecheck.exe tool.

Description: In this activity, you first access the Web page on Microsoft's site to download and install the Qfecheck.exe tool. You then run the tool to determine which security updates are properly installed in your computer. Note: The Qfecheck.exe tool is available for Windows XP, Windows 2000, and Windows 98 machines and, therefore, should be run on one of these operating systems.

1. Log on with your **AdminXX** account, where *XX* is your assigned student number. Click **Internet Explorer**.

2. Type **microsoft.com/downloads**, and then press **Enter**.

3. In the Search Microsoft.com for box at the top right of the page, type **QfeCheck.exe** and press **Enter**.

4. Select the **QfeCheck Verifies the Installation of Windows 2000 and Windows XP hotfixes** article from the results of the search.

5. Scroll down in the article to "How to Obtain QfeCheck.exe."

6. Click **Download Q282784 WXP SP1 x86 ENU.exe now**.

7. On the Windows XP Patch verification page, click **Continue** in the Validation Recommended section.

8. Select **Yes** under Validate Windows and obtain the download, and click **Continue**.

9. When the download page is displayed, click **Download** from the right side of the page. Click **Save**, select **Desktop** from the Save in drop-down list, and then click **Save** again. The download will begin immediately.

10. Close the Web page and access your desktop.

11. Double-click the **Q282784...** file on your desktop to begin the installation.

12. In the Welcome box, click **Next** to continue.

13. In the License Agreement box, select **I agree**, then click **Next**. The installation will begin immediately.

14. Click **Finish** to complete the installation and close the wizard.

15. Click **Start**, and then click **Run**.

16. Type **cmd** and press **Enter** to access the command-line tool.

17. At the command prompt, type **qfecheck.exe /v**, then press **Enter**.

18. Read the list of patches that are installed on your computer. Figure 6-5 shows the results of running the Qfecheck.exe tool.

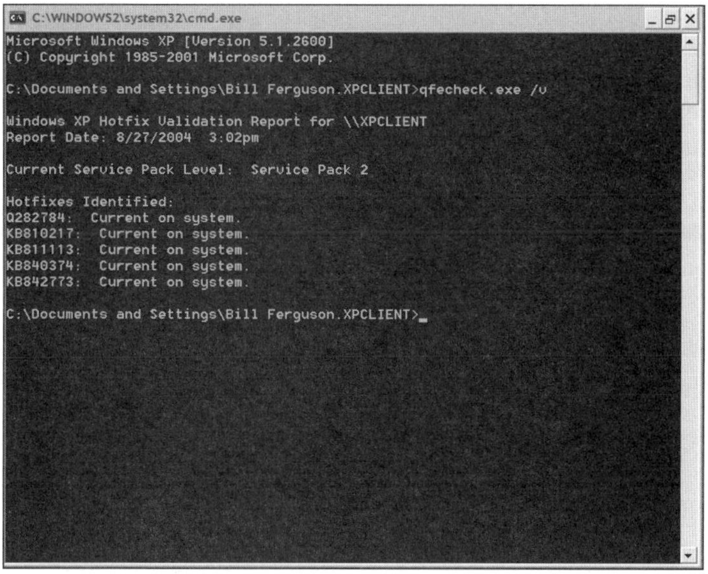

```
C:\WINDOWS2\system32\cmd.exe                                         _ 8 x
Microsoft Windows XP [Version 5.1.2600]
(C) Copyright 1985-2001 Microsoft Corp.

C:\Documents and Settings\Bill Ferguson.XPCLIENT>qfecheck.exe /v

Windows XP Hotfix Validation Report for \\XPCLIENT
Report Date: 8/27/2004  3:02pm

Current Service Pack Level:  Service Pack 2

Hotfixes Identified:
Q282784:  Current on system.
KB810217:  Current on system.
KB811113:  Current on system.
KB840374:  Current on system.
KB842773:  Current on system.

C:\Documents and Settings\Bill Ferguson.XPCLIENT>_
```

Figure 6-5   The Qfecheck.exe tool

Troubleshooting Qchain.exe

In Chapter 3, we discussed the Qchain command. Although QChain works with most Windows NT 4.0 and Windows 2000 updates, QChain.exe may not work with updates that contain binary files that are listed in the following registry key:

HKEY_LOCAL_MACHINE\System\CurrentControlSet\Control\Session Manager\KnownDLLs

This is because all Windows NT 4.0 and Windows 2000 updates earlier than SP2 use the GetFileVersionInfo function to call the version of a file. The version number is stored in memory then written to this registry key. Binary files that are listed in this registry key are loaded in memory at startup. When the update installer calls the GetFileVersionInfo function on a binary from this list, the update installer refers to the binary that is already loaded instead of the binary that is actually present in the target location. QChain affects only binary replacement operations. It does not do anything with delete operations.

The following scenario shows why QChain may not put the correct binary on the system:

- You install update packages A and B without restarting between installations.
- Both packages contain Lsasrv.dll, a file that is in the KnownDLLs list. Package A includes Lsasrv.dll version 5, package B includes Lsasrv.dll version 3, and the computer has Lsasrv.dll version 2 installed.
- When package A is installed, GetFileVersionInfo shows that the computer has Lsasrv.dll version 2. Because package A includes version 5, the update installer identifies the need for file replacement.
- The update installer moves Lsasrv.dll version 2 on the computer to a temporary location and creates a Pending File Rename Operation to delete the Lsasrv.dll file from the temporary location the next time the computer restarts.
- Package A Lsasrv.dll version 5 is copied to the computer.
- When package B is installed, GetFileVersionInfo still shows that Lsasrv.dll version 2 is installed on the computer because GetFileVersionInfo reads the version information from the Lsasrv.dll that is loaded in memory. Package B has version 3, and the hotfix therefore identifies the need for file replacement.
- The update installer moves the Lsasrv.dll that is now on the computer to a temporary location and creates a Pending File Rename Operation to delete the Lsasrv.dll from the temporary location the next time the computer restarts.
- Package B Lsasrv.dll version 3 is copied to the computer.
- QChain runs, but there are no Pending File Rename Operations for file replacement and QChain therefore does nothing.
- Because package B was installed most recently, package B Lsasrv.dll version 3 is in the correct location on the computer. Therefore, it loads into memory when the computer restarts. The Pending File Rename Operations delete both the original Lsasrv.dll version 2 and the package A Lsasrv.dll version 5. As a result, the computer now has Lsasrv.dll version 3 instead of version 5.

MANAGING SOFTWARE UPDATE DISTRIBUTION

Microsoft has developed distribution tools that can assist network administrators with all types of networks from small local area networks (LANs) to large enterprises. In this section, we will discuss the most common tools that you can use to distribute software updates, **Systems Management Server (SMS)**, **Windows Update**, and **Group Policy**.

Systems Management Server

Microsoft Systems Management Server (SMS) is designed for large enterprise environments with hundreds or even thousands of computers in multiple locations. SMS assists you in security patch management by its ability to scan computers remotely throughout your network and report the results to a central repository. The results can then be assessed and compared to determine which computers need additional patches.

SMS has many functions that assist an organization in asset management, application deployment, and so on. In this section, we will focus on the function of SMS that assists in patch management.

SMS integrates with Windows Update services and SUS. Thus, the required patches can be downloaded from the Microsoft Web site and installed on the appropriate computers.

NOTE

SMS does not detect the security update if MBSA returns a note message for that particular update. In this situation, you can use the SMS software inventory to audit the environment for file names and versions, and you can manually build collections by using the file information from the Microsoft Knowledge Base article that documents the security update.

Activity 6-5: Systems Management Server Demo

ACTIVITY

Time Required: 15 minutes

Objective: View the Systems Management Server demonstration on Microsoft's Web site regarding security patch management.

Description: In this activity, you will access Microsoft's Web site for SMS, locate the Security Patch Management demo, and view the presentation.

1. Log on with your **AdminXX** account, where *XX* is your assigned student number. Click **Internet Explorer**.

2. In the browser, type **microsoft.com/smserver**, then press **Enter**.

The demo is a pop-up. Please ensure that pop-up blockers are turned off to view it.

NOTE

3. On the top left of the page, select **Product Information**, then select **Product Overview**.

4. Scroll down the page and select **Security Patch Management**.

5. On the Security Patch Management page, select **Security Patch Management Demo**.

6. Click **Play**, then continue to click **Next** to view the demonstration. Figure 6-6 shows the demo for patch management in SMS. Note: In order for the demo to run, the browser must be configured to display flash animations. If you are using the default installation of Windows 2003, this may not be the case, and you may have to alter the settings in Internet Explorer.

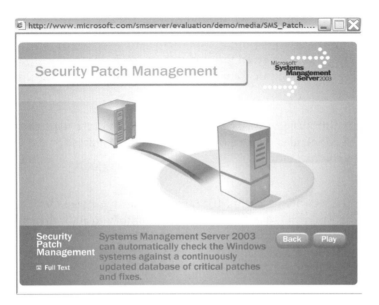

Figure 6-6   The demo for patch management in SMS

With SMS 2.0 and the SUS Feature Pack, administrators are able to easily manage security updates throughout the organization. SMS has always been able to distribute any type of software, but the SUS Feature Pack adds functionality that minimizes the security patch management process. Two features in particular that are of interest in the patch management area are the Distribute Software Updates Wizard and the Web Reports Add-in for Software Updates.

The Distribute Software Updates Wizard compares available updates with the inventory of client computers to determine missing and previously installed updates. Only the necessary updates are installed. This can reduce overhead by eliminating redundant or unnecessary updates. The Distribute Software Updates Wizard provides the following capabilities:

- Update status for all inventoried clients based on new security update information
- Review and authorization of missing updates
- Custom built packages and advertisements for each update or set of updates
- Windows Update–style notifications
- Timers that allow users to save and close applications or enable users to postpone updates

The Web Reports Add-in for Software Updates provides a patch management reporting solution, allowing inventory information and reports to be viewed from a Web browser. The preconfigured reports available from the Web Reports Add-in help track software update status for:

- Individual updates or groups of updates
- Individual computers or groups of computers
- All updates or all computers in an organization
- Patches by operating system
- Detection rate for specific updates
- Applicable updates by type

Windows Update

Microsoft maintains the Automatic Updates Web site, which contains all of the latest security updates. You can configure your Windows XP and Windows Server 2003 computers to automatically download and install the latest updates on a schedule that you specify. Alternatively, you can choose to download the updates yourself and/or install them yourself. You can configure these settings on the Automatic Updates tab in the System Properties of Windows 2000 SP3, Windows XP, and Windows Server 2003 computers.

NOTE You can also manage Automatic Updates on a Windows 2000 Professional computer with SP3 or higher installed. Management of Automatic Updates is performed through the Control Panel of the Windows 2000 Professional computer.

Figure 6-7 shows the Automatic Updates tab in System Properties.

You can efficiently customize the configuration settings of the Automatic Updates client for computers in your environment by using a variety of methods. Customizing the configuration settings allows you to control how your clients interact with some of the patch management technologies that are available from Microsoft.

Activity 6-6: Configuring Windows Update

Time Required: 15 minutes

Objective: Configure your computer for automatic updates. Because downloading updates to servers should be done in a controlled environment to a SUS server, this exercise demonstrates the client configuration. The exercise should be performed on a Windows XP machine.

Description: In this activity, you will configure your computer to automatically download and install the latest updates from the Microsoft Web site.

1. Log on with your **AdminXX** account, where *XX* is your assigned student number.

Figure 6-7 The Automatic Updates tab in System Properties

2. Click **Start**, right-click **My Computer**, and then select **Properties**.

3. Click the **Automatic Updates** tab. Note that the tab contains four options for controlling automatic updates. Examine each of the options.

4. Select the **Automatic (recommended)** option, select **Every Day** from the first drop-down list, and then select **11:00 PM** from the second drop-down list.

5. Select **OK** to save the setting and close the dialog box. Figure 6-8 shows Automatic Updates configured for every day at 11:00 p.m.

Figure 6-8 Automatic Updates configured for 11:00 p.m.

Group Policy

Although applying the Windows Update setting to one computer is not difficult, repeating that process for hundreds or even thousands of clients could get a little ... well, tedious and time-consuming. Rather than applying the setting manually to each computer, you can use Group Policy to control settings of computers in a site, domain, or organizational unit (OU) and to install software patches on computers within their defined container or containers. Group Policy to manage software updates should be used to ensure that computer systems are continually in compliance with corporate security policy and standards.

Be sure that the chain of command is followed to ensure that the update process is a smooth one. For example, the corporate and domain administrators have the ability to add Group Policy updates, the domain administrator can also disable and set new Group Policies, while a remote domain administrator can creates GPOs for automatic updates for any workstation in his OU.

In most cases, administrators will schedule the installation of new updates and computer restarts on workstations outside normal working hours. To do so, they use the Reschedule Automatic Updates scheduled installations Group Policy Object (GPO) setting, which enables computers that have missed a scheduled installation to reschedule the installation to occur when the Automatic Updates service starts. If this GPO setting is not used, then when a scheduled installation is missed because the client computer was turned off, the installation will not occur after this point, even when the computer is restarted. This creates a potential issue: If the computer is not online at the scheduled installation time, updates will never be applied.

Activity 6-7: Configuring Automatic Updates Using Group Policy

Time Required: 30 minutes

Objective: Use Group Policy to configure Automatic Updates for all computers in your domain.

Description: In this activity, you will create a Group Policy that configures the settings for Automatic Updates. You will then apply the Group Policy to all computers in your domain.

1. Log on with your **AdminXX** account, where *XX* is your assigned student number.
2. Click **Start**, select **All Programs**, and then select **Administrative Tools**.
3. Select **Group Policy Management**.
4. Click the + (plus) signs to expand your domain and then to expand the **Group Policy Objects** container.
5. Right-click the **Group Policy Objects** container, then select **New**.
6. Type **AutoUpdate**, then click **OK**.
7. Right-click the **AutoUpdate** Group Policy object, then click **Edit** to open the Group Policy Object Editor tool.
8. In the Group Policy Object Editor tool, expand **Administrative Templates** within Computer Configuration, then expand **Windows Components**.
9. On the console pane, click **Windows Update**.
10. On the details pane, right-click **Reschedule Automatic Updates scheduled installtions**, then choose **Properties**.
11. Select **Enabled**, then set to 2 the Wait after system startup (minutes) box.
12. Click **OK** to save the settings.
13. Close the **Group Policy Object Editor** tool and return to the Group Policy Management console.
14. Click and hold **AutoUpdate** Group Policy and drag it up to your domain.
15. When your domain is selected, release the mouse button, then click **OK** to link the Group Policy to the domain. Note that the Group Policy is now shown as linked to the domain. Figure 6-9 shows the settings for Windows Update in Group Policy.

Computers in the domain that are not powered up at the time that updates are run will not receive the updates and will not automatically "catch up" on their updates. If you decide to use this method, you should ensure that users leave their computers powered up at all times, or you should supplement the updates with automatic updates from Group Policy, which does have the capability to catch up with the missed updates.

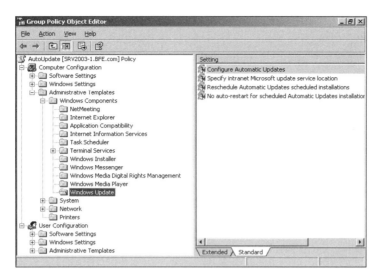

Figure 6-9   The settings for Windows Update in Group Policy

PROVIDING A CRITICAL PATCHING PROCESS

We should note here that tools are not the entire answer to staying up to date with regard to patches. You should also have a **critical patching process** in place that determines who is responsible for reporting and fixing problems associated with security patches. You can also stay in touch with the latest patches by monitoring sites such as the **CERT Coordination Center** site.

Each company should develop its own strategy, but Microsoft recommends that the following items be included in any patch management process:

- *A detailed and updated inventory of computers and software*—You can use SMS software to create and maintain this information.

- *Lab testing of software patches*—Microsoft recommends that you test the patch on a few comparable computers before rolling it out to all of your computers.

- *An established timetable or an acceptable response time*—(Administrators had 26 days of warning about the security vulnerability that the Blaster worm exploited.)

- *An established and enforced antivirus software policy*— All clients and servers should be mandated to use antivirus software . . . no exceptions.

- *A person or team that is held responsible for the proper installation and testing of all updates.*

The CERT Coordination Center was established in 1988. It is a center for Internet security expertise that is located at the Software Engineering Institute, a federally funded research and development center operated by Carnegie Mellon University. You can access the CERT Coordination Center Web page at *www.cert.org*. It contains up-to-date news about the latest security vulnerabilities and exploits and the methods that you can use to combat them. You can also read about the best practices for emergency security response.

Figure 6-10 shows the Web site for the CERT Coordination Center.

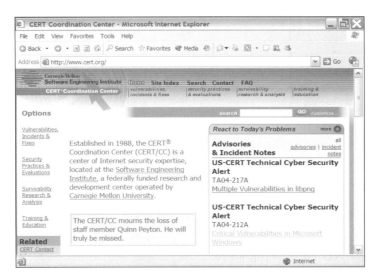

Figure 6-10   The Web site for the CERT Coordination Center

Daily routines should include the following:

- Perform an inventory on servers.
- Check the production environment for unmanaged or rogue computers.
- Check for potential system vulnerabilities.
- Check to ensure compliance with security standards and policies.
- Check sources for information about new software updates.
- Monitor the progress of software update deployment.

OPTIMIZING PATCH MANAGEMENT

In the past, many network administrators have used a reactive approach in regard to patch management. In other words, if a known security hole actually resulted in an attack that affected the network, then they would apply the patch to fix the problem. This method worked well only when attacks were few and far between.

In today's network environment the number of vulnerabilities discovered and subsequent attacks has increased to the point that the reactive approach is no longer feasible for most organizations. It has become essential to apply the patches soon after the security vulnerability is discovered and before the attack can occur. This means that specific tasks must be performed ahead of time to prevent the potential attack from having a chance to succeed. In the next section, we discuss the essential maintenance tasks that should be performed to optimize patch management in your organization. There are three primary areas of importance within security patch management that you may want to measure and improve upon:

- Improving security releases
- Improving security policy enforcement
- Improving emergency security response

Earlier, we discussed the process that should be developed and employed to ensure that patches are installed on the appropriate computers at the appropriate time. The essential maintenance tasks are really just those processes put into action. As with the critical patching process, the details will vary according to the needs of your organization, but Microsoft recommends that they include some or all of the following tasks:

- *Inventory your IT infrastructure*—The inventory should be ongoing and active so that changes are recorded at regular intervals. It should include hardware and software information.
- *Identify and monitor vulnerabilities specific to your environment*—Stay ahead of what steps might be required for your organization to resolve an issue.
- *Prioritize your computer assets*—Create a plan that includes which clients and servers receive the highest priority for a patch if all of the computers require a patch.

Enforce your security policies. You should make sure that security policies that control automatic updates and antivirus software are enforced by the software and by strict guidelines within your organization.

TROUBLESHOOTING THE PATCH MANAGEMENT INFRASTRUCTURE

It would be very nice if all of the methods of patching computers worked flawlessly the first time. It would be very nice, but it would also be asking for a little too much! You need to be familiar with the problems that can occur when you are applying patches so that you can troubleshoot the patch management infrastructure of your network.

In this section, we discuss troubleshooting patch management for the main three methods used to deploy patches on most networks: SUS, Windows Update, and Group Policy.

Troubleshooting SUS

In Chapter 5, we discussed the four phases of the patch management process. You might remember that the fourth phase involved deploying the updates. Part of this phase involves troubleshooting the process if an update fails. If the failed update has been installed in a SUS environment, then you should first cancel the approval of the update on the SUS server in order to prevent further installations, which would only compound your problems.

After you have stopped the problem from multiplying itself, you can turn your attention to the damage caused and look for a solution to the problem. For the computers that already have the update, you have only two options:

- You can remove the update using the Add or Remove Programs utility (if it is available).

- You can use the System Restore utility to revert the system back to a time before the update was installed. In some cases, however, the update cannot be uninstalled.

When time permits and you want to address the issue even further, you can examine the log files of the communication between the clients and the SUS server to attempt to determine why the update failed. The log file on a Windows XP client is located at c:\windows\windowsupdate.log. You can examine the communication between the SUS server and the client to determine whether the connection may have failed during the installation. You can then use the Microsoft Knowledge Base to find more information that you can use to troubleshoot the issue.

Figure 6-11 shows the windowsupdate.log file.

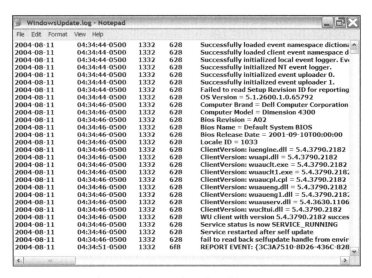

Figure 6-11   The windowsupdate.log file

NOTE   Appendix B of the SUS Deployement Guide contains a list of Software Update Services Event Log messages. It is a complete list of Event Log messages that could be reported on your server running SUS. All of these events are logged on the server to the system log.

Troubleshooting Windows Update

As you experienced for yourself earlier in this chapter, Windows Update is relatively simple to configure and manage. The only tricky part of Windows Update is that it can be controlled locally on the computer or it can be controlled through Group Policy. You should understand that Group Policies applied to the container in which the computer is located will override local computer settings. If this were to happen, the settings that you configured at the local computer would not be applied and other settings would be applied that you had no part in configuring. This would require a little troubleshooting on your part.

You can start the troubleshooting process by carefully checking the settings of the computer on the Automatic Updates tab of System Properties, then checking the settings for any Group Policies applied to the container(s) in which the computer resides.

Table 6-3 lists some of the common issues and solutions for SUS and the Automatic Updates client.

Table 6-3 SUS and Automatic Updates Client Issues

Issue	Solution
New updates do not appear on the Approve Updates page after server synchronization.	No new updates are available or the memory caches are not loading new updates. To reload, in the navigation bar, click Monitor server, Refresh.
The SUS Administration Web site is not functioning correctly.	Restart the synchronization service by clicking Start, Run, services.msc. In the results pane, right-click Windows Update Synchronization Service, Restart.
The SUS Administration Web site is not available or Automatic Updates clients cannot connect to the SUS server.	Restart Internet Information Services (IIS) by clicking Start, Run, services.msc. In the results pane, right-click World Wide Web Publishing Service, Restart.
Security enhancements in Windows Server 2003 may result in problems accessing the SUS site after you install SUS 1.0 SP1.	Ensure that http://SUSServer_computername is added to the local intranet site list. This is only necessary if the computer from which you are administering the SUS server is running Windows Server 2003.
You cannot determine if the Automatic Updates service is running.	Under Manage my computer, expand Services and Applications, then click Services. Verify that Automatic Updates appears on the list of services, double-click the Automatic Updates entry, and check the Service Status.

Table 6-3   SUS and Automatic Updates Client Issues (continued)

Issue	Solution
The Automatic Updates client is not getting updates from the SUS server.	*On the Windows client computer, ensure that the following values exist: HKEY_LOCAL_MACHINE\ Software\Policies\Microsoft\Windows\ WindowsUpdate WUServer=http://<SUSServer>, WUStatusServer=http://<YourServer>, HKEY_LOCAL_MACHINE\SOFTWARE\Policies\ Microsoft\Windows\WindowsUpdate\AU UseWUServer=dword:00000001. Update.log will have a series of log entries, for example: 2003-11-28 18:28:31 Success IUENGINE Querying software update catalog from http://intranetSUS/autoupdate/ getmanifest.asp. If entries such as this do not exist, the Automatic Updates service on that client computer has not yet attempted to query the server for updates. The client waits approximately 24 hours between attempts to query the server for updates.*

Troubleshooting Group Policy

To effectively troubleshoot patch management that is controlled by Group Policy, you must understand Group Policy. In general, when conflicting Group Policies are applied to a computer, the resulting settings will be those in the Group Policy applied to the container closest to where the computer actually resides. If Group Policies do not conflict, then the settings that are applied in both containers will be combined. There are, however, some exceptions to this rule, as we discussed in Chapter 4, which include Block Inheritance and No Override (Enforced).

Dsrevoke is a command-line tool that can be used on domain controllers that are running Windows Server 2003 or Windows 2000 Server to report the existence of all permissions for a specific user or group on a set of OUs in a domain. It is a handy troubleshooting tool that offers the option to remove from the discretionary access control lists (DACLs) of a set of OUs all permissions specified for a particular user or group. Dsrevoke provides the ability to revoke delegated administrative authority. This is helpful if you find the need to rollback or remove permissions. Dsrevoke works only on domain objects and OUs.

For patch management that is controlled through Group Policy to operate as expected, the Group Polices themselves must be configured correctly. For more information about how to troubleshoot Group Policies, refer to Chapter 4.

CHAPTER SUMMARY

- ❑ The security of software is often threatened after its initial release.

- ❑ It's extremely important that you remain up to date in regard to the security patches for your Windows operating systems.

- ❑ The MBSA tool, available from Microsoft as a free download, can assist you in scanning computers to determine security vulnerabilities.

- ❑ The MBSA tool can also scan applications such as IIS and SQL server to expose security vulnerabilities.

- ❑ The MBSA tool can perform GUI scans as well as MBSA-style and HfNetChk-style command-line scans.

- ❑ Qfecheck.exe is a command-line tool that can be used to determine which patches are properly installed on a computer.

- ❑ There are several tools from which you can choose to manage software update distribution. These include SMS, Windows Update, and Group Policy.

- ❑ The tools that you decide to use are only part of the total solution. It's equally important to put a process in place that ensures that the patches are installed in a proper and timely way on the appropriate computers.

- ❑ The process should include a detailed and updated inventory of computer hardware and software.

- ❑ You should test all updates in a lab environment whenever possible before deploying them in the production environment.

- ❑ Part of the process should be establishing a timetable and an acceptable response time.

- ❑ All processes should include an established and enforced antivirus software policy.

- ❑ All processes should specify the person or team that will be held responsible for the proper testing and installation of all updates.

- ❑ The CERT Coordination Center Web site can assist you in your organization and keeping up to date with the latest attacks and security vulnerabilities.

- ❑ You should use a proactive approach to patch management that ensures that the patches are installed very soon after a security vulnerability is discovered to prevent an attack from occurring.

- ❑ You should identify and monitor vulnerabilities specific to your environment.

- ❑ You should prioritize your computer assets to ensure that the patches are applied to the most important computers first.

- ❑ You should enforce your security policies that control automatic updates and antivirus software.

❏ If a patch that was installed from a SUS server fails, the first and most important task is to cancel the approval of that update on the SUS server.

❏ Some automatic updates can be uninstalled from a client computer using the Add or Remove Programs tool; others cannot.

❏ On Windows XP, if you cannot uninstall an automatic update that has failed, you still have the option of using System Restore to reset the computer to a time before the automatic update was applied.

❏ Windows Update can be controlled locally or through Group Policy.

❏ To effectively troubleshoot patch management that is controlled through Group Policy, you must be able to troubleshoot Group Policy itself.

KEY TERMS

CERT Coordination Center — A center for Internet security expertise that was established in 1988. CERT maintains a Web site that has the latest news about security vulnerabilities and attacks.

critical patching process — A strategy that is specific to an organization and ensures that the most critical security patches are installed properly on the appropriate computers in a timely manner.

Group Policy — A feature of Active Directory that allows administrators granular control of users and computers in sites, domains, and OUs. You can use Group Policy to control the Automatic Updates settings of hundreds or even thousands of computers.

Microsoft Baseline Security Analyzer (MBSA) — A tool that you can use to scan a Windows 2000, Windows XP, or Windows Server 2003 computer for security vulnerabilities. It is available as a free download from Microsoft's Web site.

Qfecheck.exe — A tool that you can use to determine which patches are properly installed on a computer. It enumerates all of the installed patches by their associated Microsoft Knowledge Base article.

Systems Management Server (SMS) — A Microsoft program that is designed for hardware and software inventory contol, asset management, and software distribution in large enterprise networks. You can use SMS as part of your patch management process.

Windows Update — A feature that is included in Windows 2000 SP3, Windows XP, and Windows Server 2003 computer operating systems that facilitates automatic updates from Microsoft's Windows Update Web site.

REVIEW QUESTIONS

1. Which tool can you use on a command line to identify which patches are installed properly on a computer?

    a. Qfecheck.exe

    b. MBSA command-line tool

    c. MBSA GUI tool

    d. SMS

2. If you receive an error 201 when running HfNetChk, where do you find out what the problem is?

    a. Use the F1 key

    b. The Help and Support Center of your computer

    c. Microsoft's Knowledge Base

    d. The error will automatically tell you what the problem is.

3. Which of the following does MBSA examine? (Choose all that apply.)

    a. Windows software

    b. Media Player settings

    c. Firewall settings

    d. Virus signature updates

4. On which types of operating systems can MBSA be used? (Choose all that apply.)

    a. Windows 2000

    b. Windows XP

    c. Windows 9X

    d. Windows NT 4.0

5. Which of the following applications can MBSA examine for security vulnerabilities? (Choose all that apply.)

    a. Internet Explorer

    b. Outlook Express

    c. Exchange Server

    d. Windows Explorer

6. Which type of scans can be performed using MBSA? (Choose all that apply.)

    a. GUI-based HfNetChk style

    b. Command line–based MBSA style

    c. GUI-based MBSA style.

    d. Command line–based HFNetChk style

6

7. True or false? Qfecheck.exe will warn you about any updates that you should have installed but do not currently have installed.

    a. True

    b. False

8. Which of the following does Qfecheck.exe use to enumerate patches?

    a. Registry numbers

    b. Error numbers

    c. Microsoft Knowledge Base article numbers

    d. Patch control (PC) numbers

9. Which of the following programs is specifically designed for large enterprise networks?

    a. SMS

    b. Active Directory

    c. Group Policy

    d. MBSA

10. Which of the following operating systems can use the Automatic Updates feature? (Choose all that apply.)

    a. Windows 9X

    b. Windows 2000 SP2

    c. Windows XP

    d. Windows Server 2003

11. Which of the following should be included in a critical patching process? (Choose all that apply.)

    a. A detailed and updated inventory of computers and software

    b. The Group Policy account policy setting for each OU

    c. An established and enforced antivirus policy

    d. Group Policy Block Inheritance settings for all OU administrators

12. Which of the following is the correct Web address for the CERT Coordination Center Web site?

    a. *www.cert.com*

    b. *www.cert.net*

    c. *www.cert.gov*

    d. *www.cert.org*

13. Which of the following should be included as essential maintenance tasks for patch management? (Choose all that apply.)

    a. Require backups of all patches installed on production servers.

    b. Identify and monitor vulnerabilities specific to your environment.

    c. Prioritize your efforts by installing only the patches for which prior attacks have occurred.

    d. Enforce your security policies for automatic updates and antivirus software settings.

14. Which of the following can be used to control the Windows Updates settings of a computer. (Choose all that apply.)

    a. Local System properties

    b. Group Policy

    c. NTFS permissions

    d. Share permissions to the Windows Updates folder

15. Which of the following might affect enforcement of settings for Windows Updates on a computer?

    a. Local settings could override Group Policy.

    b. Group Policy could override local settings.

    c. The domain policy could override the OU policy that contains the computers.

    d. Block Inheritance could be applied at the OU that contains the computers.

16. Which of the following security-related settings can be scanned by MBSA? (Choose all that apply.)

    a. Weak passwords

    b. Media Player settings

    c. NTFS permissions

    d. The NTFS file system

17. Which of the following are valid scan options for MBSA? (Choose all that apply.)

    a. Local computer

    b. All computers in a domain

    c. All computers in a range of domains in alphabetical order

    d. All computers in a range of IP addresses

18. Which of the following are true statements regarding an MBSA-style command-line scan performed with the MBSA tool? (Choose all that apply.)

    a. You can view the detailed results of the scan on the command line.

    b. You can view the detailed results of the scan on the MBSA GUI tool.

    c. It is more detailed when performed by default than when the scan is performed in the GUI tool.

    d. It has the same detail by default as if you had performed it in the GUI with the default settings.

19. Which is the following is the correct command for an HfNetChk–style MBSA scan?

    a. mbsacli.exe

    b. mbsaclihf.exe

    c. hfmbsacli.exe

    d. mbsacli.exe /hf

20. Which of the following is the correct command to run the Qfecheck.exe program with verbose output?

    a. qfecheck.exe /v

    b. vqfecheck.exe

    c. qfecheck.exe /verbose

    d. verbose/qfecheck.exe

21. If the user of a computer in a domain sets his computer to not accept automatic updates, but an administrator creates and applies a Group Policy to set all computers in the domain to accept automatic updates, which of the following will happen? (Choose all that apply.)

    a. The user's local settings will override the Group Policy.

    b. The Group Policy will override the user's local settings.

    c. The user's computer will accept automatic updates.

    d. The user's computer will not accept automatic updates.

22. In which container within Computer Configuration/Administrative Templates are the Windows Update settings?

    a. Windows Components

    b. System

    c. Network

    d. Windows Settings

23. Which is the correct Microsoft Web address to find information regarding Systems Management Server?

    a. *systemsmgtserv.com*

    b. *microsoft.com/smserver*

    c. *microsoft.com/sms*

    d. *systemman.microsoft.com*

24. Which of the following applications will MBSA scan for security vulnerabilities? (Choose all that apply.)

   a. Microsoft Office

   b. Outlook Express

   c. Microsoft Virtual Machine

   d. Firewall Settings

25. Which of the following types of computer operating systems can MBSA scan?

   a. Windows NT 4.0

   b. Windows Me

   c. Windows XP

   d. Windows 9X

6

CASE PROJECTS

Case Project 6-1

CASE PROJECTS

BFE Enterprises is a medium-sized company with about 1000 computers in five separate locations. Management is concerned that the computers do not have the latest security updates installed. They have asked you to recommend a few tools that they could use to check the computers for the latest security updates. Prepare a short report that outlines their options in regard to such tools.

Case Project 6-2

CASE PROJECTS

BFE Enterprises has decided to use the MBSA tool to get security vulnerability information about the computers in each of their locations. The company wants to script the tool as part of a larger script that will make more inquires of the computers. Management is asking you if they can still use the MBSA tool to view the output of the security scan. Write a short report detailing their options in regard to viewing the output created by the MBSA tool.

Case Project 6-3

CASE PROJECTS

BFE Enterprises has recently scanned all of the computers in one of its locations for security vulnerabilities. The company is in the process of training its help desk personnel to check for the latest updates on the computer, based on the Microsoft Knowledge Base article number. Management would like to install and use a simple command-line tool to accomplish this. Write a short memo explaining the tool that they should teach the help desk personnel to install and use.

Case Project 6-4

Some of the computers at BFE Enterprises are not receiving automatic updates as expected. A Group Policy that is applied to the domain is meant to control all of the computers within each of the OUs, which represent the departments of BFE. Make a list of questions that should be asked and answered to troubleshoot the problem.

Case Project 6-5

Some of the computers at BFE Enterprises are set to obtain automatic updates from the SUS server in their location, but this is not happening as expected. Meanwhile, some of the updates that have been installed from the SUS server have failed in the computers on which they were installed. The scheduled updates have not been completed for all computers. Write a list of tasks that must be accomplished. List the priority in which they should be completed.

7

PLANNING AND DEPLOYING SECURITY FOR NETWORK COMMUNICATIONS

After reading this chapter, you will be able to:

- Understand IPSec concepts
- Understand the implications of deploying IPSec
- Plan an IPSec deployment
- Understand default IPSec policies
- Configure IPSec policies
- Deploy and manage IPSec policies
- Deploy IPSec certificates

To ensure a secure IT environment, security must be addressed in all possible areas of the network. This includes the way that communication takes place in areas such as the directory service, internal network, and client configuration. Most organizations typically separate their internal network from the Internet by using firewalls and routers that block specific traffic from entering the internal network. The way many organizations do business has changed the number of ways that internal data can be accessed. Internal corporate networks now have become so complex that it is difficult to constantly protect all mission-critical data. Business applications depend on network access, and Web-based applications not only depend on Internet access but often communicate on specific ports or use specific protocols. As a result it becomes more difficult to know which ports require protection and which ports carry essential communication.

This chapter explains how to plan, deploy, implement, and maintain secure communications within your network. This includes host-to-host, virtual private networks, site-to-site, and secure server communications between other networks. It demonstrates how to use methods that allow you to control security by implementing flexible policies to adapt to any type of network. It will also explain how to secure data in the private and public environments of your network by securing packets through the use of packet filtering, encryption, and enforcing trusted communication methods.

IPSec Concepts

Internet Protocol Security (IPSec) is a set of protocols developed by the Internet Engineering Task Force (IETF). It is a framework of open standards for supporting the secure exchange of packets at the IP layer. It ensures private, secure communications over Internet Protocol (IP) networks by using cryptographic security services. IPSec is based on the following concepts:

- Protecting the contents of IP packets
- Providing packet filtering and enforcing trusted communication
- Securing communication with encryption of the information traveling the network

IPSec authorizes users, ensures that the information is traveling from and to those who are allowed to use this information, and that they are really who they claim to be. It also utilizes data integrity methods to ensure that the information is not damaged or altered in the process and that unauthorized people cannot view what is being communicated.

IPSec utilizes three main security control elements: **Authentication Header (AH)**, **Encapsulating Security Payload (ESP)**, and **Internet Key Exchange (IKE)**, which is the protocol for exchanging encryption keys. AH and ESP may be used independently of or in conjunction with each other, as you will see later in the chapter. The last piece of IPSec is **IP Compression (IPComp)**, which is used to compress raw IP data.

AH provides an authenticity guarantee for packets, by attaching a strong crypto checksum to packets. In other words, it is an identification record that includes the digital signature of the user, which is inserted in headers of all packets. The most popular bit lengths used in authentication headers are 128-bit MD5 and 160-bit SHA1 digital signatures.

ESP provides confidentiality through encryption. It provides a confidentiality guarantee for packets, by encrypting packets with encryption algorithms. The receiving end uses ESP to decrypt the contents of the encrypted packet using the preshared secret key, and protection from wiretapping or man-in-the-middle attacks is guaranteed.

If the parties do not have a preshared set of keys, IKE has to facilitate secure key exchange. This is accomplished through a protocol known as **Internet Security Association and Key Management Protocol/Oakley (ISAKMP/Oakley)**, which allows the receiver to obtain a public key and authenticate the sender using digital certificates. The security of IPSec protocols depends on the secrecy of secret keys. For secure communication to exist between locations there needs to be a way to negotiate keys in secrecy. The use of IKE makes this possible. The IPSec parties agree on a session encryption key used for encryption of the information traveling the network, typically DES or 3DES. The **Diffie-Hellman (DH) algorithm** is used to generate a session key, and the key is then safely transferred to the other party using public encryption mechanisms. You will see DES, 3DES, DH, and IKE again when configuring IPSec policies later in the chapter.

Another technique used in the IPSec suite is IPComp. In traditional dial-up connections, **Point-to-Point Protocol (PPP)** is responsible for compressing data before it gets encrypted. IPcomp provides the same type of service, compressing raw IP data prior to getting it encrypted.

WEIGHING IPSEC TRADEOFFS

Even though deploying IPSec provides greater security, there certainly are tradeoffs to consider. Deploying IPSec can affect network performance and compatibility with other services, tools, and applications. Do not deploy IPSec if the security it provides is not required. Suppose you decide that information sent between the Finance and Human Resources Departments requires higher security than information sent from the Production environment. Suppose you also decide that all private information transmitted across the Internet must be secured. When planning this type of deployment, be aware that deploying IPSec on your network increases the overall cost of administration. The exact cost cannot be predicted because it depends on various factors such as the level of application traffic. A good rule of thumb is to test your IPSec deployment in a lab first. This way you can arrive at a good estimate and then take into consideration whether the added cost is worth the added protection. This section gives you some points to look at when determining how IPSec will impact your environment, such as:

- Amount of time for connection establishment
- Computing performance
- Effect on networking inspection technologies
- Increased packet size
- Application compatibility with IPSec NAT-T
- Connectivity during cluster node addition or removal
- Effect on Active Directory and domain controller connections
- ICMP-based functionality
- Multicast and broadcast traffic functionality

IPSec increases the time it takes to initially establish authenticated connections and therefore is not recommended in situations where clients make occasional, short-lived connections. Negotiating security initially using IKE typically increases the connection time by one to three seconds, depending on policy design, network round-trip time, and the load on the systems. Make sure that you want to trade the one- to three-second increase in connection time for the added security.

The filtering and encryption of each packet uses extra resources. As the volume of IPSec traffic increases, the load placed on the network and on computer CPUs increases as well. Filters with specific source and destination IP addresses can be processed much more quickly than filters that specify a subnet or simply "Any" IP address. IPSec employs a cache algorithm that can speed up the processing of packets that match a filter. If you choose to deploy IPSec and your systems already have high loads on their CPUs, consider adding more machines or using **IPSec offload network adapters**. Offload network adapters process IPSec functions at a high rate of speed so that there is minimal performance degradation. However, these adapters generally have a maximum number of security associations (SAs) that they can support, and although IPSec offload network adapters speed up the encryption process used to secure IPSec packets, they do not speed up the filter processing time.

ESP and AH **encapsulate** IP payloads by adding a security header to every packet. The disadvantage of this is that most existing network management and diagnostic tools cannot interpret these types of packets. Some of the tools that might be affected include router and firewall access control lists, network traffic analysis and reporting tools, and Quality of Service (QoS) products. Network-based intrusion detection tools, by the nature of their design, require that network packets be inspected, modified, or both. If IPSec protocols are not used to encrypt packets, these functions can be enhanced to inspect inside the IPSec protocol header. If IPSec encryption is required for security, however, it might be difficult to maintain full network management functionality.

Using IPSec encryption adds overhead to IP packets. This reduces effective throughput and increases network utilization. Because existing networks and servers might be already operating at maximum capacity without any type of IPSec deployment, test several different IPSec policy configurations. Each policy configuration is likely to result in different performance impacts on clients and servers, and it may be necessary to increase the network bandwidth, add more CPUs, or install IPSec offload adapters to handle the increased overhead of IPSec.

Although Windows Server 2003 supports IPSec Network Address Translation Transversal (NAT-T), some applications might not work when their traffic is first protected with IPSec and then passed through a network address translator. If you are using NAT-T it is recommended that you test how your implementation of IPSec interacts with network address translators in a lab environment before deploying IPSec in your production environment.

Many clustering and load-balancing services use the same IP address for all nodes in a cluster. This creates incompatibilities with IPSec in some instances. Windows Server 2003 IPSec has proprietary extensions that allow it to work with the Network Load Balancing service and Windows Cluster Service, but support for these extensions does not exist in the current Windows 2000 and Windows XP IPSec client implementations. This can result in some loss of connectivity when you add or remove cluster nodes.

Because IPSec is based on the authentication of computers, a computer must be authenticated before it can send IPSec-protected data. Active Directory provides this authentication using the default protocol Kerberos V5. When IKE uses Kerberos V5 to authenticate, Kerberos V5 and other dependent protocols are used for communication with domain controllers. If IPSec is required from domain members to the domain controllers, authentication traffic will be blocked and IPSec communications will fail. In addition, no other authenticated connections can be made using other protocols. Because Active Directory–based IPSec policy settings are typically applied to domain members through Group Policy, no other IPSec policy settings can be applied to that domain member through Group Policy. Therefore, using IPSec for communications between domain members and domain controllers is not supported.

If you are designing an IPSec policy to secure or block Internet Control Message Protocol (ICMP) traffic, the policy might cause services and tools that rely on ICMP to measure network response times to produce misleading results. For example, tools that depend on ICMP, such as Tracert, may not work when ICMP traffic is protected by IPSec. Group Policy measures ICMP response times to determine if the connection to the domain controller is a slow link, so this may also be affected.

Because you can configure IPSec filters to block multicast and broadcast traffic, any application that uses multicast or broadcast might fail if the computer has an IPSec policy that blocks this type of traffic.

PLANNING AN IPSEC DEPLOYMENT

As demonstrated in the previous section, before deploying IPSec in your production environment you must test your deployment plan in a lab to be sure of the results. This is done after you make decisions about which computers to secure, where the security should be implemented, and how tight the security must be.

One of the best features of IPSec is that it is incredibly flexible. It can be configured for the needs of almost any network, but there are many decisions to make in regard to its configuration. Some decisions are made for you by the way that you are using IPSec or by the types of client operating systems that you are using on your network; other decisions are all yours. Table 7-1 provides some guidance for using IPSec for some of the most common security concerns.

Table 7-1   IPSec security solutions

Concern	Solution
Attacks using specific protocols or ports or Denial of Service attacks	Use IPSec traffic blocking, packet filtering, or policy filter lists allowing only traffic from trusted sources over specified protocols to specific addresses and ports.

Table 7-1   IPSec security solutions (continued)

Concern	Solution
Eavesdropping or sniffing	*Use the Encapsulating Security Payload (ESP) protocol to encrypt data with Triple Data Encryption Standard (3DES) or Data Encryption Standard (DES).*
Identity spoofing	*Use Kerberos, public key certificates, or preshared key authentication to verify the identity of computer.*
Modification of data	*Use a cryptographic checksum that incorporates a secret key to provide data integrity.*

When you are planning your deployment, there are certain situations in which the use of IPSec is not recommended. Remember that IPSec can reduce performance and increase the use of network bandwidth. In addition, using IPSec can cause application compatibility issues. As mentioned earlier, using IPSec to secure communication between domain members and their domain controllers is not recommended. This is because it reduces network performance and increases the complexity of the IPSec policy configuration and management required to actually make this work. Another use for which IPSec is not recommended is to secure all traffic in a network. Besides the reduced network performance, using IPSec for this purpose can cause issues because (1) IPSec cannot negotiate security for multicast and broadcast traffic, (2) traffic from applications that require ICMP might be incompatible with IPSec, and (3) network management functions that inspect protocol headers may not be able to function, because IPSec encapsulates and/or encrypts IP payloads.

Proper uses of IPSec are as follows:

- Packet filtering such as using IPSec with the Routing and Remote Access service to permit or block inbound or outbound traffic

- Securing host-to-host traffic on specific paths such as using IPSec to provide protection for traffic between servers or other static IP addresses or subnets

- Securing traffic to servers by requiring IPSec protection for all client computers that access a server

- Combining Layer 2 Tunneling Protocol (L2TP) and IPSec (L2TP/IPSec) for securing VPN scenarios

- Incorporating site-to-site or gateway-to-gateway tunneling when you need interoperability with third-party devices that do not support L2TP/IPSec or Point-to-Point Tunneling Protocol (PPTP) connections

NOTE   It is often necessary for a server to have a static IP address in IPSec policy filters because IPSec depends on IP addresses for establishing secure connections; therefore, it may not be possible to use dynamic IP addresses.

When planning an IPSec deployment, in a simple network structure you will be more apt to design a single IPSec policy, which may contain many rules, each one adapted for a specific type of traffic. In a large environment, many different IPSec policies may have to be designed in order to meet the security requirements of the various computer roles. Factors that can increase the number of policies required in your environment include:

- *Computer roles*—Having an environment that includes many servers with various roles and requirements can require many configurations per server.

- *Sensitivity of data traveling over the network*—Different levels of encryption may be needed to meet different levels of security needs.

- *Computer operating systems*—Some operating systems do not automatically support IPSec transport mode and require special client software to be installed.

- *Domain relationships and memberships*—IPSec configurations and authentication will depend on whether computers, servers, and domains are in the same forest or different forests, and on whether those forests trust each other.

If you have a complex environment, use IPSec only when and where it is truly needed. Use as few policies as feasible to reduce the difficulty of managing your environment. A simpler environment is less likely to produce problems and is also easier to troubleshoot if it does.

Testing the Functionality of Existing Applications and Services

You should keep in mind that the main reason for deciding to use security methods in the first place is to protect the integrity and the productivity of the network. For this reason, you should always test the applications and services that you are running on your network to make sure that they can still function with the IPSec rules that you have configured on your network. Testing successful IPSec operations is uniquely different from testing other networking components because it involves testing not only to confirm that the applications work, but also to ensure that IPSec is in fact restricting access and performing protection. There are many reasons that the application could cease to function or function with errors. Most of these involve the fact that IPSec rules can be used to filter traffic. Sometimes these filters can cause unexpected results. Besides testing IPSec's capabilities to filter port addresses and protocols, it is also important to test IPSec policy management procedures and key IT operations processes, such as:

- Importing, exporting, and remotely managing IPSec policy

- Assigning, unassigning, and changing IPSec policy to different types of computers

- Backing up, restoring, and monitoring network operations

- Deploying new domain controllers and adding new subnets to the network

- Server scaling and cross-platform capability

Application functionality testing begins with identifying and prioritizing the applications in use throughout your organization. Identify the applications that you need to test by creating an inventory of your applications, if you do not already have one, and determining the level of importance and the priority of each application, to help determine the level of testing required. This will help determine the scope of the project. After establishing priorities and examining special considerations for each application, you can develop a test plan.

Deciding Which IPSec Mode to Use

Depending on the way that you intend to use IPSec, the mode that will be used may have already been determined for you. There are basically two different types of communications that you might be securing: either communications within a network or communications between networks. Based on this fact, you can make your decision between two modes of IPSec security: **transport mode** and **tunnel mode**.

Transport Mode

You can use IPSec in transport mode to secure communications between two computers on the same network. This can be server-to-server or server-to-client communications. Once configured, IPSec provides end-to-end security based on the authentication and encryption settings that you apply. IPSec is used in situations where you require end-to-end security or you require packet filtering. IPSec can be configured to permit or block specific types of traffic based on source and destination address combinations and specific protocols and ports. In this instance, IPSec is used to block well-known ports of software so that even if a server becomes compromised, it cannot be used to compromise other computers or allow access through the well-known port. IPSec end-to-end security establishes trust and security from a unicast source IP address to a unicast destination IP address. This IPSec function is used when you want only trusted computers to access a server. In this instance, you can use IPSec to control access to all applications and services running on the server, and then choose to authenticate or encrypt all application network traffic.

Tunnel Mode

You can use IPSec in tunnel mode to secure communications between two networks. Tunnel mode is primarily used for interoperability with gateways or end systems that do not support L2TP/IPSec or PPTP VPN site-to-site connections. IPSec can also be used in tunnel mode to protect traffic end to end when one endpoint of the communication does not support IPSec. Perhaps you want to encrypt traffic end to end between two computers, but a third-party firewall or network intrusion detection system requires that traffic be decrypted.

In a gateway-to-gateway or site-to site scenario, traffic is being sent between a client computer in a vendor site and, for example, a File Transfer Protocol (FTP) server at your corporate office. Say that the vendor uses a third-party gateway and your corporate office uses a gateway running Windows Server 2003. An IPSec tunnel is used to secure traffic between the third-party gateway and the gateway running Windows Server 2003 by using static IP addresses.

What happens when you have a third-party server in an internal corporate network that does not support IPSec, an IPSec-enabled router, and a Windows Server 2003 computer in a perimeter network? In a situation like this, where one endpoint doesn't support IPSec, traffic on the path between the router and the third-party server in the internal corporate network is not secured, because the third-party server does not support IPSec. However, the tunnel rules would protect traffic between the computer running Windows Server 2003 and the IPSec-enabled router.

If the traffic must be encrypted and inspected, you can use IPSec tunnel mode to secure traffic to the inspection point. Here IPSec tunnels are used to secure traffic between a server and a third-party firewall's external interface, and then between the third-party firewall's internal interface and the other server. Traffic is decrypted for firewall inspection and then reencrypted when it is forwarded to the IPSec peer.

Planning Authentication Methods for IPSec

Authentication is a process by which entities on a network prove that they are who the say they are. Of course, you don't want everyone else to know what they said to prove it. For this reason, computers need to be able to authenticate to each other using a secure method. An authentication strategy must be well defined and implemented because authentication verifies the identity and trust of the computer at the other end of the connection. If computers cannot be properly authenticated, IPSec does not provide security. There are three main methods of authentication using IPSec. You make your choice based on the capabilities of your servers and clients and the requirements of your organization. The three main methods from which you can choose are as follows:

- Kerberos
- Certificates
- Preshared key

Kerberos V5 is the default authentication method for Windows 2000 Server and Windows Server 2003. With Kerberos, the client must prove its identity to the server, and the server must also prove its identity to the client. This is referred to as mutual authentication. Kerberos V5 can be used only with Microsoft clients later than Windows 2000 Professional. You should use Kerberos V5 when all of your clients can authenticate using Kerberos V5 and when you want to use a method that requires the least administrative effort. Figure 7-1 shows that when you open the Authentication Methods tab, Kerberos V5 is already there.

Certificates are a method of granting access to users based on their unique identification and the fact that they possess the right keys or algorithms to access the appropriate information. You issue computers a certificate as a means for them to hold on to the key and as a means for you to track the fact that they have it. Certificates can be used in situations that include access to corporate resources, external business partner communications, or computers that do not run the Kerberos V5 authentication protocol. Figure 7-2 shows where you configure certificates.

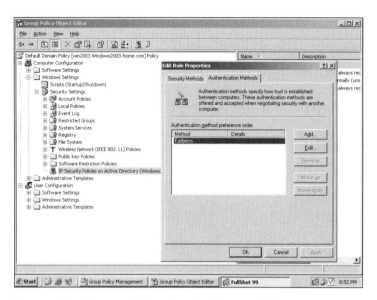

Figure 7-1   Kerberos V5 authentication method

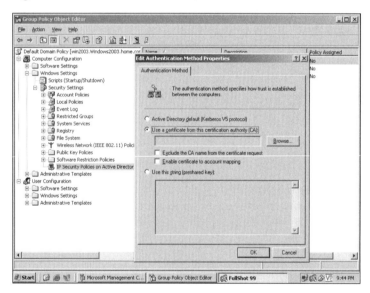

Figure 7-2   Requiring certificates for authentication

A **preshared key** is a string that you can use to authenticate computers as a last resort. You should not use a preshared key if any other authentication method is available. A preshared key is a **symmetric key**, which means that it is a shared secret key. The key is agreed upon by administrators who wish to secure the computer's communications by using IPSec. You should configure the same string on all computers that you want to authenticate. Figure 7-3 shows an example of a preshared key.

The main problem with a preshared key is that you have no way of knowing if the key is discovered. Also, the key is not specific to any individual. Therefore, an attacker could use the key to authenticate to a network, and you could not trace the attack back to an individual. In addition, the preshared key is stored in the registry in plaintext form.

Figure 7-3   Using a string to configure a preshared key

Understanding Default IPSec Policies

Windows 2003 comes with the following three default IPSec policies:

- Client (Respond Only)
- Server (Request Security)
- Secure Server (Require Security)

The Client (Respond Only) policy contains only one rule, called the default response rule. This policy does not attempt to negotiate security for any traffic. The default response rule secures communication only upon request by another computer. This policy is shown in Figure 7-4.

The Server (Request Security) default policy contains the default response rule and a second rule that allows initial incoming communication to be unsecured. This second rule also negotiates security for all outbound unicast IP traffic. This policy can be used with the Client (Respond Only) policy when you want to secure traffic by IPSec whenever possible, yet allow unsecured communication with computers that are not IPSec-enabled. This default policy is shown in Figure 7-5.

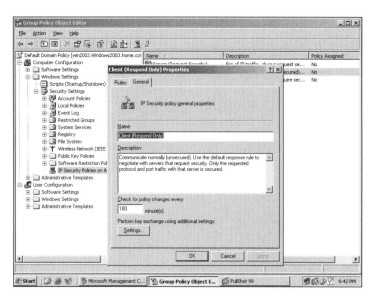

Figure 7-4   The Client (Respond Only) default policy

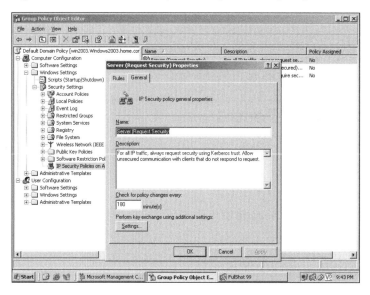

Figure 7-5   The Server (Request Security) default policy

The Secure Server (Require Security) default policy also has two rules, which consist of the default response rule and a rule that allows the initial inbound communication request to be unsecured, but requires that all outbound communication be secured. This policy requires that all connections be secured with IPSec. Any clients that are not IPSec-enabled cannot establish connections. The policy is shown in Figure 7-6.

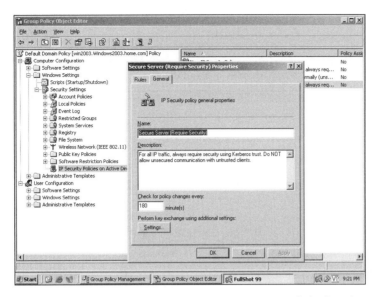

Figure 7-6   The Secure Server (Require Security) default policy

These three default IPSec policies are provided as examples only. Do not use any part of these examples as templates when creating your own IPSec policies. The example policies are overwritten during operating system upgrades and when IPSec policies are imported.

Both the Server (Request Security) and Secure Server (Require Security) default policies allow inbound unsecured communication. This allows them to be used with the Client (Respond Only) policy. The most secure type of IPSec configuration would be one that negotiates security yet doesn't receive unsecured traffic or allow communication with computers that do not recognize IPSec. In this configuration, the client computer policy must have a filter in a rule that initiates secured communication when applications on the client computer attempt outbound connections to the server. We will discuss filters a little later in the chapter.

Activity 7-1: Create an IPSec Policy

Time Required: 30 minutes

Objective: Learn how to create an IPSec policy.

Description: In this exercise, create an MMC snap-in and a new IPSec policy.

1. Log on with your **AdminXX** account, where *XX* is your assigned student number.

2. Click **Start**, **Run**, then type **mmc** in the run dialog box. Click **OK**.

3. Click **File**, **Add/Remove Snap-In**.

4. On the Standalone tab of the Add/Remove Snap-In window, click **Add**.

5. On the Add Standalone Snap-in screen, scroll down to **IP Security Policy Management**, highlight it, and click **Add**.

6. On the Select Computer or Domain screen, choose **The Active Directory domain of which this computer is a member**.

7. Click **Finish**. Click **Close** on the Add Standalone Snap-in screen. Click **OK** on the Standalone tab of the Add/Remove Snap-In window.

8. Click **IP Security Policies on Active Directory** in the left window pane. Now your MMC console is ready to configure, as shown in Figure 7-7.

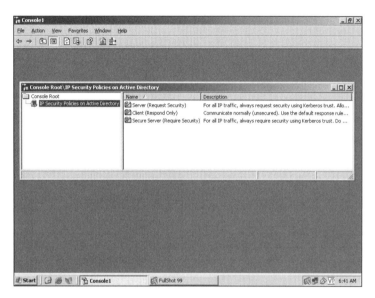

Figure 7-7   IP security MMC snap-in window

9. From the Action menu, choose **Create IP Security Policy**.

10. On the Welcome to the IP Security Policy Wizard screen, click **Next**.

11. In the IP Security Policy Name box, type **New Domain Policy**. In the description box, type a description such as **This is the new domain policy for all secured internal communication**. Choose **Next**.

12. On the Requests for Secure Communication screen, verify that the **Activate the default response rule** box is checked. Click **Next**.

13. On the Default Response Rule Authentication Method screen, verify that the **Active Directory default Kerberos V5 protocol** is chosen. Click **Next**.

14. On the Completing the IP Security Policy Wizard page, verify that the **Edit properties** box is checked. Click **Finish**.

15. On the New Domain Policy Properties page, verify that Filter Action shows **Default Response** and Authentication Methods shows **Kerberos**. Click **OK**.

16. Choose **File** from the top menu bar, choose **Save As**, then on the Save As window screen, type **IPSec** in the **File name** box. Click **Save**. Close the **MMC** window.

CONFIGURING IPSEC POLICIES BETWEEN NETWORKS AND HOSTS

Now that you have some idea of the concepts behind IPSec and what goes into planning an IPSec policy, it's time to look at how to configure those policies. How you decide to use IPSec will determine how it is configured. Remember that IKE uses mutual authentication between computers to establish trusted communications and requires the use of Kerberos V5, a public key infrastructure (PKI) certificate, or a preshared key for authentication. The two communication endpoints must have at least one common authentication method, or the communication fails. We will configure endpoints later in the chapter.

7

Configure IPSec Authentication

Only the sending and receiving computers need to be aware of IPSec because each handles security at its own end and assumes that the medium over which the communication takes place is not secure. By using peer authentication, IPSec can determine whether to communicate with another computer before the communication begins. It doesn't matter whether the computers are located near each other or across the Internet. When Windows Server 2003 IPSec performs peer authentication, it requires only mutual trust of the identities exchanged. It does not verify that the identity that is received is authorized to use a particular IP address. Table 7-2 shows which authentication method you should configure based on the access requirements.

Table 7-2   IPSec Authentication methods

Security Requirement	Authentication Method
Communication within a Windows 2000 or Server 2003 domain or between trusted Windows 2000 or Server 2003 domains	Kerberos V5
Communication outside the domain or across the Internet where Kerberos V5 is not available but CA access is	Public key certificate
Communication with computers that neither support Kerberos V5 nor have access to a CA	Preshared key

Configuring the authentication method specifies how the computers will trust each other. In other words, it specifies how they will prove their identities to each other when trying to establish a **security association (SA)**.

Activity 7-2: Configure Authentication for IPSec

Time Required: 30 minutes

Objective: Learn how to configure authentication for IPSec by using the IPSec management console to configure preshared key authentication.

Description: In this exercise, you will learn how to configure authentication for IPSec by using preshared key authentication.

1. Log on with your **AdminXX** account, where *XX* is your assigned student number.

2. Click **Start**, **Run**, then type **mmc** in the run dialog box. Click **OK**.

3. Choose **File** from the top menu, then choose **Open**. On the open screen, find the **IPsec** console you created in the last exercise and click it so that it shows in the File name box; click **Open**. The IPSec MMC console should now be open.

4. Right-click **New Domain Policy** and choose **Properties**. On the rules tab, choose **Edit**, then choose the **Authentication Methods** tab.

5. Click **Edit**, choose **Use this string (preshared key)**, and enter **ABC123QAZ** as the string. Click **OK**. You should now be back at the Authentication Methods tab, as shown in Figure 7-8.

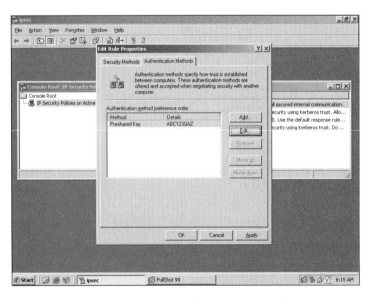

Figure 7-8   Configured reshared key authentication

6. Click **Apply**, then click **OK**. On the Rules tab, click **OK**.

7. Close the **IPSec MMC** window.

Encryption Levels

In addition to authentication, there are multiple levels of encryption that can be configured for the data itself. **Encryption** is a method whereby a plaintext message is converted to a ciphertext message so that only the recipient with the proper key can decrypt the message. There are two basic categories of computer encryption. These are symmetric key encryption and public key encryption. In symmetric key encryption, each computer has a secret key that it uses to encrypt a packet of information before it is sent to another computer. Public key encryption uses a combination of a private key and a public key. The private key is known only to your computer. The public key is given by your computer to any other computer that wants to communicate securely with it. The same key that encrypts is also used to decrypt, and when devices communicate using this technique, both machines must possess the same key. The key in public key encryption is based on a hash value. This value is calculated by using a hashing algorithm. The Diffie-Hellman (DH) algorithm can be used to generate a session key, then the key is safely transferred to the other party using public encryption mechanisms. For enhanced security, do not use Diffie-Hellman Group 1 (low). If possible, use Group 2 (medium) for interoperability with Windows 2000 and Windows XP. When you use a stronger group, the secret key that is derived from the Diffie-Hellman exchange has greater strength.

Lifetime settings determine when a new key is generated. The process of generating new keys at intervals is called dynamic rekeying or **key regeneration**. Lifetimes permit you to force the generation of a new key at a specified interval. Using multiple keys ensures that if an attacker manages to gain the key to one part of a communication, the entire communication is not compromised. Automatic key regeneration is provided by default. You can override the defaults and either specify a master key lifetime in minutes or by the number of session keys, or enable **master key perfect forward secrecy (PFS)**. Master key PFS determines how a new session key is generated. Master key PFS forces key regeneration each time. Enabling master key PFS ensures that the master key keying material cannot be used to generate more than one session key. If you decide to enable master key PFS, the session key limit will be set to 1. If you specify both a master key lifetime in minutes, and a session key limit, whichever interval is reached first will start a new key.

CAUTION   Master key PFS should be used with caution because it requires reauthentication and might impact performance. It is not required to be enabled on both peers.

The methods of encryption that are available in Windows Server 2003 are configured by clicking the General tab of an IPSec policy, then the Settings button, and finally the Methods button, as shown in Figure 7-9. You will actually go in and configure these settings shortly.

7

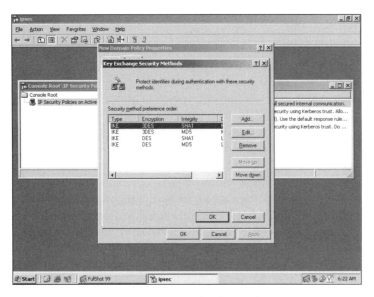

Figure 7-9   IPSec Encryption methods window

The methods of hashing and encryption that can be used are:

- *Secure Hash Algorithm (SHA)*—**Secure Hash Algorithm (SHA)** is the accepted standard for securing authentication on most government contracts. It is used as part of the Federal Information Processing Standard (FIPS). SHA is a very-high-security method that uses a 160-bit encryption key.

- *Message Digest 5 (MD5)*—**Message Digest 5 (MD5)** is used for most commercial applications. It can be used to secure authentication as well as data. This high-security method uses a 128-bit encryption key. It also has a lower performance overhead than Secure Hash Algorithm

- *Data encryption standard (DES)*—**Data encryption standard (DES)** is the lowest encryption strength of the Diffie-Hellman algorithms. It produces only a 56-bit key and is therefore not recommended for use in a high-security environment.

- *Triple DES (3DES)*—**Triple DES (3DES)** is a much stronger Diffie-Hellman algorithm. The length of the key is 64 bits, but 8 bits are used for parity. The effective key length is only 56 bits. In 3DES, three stages of DES are applied with a separate key for each stage. So the key length is 168 bits. 3DES is recommended for use in medium- and high-security networks.

Activity 7-3: Configure Encryption Methods for IPSec

Time Required: 30 minutes

Objective: Learn how to configure encryption methods for IPSec, by using the IPSec management console.

Description: In this exercise, you will learn how to configure encryption methods for IPSec through the IPSec MMC snap-in.

1. Log on with your **AdminXX** account, where *XX* is your assigned student number.

2. Click **Start**, **Run**, then type **mmc** in the run dialog box. Click **OK**.

3. Choose **File** from the top menu, and choose **Open**. On the Open screen, find the **IPSec** console you created in the last exercise and click it so that it shows in the File name box; click **Open**. The IPSec MMC console should now be open.

4. Right click on **New Domain Policy**, then choose **Properties**. On the rules tab, choose the **General** tab.

5. At the bottom of the screen, you will see a section named Perform Key exchange using additional settings. Click the **Settings** button.

6. On the Key Exchange Settings Screen (the General tab), under the section called Protect identities with IKE security methods, click the **Methods** button.

7. On the Key Exchange Security Methods screen, look at the Security method preference order. Notice that the order of security is from the strongest to the weakest.

8. The current corporate security policy requires that this be exactly the opposite. You will now use the **Move up** and **Move down** buttons to rearrange the security to fit the policy.

9. Be sure that the **IKE 3DES SHA1 Medium (2)** method is highlighted; click the **Move down** button three times, so that it is now on the bottom of the order list.

10. Next, go up one method to the **IKE DES MD5 Low (1)** method, be sure it is highlighted, and click the **Move up** button two times, so that it is now on the top of the order list.

11. Next, go down one method to the **IKE 3DES MD5 Medium(2)** method, be sure it is highlighted, and click the **Move down** button one time, so that it is now third in the order list.

12. Your screen should now have the same security method order as shown in Figure 7-10.

13. Click **OK**. Click **OK** on the **Key Exchange Settings** screen. Click **OK** on the **General** tab.

14. Close the **IPSec MMC** snap-in.

IPSec Protocols

There are two main protocols that are used when authenticating with IPSec. IPSec can protect the payload of each packet. It can protect the integrity and confidentiality of the data that it contains, or it can simply be used to ensure that the communication actually came from the original source without being tampered with during transit. Table 7-3 shows which protocol you should select depending on the requirements of your organization.

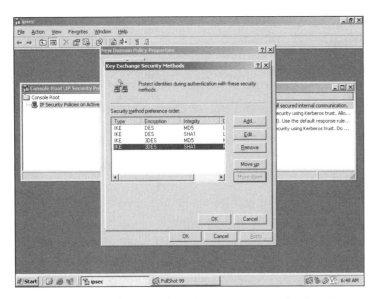

Figure 7-10   Configuring the IPSec security method order

Table 7-3   IPSec Protocol solutions

Requirement	Protocol	Solution
The data and the header need to authenticated and protected from modification, but remain readable	AH	Use in situations where data is not confidential but must be authenticated, or where network intrusion detection or firewall filtering requires traffic inspection.
Only the data needs to be protected so it is unreadable, but the IP addressing can be left unprotected	ESP	Use when data must be kept confidential, such as file sharing, database traffic, or internal Web applications that have not been adequately secured.
Both the header and data need to be protected while data is encrypted	Both AH and ESP	Use for the highest security. If possible, use ESP alone instead.

Authentication Header and Encapsulating Security Payload (ESP) can be configured for either transport mode or tunnel mode. You should remember from earlier in the chapter that transport mode IPSec is used for secure communication between client and servers in a local area network, whereas tunnel mode is used for secure communication between networks.

Authentication Header provides for authentication, integrity, and anti–replay of each packet. You should understand that this is done without encrypting the data. In other words, the data remains readable but it is protected from modification. AH uses a system of keyed hash algorithms to sign the packet to ensure its integrity. In this way, you can be assured that a packet did originate from its apparent source and that it has not been modified in transit.

This is accomplished by placing an AH header in each packet between the IP header and the IP payload, as illustrated in Figure 7-11.

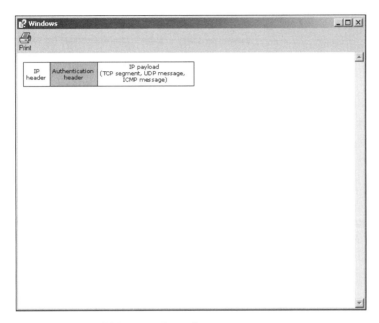

Figure 7-11 AH transport mode

With ESP, the entire packet is encapsulated into a new IP tunnel header, which contains the IP addresses of the endpoints of the tunnel. Encapsulating Security Payload provides everything that AH does and also provides for the confidentiality of the packet during transit.

In transport mode, the entire packet is not encrypted or signed; only the data in the IP payload is encrypted and signed. The authentication process ensures that the packet originated from the apparent sender, and the fact that the data was encrypted ensures that it wasn't viewed or modified during transit. This is accomplished by placing an ESP header before the IP payload and an ESP trailer after the IP payload, further encapsulating only the IP payload, as shown in Figure 7-12. Keep in mind that ESP does not sign the entire packet; only the IP payload itself is encrypted.

The concept of using AH or ESP in tunnel mode is similar to that of using transport mode, except that the packets are encapsulated twice. AH tunnel mode encapsulates an IP packet by placing an AH header between the internal IP header and the external IP header. AH then signs the entire packet for integrity and authentication. This is illustrated in Figure 7-13.

In ESP tunnel mode, the entire packet is encapsulated into a new IP tunnel header, which contains the IP addresses of the endpoints of the tunnel. IPSec tunnel mode encrypts the IP header and the payload during transit. In this way, tunnel mode provides protection for the

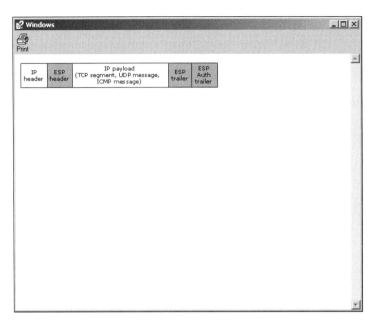

Figure 7-12   ESP transport mode

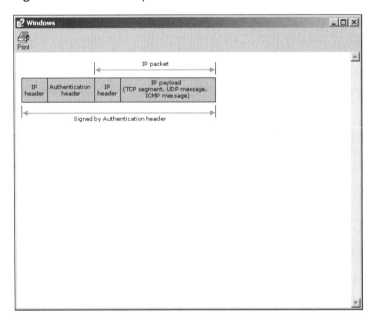

Figure 7-13   AH tunnel mode

entire packet. An entire IP packet is first encapsulated with an AH or ESP header, then the result is encapsulated with an additional IP header. This is demonstrated in Figure 7-14. The additional IP header contains the source and destination of the tunnel endpoints. Once the packet reaches the first destination at the tunnel endpoint, it can be decapsulated and then sent to the final destination by reading the IP address. This double encapsulation makes tunnel mode suitable for protecting traffic between network systems. It can be used when traffic must pass through an untrusted medium such as the Internet. It is therefore most often used with gateways or end systems that do not support Layer Two Tunneling Protocol (L2TP)/IPSec or Point-to-Point Tunneling Protocol (PPTP) connections.

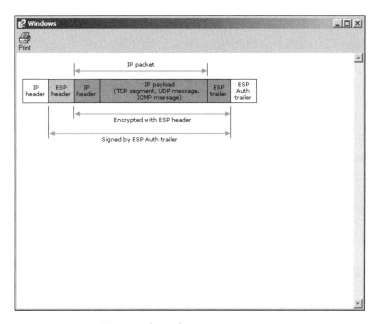

Figure 7-14   ESP tunnel mode

Activity 7-4: Configure Protocols for IPSec

Time Required: 30 minutes

Objective: Learn how to use the IPSec management console to configure the AH and ESP protocols for IPSec.

Description: In this exercise, you will learn how to configure IPSec protocols for AH only.

1. Log on with your **AdminXX** account, where *XX* is your assigned student number.

2. Click **Start**, **Run**, then type **mmc** in the run dialog box. Click **OK**.

3. Choose **File** from the top menu, and choose **Open**. On the Open screen, find the **IPSec** console you created in the last exercise and click it so that it shows in the File name box; click **Open**. The IPSec MMC console should now be open.

4. Right-click **New Domain Policy**, then choose **Properties**. On the rules tab, choose **Edit**.

5. On the Security Methods screen, choose the first method. The AH Integrity column should read <None>. Click **Edit**. On the Edit Security Method tab, choose **Custom**.

6. Click the **Settings** button. On the Custom Security Method Settings screen, check the **Data and address integrity without encryption (AH)** box.

7. In the Integrity algorithm box, select **MD5**.

8. Uncheck the **Data integrity and encryption (ESP)** box.

9. Click **OK**. On the Edit Security Method screen, click **OK.**

10. Your screen should now have the same security methods as shown in Figure 7-15. To have your screen show like the dialog box, scroll to the right.

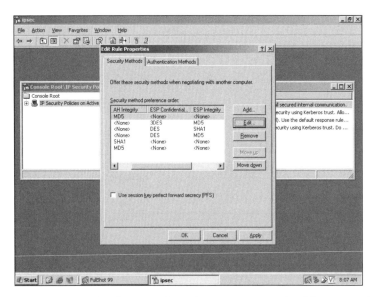

Figure 7-15   Configuring the IPSec security method for AH only

11. Click **OK**. Click **OK** on the Rules tab.

12. Close the **IPSec MMC** snap-in.

IPSec Filters

Each IPSec policy consists of one or more rules that will determine the behavior of the policy. An **IPSec filter** is a specification in the IPSec rule that is used to match IP packets to filter actions such as permit, block, or negotiate security. An IPSec rule is a statement in an IPSec policy that associates a filter list with a filter action, an authentication method, and an IPSec mode. Many IPSec rules can be defined in a single IPSec policy. The rules are configured on the Rules tab of the properties of an IPSec policy. The IPSec policy filters determine which traffic IPSec can secure.

You can use the Filter Wizard to create multiple filters in an IPSec policy rule. If you use more than one filter in a single IPSec policy rule, then you should be aware that the order that the filters are processed in is not necessarily the order in which you are viewing them. Instead, the IPSec Policy Agent reads the policy and the filters are processed into one ordered list that is sorted from the most to the least specific. You can use the IPSec Monitor console to view the filters sorted by their weight. You will work with the IPSec Monitor in the next chapter. If you change or delete a filter, the IPSec Policy Agent reorders the filters based on what remains. Because of this, you should always test applications that use IPSec after applying IPSec and after changing any filters. You may also want to use a test lab, if one is available, to test the effect of IPSec rules before assigning them in a production environment. The IPSec policy can be configured for the following rules, as shown in Figure 7-16.

- Filter list
- Filter action
- Authentication methods
- Tunnel endpoint
- Connection type

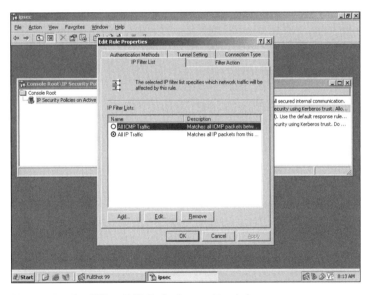

Figure 7-16   IPSec Edit Rule Properties tabs

An **IP filter list** contains one or multiple filters, and it can be shared among different IPSec policies. The filter list is configured on the IP Filter List tab in the properties of an IPSec rule. A single filter list can contain multiple predefined packet filters that allow traffic to be identified by the list. Once the traffic is identified, then the filter action can be applied. Filter lists can identify traffic based on its source, destination, and protocol. There are two predefined examples of filter lists included with Windows Server 2003:

- *All ICMP Traffic*—This filter affects any ICMP traffic that is sent and received by using the unicast IP address of any network interface on a computer and all other computers.

- *All IP Traffic*—This filter affects all IP traffic that is sent and received using the unicast IP address of any network interface on the computer to any destination IP address. Inbound broadcast and multicast traffic uses a multicast or broadcast type for the destination address so the inbound traffic is exempt. All ISAKMP traffic sent over UDP port 500 is also exempted from IPSec filtering.

A **filter action** is set for each type of traffic as identified by a filter list. The filter actions from which you can choose include Permit, Block, or Negotiate Security for the packets that match the filter list. If Negotiate Security is used, then one or more security methods can be selected. Filter actions are configured on the Filter Action tab on the properties of an IPSec rule. There are three predefined examples of filter actions included with Windows Server 2003:

- *Permit*—All traffic that matches the associated filters in the filter list is permitted.

- *Request Security*—All inbound traffic that matches the filters in the filter list is allowed unsecured. All outbound traffic that matches the filters in the filter list negotiates security. This is designed so that servers can request security for all clients, but use unsecured communication with computers that are not IPSec-enabled.

- *Require Security*—All inbound traffic that matches the filters in the filter list is allowed unsecured, and all outbound traffic that matches the filters in the filter list negotiates security. If IKE fails to receive a response and the security negotiation fails, the communication is blocked.

Each of these three filter actions allows inbound unsecured communication. This is not the most secure behavior, and it cannot be used to initiate secured communication in some trust environments. It is also not appropriate to allow inbound unsecured communication for servers that have an interface on the Internet, because it can make the servers vulnerable to a denial of service (DoS) attack. The most secure filter action is one that requires security for all inbound and outbound traffic. This filter action is created by verifying that the Accept unsecured communication, but always respond using IPSec check box, and the Allow unsecured communication with non-IPSec aware computers check box are cleared, as shown in Figure 7-17. As mentioned previously, the system will automatically process multiple filters in order of specificity, starting with the most specific.

Filter lists and filter actions are linked together to form a rule in an IPSec policy. Although you can reuse filter lists in different policies, you cannot reuse them in the same policy. Filter actions, on the other hand, can be reused by rules in the same policy as well as shared among different policies.

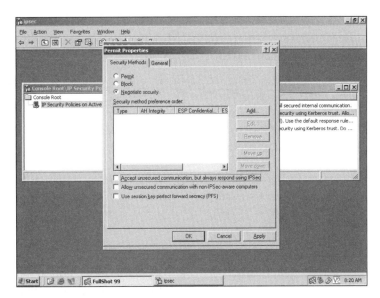

Figure 7-17 Setting a secure filter action

IPSec policy can be managed in one of two ways:

- *Create a new policy and define the set of rules for the policy, adding filter lists and filter actions as required*—When you use this method, IPSec policy is created first and then rules are added and configured. Filter lists and filter actions are added during rule creation.

- *First create the set of filter lists and filter actions, then create the policies and add rules that combine the filter lists with filter actions*—In this method, you first configure the filter lists and the filter actions. Then, you create IPSec policies, add rules that combine the proper filter list with the proper filter action, and also specify authentication methods, connection types, and tunnel settings.

You can configure one of more authentication methods to be used in main mode during negotiations. The available authentication methods (as discussed earlier) are Keberos V5, certificates, and preshared keys. You should use preshared keys only as a last resort. You can configure these using the Authentication Methods tab on the properties sheet of an IPSec rule.

When you configure a tunnel endpoint as part of a rule, you are setting up one end of a tunnel mode IPSec. You must also configure the other end of the tunnel with the same rule and its corresponding tunnel endpoint. This establishes the IP addresses that will be used when the packet is encapsulated before being sent through the tunnel. You should configure the tunnel endpoint on the Tunnel Setting tab on the properties sheet of the IPSec rule to which it applies.

The connection type specifies whether this rule applies to local area network (LAN) communications, to dial-up, or to both. This can be used to specify rules based on the inherent protocols and technologies that the connection type uses. In other words, LAN communications will certainly use different protocols than dial-up communications and will therefore require different IPSec rules as well.

You should understand that IPSec is designed to be an end-to-end security model that secures traffic between clients and servers. The IP address of the computer does not necessarily have to be the entity that is considered; rather, the system that uses the IP address is validated through an authentication process. This allows you to deploy IPSec to a computer, domain, site, or any container within your Active Directory.

NOTE   IPSec can now function through Network Address Translation (NAT). As long as the NAT is configured to allow User Datagram Protocol (UDP) traffic, the IKE protocol will detect the presence of NAT and use UDP-ESP encapsulation to allow the traffic to pass through.

In addition, because there are many ways to authenticate, IPSec can be used to secure local area network communication, wide area network communication, and remote access communication as well. This is accomplished through the configuration of IPSec policies that contain rules and filters. The rules and filters that you use will depend on what you are securing and how much protection it requires.

Activity 7-5: Using the Filter Wizard to Configure IPSec Filters

Time Required: 30 minutes

Objective: Learn how to configure a filter by using the Filter Wizard.

Description: In this exercise, you will learn how to configure an IPSec filter by using the Filter Wizard.

1. Log on with your **AdminXX** account, where *XX* is your assigned student number.

2. Click **Start**, **Run**, and type **mmc** in the run dialog box. Click **OK**.

3. Choose **File** from the top menu, then choose **Open**. On the Open screen, find the **IPSec** console you created in the last exercise and click it so that it shows in the File name box; click **Open**. The IPSec MMC console should now be open.

4. Right click on the **New Domain Policy**, then choose **Properties**. On the rules tab, click **Add**. The Security Rules Wizard opens to the Welcome to the Create IP Security Rule Wizard screen. Click **Next**.

5. On the tunnel endpoint screen, choose **This rule does not specify a tunnel**. Click **Next**.

6. On the Network Type screen, choose **All network connections**. Click **Next**.

7. On the IP Filter List screen, choose **All IP Traffic**. Click **Next**.

8. On the Filter Action screen, choose **Require Security**. Click **Next**.

9. On the Authentication Method screen, select **Active Directory default (Kerberos V5 protocol)**. Click **Next**.

10. You should now be on the Completing the Security Rule Wizard screen. Be sure the **Edit properties** box is checked. Click **Finish**.

11. This will bring you to the New Rule Properties screen, as shown in Figure 7-18. You will now configure this rule to be a bit more secure.

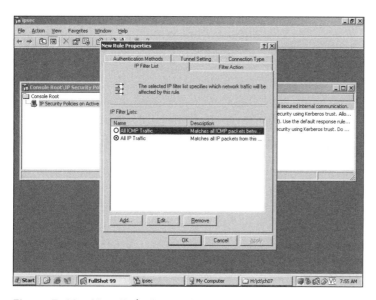

Figure 7-18   New Rule Properties screen

12. Choose the **Filter Action** tab. Click **Edit**. On the Security Methods tab, uncheck the **Accept unsecured communication, but always respond using IPSec** box. Click **Apply**, then click **OK**. Click **Close** to close the New Rule Properties screen.

13. Click **OK**. Close the **MMC** snap-in.

DEPLOYING IPSEC POLICIES

After determining your needs, building IPSec policies, and determining a plan for assigning the policies to specific areas, it's time to test the IPSec policies in a lab environment and conduct a pilot project before rolling them out for production use. Once everything works properly in a pilot environment, you can deploy the policies. IPsec policies can be deployed through a variety of methods, such as:

- Using local policy objects
- Using Group Policy Objects

- Using command-line tools
- Using scripts

Each of these methods is detailed in the following sections.

Using Local Policy Objects

Each computer running Windows Server 2003 has one local GPO, which is also known as the local computer policy. When this local GPO is used, policy settings for groups can be stored on individual computers regardless of whether they are members of an Active Directory domain. Besides Windows Server 2003 machines, you can configure the properties of IPSec and create rules using the Local Security Policy MMC on Windows 2000 Professional and all later clients as well as member servers. The local security policy is located in Administrative tools. You should be aware that any policy defined in a Group Policy overrides any policy that is deployed only to the local computer. In other words, if the computer is part of an Active Directory, the IPSec policies defined in any Group Policy that apply to its container will override its local policy. The local GPO can be overridden by GPOs assigned to sites, domains, or OUs in an Active Directory environment that have higher precedence. On a network without an Active Directory domain, the local GPO settings determine IPSec behavior because there are no other GPOs to override them. Figure 7-19 demonstrates where you configure this policy. The configuration options are the same as what you have been learning, except that the policy applies to the local machine.

 Local policy assignment is a way to enable IPSec for computers that are not members of a domain.

TIP

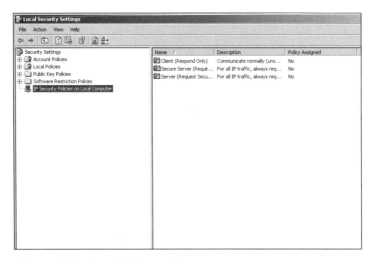

Figure 7-19   Local IPSec policy

Using Group Policy Objects

After you determine where you want to protect data and create IPSec policies for each of those areas, you must determine which IPSec policy to assign to GPOs. By using Group Policy, IPSec policies can be set on a single computer, an entire domain, an entire site, or any Active Directory organizational unit (OU). When an IPSec policy is assigned to a GPO, the IPSec policy is propagated to any computer accounts that are affected by the GPO. You can create, modify, and deploy IPSec policies using the **IP Security Policy Management console** MMC. You created this snap-in in Activity 7-1.

IPSec policies are one of the security settings in each Group Policy Object. You can use Group Policy to configure IPSec for an entire domain, an entire site, or selected organizational units. You should be aware that Group Policies are processed in the order of local, site, domain, OU, and child OU, and that any IPSec policies that conflict will be overridden by the next level of processing. In other words, the IPSec policies that will ultimately apply will be only those that are applied to the container in which the object actually resides, as well as any policies that did not conflict in the entire processing order. Assigning an IPSec policy to a GPO records a pointer to the IPSec policy inside the GPO. This causes Group Policy to detect only changes in IPSec policy assignments, not changes made within an IPSec policy after it is assigned to a GPO. The IPSec service detects changes in the related IPSec policy. This setting, called the IPSec polling interval, can be changed by setting a different value on the General tab of the properties of a policy by using the IP Security Policy Management snap-in. The setting named "Check for policy changes every:" is shown in Figure 7-20.

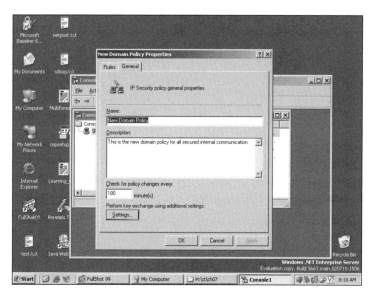

Figure 7-20 Changing the policy update value

Keep the following factors in mind when selecting GPOs for IPSec policy assignment:

- The assignment precedence for IPSec policies, from lowest to highest, is: local, site, domain, and OU. Persistent IPSec policy has the highest precedence of all, even though it is stored on the local computer.

- IPSec policies from different OUs are never merged.

- For domain-based IPSec policy, you should limit the number of rules to 10 or less.

- Create and apply an IPSec policy at the domain level to provide a baseline of IPSec protection.

- Use the Export and Import Policies commands in the IP Security Policy Management console to back up and restore the IPSec policy objects.

- Be sure to adequately test the impact of new IPSec policies before assigning them in the domain.

Using Command-Line Tools

If all of the computers on which you are running IPSec are part of the Windows Server 2003 family, then you can deploy IPSec using the **netsh ipsec command**. This method of deployment can be useful when you want to script the IPSec configuration and run the same script on multiple servers. It also provides some advanced fine-tuning for management and security that is not available in the GUI mode. There are two major types of commands from which you can choose. You make your choice based on whether you are creating a new policy that will be immediately effective or just creating a policy that can be applied later.

The IPSec context of the Netsh tool can dynamically insert new IPSec rules into the run-time system. This dynamic mode IPSec policy is part of the run-time state and is not stored; therefore, it is lost when the IPSec service is stopped either administratively or during a restart. You can use netsh ipsec dynamic commands to display the active state of IPSec and to immediately affect the configuration of the active IPSec policy. Dynamic commands are used to directly configure the security policy database (SPD). You can view the netsh dynamic commands available by accessing a command line and then typing "netsh ipsec dynamic /?" as shown in Figure 7-21.

Most dynamic commands will take effect immediately, but some require you to restart the IPSec Policy Agent or even restart the computer.

You can use netsh ipsec static commands to create, modify, and assign IPSec policies without immediately affecting the active IPSec policies. This is very much like creating a new policy and new rules within the GUI and not assigning the policy as of yet. To view the ipsec static commands, you should access the command prompt and type "netsh ipsec static /?".

The Internet Protocol Security Policies tool, Ipsecpol.exe, is a command-line tool used for configuring IPSec policies on Windows 2000. This tool runs only on Windows 2000

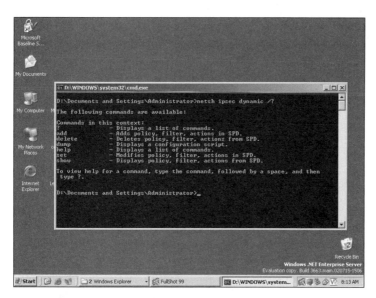

Figure 7-21   netsh dynamic commands

operating systems, and it does everything that the IPSec Microsoft Management Console (MMC) snap-in does; in fact, it is very similar to the snap-in.

IPSecPol has two modes: dynamic and static. The default mode is dynamic. One of the situations in which you may need to use this tool is in a mixed environment. Say you have a large and/or complex IPSec policy that you want to configure—IPSecPol can help you by providing a scriptable way to create that policy. Put your IPSecPol commands into a batch file, and then they can be distributed to the Windows 2000 machines. IPSecPol works similarly to netsh in that it requires that the person running the command have administrative privileges on the computer specified.

Activity 7-6: Using the Netsh Command-Line Utility

Time Required: 20 minutes

Objective: Learn how to use the netsh command to explore IPSec settings and configuration.

Description: In this exercise, you will learn how to use the Netsh command to explore IPSec settings and configuration.

1. Log on with your **AdminXX** account, where *XX* is your assigned student number.

2. Click **Start**, **Run**, then type **cmd** in the run dialog box. Click **OK**.

3. At the command prompt, type **netsh**.

4. The prompt should now be changed so that it shows: netsh>. Now type **ipsec**.

5. The prompt should be changed to show netsh ipsec>. Now type **dynamic**.

6. Once the prompt has changed, type **show all**.

7. All the IPSec information should be displayed on your screen.

8. Using the bar on the right side of the window, scroll to the top of the screen where you originally opened the command window.

9. Now scroll down and examine the IPSec parameters and the IPSec statistics. Type **exit** to exit the netsh tool. Type **exit** to close the command window.

Using Scripts

The IPSec internal infrastructure components were significantly modified for Windows Server 2003. As a result, the Netdiag.exe, IPSecpol.exe, and IPSeccmd.exe tools from earlier Windows releases do not run properly. In the last section we described how to use the Netsh tool from a command line, but in essence, the Netsh IPSec tool is a scriptable command-line method of building an IPSec policy. This can be useful in cases where a computer is not a domain member or is running an older version of Windows. Netsh IPSec can be used to create either a persistent policy or a local policy. These both are stored in the local computer registry. It can also be used to create a policy that is stored in Active Directory. If a computer is not a member of a Windows 2000 or 2003 domain, such as a standalone server, it cannot retrieve IPSec policy from Active Directory. The IPSec policy configuration for a server that does not use Active Directory can be distributed using one of the following two ways:

- By using a Netsh IPSec script, which is included as a startup script for the computer

- By using an IPSec file that can be imported from another computer through the IP Security Policy Management snap-in, or if the computer is running Windows Server 2003, the Netsh tool

The second method can be used when computers need to secure their communications, but there are not enough of them to warrant applying policies to OUs. In either case, the user or process that sets the IPSec policy must be running as a local or domain administrator. Command-line scripting using the Netsh IPSec tool is the only method of managing policy in an automated fashion because the recent Microsoft Windows Platform Software Development Kits do not contain programmable APIs for IPSec policy.

ACTIVITY

Activity 7-7: Using the Windows Scripting Host (WSH) to Create a Script File

Time Required: 45 minutes

Objective: Learn how to use the Windows Scripting Host (WSH) to create a script file.

Description: In this exercise, you will learn about scripting and how to use the Windows Scripting Host (WSH) to create a script file.

1. Log on with your **AdminXX** account, where *XX* is your assigned student number.

2. Open Internet Explorer and go to: *http://msdn.microsoft.com/library/default.asp?url=/library/en-us/dnclinic/html/scripting01142003.asp*

3. Read the article titled: WMI Scripting Primer: Part I

4. Under the section on Quick Start to WMI Scripting, create the scripts in Listings One, Two, and Three until you have the hang of creating scripts.

5. When you are finished reading the article, run the scripts you created in Listings 1 and 2. You can run the script in Listing 3, but remember if you have a large number of events, this may take a while.

6. Go to *www.microsoft.com/resources/documentation/WindowsServ/2003/standard/proddocs/en-us/Default.asp?url=/resources/documentation/WindowsServ/2003/standard/proddocs/en-us/netsh.asp*

7. Follow through the Netsh DHCP Example, creating one of your own as you go along.

8. When finished close the Internet Explorer window.

DEPLOYING IPSEC CERTIFICATES

Certificate Services can be used to automatically manage computer certificates for IPSec. Because Certificate Services is integrated with Active Directory and Group Policy, the certificate deployment process can be simplified by using configurable certificate templates, enabling certificate autoenrollment and certificate renewal. Certificate Services also allows you to use IPSec to restrict network access to a server by publishing the computer certificate as an attribute of the domain computer account.

As mentioned earlier in the chapter, IPSec can use one or more of three ways to authenticate computers. These include Kerberos V5, preshared keys, and certificates. You can use Kerberos V5 only if all of the computers to be authenticated are part of your Active Directory. You should use preshared keys only as a last resort. This means that certificates should be used the balance of the time. To be more specific, you should use certificates whenever communications include Internet access, remote access, external business partners, or computers in your network that cannot use the Kerberos V5 protocol. The use of certificates will require at least one certification authority. This authority can be set up in your own hierarchy or can be a commercial CA. You can use the certification authority and Group Policy provided by Windows Server 2003 to automatically enroll certificates for computers in your network. In this case, any computers outside of your network would require a third-party certificate authority (such as VeriSign) and manual account mapping for the certificates used. Account mapping maps the computer certificate to a particular computer account. Public key certificates should be used where security is required for access to corporate resources, external business partner communications, or computers that do not run the Kerberos V5 authentication protocol. This involves having at least one trusted root CA configured on your network and client computers having an associated computer certificate. In addition to Windows 2000 Server or Windows Server 2003 Certificate Services, IPSec supports the use of a variety of third-party X.509 public key infrastructure (PKI) systems.

Certificate Authentication Considerations

When working with certificates, realize that IKE's use of certificate authentication is compatible with various different PKI architectures. Generally, if computers have a common trusted root, or certificates that can chain through a cross-certification trust relationship, IKE authentication can be used. If you choose to use certificates for IKE authentication, define an ordered list of acceptable root CA names on the Authentication Method tab. This list controls the certificates that IKE can select. Before you apply an IPSec policy that uses certificates for authentication, make sure that all computers have the correct root CA certificates, trusted cross-certificates, and valid computer certificates, because if IKE authentication fails, you cannot retry the authentication using a different method. As always, test your PKI infrastructure with your intended IPSec policy configurations before production deployment to be sure that certificate authentication works the way you want it to. Remember that all cross-certificate trusts must be in place and working properly before you deploy the IPSec policy

CAUTION   Be sure that Certificate Services does not have the advanced option set for Enable strong private key protection. IKE authentication will not work with this option enabled, because a personal identification number (PIN) cannot be entered to access the private key during IKE negotiation.

The Certificate Process

It is important to understand how the IKE certificate process works, not only because the exam will have questions about it but also because it is a common method used to secure data communications. We will look at the negotiation process and the acceptance process, starting with the negotiation process. When IKE negotiates to use certificates for authentication, first the list of trusted roots is prepared. IKE then searches the computer store for an IPSec certificate that chains to any of the trusted CA roots identified. For each certificate chain found, several checks of the certificate chain and the computer certificate are performed. If all of these checks succeed, IKE selects the certificate chain to be sent to the IPSec peer. If any of these checks fails, IKE continues to search for another IPSec-type certificate, using the same list of root CA names. If a valid computer certificate chain is still not found, IKE retries, using the entire list of root CA names allowed by the local authentication method. If a computer certificate cannot be selected, the authentication fails.

Next we will look at the IKE certificate acceptance process. IKE receives the peer's certificate and verifies the certificate chain up to the root CAs in the appropriate authentication method of the local IPSec policy. The computer certificate Subject Name or Subject AltName is verified with the ID field passed in the IKE negotiation, and IKE verifies that the computer certificate chain does not have any trust errors. If this process is successful, additional checks are performed to verify the certificate chain. If any of these checks fails, the peer authentication fails. If certificate-to-account mapping is enabled in the IPSec policy for the certificate root CA of the peer, the mapping is performed and an access token is built for the computer account. This access token is then evaluated against the Access this computer from the network or the Deny this computer access from the network logon right defined in the Group Policy security settings. If the logon right evaluation fails, the peer authentication fails.

Certificate to Account Mapping

An administrator can control which computers are authorized to use IPSec by using **IPSec certificate-to-account mapping**. This is done by configuring Group Policy security settings and assigning either the Access this computer from the network or the Deny access to this computer from the network logon right to either individual or multiple computers. Certificate mapping enables much stronger peer authentication and can be used to restrict network access to a server.

NOTE

When you use certificate-to-account mapping, it can be used only for computer accounts that are in the same forest as the computer performing the mapping.

Certificate-to-account mapping is also used when certificates come from a PKI that is not integrated with the Active Directory structure. An example of this would be a business partner that obtains certificates from a third-party provider such as Verisign. In this instance, you can configure the IPSec policy authentication method to map certificates to a domain computer account for a specific root CA. You can also map all certificates from an issuing CA to one computer account. If the certificate-to-account mapping process is not completed properly, authentication will fail and IPSec-protected connections will be blocked, so it is important that the process be tested properly before implementation. Certificate-to-account mapping, however, does not ensure that a specific trusted computer is being allowed IPSec access.

ACTIVITY

Activity 7-8: Configure Authentication Method for Certificates

Time Required: 30 minutes

Objective: Learn how to configure authentication, using certificates.

Description: In this exercise, you will learn how to configure authentication for certificates and enable certificate-to-account mapping.

1. Log on with your **AdminXX** account, where *XX* is your assigned student number.

2. Click **Start**, **Run**, then type **mmc** in the run dialog box. Click **OK**.

3. Choose **File** from the top menu, and choose **Open**. On the Open screen, find the IPSec console you created in Activity 7-1 and click it so that it shows in the File name box; click **Open**. The IPSec MMC console should now be open.

4. Right-click **New Domain Policy**, then choose **Properties**. On the rules tab, be sure that **All IP Traffic** is checked and highlighted. Choose **Edit**, then select the **Authentication Methods** tab.

5. On the Authentication Methods tab, choose **Edit**. Select **Use a certificate from this certificate authority (CA)**. Click **Browse**.

6. Because there is not a shared certificate store, you may get an error asking if you want to select a certification authority from the certificate store on the local computer. Click **Yes**.

7. We will choose a certificate to use as an example, because your server is not configured to issue certificates. Scroll down to the bottom of the page until you find the **Windows 2003** certificate. This certificate will be available only if you have installed certificate services. If you do not have certificate services installed, you can choose the VeriSign Trust Network certificate. Click the **View Certificate** button.

8. The General tab should look similar to that shown in Figure 7-22.

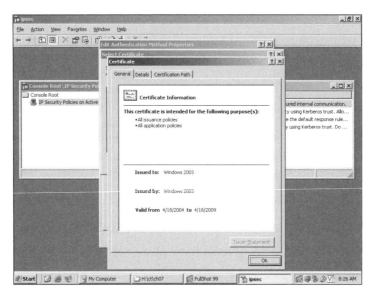

Figure 7-22   Viewing the properties of a certificate

9. Click **OK**. On the Select Certificate screen, click **OK**.

10. On the Authentication Method tab, check the **Enable certificate to account mapping** box.

11. Click **OK**. On the Authentication Methods tab, click **Apply**. Click **OK**. Click **OK** on the Rules tab. Close the **MMC** console.

CHAPTER SUMMARY

- ❏ Internet Protocol Security (IPSec) is a set of protocols developed by the Internet Engineering Task Force (IETF). It is a framework of open standards for supporting the secure exchange of packets at the IP layer. It ensures private, secure communications over Internet Protocol (IP) networks by using cryptographic security services.

- ❏ When planning an IPSec deployment in a simple network structure, you will be more apt to design a single IPSec policy, which may contain many rules, each one adapted for a specific type of traffic. In a large environment, many different IPSec policies may have to be designed in order to meet the security requirements of the various computer roles.

- ❏ There are basically two different types of communications that you might be securing: either communications within a network or communications between networks. These two modes of IPSec security are transport mode and tunnel mode.

- ❏ Authentication is a process whereby entities on a network prove that they are who they say they are. The three main methods from which you can choose are Kerberos, certificates, and preshared key.

- ❏ Encryption is a method whereby a plaintext message is converted to a ciphertext message so that only the recipient with the proper key can decrypt the message. The methods of encryption that can be used are Secure Hash Algorithm (SHA), Message Digest 5 (MD5), Data Encryption Standard (DES), and Triple DES (3DES).

- ❏ There are two main protocols that are used when authenticating with IPSec: Authentication Header and Encapsulating Security Payload (ESP), which can be configured for either transport mode or tunnel mode. Authentication Header (AH) provides for authentication, integrity, and anti-replay of each packet. Encapsulating Security Payload (ESP) mode encapsulates an IP packet with both an ESP header and IP header and an ESP trailer.

- ❏ Each IPSec policy consists of one or more rules that will determine the behavior of the policy. An IPSec filter is a specification in the IPSec rule that is used to match IP packets to filter actions such as permit, block, or negotiate security. An IPSec rule is a statement in an IPSec policy that associates a filter list with a filter action, an authentication method, and an IPSec mode.

- ❏ IPsec policies can be deployed through a variety of methods such as local policy objects, Group Policy Objects, command-line tools, and scripts.

- ❏ Certificate Services can be used to automatically manage computer certificates for IPSec. Certificate Services also allows you to use IPSec to restrict network access to a server by publishing the computer certificate as an attribute of the domain computer account.

KEY TERMS

Authentication — The process by which entities on a network prove that they are who they say they are.

Authentication Header (AH) — AH provides an authenticity guarantee for packets, by attaching a strong crypto checksum to packets.

certificate — A method of granting access to users based on their unique identification and the fact that they possess the algorithms to access the appropriate information.

Certificate Services — A service that allows the use of IPSec to restrict network access to a server by publishing the computer certificate as an attribute of a domain computer account.

Data encryption standard (DES) — The lowest encryption strength of the Diffie-Hellman algorithms. It produces only a 56-bit key and is not for use in a high-security environment.

Diffie-Hellman (DH) algorithm — An encryption algorithm used for public key encryption.

Encapsulating Security Payload (ESP) — ESP provides a confidentiality guarantee for packets, by encrypting packets with encryption algorithms.

encapsulation — The process of adding a security header to every packet to protect the packet.

encryption — A method whereby a plaintext message is converted to a ciphertext message so that only the recipient with the proper key can decrypt the message.

filter action — A setting for each type of traffic as identified by a filter list.

Internet Key Exchange (IKE) — IKE is the protocol used for exchanging encryption keys.

Internet Protocol Security (IPSec) — A set of protocols developed by the Internet Engineering Task Force (IETF) to ensure private, secure communications over Internet Protocol (IP) networks by using cryptographic security services.

Internet Security Association and Key Management Protocol/Oakley (ISAKMP/Oakley) — A protocol that allows the receiver to obtain a public key and authenticate the sender using digital certificates.

IP Compression (IPComp) — IPComp is IP compression used to compress raw IP data.

IPSec certificate-to-account mapping — An administrative tool for controlling which computers are authorized to use IPSec by configuring Group Policy security settings and assigning them to individual or multiple computers, as needed.

IPSec filter — A specification in the IPSec rule that is used to match IP packets to filter actions such as permit, block, or negotiate security.

IPSec filter list — The part of a rule that contains one or multiple filters and can be shared among different IPSec policies.

IPSec offload network adapter — An adapter that processes IPSec functions at a high rate of speed so that there is minimal performance degradation.

IP Security Policy Management console — An MMC snap-in used to create, modify, and deploy IPSec policies.

Kerberos V5 — The default authentication method for Windows 2000 Server and Windows Server 2003.

key regeneration — The process of generating new keys at specified intervals.

Lifetime settings — Settings that determine when a new key is generated.

master key perfect forward secrecy (PFS) — A key generation setting that sets the session key limit to 1, forcing key regeneration each time.

Message Digest 5 (MD5) — Encryption method used for most commercial applications. It can be used to secure authentication as well as data.

netsh ipsec command — A command-line scripting tool to configure IPSec configuration. It also provides some advanced fine-tuning for management and security that is not available in the GUI mode.

Point-to-Point Protocol (PPP) — The protocol in traditional dial-up connections that is responsible for compressing data before it gets encrypted.

preshared key — A symmetric key: a shared secret key that is agreed upon by administrators who wish to secure the computer's communications by using IPSec.

Secure Hash Algorithm (SHA) — A very-high-security method that uses a 160-bit encryption key. It is used as part of the Federal Information Processing Standard (FIPS).

security association (SA) — The combination of a negotiated key, a security protocol, and the security parameters index (SPI) used to determine the level of IPSec security.

symmetric key — A shared key method whereby the same key that is used to encrypt can also be used to decrypt.

transport mode — A mode used to secure communications between two computers on the same network.

Triple DES — A stronger Diffie-Hellman algorithm that produces a 168-bit key. It is recommended for use in medium- and high-security networks.

tunnel mode — A mode used to secure communications between two networks.

REVIEW QUESTIONS

1. Which mode of IPSec should you use to ensure security and confidentiality of data within a network?

    a. AH transport mode

    b. ESP transport mode

    c. ESP tunnel mode

    d. AH tunnel mode

2. Which two types of encryption protocols can be used to secure the authentication of computers using IPSec? (Choose all that apply.)

    a. Kerberos

    b. Certificates

    c. SHA

    d. MD5

3. Which type of authentication should you use for IPSec on an internal network if you want to set it up with the least administrative effort?

   a. Certificates

   b. Preshared keys

   c. Kerberos

   d. MD5

4. Which two types of IPSec can be used to secure communications between external sites? (Choose all that apply.)

   a. AH tunnel mode

   b. ESP tunnel mode

   c. AH transport mode

   d. ESP transport mode

5. Which type of device is usually at the endpoints of tunnel mode IPSec?

   a. Hub

   b. Switch

   c. Router

   d. Bridge

6. Which IPSec authentication method should be used only as a last resort?

   a. Certificates

   b. Preshared key

   c. Cross-certification

   d. Kerberos

7. Which 160-bit encryption method is used to secure government contracts as part of the Federal Information Processing Standard (FIPS)?

   a. SHA

   b. 3DES

   c. DES

   d. MD5

8. Which Diffie-Hellman algorithm produces a key length of 168 bits?

   a. DES

   b. 3DES

   c. MD5

   d. SHA

9. Which command can be used to create, modify, and assign IPSec policies without immediately affecting the active IPSec policies?

   a. netsh ipsec static

   b. netdiag

   c. netconfig ipsec

   d. netsh ipsec dynamic

10. Which of the following is not a point to consider when determining how IPSec will impact your environment?

   a. Amount of time for connection establishment

   b. Computing performance

   c. Connectivity during cluster node addition or removal

   d. Decreased packet size

11. Which of the following are IPSec security control elements? (Choose all that apply.)

   a. Authentication Header (AH)

   b. Encapsulating Security Payload (ESP)

   c. Internet Key Exchange (IKE)

   d. Point-to-Point Protocol (PPP)

12. If the parties do not have a preshared set of keys, IKE has to facilitate secure key exchange. This is accomplished through a protocol known as_____ .

   a. Point-to-Point Protocol (PPP)

   b. Internet Security Association and Key Management Protocol/Oakley (ISAKMP/ Oakley)

   c. Point-to-Point Tunneling Protocol (PPTP)

   d. Public Key Infrastructure (PKI)

13. Which of the following allows you to use IPSec to restrict network access to a server by publishing the computer certificate as an attribute of the domain computer account?

   a. Preshared key

   b. Kerberos

   c. Certificate Services

   d. Data Encryption Standard (DES)

14. Which of the following processes IPSec functions at a high rate of speed so that there is minimal performance degradation?

   a. IPSec filter list

   b. IPSec filter action

   c. IPSec filter

   d. IPSec offload network adapter

7

15. Which part of an IPSec policy contains filters and filter actions and controls the behavior of the policy?

    a. Authentication

    b. Rules

    c. Tunneling

    d. Encryption

16. Which of these are settings in an IPSec rule?

    a. ICMP settings

    b. Filters

    c. Connection types

    d. RAM types

17. Which IPSec rule setting defines traffic that is to be identified?

    a. Filter

    b. Filter action

    c. Tunnel endpoint

    d. Connection type

18. Which two components of a rule work together to identify packets and then make decisions that affect traffic flow and security?

    a. Kerberos V5

    b. Filters

    c. Connection types

    d. Filter actions

19. Which of the following should you use to distribute IPSec policies that affect all of the computers in a domain?

    a. AD replication

    b. Kerberos V5

    c. Group Policy

    d. Remote Installation Services

20. Which of the following tools can you use to create, manage, and deploy IPSec policies for an entire domain?

    a. Local security policy MMCs for each computer

    b. IP Security Policy Management Console

    c. netsh ipsec

    d. Active Directory Sites and Services

21. If an IPSec policy contains multiple filters, in which order are they processed?

a. Top to bottom

b. Bottom to top

c. Least specific to most specific

d. Most specific to least specific

22. Which are valid filter action settings for a filter in an IPSec policy? (Choose all that apply.)

a. Allow

b. Negotiate Security

c. Block

d. Deny

23. The most secure filter action is one that requires security for all inbound and outbound traffic. This filter action is created by making sure which two of the following options are unchecked?

a. Active Directory default (Kerberos V5 protocol)

b. Accept unsecured communication, but always respond using IPsec

c. Data integrity and encryption (ESP)

d. Allow unsecured communication with non-IPsec aware computers

24. You can create, modify, and deploy IPSec policies using which of the following?

a. Active Directory Users and Computers console

b. Group Policy Management console

c. IP Security Policy Management console

d. Active Directory Trusts and Domains console

25. Which of the following examples of filter lists is included with Windows Server 2003? (Choose all that apply.)

a. All ICMP Traffic

b. Request Security

c. Require Security

d. All IP Traffic

CASE PROJECTS

CASE PROJECTS

Case Project 7-1

Evergrow has some concern in regard to their compliance with new legislation such as the Gramm-Leach-Bliley Act and Sarbanes-Oxley. It is your job as the network administrator of the Phoenix forest to make a recommendation for securing data on the internal network.

Prepare a report for management stating which authentication and/or encryption methods you would recommend in order to make the network more secure. The network has recently been updated; all servers have Windows 2003 installed on them, and all clients are running Windows XP.

Case Project 7-2

It is your job as the network administrator to make a recommendation for securing data between the main office in Phoenix and the branches in surrounding areas. Prepare a report for management stating which authentication and/or encryption methods you would recommend to make the network more secure. The entire organization has recently been updated, and all servers have Windows 2003 installed on them; all clients are running Windows XP, and all are part of the same forest.

Case Project 7-3

Evergrow has several forests and more than 15,000 branch offices. It is your job as the network administrator to make a recommendation for securing data between the main office in Phoenix and the branches in surrounding areas. Prepare a report for management stating which authentication and/or encryption methods you would recommend to make the network more secure. The network has various different operating systems on both the clients and servers because many of the branch offices were recently acquired and have still been using their own software and hardware.

Case Project 7-4

You are the network administrator for the Evergrow Phoenix forest, which consists of several Windows 2003 domains with client computers running Windows XP Professional. You must create a solution for authentication using IPSec. You are working on an authentication method to be used between the servers and the clients in the accounting. phoenix.com domain on the internal network. You want to accomplish your task with the least administrative effort necessary. Which authentication do you choose and why?

Case Project 7-5

You are the network administrator for the Evergrow Phoenix forest, which consists of several Windows 2003 domains with client computers running Windows XP Professional. You must create a solution for encrypting network communication using IPSec. You are working on securing the communication between the servers and the clients in the accounting.phoenix.com domain on the internal network. Prepare a report for management explaining which methods can be used with IPSec to encrypt data.

CHAPTER

8

TROUBLESHOOTING IPSEC POLICIES

After reading this chapter, you will be able to:

♦ Understand default security policy container permissions

♦ Understand IPSec policy precedence

♦ Understand IPSec driver Startup modes

♦ Troubleshoot IPSec

♦ Troubleshoot IPSec across networks

♦ Troubleshoot IPSec certificates

As the previous chapter revealed, IPSec is an extremely powerful tool that can be configured with many options. As with other complex tools, there are also many possibilities for improper configuration. In order to troubleshoot errant configurations, you need to be able to recognize them, which means that you need to understand what a proper configuration looks like and how IPSec is supposed to behave in various circumstances.

In this chapter, we discuss the default security policies that are installed with IPSec and why the default security policies generally are not the best policies to use. Then we discuss the behavior of IPSec within and between networks and some tools that we can use to troubleshoot issues concerning IPSec. Finally, we discuss using IPSec in conjunction with certificates and the additional issues that are involved in troubleshooting when certificates are used.

UNDERSTANDING THE DEFAULT SECURITY POLICIES CONTAINER PERMISSIONS

Before we go into the permissions on the Security Policies container, we should review the default policies, filters, and filter lists that exist in Windows 2003. As we discussed in Chapter 7, there are three security policies that are configured by default on installations of Windows 2000 Professional and Windows XP Professional computers as well as Windows 2000 and Windows Server 2003 servers: Client (Respond Only), Server (Request Security), and Secure Server (Require Security). There are also two predefined filter lists and three predefined filter actions. All ICMP Traffic and All IP Traffic are the predefined filter lists. Permit, Request Security, and Require Security are the predefined filter lists. Filter lists and filter actions are used together to form a rule in an IPSec policy. Filter lists can be reused in different policies, but they cannot be reused in the same policy. Filter actions, on the other hand, can be reused by rules in the same policy, and they can be shared among different policies.

Remember that these are intended to be used as examples and are not intended for operational use without modification. You can use them as a starting point from which to configure your own custom IPSec policies.

By default in Windows Server 2003, Active Directory restricts Read permissions on the IP Security Policies container. This container is where domain-based IPSec policies are stored. Only members of the Domain Admins group can configure domain-based IPSec policy. Of course, you can also delegate the permissions. Only members of the Group Policy Creator Owners and the Domain Computers groups have Read permissions on the IP Security Policies container. In order to understand this more clearly, let's look at what happens when a domain controller is installed. A new installation of a Windows Server 2003 domain controller will have the following default permissions on the IP Security Policies container:

- Owner: Domain Admins
- Group: Domain Admins
- Allow domain computers: Read only
- Allow Group Policy Creator Owners: Read only
- Allow Domain Admins: Full Control

 If you run the Adprep tool to prepare for an upgrade from Windows 2000 domains and forests to Windows Server 2003, the permissions on the IP Security Policies container will change to these settings, unless you have already **NOTE**   altered the default permissions.

In the next section, we will review permissions and policy precedence. For now, keep in mind that when you create new objects in the IP Security Policies container, those objects inherit the permissions of that container. Upgrading from Windows 2000 will not modify the permissions on existing IPSec policy objects. Because Windows Server 2003 has more restrictive permissions, a member of the Domain Admins group must enable child domain computers to read the IP Security Policies container in the directory. In order for these computers to retrieve domain-based IPSec policy from Active Directory, the Local System account for each computer must have Read permissions on the IP Security Policies container. Following in that same train of thought, if computer accounts in child domains must read a parent domain-based IPSec policy, you must modify the permissions on the IP Security Policies container to allow this to happen.

The IPSec policies are a group of related directory objects, some of which can be shared between policies, so it is not a good idea to assign specific permissions for individual IPSec policies. In keeping with good security principles, you should also control permissions on the IP Security Policies container itself.

Be careful about giving Modify access permissions to the IP Security Policies container. You can restrict who can create and modify Group Policy Objects (GPOs) so that only authorized individuals can assign a domain-based IPSec policy. Because an IPSec policy administrator typically has Write access to all IPSec policies, make sure you know who has what permissions and that they are set to organization specifications.

In order to delegate permissions on the IP Security Policies container and objects, you must use the ADSI Edit tool. Delegation cannot be done by using standard delegation tools. ADSI Edit is a Windows support tool that uses the Active Directory Service Interfaces (ADSI). It can be found on the Windows Server 2003 operating system CD.

ACTIVITY

Activity 8-1: Delegate IPSec Policies

Time Required: 30 minutes

Objective: Install the ADSI Edit support tool and use it to delegate permissions on the IPSec Policies container.

Description: In this exercise, you will discover how to install the ADSI Edit tool and then use it to delegate permissions for an organizational unit (OU). Because delegation cannot be done by using standard means, you must use the ADSI tool to assign permissions. Note: Autorun must be enabled on the server. If you are using VMWare, autorun may be disabled.

1. Log on to your Windows Server 2003 computer with your **AdminXX** account, where *XX* is your assigned student number.

2. Insert the Windows 2003 CD. On the Welcome screen, select **Perform other tasks**.

3. Select **Browse this CD**. Go to the support folder and then to the tools folder.

4. Double-click on the **Suptools.msi** file.

5. On the Welcome screen, choose **Next**.

6. Choose the **I Agree** radio button for the End User License Agreement (EULA).

7. On the User Information screen, enter your **Name** in the Name box and an **Organization** in the Organization box, if you so desire. Click **Next**.

8. On the Destination directory screen, choose a directory in which to install the tools.

9. Click the **Install Now** button. Once the installation is complete, click the **Finish** button. Close the folder. Exit the CD.

10. Now you will assign permissions. Select **Start**, **Run**, type **mmc** in the run dialog box, then click **OK**.

11. When the console opens, choose **File**, **Add/Remove Snap-in**.

12. When the Add/Remove Snap-in window opens, click the **Add** button. Highlight the **ADSI Edit** snap-in, then click the **Add** button.

13. Click the **Close** button on the Standalone Snap-in screen.

14. Click **OK** on the Add/Remove Snap-in screen. Your screen should now look like Figure 8-1.

Figure 8-1 The ADSI Edit Snap-in console

15. Highlight the **ADSI Edit** object. On the Action menu, select **Connect to**. The Connection Settings dialog box opens, as shown in Figure 8-2.

16. This should show your local domain as pictured. Click **OK**. This will now connect to your local domain. Expand your domain. Expand the **DC** folder. Right-click the **Member servers OU**, and choose **Properties**.

17. Choose the **Security** tab. You will now give the local Administrators group full control over the OU. Highlight the **Administrator** group, in the Permissions for Administrators window, check the **Allow** box beside full control, as shown in Figure 8-3. Click **Apply**, then click **OK**.

18. When asked whether to save the console settings, choose to not save them. Close the console.

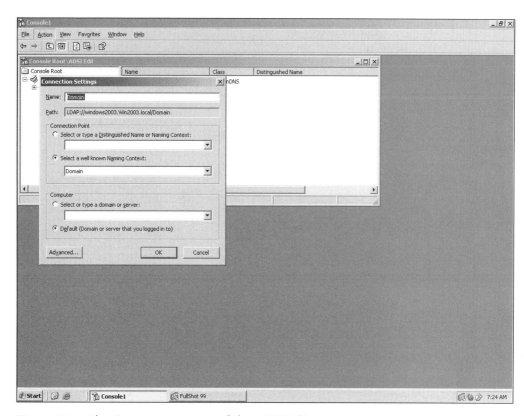

Figure 8-2   The Connect to screen of the ADSI Edit snap-in

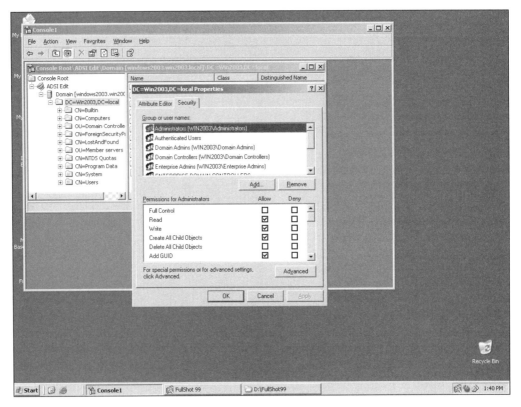

Figure 8-3   Delegating permissions for the IPSec container

UNDERSTANDING IPSEC POLICY PRECEDENCE

Because you can configure IPSec policies for a site, domain, OU, or even a single computer, understand that it is also possible to configure IPSec for multiple containers that will affect a computer. So, if a computer is in an OU that is in a domain, that is, in a site, then there are four places from which it could inherit IPSec Security Policy settings. To know how to apply IPSec policy in a such an environment, you must understand IPSec policy precedence.

Only one IPSec policy can be assigned to a computer at a time. This is different from most group policy settings because generally they are cumulative. Consequently, if there are multiple IPSec policies assigned at different levels, the last one applied is the one that takes effect. Even though only one policy can be applied, the IPSec policy uses the same precedence sequence as other group policy settings. The sequence is from lowest to highest. Let's review the order:

- *Local GPO*—Each computer has one local GPO. If the computer is not a member of a domain, this is the only place where IPSec policy can be assigned. You can also assign a local policy directly in the IP Security Policy Management snap-in or by using the Netsh IPSec command.

- *Site*—Even though IPSec policies can be assigned a the site level, this isn't always a good idea because all computers within a site must have the same security needs, which is unlikely. Another factor to keep in mind is that if the computer moves to another subnet different policies are applied and different security policies may be applied.

- *Domain*—IPSec policies are often assigned at the domain level and then superseded by more specific IPSec policies applied at the OU level.

- *OU*—Specific IPSec policies are assigned to computers contained within the OU. This is the last policy applied and this policy takes precedence. If an OU is nested within another OU, the IPSec policy assigned to the nested OU takes precedence.

Figure 8-4 shows the IPSec Policy settings on a Windows XP client computer in Local Security Policies.

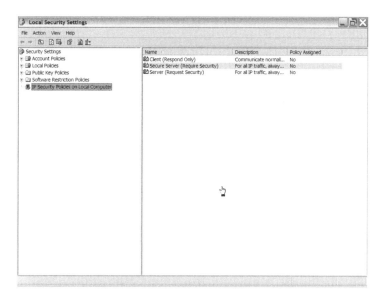

Figure 8-4 IPSec policy settings on a client computer

Although this is the default order in which policies of different types are applied, this order can be overridden by using a number of options, including *Enforced* (formerly known as *No Override*), *Block Policy Inheritance*, and *Loopback* processing. This is important to remember because routine use of these features can make it difficult to troubleshoot policies. Because it is not immediately apparent why certain settings do or do not apply, if there are issues with the IPSec policies, one of the first places you should look is in this area.

The policies will be run in the previously listed order, and the last policies that are applied will be the resulting policies. Because IPSec policies are just one setting in a group policy, either all of the IPSec policies will apply for a container or none of them will. The IPSec policies will not be "mixed and matched" from container to container. If a container has

IPSec policies listed and assigned, the policies will be run in their entirety, but if a container that is run after that container also has IPSec Policy settings, all of the settings will override all of the settings from the previous container.

When troubleshooting IPSec policies and their precedence, here is a list of items that you should remember:

- Only a single IPSec policy can be assigned at a specific level in Active Directory.
- An IPSec policy assigned to an OU takes precedence over a domain-level policy for members of that OU.
- IPSec policies from different organizational units are never merged.
- An OU inherits the policy of its parent OU unless either policy inheritance is explicitly blocked or the policy is explicitly assigned.
- Before assigning an IPSec policy to a GPO, verify the group policy settings that are required for the IPSec policy.
- Use the Enforced and Block Policy Inheritance features carefully.

When deleting policy objects, unassign the IPSec policy before you delete the policy object. The reason is that an IPSec policy might remain active even after the GPO to which it is assigned has been deleted. When this happens, computers in the Active Directory container continue to use a cached copy. In order to avoid problems, use the following procedure to properly unassign an IPSec policy and delete the GPO:

- Unassign the IPSec policy in the GPO.
- To ensure that the change is propagated, wait 24 hours.
- Delete the GPO.

Before we move on, there is one last point about troubleshooting IPSec policy precedence that we should discuss: persistent policy. To provide maximum protection against attacks during computer startup, it is highly recommended that you configure and assign a persistent IPSec policy. If you do not configure a persistent policy, the IPSec driver cannot enforce IPSec policy until domain-based or local IPSec policy is retrieved and applied.

If you create a persistent policy, this policy adds to or overrides the local or Active Directory policy and remains in effect regardless of whether other policies are applied. The purpose of persistent IPSec policies is to enhance security by providing a secure transition from computer startup to IPsec policy enforcement. In the next section, we will discuss the IPSec driver startup modes. A persistent policy can also provide backup security in the event that the IPSec policy becomes corrupt. It can also be helpful if errors occur during the application of local or domain-based IPSec policy.

When implementing a persistent IPSec policy, it is important to consider the potential impact of the persistent policy on remote management or assistance. If the only policy that is applied is the persistent IPSec policy, attempts to remotely diagnose an issue might be blocked. Remote Assistance uses TCP port 3389 for inbound TCP connections and DHCP uses port 68 for inbound UDP connections. To allow for remote management in case troubleshooting is required, it is recommended that you create appropriate permit filters when configuring a persistent IPSec policy.

Activity 8-2: Configure and Troubleshoot IPSec Persistent Policies

Time Required: 20 minutes

Objective: Configure and troubleshoot IPSec persistent policies.

Description: In this exercise, you will discover how to configure persistent policies using the Netsh command. You will then troubleshoot a remote assistance call.

1. Log on to your Windows Server 2003 computer with your **AdminXX** account, where *XX* is your assigned student number.

2. Go to **Start**, **Run**, type **cmd** in the Run dialog box, then choose **OK**.

3. At the prompt, type **netsh ipsec static set store location=persistent**.

4. Press the **Enter** key.

5. Now the machine is set for persistent IPSec policies.

6. At this point, you receive a call from the help desk, stating that they cannot access the machine. Read through the scenario described in Steps 7 through 9.

7. While helping to troubleshoot, you find that currently there are no IPSec policies configured for the OU in which the computer is located. After further investigation you look at the IPSec policies on the local computer and find the information shown is Figure 8-5.

8. From here you have deduced that there are no IPSec policies set.

9. To view the IPSec policy that is currently being applied, you can use either IP Security Monitor or the netsh ipsec dynamic show all command. Upon using the netsh show all command you find that there are persistent IPSec policies set.

10. At the command prompt that you used to determine that there are persistent policies, type **netsh ipsec dynamic set config property=bootexemptions value="tcp:0:3389:inbound UDP:0:68:inbound"**.

11. Close the **command prompt** window.

12. You call the help desk and ask them to try to connect again. This time the connection works just fine.

8

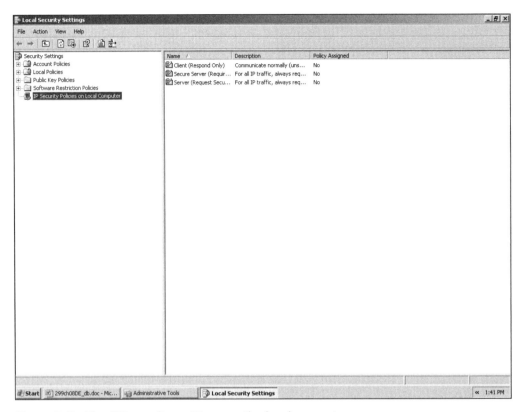

Figure 8-5   The IPSec policy settings on the local computer

UNDERSTANDING IPSEC DRIVER STARTUP MODES

You can control and troubleshoot IPSec policies by controlling the **IPSec driver startup mode** in the Services console. This can be useful for troubleshooting a problem that you suspect might be related to IPSec policies. By turning off the "master switch" of IPSec policies, you can quickly establish if the problem is related to IPSec or not.

You can control the IPSec driver in IPSec Services within the Services console of Administrative Tools. As with most services, you have three options in regard to Startup modes as follows:

- *Automatic*—With this option, the service is automatically started every time the computer is booted. Even if the service has been manually turned off, it will be restarted when the computer is booted, if this option is selected.

- *Manual*—With this option, the service is *not* automatically started when the computer is booted. However, it can be started by an administrator, if needed. Some applications can also start some services when they are in Manual mode. This is generally not the case with regard to IPSec.

- *Disabled*—With this option, the service is disabled from use. The service cannot be started until it is first enabled. This prevents the service from being started by mistake or from being started by an application.

Figure 8-6 shows the IPSec driver startup modes in the Services console.

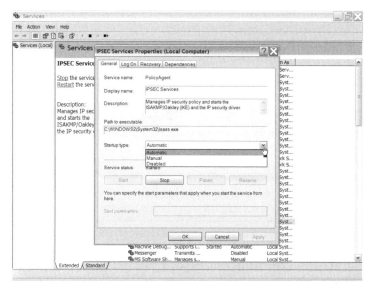

Figure 8-6 The IPSec driver startup modes in the Services console

Even though you have the option of changing the startup modes in the Services console, this just tells you whether or not the issue you are having is IPSec related. In order to really understand how IPSec policies are processed and applied, it is important to understand the modes in which the IPSec driver operates. The IPSec driver operates in one of three modes:

- Computer startup mode
- Operational mode
- Diagnostics mode

When the computer boots up, the Windows operating system loads the IPSec driver. This is the Computer startup mode. While in the Computer startup mode, the IPSec driver can perform in any one of the following capacities:

- *Permit*—The IPSec driver allows all inbound and outbound traffic. Once some type of IPSec policy is applied, the IPSec driver no longer operates in this mode.

- *Block*—The IPSec driver blocks all inbound and outbound traffic until the persistent policy is applied. Other traffic that would not be blocked is Dynamic Host Configuration Protocol (DHCP) traffic and traffic that matches any specific permit filters configured using the netsh ipsec dynamic set config bootexemptions command.

- *Stateful*—The IPSec driver permits all traffic allowed in the Block mode as well as outbound traffic initiated by the computer during startup. The stateful inbound permit filters are no longer used once the IPSec service starts and sets persistent IPSec policy. If any type of IPSec policy has been assigned to a computer, the IPSec Policy Agent sets the stateful mode for the IPSec driver by default. You can change the default startup mode for the IPSec driver by using the netsh IPSec context or by modifying the registry.

Table 8-1 describes what happens to the IPSec driver based on the startup type of the IPSec service.

Table 8-1   IPSec Driver Startup

Service Startup	IPSec Driver Startup Mode
Disabled	The IPSec driver loads in Permit mode; the IPSec driver does not filter any traffic.
Manual	The IPSec driver loads in Permit mode; the IPSec driver does not filter any traffic.
Automatic	The IPSec driver loads in a startup mode configured by the IPSec Policy Agent.

The Computer startup mode is used until the IPSec Policy Agent sets the IPSec driver into an operational mode. After the IPSec service starts, the IPSec Policy Agent can set the IPSec driver to any one of the operational modes. The operational mode that is chosen does not change the mode that the IPSec driver uses during computer startup. The operational modes are as follows:

- *Permit*—No IPSec protection is provided. This mode is used when the IPSec service is manually stopped.

- *Block*—All inbound and outbound traffic is blocked. This includes the exemptions that apply during computer startup.

- *Secure*—The IPSec Policy Agent sets the driver into Secure mode after it applies persistent policy and before it applies the Active Directory–based policy or the local policy.

You cannot use the netsh commands to configure this mode. The operational mode can be configured only by the IPSec Policy Agent.

If you are troubleshooting and start the computer in Safe mode with Networking, the IPSec service does not start. This means that no IPSec policy can be applied. However, if an IPSec policy has been assigned to the computer and the IPSec service startup type is set to Automatic, the IPSec driver remains in Computer startup mode. You can then configure specific permit filters to allow inbound traffic over specific protocols and ports.

If you are troubleshooting and have to change the IPSec driver mode to Permit to allow all inbound connections, you can either set the OperationMode registry key to a value of 0 or change the IPSec service startup type to Manual or Disabled, and then restart the computer in Safe mode with Networking again.

Activity 8-3: Examining and Disabling the IPSec Driver

Time Required: 30 minutes

Objective: Examine the **IPSec driver** in the Services console and then disable it.

Description: In this activity, you will first locate and examine the **IPSec driver** in the Services MMC. You will then disable the driver to prevent IPSec from operating on the computer.

1. Log on to your Windows Server 2003 computer with your **AdminXX** account, where *XX* is your assigned student number.

2. Click **Start**, select **Administrative Tools**, and then select **Services**; the console will open, as shown in Figure 8-7.

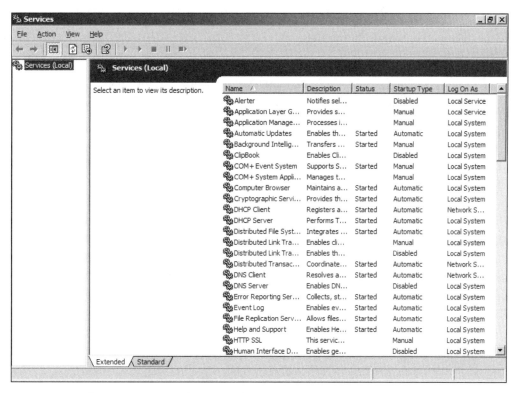

Figure 8-7   The Services console in Windows Server 2003

3. Scroll down the alphabetical listing of services and right-click **IPSEC Services**.

4. Choose **Properties**, and then examine the Startup type options by clicking on the drop-down list to the right of the **Startup type** box.

5. Select the **Dependencies** tab. Examine the services that are dependent on IpSec to see if you created issues by disabling the service.

6. To disable IPSec, choose **Disabled** as the Startup type option. If the service is started, you will also need to click the **Stop button** to terminate the service immediately.

7. Click **Apply**. Click **OK**. Close the **Services Console**.

IPSec driver event logging is disabled by default, but for troubleshooting purposes, you can enable IPSec driver event logging and specify the level of logging to provide. This will record all inbound and outbound dropped packets and other packet-processing errors in the Event Viewer system log. IPSec driver logs can record inbound and outbound per-packet drop events during Computer startup mode and operational mode. Depending on the logging level that you set, many events might be generated. This will fill the system log quickly, so it should not be used for extended periods.

ACTIVITY

Activity 8-4: Enable Logging for the IPSec Driver

Time Required: 20 minutes

Objective: Enable logging for the IPSec driver.

Description: In this activity, you will first enable logging for the IPSec services driver, then you will examine the Event Viewer system log for events. This is a method you can use for troubleshooting. Note: For this activity, the IPSEC service should be restarted. If you did not restart it after the previous exercise, do so now.

1. Log on to your Windows Server 2003 computer with your **AdminXX** account, where *XX* is your assigned student number.

2. Click **Start**, **Run**, then type **cmd** in the Run dialog box. Choose **OK**.

3. At the prompt, type **netsh ipsec dynamic set config ipsecdiagnostics 7**, as shown in Figure 8-8. This specifies that all levels of logging are to be performed.

4. Click the **Enter** key.

5. Reboot the machine. When the machine reboots. **Click Start**, **Administrative tools**, **Event Viewer**.

6. Open the **System** log file. Under the Source column, look for IPSec. You should find at least two events related the start of the IPSec driver. For example, you may find one that says the IPSec driver is starting in Bypass mode and one that says the IPSec driver has entered Secure mode.

7. When finished, close the **Event Viewer**.

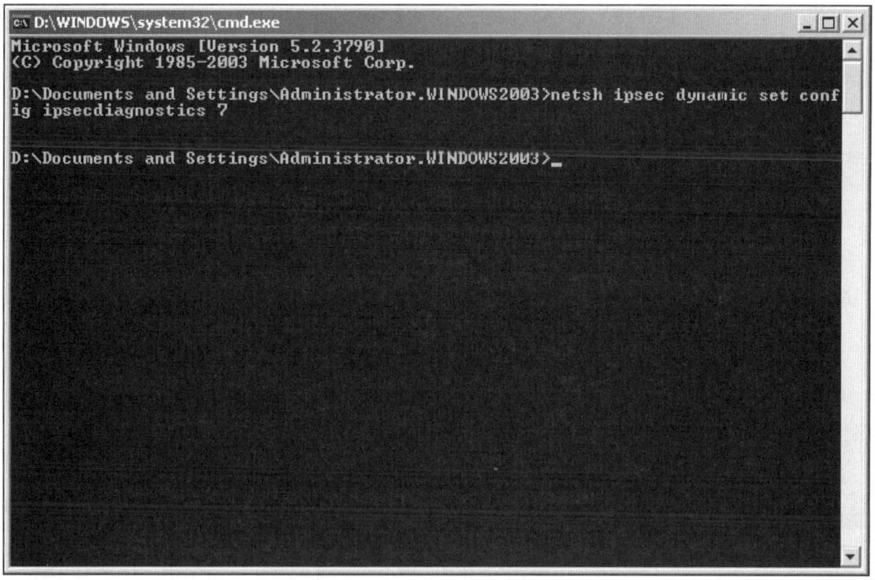

Figure 8-8   Using the Netsh command to enable logging

TROUBLESHOOTING IPSEC

As you can see, IPSec can become very complex in regard to the number of settings and to their effect on communication between computers in your network. You should be aware of the tools that are built into the Windows Server 2003 operating system that can aid you in troubleshooting IPSec. These include the **Resulting Set of Policies (RSoP)** tool, the **IP Security Monitor**, and **IPSec Logging** tools. In the following paragraphs, we will discuss each of the tools in detail.

Using RSoP

RSoP is a tool that you can use to determine the effective settings when more than one policy is applied to a computer or a user. Because the IPSec policy will be determined by the container that takes precedence (or is run last), you can determine which IPSec policy should have an effect on the computer by understanding how to use RSoP and interpret its output.

The RSoP console can be started from the Run line by typing **rsop.msc**. When you run a query in logging mode, it displays detailed IPSec policy settings for only the policy that is actually being applied. These settings include the filter rules, filter actions, authentication methods, tunnel endpoints, and connection type.

You can follow the order of precedence by understanding that the lower the number in the Precedence column, the higher the precedence of the IPSec policy. In fact, the policy with the number 1 is the only policy that is actually being applied. The policies are not merged with policies at a higher level in the Active Directory; only the policy with the highest precedence is applied, and it is applied in its entirety.

NOTE   If a local user configures IPSec policies on the connection of a computer, these policies can override the domain-level settings and the local security policy settings on the computer. In this case, the system would not detect the local security settings, so no IPSec policies will be displayed in the RSoP console.

ACTIVITY

Activity 8-5: Running RSoP to Determine Applied IPSec Policy

Time Required: 30 minutes

Objective: Run RSoP in Logging mode as part of troubleshooting IPSec, to determine the IPSec policy that is applied.

Description: In this activity, you will run RSoP in Logging mode. You will note how policies are currently being applied to the Windows Server 2003 domain controller. Next, you will assign the Server (Request Security) policy to the domain controller and run gpupdate to update the policy immediately. You will then examine the RSoP output to determine the policy that is applied and the details of the policy that is applied.

1. Log on to your Windows Server 2003 computer with your **AdminXX** account, where *XX* is your assigned student number.

2. Click **Start**, then choose **Run**.

3. On the Run line, type **rsop.msc**, and choose **OK**. This will initialize the RSoP tool in Logging mode.

4. After the policies are run, examine the Resultant Set of Policy output. In the console pane, under Computer Configuration expand **Windows Settings**, then expand **Security Settings**.

5. In the console pane, select **IP Security Policies on Local Computer**.

6. In the details pane, note that no IPSec policies are listed for the computer.

7. Close the **Resultant Set of Policy** tool.

8. Click **Start**, choose **Administrative Tools**, and then choose **Domain Controller Security Policy**.

9. In console pane of the Default Domain Controller Security Settings tool, choose **IP Security Policies on Active Directory**.

10. In the details pane, right-click the **Server (Request Security)** policy, then choose **Assign**. This will change the setting under Policy Assigned to Yes.

11. Close the **Default Domain Controller Security Settings** tool.

12. Click **Start**, then choose **Run**.

13. On the **Run** line, type **cmd** to open a command prompt.

14. On the command prompt, type **gpupdate** to immediately refresh the group policy settings on the computer. Close the command prompt when the policies are refreshed.

15. Click **Start**, then choose **Run**.

16. On the **Run** line, type **rsop.msc** and choose **OK**. This will initialize the RSoP tool in Logging mode, as shown in Figure 8-8.

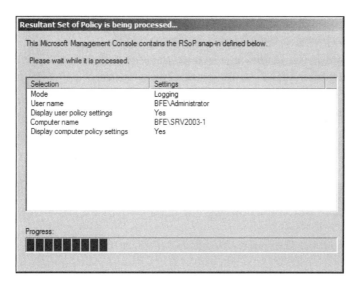

Figure 8-9 RSOP in Logging mode

17. After the policies are run, examine the Resultant Set of Policy output. In the console pane, expand **Windows Settings**, then expand **Security Settings**.

18. In the console pane, select **IP Security Policies on Local Computer**.

19. In the details pane, note that the Server (Request Security) policy is now listed.

20. Right-click on the **Server (Request Security)** policy, then choose **Properties**. Select **View** and browse the configuration tabs. Note that you can only view the settings; you cannot change settings or add settings in this tool.

Monitoring IPSec Policies by Using IP Security Monitor

You can view more detailed information about the active IPSec policy using IP Security Monitor MMC snap-in tool. You can also view statistics regarding key negotiation and authentication. There are two general categories of IPSec statistics, Main mode and Quick mode. Main mode statistics relate to the initial Internet Key Exchange (IKE) that occurs in order to establish a security association (SA) between the two computers. Quick mode statistics relate to the actual communications that occur between the computers after the SA is established. These include statistics relating to authentication as well as encryption of data packets. You can obtain a list of all of the statistics and their definitions in the Help menus of Windows Server 2003.

Auditing IKE Negotiation Successes and Failures

You can enable logging of **IKE negotiation** by enabling Audit Logon Events on the local computer. To obtain a complete log, you should enable Audit Logon Events for successes and failures. When you enable auditing, IPSec records the successes and failures for each Main mode and Quick mode negotiation and the establishment and termination of each negotiation. This information is helpful, if you need it for troubleshooting; however, it can become quite cumbersome, especially if your computer is being attacked.

You can view the success or failure of IKE negotiations in the Event Viewer security log. To view these events, enable success or failure auditing for the *Audit logon events* audit policy for your domain or local computer. If auditing is enabled for IKE events, and IKE authentication fails, event 547 is recorded. If IKE authentication succeeds, event 541 is recorded.

If you need to audit logon events on a computer running IPSec, but you don't want to audit all of the IKE events, you can disable the portion of the logging that applies to the IKE event. To disable IKE logging, you should do the following:

1. Set the HKEY_LOCAL_MACHINE\System\CurrentControlSet\Control\ Lsa\Audit\ DisableIKEAudits registry setting to a value of 1.

2. Either restart the computer or restart the IPSec service by running the **net stop policyagent** and **net start policyagent** commands at the command prompt.

NOTE   The DisableIKEAudits key does not exist by default and must be created.

CAUTION   Stopping and restarting the IPSec service can disconnect all of the computers that are using IPSec from the computer on which the IPSec service is stopped.

Configuring IPSec Logging

You can configure a computer or an entire network of computers so that you can use Event Viewer to view IPSec-related events. In particular, you can view events related to IKE events, policy change events, and IPSec driver events regarding dropped inbound and outbound packets. As demonstrated earlier in the chapter, you can use the Netsh command-line utility to control IPSec driver logging. In addition, you can send all of the IPSec logging information to a central log called the Oakley.log file. The Oakley.log file can provide a detailed trace of all IPSec transactions. How you set up the system to log IPSec-related events depends upon what type of information you need and how much information you need. In the following two sections, we discuss how to enable and disable IPSec logging in Oakley logs and Audit Policy and how to use the Netsh command-line utility to control logging of IPSec driver events.

Oakley Logs

Oakley logs are very detailed tracing logs that can be used to troubleshoot IKE interoperability under controlled circumstances. Expert knowledge of **Internet Security Association Key Management Protocol (ISAKMP)** standards and policies is required to interpret these logs. The Oakley log is stored as a file with the name *systemroot*\Debug\Oakley.log. It has a fixed size of 50,000 lines and will overwrite as necessary. A new Oakley.log file is created each time the IPSec service is started. The previous version is then stored as Oakley.log.sav. When a file becomes full without a restart of the service, the current file is saved as Oakley.log.bak and a new Oakley.log file is created. To best interpret an Oakley log, you should minimize the number of negotiations to the ones with which you are concerned and then restart the IPSec service to create a new log, which you can use to monitor the communication for a short period of time.

Here are some scenarios where IKE logging is needed and what possible solutions there are:

- *IKE failure*—Failure to negotiate IKE and the reasons for the failure are recorded in the security log as long as you enable Logon/Logoff failure audits. IKE can fail because certificate credentials do not work, or because there is an IPSec policy configuration problem.

- *IKE timeout*—IKE times out during the initial negotiation request if routers in front of the virtual private network (VPN) server do not allow User Datagram Protocol (UDP) port 500 through. When IKE times out, the audit log shows that the peer failed to reply.

In Windows Server 2003, you can enable and disable the IKE tracing that creates the Oakley.log file while the IPSec service is running.

To enable IKE tracing, type the following command at a command prompt:

```
netsh ipsec dynamic set config ikelogging 1
```

To disable IKE tracing, type the following command at a command prompt:

```
netsh ipsec dynamic set config ikelogging 0
```

In Windows 2000 and Windows XP, you can enable IKE tracing only with a registry modification.

To enable IKE tracing in Windows 2000 and Windows XP, you should do the following:

1. Set the HKEY_LOCAL_MACHINE\System\CurrentControlSet\Services\PolicyAgent\Oakley\EnableLogging DWORD registry setting to a value of 1.

2. Stop and start the IPSec services by running the **net stop policyagent** and **net start policyagent** commands at the command prompt.

You should be extremely careful when you edit the registry because incorrectly editing the registry can severely damage your system.

CAUTION

ACTIVITY

Activity 8-6: Enable Oakley Logging for IPSec

Time Required: 20 minutes

Objective: Enable Oakley logging.

Description: In this activity, you will first enable Oakley logging, then you will check to be sure that the log file exists. This is a method you use for troubleshooting.

1. Log on to your Windows Server 2003 computer with your **AdminXX** account, where *XX* is your assigned student number.

2. Click **Start**, **Run**, type **cmd** in the Run dialog box, then choose **OK**.

3. At the prompt, type **netsh ipsec dynamic set config ikelogging 1**. This specifies that logging is to be performed.

4. Click the **Enter** key.

5. Reboot the machine. When the machine reboots, right-click **My Computer**, click **Explore**, go to the Windows directory, and find the Debug folder.

6. Open the **Debug** folder. You should find two log files, as shown in Figure 8-10.

7. When finished, close the **Event Viewer**.

IPSec Driver Logging

In Windows Server 2003, you can also enable IPSec driver logging of inbound and outbound packets by using the Netsh IPSec command-line tool. Remember from an earlier exercise that to enable driver logging, you should do the following:

1. At the command prompt, type: **netsh ipsec dynamic set config ipsecdiagnostics 7**.

2. Restart the computer.

In addition, you can change the interval for writing IPSec driver packet events to the system log. By default, the IPSec driver writes events to the system log only once an hour, or after a specified threshold has been reached. For troubleshooting purposes, you can set this interval to the minimum value, 60 seconds. Changing this interval can be done with a registry edit or by using the Netsh utility.

To change the interval for writing IPSec driver packet events by editing the registry, you should do the following:

1. Set the HKEY_LOCAL_MACHINE\System\CurrentControlSet\Services\IPSec\LogInterval DWORD registry setting to **60 decimal**.

2. Restart the computer.

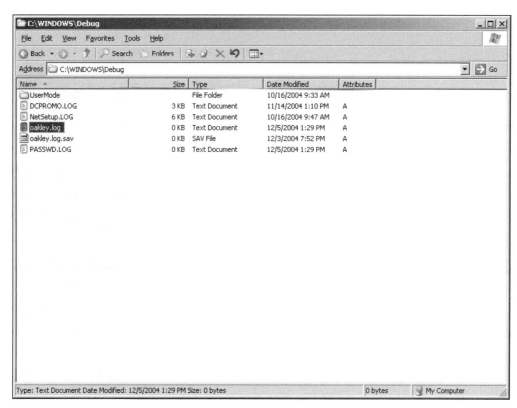

Figure 8-10   Oakley log files

CAUTION   You should be extremely careful when you edit the registry because incorrectly editing the registry can severely damage your system.

To change the interval for writing IPSec driver packet events using the Netsh utility, you should do the following:

1. At the command prompt, type **netsh ipsec dynamic set config ipsecloginterval 60**.

2. Restart the computer.

TROUBLESHOOTING IPSEC ACROSS NETWORKS

You can use IPSec to secure the entire communication channel between two computers. This means that you can secure the connections within a network as well as the connections between networks. Securing communication between two networks requires an understanding of the technologies and protocols that connect the networks. Likewise, troubleshooting IPSec across networks requires knowledge of the protocols used and how they behave between networks as well as knowledge of the tools that can be used to monitor their behavior.

In this section, we discuss the many aspects of IPSec communication across networks. In particular, we discuss using Network Monitor to view communications between network devices. We also discuss troubleshooting IPSec traffic through devices and situations that are present when communicating across networks, including Network Address Translation (NAT), port filters, protocol filters, firewalls, and router configuration.

In troubleshooting IPSec across networks, you encounter issues with certificate autoenrollment, cross-certificate trusts, and if Kerberos is being used, domain trusts between clients and servers and the permission for Kerberos traffic. These areas are important because if after IPSec policy is applied, and IKE authentication fails, communication will be blocked.

Network Monitor

Network Monitor is a component that is included with Windows Server 2003 as well as other previous Microsoft server operating systems. You can install and use Network Monitor to view IPSec communication. It includes parsers for the ISAKMP (IKE), Authentication Header (AH), and Encapsulating Security Payload (ESP) protocols. Network Monitor cannot parse encrypted portions of IPSec-secured ESP traffic when the encryption is provided by software. It can, however, process the packets if they are being encrypted and decrypted by IPSec-aware network adapters because the packets are already decrypted by the time they reach the network monitor's parsers.

Activity 8-7: Installing and Using Network Monitor on Windows Server 2003

ACTIVITY

Time Required: 20 minutes

Objective: Install the Network Monitor tool on Windows Server 2003.

Description: In this activity, you will locate Network Monitor in the Windows Components wizard of Windows Server 2003 and install the tool.

1. Log on to your Windows Server 2003 computer with your **AdminXX** account, where *XX* is your assigned student number.

2. Click **Start**, select **Control Panel**, and then select **Add or Remove Programs**.

3. Select **Add/Remove Windows Components** and scroll down to **Management and Monitoring Tools**.

4. Select the words **Management and Monitoring Tools** (do not select the check box), then click the **Details** button.

5. Within the Subcomponents of Management and Monitoring Tools, select **Network Monitor Tools**, as shown in Figure 8-11, then choose **OK**.

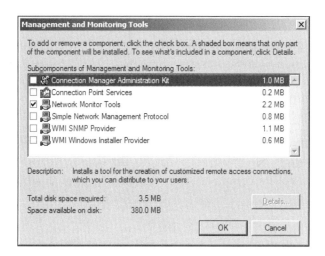

Figure 8-11   Installing Network Monitor Tools

6. Click **Next** to begin the installation. (You will need to supply the Windows Server 2003 CD-ROM if you have never installed Network Monitor on this computer before.) When the install is complete, click **Finish**.

7. To use Network Monitor, Click **Start**, point to **Settings,** point to **Control Panel**, point to **Administrative Tools**, then click **Network Monitor**.

8. Click **Capture** on the menu bar, then click **Start** to begin capturing packets.

9. You should now start to see traffic being generated on the screen.

10. Wait a few minutes, and then in the Network Monitor menu bar, click **Capture**, and then click **Stop**.

11. In the Network Monitor menu bar, click **Capture**, then click **Display Captured Data**.

12. Network Monitor displays various pieces of information about the captured frames, such as the header and delivery details, and the hexadecimal representation of the frame.

13. In the top frame, choose a frame to view. Browse through the fields and find the frame's protocol type and source address.

14. When finished, close **Network Monitor**.

Network Address Translation

Network Address Translation (NAT) is a widely used technology that allows more than one computer to share a single IP address or simply translates addresses from one network to another. Most often, NAT is used to map private IP addresses that are used on the inside of a network to public IP addresses that are registered on the Internet. This helps to conserve the public IP addresses as well as increase the security of the network, because the entities on the outside of the network are never given information about the private addressing scheme used on the inside.

Although it is possible to use a feature called Network Address Translation Traversal (NAT-T) to allow communication protected by IPSec to pass through a NAT, Microsoft does not recommend this practice with servers because of potential unintended consequences that would cause an error in the translation and lead to parties receiving traffic that they should not receive. If you require IPSec to secure communication, then Microsoft recommends that you use public IP addresses on all servers that are connected directly to the Internet. In addition, Windows XP Service Pack 2 changes XP computers so that they do not support communications with servers that are behind a NAT. You can, however, still use NAT-T to communicate, with IPSec protection, from client computer to client computer through a NAT.

Port Filters

You can configure input and output filters for Layer Two Tunneling Protocol over IPSec (L2TP). To create the filter, you must first configure the filter and then select the appropriate filter action. You must be a member of the Administrators group to perform this action. As a security best practice, Microsoft also recommends that you consider using the Run as command rather than logging on with administrative credentials.

You can also use IPSec with the NAT/Basic Firewall component of the Routing and Remote Access service or IP packet filtering to enhance IPSec to permit or block filtering of inbound or outbound traffic. One of the biggest issues that will result in errors in creating port filters is an erroneous port number. This might cause communication to be blocked or unsecured. For example, suppose that the administrator of the Web application server on the perimeter network decides to block all traffic from the Internet, except requests to TCP port 80 (HTTP) and TCP port 443 (SSL), which are used by Web services. Instead of blocking all and allowing only ports 80 and 443, the administrator allows ports 08 and 434. This will of course cause some issues for everyone, so be sure that when you use port filters you use the correct ports.

Another issue to consider is that if you are using a VPN and the client is behind any network device performing NAT, the L2TP session fails because encrypted IPSec Encapsulating Security Payload (ESP) packets become corrupted. In using VPN software, the client is most likely able to establish an L2TP session because NAT does not perform any IP address or port translation when packets originate from its own node.

Protocol Filters

IPSec rules can also be used to determine which protocols are allowed to pass through an interface. You can either configure a rule that allows all protocols except the ones that you want to block or you can configure a rule that blocks all protocols except the ones that you specifically allow. You should understand the configuration of these rules so that you can troubleshoot another administrator's rules and/or configure your own rules.

By default in Windows 2000 and Windows XP, broadcast, multicast, Kerberos, RSVP, and ISAKMP traffic is exempt from IPSec filtering. This has changed in Windows Server 2003. The default filtering exemptions have been removed except for ISAKMP traffic, and inbound multicast and broadcast traffic. To modify the default filtering behavior for Windows Server 2003 IPSec, you can use the Netsh IPSec context or modify the registry. Using the Nesth tool is a much safer way to modify the settings because changing the registry can severely affect the proper operation of the system. Use the following command to modify the default filter:

```
netsh ipsec dynamic set config ipsecexempt value={ 0 | 1 | 2 | 3}
```

Use the value of 0 only if you require compatibility with Windows 2000 and Windows XP. Use this setting with caution because if Kerberos traffic is exempted from filtering, an attacker can bypass other IPSec filters by using either UDP or TCP source port 88 to access any open port. Many port scan tools will not detect this. These tools do not allow setting the source port to 88 when checking for open ports. If you change the value for this setting, you must restart the computer for the new value to take effect.

Windows Server 2003 IPSec does not support specific filters for broadcast protocols or ports, nor does it support multicast groups, protocols, or ports. Because IPSec does not negotiate security for multicast and broadcast traffic, these types of traffic are dropped if they match a filter with a corresponding filter action to negotiate security.

 NOTE When configuring protocol filters, keep in mind that just as with ports, if protocols that are necessary are not allowed, this will prevent IPSec from functioning.

Firewalls

As you know, the purpose of a firewall is to prevent specific types of traffic from being transmitted into or out of an interface. Because IPSec involves many different types of traffic used for negotiation of security, it is quite possible that firewall filters inadvertently block IPSec negotiations from occurring. As discussed in Chapter 7, IPSec uses a few different ports, depending on the specific type of protocols that you have configured. You should ensure that the required ports are open on the firewall so that IPSec communication can take place. The following is list of the ports used by IPSec traffic:

- *UDP port 500*—Used by IKE to negotiate the security and exchange the keys
- *IP protocol 51*—Used by AH when chosen

- *IP protocol 50*—Used by ESP when chosen
- *UDP Port 4500*—Only if NAT-T will be used

You should also keep in mind that firewalls could filter some traffic that the IPSec rules do not and vice versa. The result will be a combination of the filters that have been applied at the firewall as well as those that have been applied in the IPSec rules. In other words, the two methods will not cancel each other out, but instead will be cumulative in regard to network traffic. For example, if the firewall prevents the flow of File Transfer Protocol (FTP) traffic by filtering ports 20 and 21 and an IPSec rule allows FTP traffic but blocks Simple Mail Transfer Protocol (SMTP) traffic, then the result will be that both FTP and SMTP traffic will be blocked.

You must also allow IKE to be initiated from either a source or destination IP address. ISAKMP specifies that the IKE protocol must be able to negotiate security in either direction. Stateful filtering that allows only one computer to initiate IKE to a responder typically times out and deletes the stateful inbound filter in the firewall. As a result, IKE cannot rekey IPSec security associations, and IPSec connectivity is lost. Keep this in mind when you have a situation where you are losing IPSec connectivity.

Routers

Most routers have the capability to contain access lists that either permit or deny traffic based on a protocol. These access lists can create yet another form of filtering in regard to network traffic. This additional filtering could potentially cause two problems in regard to your IPSec implementation. First, the required IPSec ports could be inadvertently blocked, thus preventing IPSec communication from taking place. Second the access lists could contain other filters that will also be cumulative in regard to their effect on network traffic. You might be blaming a problem on a potential errant IPSec configuration when the true source of the problem lies with the access list in the router. For example, Cisco routers use an implied "deny all" as a last statement in the list whenever an access list is used. If you, or another administrator, have configured a list and have not specifically allowed the required protocols to pass through the router, then your IPSec service could fail even if your IPSec configuration is correct.

TROUBLESHOOTING IPSec CERTIFICATES

As we discussed in Chapter 7, certificates are one of the three ways that users and computers can be authenticated in IPSec policies. Certificates are most useful when the users and computers are not part of your Active Directory. They are also useful for authenticating pre–Windows 2000 clients, such as Windows NT and Windows 9X clients, which cannot use the Kerberos protocol. However, if you decide to use certificates for authentication, you should be aware of the factors that might affect their use. In particular, you should understand how enterprise trust policies configured in Group Policy can be used to create certificate trust lists, which can in turn be used to validate a certificate. You should also be aware of the fact that the **Certificate Revocation List (CRL)** is the ultimate authority in a network as to whether or not a certificate is still valid but that the system can be configured to allow or to disallow a connection to occur if the CRL cannot be located.

Enterprise Trust Policies

Enterprise trust policies are a tool in Group Policy that is used for creating certificate trust lists that establish your company's trust of root CAs from other organizations. You can also use Group Policy Objects (GPOs) that are in a different Active Directory container to establish uniform trust policies for your organization. Windows provides a Certificate Trust List wizard to create new trusts or modify existing trusts. You can locate the wizard in the Computer Configuration\Windows Settings\Security Settings\Public Key Policies\Enterprise Trust node of the Group Policy Object Editor, as shown in Figure 8-12. You can start creating a new enterprise trust list by right-clicking on Enterprise Trust and then clicking on New. You can also import trust lists with the same tool.

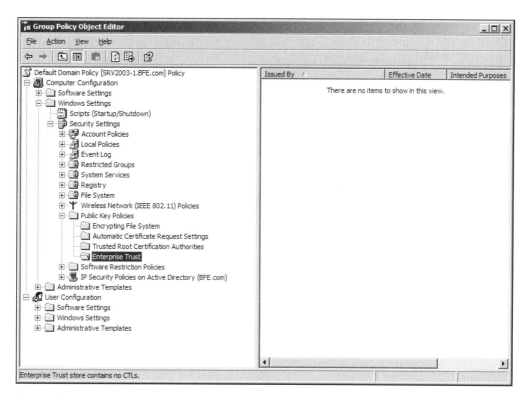

Figure 8-12   The Enterprise Trust node in Group Policy Editor

Certificate Revocation Lists

Because the CRL is the ultimate authority over whether a certificate is still valid, you cannot actually validate a certificate without checking with the CRL. Regardless of this fact, the default behavior of the system might actually let a communication continue that cannot be validated. This is so because Windows XP and Windows 2003 are configured by default to attempt to check the CRL but to deny the connection only if the CRL specifically states that the certificate is revoked. In other words, if the CRL cannot be located because of a communication error, then the connection will be allowed because the CRL cannot provide an explicit deny if you can't connect to it. By default, IPSec CRLs are automatically checked during IKE certificate authentication, but a fully successful CRL check is not required for the certificate to be accepted. However, if enhanced security is required, a fully successful CRL check is also required. CRL checking can cause delays in authentication or unnecessary failures, and some third-party Public Key Infrastructure (PKI) systems might not support it. You can use either the Netsh tool or edit the registry to reconfigure the system to disable or require strong CRL checking. To change the configuration, you should perform the following steps:

1. At the command prompt, type **netsh ipsec dynamic set config strongcrlcheck value=2**.

2. Stop and restart the IPSec service by typing **net stop policyagent** and then **net start policyagent** at the command prompt, or restart the computer.

NOTE You can also use the same command in the Netsh utility to disable IPSec CRL checking by applying a value of 0, or you can reset the system to its default by applying a value of 1.

When troubleshooting IPSec certificates, know IPSec CRL checking does not guarantee that certificate validation fails immediately when a certificate is revoked. There is always a delay between the time that the revoked certificate is placed on an updated and published CRL and the time when the computer that performs the IPSec CRL checking retrieves this CRL. Remember that the computer does not retrieve a new CRL until the current CRL has expired or until the next time the CRL is scheduled to be published. CRLs are cached in memory and in \Documents and Settings*UserName*\Local Settings\Temporary Internet Files. If a CRL cache problem occurs, restarting the computer does not resolve the problem because CRLs persist across computer restarts.

SUMMARY

- When you use IPSec policies, the order of policy inheritance is: Local, Site, Domain, Organizational Unit.

- You should configure your own policies and not just use the default policies provided by Microsoft.

- You can use the default policies as a basis for your custom-configured policies.

- When more than one group policy is applied to a computer, the settings on the last policy that runs are generally the ones that will override the settings in the other group policies; because IPSec is just one setting in a policy, the last setting that applies to IPSec will determine the IPSec policies that will be used. These policies will be used in their entirety and not mixed with any other policies or settings.

- The default order of group policy inheritance is Site, Domain, OU, and Child OU.

- You can control and troubleshoot IPSec policies by controlling the IPSec driver startup mode in the Services console.

- You can quickly isolate whether a problem is related to IPSec by disabling IPSec in the Services console.

- Resulting Set of Policy (RSoP) is a tool that you can use to determine which policy is actually applied to a computer.

- In the RSoP tool, the lower the number in the precedence column, the higher the order of precedence of the policy settings; the settings on the number 1 policy are the only ones that are actually applied.

- You can view detailed information about the active IPSec policy using the IP Security Monitor MMC snap-in tool.

- Main mode IPSec statistics relate to the initial Internet Key Exchange (IKE) that occurs in order to establish a security association (SA) between two computers.

- Quick mode IPSec statistics relate to the communications that occur between the computers after the SA is established. These include statistics relating to authentication as well as the encryption of data packets.

- Oakley logs are very detailed tracing logs that can be used to troubleshoot IKE interoperability under controlled circumstances. Expert knowledge of IKE statistics is required to interpret these logs.

- You can enable and disable IKE tracing using the netsh command-line tool or by editing the registry.

- You can enable IPSec driver logging of inbound and outbound packets using the netsh command-line tool or by editing the registry.

- You can change the interval for writing IPSec driver packet events using the netsh command-line utility.

❑ If you need to audit logon events for other reasons, but you do not want to audit all of the IKE events, then you can disable the portion of the logging that relates to the IKE events by editing the registry.

❑ You should always use great care when you edit the registry, because an improper edit could lead to being forced to reinstall the operating system.

❑ You can install and use Network Monitor to view IPSec communications, such as those using the ISAKMP, AH, and ESP protocols.

❑ Although it is possible to use Network Address Translation Traversal (NAT-T) to allow IPSec to work with a NAT, Microsoft does not recommend that it be used with servers because of the potential unintended consequence of some traffic being diverted to the wrong interface.

❑ You can use IPSec rules to filter traffic in a local area network (LAN), on a remote access connection, or both.

❑ If you use IPSec with a firewall, you should ensure that UDP port 500 is open and that the correct ports are open for your configuration of IPSec.

❑ You should understand that filtering through firewalls and access lists in a router will have a cumulative effect on how traffic is filtered in a network.

❑ You can configure enterprise trust policies for entities within your own Active Directory as well as entities external to your Active Directory.

❑ By default a certificate will be considered valid if the CRL is not available at the time the certificate is checked.

❑ You can strengthen the CRL policy so that it requires that the CRL is available at the time the certificate is checked. You can use the Netsh command-line utility to make the change.

KEY TERMS

Certificate Revocation List — A component in a Public Key Infrastructure (PKI) that is used to inform the network that a certificate is no longer considered valid. This list can be automatically published whenever changes are made.

Enterprise trust policies — A tool used for creating trust lists that establish your company's trust of root CAs from other organizations.

IKE negotiation — The communication between two computers that includes the exchange of keys and the negotiation in regard to how communication can take place.

Internet Security Association Key Management Protocol (ISAKMP) — A protocol that allows the receiver to obtain a public key and authenticate the sender using digital certificates.

IPSec driver startup mode — The "master switch" for the IPSec driver that is located in the Services console. This can be used to control the startup of IPSec and to troubleshoot IPSec-related problems.

IPSec logging — The detailed recording of IPSec-related events for the purpose of troubleshooting IPSec.

IP Security Monitor — An MMC snap-in used to monitor IPSec policies.

Network Address Translation (NAT) — A widely used technology that allows more than one computer to share a single IP address or simply translates addresses from one network to another.

Network Monitor — A component included in Windows Server 2003 that allows you to "sniff" the network and view the contents of packets flowing into and out of a computer.

Oakley logs — Detailed tracing logs that can be used to troubleshoot IKE interoperability under controlled circumstances. Interpreting these logs requires an expert knowledge of ISAKMP and standards and policies.

Resulting Set of Policy (RSoP) — A tool that you can use to determine the effective settings when more than one policy is applied to a user or a computer. The policy designated as number 1 in order of precedence is the only policy that is applied.

rsop.msc — A command used for starting the RSoP console from the Run line.

8

REVIEW QUESTIONS

1. If two Group Policies apply to the same computer, one at the domain level and the other at the OU where the computer object exists, then how will the resulting IPSec settings be determined by the system?

   a. The domain policy settings will always override the others.

   b. The OU where the computer object exists will override the other settings.

   c. The result will be a combination of the settings of both policies.

   d. The system will produce an error because the configuration is incorrect.

2. Which is the correct order of precedence in regard to Group Policies?

   a. OU, Site, Domain, Local

   b. Domain, Site, OU, Local

   c. Local, Site, Domain, OU

   d. Site, Local, Domain, OU

3. Which IPSec driver startup mode does not start IPSec when the computer is booted but does allow some applications to start the service?

   a. Manual

   b. Disabled

   c. Automatic

   d. Application controlled

4. When you are using RSoP to determine the effective settings for Group Policy, which precedence number indicates the policy that is actually applied?

   a. The highest number

   b. The lowest number (1)

   c. The settings are combined

   d. The RSoP tool does not provide precedence information.

5. Which of the following is the name of the log that provides detailed trace information of all IPSec transactions?

   a. Oakely.log

   b. IPSec.log

   c. IPDrv.log

   d. Netsh.log

6. Which tool(s) can you use in Windows 2003 to enable IKE tracing? (Choose all that apply.)

   a. Regedit.exe

   b. Netsh

   c. Active Directory Users and Computers

   d. Routing and Remote Access

7. Which tool(s) can you use in Windows Server 2003 to disable the portion of Audit Logon Events that relates to IKE events? (Choose all that apply.)

   a. Regedit.exe

   b. Netsh

   c. Routing and Remote Access

   d. Domain Security Policy

8. Which tool can you utilize to examine the packet used in IPSec communications?

   a. RSoP

   b. Domain Security Policy

   c. Network Monitor

   d. Netsh

9. True or false? Network Monitor can be used to parse IPSec ESP-secured traffic regardless of whether the encryption is provided by the software or the hardware.

   a. True

   b. False

10. Which service should you use to allow two Windows XP client computers to communicate using IPSec through network address translator?

    a. NAT-T

    b. Netsh

    c. ESP

    d. AH

11. If you are intending to connect two client computers using IPSec with ESP and NAT-T through a firewall, then which of the following ports must be open on the firewall? (Choose all that apply.)

    a. IP port 51

    b. IP port 50

    c. TCP port 4500

    d. UDP port 4500

12. Which tool should you use to create certificate trust lists for your organization?

    a. The Certificates snap-in tool

    b. Domain Security Policy

    c. Group Policy

    d. Netsh

13. If an organization has a firewall configured to filter specific ports, an IPSec policy that is also configured to filter specific ports, and routers that contain access lists that are configured to filter specific ports, then which of the following will result?

    a. The IPSec policies will override all other settings.

    b. The firewall settings will override all other settings.

    c. The three settings will cancel each other out whenever they conflict.

    d. The result will be that the combination of all of the specified ports will be filtered.

14. True or false? In its default setting, Windows Server 2003 will always ensure that a connection to the server containing the CRL can be made before accepting a certificate as valid.

    a. True

    b. False

15. Which of the following tools can you use to change the system setting in Windows Server 2003 with regard to CRL checking?

    a. Netsh

    b. Domain Security Policy

    c. Active Directory Users and Computers

    d. The Security Templates MMC snap-in tool

16. True or false? Microsoft recommends that most businesses use the default IPSec policies for their networks?
    a. True
    b. False

17. True or false? The Secure Server (Require Security) IPSec policy should be used as a basis for configuring a custom policy in a standard security network.
    a. True
    b. False

18. If the IPSec driver services setting is configured as Automatic and then manually turned off, which of the following will occur if the computer is restarted?
    a. The setting will remain at Automatic, and the service will be started.
    b. The setting will be changed to Manual, and the service will be started.
    c. The setting will remain at Automatic, but the service will not be started.
    d. The setting will be changed to Disabled.

19. Which of the following are true in regard to RSoP? (Choose all that apply.)
    a. When RSoP is in Logging mode, it displays detailed settings of only the policy that is actually applied.
    b. When RSoP is in Logging mode, it displays detailed settings for all IPSec policies on the network.
    c. RSoP can be started from the Run line by typing rsop.exe.
    d. The only way to start RSoP is through the GPMC.

20. Which command should you type on a command line to refresh group policy settings on a Windows Server 2003 computer without waiting for the refresh cycle?
    a. Secedit /refreshpolicy machine_policy
    b. gpupdate
    c. gprefresh
    d. refreshnow

21. True or false? An Oakley log is a special IPSec log that is designed to be easy to interpret and extremely user friendly.
    a. True
    b. False

22. Which tool(s) can be used to enable and disable IKE tracing without restarting the IPSec service? (Choose all that apply.)
    a. Regedit.exe
    b. Netsh
    c. Domain Security Policy
    d. System Properties

23. True or false? Microsoft recommends using NAT-T on Windows Server 2003 computers that are communicating through a NAT with IPSec.

   a. True

   b. False

24. True or false? You can establish trust lists between your company and other root CAs using the Enterprise Trust Policies tool.

   a. True

   b. False

25. To strengthen certificate security on your network, you have decided to require that the system contact the server containing the CRL before a certificate is accepted as valid. At the command prompt, you type *netsh ipsec dynamic set config strongcrlcheck value=?*. Which value should be entered instead of the question mark?

   a. 0

   b. 1

   c. 3

   d. 2

CASE PROJECTS

CASE PROJECTS

Case Project 6-1

MTC Inc. has decided to begin to use IPSec to secure communication within their computer network. They have hired you as a consultant to implement the process. The management of the company has been told that Microsoft has some default IPSec policies already configured in Windows Server 2003 and that these are sufficient for most companies' needs. Write a brief explanation of the true purpose of the default IPSec policies in Windows Server 2003 and how you intend to use them.

CASE PROJECTS

Case Project 6-2

The CIO at MTC, Inc. has some concerns about the amount of data that will be added to the Audit Logon Events portion of his security logs due to the IKE negotiation produced by IPSec. Write a brief explanation of why he should not be concerned and describe the steps that you will take to disable the IKE logging in the security log except when needed for troubleshooting.

Case Project 6-3

IT personnel at MTC, Inc. are concerned that applications that are designed to start IPSec and use the service not be able to start the service unless it is configured properly. They are asking you for your recommendation in regard to configuring the IPSec driver startup mode. Write a brief explanation of the three options for configuring the IPSec driver startup mode and the implications of each option.

Case Project 6-4

The CIO at MTC, Inc. is concerned about the result of conflicting group policies that all contain IPSec policies. His understanding of the technology is that group policy settings in multiple containers are combined to determine the result. He is very concerned that domain IPSec policies might combine with OU policies and produce some unexpected results. Write a brief explanation of regarding order of precedence and how it is related to IPSec policies.

Case Project 6-5

To further enhance security, MTC, Inc. has decided to use firewalls and router access lists in addition to IPSec filtering. The CIO is concerned that some of the security measures might somehow cancel each other out, if they are not configured properly. Write a brief summary of the expected result when multiple filtering mechanisms are used in the same network result. Include examples of protocols filtered with each of the three methods mentioned.

9

PLANNING AND DEPLOYING PUBLIC KEY INFRASTRUCTURE

After reading this chapter, you will be able to:

♦ Define certificate requirements

♦ Plan PKI group structure

♦ Plan authentication of resources

♦ Plan authorization of resources

♦ Plan, build, and manage certification authority hierarchies

♦ Select a certificate enrollment and renewal method

♦ Configure and deploy certificate authorities

♦ Configure and manage the publication of certificate revocation lists

♦ Back up and restore a certification authority

In any environment, authenticated users need access to shared resources such as file shares and printers. Previously you learned methods to secure network communication, but what about controlling and securing user access? Security planning for the network should be based on the principles that users need *access to resources* and the *network requires a secure shared infrastructure*. It is upon these two concepts that this chapter is built. This combination can provide the trust and integrity required for today's complex networking environments.

Depending on the organization, users may travel with mobile devices, desktop computers may be shared among different users, or there may be data shared with business partners, contractors, suppliers, and customers. This means that often there is valuable data relating to the organization, which is beyond its control. Somehow all this information needs to be protected, and there needs to be a way to provide confidential data exchange. The way you configure authorization for your clients and servers has an immense impact on the protection and confidentiality that you provide for network resources.

In this chapter, you will learn how to decide what types of security groups to use and plan how to manage and maintain these groups to create a secure resource authorization environment. You will also learn how to set up and operate a Public Key Infrastructure, including various aspects of configuring and managing certification authorities certificates, and keys. Finally, you will look at how to back up and restore certification authorities.

DEFINING CERTIFICATE REQUIREMENTS

Microsoft Windows Server 2003 enables secure data access based on the use of digital certificates. Before you can use digital certificates, you need to design a **Public Key Infrastructure (PKI)**. A PKI refers to a technology that includes a series of features relating to authentication and encryption. A PKI is based on a system of certificates, which are digitally signed statements that contain a public key and the name of the subject. A variety of PKI solutions can be used for purposes such as online ordering, exchanges of contracts, and remote access, but these all involve planning configuration options for one or more certification authorities and configuring certificates to meet the needs of the organization. Before you can start designing and planning a PKI, it will help if you understand how a PKI works.

Using a PKI allows an organization to publish, use, renew, and/or revoke certificates and enroll clients. Once the PKI is deployed, you can then digitally sign files such as documents and applications, secure e-mail, enable secure connections between computers, and improve user authentication through the use of smart cards.

To begin the process of designing a public key infrastructure, first identify the certificate requirements for your organization. This is done by defining the security needs of the organization. In doing so, look at whether or not you will be using any of the following:

- Digital signatures
- Secured e-mail
- Internet authentication
- Software code signing
- IP security
- Smart card logon
- Encrypted file system
- 802.1x authentication

Digital Signatures

A **digital signature** helps to guarantee the identity of the person sending the data from one point to another. The digital signature acts as an electronic signature that is used to authenticate the identity of the sender, as well as ensure that the original content sent has not been changed. You can use digital signatures even when data is distributed in plaintext, as with e-mail. In this instance, the sensitivity of the message itself may not warrant encryption, but it may be important to ensure that the data is in its original form.

Secured E-mail

Normal Internet mail is sent as plaintext with no security. This often allows intruders to penetrate mail servers and network traffic, thereby capturing sensitive information. On IP networks anyone can spoof an e-mail address. Therefore, you can never be sure who really sent a message or whether the contents of the message are valid or malicious. By using PKI, you can enhance e-mail security by using certificates to prove the identity of the sender, the origination of the mail, and the authenticity of the message. It also makes it possible to encrypt mail.

Internet Authentication

An increasing number of malicious applications, ActiveX controls, and Java applets are being downloaded and installed on computers with little or no user interaction. Authenticode technology allows software publishers to digitally sign active content. These signatures can then be used to verify both the publishers of the content and the content integrity at time of download. Authenticode relies on a certification authority structure in which a small number of commercial certificate authorities (CAs) issue software-publishing certificates.

Software Code Signing

The Internet is a key element in the growth of electronic commerce but security impacts how much and what kinds of information users are willing to share across the Internet. For Internet transactions to be secure, the data that is transferred needs to be encrypted and clients need a way to verify the identity of the servers they are communicating with. Using cryptographic signatures and certificates, clients and servers can more securely verify identities, establishing a security context to determine what resources the client is allowed or not allowed to use on the server.

IP Security

Remember from Chapter 7 that IPSec is a suite of protocols that allows encrypted and/or digitally signed communication, depending on the needs of the organization. IPSec can provide end-to-end security or provide security to and from selected gateways. IPSec provides end-to-end security by encrypting or signing the packets so that they can be decrypted only by the recipient entity. If you use public key technology in conjunction with IPSec, you can create a more scalable distributed trust architecture in which IPSec devices can mutually authenticate each other, yielding a higher level of security than IPSec without a PKI.

Smart Card Logon

Smart cards enhance the security of your organization by allowing you to store extremely strong credentials. Having a physical **smart card** for authentication can virtually eliminate the potential for spoofing the identities of your users across a network. Using smart cards for logon is one of the most persuasive reasons for implementing a PKI. When smart card logon is enabled, the system recognizes the smart card insertion as a means to initiate a logon. The user is then prompted for the smart card PIN code, which controls access by using the private key stored on the smart card. The smart card also contains a copy of the certificate of the user. You can also use smart card applications in combination with virtual private networks, in certificate mapping, and in e-commerce.

Encrypted File Systems

An **Encrypted File System (EFS)** allows users and services to encrypt their data. This prevents the data from being viewed, and it provides for data recovery should another means be needed to access this data. EFS allows recovery agents to configure public keys that can be used to enable file recovery. You do not need to have a PKI to use EFS, but the use of public keys improves the manageability of EFS. While EFS does require certificates to exist for the user encrypting the file or folder and will, if necessary, issue a certificates to the user, in a Windows domain environment, it is recommended that EFS be used in conjunction with a PKI.

802.1x Authentication

A growing number of facilities such as coffee shops and retail stores are implementing wireless network access. This creates the challenge of ensuring that only authenticated users can access the wireless network and the data transmitted across the wireless network cannot be intercepted. PKIs combined with the IEEE 802.1x standard provide centralized user identification, authentication, and dynamic key management for network access to 802.11 wireless networks and to wired Ethernet networks.

PLANNING PKI GROUP STRUCTURE

The status of a public key certificate is determined by way of a process called chain building. **Chain building** is the creation of a trust chain, or certification path, from the end certificate to a root CA that is trusted by the security principal. Before that trust chain or certification path can be built, you need to identify the categories of users, computers, and services that will use these certificate services. Certificate use might be based on job function, location, organizational structure, or a combination of all three. Therefore, the Active Directory structure should be evaluated.

Deciding Which Types of Groups to Use

A large part of Windows Server 2003 is based on Active Directory. When creating your Active Directory architecture, you must carefully consider the various types of boundaries defined such as the forest, domain, site topology, and permission delegation. Although these boundaries are automatically established during Active Directory installation, the permission boundaries have to be reviewed and changed to meet the organizational requirements and policies. The object of designing Active Directory is to create a securely structured organization that can grow without having to redesign the layout unless there are major changes to the environment, such as a merger or acquisition. It is by these structured boundaries that your group organization will be established. In order to keep a proper balance between security and administrative functions, permission delegation boundaries can be broken down further into security boundaries and administrative boundaries.

Security boundaries help define the independence or separation of different groups within an organization. The forest is the true security boundary. Microsoft recommends creating separate forests rather than separate domains. This arrangement keeps your environment secure from rogue administrators and other potential threats. A domain is the management boundary of Active Directory. The domain boundary will provide contained management of services and data within each domain of the organization.

In addition to the security boundaries established, your organization may need to consider dividing the administrative control of services and data within the current Active Directory design. These are called **administrative boundaries**. You must determine the different administrative levels required. At this point, you may want to consider what types of administrators you will need. Generally, the administrators can fall into one of two categories:

- *Service administrators*—Service administrators are responsible for configuring and delivering the directory service.

- *Data administrators*—Data administrators are responsible for managing data stored in Active Directory or on computers joined to Active Directory.

Creating groups gives administrators a way to segment specific groups of users, security groups, or servers into containers for administration. When you create an Active Directory group, you can define it as either a security or a distribution group. **Security groups** can be assigned permissions to resources through access control entries (ACEs). User rights are applied to security groups to determine what members of that group can do within the scope of a domain or forest. Be aware that user rights are automatically assigned to some security groups at the time that Active Directory is installed. For example, a user who is added to the Backup Operators group has the ability to back up and restore files and directories located on each domain controller in the domain.

Distribution groups are used for membership purposes only. These are actually an extension of Microsoft Exchange distribution lists. Distribution groups are not security-enabled, meaning that they cannot be listed in discretionary access control lists (DACLs). If you need a group for controlling access to shared resources, create a security group. Security groups can be members of distribution groups, but distribution groups cannot be members of security groups. A group can be converted from a security group to a distribution group, and vice versa, only if the domain functional level is set to Windows 2000 native or higher. We will discuss domain functional level in the section on nested groups.

NOTE

A security group can also be used as an e-mail entity. Even though it is a security group, it can be used as a distribution group. This does not work the other way around; a distribution group cannot be used as a security group.

In Windows 2000 and Windows Server 2003, you can assign management of a group to a group if you understand how to use the Active Directory Service Interfaces (ADSI) edit tool to change the value of the Managed By attribute, and you know the permissions to set. In Windows Server 2003, the Managed By tab in Active Directory Users and Computers includes a new check box that lets the group manager update group membership. You will work with this check box in the next activity.

ACTIVITY

Activity 9-1: Creating Security and Distribution Groups

Time Required: 45 minutes

Objective: Learn the difference between security and distribution groups by creating one of each type of group. You will then allow the manager to update each the group list.

Description: In this activity, you create both a security and a distribution group and allow the manager to update the group list.

1. Log on with your **AdminXX** account, where *XX* is your assigned student number.

2. Go to **Start**, **All Programs**, **Administrative Tools**, **Active Directory Users and Computers**.

3. Expand your domain. Right-click the **Member Servers** container, choose **New**, **Group**.

4. In the Group name box, type **Testers**, then set the Group Scope to **Domain local**. Verify that the Security radio button is selected for the Group type.

5. Click **OK**. Select the Member Servers container on the left side of the screen. The group should now appear in the right side of the screen, as shown in Figure 9-1.

6. Right-click the **Testers** group, then choose **Properties**. On the General tab, in the Description box, type **This is the local domain software testers group**. Select the Members tab, then click **Add**. On the Select Users, Contacts, Computers or Groups screen, click the **Advanced** button. Under Common Queries, click **Find Now**. All the users and groups are now shown in the bottom list box.

7. Select **Administrator**. While holding down the **CTRL** key, find your account and select that one as well. Click **OK**.

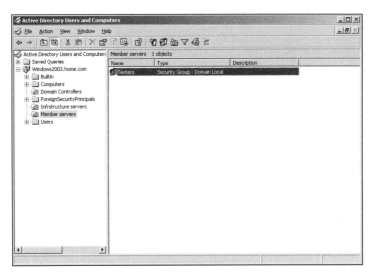

Figure 9-1   Creating a security group

8. On the Select Users, Contacts, Computers or Groups screen, click **OK**.

9. Click the **Managed By** tab. Click the **Change** button. On the Select User or Contact screen, click on the **Advanced** button. Under Common Queries, click **Find Now**. All the users and groups are now shown in the bottom list box.

10. Choose the **Administrator** account, then click **OK**. On the Select User or Contact screen, click **OK**. Check the **Manager can update membership list** box. Click **Apply**. Click **OK**.

11. Expand your domain. Right-click the **Member Servers** container, then choose **New**, **Group**.

12. In the Group name box, type **QA Testers** and verify that the group scope is set to **Global**. Change the radio button for the group type to **Distribution**. Set the group scope to Universal.

13. Click **OK**. The group should now appear in the right side of the screen, as shown in Figure 9-2.

14. Select, then right-click the **QATesters** group, then choose **Properties**. On the General tab, in the Description box, type **This is the global QATesters distribution group**. In the E-mail box, type **QATesters@Windows2003.com**.

15. Select the Members tab, then click **Add**. On the Select Users, Contacts, Computers or Groups screen, click the **Advanced** button. Under Common Queries, click **Find Now**. All the users and groups are now shown in the bottom list box.

16. Select **Administrator**. While holding down the **CTRL** key, find your account and select that one as well. Click **OK**.

17. On the Select User, Contacts, Computers or Groups screen, click **OK**.

9

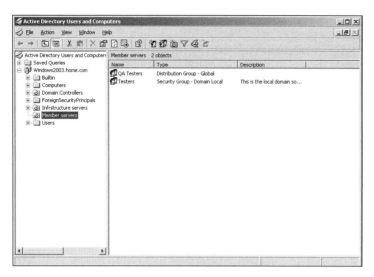

Figure 9-2   Creating a distribution group

18. Click the **Managed By** tab. Click the **Change** button. On the Select Users or Contact screen, click the **Advanced** button. Under Common Queries, click **Find Now**. All the users and groups are now shown in the bottom list box.

19. Choose the **Administrator account**, then click **OK**. On the Select User or Contact screen, click **OK**. Check the **Manager can update membership list** box. Click **Apply**. Click **OK**.

20. Close the **Active Directory Users and Computers** window.

Planning Security Group Scope

Groups are distinguished by their scope and type. The **group scope** determines the level to which the group is applied within a domain or forest. There are three group scopes: universal, global, and domain local. The **group type** determines whether a group can be used to assign permissions from a shared resource for security groups or if a group can be used for e-mail distribution lists only for distribution groups.

Beginning with Windows 2000, Microsoft added hierarchical abilities to the group concept by allowing nesting. Group nesting will be discussed in further detail in the next section. Nesting allows one group to contain other groups in its scope of authority. A group's scope dictates who can be a member of the group and what resources the group has access to, and the domain or forest functional level will affect which group scopes can be used.

Members of universal groups can include other groups and accounts from any domain in the domain tree or forest and can be assigned permissions in any domain in the domain tree or forest. Members of global groups can include other groups and accounts only from the domain in which the group is defined and can be assigned permissions in any domain in the forest. Members of domain local groups can include other groups and accounts from Windows 2003, Windows 2000, or Windows NT domains and can be assigned permissions only within a domain.

Domain and forest functionality levels are new to Windows Server 2003 Active Directory. If you have experience in Windows 2000, recall that you could set a server to run in either mixed mode or native mode. This concept has been built upon in Windows 2003 and allows different levels of domain functionality and forest functionality, depending on your environment. If all domain controllers in your domain or forest are running Windows Server 2003, you can set the functional level to Windows Server 2003, which allows all functional features. If Windows NT 4.0 or Windows 2000 domain controllers are included in your domain or forest with domain controllers running Windows Server 2003, these features are limited and the domain functionality must be set accordingly. Domain controllers running Windows 2000 Server are unaware of domain and forest functionality. Four domain functional levels are available: Windows 2000 mixed, which is the default; Windows 2000 native; Windows Server 2003 interim; and Windows Server 2003. By default, domains operate at the Windows 2000 mixed functional level.

Table 9-1 lists the group scopes and describes how they work under certain domain functionality levels.

Table 9-1 Group Scope Functionality

Domain Functionality	Domain Local Scope	Global Scope	Universal Scope
Domain functional level set to Windows 2000 Native or Windows 2003	Members of domain local scope can include accounts, global groups, and universal groups from any domain, as well as domain local groups from the same domain.	Members of global groups can include accounts and global groups from the same domain.	Members of universal groups can include accounts, global groups, and universal groups from any domain.
Domain functional level set to Windows 2000 mixed	Members of domain local scope can include accounts, global groups from any domain as well as domain local groups from the same domain.	Members of global groups can include accounts from the same domain.	Security groups with universal scope cannot be created.

The following list gives you some guidelines on when to use which types of groups.

- *Groups with domain local scope*—Groups with domain local scope are used to define and manage access to resources within a single domain.

- *Groups with global scope*—Groups with global scope are used for daily maintenance objects, such as user and computer accounts. Groups with global scope are not replicated outside of their own domain so these types of accounts can be changed frequently without generating replication traffic to the global catalog.

- *Groups with universal scope*—Groups with universal scope are used to manage groups that cross domains. Group membership of universal scope should not change frequently, because changes cause the entire membership of the group to be replicated to every global catalog in the forest. Do not put users directly in universal groups.

Planning Nested Group Structure

Placing every account into a single organizational resource group is not an effective solution because it requires the creation and maintenance of a large number of membership links. **Nested groups** allow you to provide access to resources with very little maintenance. Security group nesting occurs when one security group is made a member of another security group. The nested group inherits all of the privileges and permissions that are granted to the parent. The purpose of nested groups is to consolidate group management by lowering the number of times permissions are granted and the replication traffic that is caused by group membership changes. Nesting options depend on the domain functionality level. If your domain is operating at the Windows 2000 mixed functional level, then you can add global groups only to local groups. When the domain is operating at the Windows Server 2003 functional level, you can nest global groups within other global groups. This allows greater flexibility in managing security groups.

To use nested groups, administrators typically create a hierarchy that contains several account groups that represent the managerial divisions of the organization. This could start at the top with a generic group such as employees. The next level might contain groups that represent major divisions of the organization such as administration, management, and so on. The groups at this level would also be members of the employees group but would have additional access to shares and other resources appropriate to the division it represents. Within a division, the next level might represent departments. Within a department, the structure can be organized into additional security groups as required. With a nested group hierarchy such as this, you can give a new employee immediate access to the resources required by placing that person in a specific group.

Recall that there are four domain functional levels available: Windows 2000 mixed, which is the default; Windows 2000 native; Windows Server 2003 interim, which is available only when upgrading Windows NT Server to Windows Server 2003; and Windows Server 2003. Your nesting options depend on which domain functional level your Windows Server 2003 domain is set to. Security groups in a Windows 2000 mixed domain are restricted. A domain must be configured at the Windows 2000 native or Windows Server 2003 functional level for global groups to be nested within global groups or for domain local groups to be nested within domain local groups.

NOTE Security groups with universal scope cannot be created in mixed mode because universal scope is supported only in domains in which the functional level is set to native mode or 2003 mode.

The default group membership limitation is 120 groups. A user's Kerberos access token is built primarily from the security identifiers (SIDs) of the groups to which the user belongs. Because this token contains the security identifiers (SIDs) for each group of which the user is a member, uncontrolled group nesting may result in access token size problems. It is important that you keep the nesting of groups under control and that there be some type of policy in place as to how deep nesting can go. If there is not a nesting policy in place, it becomes difficult to know exactly which permissions members of nested groups might inherit. Although there may be concerns with the number of groups a user can be a member of, there aren't any limitations as to the number of users in a group.

Table 9-2 provides a recap of the domain functionality level features.

Table 9-2 Domain Functionality Level Features

Feature	Windows 2000 Mixed	Windows 2000 Native and Windows Server 2003
Creation of universal groups	Available for distribution groups only	Allows both security and distribution groups
Group nesting	Available for distribution groups and domain local groups, which can contain global groups	Allows full group nesting
Converting groups	No group conversions allowed	Allows for conversion between security groups and distribution groups
SID history	No SID history migration	Allows for migration of security principals from one domain to another

In addition to domain functionality, the forest functionality level can be set. Forest functionality enables features across all the domains within your forest. Three forest functional levels are available: Windows 2000, which is the default; Windows Server 2003 interim; and Windows Server 2003. By default, forests operate at the Windows 2000 functional level, which then can be raised to Windows Server 2003. The Windows Server 2003 interim level is used when your first Windows NT 4.0 domain becomes the first domain in a new Windows Server 2003 forest.

CAUTION Once the forest functional level has been raised, domain controllers running earlier operating systems cannot be introduced into the forest. Domain controllers running Windows 2000 Server cannot be added to the forest if the functional level to set to Windows Server 2003.

PLANNING AUTHENTICATION

One of the most essential parts of an organization's security strategy is verifying the identity of clients and granting them appropriate access to resources based on that identity. You can prevent attackers and malicious users from accessing sensitive information by creating a stringent authentication strategy for your organization. This involves evaluating your existing infrastructure and establishing standards for network authentication based upon user needs.

Before establishing an authentication strategy for your organization, become familiar with your current environment. This includes how the organization is structured; what users, computers, and services require authentication; and what applications and services are in use. In order to help you with this, Microsoft has created an Authentication Strategy Planning sheet. It is called DDSAUT_1.doc and can be found by downloading the Job Aids Designing and Deploying Directory and Security Services.zip file at: *www.microsoft.com/downloads/ details.aspx?FamilyID=edabb894-4290-406c-87d1-607a58fc81f0&DisplayLang=en#filelist* or going to *www.microsoft.com/windowsserver2003/techinfo/reskit/deploykit.mspx* and clicking the Job Aids for the Windows Server 2003 Deployment Kit. If you choose not to use the planning sheet, be sure that you take the following into consideration when planning authentication for your environment:

- The number of domain controllers needed to accommodate your users' authentication requests

- The type of network connectivity between site locations that could affect the ability of users to authenticate

- The location of CAs that are available for certificate validation and issuance

- The number of users, groups, and computers within the organization and where the computers are located

- The number of clients and servers that are running versions of Windows earlier than Windows 2000 or other operating systems

- The number and locations of mobile users or business partners who access the network

- The number and location of smart card users currently in your organization and an estimate of how many might require smart cards in the future

If your environment includes more than one forest, or if your organization needs to share information with other Kerberos clients and servers, you'll need to support those relationships and resources. Do this by establishing trust relationships and by creating Active Directory accounts as appropriate.

Trust Relationships

Since an authentication strategy may entail securing communication across domains, it is important that you understand how trusts work in Windows 2003. Although you should be familiar with trust relationships by now, we will do a quick review and create one in an activity to refresh your memory. Communication between domains occurs through trusts. **Trusts** are authentication mediums that allow users in one domain to access resources in another domain. By default, two-way, transitive trusts are created in a Windows Server 2003 forest. A **two-way trust** is a trust relationship between two domains in which both domains trust each other. A **transitive trust** is a trust relationship that passes throughout a group of domains, forming a relationship between one domain and all other domains that trust that domain. All parent-child trusts are two-way, transitive trusts. The default two-way, transitive trusts that exist are between domains within the same tree or between trees in a forest and the forest root. Transitive trusts are required for Kerberos-based authentication and Active Directory replication.

In addition to the default trust types created, four other types of trusts can be created using the New Trust Wizard or the Netdom command-line tool. These trusts are as follows:

External—This is a nontransitive, one- or two-way trust used to provide access to resources located on a Windows NT 4.0 domain or a domain located in a separate forest that is not joined by a forest trust.

Realm—This trust is used to form a trust relationship between a non-Windows Kerberos realm and a Windows Server 2003 domain. It can be either transitive or nontransitive and one-way or two-way. A realm trust is used for cross-platform interoperability with other Kerberos V5 versions such as *UNIX* and MIT implementations.

Forest—This is a transitive, one- or two-way trust used to share resources between forests. If each forest trust is a two-way trust, authentication requests made in either forest can reach the other forest. Forest trusts are useful for organizations during mergers or acquisitions. They can also be used for business extranets.

Shortcut—This is a transitive, one- or two-way trust used to improve user logon times between two domains within a forest. Shortcut trusts may be necessary when many users in a domain regularly log on to other domains in a forest. Essentially, a shortcut trust shortens the authentication route traveled between domains located in two separate trees.

Each trust relationship within a particular domain is represented by trusted domain objects (TDOs). Whenever a trust is established, a unique TDO is created and stored in the System container within its domain. A TDO contains attributes such as the trust transitivity, type, and reciprocal domain names. Forest trust TDOs store additional attributes to identify all of the trusted namespaces from the partner forest.

Activity 9-2: Creating a Realm Trust

Time Required: 25 minutes

Objective: Use the New Trust Wizard to review the difference between the various types of trusts and create a trust.

Description: In this activity, you will check the domain functionality level and create a one-way, nontransitive, realm trust. Note: When entering the password in this exercise, the operating system will require a strong password and will reject the entry otherwise.

1. Log on with your **AdminXX** account, where *XX* is your assigned student number.

2. Go to **Start**, **All Programs**, **Administrative Tools**, **Active Directory Domains and Trusts**.

3. Right-click your domain, then choose **Properties**. On the General tab, make note of the Domain functional level and the Forest functional level.

4. Select the **Trusts** tab. Choose the **New Trust** button. The Welcome to the New Trust Wizard should open, as shown in Figure 9-3.

Figure 9-3 Creating a New Trust Wizard

5. Click **Next**. In the Name box on the Trust Name screen, type **Production**.

6. Click **Next**. On the Trust Type screen, under Trust Type it should say that the name is not a valid Windows domain and ask if it is a Kerberos V5 realm. Choose the **Realm trust** radio button in the Select the appropriate trust type area.

7. Click **Next**. On the Transitivity of Trust screen, choose the **Nontransitive** radio button. Click **Next**.

8. On the Direction of Trust screen, select the **One-way incoming** radio button. Click **Next**.

9. On the Trust Password screen, type a password of your choice in the Trust password box. Type the same password in the Confirm trust password box. Note: the password will need to be complex or you will be prompted to enter another password. Click **Next**.

10. Review your choices to be sure that everything is correct on the Trust Selections Complete screen. Click **Next**.

11. The Completing the New Trust Wizard screen will appear, and you should have a yellow warning telling you that before the trust can function, it must also be created in the other domain.

12. Click **Finish**. The trust you just created should appear in the Domains that trust this domain box, as shown in Figure 9-4.

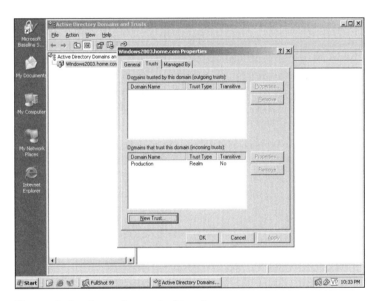

Figure 9-4   A newly created trust

13. Click **OK**. Close the **Active Directory Domains and Trusts** window.

Authentication Protocols

Authentication verifies that an individual or object is who or what it claims to be. Whenever a client requests access to a server, an authentication protocol is used to validate the identity of the client to the server. A domain controller running Windows Server 2003 authenticates users and applications using one of either Kerberos V5 or **NT LAN Manager (NTLM)**. Kerberos is the default authentication method for Windows 2000 Server and Windows Server 2003. With Kerberos, the client must prove its identity to the server, and the server must also prove its identity to the client. This is referred to as **mutual authentication**. Kerberos can be used only with Microsoft Windows 2000 Professional clients or later. When clients require authentication across domains, the client requests a ticket from a domain controller in its account domain to the server in the trusting domain. A Kerberos ticket contains both encrypted and unencrypted information, including an encrypted password that confirms the user's identity to the requested service. This ticket is issued by an intermediary trusted by the client and the server. The client presents this trusted ticket to the server in the trusting domain for authentication.

You should use Kerberos when all of your clients can be authenticated using Kerberos and when you want to use a method that requires the least administrative effort. If any computer involved in a transaction does not support Kerberos V5, the NTLM protocol will be used. NTLM is a challenge/response authentication and was the default authentication protocol for earlier versions of Windows. When a client tries to access resources on a server in another domain using NTLM authentication, the server containing the resource must contact a domain controller in the client account domain to verify the account's credentials. The NTLM2 protocol can be used for Windows 95, Windows 98, or Windows 98 Second Edition clients. The LAN Manager protocol was used for early Microsoft operating systems. You can use the LAN Manager Authentication Level to set a level that specifies whether certain authentication protocols are available for network communication. This is done by setting the value of the LM Compatibility Level in the registry.

 NOTE If you use Registry Editor incorrectly, you may cause serious problems that may require you to reinstall your operating system. Use the Registry Editor with extreme caution.

Figure 9-5 shows where you edit the setting. The valid range for the value is 0–5.

The following list describes each of the values of the LMCompatibilityLevel key and how they are used for authentication:

- *Level 0*—This setting allows clients to use LM and NTLM authentication, and never use NTLM 2 session security. Domain controllers accept LM, NTLM, and NTLM 2 authentication.

- *Level 1*—This setting allows clients to use LM and NTLM authentication, and use NTLM 2 session security if the server supports it. Domain controllers accept LM, NTLM, and NTLM 2 authentication.

- *Level 2*—Using this setting, the clients use only NTLM authentication, and use NTLM 2 session security if the server supports it. Domain controllers accept LM, NTLM, and NTLM 2 authentication.

- *Level 3*—Under this setting, clients use NTLM 2 authentication, and use NTLM 2 session security if the server supports it. Domain controllers accept LM, NTLM, and NTLM 2 authentication.

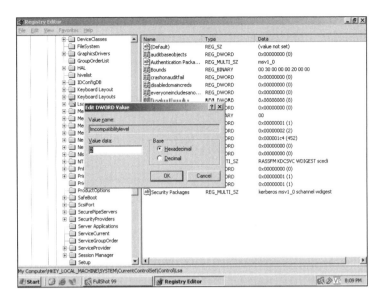

Figure 9-5   Setting NTLM authentication

- *Level 4*—This setting allows clients to use NTLM authentication, and use NTLM 2 session security if the server supports it. Domain controllers accept only NTLM and NTLM 2.

- *Level 5*—With this setting, clients use NTLM 2 authentication and NTLM 2 session security if the server supports it. Domain controllers accept only NTLM 2 and refuse LM and NTLM responses.

Due to advances in password-cracking tools and hardware capabilities, LAN Manager authentication encryption is more susceptible to attack than newer forms of encryption. Therefore, it is important to restrict the use of LAN Manager authentication whenever possible. If you must support LAN Manager authentication, you can increase network security by enabling support of NTLMv2 whenever possible.

Multifactor Authentication

Multifactor authentication is one of the most popular methods to increase the reliability of authentication. It works on the premise that a user can prove his identity in three ways as follows:

Something he or she knows—For example, a password or a personal identification number (PIN) for a smart card can be used.

Something he or she has—For example, the possession of the smart card itself can be used.

Something he or she is—For example, a fingerprint or retinal scan can be used.

Multifactor authentication is the combining of two or even three of these factors for proof of identification. The advantage of this method is that it is more secure than authentication from a single factor. The only disadvantage is that it is less convenient for the user who has to provide the additional methods of authentication. This type of authentication is used with smart cards. A smart card contains a public key certificate. In order to unlock the certificate, the user must supply a password or PIN. This combination makes it much more difficult for an attacker to gain access to network resources. In order to decide whether smart card authentication is appropriate for your organization, take the following items into consideration:

- *Cost*—There is an initial cost for the purchase of smart cards and smart card readers, as well as administrative costs for preparing and distributing the cards.

- *Infrastructure*—Since PKI is required for smart card authentication, the internal infrastructure must be able to support this type of authentication.

- *Administrative overhead*—Smart cards cannot be replaced easily if lost or forgotten.

- *Remote connections*—Users might experience longer logon times when they use smart cards, especially over slow dial-up connections.

Many organizations choose to deploy smart cards only to administrators or users who have access to extremely sensitive data because of the equipment costs and administrative overhead.

Authentication for Web Users

Many organizations share data with business partners, customers, and suppliers through the use of extranets. Extranets are quickly becoming a primary means of communication among companies that work together. This of course also opens up the organization to malicious activity. To ensure that the network and the users' credentials are protected, select the strongest authentication method possible. The authentication methods that you select will depend on the operating system of clients accessing your Web servers and the method you choose to protect the users' credentials.

The following authentication methods are used for Web site authentication:

- *Anonymous authentication*—Allows anonymous users the right to log on locally. This method provides a great deal of flexibility and allows you to set up different anonymous accounts for different Web sites, virtual directories, directories, and files.

- *Basic authentication*—Supported by most Web servers and Web browsers. Users must enter credentials, allowing you to track access based on the user ID. This method is commonly used when you cannot guarantee that the user's browser supports integrated Windows authentication, and you must authenticate the user through a proxy server.

- *Digest authentication*—This method does not send the password in cleartext and can be used through proxy servers.

- *Advanced Digest authentication*—A newer version of Digest authentication that was introduced with Windows XP Professional, where the client uses a hash of the password.

- *Integrated Windows authentication*—Primarily used for intranet situations, either NTLM authentication or Kerberos authentication and the current credentials of the logged on user are used to authenticate to the Web server.

- *Certificate authentication*—Used to allow both servers and clients to authenticate each other.

In addition to authentication, you can also encrypt the data that is transferred between the client and the Web server. Based on the type of client that might access the Web server, Secure Sockets Layer (SSL), IPSec, or a virtual private network (VPN) can be used. SSL and VPNs are discussed in the next chapter. The rule of thumb when planning for these methods is that SSL is used when the client computers are not a part of your organization, and you want to avoid installing any files on the client computers. IPSec is used when you are creating an intranet or an extranet and the client computers are a part of your organization or a partner's organization. When using IPSec, certificates may be installed on the client computers, so they should have high-speed persistent connections to your private network. A VPN is used similarly to IPSec, except that the client computers are connecting over direct or dial-up Internet connections instead of directly to your network.

Some organizations may require more advanced authentication solutions to meet their user access needs. Often Web-based clients use browser applications to access data stored on back-end servers. In these instances, you must plan and implement more complex authentication strategies, such as delegation, constrained delegation, and protocol transfer, to allow those clients to access the requested services in a secure manner.

Delegated Authentication

Delegated authentication occurs when a network service accepts a request from a user then assumes that user's identity in order to initiate a new connection to a second network service. In this case, front-end servers, such as Web servers are responsible for handling client requests, and back-end servers such as large databases are responsible for storing information. This works by establishing a service or computer as trusted for delegation, that service or computer receives a ticket for the user making the request, and then the service or computer accesses the information the user requested. Requiring that all data be accessed through credentials that are delegated to the server on behalf of the client ensures that the server cannot be compromised and then used to gain access to information on other servers. Delegated authentication is useful on applications where Internet Information Services (IIS) supports a Web interface to a database running on another computer. An example of this would be Web enrollment support pages for an enterprise certification authority when the pages are installed on a separate Web server.

To delegate this right, assign the Enable computer and user accounts to be trusted for delegation user right to the selected individuals. Users who are assigned the right to enable delegated authentication can assign the Trusted for delegation right to computer and service accounts that are used to serve users information that is stored on back-end servers that must be accessed securely.

The user account that is requesting the resource must not be marked as sensitive because this denies the right to delegation.

CAUTION

Microsoft recommends that you deny the right to participate in delegated authentication for computers that are not physically secure. Because domain administrator accounts have access to sensitive resources, it is also recommended that you deny the right to participate in delegated authentication for these accounts as well.

Another method of delegation is constrained delegation. Constrained delegation allows administrators to specify particular services from which a computer that is trusted for delegation can request resources. Before you enable constrained delegation, separate critical data that must be kept secure from data that requires frequent access. For example, if your organization maintains an e-commerce Web site, isolate customer credit cards numbers and internal billing information from order status information that customers access frequently.

To help in planning with this type of authentication, Microsoft has created a Supplemental Authentication Strategies document. It is called DSSAUT_4.doc and can be found by downloading the Job Aids Designing and Deploying Directory and Security Services. zip file at: *www.microsoft.com/downloads/details.aspx?FamilyID=edabb894-4290-406c-87d1-607a58fc81f0&DisplayLang=en#filelist* or going to *www.microsoft.com/windowsserver2003/techinfo/reskit/deploykit.mspx* and clicking the Job Aids for the Windows Server 2003 Deployment Kit.

Activity 9-3: Delegating Authentication

Time Required: 25 minutes

ACTIVITY

Objective: Learn how to restrict delegated authentication and enable delegation.

Description: In this activity, you will learn how to restrict delegated authentication and enable delegation.

1. Log on with your **AdminXX** account, where *XX* is your assigned student number.

2. Go to **Start**, **All Programs**, **Administrative Tools**, **Active Directory Users and Computers**, expand the **Users** folder, right-click the **Administrator account**, and select **Properties**.

3. On the **Account** tab, under **Account options**, select the **Account is sensitive and cannot be delegated** check box, as shown in Figure 9-6.

4. Click **OK**.

5. In **Active Directory Users and Computers**, double-click the Domain Controllers folder.

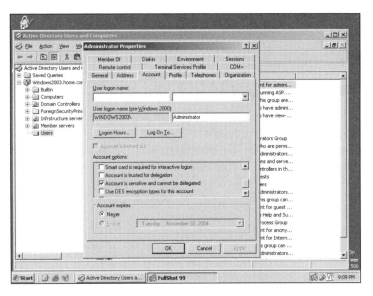

Figure 9-6   Restricting delegated authentication

6. Right-click the server computer account on the right side of the screen and select **Properties**.

7. On the **General** tab, select **Trust computer for delegation**.

8. Click **OK**.

9. Close the **Active Directory Users and Computers** window.

PLANNING AUTHORIZATION

Authorization is the process of verifying that an authenticated party has the permission to access a particular resource. This is the layer of security control following authentication. When a user logs on, that user does not automatically have access to the resources he or she requires. Users must be authorized to access resources. You want to be sure the users have access to what they need, but only at the level they need. Often a large group of users has the same need for access to a network resource. For example, all users in the financial department might need access to a specific high-speed printer. You can easily manage access by putting every member of the financial department into a security group that is authorized to access that printer. Security groups are crucial to proficiently controlling access, and they will be the main component of your authorization strategy. Before moving on, be sure you understand what security groups are and how they should be used. Prior to designing a resource authorization strategy, you also need to be familiar with trust relationships, domain and forest functional levels, and some basic security principles, which we have already covered. When planning authorization methods for your environment, you must also consider policies for security group management, including who is allowed to create security groups, and how they are named, nested, and administered. By applying this information appropriately to your organization, you can design a resource authorization strategy that is scalable, easy to maintain, and cost-effective.

Configuring Access Control Lists (ACL)

You can select one of several resource authorization methods to enable users to access shared resources in your organization. It is important to select the method that is the most appropriate for the environment and for the specific resource to be accessed. Depending on the needs of your organization, you can choose to apply any or all of the following authorization methods:

- User/ACL method
- Account group/ACL (AG/ACL) method
- Account group/resource group (AG/RG) method
- Role-based method

When using the User/ACL method, the resource owner adds security principal accounts directly to the resource ACL. The ACL is then configured to allow permissions for each security principal.In other words, the user creates a share and then determines who has access to it. Keep in mind the differences between share permissions and NTFS permissions. Remember that a shared resource refers to any resource that is made available to network users, such as folders, files, and printers. You can control access to shared resources with a variety of methods. You can use share permissions that restrict a shared resource's availability over the network to only certain users. These are simple to apply and manage. Or, you can use access control, which is a security mechanism that determines which operations a user, group, service, or computer is authorized to perform on the NTFS file system.

This might work for small organizations with few users and little resources. However, this approach does not scale well and is impractical for larger organizations because access to resources is inconsistent from one user to the next, and there is no way to know which resources a user has access to without extensive tracking.

With the Account group/ACL method, security groups are added to the resource ACL. The access permissions are then set for the groups. The Account group/ACL method is a more scalable solution because security groups can be nested. If groups from multiple domains or from multiple forests require the same permissions, they can be grouped together in one security group, and you can add this security group to the resource ACL. This can create more administrative overhead if access is unique to resources for just a few individuals, thus creating a greater number of groups.

The Account group/resource group method is used when users with similar access needs are grouped into account groups, and the account groups are added to a resource group that is granted specific resource access permissions. This method is most suitable for large organizations with many shared resources. It is scalable and can be maintained in various environments and at various domain functional levels. It is most useful when you cannot nest groups because your domains are at Windows 2000 mixed functional levels.

With role-based authorization, users with similar roles are authorized to perform predefined tasks. This allows you to apply granular control over access based on the tasks performed in your organization. To use role-based authorization, your environment must be operating at the Windows Server 2003 domain functional level.

Planning the Assignment of User Rights

The assignment of user rights is a security option that applies to user accounts. User rights define capacity at the local level. The user rights assignment is twofold: it can grant specific privileges and it can grant logon rights to users and groups in your computing environment. Logon rights control who and how users log on to the computer, such as the right to log on to a system locally, whereas privileges allow users to perform system tasks such as the right to back up files and directories. Although user rights can apply to individual user accounts, they are best administered by using group accounts. Keep in mind that privileges and permissions are different and sometimes privileges can override permissions set on an object. For example, a user logged on to a domain account as a member of the Backup Operators group has the right to restore files and folders. This requires the capability to read files on which their owners may have set permissions that explicitly deny access to all users. The user right assignment allows the backup operator to bypass file and directory permissions when restoring backed-up files and directories.

NOTE Windows Server 2003 has three built-in local accounts used as logon accounts for different services: Local System, Local Service, and Network Service. These accounts are used by system processes, should never have a user assignment, and should not have the default setting changed.

Planning the Requirements for Digital Signatures

Digital signatures are used to ensure message integrity and authenticity. The process of digitally signing information involves transforming the information along with some secret information held by the sender, into a tag called a signature. A process called a hash function is used in both creating and verifying a digital signature. A hash function is an algorithm that creates a digital representation or fingerprint in the form of a hash value. Any change to the message produces a different hash result when the same hash function is used. The use of digital signatures involves two processes, one performed by the signer and the other by the receiver of the digital signature. In essence a digital signature is actually the encrypted hash, decrypted by the recipient, and then compared to the hash calculated by the recipient that provides message integrity and authenticity.

A digital signature is used to make sure the data has not been altered since it was signed and confirms the identity of the person or entity who has signed the data. Digital signatures use public key cryptography, which employs an algorithm using two different keys, one for creating a digital signature and another for verifying the signature. To verify a digital signature, the verifier must have access to the signer's public key and have assurance that it corresponds to the signer's private key. In order to use digital signatures, the organization must have PKI in place.

Should your organization require implementation of digital signatures, your planning process should take the following into consideration:

- Interoperablity with PKI-generated certificates
- Security and cost
- How the signing and verifying process will work
- How the signature data will be stored
- Performance issues

PLANNING, BUILDING, AND MANAGING CERTIFICATION AUTHORITY HIERARCHIES

Once you identify the certificate requirements for your organization and have identified the categories of users, computers, and services that will use certificate services, you can plan how they will be authorized and authenticated. Once this is accomplished, you can begin to look at configuring certificates and certification authorities (CAs), developing support procedures, and establishing a system of checks and balances for administrative authority of your PKI. To support the certificate-based needs of your organization, you must establish a structure of CAs that are responsible for issuing, validating, renewing, and revoking certificates as needed. In doing so, decisions will have to be made about the location of the root certification authorities, whether to use internal or third-party certificates, and the number, type, and roles of the CAs.

Certification Authority Hierarchies and Roles

A single Windows Server 2003 computer with Certificate Services installed can be used to issue certificates for multiple purposes on your network, but best practices dictate that you should use a hierarchy of certificate servers that trust one another and authenticate certificates belonging to one another. Within this infrastructure, a final authority, called a **root CA**, certifies other certification authorities to publish and manage certificates within the organization. There are different types of hierarchies and roles that can be used for CAs. Here are three types of hierarchical models that can be used:

- *Rooted trust model*—In a rooted trust model, a CA is either a root or a subordinate. You can use offline root CAs for the highest level of security.
- *Cross-certification trust model*—In a cross-certification trust model, every CA is both a root and a subordinate.

- *Hybrid trust model*—Hybrid trust models combine elements of both the rooted and cross-certification trust models.

In addition to a hierarchy, you may choose either an **enterprise CA**, which is integrated with Active Directory or a **standalone CA**. Enterprise CAs use certificate templates. When a certificate is issued, the enterprise CA uses information in the certificate template to produce a certificate with the proper attributes for that certificate type.

When you employ a CA hierarchy, the best practice is to use a standalone root CA. This enables you to keep the standalone CA offline and physically protected in a locked vault. You should avoid the use of an offline enterprise CA because it cannot maintain its integration with Active Directory when offline so it would never be up to date. If you have a root CA that is kept offline, it is secure against any type of attack, so its certificates cannot be compromised. You can always bring it online for only the brief interval needed to issue certificates for intermediate or issuing CAs when needed.

Besides choosing a hierarchical model, there are roles that can be chosen for CAs. These include:

- *Intermediate CA*—An intermediate CA certifies lower-level CAs to issue certificates.
- *Rudimentary CA*—Issues certificates for very basic operations, for instance, user authentication without an identity check.
- *Basic-security CA*—Issues certificates to users and computers that do not have special security requirements.
- *Medium-security CA*—Issues certificates to users and computers that meet special security requirements.
- *High-security CA*—Issues certificates to users or computers that meet especially high security requirements and whose identities must be verified by means of some physical credential.

Standalone CAs are primarily used in intermediate and rudimentary roles, while Enterprise CAs are primarily used for basic-, medium-, and high-security roles.

Rooted Trust Model

In a **rooted trust model**, the root CA has a self-signed certificate, and that CA issues a certificate to all direct subordinate CAs. The subordinate CAs in turn issue certificates to their subordinate CAs or issuing CAs. A subordinate CA is trusted based on the signature of its parent, as shown in Figure 9-7.

NOTE

Only one root CA exists in this hierarchy. You may have any number of intermediate and issuing CAs, but only one root CA. The root CA is always installed first and is always the most trusted authority.

CAs in a rooted trust hierarchy can be online or offline. This allows great flexibility in how you deploy and manage your PKI. The private key of a CA can be protected by taking the

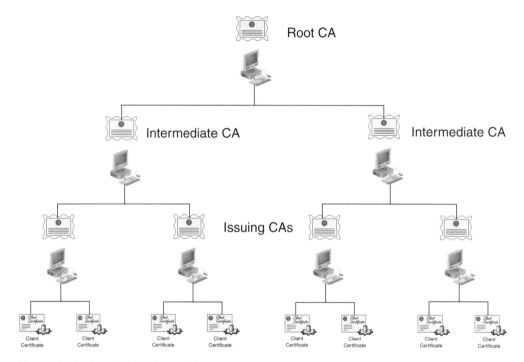

Figure 9-7   Rooted trust model

CA offline. Rooted trust hierarchies are more scalable and easier to administer than other hierarchies because each CA serves a single role within the hierarchy and is not dependent on other CAs. You can add a new CA to a rooted trust hierarchy by enrolling it to a CA anywhere in the trust hierarchy. Rooted trust hierarchies can fall into two subcategories:

- *Two-tier CA hierarchy*—This hierarchy consists of a root CA that issues certificates to one or more subordinate CAs. Each subordinate CA may be dedicated to a single type of certificate, such as smart card or EFS, or to an organizational site location.

- *Three-tier CA hierarchy*—This hierarchy consists of a root CA that issues certificates to one or more intermediate CAs, which in turn issue certificates to issuing CAs. The intermediate CAs are located in different geographical sites, and the issuing CAs are dedicated to certificate types.

Any CA in a rooted trust hierarchy is either a root or a subordinate but never both. Each CA is responsible for processing requests, issuing certificates, revoking certificates, and publishing CRLs and can be managed independently by personnel in different parts of an organization. You can add a new CA to a rooted trust hierarchy by enrolling it to a CA anywhere in the trust hierarchy. If you create a new trust hierarchy, it needs to trust the root CA of the new PKI in order to trust all the subordinate CAs in the new hierarchy.

Numerous products and services offered by major software vendors, including Microsoft, support rooted trust hierarchies. To better protect Microsoft customers from security issues that are related to the use of PKI certificates, Microsoft maintains the Microsoft Root Certificate Program. This program defines and standardizes the criteria that the CAs must meet to be included in Microsoft products. For more information about the Microsoft Root Certificate Program, visit the following Microsoft Web site: *www.microsoft.com/technet/security/news/rootcert.mspx*.

In addition, you can see which trusted certificates are automatically installed by right-clicking Internet Explorer, choosing Properties, selecting the Content tab, selecting the Certificates tab, then choosing the Trusted Root Certificate Authorities tab.

Cross-Certification Model

If your organization has many distributed divisions, you might not be able to establish a single, trusted root. Cross-certification creates a shared trust between two CAs that do not have the same root CA. A **cross-certification model** is one in which all CAs are self-signed, and trust relationships between CAs are based on cross-certificates. Cross-certificates are special certificates that are used to establish these trusts between unrelated CAs. The trusts shown in Figure 9-8 are bidirectional. This means that the first CA issued a cross-certificate of trust to the second CA, and the second CA issued a cross-certificate of trust to the first CA, and so on down the line.

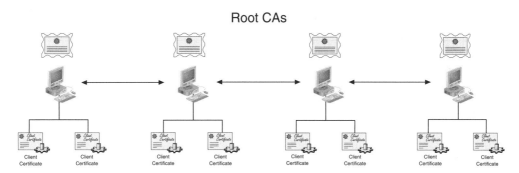

Figure 9-8 Cross-certification model

Cross-certification does not need to be bidirectional, and a cross-certifying CA does not need the cooperation of the CA being certified. A CA can create a cross-certificate without the knowledge of another CA because all that CA needs is the public key certificate of the second CA. This is known as *unilateral cross-certification*, where one CA cross-certifies another CA but not the reverse. Full trust between cross-certified CAs also means that the client trusts all certificates issued by the other CA, regardless of the purpose of the certificate.

The advantages to using cross-certification include low cost and greater flexibility because you can cross-certify at any level in the hierarchy. If you need to share information in two different divisions of an organization, the two divisions should cross-certify CAs that are lower in the CA hierarchy for better security. Cross-certification requires greater administrative overhead than other trusted root models and increases the risk that outsiders might unintentionally be given access to internal resources.

Using Third-Party Certificate Authorities

If your organization conducts most of its business with external customers and clients, you may want to consider outsourcing certificate issuance and management processes by using a third-party CA such as Verisign or Thawte. This is especially true if a majority of the business is Web-based. This allows customers a greater degree of confidence when conducting secure transactions with the organization because they tend to be more trusting of third-party names they are familiar with. This also allows the organization to take advantage of the provider's understanding of the technical, legal, and business issues associated with certificate use, while allowing the organization to concentrate on developing an internally managed PKI. Although this type of arrangement is more convenient, it can involve a high per-certificate cost, allow less flexibility in configuring and managing certificates, and autoenrollment is not possible. Depending on your organizational requirements, you might need to use both internal and third-party CAs.

Installing Certification Authority Roles

Using multiple CAs is an excellent way to ensure that your infrastructure can support enterprise scalability. This provides greater reliability, greater scalability, and improved availability. After you have designed the trust hierarchy for your organization, you must define the roles for your CAs and install them. The procedure for installing a CA depends on its position in the hierarchy, but you always begin by installing the root CA on a standalone server. Then you continue by installing as many intermediate CAs as are necessary, and finally you install the issuing CAs.

Root CAs

If you are installing only a single CA, you can use either an enterprise root CA or standalone root CA. A root CA is the CA that is at the top of a certification hierarchy and must be trusted unconditionally by clients in your organization. Whether you use enterprise or standalone CAs, you need to designate a root CA. Because there is no higher certifying authority in the certification hierarchy, a root CA serves as the foundation upon which you base your certification authority trust model. It guarantees that the subject public key belongs to the subject identity information that is contained in the certificates it issues. The root CA is the most important CA in your hierarchy. If your root CA is compromised, every other CA and certificate in your hierarchy might have been compromised. You can increase the security of the root CA by keeping it offline and using subordinate CAs to issue certificates to other subordinate CAs or to end users.

An enterprise root CA stores its information in Active Directory and must be installed on a domain controller. After you have installed the root CA, you should configure the online location of the certificate revocation list (CRL). You should do this before installing any subordinate CAs because the root CA includes the location information for CRLs on any certificates that it issues. Subordinate CAs then include this information on their certificates. Applications must be aware of the location of the CRL so that they can check certificates presented to them to ensure their validity; otherwise, a security risk could be presented by a revoked certificate. Moreover, many applications will not work if they do not have the proper information available to them regarding the CRL. We discuss the CRL in further detail later in this chapter.

Activity 9-4: Install a Root CA

Time Required: 15 minutes

Objective: Learn how to install a root CA.

Description: In this activity, you will learn how to install a root CA. Note: To install the root CA on a standalone server, you need to have Internet Information Services (IIS) 6.0 installed. You will work with a partner for this exercise. This exercise is to be done only on one machine.

1. Log on with your **AdminXX** account, where *XX* is your assigned student number.

2. Go to **Start, Settings, Control Panel, Add or Remove Programs.** Select **Add/Remove Windows Components**.

3. In the **Windows Components Wizard**, select the **Certificate Services** check box.

4. Click **Yes** to accept the warning that the computer name and domain membership cannot be changed. Then click **Next**.

5. On the CA Type page, click **Stand-alone root CA**, then click **Next**.

6. On the CA Identifying Information page, enter **CARoot** in the Common name box, then click **Next**.

7. On the Certificate Database Settings page, accept the default locations for the certificate database, certificate database log, and shared folder, as shown in Figure 9-9. Then click **Next**.

8. Click **Yes** to temporarily stop IIS.

9. If the Windows Server 2003 CD-ROM is not in the CD-ROM drive, insert it when requested. When the CD starts, if necessary, click **OK**.

10. You are informed that Active Server Pages (ASPs) must be enabled in IIS to enable Web enrollment services. Click **Yes** to proceed.

11. When the completion page appears, click **Finish**.

12. Close the **Add or Remove Programs** window.

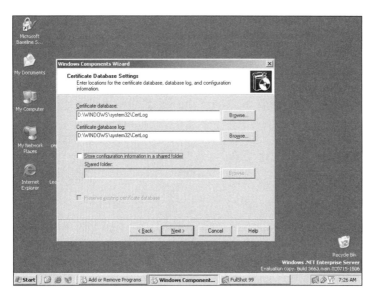

Figure 9-9 Selecting certificate database settings

Intermediate CAs

When you have installed a root CA and configured the online location of its CRL, you are ready to proceed with installing as many intermediate CAs as your security infrastructure requires. CAs that are not root CAs are considered subordinate. The first subordinate CA in a hierarchy obtains its CA certificate from the root CA. These subordinate CAs are referred to as intermediate CAs. An **intermediate CA** is subordinate to a root CA, but also serves as a higher certifying authority to one or more subordinate CAs. An intermediate CA can also be referred to as a policy CA because it is typically used to separate classes of certificates that can be distinguished by policy. To install an enterprise subordinate CA, you must be a member of the Domain Admins and the Enterprise Admins group and have access to permissions on the DNS server, the Active Directory database, and the CA server.

Activity 9-5: Install an Intermediate CA

Time Required: 45 minutes

Objective: Learn how to install an intermediate CA.

Description: In this activity, you will learn how to install an intermediate CA from an offline root CA. You will work with a partner for this exercise so that you will be using two servers. The server will require IIS and Active Directory to be installed. The first 12 steps are to be done on the machine that is not the root CA. Note: To complete this activity, you must enable the session state option in IIS. For directions on how to do so, scroll to the end of the exercise.

1. Log on with your **AdminXX** account, where *XX* is your assigned student number.

2. Go to **Start**, **Control Panel**, **Add or Remove Programs**. Select **Add/Remove Windows Components**.

3. In the Windows Components Wizard, select the **Certificate Services** check box.

4. Click **Yes** to accept the warning that the computer name and domain membership cannot be changed, then click **Next**.

5. On the CA Type page, select **Stand-alone subordinate CA**, then click **Next**.

6. On the CA Identifying Information page, type **SubordinateCA** in the Common name box. This name is combined with the distinguished name suffix and displayed as the preview of the distinguished name. Click **Next**.

7. Accept the locations for the certificate database and log. Click **Next**.

8. On the CA Certificate Request page, select **Save the request to a file**. Make a note of where the file saved to, then click **Next**. You need to select this option because you are keeping the root CA offline.

9. Click **Yes** to temporarily stop IIS.

10. If the Windows Server 2003 CD-ROM is not in the CD-ROM drive, insert it when requested.

11. You are informed that the Certificate Services installation is incomplete. Read the message and click **OK**. If you are prompted to enable ASP, click **Yes**.

12. When the completion page appears, click **Finish**.

13. Copy the certificate request file to a floppy disk, then insert this floppy into the offline root CA. Find the certificate request file, right-click the file, choose **Open**, choose **Select the program from a list**, click **OK**, select **Notepad**, then click **OK.**

14. At the offline root CA, click **Start**, **Run**, and type **http://localhost/certsrv**. This opens the Certificate Services Web page in Internet Explorer, as shown in Figure 9-10.

15. Select the **Request a certificate** link.

16. Select the **Advanced Certificate Request** link.

17. Select the **Submit a certificate request by using a base-64-encoded CMC or PKCS #10 file, or submit a renewal request by using a base-64-encoded PKCS #7** file link.

18. In Notepad, copy the text of the certificate request file (do not include the "BEGIN/END REQUEST" lines), then paste this text into the **Saved Request** field of the Certificate Services Web page. Then click **Submit**. Certificate Services informs you that the certificate request has been received and that you must wait for an administrator to issue the certificate. Note: If you receive an error stating that the Certificate server failed to create the request, you must enable the session state option in IIS.

19. To issue the certificate, click **Start**, **Administrative Tools**, **Certification Authority**. In the Certification Authority snap-in, expand the CA and select **Pending Requests**. This displays the certificate request in the details pane.

9

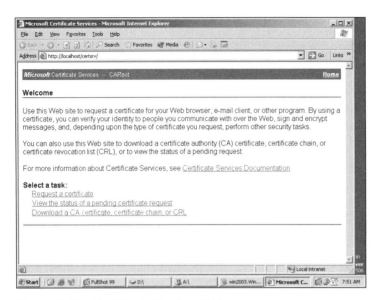

Figure 9-10 Certificate Services Web page

20. Right-click the certificate request and choose **All Tasks**, **Issue**.

21. In Internet Explorer, return to the home page *http://localhost/certsrv* and select the **View the status of a pending certificate request** link.

22. On the View the Status of a Pending Certificate Request page, select the link to the certificate request. You should be taken to the Certificate Issued page. Click **Download certificate**.

23. On the File Download page that appears, click **Save** to save the .cer file to the floppy disk.

24. Insert the floppy disk in the subordinate CA. On this computer, click **Start**, **Administrative Tools**, **Certification Authority** to open the Certification Authority snap-in. This displays the CA with the identification name you specified earlier in this procedure. It appears with a red mark that signifies it is not yet valid.

25. Right-click the CA and choose **All Tasks**, **Install CA Certificate**.

26. Navigate to the .cer file and double-click it. If you receive a message that the root certificate is untrusted, click **OK**.

27. The certificate is installed and Certificate Services starts. The red mark changes to a green check mark, signifying that the CA is operational. If this does not occur, right-click the CA and choose **All Tasks**, **Start Service**. To enable the application session state, click **Start**, **Programs**, **Administrative tools**, then **IIS Manager**. Expand the Web Sites folder. Right-click the **Default Web Site**, then choose **Properties**. On the Home Directory tab, in the Application settings area, click **Configuration**. Click the **Options** tab, check the **Enable session state** box. Click **OK**. Click **OK** again. Right-click your server, select **All Tasks**, then restart IIS.

Issuing CAs

The next level in the CA hierarchy usually contains the **issuing CA**. The issuing CA issues certificates to users and computers. Sometimes CA hierarchies, the lowest level of subordinate CAs is replaced by rudimentary CAs, which can act as intermediaries for a CA. RAs merely process transactions on behalf of the CA.

Installing an issuing CA is similar to installing an intermediate CA. However, because the intermediate CA is online, you can select the Send the request directly to a CA already on the network option in Step 8 of the previous procedure. Then proceed as follows:

1. Type in or browse to the computer on which you installed the intermediate CA. Also type the name of this CA in the Parent CA list box if it is not available. Then click Next.

2. Click Yes to temporarily stop IIS.

3. Insert the Windows Server 2003 CD-ROM when prompted.

4. Click Yes to enable Active Server Pages.

5. Click Finish when the completion page appears.

As you can see from the steps above, it is less complicated to install a CA from an online CA than from an offline CA but keep in mind that storing the root CA offline is much more secure.

9

SELECTING A CERTIFICATE ENROLLMENT AND RENEWAL METHOD

Once you have a certificate hierarchy in place and have chosen roles for the CAs, you can begin to define the certificate enrollment options that you need to meet the requirements of your users, as well as the security needs of your organization. Enrollment involves either configuring permissions to establish which security principals have Enroll permissions for specific certificate templates or appointing a certificate administrator who reviews each certificate request and issues or denies the request based on the information provided. Whether you choose to generate certificate requests automatically or manually depends on the types of certificates that you intend to use and the number and type of clients that you enroll.

Automatic versus Manual Requests

Microsoft Certificate Services allows you the flexibility to process certificate requests manually or automatically. Essentially, manual requests are made if administrative approval is required, and automatic requests are made if no approval is necessary. When you want all users or computers to use a certain type of certificate, it is not realistic to require that each certificate be requested individually. Autoenrollment is most useful for issuing and renewing computer and IPSec certificates. But there may be circumstances in which you might want to have users or an administrator request certain high-security certificates. For example, if you had to issue certificates used for digital signing or administrative tasks only when needed, manual requests would be a better choice. Manual requests and approvals can improve administrative control over certificates, especially if certificate use is not limited by a user or computer OU, or security group membership.

Should you choose automatic enrollment, the following methods are available:

- *Certificate autoenrollment and renewal*—Allows you to automatically issue certificates, based on a combination of Group Policy settings and certificate templates
- *Certificate Request Wizard and Certificate Renewal Wizard*—Allows the use of a wizard to request a certificate from an active enterprise CA
- *Web enrollment support pages*—Provides a Web-based user interface to a CA
- *Smart card enrollment station*—Advanced version of the Web enrollment that allows trusted administrators to enroll for smart card certificates

Users can request a certificate either manually or automatically. If manually requested, it is held until an administrator approves it. If autoenrollment is required, it is held until the verification process is completed. Most of the time, you choose the same method for certificate approval that you choose for certificate requests; however, there may be cases in which you decide to approve automatically a certificate request that was generated manually or manually approve certificate requests that were automatically generated.

Configuring and Deploying Certificate Authorities

Like any other server, a root or subordinate CA must be configured before it can issue certificates. First, the **Authority Information Access (AIA)** and **CRL distribution point (CDP) extensions** should be configured. The AIA extension specifies where to find up-to-date certificates for the CA. The CDP extension specifies where to find up-to-date CRLs that are signed by the CA. These extensions apply to all certificates that are issued by that CA. In addition, you will also need to configure certificate revocation, key archival, and key recovery. Configuring these options ensures that the number of failures due to unverified certificate chains or certificate revocations is reduced. This helps eliminate issues that can result in unsuccessful VPN connections, failed smart card logons, or unverified e-mail signatures.

The certificate templates available with an enterprise CA in Windows 2000 Server and Windows Server 2003 provide the default contents of all certificates that can be requested from a Windows enterprise CA. These certificate templates are stored in Active Directory and cannot be used with standalone CAs.

Configuring Certificate Templates

Certificate Services provides certificate templates to simplify the process of requesting and issuing certificates for various purposes. Each template contains the rules and settings that must be in place to create a certificate of a certain type. Certificate templates can serve a single purpose or multiple purposes. Single-purpose templates generate certificates that can be used for a single application. Multipurpose templates generate certificates that can be used for a number of applications, for example, a user certificate that can be used for both user authentication and EFS encryption.

Windows 2000 and Windows Server 2003 Standard Edition support only version 1 templates. Version 1 templates are the same as those provided with Windows 2000. They are read-only and can be used with client computers running Windows 2000 and later. Windows Server 2003 Enterprise Edition supports version 2 templates. Version 2 templates are new to Windows Server 2003. They are editable and support certificate autoenrollment. They can be used only on client computers running Windows XP or Windows Server 2003. When you duplicate a version 1 template, the duplicated template is version 2 and can be edited and used for certificate autoenrollment.

Certificate templates are available only on enterprise root and subordinate CAs. They are stored in Active Directory and are available to every enterprise CA in the forest, including those that are subordinate to an offline standalone root CA. The Certificate Templates MMC snap-in provides administrators with the capability to:

- Create additional templates by duplicating and modifying existing templates

- Modify template properties such as validity and renewal periods, cryptographic service provider (CSP), key size, and key archiving

- Configure policies applied to certificate enrollment, issuance, and application

- Allow the autoenrollment of certificates based on Windows Server 2003 version 2 templates

- Configure access control lists (ACLs) on certificate templates

When newly installed, the CA can issue certificates based on a limited set of templates, as listed in the Certificate Templates node of the Certification Authority snap-in. When configuring an issuing CA, you should include only those certificate templates that the CA will be issuing, so you may need to remove unnecessary templates. You can control the issuance of certificate requests in three ways:

- Configuring permissions on the template from the Security tab

- Preventing the CA from issuing that certificate type by deleting the template

- Configuring the permissions on the CA

Restrict permissions on your CAs to prevent unauthorized access. In general, no need exists for users to request certificates from root CAs and intermediate CAs. Only users who require the type of certificate issued by a given issuing CA should have permissions to templates on that CA, and only to the types of templates that they need. Configure the discretionary access control list (DACL) for each template so that only the required security principals have Enroll and Read permissions for particular templates.

Activity 9-6: Create a Certificate Template

Time Required: 25 minutes

Objective: Learn how to use the MMC Certificate Templates snap-in to create a certificate template.

Description: In this activity, you will learn how to create a certificate template by using the Certificate Templates MMC snap-in.

1. Log on with your **AdminXX** account, where *XX* is your assigned student number.

2. Go to **Start**, **Run**, then in the run box type **MMC**. Press **Enter**.

3. When the MMC console opens, choose **File**, **Add/Remove Snap-in**.

4. On the Standalone tab of the Add/Remove Snap-in screen, choose **Add**.

5. On the Add Standalone Snap-in screen, choose **Certificate Templates**, then click **Add**.

6. On the Add Standalone Snap-in screen, click **Close**. Then click **OK** on the Add/Remove Snap-in screen.

7. Double-click **Certificate Templates** on the left side of the screen. Your screen should display all the available templates along with additional parameters, as shown in Figure 9-11.

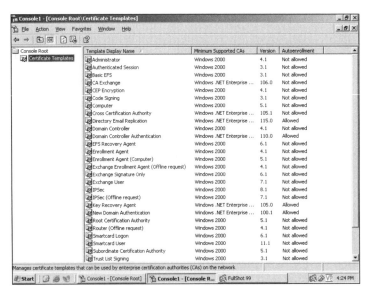

Figure 9-11   Available certificate templates

8. Highlight the **Domain Controller Authentication template**. Right-click the template and choose **Duplicate Template**.

9. On the General tab, In the Template display name text box, type **New Domain Authentication template**.

10. Under Validity period, change the 1 to **2**. Change the Renewal period to **2 months**.

11. On the Issuance Requirements tab, under Require the following for enrollment, Check the **CA certificate manager approval** box.

12. Click **Apply**, then click **OK**.

13. Close the **Console** window. Do not save the settings.

CONFIGURING AND MANAGING THE PUBLICATION OF CERTIFICATE REVOCATION LISTS

All certificates have specified lifetimes. However, in some situations, you might need to invalidate or revoke a certificate before it has reached the end of its lifetime. For example, you might choose to revoke certificates because an unauthorized user has gained access to the private key of the certificate or the CA itself. Perhaps the CA that issued the certificate is no longer operating. When you revoke a certificate, the revoked certificate is published in the **certificate revocation list (CRL)**. Because CRLs are valid only for a limited time, PKI clients need to retrieve a new CRL periodically. PKI applications look in the CRL distribution point extension for a URL that points to a network location from which the CRL can be retrieved. This point is the CRL distribution point. The system account writes the CRL to its distribution point. You can modify the CRL distribution point by using the Certification Authority MMC snap-in.

Because the CRL path is included in every certificate, you must define the CRL location along with the access path before deploying certificates. If an application performs revocation checking and a valid CRL is not available on the local computer, it rejects the certificate. Windows Server 2003 includes two types of CRLs: base CRLs and delta CRLs. **Base CRLs** include a complete list of revoked certificates. If the organization issues a large number of certificates the base CRL can consumes a large amount of network bandwidth when replication occurs. Because CRLs can become long, Windows Server 2003 has added the concept of a **delta CRL**, which is a list of certificates that have been revoked since the last publication of a full CRL. By using delta CRLs, you can publish CRL information more frequently with less replication traffic. Delta CRLs are published on a differential basis. In other words, each delta CRL includes all revoked certificates since the previous full CRL was published.

9

Activity 9-7: Specify a CRL Publication Interval and Download the CRL

Time Required: 45 minutes

Objective: Learn how to use the MMC Certificate Authority snap-in to specify a CRL publication interval, view the CRL, and then obtain a copy of the CRL.

Description: In this activity, you will learn how to use the MMC Certificate Authority snap-in to specify a CRL publication interval, view the CRL, and then obtain a copy if the CRL.

1. Log on with your **AdminXX** account, where *XX* is your assigned student number.

2. Go to **Start**, **Run**, then in the run box type **MMC**. Press **Enter**.

3. When the MMC console opens, choose **File**, **Add/Remove Snap-in**.

4. On the Standalone tab of the Add/Remove Snap-in screen, choose **Add**.

5. On the Add Standalone Snap-in screen, choose **Certification Authority**, then click **Add**.

6. On the Certification Authority window, be sure the **Local computer** radio button is selected. Click **Finish**.

7. On the Add Standalone Snap-in screen, click **Close**. Then click **OK** on the Add/Remove Snap-in screen.

8. Expand the Certificate Authority on the left side of the screen. Your CA should appear with a green check mark on it. If it does not, right-click it, select All Tasks, and choose **Start Service**.

9. Expand your CA, right-click Revoked Certificates, and choose **Properties**.

10. On the CRL publishing Parameters tab of the Revoked Certificates Properties dialog box, change the CRL publication interval to **2 Weeks**, check the **Publish Delta CRLs** check box, if necessary, and then change the delta CRL publication interval to **2 Days**. Note: If you want to view current CRLs, select the **View CRLs** tab and click **View CRL** button.

11. Click **Apply**, then click **OK**. Close the MMC window. Do not save the console settings.

12. Next you will obtain a copy of the CA certificate and CRLs from the Certificate Services Web pages. Click **Start**, **Run**. In the run box, type **http://localhost/certsrv**.

13. On the home page, select the **Download a CA certificate, certificate chain, or CRL** link. Your screen should now look like Figure 9-12.

14. Select **Download latest base CRL**. On the File Download page that appears, click **Save** and specify a location for the CRL in the Save As dialog box that appears.

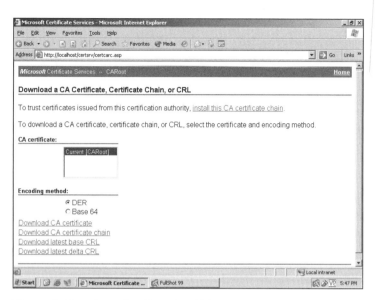

Figure 9-12 Downloading the CRL

15. Copy the certificate request file to a floppy disk. This floppy can then be inserted in the offline root CA and the CRL copied.

16. Close the Web page when finished.

Configuring Archival and Recovery of Keys

As part of your certificate management plan, you need to evaluate the potential consequences of loss of public keys and create a strategy for archival and key recovery. You can configure Windows Server 2003 Enterprise Edition to archive the private keys of certificates at the time of issuance. Such an archive enables you to recover the key should it be lost at any time by accidental deletion, corruption, or system failure. Key recovery allows a trusted agent to gain access to user private keys. For this reason, it is best to use key recovery only if your organization permits a person other than the original requester to have access to the private key of another user.

When you have configured key archival, a user or computer requesting a certificate provides his or her private key to the CA, which stores this key in its database, in case later recovery is required. You can archive keys only at an enterprise CA server running Windows Server 2003 Enterprise Edition. Standalone CAs and CAs on servers running Windows Server 2003 Standard Edition do not support key archival. A level of danger exists in the archival of keys, especially private keys associated with identification or digital signatures. Unauthorized users could recover archived keys and use them for improper purposes such as the impersonation of legitimate users on the network. In addition, only highly trusted individuals should be granted the privilege of archiving and recovering keys. By default, Certificate Services does not archive private keys.

After you have configured key archival, you can recover a lost key as required by performing key recovery and importing the recovered private key. Windows Server 2003 includes a new certificate template to support the key recovery agent role. By default, only an enterprise administrator or a domain administrator can request a key recovery agent certificate. You must also select an encryption key length for the key recovery agent certificate. An encryption key of 2048 bits satisfies most security needs. You must mark the keys as exportable to enable the key recovery agent to export the private keys from the local store of the workstation to a floppy disk for safe storage. The default key recovery agent certificate template requires manual approval of requests for key recovery agent certificates. It is best if a certificate manager manually approves all key recovery agent certificate requests.

Key recovery can also be done by the use of the **certutil** tool, which is a command-line utility included with Windows Server 2003 Certificate Services that performs a large number of certificate management tasks. The certutil command will be explained in further detail in Chapter 12. You can also use the key recovery tool, krt.exe, included in the Windows Server 2003 Resource Kit.

Deploying and Revoking Certificates for Users, Computers, and CAs

A PKI cannot be effective and secure unless an organization includes in their plan strategies for enrolling and renewing certificates and mapping certificates to user accounts in addition to revoking certificates, distributing CRLs, and using key recovery. After you have configured templates for the types of certificates your company needs to deploy, it is a simple matter to make these certificate templates available to users through the Certification Authority snap-in, as shown in Figure 9-13.

Many organizations base their certificate enrollment and renewal methods on the level of security associated with each type of certificate and the volume of certificate requests that they anticipate. You can automate the deployment of computer certificates by configuring Group Policy to automatically assign the necessary computer certificates.

 NOTE   This is new to Windows XP and Windows Server 2003 and is referred to as autoenrollment of certificates. **Autoenrollment** is the ability to automatically enroll users and computers for certificates, retrieve existing certificates, and renew expired certificates without user interaction.

Autoenrollment is the preferred enrollment method for e-mail and EFS certificate requests, which represent the majority of certificate activity. Because only clients who have already been authenticated by the network can request these certificates, the risks associated with the use of these certificates are relatively low. Manual approval should be required for all certificates that are needed to perform network administration or software development and those issued to joint venture partners.

You can autoenroll only certificates that are based on version 2 templates. In addition, the client computer must be integrated into Active Directory, the enterprise CA must be hosted

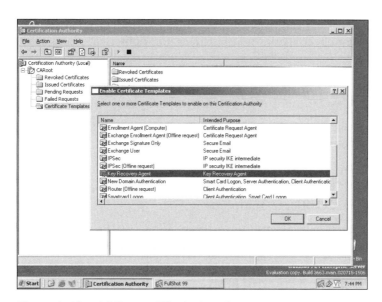

Figure 9-13   Adding certificate templates

on a server running Windows Server 2003 Enterprise Edition, and users require the Read, Enroll, and Autoenroll permissions in order to autoenroll certificates.

Activity 9-8: Configure Autoenrollment Using Group Policy

Time Required: 45 minutes

Objective: Learn how to configure autoenrollment for clients using Group Policy.

Description: In this activity, you will learn how to configure autoenrollment for clients using Group Policy. Note: To complete this exercise the certificate authority must be configured as an enterprise CA.

1. Log on with your **AdminXX** account, where *XX* is your assigned student number.

2. Go to **Start**, **Run**. In the run box, type **MMC**. Press **Enter**.

3. When the MMC console opens, choose **File**, **Add/Remove Snap-in**.

4. On the Standalone tab of the Add/Remove Snap-in screen, choose **Add**.

5. On the Add Standalone Snap-in screen, choose **Certification Authority**, then click **Add**.

6. On the Certification Authority window, be sure that the **Local computer** radio button is selected. Click **Finish**.

7. On the Add Standalone Snap-in screen, click **Close**. Then click **OK** on the Add/Remove Snap-in screen.

8. Expand the Certification Authority on the Left side of the screen. Your CA should appear with a green check mark on it. If it does not, right-click it and choose **Start Service**.

9. Expand your **CA**, right-click **Certificate Templates**, then choose **Manage**.

10. Right-click the **New Domain Authentication template**, then choose **Properties**.

11. On the Security tab, choose **Authenticated Users** and grant the group the **Read**, **Enroll**, and **Autoenroll** permissions. Click **Apply**. Click **OK**.

12. Close the **Manage Certificate Templates** window.

13. In the Certification Authority snap-in, enable the certificate template by highlighting then right-clicking **Certificate Templates**.

14. Choose **New**, **Certificate Template to Issue**. When the Enable Certificates Templates dialog box opens, choose the **New Domain Authentication** template, then click **OK**.

15. Close the **Certification Authority MMC**. Don't save the changes.

16. Go to **Start**, **Administrative Tools**, **Group Policy Management**.

17. Right-click the **Infrastructure Server** container and select **Create and Link a GPO here**.

18. In the New GPO Name box, type **Autoenrollment**. Click **OK**.

19. Right-click the Autoenrollment policy and choose **Edit**.

20. Expand the **Computer Configuration\Windows Settings\Security Settings\Public Key Policies** node so that you can see Autoenrollment settings on the right side of the screen, as shown in Figure 9-14.

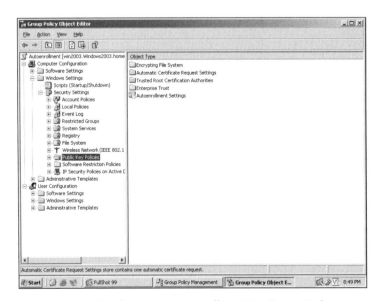

Figure 9-14   Configuring autoenrollment in Group Policy

21. Right-click **Autoenrollment Settings**, choose **Properties**, and verify that the **Enroll certificates automatically** radio button is selected. Check the **Update certificates that use certificate templates** box.

22. Click **Apply**, then click **OK**. Close the window and the **Group Policy Management** console.

You may need to revoke a certificate for various reasons such as the compromising of the certificate or termination of the user to whom the certificate was issued. To revoke a certificate, select the Issued Certificates node of the Certification Authority snap-in. Right-click the certificate to be revoked and select All Tasks, Revoke Certificate. Select a reason code from those displayed in the drop-down list of the Certificate Revocation dialog box, as shown in Figure 9-15, then click Yes. The certificate is removed from the Issued Certificates list and added to the Revoked Certificates list and the CRL.

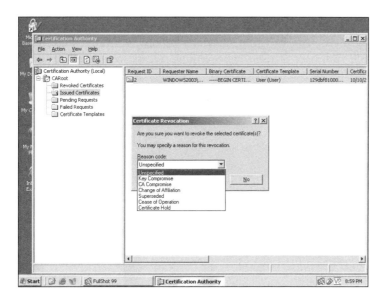

Figure 9-15   Revoking a certificate

 If you are unsure about the validity of a certificate, you should specify the Certificate Hold reason when revoking it. Specifying this reason provides you with an option to unrevoke the certificate later.

Mapping Certificates to User Accounts

You can map certificates issued to a user to the user's account, as shown in Figure 9-16. This creates an association between the certificate and the account. When a certificate is mapped and a user presents the certificate, Windows looks at the mapping to determine which account a user should be logged on to. You need to use certificate mapping for many types of certificates, such as those used for smart card logons. Certificate mapping allows you to provide a more secure method for user authentication. A server application can authenticate the user by means of this certificate. When certificate mapping is enabled, users are authenticated in Active Directory on the authority of the mapped certificates, and they are granted rights and permissions based on the authentication.

The following two ways of certificate mapping are possible:

- *One-to-one mapping*—Maps a single certificate to a single user account. This enables users to connect to a company's secure intranet Web pages from anywhere by providing his or her client certificate. The user can then log on to his or her user account and receive normal access. Use one-to-one mapping when you have a relatively small number of clients.

- *Many-to-one mapping*—Maps several certificates to a single user account. You can map any certificate with the same subject to the user account regardless of the certificate's issuer, or any certificate that has the same issuer to the user account regardless of the certificate's subject. Many-to-one mapping is useful for authenticating large numbers of users who require access to a given resource on your network, such as an internal Web site.

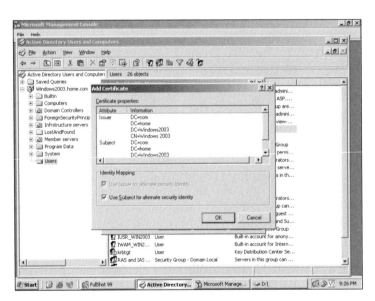

Figure 9-16 Mapping a certificate

You can use either IIS or Active Directory to create mapping. IIS mapping can be configured for each Web server. This type of mapping is useful for a limited number of mappings or different mapping on each Web server. With Active Directory mapping, the IIS server receives a certificate from the user, then passes it on to Active Directory, which maps it to a Windows user account. The IIS server then logs on to the account. Active Directory mapping should be used when the account mappings are identical on all IIS servers. It is easier to maintain than IIS mapping because you have to create the mapping in only one location.

BACKING UP AND RESTORING THE CA

As with any other server, you need to back up the CA server regularly so that you can recover it should any type of disaster occur. The recommended method for backing up a CA is to use the Backup utility to back up the entire server, including the system state that contains the CA's data. At the same time, you should back up IIS because the proper functioning of the certificate server depends on the Web enrollment pages. It is also possible to back up and restore a CA using the Certification Authority snap-in, but this backup method is intended for use only in special cases where you do not want to back up the entire server on which the CA is installed.

9

When the need arises to restore the CA, the IIS metabase must also be restored if it has been damaged or lost, otherwise IIS will fail to start and the Certificate Services Web pages will fail to load. If the CA database logs are manually deleted before the restore, the CA will be restored to the point in time that the backup was performed; otherwise, the CA will be restored, the database logs will be replayed, and the changes made since the last backup will be applied to the database.

Backing Up and Restoring Certificate Storage

Certificates are stored in **certificate stores**, which are located in a protected area of the registry. A series of certificate stores can exist for each user, computer, and entity. Each certificate store can be accessed via the Certificates snap-in. You can back up Certificate Services by itself by using the Certification Authority. When you use this method, you need to specify an empty backup folder in which to store the backup. You can specify a nonexistent folder, and the Backup Wizard will verify that you want to create the folder. Certificate Services also provides a Restore Wizard. This can be done through the Certification Authority snap-in in a similar manner to how the backup is performed. You will have to supply a password when backing up the public and private keys and CA certificate. This same password will be used to restore the CA. After performing the initial full backup of the CA, you can do incremental backups. If using the incremental method, you must restore the full backup first and then each incremental backup in the order that they were created.

You can use the Certificate Export and Import Wizards to back up and restore certificates with their associated private keys. You should do this to ensure that they are available for recovery or to move them to a different computer. When exporting the certificate, you should export the private key unless you are simply providing someone with a copy of the certificate. The key can be exported to several different file formats. When importing the certificate, on the Certificate Store page, ensure that the certificate is imported to the correct store.

You can also back up part of the CA by using the following certutil commands:

- *certutil -backup*—Backs up the database and the log files only
- *certutil -backupkey*—Individually backs up the CA certificate and the keys
- *certutil -backupdb*—Archives the database

These backup procedures are appropriate for a restore operation that repairs a damaged CA, assuming that the CA is correctly configured. These commands will not back up any of the CA configuration or role separation information in the registry. Keep in mind that a backup procedure may not work as expected, so it is recommended that regularly scheduled tests of restore operations be performed to ensure that the backup procedure is working properly.

Handle the backup data with caution at all times. Store it securely if the private CA key is part of your backup.

NOTE

CHAPTER SUMMARY

- ❏ Using PKI allows an organization to publish, use, renew, and/or revoke certificates and enroll clients. Once PKI is deployed, you can then digitally sign files such as documents and applications, secure e-mail, enable secure connections between computers, and improve user authentication through the use of smart cards.

- ❏ Security boundaries help define the independence or separation of different groups within an organization. In addition to the security boundaries established, your organization may need to consider establishing administrative boundaries.

- ❏ A group's scope dictates who can be a member of the group and what resources the group has access to, and the domain or forest functional level will affect which group scopes can be used. Nested groups allow you to provide access to resources with very little maintenance.

- ❏ Trusts are authentication media that allow users in one domain to access resources in another domain. By default, two-way, transitive trusts are created in a Windows Server 2003 forest. Transitive trusts are required for Kerberos-based authentication and Active Directory replication.

- ❏ Authentication verifies that an individual or object is who or what it claims to be. A domain controller running Windows Server 2003 authenticates users and applications using either Kerberos V5 or NTLM.

- ❏ Authorization is the process of verifying that an authenticated party has the permission to access a particular resource. This is the layer of security control following authentication. You want to be sure that users have access to what they need, but only at the level they need.

- ❏ Digital signatures are used to ensure message integrity and authenticity. A digital signature is used to make sure that the data has not been altered since it was signed and confirms the identity of the person or entity who signed the data.

❏ To support the certificate-based needs of your organization, you must establish a structure of CAs that are responsible for issuing, validating, renewing, and revoking certificates as needed.

❏ Using multiple CAs is an excellent way to ensure that your infrastructure can support enterprise scalability. This provides greater reliability, greater scalability, and improved availability. After you have designed the trust hierarchy for your organization, you must define the roles for your CAs and install them.

❏ Enrollment involves either configuring permissions to establish which security principals have Enroll permissions for specific certificate templates or appointing a certificate administrator who reviews each certificate request and issues the certificate or denies the request based on the information provided.

❏ Certificate Services provides certificate templates to simplify the process of requesting and issuing certificates for various purposes. Each template contains the rules and settings that must be in place to create a certificate of a certain type.

❏ As part of your certificate management plan, you need to evaluate the potential consequences of loss of public keys and create a strategy for archival and key recovery. Archiving enables you to recover the key should it be lost at any time by accidental deletion, corruption, or system failure.

❏ Autoenrollment is the preferred enrollment method for e-mail and EFS certificate requests, which represent the majority of certificate activity. Manual approval should be required for all certificates that are needed to perform network administration or software development, as well as those issued to joint venture partners.

❏ You can map certificates issued to a user to the user's account. Certificate mapping allows you to provide a more secure method for user authentication. You need to use certificate mapping for many types of certificates, such as those used for smart card logons.

KEY TERMS

administrative boundaries — Boundaries dividing the administrative control of services and data within the current Active Directory design.

authentication — The process of verifying that an individual or object is who or what it claims to be.

authorization — The process of verifying that an authenticated party has the permission to access a particular resource.

Authority Information Access (AIA) — An extension that specifies where to find up-to-date certificates for the CA.

autoenrollment — The ability to automatically enroll users and computers for certificates, retrieve existing certificates, and renew expired certificates without user interaction.

base CRLs — A complete list of revoked certificates.

certificate revocation list (CRL) — When you revoke a certificate, the revoked certificate is published in this list.

certificate stores — A protected area of the registry where certificates are stored.

certutil tool — A command-line utility included with Windows Server 2003 Certificate Services that performs a large number of certificate management tasks.

chain building — The building of a trust chain, or certification path, from the end certificate to a root CA that is trusted by the security principal.

CRL distribution point (CDP) extension — An extension that specifies where to find up-to-date CRLs that are signed by the CA.

cross-certification model — A model in which all CAs are self-signed and trust relationships between CAs are based on cross-certificates.

delegated authentication — Delegation that occurs when a network service accepts a request from a user, then assumes that user's identity in order to initiate a new connection to a second network service.

delta CRL — A list of certificates that have been revoked since the last publication of a full CRL.

digital signature — A digital signature acts as an electronic signature that is used to authenticate the identity of the sender, as well as ensure that the original content sent has not been changed.

distribution groups — Groups that are used for membership purposes only. These are actually an extension of Microsoft Exchange distribution lists.

Encrypting File System (EFS) — A method that allows users and services to encrypt their data.

enterprise CA — A certificate authority that is integrated with Active Directory.

group scope — The scope of a group determines the level to which the group is applied within a domain or forest.

group type — The group type determines whether a group can be used to assign permissions from a shared resource for security groups or if a group can be used for e-mail distribution lists only for distribution groups.

intermediate CA — A CA subordinate to a root CA, but that also serves as a higher certifying authority to one or more subordinate CAs.

issuing CA — The CA that issues certificates to users and computers.

Multifactor authentication—The combining of two or even three of these factors for proof of identification.

Mutual authentication — An authentication method in which the client must prove its identity to the server and the server must also prove its identity to the client.

nested groups — Group nesting occurs when one security group is made a member of another security group.

NT LAN Manager — This is an authentication protocol used by Windows operating systems.

Public Key Infrastructure (PKI) — A technology that includes a series of features relating to authentication and encryption, which is based on a system of certificates.

root CA — A final authority that certifies other certification authorities to publish and manage certificates within the organization.

rooted trust model — A model in which the root CA has a self-signed certificate, and the CA issues a certificate to all direct subordinate CAs.

security boundaries — Boundaries that define the independence or separation of different groups within an organization.

security groups — Groups can be assigned permissions to resources through access control entries (ACEs).

smart card — A physical card inserted as a means to initiate a logon. The user is then prompted for the smart card PIN code, which controls access by using the private key stored on the smart card.

standalone CA — A certificate authority that is not integrated with Active Directory.

transitive trust — A trust relationship that passes throughout a group of domains, forming a relationship between one domain and all other domains that trust that domain.

trust — An authentication medium that allow users in one domain to access resources in another domain.

two-way trust — A trust relationship between two domains in which both domains trust each other.

REVIEW QUESTIONS

1. You have configured Certificate Services on a server in your domain. Several users attempt to enroll for a user certificate but receive a message that the template was not found. What should you do?

   a. Include a group containing the required users in the access control list (ACL) for the User Certificate template.

   b. Create a duplicate of the User Certificate template and specify the autoenroll permission for the Authenticated Users group.

   c. Configure the Web enrollment pages to use basic authentication.

   d. Configure the automatic certificate request policy in a GPO linked to the domain.

2. You have deployed a three-tier CA hierarchy. Which of the following types of CAs would you expect to be issuing smart card certificates to users in the forest? (Choose all that apply.)

   a. Enterprise root CA

   b. Enterprise subordinate CA

   c. Standalone root CA

   d. Issuing enterprise CA

3. You have been asked to install and configure an enterprise CA so users with the proper permissions can use the enrollment Web pages. Which of the following must be available for you to accomplish this task? (Choose all that apply.)

   a. DHCP

   b. DNS

   c. Active Directory

   d. IIS

4. You need to set a rule for mapping these certificates to allow the workers to view Web pages. How should you proceed?

   a. Configure one-to-one mapping of the certificates

   b. Configure many-to-one mapping of the certificates

   c. Configure one-to-many mapping of the certificates

   d. Configure user principal name mapping instead

5. Which of the following types of CAs should you keep offline as a safeguard against certificate compromise?

   a. Enterprise root

   b. Standalone root

   c. Intermediate

   d. Issuing

6. You are planning to install Certificate Services as a standalone root CA on a computer running Windows Server 2003. Which of the following should you install before you install Certificate Services?

   a. Active Directory

   b. DNS

   c. Exchange Server

   d. IIS

7. You have configured Certificate Services to publish a base CRL every Monday at 6 p.m. and a delta CRL daily at 6 p.m. On Friday morning, a financial application needs to check the CRL to ensure that a new user's certificate is valid. Which of the following CRLs does the application check?

   a. The base CRL and each delta CRL published from Tuesday to Thursday

   b. The base CRL and Thursday's delta CRL

   c. The base CRL and Friday's delta CRL

   d. Thursday's delta CRL only

8. Which of the following features of IIS needs to be enabled so that Web enrollment services can work properly?

   a. Active Server Pages (ASPs)

   b. File Transfer Protocol (FTP)

   c. Host headers

   d. Server certificates

9. Which of the following actions are possible with version 2 certificate templates but not with version 1 templates? (Choose all that apply.)

   a. Specification of the level of user interaction possible during certificate enrollment

   b. Specification of the Enroll permission for users and groups requiring certificates

   c. Specification of the Autoenroll permission for users and groups requiring certificates

   d. Specification of the purpose of the certificate

10. Which of the following are required to enable the autoenrollment of users and computers for certificates? (Choose all that apply.)

   a. The certificate server must be hosted on a server running Windows Server 2003 Enterprise Edition.

   b. The user or group must have the Read, Enroll, and Autoenroll permissions.

   c. A GPO needs to be configured for automatic enrollment of user and computer certificates.

   d. Client computers must be integrated into the Active Directory domain.

11. Which of the following certutil commands individually backs up the CA certificate and the keys?

   a. certutil –backupdb

   b. certutil –backupkey

   c. certutil –backup

   d. certutil –backupdata

12. Which of the following determines the level to which the group is applied within a domain or forest?

   a. Group type

   b. Group nesting

   c. Group scope

   d. Group membership

13. Which of the following allows one group to contain other groups in its scope of authority?

   a. Security groups

   b. Nested groups

    c. Distribution groups

    d. User groups

14. Which of the following groups can be used for e-mail distribution lists?

    a. Only distribution groups

    b. Only security groups

    c. Neither one; you must use Microsoft Exchange groups

    d. Both security and distribution groups

15. Which of the following is considered the true security boundary?

    a. The forest

    b. The OU

    c. The site

    d. The domain

16. Which of the following occurs when a network service accepts a request from a user then assumes that user's identity in order to initiate a new connection to a second network service?

    a. Certificate authentication

    b. Digest authentication

    c. Anonymous authentication

    d. Delegated authentication

17. Which of the following authentication methods is supported by most Web servers and Web browsers and is commonly used when you cannot guarantee that the user's browser supports integrated Windows authentication?

    a. Certificate authentication

    b. Basic authentication

    c. Anonymous authentication

    d. Digest authentication

18. Which of the following is the process of verifying that an authenticated party has the permission to access a particular resource?

    a. Encryption

    b. Authentication

    c. Authorization

    d. Certification

19. Which of the following is based on a system of certificates, which are digitally signed statements that contain a public key and the name of the subject?

    a. CRL

    b. PKI

    c. EFS

    d. DNS

20. Which of the following is a list of certificates that have been revoked since the last publication of a full CRL?

    a. Base CRL

    b. Incremental CRL

    c. Differential CRL

    d. Delta CRL

21. Which if the following allows users and services to encrypt their data and provides for data recovery should another means be needed to access this data?

    a. CA

    b. EFS

    c. CRL

    d. DHCP

22. Which of the following are true about version 2 templates? (Choose all that apply).

    a. They are read-only.

    b. They are new to Windows Server 2003.

    c. They are editable and support certificate autoenrollment.

    d. They are the same ones provided with Windows 2000.

23. Certificate templates are available on which of the following CAs? (Choose all that apply.)

    a. Enterprise root

    b. Standalone root

    c. Enterprise subordinate

    d. Standalone issuing

24. You can archive keys at an enterprise CA server running which of the following operating systems?

    a. Windows Server 2003 DataCenter Edition

    b. Windows Server 2000 Standard Edition

    c. Windows Server 2003 Standard Edition

    d. Windows Server 2003 Enterprise Edition

9

25. Key recovery can also be done by the using which of the following tools? (Choose all that apply.)

a. ntbackup

b. msbacli.exe

c. certutil

d. krecover utility

Case Projects

Case Project 9-1

Evergrow is currently running Windows XP on all client computers. Management would like to implement a PKI infrastructure. To begin the process of designing a public key infrastructure, you will need to identify the certificate requirements for your organization by defining the security needs of the organization. Explain how you will determine the needs of the organization and begin planning a PKI.

Case Project 9-2

You are the network administrator at Evergrow. You have a forest and several domains. All servers are using Windows Server 2003. Evergrow is in the midst of acquiring another company that will have to be merged with the current forest structure that is in place. This company has four Windows 2000 domains. When you designed the Active Directory structure for the organization, it was done so that the company could grow without having to redesign the layout but you didn't expect to have any Windows 2000 servers in place. Currently you have universal groups, global groups, and domain local groups in place. Explain how this merger will affect the group scopes that you have created and how they work under the various domain functionality levels.

Case Project 9-3

You are the network administrator at Evergrow. You have just merged with another company and have a forest and several domains. The servers are using Windows Server 2003 and Windows 2000. The client machines are varied and have installed Windows 98, NT Workstation, 2000 Professional, and Windows XP. You have been given the task of establishing an authentication strategy for your organization. Management requests that this be done within the week. You have 50 servers and 6500 clients. Prepare a list of the items that should be taken into consideration when planning authentication for your environment and determine if this task can be done in the time period specified by management.

Case Project 9-4

You are the network administrator at Evergrow. You have just merged with another company and have a forest and several domains. The servers are using Windows Server 2003 and Windows 2000. You have been given the task of establishing an authorization strategy for your organization. When planning authorization methods for your environment, you must also consider policies for security group management, including who is allowed to create security groups and how they are named, nested, and administered. You have completed this part and are ready to move on. Explain the various resource authorization methods available to enable users to access shared resources in your organization. Then choose one and explain why you have made this choice.

Case Project 9-5

You are the network administrator at Evergrow. Management has asked you to evaluate implementing certificates as a way to secure the network. You know that a single Windows Server 2003 computer with Certificate Services installed can be used to issue certificates for multiple purposes on your network, but best practices dictate that you should use a hierarchy of certificate servers that trust one another and authenticate certificates belonging to one another. In order to justify the cost of additional servers, explain the various types of hierarchies and the roles that can be used when implementing a certificate structure.

Case Project 9-6

You are the network administrator at Evergrow. You are implementing certificates as a way to secure the network. Prepare a plan for implementing and revoking certificates and backing up the certificate stores. Include in your plan whether or not you will use autoenrollment, whether you will use a base or delta CRL, and which method you will use to back up the certificates.

CHAPTER

10

PLANNING AND DEPLOYING AUTHENTICATION FOR REMOTE ACCESS USERS

After reading this chapter, you will be able to:

♦ Deploy and manage SSL certificates

♦ Configure a Web server for SSL certificates

♦ Configure a client for SSL certificates

♦ Determine certificate renewal

♦ Configure security for Remote Access users

♦ Provide Remote Access over a VPN

♦ Manage client configuration for Remote Access security

In such a mobile world, chances are that you have users who travel frequently or need to access your network from home or other locations. In addition, you may share resources on your network with other organizations. This may leave your systems vulnerable; therefore, it is important to secure your authentication process to protect your system against many types of security threats. This includes abuse of system access rights, impersonation of authenticated users, and hacking tools.

Proper security safeguards on your Web and Remote Access servers can help reduce or eliminate some of the aforementioned security threats. The use of certificates to authenticate servers and clients was explained in the last chapter. This knowledge can be extended to your Web servers and clients as well as wireless clients. In addition, you can secure the servers that service dial-in users and remote connections. In the process, you must ensure that these authentication policies interoperate with the authentication policies that are already in place on the internal infrastructure of the network.

This chapter explains how to plan and deploy authentication for remote users while keeping your internal network secure. This includes deploying, managing, and configuring SSL certificates. It demonstrates how to configure security and authentication for remote access users. It will also guide you through configuring and troubleshooting virtual private network protocols. Finally, it will explain how to manage client configuration for remote access security.

DEPLOYING AND MANAGING SSL CERTIFICATES

In many businesses, the day-to-day operations of an organization depend on applications that are running on Internet Information Services (IIS) 6.0 Web servers. Because many of these may be mission critical, an organization's Web servers, sites, and applications need to be highly secured. For these reasons, IIS 6.0 is not installed by default on Windows Server 2003, Standard Edition, Enterprise Edition, and Datacenter Edition. In addition, when IIS 6.0 is installed, it is installed in a highly secure and locked configuration. Features such as Active Server Pages (ASP), ASP.NET, Common Gateway Interface (CGI) scripting, FrontPage 2002 Server Extensions, and Web-based Distributed Authoring and Versioning (WebDAV) do not work by default.

Using authentication with IIS is critical if your Web server contains resources that are not meant for anonymous or public access, but approved users must be able to access the Web server over the Internet. Although we will concentrate on the certificate authentication in this section, Table 10-1 shows the various methods and security levels used for authentication in IIS 6.0 as a quick reference and review.

Table 10-1   IIS Authentication Methods

Method	Security Level
Anonymous authentication	None
Basic authentication	Low
Digest authentication	Medium
Advanced Digest authentication	Medium
Integrated Windows authentication	High
Certificate authentication	High
.NET Passport authentication	High

To encrypt confidential information exchanged between the Web server and the client, the **Secure Sockets Layer (SSL)** protocol can be used with IIS 6.0. SSL is a public key–based security protocol that is used by Internet services and clients for authentication, message integrity, and confidentiality. The SSL process uses certificates for authentication, and encryption for message integrity and confidentiality. To establish encrypted communications using SSL, you must have a valid server certificate installed. Certificates include keys that are used to establish an SSL-encrypted connection. The certificate-based SSL features in IIS consist of a server certificate, a client certificate, and various digital keys. The World

Wide Web Publishing Service (WWW service) on your Web server uses a key pair to negotiate an encrypted connection with the client browser.

You can use Certificate Services to create certificates, or you can obtain certificates from a mutually trusted third-party organization called a certification authority (CA). This process, which is similar to the process we described in Chapter 9, can be used with both the Hypertext Transfer Protocol over Secure Sockets Layer (HTTPS) and the LDAPS protocols.

HTTPS

SSL works by establishing a secure channel using Public Key Infrastructure (PKI). This can eliminate a vast majority of attacks such as session hijackings and information theft. HTTPS is technology that encrypts individual messages in Web communications rather than establishing a secure channel. It is a popular e-commerce technology and is used for secure online shopping. Basic Web connectivity using the Hypertext Transfer Protocol (HTTP) occurs over TCP port 80. When the SSL protocol is used, it communicates on port 443. All URLs that are SSL-secured have to begin with the https:// prefix instead of the http:// prefix. HTTPS was originally created by the Netscape Corporation and used a 40-bit RC4 stream encryption algorithm to establish a secured connection encapsulating data transferred between the client and Web server, although it can also support the use of X.509 digital certificates to allow the user to authenticate the sender. Now, 128-bit encryption keys are available; they have become the accepted level of secure connectivity for online banking and electronic commerce transactions.

During this process, the client connects to the Web site using the HTTPS protocol and port 443. The server sends the client a copy of its certificate containing its public key. At this point, the client creates a unique session key and keeps a copy of the key unencrypted. It creates another copy of the key encrypted with the public key that it received from the server. The server and the client communicate using the same encryption key. At the termination of the session, the keys are discarded and never used again. At least one new session key is created for every session.

LDAPS

You can also use SSL to encrypt Active Directory traffic. The Lightweight Directory Access Protocol (LDAP) is used to read from and write to the Active Directory. By default, the traffic is transmitted unsecured, but you can secure it using LDAP over SSL/Transport Layer Security (TLS), or LDAPS. You can enable LDAPS by installing a properly formatted certificate from either a Microsoft certification authority (CA) or a non-Microsoft CA. LDAPS communication occurs over port TCP 636. LDAPS communication to a global catalog server occurs over TCP 3269. When connecting to ports 636 or 3269, SSL/TLS is negotiated before any LDAP traffic is exchanged. Installing a valid certificate on a domain controller permits the LDAP service to listen for, and automatically accept, SSL connections for both LDAP and global catalog traffic. There is no user interface for configuring LDAPS.

10

ACTIVITY

Activity 10-1: Check LDAP Communication

Time Required: 10 minutes

Objective: Learn how to use the ldp.exe command to check LDAP communication over ports 636 and 3269.

Description: In this exercise, you will learn how to use the lpd.exe command to check LDAP communication over ports 636 and 3269. Note: Windows Support Tools must be installed to complete Activity 10-1.

1. Log on with your **AdminXX** account, where *XX* is your assigned student number.

2. Click **Start**, **Run**, and type **ldp.exe** in the run dialog box. Click **OK**.

3. Choose the **Connection** menu and click **Connect**.

4. Type the name of the domain controller to connect to in the **Server** name box, such as your local domain or the domain of the instructor.

5. Type **636** in the **Port** box. Click **OK**.

6. Your screen should look similar to the one shown in Figure 10-1. Notice that the upper-left corner on the very top of the window shows ssl://.

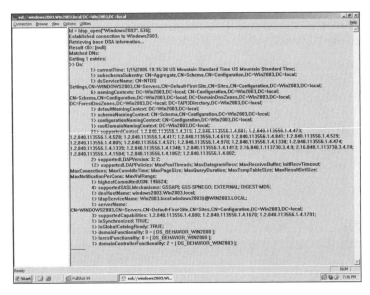

Figure 10-1   LDAP communications on port 636

7. Choose the **Connection** menu and click **Disconnect**.

8. Choose the **Connection** menu and click **Connect**.

9. The name of the domain controller should still be in the Server box.

10. Type **3269** in the **Port** box. Click **OK**.

11. Notice that the upper-left corner on the very top of the window shows gcssl://.

12. Choose the **Connection** menu, then click **Disconnect**. Choose the **Connection** menu, and click **Exit**.

Wireless Networks

You can secure communications when performing administration on wireless access points (AP) by leveraging protocols such as Secure Shell (SSH) or HTTP with SSL or TLS. A wireless AP can implement access control functions to allow or deny access to the network and provides the capability of encrypting wireless traffic. It also has the means to query an authentication and authorization service for authorization decisions and securely exchange encryption keys with the client to secure the network traffic.

As a general rule, SSL is not as flexible as IPSec from an application perspective, but is more flexible for access from any location. One must determine the usage requirements for each class of user and determine the best approach. Table 10-2 shows the advantages and disadvantages of using SSL for your wireless communications.

10

Table 10-2   SSL Advantages and Disadvantages

SSL Advantages	SSL Disadvantages
Provides a solution for access from anywhere, especially home PCs, mobile phones, and public access devices	Limited client-server application support (many port forwarded applications must be individually developed)
Less costly to deploy and maintain	Access control issues on public access devices such as kiosks and so on
More control over data files	Can be restrictive for power users
Wide range of support for Macintosh, Linux, UNIX, PDAs, and mobile phones	
Mature technology	

CONFIGURATION OF THE WEB SERVER FOR SSL CERTIFICATES

Encryption is used to protect the private information that clients exchange with a server, such as credit card numbers or phone numbers. When you enable SSL encryption, you can prevent unauthorized individuals from understanding the original content of your transmissions. Encrypted transmissions can significantly reduce transmission rates and server performance. Therefore, to maintain the performance level of your Web server, consider using SSL encryption only for sensitive information, such as financial transactions.

When you require users to establish an encrypted channel with your server, this requires both the user's Web browser and your Web server to support the encryption scheme used to secure the channel.

Server certificates provide a way for users to confirm the identity of your Web site before they transmit personal information, such as a credit card number. A server certificate contains detailed identification information, such as the name of the organization that is affiliated with the server content, the name of the organization that issued the certificate, and a public key that is used to establish an encrypted connection. This information helps to assure users of the authenticity of Web server content and the integrity of the SSL-secured connection.

Remember from earlier in the chapter that after establishing a link, a special session key is used by both your Web server and the user's Web browser to both encrypt and decrypt information.

For example, when an authenticated user attempts to download a file from a Web site requiring a SSL-secured channel, your Web server uses a session key to encrypt the file and related HTTP headers. After receiving the encrypted file, the Web browser then uses a copy of the same session key to recover the file.

Activity 10-2: Configure a Server for an SSL Certificate

Time Required: 30 minutes

Objective: Learn how to configure your server for SSL certificates using the IIS Manager tool.

Description: In this exercise, you will learn how to configure your server for SSL certificates using the IIS Manager tool. Note: Active Directory, IIS, and Certificate Services need to be installed on the machine. (You should have already done this in previous chapters.)

1. Log on with your **AdminXX** account, where *XX* is your assigned student number.

2. Click **Start**, **Administrative Tools**, **Internet Information Services (IIS) Manager**. Expand your server. Expand the **Web Sites** folder.

3. Right-click the **Default Web Site**. Choose **Properties**. Choose the Directory Security tab. In the Secure communications section, select the **Server Certificate** button.

4. The Welcome to the Web Server Certificate Wizard screen should open, as shown in Figure 10-2. Click **Next**.

5. On the Server Certificate screen, choose the **Create a new certificate** radio button, if necessary. Click **Next**.

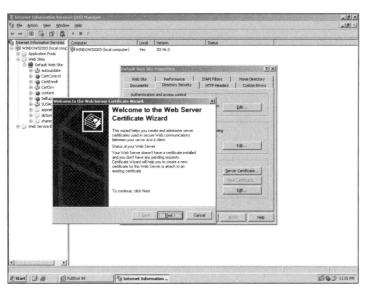

Figure 10-2   Web Server Certificate Wizard screen

6. On the Delayed or Immediate Request screen, choose the **Send the request immediately to an online certification authority** radio button. Click **Next**.

7. On the Name and Security Settings screen, type **Default Web Site SSL certificate** in the Name box. Leave the Bit length at 1024. Click **Next**.

8. On the Organization Information screen, type your class name, such as **CNT 1250** in the Organization name box. Type **Web servers** in the Organizational unit name box. Click **Next**.

9. On the Your Site's Common Name screen, the Common name box should default to your server name. If it does not, type your server name in the box. Click **Next**.

10. On the Geographical Information screen, Country should default to **US**. Type your state and city in the respective boxes. Click **Next**.

11. On the SSL Port screen, the **SSL port this web site should use** box should default to port 443. If it does not, type 443 in the box. Click **Next**.

12. On the Choose a Certification Authority screen, the Certification authorities box should default to your server, provided that you still have certificate services installed from the last chapter. If there is not a default server in the Certification authorities box, use the drop-down list arrow and select one. Click **Next**.

13. You should now be on the Certificate Request Submission screen, and the information should look similar to that in Figure 10-3. Click **Next**.

14. When the Completing the Web Server Certificate Wizard screen appears, click **Finish**.

10

Figure 10-3 Certificate Request Submission screen

15. Click **OK** on the Default Web Site Properties page. Choose **File** from the toolbar menu, then click **Exit** to close the IIS Manager screen.

When you set security properties for a specific Web site, you automatically set the same security properties for directories and files belonging to that site, unless the security properties of the individual directories and files have been previously set. When you attempt to change security properties for your Web site, the Web server will prompt you for permission to reset the properties of individual directories and files. If you choose to reset these properties, your previous security settings will be replaced by the new settings.

Once you have a certificate issued, you can configure your Web site to require SSL certificates for the clients. You can configure your Web server to require a 128-bit minimum session-key strength for all SSL-secured communication sessions. If you set a minimum 128-bit key strength, however, users attempting to establish a SSL-secured communications channel with your server must use a browser capable of communicating with a 128-bit session key. Client configuration for SSL certificates will be discussed in the next section of this chapter; however, in the next activity we will look at the server configuration of this as well as the configuration of a certificate trust list (CTL).

You can configure computers running Windows Server 2003 with IIS 6.0 to accept certificates from a predefined list of certification authorities (CAs). For example, you might create a different list of trusted certification authorities for each department on your network. IIS would accept only client certificates supplied by certification authorities in the CTL for that department. Each Web site can be configured to accept certificates from a different list by using CTLs. You can automatically verify client certificates against the CTL.

You can use the Certificate Trust List Wizard to create and edit CTLs and to add new root certificates to your CTLs.

ACTIVITY

Activity 10-3: Configure a Server to Accept Clients Using a SSL Certificate and Certificate Trust List

Time Required: 45 minutes

Objective: Learn how to configure your server for client SSL certificates and verify them against a certificate trust list using the IIS Manager tool.

Description: In this exercise, you will verify that the certificate you requested in the last activity was indeed issued, import it, and learn how to configure your server to accept client SSL certificates and verify them against a certificate trust list using the IIS Manager tool.

1. Log on with your **AdminXX** account, where *XX* is your assigned student number.

2. Click **Start**, **Administrative Tools**, **Certification Authority**. Expand your server. Select the Issued Certificates folder. Verify that the Web Server Certificate you requested in the last exercise has been issued. Choose the **File** menu from the toolbar, then choose **Exit**.

3. Click **Start**, **Run**, type **mmc** in the Open box, and click **OK**. In the console window, click the **File** menu, then choose **Add/Remove Snap-in**. On the Standalone tab, click **Add**.

4. On the Add Standalone Snap-in screen, choose **Certificates**, then click **Add**.

5. On the Certificates Snap-in screen, select the **Computer account** radio button. Click **Next**.

6. On the Select Computer screen, select the **Local computer (the computer this console is running on)** radio button. Click **Finish**.

7. Click **Close** on the Add Standalone Snap-in screen. Click **OK** on the Standalone screen.

8. Expand the **Certificates** icon on the left side of the screen. Expand the **Personal** folder. Select **Certificates**. On the right side of the screen, highlight the Web certificate you just issued. Right-click, then choose **All Tasks**, **Export**.

9. The Welcome to the Certifcate Export Wizard screen opens. Click **Next**.

10. On the Export Private key screen, under Do you want to export the private key with the certificate?, be sure that the radio button has defaulted to **No, do not export the private key**. Click **Next**.

11. On the Export File Format screen, be sure that the **DER encoded binary X.509 (.CER)** radio button is selected. Click **Next**.

12. On the File to Export screen, type **Web** in the File name box. Click **Next**. Click **Finish**.

10

13. You will get a message telling you that the export was successful. Click **OK**.

14. Expand the **Trusted Root Certification Authorities** folder. Right-click the **Certificates** folder and choose **All Tasks, Import**.

15. The Welcome to the Certificate Import Wizard screen should appear, as shown in Figure 10-4. Click **Next**.

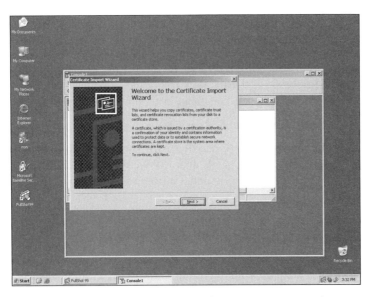

Figure 10-4 Welcome to the Certificate Import Wizard screen

16. On the File to Import screen, in the File name box, choose the **Browse** button. Navigate to the Administrator.Yourserver folder. At the bottom of the open screen, you should find the Web.cer certificate; highlight it. Click **Open**. Click **Next**.

17. On the Certificate Store page, the radio button should default to **Place all certificates in the following store**, and the Trusted Root Certification Authorities should show in the Certificate store box. Click **Next**.

18. On the Completing the Certificate Import Wizard screen, click **Finish**.

19. You will receive a message saying that the import was successful. Click **OK**. Close the console. When asked about saving the console settings, click **No**.

20. Click **Start, Administrative Tools, Internet Information Services (IIS) Manager**. Expand your server. Expand the **Web Sites** folder.

21. Right-click the **Default Web Site**. Choose **Properties**. Choose the Directory Security tab. In the Secure communications section, select the **View Certificate** button. Select the **Certification Path** tab. Check the **Certificate status** box to be sure that it says This certificate is OK. Click **OK**.

22. On the Directory Security tab, in the Secure communications section, select the
    Edit button. On the Secure Communications screen, check the **Require secure
    channel (SSL)** box.

23. Under the Client certificates section, choose the **Require client certificates** radio
    button.

24. Check the **Enable certificate trust list** box. Click **New**.

25. The Welcome to the Certificate Trust List Wizard should appear, as shown in Figure
    10-5. Click **Next**.

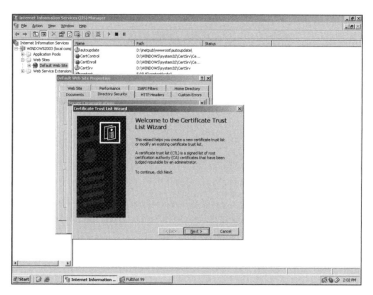

Figure 10-5   Welcome to the Certificate Trust List Wizard screen

26. On the Certificates in the CTL screen, choose **Add from Store**. When the Select
    Certificate screen comes up, find the certificate you just imported, highlight it, and
    click **OK**.

27. On the Certificates in the CTL screen, click **Next**. On the Name and Description
    screen, in the Friendly name box, it should default to **New IIS CTL**. Click **Next**.

28. On the Completing the Certificate Trust List Wizard screen, review the information,
    then click **Finish**.

29. You will get a message that the Certificate Trust List wizard succeeded. Click **OK**.
    On the Secure Communications screen, click **OK**. On the Default Web Site Proper-
    ties screen, click **Apply**, then click **OK**. Close the **IIS Manager** console.

Self-Issued Certificates

As you saw in Activity 10-2, you can use the Web Server Certificate Wizard to generate a certificate request from an online certification authority such as Microsoft Certificate Services. Depending on your organization's needs and relationship with its Web site users, you can issue your own server certificates. In cases where departments such as employee payroll or benefits use the corporate intranet, it might be in the organization's best interest to run a certificate service and assume responsibility for validating identification information and issuing server certificates.

The following considerations should be taken into account when deciding whether to issue your own server certificates:

- Microsoft Certificate Services can accommodate different certificate formats and provide for auditing and logging of certificate-related activity.
- Evaluate the cost of each by comparing the cost of issuing your own certificates against the cost of buying a certificate from a certification authority.
- Keep the learning curve in mind. Your organization will require an initial adjustment period to learn, implement, and integrate Certificate Services with existing security systems and policies.
- If outside vendors are connecting to your servers, evaluate the willingness of these clients to trust your organization as a certificate supplier.

The success of certificate authentication depends on whether the party receiving a certificate trusts the authority who issued the certificate and that the authority correctly verified the certificate owner's identity. Should your vendors, business partners, or clients have any doubt about trusting in your certificates, you should consider using a third-party commercial issuer. In addition, as a rule of thumb, if you don't control the client computer then use Public CAs.

Publicly Issued Certificates

If a user logging on to your company's Web site notices that the certificate issued is issued from your organization rather than a well-known certificate authority, the user might be hesitant to provide credit card information. This might be especially true if your company is new and not well known. If this is the case, consider obtaining a server certificate from a certification authority. You can obtain a certificate from a mutually trusted, third-party commercial organization such as VeriSign or Thawte. The primary responsibility of the CA is to confirm the identity of the party that is seeking a certificate, thus ensuring the validity of the identification information that is contained in the certificate.

Before issuing a certificate, the CA requires you to provide identification information, such as name, address, and organization. The extent of the information required can vary with the identification requirements of the certificate authority. This information might require a personal interview with the CA as well as the endorsement of a notary. Depending on the level of identification assurance offered by your server certificate, you can expect to wait anywhere from several days to several months for the certification authority to approve your request and send you a certificate file.

NOTE

If you use a third-party commercial organization, be sure to check the renewal on the certificate.

When you use a third-party commercial organization for certificates, they must be renewed on a regular basis, usually every one or two years. Be cognizant of this fact, because the commercial organization may not send a renewal notice and the certificate could expire without your knowing it. When this happens, the connecting client will be told that the certificate has expired and will be asked if he or she wants to continue. For an organization that does much of its business over the Internet, this could cause a confidence issue with clients and be a source of lost revenue.

Whether you choose to issue your own certificates or obtain them from a third-party commercial issuer, keep in mind the following general rules about Web certificates:

- Each Web site can have only one server certificate assigned to it.
- One certificate can be assigned to multiple Web sites.
- You can assign multiple IP addresses per Web site.
- You can assign multiple SSL ports per Web site.

10

CONFIGURATION OF THE CLIENT FOR SSL CERTIFICATES

With SSL, your Web server also has the option of authenticating users by checking the contents of their client certificates. **Client certificates** are electronic documents that contain certificate information about clients. These certificates, like server certificates, contain not only certificate information but also public encryption keys that form part of the SSL security feature of IIS. You can use client certificate authentication, along with SSL encryption, to implement a method for verifying the identity of your users. The public keys from the server and the client certificates make encryption and decryption of transmitted data possible over an open network such as the Internet. Certification authorities may offer different types of client certificates, which contain differing amounts of information, depending on the level of authentication that is required. The typical client certificate contains the following items of information:

- The identity of the user
- The identity of the certification authority
- A public key used for establishing encrypted communications
- Validation information, such as an expiration date and serial number

Your Web server cannot process client certificates unless you have previously installed a server certificate and enabled your server's communication security features, much like you did in the last activity.

The exact configuration of the client will vary based on the type of client. Microsoft Internet Explorer browsers are configured to use SSL on the Advanced Internet Options within the Security category, as shown in Figure 10-6. The client will also need a digital certificate, which can be autoenrolled through Group Policy and your CA or assigned by a third party.

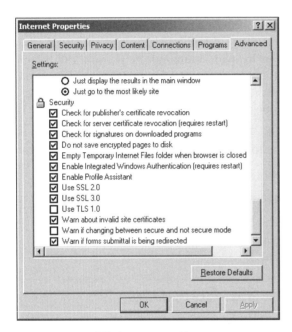

Figure 10-6   SSL browser options

Although you can require users attempting to access your Web site to log on with a client certificate, requiring a client certificate does not reliably protect your content from unauthorized access. Any user with a valid and trusted client certificate can establish a connection and access your resources. To protect your Web content from unauthorized access you must do one of the following:

- Use Basic, Digest, or Integrated Windows authentication, in addition to requiring a client certificate.

- Create a Windows account mapping for client certificates.

CERTIFICATE RENEWAL

Microsoft Certificate Services provides the flexibility to process certificate requests manually or automatically. Essentially, manual requests are made if administrative approval is required and automatically if no approval is necessary. Many organizations base their certificate enrollment and renewal methods on the level of security associated with each type of certificate and the volume of certificate requests that they anticipate. You can automate the deployment of computer certificates by configuring Group Policy to automatically assign the necessary computer certificates. This is done through autoenrollment, which was outlined in Activity 9-8.

The security and renewal requirements for your certificates should be based on the following factors:

- The value of the network resources protected by the CA trust chain
- The degree to which you trust your certificate users
- The amount of administrative effort that you are willing to devote to certificate renewal and CA renewal
- The business value of the certificate

The validity period of certificates depends on the organization's requirements as well as the aforementioned requirements. Table 10-3 outlines some of Microsoft's recommendations for the validity period for different CA types. Microsoft also offers a worksheet called Windows Server 2003 Certificate Lifecycle Plan (DSSPKI_3.doc) that can be used to plan a renewal strategy.

Table 10-3 Recommendations for Validity Periods

Certificate Purpose	Certificate Life	Renewal Recommendation
Enterprise CA s for medium security certificates	5 years	Renew every 3 years. Renew by using a new key at least every 5 years.
Enterprise CA s for high security certificates	5 years	Renew with new key at least every 4 years.
Enterprise CA for external certificates	5 years	Renew at least every 4 years. Renew by using a new key at least every 5 years.
Secure mail and secure browser certificates	1 year	Renew by using a new key at least every 2 years.
Smart card certificates	1 year	Renew by using a new key at least every 2 years.
Administrator certificates	1 year	Renew by using a new key at least every 2 years.
Secure Web server certificates	2 years	Renew by using a new key at least every 2 years.

Keep in mind that these are recommendations for self-issued certificates. If you are using third-party commercial certificates, you will have to be aware of the renewal dates so that they don't expire. Remember that these are only recommendations, and your organization's needs may warrant different actions. For example, you might trust temporary users less than you trust normal business users, and therefore you might set shorter lifetimes on the certificates of temporary users and require stricter controls for their renewal. Your organization may want to place tighter restrictions on certificates used to validate critical data such as purchase contracts than you place on certificates for routine e-mail. On the other hand, to reduce the administrative effort required to renew CAs, you can specify long, safe lifetimes for your certification trust hierarchies.

CONFIGURING SECURITY FOR REMOTE ACCESS USERS

One of the big issues an organization faces is how to provide authentication and authorization for dial-up, VPN, and wireless access to their network in a safe and secure manner. In addition, organizations that outsource network access, perform joint ventures with other organizations, or hire outside contractors for a majority of their work, require the authentication of user accounts from outside of the private network.

Microsoft has included a product that works with standards-based implementations of the Remote Authentication Dial-In User Service (RADIUS) protocol, so that you can use it with any standards-compliant RADIUS client, server, or proxy server. The process of deploying the Internet Authentication Service (IAS) component of Windows Server 2003 is an integral part of an authentication solution and will be discussed in further detail in the next chapter. To provide a secure and reliable remote access solution you should carefully plan then test your remote access design. This includes deciding whether to deploy a dial-up network, a VPN, or a combination of both. Often your remote access solution will involve elements of both. To properly plan and deploy remote access authentication and enhance the security of your network, it is important to review the protocols that can be used for this purpose.

Password Authentication Protocol

Password Authentication Protocol (PAP) is an older, simple remote access authentication protocol. PAP uses a two-way handshake to provide for user authentication in which the server asks for the credentials and the user supplies them. With PAP, the user's credentials are sent over the wire in cleartext and can be easily sniffed by an attacker. PAP is strongly discouraged because passwords can easily be read from the Point-to-Point Protocol (PPP) packets exchanged during the authentication process. PAP cannot be used with Microsoft Point-to-Point Encryption (MPPE) and is currently used only by older UNIX-based servers that do not support any other authentication protocols.

NOTE A Windows XP remote access client will terminate a connection if the connection is configured to require a secured password, and the client connects to a server that is configured only for PAP.

Challenge Handshake Authentication Protocol

The **Challenge Handshake Authentication Protocol (CHAP)** can be used to provide on-demand authentication within an ongoing data transmission. CHAP uses a one-way hashing function that first involves a service requesting a CHAP response from the client. The client creates a hashed value that is derived using the message digest (MD5) hashing algorithm and sends this value to the service, which also calculates the expected value itself. The server, referred to as the authenticator, compares these two values, and if they match, the transmission continues. This process is repeated at random intervals during a data transaction session. In other words, the remote access server knows the password, but it does not ask the client for the password. Instead, the remote access server sends a challenge message that is encrypted so that the client will be able to decrypt the challenge only if the client actually has the password. The client then decrypts the challenge using its password and a hash algorithm; after this, the client sends the result back to the server. The server compares the result with its own decryption of the challenge using the same password.

CHAP functions PPP connections. Just as with PAP, you cannot use CHAP authentication when using MPPE. There are also two forms of CHAP that are Microsoft-specific: MS-CHAP and MS-CHAPv2.

Microsoft Challenge Handshake Authentication Protocol

If you intend to use PPTP VPN connections, they require the use of the Microsoft Challenge Handshake Authentication Protocol (MS-CHAP), Microsoft Challenge Handshake Authentication Protocol version 2 (MS-CHAP v2), or Extensible Authentication Protocol Transport Layer Security (EAP-TLS) authentication protocols. Only these three authentication protocols provide a means to generate the same encryption key on both the VPN client and the VPN server.

Microsoft Challenge Handshake Authentication Protocol uses the same type of challenge/response mechanism as CHAP but it uses a nonreversible encrypted password. Since MPPE uses this encryption key as a basis for encrypting all PPTP data sent over the VPN connection, MPPE can be used with MS-CHAP

MS-CHAPv2

Microsoft Challenge Handshake Authentication Protocol version 2 uses a challenge/response mechanism, but it is much more sophisticated than that of MS-CHAP. With MS-CHAP v2, the server must first prove to the client that it knows the correct password that the client should send. Then, the client answers the challenge of the server to

10

provide the proof that it has the password. During this process, separate cryptographic keys are generated for transmitted and received data during the authentication process. MS-CHAP v2 is supported by client computers running Windows XP, Windows 2000, Windows 98, Windows Millennium Edition (ME), and Windows NT version 4.0. A dial-up connection typically uses MS-CHAP v2 as the user authentication method to authenticate the router, along with MPPE for data encryption.

 Windows 95 clients support MS-CHAP v2 for VPN connections, but not for dial-up connections.

NOTE

Remember that MSCHAP and MSCHAP v2 are password-based authentication protocols. If you are not using certificates or smart cards, it is a better choice to use MS CHAP v2. This is a stronger authentication protocol than MS CHAP. In addition, be sure to enforce the use of strong passwords on your network, if you are using a password-based authentication protocol.

Extensible Authentication Protocol

The **Extensible Authentication Protocol (EAP)** is an extension to PPP. It is an arbitrary authentication mechanism that authenticates a remote access connection. The exact authentication scheme to be used is negotiated by the remote access client and the authenticator, which could be either a remote access server or a RADIUS server. To be more specific, the authentication mechanism is not chosen during the link establishment phase. Instead, the EAP negotiation is performed during the connection authentication phase. Once the connection authentication is established, the use of an EAP type is negotiated. Once the EAP type is agreed upon, EAP allows for an open-ended conversation between the remote access client and the remote access server that can vary based on the parameters of the connection. The conversation consists of requests for authentication information and the responses, which are dependent upon the EAP type. Routing and Remote Access includes support for EAP-TLS and Message Digest-5 Challenge (MD-5 Challenge) by default.

EAP-MD5

Message Digest-5 Challenge can be used to authenticate the credentials of remote access clients by using username and password–based security systems. It can also authenticate the integrity of the message. MD-5 Challenge uses the same challenge handshake protocol as CHAP. Like CHAP, EAP-MD5 requires that local or domain passwords are stored in a reversibly encrypted form. The difference is that the challenges are sent as EAP messages. Once the connection authentication phase is reached, the authenticating server sends an EAP-Request message requesting the identity of the client. Once the client sends its username as an EAP-Response message, the server sends an EAP-Request message containing the MD-5 Challenge string. The client then sends the MD-5 hash of its username and password to the server as an EAP-Response message. Provided the server receives a proper response, the client gets a success message.

EAP-TLS

The **Transport Layer Security protocol** is based on SSL. The **Extensible Authentication Protocol–Transport Layer Security authentication protocol (EAP-TLS)** is designed for use with a certificate infrastructure and either certificates or smart cards. You can use Certificate Services in Windows Server 2003 as the CA for your organization, or you can use a third-party CA when you deploy EAP-TLS as your authentication method. With EAP-TLS, the VPN client sends its user certificate for authentication, and the authenticating server for the VPN server sends a computer certificate for authentication.

TLS provides authentication, data integrity, and data confidentiality services. This is the strongest authentication method, because it does not rely on passwords. EAP-TLS is supported only on servers that are running Routing and Remote Access, that are configured to use Windows Authentication, and that are members of a domain.

Remember from Chapter 8 that preshared keys can also be used. The preshared key is shared among the recipients of encrypted messages. You should not use a preshared key if any other authentication method is available. There are a couple of disadvantages of using a preshared key. The same key that is used to encrypt is also used to decrypt. Therefore, it is an inherent security risk, because if the key is compromised, an attacker could use the key for authentication to a network. In addition, the preshared key is stored in the registry in plaintext.

Activity 10-4: Configure Dial-in Server for MS-CHAP v2 Authentication

ACTIVITY

Time Required: 30 minutes

Objective: Learn how to configure authentication for remote connections to use MS-CHAP v2 for dial-in connections.

Description: In this exercise, you will learn how to enable Routing and Remote Access to use MS-CHAP v2 for dial-in connection authentication.

1. Log on with your **AdminXX** account, where *XX* is your assigned student number.

2. Click **Start**, **Administrative Tools**, **Routing and Remote Access**. Highlight your server. Your screen should look like Figure 10-7. Note: If RRAS has already been configured, go to the Action menu and choose **Disable Routing and Remote Access**.

3. Go to the **Action** menu, and choose **Configure and Enable Routing and Remote Access**.

4. On the Welcome to the Routing and Remote Access Server Setup Wizard screen, click **Next**.

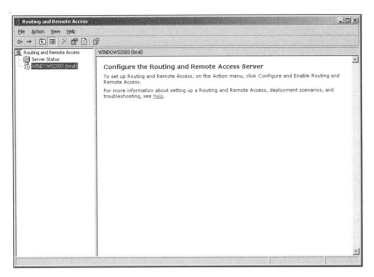

Figure 10-7   Configure Routing and Remote Access Server screen

5. On the Configuration screen, select the **Remote access (dial-up or VPN)** radio button if necessary. Click **Next**.

6. On the Remote Access screen, check the **Dial-up** box. Click **Next**.

NOTE   If you are connected to more than one network you may encounter a screen asking you to select the network. Should this happen, your instructor will instruct you which network to choose.

7. On the IP Address Assignment screen, select the **From a specified range of addresses** radio button. Click **Next**.

8. On the Address Range Assignment screen, select the **New** button. When the New Address Range box opens, type **192.168.100.1** in the Start IP address box. Type **192.168.100.254** in the End IP address box. The Number of addresses box should show **254**. Click **OK**. Click **Next**.

9. On the Managing Multiple Remote Access Servers screen, leave the default radio button selected, **No, use Routing and Remote Access to authenticate connection requests**. Click **Next**.

10. On the Completing the Routing and Remote Access Server Setup Wizard screen, review the information, then click **Finish**.

11. You may receive a message telling you to configure the DHCP Relay Agent with the IP address of your DHCP server. Click **OK**. The Routing and Remote service will start. Your screen should now look like Figure 10-8.

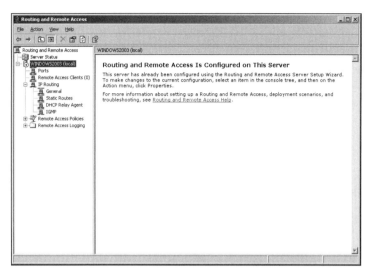

Figure 10-8   Configured Routing and Remote Access

10

12. On the left side of the screen, click **Remote Access Policies**. The right side of the screen should show two policies. Right-click **Connections to Microsoft Routing and Remote Access server** and choose **Properties**.

13. Select the **Edit Profile** button. On the Edit Dial-in Profile screen, choose the **Authentication** tab.

14. Uncheck the **Microsoft Encrypted Authentication (MS-CHAP)** box. Uncheck the **User can change password after it has expired** box under MS-CHAP v2. Your screen should look like Figure 10-9.

15. Click **Apply**. Click **OK**. Click **OK** on the Settings screen. Choose **File** and **Exit** to close the console.

In regard to using these methods to secure your remote communications, you should use the most secure protocols that your network access servers and clients can support. If you need a high level of security, configure the remote access server and the authenticating server to accept only a few very secure authentication protocols. On the other hand, if flexibility is more important than maintaining a high level of security, configure the authenticating server to accept a less secure authentication protocol as you just did in Activity 10-4.

Multifactor Authentication

The best possible authentication solution involves a combination of other methods. A multifactor solution like this might include the use of a smart card token storing biometric values that are compared to those of the user, who might also be asked to enter a valid password. The difficulty involved in gaining unauthorized access increases as more types of authentication are used, though the difficulty for users wishing to authenticate themselves is

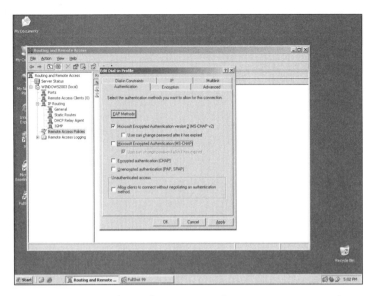

Figure 10-9   Configured Routing and Remote Access Authentication policy

also increased. Administrative overhead and cost of support also increase with the complexity of the authentication scheme, so a solution should be reasonable based on the sensitivity of data being secured.

Multifactor authentication works on the premise that a user can prove his identity in three ways:

- Something he knows—which could be a password or a personal identification number (PIN)

- Something he has—such as possessing a smart card or access card

- Something he is—which usually is some type of biometric identification such as a fingerprint or retinal scan

Multifactor authentication combines two or even three of these factors for proof of identification. This method is more secure than authentication from a single factor, but it is inconvenient for users and often they find biometric processes intrusive.

Providing Remote Access over a VPN

In a **virtual private network (VPN)** solution for remote access, users connect to your corporate network over the Internet. You will find VPN solutions in organizations with widespread remote access requirements. A VPN is a method of communicating through a nonsecure medium in a secure way. The nonsecure medium is usually the Internet. The process of communicating through the Internet with a protocol that keeps the communication secure is called tunneling. VPNs use a combination of tunneling, authentication, and encryption technologies to create secure connections. VPNs are attractive because they reduce remote access expenses by using the existing Internet infrastructure. A VPN solution can be used to partially or entirely replace an in-house, dial-up remote access infrastructure. Administrative overhead is reduced with a VPN because the Internet service provider (ISP) is responsible for maintaining the connectivity once the user is connected to the Internet. VPNs offer the following benefits:

- Using the Internet as a connection medium saves long-distance phone expenses and requires less hardware than a dial-up networking solution does.

- Authentication prevents unauthorized users from connecting, and using strong encryption methods make it extremely difficult for a hacker to read the data sent across a VPN connection.

Because a VPN remote access solution routes data over a packet-switched connection, security is an important part of your VPN remote access server design. When designing security for your VPN remote access server solution, the following steps give you an idea of the procedure:

1. Choose a VPN protocol.

2. Decide which authentication protocols are needed.

3. Pick the extent and level of encryption that will be used.

4. If organizational needs warrant the use of certificates, plan a certificate infrastructure that supports client authentication for remote access.

5. Consider enhancing security by using remote access account lockout.

The security of a VPN is based on the tunneling and authentication protocols that you use and the level of encryption that you apply to VPN connections. Windows Server 2003 supports both Point-to-Point Tunneling Protocol (PPTP) and Layer Two Tunneling Protocol (L2TP), but not all client operating systems support them. We will discuss these tunneling protocols and client operating systems shortly. Keep in mind that the tunneling protocols themselves are only one part of the system that makes secure communication through a nonsecure medium possible. To effectively configure and troubleshoot a VPN, you should be familiar with the role an ISP plays in your VPN solution.

Internet Service Providers

To access the Internet, either your organization registers an IP address with an approved registration organizations and maintains its own DNS server and DNS resolution, or the organization uses a DNS server and equipment that has been registered by someone else, namely an ISP. Outsourcing part or all of a remote access solution through a contract with an ISP may provide your organization significant cost savings by minimizing both setup and operations costs, especially if the organization is large and has many business partners or users requiring remote access. In addition, if you purchase a wholesale contract with an ISP, you can require that the ISP provide a guaranteed level of service for some or all components of your remote access solution. Many ISPs offer a level of service that is equal to those of dial-up wide area network (WAN) connections. An ISP can also provide access to an extensive network of connections across a wide geographical area for a fixed cost. Therefore, if you are deploying a dial-up networking solution, consider outsourcing your deployment to avoid long-distance charges as well as increasing your service level.

Client Operating Systems

Windows Server 2003 supports two VPN protocols: PPTP and Layer Two Tunneling Protocol with Internet Protocol security (L2TP/IPSec). Depending on the needs of the organization, your choice of clients may be limited or your choice of tunneling protocols may be limited. The planning of a VPN design will be determined by which VPN protocol best meets your requirements and provides the degree of security that you desire for the clients that are accessing your network. Table 10-4 compares client support for PPTP and L2TP/IPSec.

Table 10-4   Comparison of Client Support for Tunneling Protocols

PPTP	L2TP/IPSec
Windows 2000	Windows 2000
Windows XP	Windows XP
Windows NT Workstation	Mls2tp.exe must be installed for Windows NT Workstation
Windows ME	Mls2tp.exe must be installed for Windows ME
Windows 98	Mls2tp.exe must be installed for Windows 98

A supported tunneling protocol can be configured in the Networking tab of the connection properties of the client as shown in Figure 10-10.

CAUTION

When a VPN client connects and creates a new default route, Internet sites that have been accessible are no longer accessible. This poses no problem for VPN remote access users who require access only to the organization's network. However, it is not acceptable for remote users who need access to the Internet while they are connected to the organization's network.

Using Point-to-Point Tunneling Protocol

Point-to-Point Tunneling Protocol allows tunneling that works at Layer 2 of the OSI model and enables a single point-to-point connection. There are two main connection types where PPTP may be used: over the Internet (such as VPN) or via a dial-up connection. PPTP technology embeds its own network protocol within the TCP/IP packets carried by the Internet. After the PPTP tunnel is created, user data is transmitted between the client and PPTP server. PPTP VPN connections require the use of the MS-CHAP, MS-CHAP v2, or EAP-TLS authentication protocols. These authentication protocols provide a mechanism to generate the same encryption key on both the VPN client and the VPN server.

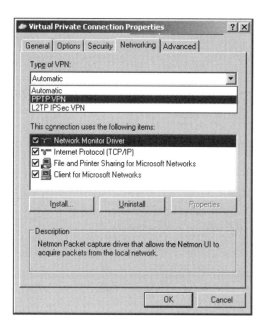

Figure 10-10   Configuring a client tunneling protocol

PPTP is easy to implement and administer but not the most secure method available. When used with MS-CHAP v2 for password-based authentication and strong passwords, PPTP is more secure. If you need stronger authentication for PPTP connections, you can implement a PKI using smart cards or certificates along with EAP-TLS. PPTP can be used by all Microsoft clients and has MPPE (which encrypts data between two Microsoft systems) built in.

Using Layer Two Tunneling Protocol

Layer Two Tunneling Protocol (L2TP) is extension of the PPP protocol, created by combining the best qualities of PPTP and Layer 2 Forwarding (L2F). L2TP is a Datalink extension of PPP that sets up a single point-to-point connection between two computers. L2TP/IPSec provides data integrity, data origin authentication, data confidentiality, and replay protection for each packet. Since L2TP defines its own tunneling protocol, it requires support on the routers of the ISP, but it can encapsulate PPP packets for transmission over protocols like X.25, Frame Relay, and ATM tunnels. It is protocol-independent and includes an authentication mechanism. For L2TP/IPSec connections, you can use any user authentication protocol, because the authentication occurs after the VPN client and VPN server have established a secure communication channel.

L2TP/IPSec uses PPP user authentication methods and IPSec encryption to encrypt IP traffic. It combines certificate-based computer authentication with PPP-based user authentication. L2TP/IPSec can be used only by Windows 2000 Professional and newer clients. If you intend to use L2TP/IPSec with older operating systems, such as Windows 98 or Windows NT Workstation4.0, download and install the Microsoft L2TP/IPSec VPN Client found at *www.microsoft.com/windows2000/server/evaluation/news/bulletins/l2tpclient.asp.*

Although PPTP is widely supported, easily deployed, and works with most network address translators (NATs), for the highest level of security, use a remote access VPN based on L2TP/IPSec with certificate-based IPSec authentication and Triple-DES for encryption. Should you choose to use a PPTP-based VPN solution, it is best to use MS-CHAP v2 as the authentication protocol. When you are choosing an authentication protocol for VPN connections, keep the following in mind:

- When using smart cards or certificates, use EAP-TLS authentication protocol for both PPTP and L2TP connections.

- When using a password-based authentication protocol, choose MS-CHAP v2, then use Group Policy to enforce strong passwords.

- Always use the most secure protocols that your network access servers and clients can support.

Network Address Translation Devices

The idea behind **network address translation (NAT)** is to keep private network addresses private while reducing the cost and use of public addresses. NAT devices work by translating the IP addresses and Transmission Control Protocol/User Datagram Protocol (TCP/UDP) port numbers of packets that are forwarded between a private network and the Internet, thereby preventing other users on the Internet from knowing the real address of your private network. A nice side benefit is that it also allows you to use one public address to provide Internet access to many users simultaneously, reducing organizational costs for public IP addresses.

Because of their encryption mechanisms, some tunneling protocols have issues when combined with NAT. PPTP with its built-in MPPE encryption is able to interoperate with NAT. If you are using a NAT device with your VPN remote access server solution, your plan for remote access must include the required setup for placing VPN clients behind the NAT device. When a VPN client that uses a PPTP connection is behind a NAT device, the NAT device must include a NAT editor that can translate PPTP traffic. This editor is included in the NAT/Basic Firewall routing protocol component of the Routing and Remote Access service.

PPTP is the recommended protocol when tunneling with NAT using Microsoft servers earlier than Windows Server 2003. Although L2TP does not have an inherent encryption mechanism, L2TP uses IPSec for the encryption. Keep in mind that devices that support NAT may not support it for tunneling with L2TP using IPSec encryption. For example, Microsoft servers prior to Windows Server 2003 could not use IPSec and NAT together. Windows Server 2003 allows IPSec to be used through a NAT device with a new service called IP NAT Traversal.

IP NAT Traversal

One of the issues with deploying L2TP with IPSec is that when IPSec peers are located behind a NAT device, IPSec thinks that packets sent across the NAT device have been tampered with and discards them. Realizing that this was an issue, some of the leading technology companies created a new technology known as **IPSec NAT Traversal (NAT-T).** NAT-T enables IPsec VPNs to work with NAT devices. Because Windows Server 2003 NAT devices support NAT-T, traffic can be secured by IPSec, while also being translated by a NAT device. IPSec NAT-T works by providing UDP encapsulation of IPSec packets to enable Internet Key Exchange (IKE)− and Encapsulating Security Payload (ESP)− protected traffic to pass through the NAT device. To use NAT-T, both the remote access VPN client and the remote access server must support IPSec NAT-T. With Windows Server 2003, this should not be an issue because NAT-T is supported by the server as well as the Microsoft L2TP/IPSec VPN client.

To recap VPN client use with NAT:

- PPTP-based VPN clients can be located behind a NAT device if the NAT includes an editor that can translate PPTP such as the NAT/Basic Firewall routing protocol component of the Routing and Remote Access service.

- If you locate L2TP/IPSec-based clients or servers behind a NAT device, both client and server must support IPSec NAT Traversal.

Activity 10-5: Configure a Routing and Remote Access Server for NAT

Time Required: 30 minutes

Objective: Learn how to configure a Routing and Remote Access server for NAT.

Description: In this exercise, you will learn how to enable Routing and Remote Access to use the server as a NAT device.

1. Log on with your **AdminXX** account, where *XX* is your assigned student number.

2. Click **Start**, **Administrative Tools**, **Routing and Remote Access**. Highlight your server, choose the **Action** menu, and choose **Disable Routing and Remote Access**. If a dialog box appears, click **Yes**.

3. Go to the **Action** menu, then choose **Configure and Enable Routing and Remote Access**.

4. On the Welcome to the Routing and Remote Access Server Setup Wizard screen, click **Next**.

5. On the Configuration screen, select the **Network Address Translation (NAT)** radio button. Click **Next**.

NOTE

If you are connected to more than one network you may encounter a screen asking you to select the network. Should this happen, your instructor will instruct you which network to choose.

6. On the NAT Internet Connection screen, check that the **Create a new demand-dial interface to the Internet** radio button is selected and the **Enable security on the selected interface by setting up Basic Firewall** box is checked. Click **Next**.

7. On the Ready to Apply Selections screen, click **Next**. The Routing and Remote Access service should start and the Demand Dial Interface Wizard should appear, as shown in Figure 10-11. Click **Next**.

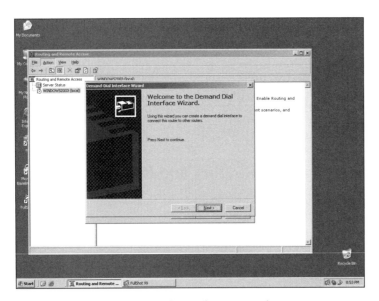

Figure 10-11   Demand Dial Interface Wizard

8. On the Interface Name screen, type **Windows 2003 local** in the Interface name box. Click **Next**.

9. On the Connection Type screen, select the **Connect using virtual private networking (VPN)** radio button. Click **Next**.

10. On the VPN Type screen, select the **Layer 2 Tunneling Protocol (L2TP)** radio button. Click **Next**.

11. On the Destination Address screen, in the Host name or IP address box, type **external.com**. Click **Next**.

12. On the Protocols and Security screen, check the **Add a user account so a remote router can dial in** check box. Click **Next**.

13. On the Dial In Credentials screen, in the Password box, type **y&er546lq$**, and in the Confirm password box, type **y&er546lq$**. Click **Next**.

14. On the Dial Out Credentials screen, in the User name box, type **dialout**. In the Domain box type the name of your domain. In the password box, type **pl%02@bz**. In the confirm password box, type **pl%02@bz**. Click **Next**.

15. You should now be on the Completing the Demand-Dial Interface Wizard screen, as shown in Figure 10-12. Click **Finish**.

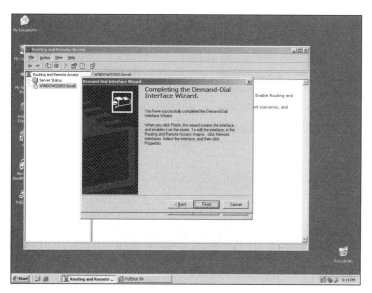

Figure 10-12   Completing the Demand-Dial Interface Wizard screen

16. The Summary screen should now appear, showing that you configured NAT and a basic firewall for the Internet interface on your local server. Click **Finish**.

17. Expand the **IP Routing** node on the left side of the screen if necessary. Highlight **NAT/Basic Firewall**. Verify that your server shows on the right side of the screen.

18. Choose **File**, **Exit** to close the RRAS window.

Routing and Remote Access Servers

To configure the server as a dial-up and VPN server, you will need to configure the Routing and Remote Access service on Windows Server 2003. By now, you should be familiar with this process, because we have been doing just that in the last few activities. When deciding on a remote access solution, you should evaluate your remote access needs, and then make a decision based on the benefits and features of both dial-up and VPN remote access. Your organization may choose to use a single method for remote access or deploy both. For obvious reasons, Microsoft recommends that the domain controller and the server running Routing and Remote Access operate on separate servers. When you deploy a remote access server solution, there are several steps that are to be taken. For example, if you deploy a VPN solution, these steps are to be followed:

1. Configure the server as a VPN remote access server.

2. Configure routing on the VPN server.

3. Implement security.

4. If required, install certificates.

5. Configure the remote access policy for the VPN server.

6. Configure remote access account lockout if necessary.

As a security measure, you can use remote access account lockout on remote access accounts. Although this is used as a security feature, keep in mind that if a malicious user intentionally forces an account or several accounts to be locked out, authorized users will be unable to create remote access connections. Remote access account lockout can be configured only in the registry of Windows Server 2003. This is done by modifying the following subkey in the registry on the server that authenticates remote access requests, as shown in Figure 10-13:

HKEY_LOCAL_MACHINE\SYSTEM\CurrentControlSet\Services\RemoteAccess\ Parameters\AccountLockout

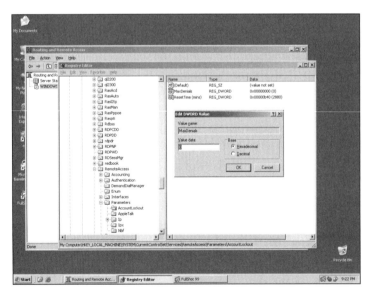

Figure 10-13   Configuring remote access account lockout

NOTE Although Windows Server 2003, Standard Edition can accept 1000 concurrent VPN connections, Windows Server 2003, Web Edition accepts only one VPN connection at a time.

Generally, a remote access server will carry a heavy load. As noted before, there is a limit to the number of connections that a server can handle. When planning deployment of remote access servers, there are several options to increase the server performance. These options include upgrading the server hardware, increasing the amount of RAM, and using separate remote servers. Starting with upgrading the server hardware, here are some guidelines:

For dial-up networking:

- A modem or a multiport adapter and access to an analog telephone line. For a large number of clients, install modem bank equipment and multiple phone lines.

- For each modem, a server serial port or for modem banks, a multiport serial adapter or a high-density combination card.

- Consider using multiport serial boards to offload processing from the remote access server.

For a VPN:

- Use network adapters capable of IPSec hardware offloading for interfaces on the public network.

- Configure all devices to 100 Mbps full duplex.

- Private network interfaces and data servers and routers that remote access clients will access should be directly connected to a high-capacity switch.

If you will not handle more than 1000 concurrent calls, 512 MB of RAM is adequate. However, if the need is greater, for every 1000 concurrent calls, provide an extra 128 MB of RAM, plus a base of 128 MB more for remote access and related services. If there is a large number of clients using remote access, consider increasing availability, security, and performance by using redundant servers for increased availability and network load balancing for increased availability and performance.

In addition, if one or more groups require a high-priority access, using separate remote access servers for these groups may be the proper solution.

VPN Router Placement in Relation to Firewalls

Firewalls protect your network by filtering incoming and outgoing traffic. They examine each packet to determine what type of packet it is, and then make a decision whether to forward the packet or discard it. How you configure firewall filters and the filters on the VPN router depends on the position of the VPN router relative to the firewall. Many organizations have a **demilitarized zone (DMZ)** or perimeter network. A DMZ or perimeter network is the last of your networks that traffic would traverse on the way to the Internet or the first of your networks that traffic would traverse on the way into your internal network. A DMZ can be viewed as a layer of privacy between corporate infrastructure and the Internet, exposing only those systems that have to be known to the public. The DMZ often hosts the corporation's WWW and FTP sites, e-mail, external DNS (Domain Name Service), and similar devices. If your organization already uses a DMZ, you can add your VPN router to the existing set of servers here. If not, your organization should consider this type of setup.

Even though it is possible to place the VPN router in front of the firewall with the VPN router attached to the Internet, this is not common. A more common configuration is to place the VPN router behind the firewall and attach the firewall to the Internet, which is the recommended method. Placing the VPN router behind the firewall allows you to configure the firewall with input and output filters on the firewall's Internet and DMZ interfaces, thereby restricting traffic to the VPN server.

If it is decided that the VPN server will be placed behind the firewall, configure the Internet interface on the firewall with inbound and outbound filters that allow traffic to the VPN server. Then for an added layer of security, configure the perimeter network interface on the VPN server with PPTP or L2TP/IPSec packet filters. If you choose to place the VPN server in front of the firewall, configure inbound and outbound filters on the VPN server to allow only VPN traffic to and from the IP address of the VPN server's Internet interface.

Because many filtering decisions are made based on the source and destination ports of the packet, you should make sure that the appropriate port is open to allow your tunneling protocols to operate. Table 10-5 can be used as guidance for the VPN placement and ports to be opened.

Table 10-5 Comparison of Port Configuration Based on Firewall Placement

Filter	VPN Server behind a Firewall	VPN Server in Front of a Firewall
PPTP inbound	TCP destination port 1723 on the firewall's Internet interface and the perimeter network interface	TCP destination port 1723
PPTP outbound	TCP source port 1723 on the firewall's Internet interface and the perimeter network interface	TCP source port 1723
L2TP/IPSec inbound	UDP destination port 500 and UDP destination port 4500 on the firewall's Internet interface and the perimeter network interface	UDP destination port 1701 UDP destination port 500
L2TP/IPSec outbound	UDP source port 500 and UDP destination port 4500 on the firewall's Internet interface and the perimeter network interface	UDP source port 1701 UDP source port 4500

MANAGING CLIENT CONFIGURATION FOR REMOTE ACCESS SECURITY

So far we have discussed much about the server configuration and requirements of the server, but what about the clients? To allow remote users to connect to your network using virtual private networking or dial-up networking, you will need to configure each client to connect to the remote access dial-up or VPN servers. You can either use the native connection features in Windows to configure clients or use a managed client solution, such as Connection Manager and its components, to create and distribute a custom service profile.

Overview of Remote Access Client Deployment

Windows Server 2003 has built-in tools to assist you in managing client access to a remote access server. These tools allow you to select the type of connection, encryption, and authentication that you will allow to make successful connections. It is possible to manually configure remote access connections using the native network connection capabilities in Windows. These native capabilities are best suited for when there are few users connecting to the network. This type of connection is relatively simple to set up when there are a small number of clients, however, when you are administering a large network with many remote access users with different needs, this becomes unmanageable. Connection Manager is a managed remote access solution that enables a network administrator to preconfigure remote access clients. The configuration can include a custom appearance and an updatable phone book that supplies users with dial-up access numbers.

Remote Access Policy

With remote access policy, a user can be allowed or denied access based on many factors including their connection type, security group membership, or the time of day that they are attempting to make the connection. A **remote access policy** is a collection of conditions and settings that define authorization and access privileges for connection attempts. Remote access policies consist of three components that work together to allow or deny the connection. You can configure multiple remote access policies on a single server.

 If multiple policies are configured, they will be processed in order from the top down. You should place the policy that is most specific at the top of the list.

NOTE

Remote Access Policy has a default remote access policy named Connections to Microsoft Routing and Remote Access server. This policy has preset configured packet filters to the remote access policy profile settings for the VPN connection to allow only inbound traffic that originates from remote access clients.

Conditions

Remote access policy conditions are attributes that must be met in order to satisfy the policy. They are the first component that is checked on a connection attempt. They are checked only at the initial time of the connection attempt. Conditions might include day and time restrictions, connection types, and security group memberships. If you set multiple conditions on the same remote access policy, then all of the conditions must be met to satisfy the policy.

A policy can be configured to accept or deny the connection based on the conditions. In other words, if the conditions state that a user must be in the Developers group to satisfy the policy and the user is in the Developers group, then the policy is satisfied. However, if that policy states that all users who satisfy it are denied access, then the users in the Developers group would be denied access because they met the conditions of the policy.

Permissions

The Dial-in permissions of the user are checked after the conditions, assuming that a condition to deny has not already been met. If your domain is in at least a Windows 2000 native mode functional level then the Dial-in permissions for the user can be set to Allow, Deny, or Control Access through Remote Access Policy. If your domain is in a lower functional level, then the Control access through Remote Access Policy option is not available. If you set the permissions to Allow, then the user is connected because he or she already met the conditions earlier. If you set the permissions to Deny, then the user is denied access even though he or she met the conditions earlier. If you set the permissions to Control access through Remote Access Policy, then the user's connection will be accepted or denied based on the next step. Even when remote access permission is allowed, the connection attempt still can be denied on the basis of other user account properties, such as callback options configured on the Dial-in tab, or it can be denied on the basis of remote access policy conditions or profile settings.

Profiles

If you set the user permissions to Control access through Remote Access Policy, then the profile settings on the policy must be met in order to obtain and to continue a connection. Profiles are checked after conditions. Profile settings that you can select include day and time restrictions, idle-timeouts, session-timeouts, encryption, authentication, connection types, and many more. If you set multiple profile settings in a remote access policy, then the user must meet and continue to meet the restrictions that you set.

ACTIVITY

Activity 10-6: Create a New Remote Access Policy

Time Required: 15 minutes

Objective: Learn how to create and configure a remote access policy.

Description: In this exercise, you will learn how to create and configure a new remote access policy.

1. Log on with your **AdminXX** account, where *XX* is your assigned student number.

2. Click **Start**, **Administrative Tools**, **Routing and Remote Access**.

3. Click **Remote Access Policies**, then right-click it and select **New Remote Access Policy**.

4. On the Welcome to the New Remote Access Policy Wizard screen, click **Next**.

5. On the Policy Configuration Method screen, select the **Use the wizard to set up a typical policy for a common scenario** radio button, if necessary. In the Policy name box, type **New Remote Policy**. Click **Next**.

6. On the Access Method screen, select the **VPN** radio button, if necessary. Click **Next**.

7. On the User or Group Access screen, select the **Group** radio button. Click the **Add** button. Type **Domain Users** in the Enter the object names to select box. Click **OK** to close the Select Groups dialog box. Click **Next**.

8. On the Authentication Methods screen, check the **Extensible Authentication Protocol (EAP)** box. Under Type (based on method of access and network configuration), use the drop-drown box and select **Smart Card or other certificate**. Click **Next**.

9. On the Policy Encryption Level screen, uncheck the **Basic encryption (IPSec 56-bit DES or MPPE 40-bit)** box and the **Strong encryption (IPSec 56-bit DES or MPPE 56-bit)** box. Click **Next**.

10. On the Completing the New Remote Access Policy Wizard screen, review the information, then click **Finish**.

11. Your screen should now look like Figure 10-14.

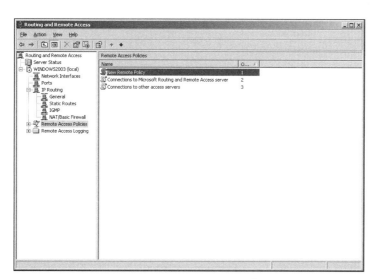

Figure 10-14   New remote access policy

12. Select the **File** menu, then choose **Exit** to close the console.

Connection Manager Administration Kit

You can use a component of the Microsoft Windows Server 2003 operating systems, **Connection Manager**, to provide customized remote access to your network through a dial-up or a VPN connection. Connection Manager actually consists of three different pieces:

■ The Connection Manager client, which provides a simplified way of connecting to a remote network.

■ The Connection Manager Administration Kit (CMAK), which allows the administrator to create and configure the service profile by creating a small, self-installing package.

■ Connection Point Services (CPS), which allows you to create and maintain phone books.

In this section you will work with the **Connection Manager Administration Kit**. CMAK is a wizard that guides you through the process of building profiles customized for your business. You can use CMAK to fully customize a connection and provide additional functionality for a user. There are many new features on the CMAK Wizard for Windows Server 2003, including the following:

■ Provide routing table updates that apply only while clients are connected to your server (split tunneling).

■ Automatically configure Internet Explorer proxy settings for a client computer.

■ Enable clients to choose which VPN server to use when they make a connection.

■ Automatically run applications on the client computer or on the server at the time of the connection.

Customizing Connection Manager

You can use the CMAK Wizard to create a custom service profile and then distribute this file to your users, so that when they double-click the file, it installs a service profile customized with the information you entered in the CMAK Wizard. The Connection Manager client then allows users to dial in to the organization or to complete a VPN connection, based on the information provided in the CMAK Wizard.

Connection Manager also has the ability to run custom actions at various points when establishing a connection. By taking advantage of custom actions, you can eliminate potential sources of calls to the help desk or connection issues for your users. The CMAK Wizard is used to include custom actions in your service profile, such as automatically starting programs when users connect. Custom actions are quite flexible and can include batch files, executable files, and dynamic link libraries (DLLs), or they can use installed or distributed programs. Here is a list of the custom actions that can be performed:

- Preinitialization actions
- Preconnect actions
- Predial actions
- Pretunnel actions
- Postconnect actions
- Disconnect actions
- On cancel actions
- On error actions

Examples of uses for these actions would be using preconnect actions to start an e-mail program, using a postconnect action to download the latest virus signatures, or using an error action to point the user to custom help files.

The CMAK is very versatile and allows you to apply your own branding to the client by using custom graphics, icons, menu items for the notification area shortcut, help, and license agreement. You can also configure additional customization by selecting the Advanced Customization check box in the Ready to Build the Service Profile page of the CMAK Wizard.

10

ACTIVITY

Activity 10-7: Use CMAK to create a Service Profile

Time Required: 45 minutes

Objective: Learn how to use the CMAK to create a service profile for dial-in users.

Description: In this exercise, you will learn how to install and use the CMAK to create a service profile for VPN users. Note: Microsoft Baseline Security Analyzer must be installed to complete Activity 10-7.

1. Log on with your **AdminXX** account, where *XX* is your assigned student number.

2. Click **Start**, **Control Panel**, **Add or Remove Programs**, **Add/Remove Windows Components**, highlight **Management and Monitoring tools**, click **Details**, then check the **Connection Manager Administration Kit** and **Connection Point Services** boxes. Click **OK**. Click **Next**.

3. If asked to insert the CD, do so and click **OK**. When you receive the Optional Networking Components screen, click **Yes**.

4. On the Completing the Windows Components Wizard screen, click **Finish**.

5. Close the **Add or Remove Programs** screen.

6. Click **Start**, **Administrative Tools**, **Connection Manager Administration Kit**.

7. On the Welcome to the Connection Manager Administration Kit Wizard screen, click **Next**.

8. On the Service Profile Selection screen, select the **New profile** radio button. Click **Next**.

9. On the Service and File Names screen, type your class name, such as **CNT 1310** in the Service name box. In the File name box, type **VPN**. Click **Next**.

10. On the Realm Name screen, select the **Add a realm name to the user name** radio button, then select the **Suffix** radio button. Type **Windows.com** in the Realm name box. Click **Next**.

11. On the Merging Profile Information screen, click **Next**.

12. On the VPN Support screen, check the **Phone book from this profile** box. Select the **Always use the same VPN server** radio button. Type **192.168.100.10** in the information box. *Note:* The IP address that you use here may be different than the one specified. Check with your instructor to verify which address you should use. Click **Next**.

13. On the VPN Entries screen, click the **Edit** button. Select the Security tab, in the drop down Security settings box, select **Use advanced security settings**. Click the **Configure** button next to Advanced Security Settings.

14. On the Advanced Security Settings screen, select the **Use Extensible Authentication Protocol (EAP)** radio button. In the drop-down list box, select the **Smart Card or other certificate (encryption enabled)** option. Under the VPN strategy area, use the drop-down list box to select **Only use Layer Two Tunneling Protocol (L2TP)**, as shown in Figure 10-15. Click **OK**. Click **OK**. Click **Next**.

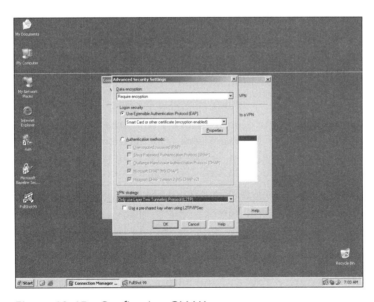

Figure 10-15   Configuring CMAK

15. On the Phone Book screen, uncheck the **Automatically download phone book updates** box. Click **Next**.

16. On the Dial-up Networking Entries screen, click **Next**.

17. On the Routing Table Update screen, click **Next**.

18. On the Automatic Proxy Configuration screen, click **Next**.

19. On the Custom Actions screen, next to Action type, choose **Post-connect** from the drop-down menu. Select the **New** button.

20. On the New Custom Action screen, in the Description box, type **MBSA**. In the Program to run box, click the **Browse** button. Use the Look in drop-down list box to find **Program files, Microsoft Baseline Security Analyzer, mbsa.exe**. Click **Open**. Uncheck the **Program interacts with the user box**, so that your screen looks like Figure 10-16. Click **OK**. Click **Next**.

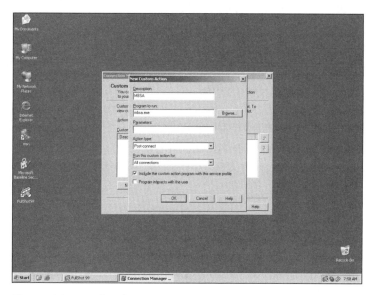

Figure 10-16 Configuring a custom action

21. On the Logon Bitmap screen, click **Next**.

22. On the Phone Book Bitmap screen, click **Next**.

23. On the Icons screen, click **Next**.

24. On the Notification Area Shortcut Menu screen, click **Next**.

25. On the Help File screen, click **Next**.

26. On the Support Information screen, in the Support information box, type 1-800-FOR-HELP. Click **Next**.

27. On the Connection Manager Software screen, click **Next**.

28. On the License Agreement screen, click **Browse**. In the Look in box, navigate to the **WINDOWS, System32** folder and choose the **eula.txt** file. Click **Open**. Click **Next**.

29. On the Additional Files screen, click **Next**.

30. On the Ready to Build the Service Profile screen, click **Next**.

31. The Profile will build and then display the Completing the Connection Manager Administration Kit Wizard screen. Click **Finish**.

Deploying Remote Access Clients

Although Windows XP provides users with the flexibility to configure their own dial-up client connection using the New Connection Wizard, you can create a prepackaged and preconfigured dial-up client connection for installation on your users' computers as you just did in Activity 10-7. Large remote access deployments can be complex and difficult to manage without tools to centrally configure dial-up clients.

Using the CMAK can automate the client configuration process and eliminate the need for clients to configure separate connections and manage separate logins. There are several ways to distribute your client configuration once you have completed the service profile.

- Distribute CDs or floppy disks containing your self-installing Connection Manager package.
- Send a service profile through e-mail to your users.
- Set up a Web site where users can download the service profile.
- Install the service profile on each client individually.
- Use a combination of distribution methods.

Chapter Summary

- To encrypt confidential information exchanged between the Web server and the client, the SSL protocol can be used with IIS 6.0. SSL is a public key–based security protocol that is used by Internet services and clients for authentication, message integrity, and confidentiality. The SSL process uses certificates for authentication, as well as encryption for message integrity and confidentiality.

- You can configure computers running Windows Server 2003 with IIS 6.0 to accept certificates from a predefined list of certification authorities. For example, you might create a different list of trusted certification authorities for each department on your network. IIS would accept only client certificates supplied by certification authorities in the CTL for that department.

- Even though it is possible to place the VPN router in front of the firewall with the VPN router attached to the Internet, this is not common. A more common configuration is to place the VPN router behind the firewall and attach the firewall to the Internet, which is the recommended method. Placing the VPN router behind the firewall allows you to configure the firewall with input and output filters on the firewall's Internet and DMZ interfaces, thereby restricting traffic to the VPN server.

❏ As a security measure, you can use remote access account lockout on remote access accounts. Although this is used as a security feature, keep in mind that if a malicious user intentionally forces an account or several accounts to be locked out, authorized users will be unable to create remote access connections.

❏ With remote access policy, users can be allowed or denied access based on many factors including their connection type, security group membership, or the time of day that they are attempting to make the connection.

❏ Windows Server 2003 supports two VPN protocols: Point-to-Point Tunneling Protocol and Layer Two Tunneling Protocol with Internet Protocol Security (L2TP/IPSec).

❏ The best possible authentication solution involves a combination of methods. A multi-factor solution like this might include the use of a smart card token storing biometric values that are compared to those of the user, who might also be asked to enter a valid password.

❏ The idea behind network address translation is to keep private network addresses private, while reducing the cost and use of public addresses. NAT devices work by translating port numbers of packets that are forwarded between a private network and the Internet.

❏ PPTP-based VPN clients can be located behind a NAT device if the NAT device includes an editor that can translate PPTP such as the NAT/Basic Firewall routing protocol component of the Routing and Remote Access service. If you locate L2TP/IPSec–based clients or servers behind a NAT device, both client and server must support IPSec NAT traversal.

❏ You can use the CMAK Wizard to create a custom service profile and then distribute this file to your users, so that when they double-click the file, it installs a service profile customized with the information you entered in the CMAK Wizard.

10

KEY TERMS

Challenge Handshake Authentication Protocol (CHAP) — An authentication protocol that can be used to provide on-demand authentication within an ongoing data transmission. CHAP uses a one-way hashing function that first involves a service requesting a CHAP response from the client.

client certificates — Electronic documents that contain certificate information about clients. These certificates contain not only certificate information but also public encryption keys that form part of the SSL security feature of IIS.

Connection Manager — A component of Windows 2003 used to provide customized remote access to your network through a dial-up or a virtual private network (VPN) connection.

Connection Manager Administration Kit (CMAK) — A part of Connection Manager managed by a wizard that guides you through the process of building profiles customized for your business. You can use CMAK to fully customize a connection and provide additional functionality for a user.

demilitarized zone (DMZ) — Also called a perimeter network, the DMZ is the last of your networks that traffic will traverse on the way to the Internet or the first of your networks that traffic will traverse on the way into your internal network. A DMZ can be viewed as a layer of privacy between corporate infrastructure and the Internet, exposing only those systems that have to be known to the public.

Extensible Authentication Protocol (EAP) — An extension of Point-to-Point Protocol (PPP). It is an arbitrary authentication mechanism that authenticates a remote access connection.

Extensible Authentication Protocol-Transport Layer Security (EAP-TLS) — An authentication protocol that is designed for use with a certificate infrastructure and either certificates or smart cards.

Firewalls — Protect your network by filtering incoming and outgoing traffic. They examine each packet to determine what type of packet it is and then make a decision whether to forward the packet or discard it. How you configure firewall filters and the filters on the VPN router depends on the position of the VPN router relative to the firewall.

IPSec NAT Traversal (NAT-T) — A process that works by providing UDP encapsulation of IPSec packets to enable Internet Key Exchange (IKE) and Encapsulating Security Payload (ESP)−protected traffic to pass through the NAT.

Layer Two Tunneling Protocol (L2TP) — An extension of the PPP protocol created by combining the best qualities of PPTP and Layer 2 Forwarding (L2F). L2TP is a datalink extension of PPP that sets up a single point-to-point connection between two computers.

L2TP/IPSec — L2TP/IPSec uses PPP user authentication methods and IPSec encryption to encrypt IP traffic. It combines certificate-based computer authentication with PPP-based user authentication.

Microsoft Challenge Handshake Authentication Protocol (MS-CHAP) — A protocol that uses the same type of challenge/response mechanism as CHAP but it uses a nonreversible encrypted password. MPPE uses this encryption key as a basis for encrypting all PPTP data sent over the VPN connection.

Microsoft Challenge Handshake Authentication Protocol version 2 (MS-CHAP v2) — A protocol that uses a challenge/response mechanism but is much more sophisticated than MS-CHAP. With MS-CHAP v2, the server must first prove to the client that it knows the correct password that the client should send.

Message Digest-5 Challenge — MD5 can be used to authenticate the credentials of remote access clients by using username and password–based security systems. It can also authenticate the integrity of the message. MD-5 Challenge uses the same challenge handshake protocol as CHAP.

network address translation (NAT) — A device that works by translating the IP addresses and Transmission Control Protocol/User Datagram Protocol (TCP/UDP) port numbers of packets that are forwarded between a private network and the Internet, thereby preventing other users on the Internet from knowing the real address of a private network.

Password Authentication Protocol (PAP) — An older, simple remote access authentication protocol. PAP uses a two-way handshake to provide for user authentication in which the server asks for the credentials and the user supplies them.

Point-to-Point Tunneling Protocol (PPTP) — A protocol that allows tunneling at Layer 2 of the OSI model and enables a single point-to-point connection.

remote access policy — A collection of conditions and settings that define authorization and access privileges for connection attempts. Remote access policies consist of three components that work together to allow or deny a connection.

Secure Sockets Layer (SSL) — A protocol that can be used with IIS 6.0. SSL is a public key–based security protocol that is used by Internet services and clients for authentication, message integrity, and confidentiality.

Transport Layer Security (TLS) protocol — A protocol based on Secure Sockets Layer (SSL).

virtual private network (VPN) — A method for allowing remote access users to connect to a corporate network over the Internet.

REVIEW QUESTIONS

10

1. Which of the following secure Internet communication uses port 443?

   a. CHAP

   b. SSL

   c. TLS-EAP

   d. MS-CHAP

2. Which are not elements of SSL communication? (Choose all that apply.)

   a. Public Keys

   b. Certificates

   c. CHAP

   d. MD5

3. Which encryption protocol is used only by Microsoft clients and servers?

   a. CHAP

   b. MD5

   c. MMPE

   d. MS-CHAP

4. Which of the following are forms of EAP authentication? (Choose all that apply.)

   a. CHAP

   b. TLS

   c. MD5

   d. PPTP

5. Which tunneling protocol is used only with Windows 2000 Professional and newer clients?

   a. PPP

   b. MS-CHAP

   c. L2TP

   d. CHAP

6. Which of the following may be used in multifactor authentication? (Choose all that apply.)

   a. Retinal Scan

   b. Smart Cards

   c. IPSec

   d. Fingerprints

7. Which tunneling protocol may have issues when being used through a NAT?

   a. PPTP

   b. L2TP

   c. Triple DES

   d. MD5

8. Which of the following ports on a firewall should be open to allow for L2TP/IPSec inbound or outbound tunneling? (Choose all that apply.)

   a. TCP 1723

   b. UDP 1701

   c. UDP 500

   d. UDP 4500

9. Which of the following ports on a firewall should be open to allow for PPTP inbound or outbound tunneling?

   a. TCP 1723

   b. UDP 1701

   c. UDP 500

   d. UDP 4500

10. Which authentication protocol sends the user's credentials in cleartext?

   a. CHAP

   b. MS-CHAP

   c. PPTP

   d. PAP

11. Which Microsoft clients support MS-CHAPv2 on dial-up connections? (Choose all that apply.)

   a. Windows 95

   b. Windows XP

   c. Windows 98

   d. Windows NT workstation

12. Smart cards use which of the following types of EAP authentication?

   a. TLS

   b. MD5

   c. RADIUS

   d. PEAP

13. Which tool provides a wizard that can assist you in building profiles and proxy settings that are customized for your users to either dial in with or use over a VPN?

   a. Routing and Remote Access service

   b. Connection Manager Administration Kit

   c. Certificate Services

   d. Internet Information Services manager

10

14. Which of the following components of remote access policy are checked at the beginning of a session?

   a. Conditions

   b. Profiles

   c. Exceptions

   d. Permissions

15. Which type of Internet communication is secured using digital certificates?

   a. SSL

   b. HTTP

   c. PPTP

   d. PAP

16. Which of these settings in a CMAK are custom actions? (Choose all that apply.)

   a. Preconnect

   b. Pretunnel

   c. Disconnect

   d. Error

17. Which are ways to distribute a client configuration once you have completed the CMAK service profile? (Choose all that apply.)

    a. Through e-mail

    b. Through a Web site

    c. Through a .msi file

    d. On a CD or floppy disk

18. Which of the following authentication protocols can be used by all clients, no matter what operating system they are using?

    a. MS-CHAP v2

    b. MS-CHAP

    c. CHAP

    d. MPPE

19. Which of the following can you use SSL to encrypt? (Choose all that apply.)

    a. Active Directory traffic

    b. Database services

    c. Web communications

    d. File services

20. Which of the following are some general rules that apply for using Web certificates? (Choose all that apply.)

    a. You can assign only one SSL port per Web site.

    b. Each Web site can have only one server certificate assigned to it.

    c. Only one certificate can be assigned to each Web site.

    d. You can assign multiple IP addresses per Web site.

21. VPNs use a combination of which of the following technologies to create secure connections? (Choose all that apply.)

    a. Authorization

    b. Tunneling

    c. Encryption

    d. Authentication

22. The security and renewal requirements for your certificates should be based on which of the following factors? (Choose all that apply.)

    a. The value of the network resources protected by the CA trust chain

    b. The degree to which outside vendors would trust your certificate users

    c. The amount of administrative effort that you are willing to devote to certificate renewal and CA renewal

    d. The personal value of the certificate

23. If multiple policies are configured, they will be processed in which of the following orders?

    a. From least specific to most specific

    b. From the bottom up

    c. From the top down

    d. According to the order in which they were made

24. Windows Server 2003 supports which of the following VPN protocols?

    a. PPTP

    b. FTP

    c. HTTP

    d. L2TP/IPSec

25. Which of the following are benefits of using a VPN? (Choose all that apply.)

    a. It saves on long-distance phone calls.

    b. Authentication can prevent unauthorized users from connecting.

    c. With remote access account lockout, users may be unable to create remote access connections.

    d. Using the Internet as a connection medium requires less hardware than a dial-up networking solution.

10

CASE PROJECTS

Case Project 10-1

Evergrow, a large, national institution that specializes in banking and financial services, has some concern in regard to their remote user access. Currently there are about 300 dial-up users who are using various operating systems from home that range from Windows 95 to Windows XP. It is your task to formulate a plan to secure these communications. The network has recently been updated, and all servers have Windows 2003 installed on them. Present a written plan to management to show how you propose to secure the remote access communications, including which protocol you would use and why.

Case Project 10-2

It is your job as the network administrator to make a recommendation for securing data between the main office in Phoenix and the branches in surrounding areas. The company wants to use a dial-in solution because the branches are all local. Prepare a report for management stating what authentication and/or encryption methods you would recommend to make this type of network access more secure. The entire organization has recently been updated, and all servers have Windows 2003 installed on them; all clients are running Windows XP, and all are part of the same forest.

Case Project 10-3

Evergrow has several forests and more than 15,000 branch offices. It is your job as the network administrator to make a recommendation for securing data between the main office in Phoenix and the branches in other states. The company wants to use a VPN solution because the branches are not all local and they want to save money on long-distance phone calls. Prepare a report for management stating what authentication and/or encryption methods you would recommend to make the network more secure. The network has various operating systems on both the clients and servers because many of the branch offices were recently acquired and are still using their own software and hardware.

Case Project 10-4

You are the network administrator for the Evergrow Phoenix forest, which consists of several Windows 2003 domains with client computers running Windows XP Professional. A large portion of your business is done through the company's Web servers, with both external clients and internal applications. You are working on an SSL implementation method to be used for both external clients connecting to the Web servers in the DMZ and the internal employees using the intranet. You want to make this the most secure method possible. Prepare a report for management stating what authentication and/or encryption methods you would recommend to make the SSL solution work. Explain why you have chosen these methods.

Case Project 10-5

You are the network administrator for the Evergrow Phoenix forest, which consists of several Windows 2003 domains with 15,000 client computers running Windows XP Professional. You must create a solution for standardizing the way that the clients access information. You have put a VPN solution in place but need to find a way to get the clients under control. Prepare a report for management explaining how you can use CMAK to make this feat possible.

11

PLANNING AND CONFIGURING SECURITY FOR WIRELESS NETWORKS

After reading this chapter, you will be able to:

♦ Understand WLAN technology

♦ Close inherent security risks for WLANs

♦ Plan groups and group policies for wireless access

♦ Plan authentication for a wireless network

♦ Use encryption on a wireless network

♦ Configure SSL certificates for wireless networks

♦ Work with wireless access policies

♦ Configure servers and access points for wireless support

♦ Configure wireless support for client computers

If communication security is lax, an otherwise successful organization can virtually be destroyed. This holds true not only in wired network communications, but also in wireless communications as well. The recent advances in wireless networking technology have enabled individuals to easily connect to networks from virtually anyplace. Many organizations are taking advantage of the simplicity of setting up wireless LANs (WLANs), thereby allowing for mobility and portability of computers and other devices located within the organization. Public access points in locations such as coffee shops, kiosks, and airports permit users to send and receive data from many places that would have been impossible not too many years ago. Along with this convenience comes an increased chance of unauthorized access to the networks as well as the data they contain.

Securing wireless communications is crucial to surviving in the world of technology. This chapter gives you an understanding of the basic principles surrounding wireless networking security. It describes how to use the networking services the Microsoft Windows Server 2003 operating system provides to deploy a secure and manageable WLAN infrastructure within an enterprise environment. It will also guide you through planning and configuring authentication and authorization for wireless networks as well as configuring Secure Sockets Layer (SSL) certificates and encryption.

UNDERSTANDING WLAN TECHNOLOGY

The technologies for wireless devices have evolved quickly over the past several years. Ever since the first wireless transmissions took place more than a century ago, there has been a push to manage the public airwaves responsibly. During that time, frequency bands have been divided up to accommodate the various user categories such as the military, broadcasters, and amateur radio operators. One of the issues with the current wireless technology is that it is a broadcast signal. This means that a wireless device advertises its presence, making it easy for an intruder to pick up and monitor. The airwaves are out there for the taking. In order to prevent this from happening, some standards have been put into place. The WLAN solution provided by Windows XP and Windows Server 2003 is based on IEEE standards 802.11 and 802.1x.

802.1x Standard

802.1x is a standard developed by IEEE for WLANs. The 802.1x standard is a port-based authentication framework for access to Ethernet networks. Although this standard is designed for wired Ethernet networks, it applies to 802.11 WLANs as well. This port-based network access control uses the physical characteristics of the switched LAN infrastructure to authenticate devices attached to a LAN port. It requires three roles in the authentication process: a device requesting access, an authenticator, and an authentication server. 802.1x allows scalability in wireless LANs by allowing centralized authentication of wireless users or stations. The standard is flexible enough to allow multiple authentication algorithms, and it is an open standard.

802.11 Standard

IEEE 802.11 specifies a technology that operates in the 2.4 through 2.5-GHz band. Wireless networks in common use operate according to the specifications of the IEEE 802.11 standards, which are defined at the Data Link layer of the Open Systems Interconnection (OSI) model. In this standard, there are two different ways to configure a network: ad hoc and infrastructure. In the ad hoc network, computers are brought together to form a network on the fly. The 802.11 standard also places specifications on the parameters of both the physical and media access control (MAC) layers of the network.

The 802.11 standard defines an **access point (AP)** as a device that functions as a transparent bridge between the wireless clients and the existing wired network. The access point contains at least one interface to connect to the existing wired network, and transmitting equipment to connect with the wireless clients. It also contains IEEE 802.1D bridging software, to act as a bridge between wireless and wired Data Link layers. Table 11-1 lists the current and future WLAN standards under 802.11.

Table 11-1   802.11 Standards

Standard	Description
802.11a	Uses Orthogonal Frequency Division Multiplexing (OFDM), which offers significant performance benefits compared with the more tradi-tional spread-spectrum systems. OFDM is a modulation technique for transmitting large amounts of digital data over radio waves. Capacity per channel is 54 Mbps with real throughput at about 31 Mpbs. It oper-ates at a frequency of 5 GHz, which supports eight overlapping channels.
802.11b	The most popularly used 802.1x technology. Uses Direct Sequence Spread Spectrum (DSSS). Capacity per channel is 11 Mbps with real throughput at about 6 Mpbs. It operates at a frequency of 2.4 GHz, which supports three nonoverlapping channels.
802.11d	Aims to produce versions of 802.11b that are compatible with other frequencies, so it can be used in countries where the 2.4-GHz band is not available.
802.11e	Will add Quality of Service (QoS) capabilities to 802.11 networks. It uses a Time Division Multiple Access (TDMA) scheme and adds extra error correction.
802.11f	Improves the handover mechanism in 802.11, so users can maintain a connection while roaming. It is aimed at giving network users the same roaming freedom that cell phone users have.
802.11g	This is a combination of 802.11a and 802.11b. It can use either Direct Sequence Spread Spectrum (DSSS) or Orthagonal Frequency Division Multiplexing (OFDM). Capacity per channel is 54 Mbps with real throughput at about 12 Mpbs. It operates at a frequency of 2.4 GHz.
802.11h	Attempts to improve on 802.11a by adding better control over radio channel selection and transmission power.
802.11i	Deals with security. This is an entirely new standard based on the Advanced Encryption Standard (AES). This standard has a feature called Robust Security Network (RSN), which defines two security methodologies. The first is for legacy-based hardware using RC4, and the second one is for new hardware based on AES.
802.11j	Allows 802.11a and HiperLAN2 networks to coexist in the same airwaves.

11

NOTE   Although devices that support the 802.11a standard are generally incompatible with those that support 802.11b, some devices are equipped to support either 802.11a or 802.11b. The newest standard, 802.11g, allows 802.11b and 802.11g devices to operate together on the same network. This standard was created specifically for backward compatibility with the 802.11b standard.

Benefits of Wireless Networks

The benefits of WLAN technology are many. Probably the most obvious benefit is the increased flexibility and mobility that is created when using WLANs. Employees can freely move around the organization without disconnection from the network. Here are some examples of how wireless networking can benefit an organization:

- Inventory taking is more convenient when employees can freely walk around the warehouse or organization.

- Devices like personal digital assistants (PDAs) and Tablet PCs can be used in hospital wards to track patients and doctor visits.

- Mobile workers moving between offices and telecommuters coming into the office can more easily connect to the LAN from almost anywhere.

- Online information is always available for research or information retrieval.

- Production on manufacturing shop floors can more readily be evaluated.

- Wireless network infrastructure can be moved to a new building relatively easily.

- The cost of providing network access to buildings is substantially lowered.

Given all of the obvious benefits, the security drawbacks of WLANs would need to be fairly severe to undermine their appeal. Unfortunately, this is more often than not the case. Many WLANs deployed to date have no security enabled at all. If you intend to deploy wireless devices, you need to know how to close these security risks.

CLOSING INHERENT SECURITY RISKS FOR WLANS

Wireless devices present a whole new set of threats, never mind the fact that many times network administrators may be unaware of their presence. The most obvious risks concerning wireless networks are theft and rogue devices. Most cell phones, text pagers, PDAs, and wireless network cards are small enough that they can be easily lost or stolen. Because they are simple to conceal and contain valuable information about a company, they have become favorite targets of intruders. Wireless LANs can be subject to session hijacking and man-in-the-middle attacks. Additional risks remain because anyone can purchase an access point and set it up. The dangers of broadcasting your unprotected corporate network data to anyone who happens to be in the vicinity might seem obvious, but a surprising number of WLAN installations still exist without any security enabled. Just as with firewalls, routers, and switches, wireless devices need to be properly secured. The best ways to do this include enforcing authorization and authentication and encrypting data.

Security Problems with WLANs

Wireless access points, when set up right out of the box have no security. They also broadcast their presence. So in essence, they say, "Hey, my name is *xxx*. Here I am!" In addition, the free availability of 802.11 network audit tools like AirSnort and NetStumbler means that breaking into wireless networks configured with weak security is now quite easy. These tools can be used to check wireless security by identifying unauthorized clients or access points, as well as verifying encryption usage. There are also tools available that come in the form of management software. To eliminate existing 802.11 shortcomings and to help improve the image of wireless technology on the market, the Institute of Electrical and Electronics Engineers (IEEE) together with Wireless Ethernet Compatibility Alliance (WECA) proposed standards for significantly improved user authentication and media access control mechanisms.

Here are some additional inherent risks associated with wireless networks:

- 802.1x transmissions generate detectable radio-frequency traffic in all directions. Persons wishing to intercept the data transmitted over the network may use many solutions to increase the distance over which detection is possible, including the use of metal tubes such as a Pringles or large tomato juice can.

- Without the use of an encryption standard of some type, data is passed in cleartext form. Even though technologies such as Wired Equivalent Privacy (WEP) encrypt the data, they still lack good security, and a determined listener can easily obtain enough traffic data to calculate the encryption key in use.

- Because the authentication mechanism is one-way, it is easy for an intruder to wait until authentication is completed and then generate a signal to the client that tricks the client into thinking it has been disconnected from the access point; meanwhile the intruder begins to send data traffic, pretending to be the original client.

- The request for connection by the client is a one-way open broadcast. This gives an intruder the chance to act as an access point to the client, and as a client to the real network access point. This allows an intruder to watch all data transactions between the client and access point, then modify, insert, or delete packets at will.

- A popular pastime involves driving around with a laptop system configured to listen for open wireless access points, which is known as **wardriving**. Several Web sites provide detailed information for unsecured networks. These sites provide locations, sometimes on city maps for the convenience of others looking for open access links to the Internet. This is an attractive method not only to capture data from networks, but also to connect to someone else's network, use that person's bandwidth, and pay nothing for it.

- A method is also being used to mark buildings, curbs, and other landmarks, indicating the presence of an available access point and its connection details by utilizing a set of symbols and shorthand. This is called **warchalking**.

Wireless security comes in two major varieties today: Wired Equivalent Privacy (WEP) and Wi-Fi Protected Access (WPA). Both include methods to encrypt wireless traffic between wireless clients and APs. WEP has been included in 802.11-based products for some time and includes a strategy for restricting network access and encrypting network traffic based upon a shared key. A company can protect itself by implementing the following:

- *Enabling WEP*—Nearly all Wi-Fi certified product ships with basic encryption capabilities. 40-bit key WEP just is not enabled by default. When WEP is enabled it is designed to provide the same level of security as that of a wired LAN.

- *Changing default access point administration passwords*—any devices right out of the box do not even have a password on the Administrator account. Programs like AirSnort identify the manufacturer based on the MAC address, so if you change only the SSID, chances are that an informed hacker can easily gain access.

- *Changing default Service Set Identifiers (SSIDs)*—Don't change the SSID to reflect your company's main names, divisions, products, or address. This just makes you an easy target. Keep in mind that if an SSID name is enticing enough, it may attract hackers.

- *Disabling broadcast SSID*—By default, broadcast SSID is enabled. This means that it will accept any SSID. When you disable this feature, the SSID configured in the client must match the SSID of the access point.

- *Separating the wireless network from the wired network*—Consider using an additional level of authentication, such as RADIUS, before you permit an association with your access points. The wireless clients can be separated, so the connections can not only use RADIUS authentication, but can also be logged.

- *Putting the wireless network in an Internet-access-only zone or a demilitarized zone (DMZ)*—Put your wireless access points in a DMZ and have your wireless users tunnel into your network using a VPN. This will require extra effort in setting up a VLAN for your DMZ, but this solution adds a layer of encryption and authentication that could make a wireless network suitable for sensitive data.

- *Disabling DHCP within the WLAN to keep tighter control over users*—Consider assigning static IP addresses for your wireless network. This creates more administrative overhead to manage, but it makes it harder to access your network.

- *Enabling MAC address filtering on access points to limit unauthorized wireless NICs*—Many access points allow you to control access based on the MAC address of the NIC attempting to associate with it. If the MAC address of the NIC isn't in the table of the access points, the network won't allow access. Although there are ways of spoofing a MAC address, this takes an additional level of sophistication.

As a network administrator, you should periodically survey your site using a tool such as NetStumbler or AirSnort to see if any rogue access points are installed on the network. In addition, take a notebook equipped with a wireless sniffer and an external antenna outside your office building. Check to see what information inside your building can be accessed by someone parked in the parking lot or across the street.

PLANNING GROUPS AND GROUP POLICY FOR WIRELESS ACCESS

The user and computer accounts in Active Directory will be used for authentication and authorization of wireless users. We will discuss authentication and authorization later in the chapter. Active Directory also contains the Group Policy settings that govern wireless connections such as the information regarding enrollment for users and computer certificates for wireless clients and the Wireless Network Policies settings. There are two ways of doing this: users and computers could be placed in an organizational unit (OU) that will be linked to a wireless group policy object or you could use security groups within remote access policy.

If you are using an OU with Group Policy, to plan for the Active Directory configuration of your wireless clients, first identify the user and computer accounts for wireless users. If you are using security groups within remote access policy, create the group and add the users to the group that will be used along with a remote access policy. Then determine how to set the remote access permission on the user and computer accounts. If the Active Directory functional level is set to Windows Server 2003 mode, you can use universal groups and nested global groups. For example, you might create global groups of wireless users and then nest them in a universal group named Wireless, as shown in Figure 11-1.

11

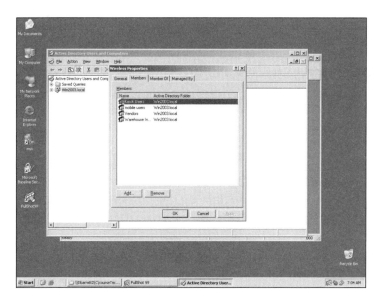

Figure 11-1   Nested wireless group

Later in the chapter, you will configure a group policy for wireless users. For now, though, you should be aware of the following about wireless group policy in general:

- If a domain policy for wireless configuration exists, the local user cannot disable or remove the domain policy.

- The wireless network configuration settings that are defined in Group Policy Objects (GPOs) take precedence over user-defined settings. The only exception to this is the list of preferred networks, where the policy-defined list is merged with the user-defined list.

- When a Group Policy change occurs, the Wireless Configuration service breaks the current association only if the new policy takes precedence. In all other cases, the association does not change.

- If a GPO that contains wireless network policies is deleted, the Wireless Configuration service clears its policy cache, initiates and processes a soft reset, and then reverts to the user-configured settings.

You can simplify Wireless Network policy management by creating a single GPO and applying it to the domain object. Many organizations will find the need to the create only one Wireless Network Policy GPO but will choose to create it and apply it to a location other than the domain object.

PLANNING AUTHENTICATION FOR A WIRELESS NETWORK

User authentication is a natural choice when considering identification to WLAN infrastructure. However, in most cases, you will also want to implement computer authentication to ensure a complete solution. Computer authentication is recommended, and by default, authentication is set to Enabled. Any wireless device that is located within range of your access point can theoretically connect to your network. Such a connection can even come from outside the building, as stated earlier in the chapter. You need to ensure that secure authentication policies are in effect that permit only authorized users to connect to your WLAN.

This first stage of authentication proves that the device is authorized to connect to the network. Once this is established, the user can be authenticated in the same way that they would when accessing a wired LAN. The following three means of wireless authentication are currently used:

- *Open authentication*—**Open authentication** allows access to anyone providing the correct SSID or WEP key for the access point. This method provides only minimum protection and should be used with an additional protection mechanism.

- *Shared key authentication*—**Shared key authentication** is similar to a challenge-response authentication process. The client sends a request for access to the access point, which returns a challenge. The client returns an encrypted response. It is also known as shared secret authentication, because the client computer needs only this shared secret to authenticate itself.

- *802.1x authentication standard*—**802.1x authentication standard** is an extension of the Point-to-Point Protocol (PPP) that relies on the **Extensible Authentication Protocol (EAP)** for its authentication needs. EAP is a challenge-response protocol that can be run over secured transport mechanisms. It is a flexible authentication technology and can be used with smart cards, one-time passwords, and public key encryption.

EAP messages are encapsulated into 802.1x packets and are marked as EAP over LAN (EAPOL). Once the client sends a connection request to a wireless access point, the authenticator marks all initial communication with the client as unauthorized, and only EAPOL messages are accepted in this mode. All other types of communication are blocked until credentials are verified with an authentication server. Upon receiving an EAPOL request from the client, the wireless access point requests log-on credentials and passes them on to an authentication server. **Remote Authentication Dial-In User Service (RADIUS)** is usually employed for authentication purposes; however, 802.1x does not make it mandatory. If the server successfully validates the credentials, communication can begin; otherwise, the session request is rejected. To provide the highest level of security, use a version of EAP that provides mutual authentication, such as EAP-MS-CHAP v2, EAP-TLS, or EAP-MD5. To ensure the highest level of security for a WLAN in a corporate enterprise environment, use 802.1x with EAP-TLS authentication, a PKI, and RADIUS. The wireless clients must support 802.1x in a WLAN deployment using EAP-TLS. Windows Server 2003 uses the 802.1x standard for authenticating access to wired Ethernet networks and wireless 802.11 networks. This standard provides support for EAP used in conjunction with several different authentication methods for wireless computers:

- *EAP-TLS*—Uses certificate-based mutual authentication, negotiation of the encryption method, and encrypted key determination between the client and the authenticating server.

- *EAP-MS-CHAP v2*—Provides mutual authentication-based on password-based user and computer authentication. Both server and client must prove knowledge of the user's password for successful authentication.

- ***Protected EAP (PEAP)***—Provides several additional benefits within TLS, including an encrypted authentication channel, dynamic keying material from TLS, fast reconnect using cached session keys, and server authentication that protects against the setup of unauthorized access points. PEAP was codeveloped by Cisco, Microsoft Corp., and RSA Security Inc.

Figure 11-2 shows where to configure these options in the wireless policy.

You can use PEAP along with EAP-TLS, EAP-MS-CHAP v2, and non-Microsoft EAP authentication methods; however, PEAP is not supported for use with EAP-MD5. As well as providing encrypted authentication, PEAP creates a session key that is used to derive data encryption keys that protect data being sent between the client and the access point during the session.

11

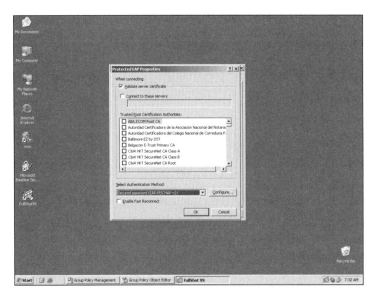

Figure 11-2 EAP authentication methods

The access point must support the authentication method that you select. For example, the access point must support 802.1x. If you choose EAP-TLS, all computers must support it, which includes the servers. In other words, your servers and wireless clients must support the authentication method you plan to deploy. Whether you choose EAP-TLS, or PEAP as the authentication method over 802.1x, both your RADIUS server and your wireless clients need to support it. It is recommended that you permit certificate autoenrollment for users and computers when you use EAP-TLS.

Certificate-based protocols, such as EAP-TLS and PEAP, perform a CPU-intensive public key operation upon initial logon. For subsequent logons, they use a cached credentials strategy called **fast reconnect**. Fast reconnect is used until the cache expires, which is set to 8 hours by default. The fast reconnect ability allows roaming users to maintain their connection when moving between different access points on the same network, as long as each access point is configured as a client of the same RADIUS server, and fast reconnect is configured on both the client and the server. This reduces time delays and resource requirements associated with the reconnection. Full reauthentication occurs when wireless clients associate to access points that use a different IAS server than was previously used. This roaming reauthentication happens only once between each client and IAS server and is transparent to the end user when EAP-TLS is used. The client can cache TLS session keys for more than one RADIUS server.

When planning wireless authentication methods, there should be a balance between the required level of security and the ease of deployment. For instance, PEAP with EAP-MS-CHAP v2 requires less effort to deploy because certificates or smart cards are not needed, yet PEAP with EAP-TLS will provide a higher level of security because of the use of certificates and smart cards. EAP-TLS can support one-way authorization or unauthenticated access when a client does not send credentials. If a network access client does not provide credentials, IAS determines whether unauthenticated access is enabled in the remote access policy that matched the connection attempt. There may be time when you use unauthenticated EAP-TLS. EAP-TLS unauthenticated access provides a means to grant guest access for a wireless client that does not have a certificate installed. This type of access can be useful when you want to grant guest access to visitors such as consultants. The unauthenticated users can be redirected to a specific virtual LAN (VLAN), providing limited network access to allow visitors access to an unsecured VLAN outside of the corporate firewall, giving them Internet access and the ability to connect back to their own organizations.

ACTIVITY

Activity 11-1: Install IAS and Configure It for Wireless Authentication

Time Required: 45 minutes

Objective: Learn how to configure IAS on your server, obtain a certificate, and register the server on the network.

Description: In this exercise, you will learn how to configure IAS on your server, obtain a certificate, and register the server on the network.

1. Log on with your **AdminXX** account, where *XX* is your assigned student number.

2. Click **Start**, **Control Panel**, **Add or Remove Programs**, **Add/Remove Windows Components**, highlight **Networking Services**, click **Details**, then check the **Internet Authentication Service** box. Click **OK**. Click **Next**.

3. If asked to insert the CD, do so and click **OK**. If you receive the Optional Networking Components screen, click **Yes**.

4. On the Completing the Windows Components Wizard screen, click **Finish**.

5. Close the **Add or Remove Programs** screen.

6. Click **Start**, **Administrative Tools**, **Internet Authentication Service**.

7. On the Action menu, choose **Register Server in Active Directory**.

8. You may receive a message asking if you wish to authorize this computer to read users' dial-in properties from the domain. Click **OK**.

9. On the Server registered message, click **OK**.

10. Close the **Internet Authentication Service** screen.

11. Click **Start**, **Run**. In the Open box type **mmc**. Click **OK**.

12. On the Console Root screen, choose **File**, **Add/Remove Snap-in**. On the Stand-alone tab, click **Add** and highlight the **Certificates** Snap-in. Click **Add**.

13. On the Certificates Snap-in screen select the **Computer account** option button. Click **Next**. On the Select the Computer You Want This Snap-in to Manage screen,

11

select the **Local computer (the computer this console is running on)** radio button. Click **Finish**.

14. Click **Close** on the Add Standalone Snap-in screen. Click **OK** on the Add/Remove Snap-in screen.

15. Expand the Certificates node on the left side of the screen. Highlight the Personal folder. Right-click the folder and choose **All Tasks**, **Request New Certificate**. The Welcome to the Certificate Request Wizard should appear, as shown in Figure 11-3. Click **Next**.

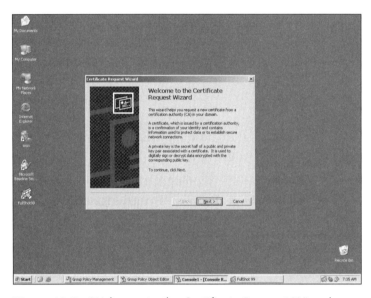

Figure 11-3   Welcome to the Certificate Request Wizard screen

16. On the Certificate Types screen, in the Certificate types box, highlight **Domain Controller Authentication**. Click **Next**.

17. On the Certificate Friendly Name and Description page, type **Wireless–IAS** in the Friendly name box. Type **This certificate will be used for wireless clients through IAS** in the Description box. Click **Next**.

18. On the Completing the Certificate Request Wizard screen, click **Finish**.

19. You will receive a message saying that the certificate request was successful. Click **OK**. Close the console. When asked about saving the console settings, click **No**.

20. Click **Start**, **Administrative Tools**, **Certification Authority**. Expand your server. Select the Issued Certificates folder. Check to be sure that the certificate you just requested has been issued.

21. Click **Start**, **Run**. In the Open box type **mmc**. Click **OK**.

22. On the Console Root screen, choose **File**, **Add/Remove Snap-in**. On the Stand-alone tab, click **Add** and highlight the **Certificates** Snap-in. Click **Add**.

23. On the Certificates Snap-in screen, select the **Computer account** option button. Click **Next**. On the Select the Computer You Want This Snap-in to Manage screen, select the **Local computer (the computer this console is running on)** option button. Click **Finish**.

24. Click **Close** on the Add Standalone Snap-in screen. Click **OK** on the Add/Remove Snap-in screen.

25. Expand the Certificates node on the left side of the screen. Expand the Personal folder, select the **Certificates** folder. Highlight the **Wireless-IAS** certificate, right-click the certificate, choose **All Tasks**, **Export**.

26. The Welcome to the Certificate Export Wizard opens. Click **Next**.

27. On the Export Private Key screen, under Do you want to export the private key with the certificate?, be sure that the option button has defaulted to **No, do not export the private key**. Click **Next**.

28. On the Export File Format screen, be sure that the **DER encoded binary X.509 (.CER)** option button is selected. Click **Next**.

29. On the File to Export screen, type **Wireless-IAS** in the File name text box, as shown in Figure 11-4. Click **Next**. Click **Finish**.

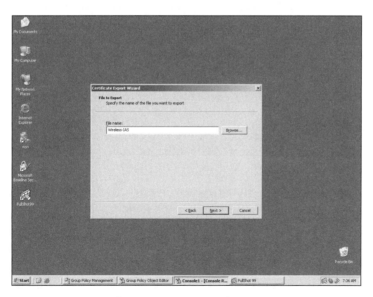

Figure 11-4   Certificate Export Wizard

30. You will get a message telling you that the export was successful. Click **OK**.

31. Right-click the **Trusted Root Certification Authorities** folder and select **All Tasks**, **Import**.

32. The Welcome to the Certificate Import Wizard screen appears. Click **Next**. On the File to Import screen, click the **Browse** button. The **Wireless-IAS.crt** file should be in the Look in list box. When locating the certificate, the name will be different because Wireless-IAS is only the friendly name and not the exact name. Highlight it and click **Open**. Click **Next**.

33. On the Certificate Store screen, be sure that the **Place all certificates in the following store** option button is selected. Verify that the Certificate store text box shows **Trusted Root Certification Authorities**. Click **Next**.

34. On the Completing the Certificate Import Wizard screen, click **Finish**.

35. You will receive a message that the import was successful. Click **OK**.

36. Close the console. When asked to Save console settings, click **No**.

Using VPN Technology

Using virtual private network (VPN) technology to protect WLAN traffic has been a popular approach for high-security environments. Many organizations rely on the tried and trusted VPN technologies to protect the confidentiality of data sent over the Internet. When the vulnerabilities of static WEP were discovered, VPN was proposed as the best way to secure data traveling over a WLAN. Although VPN is a great solution to securely travel through a network such as the Internet, it is not necessarily the best solution for securing internal WLANs. A VPN offers little or no additional security compared with 802.1x solutions. Implementing a VPN for a WLAN presents the following challenges:

- Because all WLAN client access is funneled through the VPN server, it can become a bottleneck. Many VPN devices will be unable to cope with more than a few hundred clients.

- The VPN authentication method may not be as secure as you think. Many VPN implementations rely on a preshared key authentication, which is the same security flaw as static WEP keys.

- A separate user VPN or Remote Access Service (RAS) logon is required in addition to the standard network or domain logon.

- Because the logon is only user-initiated, an idle, logged-off computer cannot be remotely managed or monitored. This could affect the ability of the computer to receive Group Policy settings.

- More sophisticated policy-based access controls may be needed, especially if users are allowed to roam between access points.

- Depending on the VPN solution chosen, the cost of the client software licenses can be prohibitive.

- VPN is a great technology for remote access to networks, but it is not meant to work alone to protect WLAN traffic. However, it does offer these advantages:

  - Because most organizations already have a VPN solution deployed, users and IT staff are familiar with its use and configuration.

  - VPN data protection normally uses software encryption as opposed to hardware-based encryption.

  - Because VPN protection is independent of WLAN hardware, in some instances, you find the cost is less.

VPN servers can utilize the RADIUS components. The VPN servers pass the clients' authentication requests to the RADIUS infrastructure. This solution leverages the existing infrastructure and centralized account management yet still leaves the access policy control up to the network administrator. Additional enhancements, such as smart card–based user authentication can be an extra layer of protection as you learned in the last chapter.

Using Wireless Access Points with a RADIUS Infrastructure

The **Internet Authentication Service (IAS)** in Microsoft Windows Server 2003 is the Microsoft implementation of a RADIUS server and proxy. IAS performs authentication, authorization, and accounting of various types of network connections. When used as a RADIUS proxy, IAS can forward RADIUS requests to another RADIUS server. As mentioned earlier, IAS can be used in conjunction with VPN servers. It can also be used with wireless access points (WAPs).

You can set up WAPs as RADIUS clients, and then configure them to send access requests to a central RADIUS server running IAS. When planning for IAS authentication, the availability of IAS servers to WAPs determines the availability of the WLAN to end users. Therefore, when setting up a RADIUS infrastructure, you should ensure that two or more IAS servers are available for WAPs at all times. Most modern WAPs include the ability to configure a total of four Radius servers, two for authentication and two for accounting. This way, the loss of a single RADIUS server will not affect service to WLAN clients. If you are planning on using IAS as an authentication solution for your wireless clients, be sure that you follow recommended guidelines for hardware requirements and redundancy to ensure continued connectivity for clients.

Another consideration when planning authentication is the logging of events. Successful and rejected authentication events generated from devices and users attempting to access the WLAN are recorded in IAS in the Windows Server 2003 system event log by default.

NOTE

Successful WLAN access events will rapidly fill the system event log and may not be necessary for security purposes if RADIUS authentication request logging is enabled.

In order to refresh 802.11 WEP session encryption keys, wireless clients can be forced to reauthenticate themselves to the RADIUS servers. In fact, some WAP models include features to perform timed WEP session key refresh without the need to force clients to perform frequent reauthentication. This is done at timed intervals and is vendor-specific. Table 11-2 can help in the planning considerations for how your IAS servers will service client requests.

Table 11-2   Authentication Types

Authentication Point	Authentication Process
Initial authentication of computer	Client must perform a full authentication with IAS.
Initial authentication of user	Client must perform a full authentication with IAS.
Reauthentication of device when roaming between WAPs	Client performs a full authentication once with each IAS server, then uses fast reconnect for additional authentications.
Reauthentication of user when roaming between WAPs	Client performs a full authentication once with each IAS server, then uses fast reconnect for additional authentications.
Timed reauthentication of computer	Client uses a cached authentication with IAS.
Timed reauthentication of user	Client uses a cached authentication with IAS.

Using proper authentication can prevent anyone who has a compatible WLAN adapter from gaining access to the network. To further secure your wireless transmissions, the data being sent between the wireless devices and the AP should be encrypted. IAS provides enhanced security for WLANs by providing dynamic encryption keys through certificate-based authentication protocols such as EAP-TLS.

Activity 11-2: Configure IAS for a Remote RADIUS Server Group

Time Required: 30 minutes

Objective: Learn how to configure your IAS server for remote access through RADIUS server groups and configure a new connection policy.

Description: In this exercise, you configure your IAS server for remote access through RADIUS server groups and configure a new connection policy.

1. Log on with your **AdminXX** account, where *XX* is your assigned student number.

2. Click **Start**, **Administrative Tools**, **Internet Authentication Service**. Expand the **Connection Request Processing** folder.

3. Right-click **Remote RADIUS Server Groups**, then select **New Remote RADIUS Server Group**. The Welcome to the New Remote Access Policy Wizard screen should appear, as shown in Figure 11-5. Click **Next**.

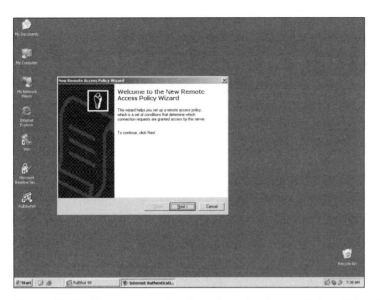

Figure 11-5   Welcome to the New Remote Access Policy Wizard screen

11

4. On the Group Configuration Method screen, select the **Custom** option button. In the Group name box, type **Wireless RADIUS**. Click **Next**.

5. On the Add Servers screen, click **Add**. In the Server box type **192.168.200.10**, click **Apply**, and then click **OK**.

6. On the Add Servers screen, click **Next**. The Completing the New Remote RADIUS Server Group Wizard screen will appear. Verify that the **Start the New Connection Request Policy Wizard when this wizard closes** box is checked. Click **Finish**.

7. The Welcome to the New Connection Request Policy Wizard screen should appear, as shown in Figure 11-6. Click **Next**.

8. On the Policy Configuration Method screen, select the **A custom policy** option button. Type **Wireless connections** in the Policy name box, then click **Next**.

9. On the Policy Conditions screen, click **Add**. On the Select Attribute screen, select the **Client-Friendly-Name** attribute, then click **Add**.

10. On the Client-Friendly-Name screen, type **Wireless** in the Type a word or wild card box. Click **OK**. Click **Next**.

11. On the Request Processing Method screen, click the **Edit Profile** button. Select the Accounting tab, check the **Record accounting information on the servers in the following remote RADIUS server group** box. Click **Apply**, and then click **OK**.

12. On the Request Processing Method screen, click **Next**. On the Completing the New Connection Request Processing Policy Wizard screen, review the information, and then click **Finish**.

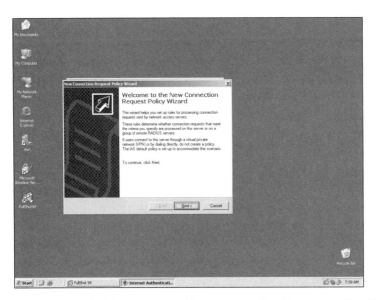

Figure 11-6   Welcome to the New Connection Request Policy Wizard screen

13. Highlight Connection Request Policies on the left side of the screen if necessary. Verify that the wireless connection policy you just created shows on the right side of the screen.

14. Choose **File**, **Exit** to close the IAS configuration screen.

USING ENCRYPTION ON A WIRELESS NETWORK

Encryption of data traveling across the wireless network is of paramount importance. Current encryption for wireless networks often leaves a bit to be desired. It gives you a comforting feeling without actually delivering much. Although using **Wired Equivalent Privacy (WEP)** is much better than no encryption at all, it's important to understand its limitations so that you have an accurate picture of the consequences and what you must do to properly protect your wireless environment. It is also important to know what part technologies such as 802.1x and IPSec play in securing your wireless network and how to get the maximum security possible from all three.

IPSec and Wireless Networks

Although IPSec by itself does not control access to the WLAN, it can, however, be used in conjunction with 802.1x to provide security for data being sent to client computers that are roaming between access points on the same network. For better security, segment the wireless network by placing a firewall between the WLAN and the remainder of the network. Because IPSec is a solution to the problem of securely authenticating and encrypting network IP packets, you can use IPSec to provide strong security between a

RADIUS server and a domain controller, or to secure traffic to a partner organization's RADIUS servers. Many of the VPN solutions use IPSec, and like a VPN, IPSec is an excellent solution in many circumstances; it should not, however be, a direct alternative for WLAN protection implemented at the network hardware layer. If you use IPSec, keep the following in mind:

- IPSec uses computer-level authentication only, although some IPSec implementations on non-Windows platforms use user-only authentication.
- Managing IPSec policies can be complex for a large organization.
- For total security, all end-to-end traffic should be encrypted. When devices are used that are not IPSec-capable, traffic will appear in cleartext.
- IPSec encryption processing overhead load is often absorbed by the server or client, unless special network cards are used.

In addition to the various versions of EAP or IPSec, 802.1x can also be used with **Light EAP (LEAP)**. LEAP combines centralized two-way authentication with dynamically generated Wireless Equivalent Privacy keys, or WEP keys. LEAP was developed by Cisco for use on WLANs that use Cisco 802.11 wireless devices. It features mutual authentication; secure session key derivation; and dynamic per user, per session WEP keys. However, because it uses unencrypted challenges and responses, LEAP is vulnerable to dictionary attacks. Still when LEAP is combined with a rigorous user password policy, it can offer strong authentication security without the use of certificates. LEAP can authenticate the user only to the WLAN, not the computer. Without computer authentication, machine group policies will not execute correctly, software installation settings, roaming profiles, and log-on scripts may all fail, and users cannot change expired passwords.

NOTE LEAP is a proprietary EAP method because it requires the use of a Cisco AP. Wired Equivalent Privacy.

WEP is the most basic form of encryption that can be used on 802.11-based wireless networks to provide privacy of data sent between a wireless client and its access point. Until recently, many wireless networks were based on the IEEE 802.11 standard, which had serious data transmission security shortcomings. When this standard was put into place, the 802.11 committee adopted an encryption protocol called WEP. In order to discuss WEP's shortcomings, it is necessary to understand how it operates. WEP uses a stream cipher called RC4 for encryption. RC4 uses a shared secret key to generate a long sequence of bytes from what is called a generator. This stream is then used to produce the encrypted ciphertext. Early 802.11b networks used 40-bit encryption because of government restrictions. Hackers can crack a 40-bit key in a few hours. It is much easier to break RC4 encryption if a second instance of encryption with a single key can be isolated. In other words, the weakness is that the same keys are used repeatedly.

In some cases, WEP uses a 104-bit key to protect data against unauthorized access. You can configure the key that WEP uses in Windows XP and Windows Server 2003. Although utilities exist that can crack WEP encryption, you can still provide a moderate level of security by using WEP, particularly if you change the encryption keys frequently. This weakness may be improved with newer standards such as the Temporal Key Integrity Protocol (TKIP), which involves time-changing encryption keys and Wi-Fi protected access (WPA), which combines TKIP with Message Integrity Code (MIC) to protect against forgery attacks.

WEP can work with either open-system or shared-key authentication. We discussed these two authentication methods in the last section. You should use WEP only in cases where only minimal security is required, or if your hardware or software does not support 802.1x.

802.1x Framework

Earlier in the chapter, we discussed using the 802.1x framework for authenticating access to a network. In addition to providing port-based network access control for authentication, 802.1x also provides encryption of data. 802.1x works along with EAP to provide data encryption. Because EAP is a pluggable authentication method, there are a number of different EAP types to choose from. Remember that EAP-MS-CHAP v2, EAP-TLS, or EAP-MD5 can be used to provide data encryption after a client has been authenticated to the wireless network. EAP types natively use encryption to protect the authentication conversation and can dynamically generate the keys used for encryption during the process. 802.1x with EAP-TLS is one of the most popular and secure EAP methods for use with 802.1x. It requires public key certificates on the client and RADIUS server. Some of the benefits based on this option include the following:

- It allows computer-based and user-based access control to the network so that unauthorized users cannot log on to an authorized computer.

- It creates a transparent network user experience, which may not be so with VPN- and IPSec-based alternatives.

- It allows for an unattended computer to download Group Policy and be remotely managed and monitored.

- Because network traffic is not all channeled through one central server, network bottlenecks can be eliminated.

- It is based on IEEE and IETF standards, so no proprietary equipment is needed, and it offers broad support across client platforms and network vendors.

You should use 802.1x encryption wherever possible. Microsoft also provides support for using 802.1x with PEAP. Support for PEAP is widespread in the industry, and Microsoft Windows XP SP2 and Pocket PC 2003 have built-in support for PEAP. In addition, MS-CHAP v2 can be used to do secure password authentication within PEAP.

USING SSL CERTIFICATES WITH WIRELESS NETWORKS

Chapter 10 discussed SSL Certificates and their configuration. The SSL process uses certificates for authentication, and encryption for message integrity and confidentiality. The certificates include keys that are used to establish an SSL-encrypted connection. You can maintain secure communications when performing administration on WAPs by using protocols such as Secure Shell (SSH) or HTTP with SSL or TLS.

Many people think of TLS and SSL as protocols that are used with Web browsers to browse the Internet more securely. However, they are also general-purpose protocols that can be used whenever authentication and data protection are necessary. For example, you can use TLS/SSL for:

- SSL-secured transactions with an e-commerce Web site
- Authenticated client access to an SSL-secured Web site
- Remote access
- SQL and/or e-mail access

You can use this technology to provide authentication and data protection when users remotely log on to Windows-based systems or networks. Users can more securely access their e-mail or enterprise applications, reducing the risk of exposure of the information to anyone on the Internet. The security benefits of using TLS/SSL on regular or wireless networks include mutual authentication, communication privacy, and communication integrity.

Understanding Certificates and Certificate Templates

Throughout the chapters we have discussed several different types of certificates. It is possible to combine a number of different usages onto a single certificate so that you can use one certificate to sign e-mail, log on to the network, and grant access to an application. Combining certificate usages allows lower management and storage overhead on the certificate and directory servers. However, the IAS server certificates are considered medium-assurance certificates. The threat posed by an unauthorized server certificate is much greater than that posed by an illegitimate client certificate. For this reason, Microsoft recommends not combining them with usages for standard-assurance applications. Figure 11-7 shows the recommended structure for issuance of wireless certificates.

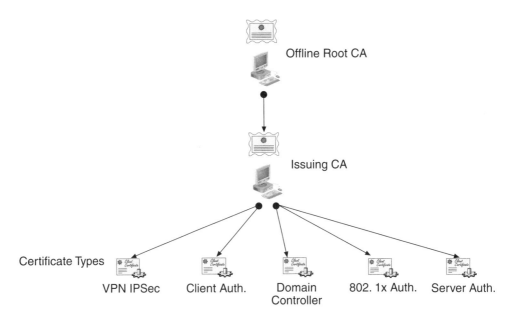

Figure 11-7 Recommended certificate structure

To help control the usage of a certificate outside its intended purpose, restrictions are automatically placed on certificates. **Key usage** is a restriction method and determines what a certificate can be used for. This allows the administrator to issue certificates that can be used for only specific tasks or certificates for a broad range of functions. Both EAP-TLS and PEAP use certificates for server authentication. In addition, applications will often expect certificates to be configured in a precise way. The application will at least require that the key usage has been correctly defined. If you are issuing certificates that include both application policy and **Enhanced Key Usage (EKU)** extensions, ensure that the two extensions contain identical object identifiers. Similarly, when EAP-TLS is configured as the authentication method for wireless clients, the IAS server certificate contains the server authentication purpose in the EKU extension of its certificate to identify itself to the client. To determine whether a certificate contains the appropriate purposes in the EKU extension, double-click the certificate in the details pane of the Certificates Snap-in. On the Details tab of the dialog box that appears, scroll to locate the EKU extension and double-click this extension. The lower panel of the dialog box shows the purposes assigned to the certificate, as shown in Figure 11-8.

Users and clients may also use certificates, depending on the type of authentication specified. The client uses a certificate from a smart card or the local certificate store to validate itself at the IAS server. The client's certificate must contain the client authentication purpose in the EKU extension. If PEAP is being used with EAP-MS-CHAP v2, the mutual authentication process is similar, except that the user employs a username and password.

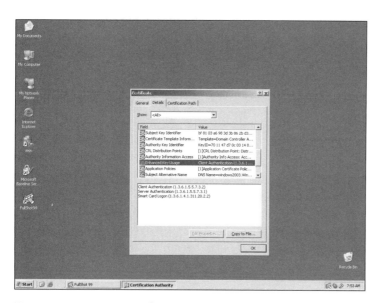

Figure 11-8 Server authentication purpose

Certificate templates provide considerable benefits by easing the management of multiple certificate types especially across multiple CAs. In contrast to the root CA, the issuing CA requires additional capabilities of Windows Server 2003 Enterprise Edition to support editable certificate templates and user certificate autoenrollment. Windows Server 2003, Standard Edition, supports only **version 1 templates**. Windows Server 2003, Enterprise Edition and Datacenter Edition support both version 1 and **version 2 templates**.

Remember that version 1 templates are read-only, so the certificate purposes under Enhanced Key Usage are hard-coded and cannot be modified. Rather than edit the original templates, make copies of the built-in templates and edit the copies to arrive at the required settings. This allows you to easily revert to the built-in templates if needed, knowing that they have not been modified. When configuring an SSL certificate for wireless networks, you must create this certificate from a template that includes these extensions for both the server and the client, as shown in Figure 11-9.

In the case of a version 2 template, the Enhanced Key Usage extension is known as application policies. If necessary, you can click the Edit button to add additional purposes, as shown in 11-10. Then click Add to display the Add Application Policy dialog box, from which you can select any of the additional certificate purposes or create a new purpose.

Remember that you can duplicate a version 1 certificate template to make a version 2 template, which then can be modified. You can add certificate purposes to the copied template as necessary. Version 1 templates are provided for backward compatibility and support many general needs for subject certification. They are created by default when a certification authority is installed and cannot be modified or removed.

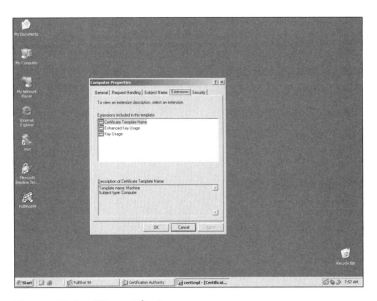

Figure 11-9   SSL certificate purposes

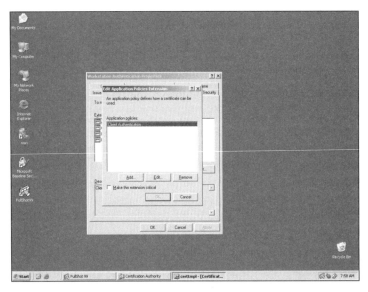

Figure 11-10   Editing the application policies extension

Configuring the IAS Server for Certificates

The security of a certificate is also known as its **assurance level**. It measures the strength that binds the subject of the certificate to the certificate itself. It is a gauge of how confident you can be that the object using the certificate is really the same as the subject named in the certificate. This assurance level is an evaluation of:

- The thoroughness of the registration and certificate enrollment process
- The way in which the private key is stored

If you do not want any stronger assurance from a certificate than that it belongs to an authorized domain user, then domain credentials are completely acceptable as the registration evidence to enroll a certificate. Configuration of the IAS server to use certificates to authenticate wireless clients is similar to any other certificate request. You can connect to the Certificate Request Web pages at the CA server to request and install a certificate on the IAS server. If you are using RADIUS, the server must support the EAP-TLS authentication protocol, which is used in certificate-based security environments. In addition, EAP-TLS is required if you are using smart cards for network access authentication. The RADIUS server also must support the PEAP-MS-CHAP v2 authentication protocol, which is used in password-based security environments.

After you have obtained and installed the certificate on the IAS server, you can configure a limited amount of properties from the Certificates Snap-in. We won't go too far into detail here because you have already issued a certificate for the server in an activity earlier in the chapter. It is worth mentioning the fact that once you have the access points and clients configured, you can monitor your wireless access by using the MMC.

You can automatically enroll users and computers for EAP-TLS or EAP-MS-CHAP v2 certificates by adding them to security groups in Active Directory Users and Computers. This method is preferred for lowering the certificate management overhead. You can use autoenrollment even when a certificate requires manual approval. The certificate will not be issued immediately, but a request will be submitted to the CA, and the enrollment will be completed after the request is approved. Autoenrollment requires that the Read, Enroll, and Autoenroll permissions have been configured on the appropriate version 2 certificate templates.

Manual offline enrollment is used for all certificate enrollment and renewal at the root CA. Manual offline enrollment involves generating the request as a file, taking it to the CA, submitting the request by using the Certification Authority management console, and retrieving it by using the management console.

Some scenarios are more complex, and neither autoenrollement nor manual enrollment will work. For example, a certificate request needs to be signed by a third party before submission to the CA. Autoenrollment is also not possible in any case where you need to define the subject name or alternate subject name in the certificate request rather than allow Active Directory to generate it.

11

PLANNING WIRELESS ACCESS POLICIES

In trying to keep a secure environment, it is often difficult to prevent visitors from using wireless laptops or employees from adding unauthorized wireless devices to the network. Group Policy in Windows Server 2003 enables you to create access policies that control the use of your wireless network and create a remote access policy using a RADIUS server, such as the Microsoft Internet Authentication Service (IAS) server. For example, the RADIUS server checks the client credentials against the directory. If the client is successfully authenticated, the RADIUS server decides whether to authorize the client to use the WLAN. It can use information such as group membership together with access policy to either grant or deny access to the client. The RADIUS relays the access decision to the AP. As you can see, planning an access policy involves several factors, so when planning your policy, consider the following factors:

- Which users, groups, and computers are allowed to access the WLAN
- Which domains or organizational units should have wireless access
- Where and when users can access the WLAN
- What authentication methods will be used
- What type of network security will be used

You should create a wireless access policy that matches your company's security policies while granting users the level of access needed to perform their duties. Create the minimum number of policies needed to achieve a goal that allows for flexible and simple management of network access. In fact, most organizations will find the need to create only one wireless network policy GPO, but will choose to create it and apply it to a location other than the domain object such as an OU.

Using Group Policy to Create a Wireless Access Policy

New to Windows Server 2003 is the ability to create a wireless network policy in Group Policy. Windows provides the Wireless Network Policy Wizard to assist you in creating your policy. Because we already discussed some of the considerations for formulating a wireless access policy, it is time to create one. Remember that most organizations create only one wireless policy, because, as with all policies, the more you have, the more complicated management of these policies becomes.

Activity 11-3: Create a Wireless Access Policy in Group Policy

Time Required: 30 minutes

Objective: Learn how to create and configure a wireless access policy and add an access connection point in Group Policy.

Description: In this exercise, you will create a wireless container, then create and configure a wireless access policy in Group Policy.

1. Log on with your **AdminXX** account, where *XX* is your assigned student number.

2. Click **Start**, **Administrative Tools**, **Active Directory Users and Computers**. Select your domain. From the menu bar choose **Action**, **New**, **Organizational Unit**.

3. On the New Object screen in the Name box, type **Wireless**, then click **OK**.

4. Right-click the Wireless OU, select **New**, **Group**. In the Group name box, type **Wireless**. Verify that the Group scope **Global** option button is selected. Click **OK**.

5. Click **Start**, **Run**, type **mmc** in the Open box, click **OK**. In the console window, choose **File**, **Add/Remove Snap-in**. On the Standalone tab, click **Add**.

6. On the Add Standalone Snap-in screen, choose **Group Policy Management**, and click **Add**.

7. Click **Close** on the Add Standalone Snap-in screen. Click **OK** on the Standalone screen.

8. Expand the **Group Policy** node of your Forest, Domain, until you find **Wireless.** Right-click the OU and select **Link an Existing GPO**.

9. On the Select GPO screen, in the Group Policy objects box, choose **Default Domain Controllers Policy**, and click **OK**.

10. Right-click the **Default Domain Controllers Policy** under the Wireless GPO, then select **Edit**.

11. Expand **Computer Configuration**, **Windows Settings**, **Security Settings**, right-click **Wireless Network (IEEE 802.11) Policies**, as shown in Figure 11-11. Select **Create Wireless Network policy**. Note: If this option is not present, select **Refresh**. Then right-click **Wireless Network (IEEE 802.11) Policies** again.

12. On the Welcome to the Wireless Network Policy Wizard screen, click **Next**.

13. On the Wireless Network Policy Name page of the wizard, type **Wireless** in the Name text box and **This policy defines the requirements for the objects in the Wireless OU** in the Description text box. Click **Next**.

14. On the Completing the Wireless Network Policy Wizard screen, ensure that the **Edit Properties** box is checked, and then click **Finish**.

15. On the General tab of the Wireless Properties dialog box that appears, select the drop-down list box next to Networks to access, choose **Access point (infrastructure) networks only**, as shown in Figure 11-12.

16. On the Preferred Networks tab, click **Add**. On the Network Properties tab, type **Warehouse** in the Network name (SSID) text box and **This is the Warehouse access point** in the Description text box.

11

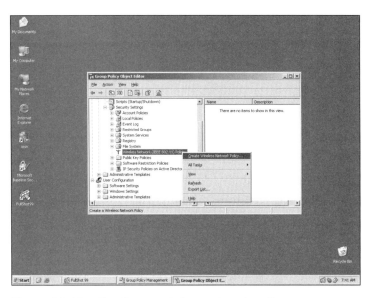

Figure 11-11 Creating a wireless network policy

17. Select the **IEEE 802.1x** tab and verify that the **Authenticate as guest when user or computer information is unavailable** check box is not checked. Click **OK**.

18. Click **OK** on the Preferred Networks tab. Close the **GPO Editor** screen. Choose **File**, **Exit** to close to console. When asked to save the console settings, click **No**. Close the Active Directory Users and Computers window.

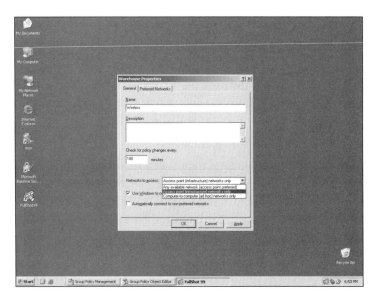

Figure 11-12 Configuring a wireless network policy

Configuring Wireless Access by Using IAS Server

IAS server allows you to control the authentication of users who are accessing multiple access points by means of a single server. Installing IAS on a domain controller rather than a member server allows direct authentication of a user in Active Directory without the need to cross the network to a domain controller. By using IAS as your RADIUS server and Active Directory as your directory service, you can provide a single sign-on solution. IAS uses Active Directory as its user accounts database, and the same set of credentials is used to control the network, to log the user on to an Active Directory domain, and to control access to resources in the domain. IAS in Windows Server 2003 supports a number of network access situations such as:

- Wireless and wired access
- VPN and dial-up access
- Extranet and Internet access

IAS provides enhanced security for WLANs by performing as a RADIUS server for 802.1x WAPs and client devices and by providing dynamic encryption keys through certificate-based authentication protocols, such as EAP-TLS. You can deploy IAS servers to function as a RADIUS server, a RADIUS proxy, or both. WLAN access management usually requires only a RADIUS server, but if your organization plans to use wireless network infrastructure to service users and devices from multiple Active Directory forests, you will also need a RADIUS proxy server role to route requests to separate RADIUS servers in each forest.

IAS remote access policies can either allow or deny connections. A policy contains a set of criteria against which each connection attempt is matched. As with other remote access policies, you can specify additional criteria for acceptance or rejection of connection attempts in the profile associated with each access policy. Right-click the policy in the details pane of the IAS Snap-in and choose Properties to access the dialog box shown in Figure 11-13. From here, you can add additional policy conditions or specify additional conditions in the profile associated with the policy.

You can use custom security groups to restrict which users and computers are allowed access to the WLAN. If you want all of your domain users and computers to be able to access the WLAN, simplify administration by adding the Domain Users and Domain Computers groups to these custom security groups. Connection restriction profiles are unique to each remote access policy, so if multiple types of connection restriction profiles are required, so are multiple remote access policies.

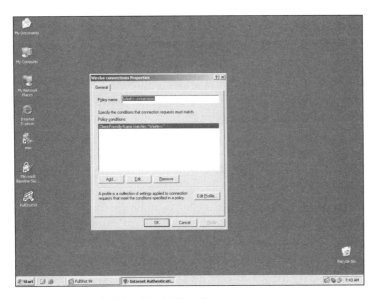

Figure 11-13   Editing the IAS policy

Activity 11-4: Configure the IAS Server to Accept RADUIS Clients and Create a New Remote Access Policy

Time Required: 30 minutes

Objective: Learn how to configure the IAS server to accept RADIUS clients and to create a remote access policy.

Description: In this exercise, you will learn how to configure the IAS server to accept RADIUS clients and to create a remote access policy.

1. Log on with your **AdminXX** account, where *XX* is your assigned student number.

2. Click **Start**, **Administrative Tools**, **Internet Authentication Service**.

3. In the console tree, right-click **RADIUS Clients** and choose **New RADIUS Client**.

4. In the New RADIUS Client dialog box, type **Warehouse1** in the Friendly name text box and **192.168.0.90** in the Client address (IP or DNS) text box, and then click **Next**.

5. On the Additional Information screen, in the Client-Vendor list box be sure that **RADIUS Standard** shows. Type **QW#RTE>*&** in the Shared secret and Confirm shared secret text boxes, and then click **Finish**.

6. In the console tree of the IAS Snap-in, right-click **Remote Access Policies** and select **New Remote Access Policy**.

7. On the Welcome to the New Remote Access Policy Wizard screen, click **Next**.

8. On the Policy Configuration Method screen, select the **Set up a custom policy** option button. In the Policy name text box, type **Warehouse clients**. Click **Next**.

9. On the Policy Conditions screen, click **Add**. On the Select Attribute screen, select **Windows-Groups**, click **Add**.

10. On the Groups page, click **Add**. In the Enter the object names to select text box, type **Wireless**. Click **OK**. Click **OK**.

11. On the Policy Conditions screen, click **Next**. On the Permissions screen, choose the **Grant Remote access permission** option button. Click **Next**.

12. On the Profile screen, choose the **Edit Profile** button. On the Authentication tab, select the **EAP Methods** button. On the Select EAP Providers screen, click **Add**.

13. On the Select EAP Providers screen, click **Add**. On the Add EAP screen, choose **Protected EAP (PEAP)**. Click **OK**.

14. On the Select EAP Providers screen, click the **Edit** button. On the Protected EAP Properties screen, click **Add**.

15. Select the **Smart Card or other certificate** authentication method on the Add EAP screen. Click **OK**. On the Protected EAP Properties screen, highlight **Smart card or other certificate** in the EAP Types box, then select the **Move Up** button.

16. Check the **Enable Fast Reconnect** box so that your screen now looks like Figure 11-14. Click **OK**. Click **OK**.

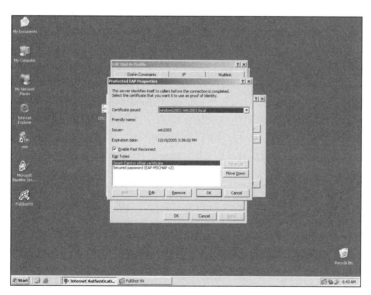

Figure 11-14 Configuring PEAP

17. On the Edit Dial-in Profile screen, click **Apply**, and then click **OK**. If a Dial-in Settings information dialog box opens with a message pertaining to viewing the Help topics for authentication methods, click **No**. On the Profile screen click **Next**, then click **Finish** to complete the wizard.

18. Choose **File**, **Exit** to close to console.

Windows Server 2003 Standard Edition can be configured with a maximum of 50 RADIUS clients and a maximum of 2 remote RADIUS server groups. You can also define a RADIUS client by using a fully qualified domain name or an IP address, but you cannot define groups of RADIUS clients by specifying an IP address range. With Windows Server 2003, Enterprise Edition and Datacenter Edition, you can configure an unlimited number of RADIUS clients and remote RADIUS server groups, along with configuring RADIUS clients by a specific IP address range.

CONFIGURING SERVERS AND ACCESS POINTS FOR WIRELESS SUPPORT

We have already discussed the WEP and 802.1x encryption methods used in wireless networks, and in an earlier activity you created a policy for the server; however, we didn't go into detail on how to configure your servers to use these encryption methods. These next two sections will cover these options.

Enabling WEP

WEP encrypts data across the wireless network using a network key that can be automatically provided for clients. Recall that WEP encryption uses a shared-secret key and the RC4 encryption algorithm. The access point (AP), and all stations that connect to it, must use the same shared key. For each packet of data sent in either direction, the transmitter combines the contents of the packet with a checksum of the packet. Once you have created a wireless network policy in Group Policy, you can configure WEP. Figure 11-15 shows the options available for configuration.

In general, you should avoid using a shared key, because if that key is compromised, it means that an attacker can eavesdrop on your traffic or join your network. If it is available, use 128-bit WEP and change the keys frequently. The WEP standard doesn't provide for any way to automatically change keys. As a result, you can only rekey an access point (AP) and its stations manually, unless the access points that can provide dynamic WEP keys and wireless clients can support them. If this is the case, select the The key is provided automatically option to provide dynamic WEP keys.

Besides enabling WEP on the WAP, the configuration area of WAPs that is most vital is changing the default settings. Right out of a box, most WAPs are not secure. WAPs broadcast their **service set identifier (SSID).** The SSID is the name designated for a specific wireless local area network. The SSID's factory default setting is usually default. The SSID can be easily changed to connect to an existing wireless network or to establish a new wireless network. This is an action you certainly want to take. Changing default SSIDs helps protect your network. Leaving the default SSID and password on a WAP is like using admin and

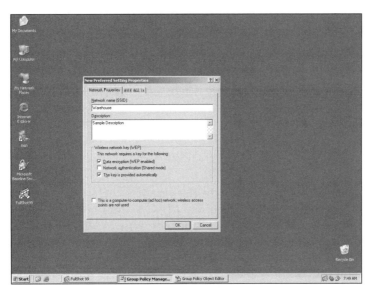

Figure 11-15   WEP configuration options

11

password for the login and password on a server. Many devices right out of the box do not even have a password on the Administrator account.

You can use MAC filters to allow or deny LAN computers access to the network, according to their MAC addresses. Enabling MAC address filtering on access points limits unauthorized wireless NICs. Many access points allow you to control access based on the MAC address of the NIC attempting to associate with it. If the MAC address of the NIC isn't in the table of the access point, it won't allow access.

ACTIVITY

Activity 11-5: Configuring Wireless Access Points

Time Required: 15 minutes

Objective: Learn how to change the default settings and configure a wireless access point.

Description: In this exercise, you will learn how to change the default settings and configure a wireless access point. Note: In this exercise a D-Link WAP was used; depending on the manufacturer of the device, the location of the settings may be different, but they basically all have similar features.

1. Log on with your **AdminXX** account, where *XX* is your assigned student number.

2. Open Internet Explorer. Choose **File**, **Open**. In the Open dialog box type the default address of the WAP. In the case, it is **192.168.0.1**. Click **OK**.

3. You may receive a pop-up box asking for a login and password. Type in the proper information, and then click **OK**.

4. Find the tab that contains the WAP setting information. In this case it is the Wireless Settings tab. On the Wireless Settings tab, in the SSID list box, change the default to

warehouse. Change the SSID broadcast option button to **Disabled**. Change the Security option button from **None** to **WEP**. Click on the **Apply** check mark at the bottom of the screen. Note: Write down the WEP key, because you will need it for the next exercise.

5. The device will restart itself. Find the tab where the password can be changed. For the D-Link model we are using, it is the Tools tab. Click the **Tools** tab. In the Administrator Settings area, in the New Password text box, type in an appropriate complex password, such as **Qn&%>P8t**, and then type the same password in the Confirm Password text box. Click on the **Apply** check mark at the bottom of the screen.

6. Locate the area where filters can be set. In this case, it is the Advanced tab. On the Advanced tab in the Filters section, select the **MAC Filters** option button. In the MAC filters area, choose **Only allow computers with MAC address listed below to access the network**, as shown in Figure 11-16. In the Name text box, type the name of the first client machine you want to be able to access the WAP, and then type the MAC address in the MAC address section. Do this for all computers accessing the WAP. When you are finished, click on the **Apply** check mark at the bottom of the screen.

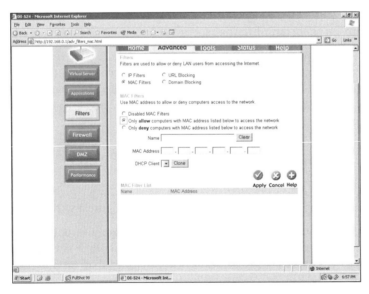

Figure 11-16   Configuring MAC filtering

Enabling 802.1x

802.1x is the recommended method of authentication and encryption for enhanced security on computers running Windows XP and Windows Server 2003. The use of 802.1x offers an effective solution for authenticating and controlling user traffic to a protected network, as well as dynamically varying encryption keys. 802.1x ties EAP to both the wired and wireless LAN media and supports multiple authentication methods, such as token cards, Kerberos, one-time passwords, certificates, and public key authentication. You configure 802.1x encryption from the IEEE 802.1x tab of the Edit Properties dialog box. This is shown in Figure 11-17.

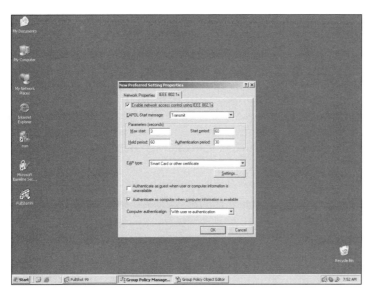

Figure 11-17   IEEE 802.1x configuration tab

Most WAPs have a configuration mode of **Wi-Fi Protected Access (WPA)**. WPA authorizes and identifies users based on a secret key that changes automatically at a regular interval. WPA uses TKIP (Temporal Key Integrity Protocol) to change the temporal key every 10,000 packets. This ensures much greater security than the standard WEP security.

CONFIGURING WIRELESS SUPPORT FOR CLIENT COMPUTERS

The wireless client must establish its credentials with the Authenticating server before wireless network access is established. When the client computer is in range of the WAP, it tries to connect to the WLAN that is active on the WAP. If the WAP is configured to allow only secured or 802.1x-authenticated connections, the WAP issues a challenge to the client. The AP then sets up a restricted channel that allows the client to communicate only with the RADIUS server. The RADIUS server will accept a connection only from a trusted WAP or one that has been configured as a RADIUS client on the Microsoft Internet Authentication Service (IAS) server and that provides the shared secret for that RADIUS client. The RADIUS server validates the client credentials against the directory. If the client is successfully authenticated, the RADIUS server decides whether to authorize the client to use the WLAN. If the client is granted access, the RADIUS server transmits the client master key to the WAP. The client and WAP now share common key information that they can use to encrypt and decrypt the WLAN traffic passing between them. This process should seem familiar to you because you have already configured most of these options throughout the chapter. Configuration of Windows client computers depends on the operating system. We will discuss configuring Windows XP, Windows 2000, and Windows CE computers for wireless networking in the next few sections.

Windows XP

Wireless Auto Configuration dynamically selects the wireless network to which a connection is attempted, based on either configured preferences or default settings. Computers running Windows XP support **Wireless Zero Configuration**, which enables these computers to automatically connect to available wireless networks. By default, Windows XP client computers can choose from available wireless networks and connect automatically without the need for user action. Wireless Zero Configuration automatically configures items such as TCP/IP settings, DNS server addresses, IAS server addresses, and so on. Wireless Zero Configuration also includes support for 802.1x authentication and encryption. Here are the default preferences for zero configuration using IEEE 802.1x authentication:

- Infrastructure before ad hoc mode, and computer authentication before user authentication.

- WEP authentication attempts to perform an IEEE 802.11 shared key authentication if the network adapter has been preconfigured with a WEP shared key, otherwise the network adapter reverts to the open system authentication.

- Although the IEEE 802.1x security enhancements are available in Windows XP Professional, the network adapters and access points must also be compatible with this standard for deployment.

Although you can change the default settings to allow, for example, guest access, which is not enabled by default, never turn on Guest access on a laptop using Wireless Zero Configuration. An unauthorized user could establish an ad hoc connection to the laptop and gain access to confidential information on the laptop.

You can access additional options by manually configuring Windows XP computers for wireless networks. Figure 11–18 shows the Smart Card or other Certificate Properties dialog box for configuring the system for use with a smart card or certificate.

Windows 2000

Computers running Windows 2000 do not support Wireless Zero Configuration. You can configure a wireless network card for connection using EAP-TLS or PEAP authentication just as you can when configuring Windows XP computers. Only Windows XP computers natively support IEEE 802.1x authentication. Microsoft provides an 802.1x Authentication Client download that allows Windows 2000 computers to use the 802.1x standard, which can be found at *www.microsoft.com/windows2000/server/evaluation/news/bulletins/8021xclient.asp*. Microsoft also provides 802.1x authentication clients for Windows 98 and Windows NT 4.0 Workstation to customers with Premier and Alliance support contracts.

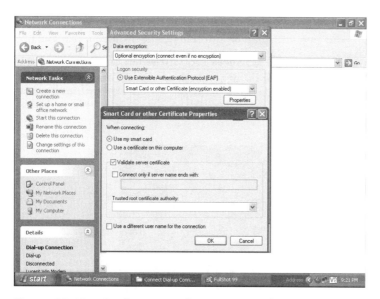

Figure 11-18   Configuring a client smart card or certificate

Windows CE

Palm-top computers running Windows CE .NET include Wireless Zero Configuration and similar manual configuration options to those found on Windows XP. They support 802.11a and Native Wireless Fidelity (Wi-Fi). Older Windows CE palm-top computers can also be configured for wireless networking. Settings and configurations are similar to those for Windows 2000.

Because of the differences in configuration and the ability to use Wireless Zero Configuration, when configuring client policies place Windows XP computers into a separate OU. Define policies that apply only to these computers in a GPO linked to this OU, and policies that apply to Windows 2000 computers in a GPO linked to the OU in which these computers are located.

Activity 11-6: Configuring a Wireless Client

Time Required: 15 minutes

Objective: Learn how to change the default settings and configure a wireless client.

Description: In this exercise, you will learn how to change the default settings and configure a wireless client. Note: In this exercise you will use Windows XP with a wireless network card installed.

1. Log on with your **AdminXX** account, where *XX* is your assigned student number.

2. Click **Start**, **Control Panel**, **Network Connections**, **Wireless Network Connection**. On the General tab, select Properties. Upon installation of the wireless

network card, it should automatically create a wireless connection icon in Network Connections. If it did not, you may have to create the connection manually.

3. On the Properties tab, click the **Wireless Networks** tab. In the Preferred Networks section, click **Add**, and in the SSID dialog box, type **warehouse**.

4. Check the **Data Encryption (WEP enabled)** check box, as shown in Figure 11-19, and click **OK**.

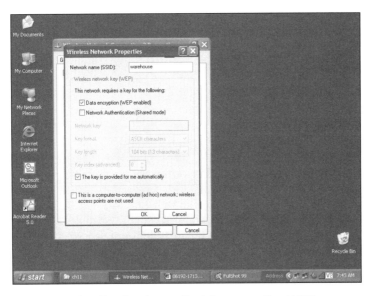

Figure 11-19 Configuring a client to access the WAP

5. Click **OK** to close the properties window, and then click **Close** to close the connection.

CHAPTER SUMMARY

◻ Wireless networks in common use operate according to the specifications of the IEEE 802.11 standards, which are defined at the Data Link layer of the OSI model. 802.1x is a standard developed by IEEE for WLANs. It employs port-based network access control. This port-based network access control uses the physical characteristics of the switched LAN infrastructure to authenticate devices attached to a LAN port.

◻ To plan for the Active Directory configuration of your wireless clients, first identify the user and computer accounts for wireless users. Next, add them to a group that will be used along with a remote access policy. Then determine how to set the remote access permission on the user and computer accounts. If the Active Directory functional level is set to native mode, you can use universal groups and nested global groups.

❏ When planning wireless authentication methods, there should be a balance between the required level of security and the ease of deployment. For instance, PEAP with EAP-MS-CHAP v2 requires less effort to deploy because certificates or smart cards are not needed, yet PEAP with EAP-TLS will provide a higher level of security because of the use of certificates and smart cards.

❏ When the vulnerabilities of static WEP were discovered, VPN was proposed as the best way to secure data traveling over a WLAN. Although VPN is a great solution to securely travel through a network such as the Internet, it is not necessarily the best solution for securing internal WLANs. A VPN offers little or no additional security compared with 802.1x solutions.

❏ The IAS in Microsoft Windows Server 2003 is the Microsoft implementation of a RADIUS server and proxy. IAS performs authentication, authorization, and accounting of various types of network connections. When used as a RADIUS proxy, IAS can forward RADIUS requests to another RADIUS server.

❏ Although using WEP is much better than no encryption at all, it's important to understand its limitations so that you have an accurate picture of the consequences and what you must do to properly protect your wireless environment. It is also important to know what part technologies such as 802.1x and IPSec play in securing your wireless network and how to get the maximum security possible from all three.

❏ IAS provides enhanced security for WLANs by performing as a RADIUS server for 802.1x WAPs and client devices and providing dynamic encryption keys through certificate-based authentication protocols, such as EAP-TLS. You can deploy IAS servers to function as a RADIUS server, a RADIUS proxy, or both.

❏ Many people think of TLS and SSL as protocols that are used with Web browsers to browse the Internet more securely. However, they are also general-purpose protocols that can be used whenever authentication and data protection are necessary.

❏ The IAS server certificates are considered medium-assurance certificates. The threat posed by an unauthorized server certificate is much greater than that posed by an illegitimate client certificate. For this reason, Microsoft recommends not combining them with usages for standard-assurance applications.

❏ You can automatically enroll users and computers for EAP-TLS or EAP-MS-CHAP v2 certificates by adding them to security groups in Active Directory Users and Computers. This method is preferred for lowering the certificate management overhead. You can use autoenrollment, even where a certificate requires manual approval.

❏ 802.1x is the recommended method of authentication and encryption for enhanced security on computers running Windows XP and Windows Server 2003. The use of 802.1x offers an effective solution for authenticating and controlling user traffic to a protected network, as well as dynamically varying encryption keys. 802.1x ties EAP to both the wired and wireless LAN media and supports multiple authentication methods, such as token cards, Kerberos, one-time passwords, certificates, and public key authentication.

11

❑ Computers running Windows 2000 do not support Wireless Zero Configuration without an added authentication client from Microsoft.com. You can configure a wireless network card for connection using EAP-TLS or PEAP authentication just as you can when configuring Windows XP computers. Only Windows XP computers natively support IEEE 802.1x authentication.

KEY TERMS

802.1x — A standard developed by IEEE for wireless local area networks. It employs port-based network access control.

802.1x authentication standard — An authentication standard that relies on the Extensible Authentication Protocol for its authentication needs.

access point (AP) — A device that functions as a transparent bridge between the wireless clients and the existing wired network.

assurance level — The security of a certificate. It measures the strength that binds the subject of the certificate to the certificate itself.

certificate templates — Ease the management of multiple certificate types especially across multiple CAs.

Enhanced Key Usage (EKU) — The certificate extension that lists the purpose of the certificate.

Extensible Authentication Protocol (EAP) — A challenge-response protocol that can be run over secured transport mechanisms.

fast reconnect — A cached credentials strategy allowing for subsequent logon until the cache expires, which is set to 8 hours by default.

Internet Authentication Service (IAS) — Microsoft's implementation of a RADIUS server and proxy. IAS performs authentication, authorization, and accounting of various types of network connections.

Key usage — A restriction method that determines what a certificate can be used for. This allows the administrator to issue certificates that can be used for only specific tasks or for a broad range of functions.

Light EAP (LEAP) — A protocol that combines centralized two-way authentication with dynamically generated Wireless Equivalent Privacy keys, or WEP keys. LEAP was developed by Cisco for use on WLANs that use Cisco 802.11 wireless devices.

open authentication — An authentication method that allows access to anyone providing the correct service set identifier (SSID) or Wired Equivalent Privacy (WEP) key for the access point.

Protected EAP (PEAP) — An authentication protocol that protects data being sent between the client and the access point during the session, which was codeveloped by Cisco, Microsoft Corp., and RSA Security Inc.

Remote Authentication Dial-In User Service (RADIUS) — An authentication server usually employed for authentication purposes.

service set identifier (SSID) — The name designated for a specific wireless local area network.

shared key authentication — An authentication method similar to a challenge-response authentication process.

version 1 templates — Read-only certificate templates used for backward compatibility.

version 2 templates — An editable template for configuring certificates.

warchalking — A method used to mark buildings, curbs, and other landmarks indicating the presence of an available access point and its connection.

wardriving — The process of driving around with a laptop system configured to listen for open wireless access points.

Wired Equivalent Privacy (WEP) — The most basic form of encryption that can be used on 802.11-based wireless networks to provide privacy of data sent between a wireless client and its access point.

Wi-Fi Protected Access (WPA) — Authorizes and identifies users based on a secret key that changes automatically at a regular interval.

Wireless Zero Configuration — Configuration option which enables computers to automatically connect to available wireless networks.

REVIEW QUESTIONS

11

1. Which of the following authentication methods support the use of PEAP? (Choose all that apply.)

    a. EAP-TLS

    b. EAP-MS-CHAP

    c. EAP-MS-CHAP v2

    d. EAP-MD5

2. After implementing a WLAN policy, users report that they are unable to access the WLAN. The WLAN is set up with specified access points located in different areas of the company's office building. Which of the following are possible reasons for this problem? (Choose all that apply.)

    a. The administrator has specified access to infrastructure networks only.

    b. The administrator has cleared the Use Windows to configure wireless network settings for client's option.

    c. The administrator has cleared the Automatically connect to non-preferred networks option.

    d. The administrator has not specified any wireless networks on the Preferred Networks tab of the policy's Properties dialog box.

3. You have installed an IAS server and obtained a certificate for this server from the company's enterprise root CA server. How do you ensure that this certificate is used to authenticate the server to clients connecting to the WLAN, but not for client authentication?

   a. On the General tab of the Certificate Properties dialog box, select the Disable all purposes for this certificate option.

   b. On the General tab of the Certificate Properties dialog box, select Enable only the following purposes. Ensure that Server Authentication is selected and Client Authentication is cleared.

   c. On the Cross-Certificates tab of the Certificate Properties dialog box, clear the Specify additional Cross-Certificate download locations option.

   d. The certificate is used for server authentication purposes only by default.

4. Only 802.1x authentication and encryption is enabled on your WLAN. How should you configure the Group Policy Properties dialog box?

   a. Select the Data Encryption (WEP enabled) check box.

   b. Clear the Data Encryption (WEP enabled) check box.

   c. Select the Network authentication (Shared mode) check box.

   d. Select the Enable network access control using IEEE 802.1x check box.

5. Which of the following operating systems support Wireless Zero Configuration? (Choose all that apply.)

   a. Windows Server 2003

   b. Windows 2000

   c. Windows 98

   d. Windows XP

6. Which of the following authentication methods provides only minimum protection?

   a. Open authentication

   b. Shared key authentication

   c. 802.1x authentication with EAP-TLS

   d. 802.1x authentication with EAP-MS-CHAP v2

7. You are using shared key authentication for authenticating users to your wireless access point. Which of the following data encryption standards should you choose?

   a. 802.1x

   b. IPSec

   c. WEP

   d. EAP

8. Which of the following would you use to provide an encrypted authentication channel and fast reconnect using cached session keys?

   a. Shared key authentication

   b. EAP-TLS

   c. EAP-MS-CHAP v2

   d. PEAP

9. Your corporate policy requires a port-based access control method that works along with EAP-TLS and EAP-MD5 authentication methods. Which of the following should you choose?

   a. WEP

   b. 802.1x

   c. IPSec

   d. IAS

10. You are using an IAS server to authenticate users connecting to your network from wireless access points. Which of the following should you configure as clients of the IAS server?

    a. Users requiring wireless access to the network

    b. Computers used for wireless access to the network

    c. Access points from which wireless users access the network

    d. Active Directory domain controllers

11. Which of the following are benefits of using a RADIUS server to authenticate wireless connections to your network? (Choose all that apply.)

    a. RADIUS provides centralized authentication, authorization, and accounting services.

    b. RADIUS can authenticate users accessing the network from multiple access points.

    c. RADIUS provides data encryption as well as authentication to wireless clients.

    d. RADIUS provides a secure authentication service without the need for a certificate.

12. Which of the following must you do to in a WLAN policy to enable users to access the WLAN from a wireless access point? (Choose all that apply.)

    a. Specify and configure a certificate for each wireless access point.

    b. Define the users or groups permitted to access the WLAN.

    c. Specify and configure a data encryption type for the policy.

    d. Specify and configure the EAP type for the policy.

11

13. Which of the following are security benefits of using SSL on wireless networks? (Choose all that apply.)

    a. SSL provides one policy that determines the authentication of users accessing the network from multiple access points.

    b. SSL validates the identities of both the server and client computers.

    c. SSL encrypts all information sent between the server and client computers.

    d. SSL ensures that information sent between the server and client computers has not been altered in transit.

14. Which of the following encryption strengths can be used in a WEP-based WLAN? (Choose all that apply.)

    a. 40 bits

    b. 64 bits

    c. 128 bits

    d. 104 bits

15. Which of the following is a benefit of using IAS server to control authentication of users to a WLAN?

    a. IAS provides a stronger level of authentication and encryption of data being transmitted across the WLAN than 802.1x.

    b. IAS allows for mutual authentication of both the server and client computers creating a wireless connection.

    c. IAS allows you to control authentication of users accessing multiple access points by means of a single server.

    d. IAS allows roaming users to maintain their connection when moving between different access points on the same network.

16. You are configuring a Windows XP Professional client computer manually to authenticate to a WLAN using a username and password. Which of the following options should you specify in the Properties dialog box?

    a. On the Wireless Networks tab, select the network to which you want to authenticate, and then click Configure. Then select Secured Password (EAP-MS-CHAP v2).

    b. On the Authentication tab, select Enable network access control using IEEE 802.1x and Protected EAP, and then click Properties. Then select Secured Password (EAP-MS-CHAP v2).

    c. On the Wireless Networks tab, select the network to which you want to authenticate, and then click Configure. Then select Smart Card or other Certificate.

    d. On the Authentication tab, select Enable network access control using IEEE 802.1x and Protected EAP, and then click Properties. Then select Smart Card or other Certificate.

17. Which of the following would you use to provide certificate-based mutual authentication and use of smart cards for user logon?

   a. EAP-TLS

   b. Shared key authentication

   c. EAP-MS-CHAP v2

   d. PEAP

18. Which of the following is not an accurate statement about EAP-MS-CHAP v2?

   a. EAP-MS-CHAP v2 provides mutual authentication based on password-based user and computer authentication.

   b. EAP-MS-CHAP v2 is used along with Protected EAP (PEAP) to provide benefits such as an encrypted authentication channel and fast reconnect using cached session keys.

   c. EAP-MS-CHAP v2 can be used with Internet Authentication Service (IAS) to provide a centralized authentication mechanism for clients accessing the WLAN.

   d. EAP-MS-CHAP v2 provides mutual authentication based on smart card–based user and computer authentication.

19. Which of the following is not an accurate statement about 802.1x authentication?

   a. 802.1x provides port-based network access control for authenticating clients to the WLAN.

   b. 802.1x provides both authentication and data encryption services.

   c. 802.1x is especially useful to provide strong security between an IAS server and a domain controller when these services are provided by different servers.

   d. 802.1x works together with EAP-MS-CHAP v2, EAP-TLS, or EAP-MD5 to provide data encryption after the client has connected to the WLAN.

20. Which of the following operating systems does not require a Microsoft 802.1x Authentication Client to use 802.1x authentication and encryption?

   a. Windows 98

   b. Windows XP

   c. Windows NT 4.0

   d. Windows 2000

21. You are using SSL certificates to secure communications between client computers and Web servers. Which of the following options would you choose to ensure that no client computers can communicate with servers unless they have certificates available?

   a. Accept client certificates

   b. Require client certificates

   c. One-to-many mapping

   d. Many-to-one mapping

11

22. A company can protect its wireless network by doing which of the following? (Choose all that apply.)

    a. Changing default access point administration passwords

    b. Changing default service set identifiers (SSIDs)

    c. Putting the wireless network in an Internet-access-only zone or a demilitarized zone (DMZ)

    d. Disabling WEP

23. Which of the following means of wireless authentication are currently used? (Choose all that apply.)

    a. Open authentication

    b. Shared key authentication

    c. Password authentication

    d. 802.1x authentication standard

24. Which of the following is not an 802.11 standard?

    a. 802.11a

    b. 802.11i

    c. 802.11m

    d. 802.11b

25. Which of the following are inherent risks associated with wireless networks? (Choose all that apply.)

    a. 802.1x transmissions generate detectable radio-frequency traffic in all directions.

    b. Without the use of an encryption standard of some type, data is passed in cleartext form.

    c. The request for connection by the client is a two-way protected broadcast.

    d. Wireless LANs can be subject to session hijacking and man-in-the-middle attacks.

CASE PROJECTS

Case Project 11-1

You are the network administrator for the Evergrow forest that consists of several Windows Server 2003 domains with client computers running Windows XP Professional. You are planning the authentication method for wireless clients. Many of the users have laptops to do inventory and often move around from department to department. You want these roaming users to maintain their connection when moving between different access points on the same network. Management wants you to submit a written plan on how you will accomplish this. Prepare a report that nontechnical people can understand.

Case Project 11-2

You are the network administrator for the Preplogic forest that consists of several Windows Server 2003 domains with client computers running Windows XP Professional. Your manager has asked you to implement a wireless encryption solution that will provide a strong level of security for data being transmitted across your WLAN among several departments. You are to use a port-based access control method that works along with the EAP-TLS and EAP-MD5 authentication methods. Prepare a plan for your manager with the solution you think would best work for this situation.

Case Project 11-3

You are the network administrator for the Test domain that consists of a Windows Server 2003 domain with client computers running Windows XP Professional. You are responsible for configuring a wireless security policy in Active Directory to restrict users access on the WLAN. The WLAN is set up with specified access points located in various areas of the building. Management has received an anonymous letter revealing some proprietary information obtained via drive-by hacking. Based on the information shown in Figure 11-20, prepare a report for management explaining what you will change in the GPO to prevent this from happening in the future.

11

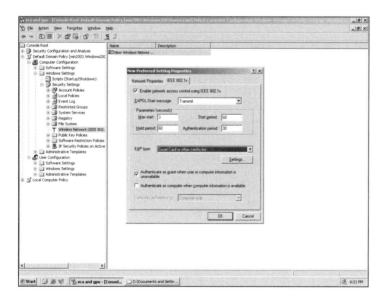

Figure 11-20   Wireless GPO settings

Case Project 11-4

You are the network administrator for the Test domain that consists of a Windows Server 2003 domain with client computers running Windows XP Professional. You are responsible for configuring a wireless security policy. You want to automatically enroll users and computers for EAP-TLS certificates. How will you accomplish this?

Case Project 11-5

You are the network administrator at Evergrow. You are the network administrator for the Test domain that consists of a Windows Server 2003 domain with client computers running Windows XP Professional. You are responsible for configuring digital certificates. You are using SSL connections between clients and the Web servers. Explain to management how the process of SSL authentication works.

CHAPTER

12

TROUBLESHOOTING PKI, REMOTE ACCESS, AND WIRELESS POLICIES

After reading this chapter and completing the exercises, you will be able to:

♦ Troubleshoot authorization and authentication

♦ Troubleshoot certificate revocation lists

♦ Troubleshoot remote access

♦ Troubleshoot wireless access

A s much as we would like to believe that if we plan and configure everything properly, once the network is set up, it will run trouble free. However, things will go wrong, systems will crash, and applications will hang. This is part of everyday life for a network administrator. Vendors constantly update their operating systems, software, drivers, and equipment. As a result, the network will continually change. More complex network environments mean that the potential for connectivity and performance problems in networks is high, and the source of the problem is often hard to pin down. You must ensure that users have ongoing access by making sure that if something happens, you have a plan so that the normal course of business operations is not interrupted. To have as little downtime as possible, you must be proactive in managing the environment and know how to effectively troubleshoot any issues that may arise.

Troubleshooting skills are acquired through experimentation and experience. You cannot learn the resolution to every problem that exists. You can, however, learn a methodology to diagnose nearly every problem in a systematic and logical manner. This includes having good resources handy. This chapter will guide you through preventing problems by being proactive in avoiding issues that can arise, show you areas of concern that will help with troubleshooting, and expose you to related tools and resources that are available to help make this process easier. It will start with troubleshooting Public Key Infrastructure (PKI) group structure, authentication, and authorization. It will then move on to discuss troubleshooting certificate structures, including autoenrollment. From there, we will move on to remote access issues and what logs are important in troubleshooting this area. Finally, we will look at wireless access troubleshooting tools.

TROUBLESHOOTING AUTHORIZATION AND AUTHENTICATION

In Chapter 9, you learned that PKI refers to a technology relating to authentication and encryption that is based on a system of certificates. Using PKI allows an organization to publish, use, renew and revoke certificates as well as enroll clients. A PKI infrastructure is intertwined with Active Directory because in a Windows Server 2003 domain environment, the "Active Directory" directory service is the most likely publication point for certificates issued by Windows Server 2003–based certificate authorities (CAs). Active Directory stores not only user credentials but also access control information. Users who log on to the network obtain both authentication and authorization to access system resources.

Active Directory also allows administrators to create group accounts, allowing system security and accounts to be managed more efficiently. Once group accounts are set up, you can use Group Policy in Windows to distribute certificates to subjects automatically, establish common trusted certification authorities, and manage recovery policies. It is here at the group structure that we will begin to look at PKI troubleshooting.

Troubleshooting Group Structure

Many basic network services and configuration decisions involve creating and defining explicit boundaries, securing network traffic, and securing your servers. The way that you plan your domains, forests, and organizational units plays a critical role in defining your network's security boundaries. This relationship might sometimes be based on administrative requirements; at other times, the relationship might be defined by operational requirements such as geographical location and controlling replication. In addition, if you have multiple forests, you need to plan the logical trust relationships between forests that allows pass-through authentication.

Groups help properly plan a secure environment by allowing administrators to separate users into groups that can be granted permissions and are used in the creation of certificate policies. Groups and Group Policy are common areas where you will regularly have to troubleshoot.

Security Groups

In prior versions of Microsoft Windows Server, there really was no way to tell what the results of various applied permissions were. The **Effective Permissions** tab is a new advanced option in Windows Server 2003. It lets you see all of the permissions that apply to a security principal for a given object, including the permissions resulting from memberships in security groups. In Chapter 2 you installed the Group Policy Management console. It can be accessed by clicking Start, Administrative tools, and Group Policy Management. The Effective Permissions tab is located on the right side of the screen.

This tab is shown in Figure 12-1.

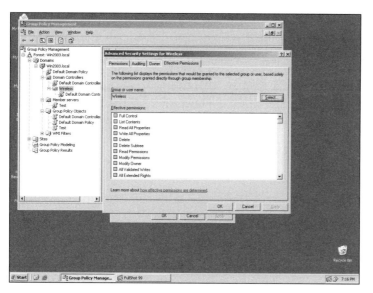

Figure 12-1   Effective Permissions tab

The Group Policy Management console, which is new to Windows Server 2003, is also a good source of information when troubleshooting. The Group Policy Management console can be accessed by clicking Start, Run; typing mmc in the Open box; and selecting the Group Policy Management console Snap-in. The Settings tab will display all the configured settings for the policy, as shown in Figure 12-2.

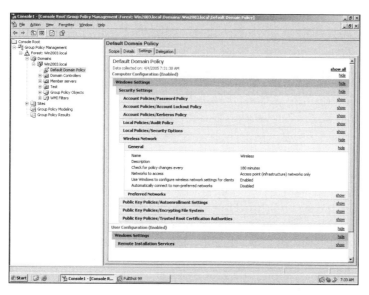

Figure 12-2   Group Policy Settings tab

In addition to permissions, **inheritance** is another area that you may need to examine if policies for groups do not work properly. Inheritance allows administrators to easily assign and manage permissions. This feature automatically causes objects within a container to inherit all the inheritable permissions of that container. Only permissions marked to be inherited will be inherited. When you set permissions on a parent folder, new files and subfolders created in the folder inherit these permissions. If the file or folder has inherited permissions from the parent folder, there are three ways to make changes to inherited permissions:

- Make the changes to the parent folder so that the file or folder will inherit the permissions.

- Select the opposite permission to override the inherited permission.

- Clear the Allow inheritable permissions from parent to propagate to this object check box so that the file or folder will no longer inherit permissions from the parent folder.

If neither Allow nor Deny is selected for a permission, then the group or user may have obtained the permission through group membership. If the group or user has not obtained the permission through membership in another group, then the group or user is implicitly denied the permission.

Block Policy inheritance and No Override are also features that can be used to control which policies apply. A No Override attribute has precedence over all of the policies that are applied thereafter. Any GPO (Group Policy Object) that is linked to a site, domain, or OUs (organizational units) can be set to No Override with respect to that container so that none of its policy settings can be overridden. When more than one GPO has been set to No Override, the one that is highest in the Active Directory hierarchy takes precedence. Remember that you cannot select which policies you block when you use Block Policy inheritance. Blocking does not affect local GPOs. The Block Policy Inheritance option blocks all group policy settings that would filter down to the site, domain, or OU from a parent, no matter what GPO those settings originate from, but it will not block Group Policy settings from GPOs that are linked directly to the site, domain, or OU. Inheritance information for Group Policy can be found on the Inheritance tab of the policy, as shown in Figure 12-3.

Besides using the Effective Permissions tab, you can use several command-line tools to view the existence of all permissions for a specific user or group on a set of OUs in a domain. **Dsrevoke** can be used on domain controllers that are running Windows Server 2003 or Windows 2000 Server. It can also be used to remove all permissions specified for a particular user or group. Dsrevoke is meant to complement the functionality provided by the Delegation of Control Wizard by providing the ability to revoke delegated administrative authority. There are some caveats in using Dsrevoke. It works only on domain objects and OUs and removes only permissions. If a role has user rights applied, you must manually remove them by modifying the appropriate Group Policy.

Figure 12-3   Group Policy Inheritance tab

12

ACTIVITY

Activity 12-1: Use Dsrevoke to View Permissions

Time Required: 30 minutes

Objective: Install the Dsrevoke tool, delegate permissions on an OU, and then use the Dsrevoke tool to view permissions on the OU.

Description: In this exercise, you will discover how to install the Dsrevoke tool, delegate permissions on an OU, and then use the Dsrevoke tool to view permissions on the OU.

1. Log on to your Windows Server 2003 computer with your **AdminXX** account, where *XX* is your assigned student number.

2. Open Internet Explorer. Go to **http://www.microsoft.com/downloads/details.aspx?FamilyID=77744807–c403–4bda–b0e4–c2093b8d6383&displaylang=en**.

3. In the Validation Recommended box, click **Continue**.

4. In the Validate Windows and obtain the download section, select the **No, do not validate Windows at this time, but take me to the download** radio button, and click **Continue**.

5. Scroll down to the bottom of the page and click the **dsrevoke.exe** file. When the File Download box opens, click the **Save** button, choose a file location to download, and click **Save**. Click **Close**.

You should also download the Dsrevoke.doc file so that you have reference material on how to use this utility.

NOTE

6. Go to **Start**, **Administrative Tools**, **Active Directory User and Computers**. Expand and highlight your domain, and from the **Action** menu, choose **New, Organizational Unit**. On the New Object screen, in the Name box, type **Test**. Click **OK**.

7. Highlight the Users folder, and from the **Action** menu, choose **New, Group**. On the New Object - Group screen, in the Group name box, type **Developers**. Select the **Domain local** radio button and the **Security** radio button if necessary, then click **OK**.

8. Right-click the **Test** OU and select **Delegate Control**. The Welcome to the Delegation of Control Wizard screen will open, as shown in Figure 12-4. Click **Next**.

Figure 12-4   Welcome to the Delegation of Control Wizard screen

9. On the Users or Groups screen, click **Add**. On the Select Users, Computers, or Groups screen, in the Enter the object names to select box, type **Developers**. Click **OK** and click **Next**.

10. On the Tasks to Delegate screen, check the **Create, delete, and manage user accounts, Read all user information** and the **Generate Resultant Set of Policy (Planning)** boxes. Click **Next**.

11. On the Completing the Delegation of Control Wizard screen, Click **Finish**.

12. On the Active Directory Users and Computers screen, choose **File**, **Exit** to close the window.

13. Go to **Start**, **Run** and in the Run box, type **cmd**. Click **OK**.

14. At the command prompt, navigate to the directory where you saved the dsrevoke file. Type **dsrevoke /report "Yourdomainname\Developers"**. Press **Enter**.

15. The Permissions for the Testers should show, as demonstrated in Figure 12-5.

Figure 12-5   Using Dsrevoke to display permissions

16. At the command prompt, type **Exit** to close the window.

Nested Groups

Security group nesting occurs when one security group is made a member of another security group. The nested group inherits all of the privileges and permissions that are granted to the parent. Nested groups are used to consolidate group management by reducing the number of times permissions are granted and reducing replication traffic that is caused by replication of group membership changes. In other words, nested groups allow you to provide access to resources with minimum maintenance.

Four domain functional levels are available: Windows 2000 mixed, which is the default; Windows 2000 native; Windows Server 2003 interim; and Windows Server 2003. Your nesting options depend on which domain functional level your Windows Server 2003 domain is set to. Security groups in a Windows 2000 mixed domain are restricted. A domain must be configured at the Windows 2000 Native or Windows Server 2003 functional level for global groups to be nested within global groups or for domain local groups to be nested within domain local groups. Remember from Chapter 9 that the default group membership limitation is 120 groups, and uncontrolled group nesting may result in access token size problems. Additionally, it becomes difficult to know exactly which permissions members of nested groups might inherit. Group nesting is available in Windows 2000 mixed mode for distribution groups and domain local groups. For Windows 2000 Native and Windows Server 2003, full group nesting is permitted.

Troubleshooting Authorization

In Chapter 9, you learned that authorization is the process of verifying that an authenticated party has the permission to access a particular resource. This is the layer of security control following authentication. Security in the Microsoft Windows Server 2003 operating system controls the use of system and network resources through the interrelated mechanisms of authentication and authorization. When a user logs on, that user does not automatically have access to the resources they require. Users must be authorized to access resources.

Remember that there is a difference between NTFS (New Technology File System) permissions and share permissions. Shared resources are resources available to users and groups other than the resource's owner. Shared resources are assigned permissions that enable the resource's owner to enforce access control by either denying access to unauthorized users or limiting the extent of access provided to authorized users. After a folder is shared, you can protect the shared folder by specifying one set of share permissions for all files and subfolders of the shared folder. **Share permissions** are set in much the same way file and folder permissions are set in NTFS. With **NTFS permissions**, you also have the choice of assigning special permissions to groups or users. Special permissions are permissions on a more detailed level.

Share permissions apply globally to all files and folders in the share and have no effect on users accessing the contents of a shared folder when the shared folder is on a local disk.

NOTE

Deny permissions should be used only for special cases, such as excluding a subset of a group that has Allowed permissions, or excluding one, special permission when you have already assigned Full Control to a user or group. Inappropriately set permissions can deny valid users access to required files and directories. User File Permissions, or **Perms**, is a command-line tool that displays user access permissions for a file or directory on an NTFS file system volume by querying the permissions associated with a specific access control entry (ACE).

ACTIVITY

Activity 12-2: Use Perms.exe to View File Permissions

Time Required: 30 minutes

Objective: Install the Perms tool and use it to view permissions on a file.

Description: In this exercise, you will discover how to download and install the Windows 2003 Resource Kit tools. You will then use the Perms tool to view permissions on a file.

1. Log on to your Windows Server 2003 computer with your **AdminXX** account, where *XX* is your assigned student number.

2. Open Internet Explorer. Go to **http://www.microsoft.com/downloads/details.aspx?FamilyID=9D467A69-57FF-4AE7-96EE-B18C4790CFFD&displaylang=en**.

3. This is the Windows Server 2003 Resource Kit Tools page. On the right side of the page, click the **Download** button. When the File Download box opens, click the **Save** button. If the download box doesn't open, then click the **Start download** link, choose a file location to download, and click **Save**.

4. When the download is complete, click **Open**. On the Welcome to the Windows Resource Kit Tools Setup Wizard screen, click **Next**.

5. On the End-User License Agreement screen, select the **I Agree** radio button. Click **Next**.

6. On the User Information screen, type your name in the Name box and your school in the Organization box. Click **Next**.

7. On the Destination Directory screen, accept the default location or choose a directory where you want to install the tool, then click the **Install Now** button.

8. When the install is finished, on the Completing the Windows Resource Kit Tools Setup Wizard screen, click **Finish**.

9. Double-click **My Computer** on the Start menu. Double-click the **root drive** where Windows Server is installed, such as C:, double-click **Program Files**, then double-click **Cmak**.

10. Right-click **cmak.exe**, click **Properties**, then click the **Security** tab. Click **Add**.

11. On the Select Users, Computers, or Groups screen, in the Enter the object names to select box, type **Testers**. Click **OK**.

12. In the Permissions for Testers area, check the **Allow** box next to Modify. Note that this will automatically check the Write box. Click the **Advanced** button.

13. On the Permissions tab, select the Edit button. In the Permissions area, check the **Allow** box next to Take Ownership. Click **OK**. Click **Apply**. Click **OK**.

14. Click **Apply**, then click **OK**. You should now be back to the Explorer window. Click **File**, **Close**.

15. Click **Start, Run**; in the Run box, type **cmd** and click **OK**.

16. At the command prompt, type **perms Testers "C:\Program Files\CMAK\cmak.exe"** and press **Enter**. Note: if your install is in a different root directory, you may need to use a letter other than C:.

17. The file permissions for the Testers group on the cmak.exe file should be displayed, as shown in Figure 12-6.

18. At the command prompt, type **exit** to close the window.

12

Figure 12-6 Using perms to display file permissions

User Rights Assignments

As you learned in earlier chapters, user rights are applied to security groups to determine what members of that group can do within the scope of a domain or forest. The user rights assignment can grant specific privileges and can grant logon rights to users and groups. User rights are assigned by administrators to individual users or groups as part of the security settings for the computer. Although user rights can be managed centrally through Group Policy, they are applied locally. User rights are automatically assigned to some security groups at the time Active Directory is installed to help administrators define a person's administrative role in the domain. You can assign user rights to security groups, using Group Policy, to help delegate specific tasks. You should always use discretion when assigning delegated tasks because an untrained user assigned too many rights on a security group can potentially cause significant harm to your network. The following two user rights assignments may be the source of issues:

- *Allow log on locally*—This right allows a user to start an interactive session on the computer. Users who do not have this right can start a remote interactive session on the computer if they have the Allow logon through Terminal Services right. For domain controllers, only grant this right to the Administrators group. For other server roles, add Backup Operators and Power Users.

- *Back up files and directories*—This user right allows the user to circumvent file and directory permissions to back up the system. Limit this right to staff who need to be able to back up data as part of their daily job responsibilities.

Troubleshooting Authentication

The user authentication method that you implement depends on the operating systems that your clients are running and the level of security that you require for your network. For example, you might require passwords, certificates, or smart cards for user authentication, depending on your organization's security needs. The logon process begins when a user enters credentials in the form of a username and password into the Log On to Windows dialog box or when the user inserts a smart card into the smart card reader. The authentication process confirms the user's identification to the security database on the user's local computer or to an Active Directory domain. Assuming that these credentials are acceptable, the system creates an access token for the user. From there, how you troubleshoot issues will depend on the authentication method you are using.

Kerberos is the default authentication protocol, so any issue related to authentication, such as console logon, network logon, access to network resources, or remote access, might indicate some sort of Kerberos error. For Kerberos authentication to occur, there must be TCP/IP network connectivity between the client, the authenticating domain controller, and the target server. If you use a firewall, be sure that TCP port 88 and UDP port 88 are open. They are used by the Kerberos ticket-granting service.

The following tools, which are found in the Windows Server 2003 Resource Tools Kit, are helpful in troubleshooting Kerberos-related authentication and delegation issues:

- *Kerbtray*—A utility that can be used to view the Kerberos tickets in the cache on the current computer
- *Klist*—A command-line tool similar in functionality to Kerbtray but that also allows you to view and delete Kerberos tickets
- *Setspn*—A command-line tool that allows you to manage the Service Principal Names (SPN) directory property for an Active Directory service account

Authentication issues may also arise that are associated with SSL certificates. To troubleshoot these issues, first confirm whether you can telnet to port 443 on the IP addresses of the client and server computer. There is no sense troubleshooting the certificate if you can't access the port. If you can telnet to 443, check the certificates attribute using the browser's View Certificate dialog box. Check the certificate's effective and expiration dates, whether the common name is correct, and also what the **Authority Information Access (AIA)** or CRL (certificate revocation list) distribution point is. The AIA extension specifies where to find up-to-date certificates for the CA. Then confirm that you can browse the directory for those AIA/CRL points successfully. If you are using a custom client application instead of a browser to access an SSL-enabled Web site that requires client certificates, check that the client certificate is located in the correct store that the client application accesses. The Certificate Services MMC Snap-in can be used to examine the contents of certificate stores.

Another source of authentication issues is access to Web pages, applications, and sites. If you are using Windows authentication, verify that the account providing the context is able to be authenticated by the remote computer. You may want to consider enabling just Basic authentication and manually log on to ensure you know what principal is being authenticated. Restart IIS to ensure that log on sessions aren't being cached. If you are using Integrated Windows authentication, check browser settings and the Web content zone. Within User Authentication ensure that the Logon setting is set correctly for your application. Test your system with a simple Web page that displays security context information. If this fails, enable auditing on the requested file and check the Security event log. Examine the log for invalid usernames or invalid object access attempts. If you see an error message that indicates that the logon has failed for NT AUTHORITY\ ANONYMOUS, this indicates that the identity on the Web server does not have any network credentials and is attempting to access the remote computer. Identify which account is being used by the Web application for remote resource access and confirm that it has network credentials.

Activity 12-3: Use Klist.exe to View Kerberos Authentication

Time Required: 10 minutes

Objective: Use the Klist tool to view Kerberos authentication on a server.

Description: In this exercise, you will use the Klist tool to view Kerberos authentication on a server.

To use Klist to view tickets, you must run the tool on a computer that is a member of a Kerberos realm.

NOTE

1. Log on to your Windows Server 2003 computer with your **AdminXX** account, where *XX* is your assigned student number.

2. Click **Start**, **Run**, and in the Run box type **cmd** and click OK.

3. At the command prompt, type **Klist tickets** and press **Enter**. This will display the cached session tickets on the machine.

4. At the command prompt, type **Klist tgt** and press **Enter**. This will display information on the ticket granting ticket (TGT). A TGT enables the authentication service to safely transport the requestor's credentials to the ticket-granting service. Your screen should look similar to the one shown in Figure 12-7.

5. At the command prompt, type **exit** to close the window.

Figure 12-7   Using Klist to view Kerberos authentication tickets

12

TROUBLESHOOTING CRLs

All certificates have specified lifetimes, but you can invalidate or revoke a certificate before it has reached the end of its lifetime. When you revoke a certificate, the revoked certificate is published in the CRL. Because CRLs are valid only for a limited time, PKI clients need to retrieve a new CRL periodically. A CRL is valid for a period that is approximately 10 percent longer than its publication period, which is one week by default. Revoking a CA certificate revokes all certificates issued by this CA. Any application that obtains a CRL showing that the parent certificate has been revoked will reject these certificates. If an application performs revocation checking and a valid CRL is not available on the local computer, it rejects the certificate. There are several CRL-related problems that you might encounter. The following information will help you in troubleshooting these problems:

- Applications that check the CRL must be able to access all CRLs in the CA hierarchy. If you are employing an offline root CA, configure an online location before any certificates are issued and ensure that a copy of its CRL is made available at this location.

- Be sure that copies of the CRLs are published to URLs or file locations that the applications can access, because applications must be able to locate the current CRL and delta CRL.

- Change the location of a CRL only when it is absolutely necessary. When you change the location of a CRL, information on the new location is not added to certificates published prior to the change.

- During smart card logon, the client validates the domain controller certificate and the domain controller validates the user certificate. If either validation fails, the smart card logon process will fail.

- When changes occur to the CRL or delta CRL, they are not reflected in the context of the user or computer until expiration of a cached CRL or delta CRL. As a result, information on revoked certificates may not be immediately available. To alleviate this problem, use a short delta CRL publication interval.

- By default, enrollees are allowed to read CA properties and CRLs and can request certificates. On an Enterprise CA, a user must also have Read and Enroll permissions on the certificate template to request a certificate.

Certutil.exe

Certutil is a tool for troubleshooting problems associated with certification authorities. It is a command-line program that is installed as part of Certificate Services used to export and display CA configuration information, configure Certificate Services, back up and restore CA components, and verify certificates, key pairs, and certificate chains.

Table 12-1 lists some of the information provided by Certutil.exe.

Table 12-1   Information Provided by Certutil.exe

Certutil Parameter	Purpose
-schema	Display Certificate schema
-getconfig	Get the CA configuration string
-RecoverKey	Retrieve the archived private key
-revoke	Revoke certificates
-dsPublish	Publish a Certificate or CRL
-verify	Determine if a certificate is valid
-resubmit	Resubmit pending requests
-deny	Deny pending requests
-pulse	Pulse autoenrollment events
-decodehex	Decode files based on hexadecimal encoded files
-shutdown	Shut down certificate services
-backupDB	Back up the Certificate Services database
-SCInfo	Display smart card information
-error	Display error message text for a specified error code
-ImportKMS	Import user keys and certificates into server database for key archival
-get reg	Display certification authority registry settings
-vroot	Create or remove Certificate Services Web virtual roots and file shares

When using Certutil, you may have to restart the certification authority for these changes to take effect. In addition, some of these configurations may require changes to the registry.

Incorrectly editing the registry may severely damage your system. Before making changes to the registry, you should back up any valued data on the computer.

Besides the Certutil tool, the **Key Recovery Tool (KRT)** can be used with Certificate Services. By default, Certificate Services does not archive private keys, but it has the capability to. Archiving enables you to recover the key should it be lost by accidental deletion, corruption, or other means. KRT is a GUI tool that enables a **key recovery agent (KRA)** with appropriate permissions to recover private keys from a Windows Server 2003 CA. The process of using a KRA can be somewhat difficult to manage at a command line, so KRT provides a simple utility to locate and recover private keys. Certutil must be installed for KRT to work. On computers running Windows XP Professional, Certutil is installed via the Windows Server 2003 Administration Tools Pack.

Activity 12-4: Use Certutil.exe to View Certificates

12

Time Required: 10 minutes

Objective: Use the Certutil command to display certificate information.

Description: In this exercise, you will discover how to use the Certutil command to display certificate information.

1. Log on to your Windows Server 2003 computer with your **AdminXX** account, where *XX* is your assigned student number.

2. Click **Start**, **Run**. In the Run box, type **cmd** and click **OK**.

3. At the command prompt, type **Certutil**. Press **Enter**. Certutil will display basic certificate configuration information, as shown in Figure 12-8.

4. At the command prompt, type **Certutil /?|more**. Press **Enter**. This will display all the commands available. Press **Enter** until you are back at the command prompt.

5. At the command prompt, type **Certutil –CAInfo**. Press **Enter**. This will display information on the certificates issued by the CA.

6. At the command prompt, type **exit** to close the window.

Figure 12-8   Using certutil to display certificate information

Activity 12-5: Use Krt.exe to Recover Certificates

Time Required: 45 minutes

Objective: Configure the server for key recovery and then use the Krt.exe tool to recover a lost key.

Description: In this exercise, you will discover how to configure a certificate template for key recovery and then use the Krt.exe tool to recover a lost key. Note: To complete this exercise you must have the Windows Server 2003 Resource Kit tools installed.

1. Log on to your Windows Server 2003 computer with your **AdminXX** account, where *XX* is your assigned student number.

2. Click **Start**, **Run,** type **certtmpl.msc** in the Open box, and then press **Enter**. Highlight **Certificate Templates.** In the details pane, right-click **Key Recovery Agent** and choose **Properties**.

3. Select the **Issuance Requirements** tab, and uncheck the **CA certificate manager approval** box. Click **OK**. Close the console.

4. Click **Start**, **Administrative Tools**, **Certification Authority**. Double-click your server, right-click **Certificate Templates,** and select **New, Certificate to Issue.**

5. On the **Enable Certificate Templates** screen, select **Key Recovery Agent**. Click **OK**. Close the **Certification Authority**.

6. Click **Start**, **Run,** in the Open box, type **mmc**, and click **OK**. On the **File** menu, select **Add/Remove Snap-in.** On the Add/Remove Snap-in screen, click **Add**. On the Add Stand-alone Snap-in screen, click **Certificates,** and click **Add.**

7. On the Certificates snap-in screen, select the **My user account** radio button, then click **Finish**. Click **Close**, then click **OK**.

8. Double-click **Certificates – Current User.** Right -click **Personal,** and select **All Tasks, Request New Certificate.**

9. On the Welcome to the Certificate Request Wizard screen, click **Next**. On the Certificate Types screen, select **Key Recovery Agent**, and click **Next.** On the Certificate Friendly Name and Description screen, in the Friendly name box**, type Key Recovery,** and click **Next.**

10. On the Completing the Certificate Request Wizard screen, click **Finish**. On the Certificate Request Wizard pop-up box, select **OK.** Close the console without saving changes.

11. Click **Start, Administrative Tools, Certification Authority.** Right-click your server, and select **Properties.** Select the **Recovery Agents** tab, and click the **Archive the key** radio button.

12. In the Number of recovery agents to use box, verify that the **Number of recovery agents to use** has defaulted to **1.**

13. Under key recovery agent certificates: click **Add**, select the certificate listed, and click **OK**. Click **OK.** If prompted to restart the CA, click **Yes.** Close the console.

14. Click **Start, Run,** in the Open box, type **mmc**, click **OK**. On the **File** menu, select **Add/Remove Snap-in.** On the Add/Remove Snap-in screen, click **Add**. On the Add Stand-alone Snap-in screen, click **Certificate Templates,** and click **Add.** Click **Close**, and click **OK.**

15. Highlight **Certificate Templates,** right-click the **User** template, and select **Duplicate Template.** In the **Properties** of New Template dialog box, on the **General** tab, type **ArchUser** in the **Display name** box. On the **Request Handling** tab, enable the **Archive subject's private key** option.

16. Click **Start, Administrative Tools, Certification Authority.** Highlight your server, right-click **Certificates Templates**, select **New**, and select **Certificate to Issue.**

17. On the **Enable Certificate Template**, select **ArchUser** and then click **OK.** Close the **Certification Authority**.

18. Click **Start, Administrative Tools, Active Directory Users and Computers.** Highlight your server, right-click the **Users** container, and select **New User.** Enter the information as follows:

   - First name: **Archive**
   - Last name: **User**
   - User logon name: **ArchiveUser**
   - Password: **Password**

12

- Member of: **Server Operators**

- Email: **Archiveuser@yahoo.com**

19. Click **Next**, and click **Finish**. Double-click the **ArchiveUser** account, and then select the **Member of** tab. Click **Add**, in **Select Groups**, type **Server Operators**, click **Check Names**, and then click **OK**. Click **OK** to close the **User Properties**. Close **Active Directory Users and Computers** and log off the machine.

20. Log in to the network as **ArchUser**. Click **Start**, **Run,** in the Open box, type **mmc**, and click **OK**. On the **File** menu, select **Add/Remove Snap-in.** On the Add/Remove Snap-in screen, click **Add**. On the Add Stand-alone Snap-in screen, click **Certificates,** click **Add,** and click **OK.**

21. Double-click **Certificates – Current User.** Right-click **Personal**, and select **All Tasks, Request New Certificate.**

22. On the Welcome to the Certificate Request Wizard screen, click **Next**. On the Certificate Types screen, select **ArchUser**, and click **Next.** On the Certificate Friendly Name and Description screen, in the Friendly name box**, type ArchUser**, and click **Next.**

23. On the Completing the Certificate Request Wizard screen, click **Finish**. On **Certificate Request Wizard**, click **Install Certificate**, and click **OK**. Close the new console without saving changes. Close all windows and log off of the computer.

24. Log on as Administrator. Click **Start, Administrative Tools, Certification Authority.** Highlight your server, right-click **Issued Certificates**, double-click the **ArchUser** certificate, select the **Details** tab. Write down the serial number of the certificate. Close the **Certificate Authority**.

25. Go to the directory where you have installed the Resource Kit tools.

26. Double-click **Krt.exe**. The Key Recovery Tool GUI will open. Under search criteria, select **certificate serial number** from the drop-down box, type the **serial number** in the value box, and click **search**.

27. The certificate will show up in the certificates area. Select the certificate and click **Recover**.

28. Close the **Key Recovery Tool**.

Troubleshooting Autoenrollment

The more keys and certificates that are used by a CA, the more its performance will be affected by service restarts as each certificate and key must be validated. Besides enrollment issues, latency occurs with **autoenrollment** events. Before we go into the actual autoenrollment troubleshooting, we will discuss latency issues so that you are aware that this condition exists. When the autoenrollment event occurs, several operations are triggered:

1. Verification of the current certificate against the autoenrollment object, and reenrollment, if necessary

2. Downloading of root certificates from the Active Directory–based enterprise root certificate store to the local enterprise root certificate store

3. Downloading of enterprise CA certificates from the Active Directory–based certificate store to the local certificate store

For example, if a newly installed enterprise CA has issued a smart card logon certificate, then domain controllers processing the logon request may not be aware of the new CA. To remedy this, pulse the autoenrollment event on the domain controller. This can be done by using the **DSStore** utility to pulse the event manually. An alternative to remedy this is to wait for replication and autoenrollment to take place, which can take up to 8 hours.

Remember that you can only autoenroll certificates that are based on version 2 templates. Accordingly, only version 2 certificates support autoenrollment. Client computers must be integrated into Active Directory, and the enterprise CA must be hosted on a server running Windows Server 2003 Enterprise Edition. Users require the Read, Enroll, and Autoenroll permissions to autoenroll certificates. Table 12-2 lists some of the issues and their resolutions associated with autoenrollment.

12

Table 12-2   Troubleshooting Autoenrollment and Certificate Services

Problem	Resolution
Autoenrollment is enabled, but clients do not automatically enroll for certificates.	Use Gpupdate to force immediate replication of Group Policy.
Clients are unable to obtain certificates by means of autoenrollment.	Set user permissions to Allow for Read, Enroll, and Autoenroll.
Computers are not automatically enrolling for certificates after renewing the CA.	Link a GPO to the appropriate Active Directory container in which the automatic certificate request policy is configured.
Template is not found when enrolling for a certificate in a child domain.	Set the permissions for the template to include the child domain accounts.
Certificate template names appear as a string of characters.	Close and reopen the Certificates Snap-in.

Table 12-2 Troubleshooting Autoenrollment and Certificate Services (continued)

Problem	Resolution
Some CAs on the network still have the original version after modifying a certificate template.	Use Active Directory Sites and Services to force replication or wait until replication has taken place.
Web enrollment pages installed on a server other than the certificate server do not work.	Configure the pages to use basic authentication, and then use SSL to protect the passwords.
Users are unable to log on to the CA Web pages.	Modify the default security permissions so that the user account has the user right to log on to the server.
Either no certificates or invalid certificates are generated by the CA Web pages.	Configure IIS to use an authentication method other than anonymous.
User cannot log on with a smart card due to missing or incorrect password, because the computer account in the primary domain is missing or the password on the account is incorrect.	Verify that the root CA's certificate is in the Trusted Root Certification Authorities store, verify that the domain controller has been issued a certificate that can be verified to a trusted root, and ensure that the domain computer account is enabled.
The encryption private key option has been configured from the Request Handling tab but Certificate Services is not archiving the private key.	Specify the Signature and Encryption option on the Request Handling tab.

TROUBLESHOOTING REMOTE ACCESS

You can use the Remote Access diagnostic functions available in the Windows Server 2003 to collect detailed logs and information about a remote access connection. Log files are one of the best sources of information when it comes to troubleshooting. With log file analysis tools, it's possible to get a good idea of what actually happened before, during, and after a remote access connection. It is a good idea to always start by consulting the Windows event and security logs. Diagnostics can be set from the Diagnostics tab of the properties of the connection in the Network Connection folder, or you can run specific diagnostics by typing the netsh ras diagnostics command at the command line. You first became familiar with the netsh command in Chapter 8.

Authentication and Accounting Logging

Authentication and accounting logging is particularly useful for troubleshooting remote access policy issues. AVPN server running Windows Server 2003 with Windows accounting enabled supports the logging of information for remote access and site-to-site VPN connections in local logging files. Authentication and accounting logging information is used to track remote access usage and authentication attempts. This logging is separate from the events recorded in the system event log, which we will discuss later in the chapter. To configure authentication and accounting logging, you must first enable either Windows Authentication or Windows Accounting. The log files are stored in the %SYSTEMROOT%\System32\LogFiles folder. The log files are saved in a format that any database program can read, so the log files can either be exported or accessed directly for analysis. You configure accounting or authentication logging and log file settings from the properties of the Local File method within the Remote Access Logging folder in the Routing and Remote Access Snap-in, as shown in Figure 12-9. If your RADIUS server is also running IAS, then authentication and accounting information is logged in log files stored on the IAS server as well.

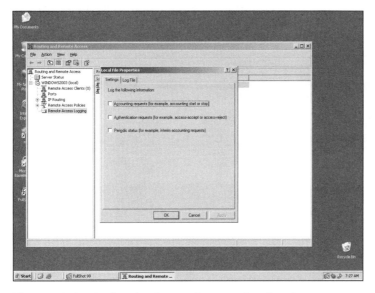

Figure 12-9   Authentication and accounting logging

Audit Logging and Oakley Logging for L2TP/IPSec Connections

A fast and simple method to troubleshoot unsuccessful L2TP/IPSec connections is to use the Audit Logging feature to monitor IPSec-related events. You can also audit IKE and policy change events and display these events in the security event log by configuring the auditing of logon and policy change events for success and failure Local Security Policy settings, or Group Policy Object Editor can be used to verify that security auditing is enabled, so you can ensure that the success and failure of IKE negotiations are recorded. Remember that the default auditing policy setting for domain controllers is *No Auditing.* This means that even if auditing is enabled in the domain, the domain controllers do not inherit auditing policy locally.

You can enable the Oakley log to record all ISAKMP main mode or quick mode negotiations. The Oakley log tracks events related to IKE negotiations and is recorded in the %SYSTEMROOT%\Debug\Oakley.log file. This log records Internet Security Association Key Management Protocol (ISAKMP) main mode and quick mode negotiations. The log has a set size of 50,000 lines and overwrites when necessary. A new Oakley.log file is created each time the IPSec service is started, and the previous version of the Oakley.log file is saved as Oakley.log.sav. As the Oakley.log file becomes full, a new Oakley.log file is created with the current one saved as Oakley.log.bak.

Oakley logging is used exclusively with L2TP/IPSec data transmission. The Oakley log is not enabled by default. To enable Oakley logging, set the HKEY_LOCAL_MACHINE\SYSTEM\CurrentControlSet\Services\PolicyAgent\Oakley\EnableLogging DWORD registry value to 1, as shown in Figure 12-10.

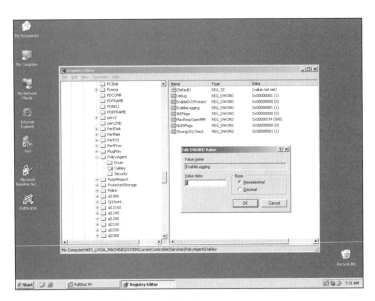

Figure 12-10   Enabling Oakley logging

To activate the new registry setting after modifying its value, stop and start the IPSec Policy Agent and related IPSec services. This is done by running the net stop policyagent and net start policyagent commands at the command prompt. If you are restarting the IPSec service on a computer that is running Windows Server 2003 and the Routing and Remote Access service, any IPSec configuration for L2TP will be lost. For example, if you are restarting the IPSec service while an L2TP/IPSec VPN tunnel is connected, the tunnel will lose connectivity and must be reconnected when the IPSec service is restarted. Therefore, you must stop and restart the Routing and Remote Access service, as well as the IPSec service. A PPTP tunnel, on the other hand, does not use IPSec and therefore will stay connected if you stop the IPSec service.

Event Logging

You can use **event logging** to record remote access server errors, warnings, and other detailed information in the system event log. You can enable event logging on the Logging tab on the properties of a remote access server, as shown in Figure 12-11.

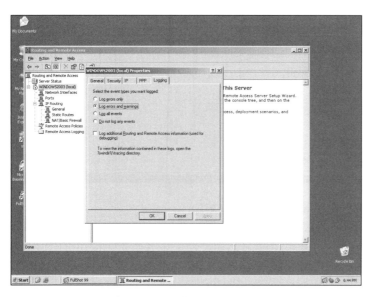

Figure 12-11   Enabling event logging

You should already be familiar with event logging. It is typically used for troubleshooting or for notifying network administrators of unusual events. The system event log provides information on errors from services that provide authentication. For example, there might be Kerberos errors showing that the Kerberos protocol was being used when a logon failure happened. The event log also provides information on remote access connections. You can use event logging to record remote access server errors, warnings, and other detailed information in the system event log.

In addition to the settings that are configurable through the graphical user interface, you can now delegate access to event logs. This is new in Windows Server 2003. The feature allows you to customize the permissions on each event log on a computer by editing the value in the registry. The ACL is stored as a string in a Reg_SZ value called CustomSD for each event log.

PPP Logging

PPP logging is used to troubleshoot the functions and PPP control messages during a connection. This log is a valuable source of information when you are trying to understand why a PPP connection failed. You may already be familiar with the PPP log. This log, which was configured from the PPP tab of the RAS Server Properties tab in some of the earlier

Microsoft server operating systems, has been replaced by the tracing function beginning with Windows Server 2000. By default, the PPP log is stored as the ppp.log file in the %SYSTEMROOT%\Tracing folder. PPP logging creates a log file of the PPP control messages that are sent and received during a PPP connection. **Tracing** records the sequence of programming functions called during a process to a file. Figure 12-12 shows the partial contents of a PPP log.

```
PPP.LOG - Notepad
File Edit Format View Help
[164] 02-11 19:55:20:015: PortName: COM3
[164] 02-11 19:55:20:015: Starting PPP on link with IfType=0xffffffff,IPIf=0xffffffff,IPXIf=0xffffffff
[164] 02-11 19:55:20:015: RasGetBuffer returned 960d828 for SendBuf
[164] 02-11 19:55:20:015: FsmInit called for protocol = c021, port = 12
[164] 02-11 19:55:20:015: ConfigInfo = 83034a
[164] 02-11 19:55:20:015: APs available = 5e
[164] 02-11 19:55:20:015: FsmReset called for protocol = c021, port = 12
[164] 02-11 19:55:20:015: Inserting port in bucket # 12
[164] 02-11 19:55:20:015: Inserting bundle in bucket # 10
[164] 02-11 19:55:20:015: FsmOpen event received for protocol c021 on port 12
[164] 02-11 19:55:20:015: FsmThisLayerStarted called for protocol = c021, port = 12
[164] 02-11 19:55:20:015: FsmUp event received for protocol c021 on port 12
[164] 02-11 19:55:20:031: <PPP packet sent at 02/12/2005 02:55:20:015
[164] 02-11 19:55:20:031: <Protocol = LCP, Type = Configure-Req, Length = 0x19, Id = 0x0, Port = 12
[164] 19:55:20:031: <C0 21 01 00 00 17 02 06 00 00 00 00 05 06 70 4C |.!............pL|
[164] 19:55:20:031: <1B 85 07 02 08 02 0D 03 06 00 00 00 00 00 00 00 |................|
[164] 02-11 19:55:20:031:
[164] 02-11 19:55:20:031: InsertInTimerQ called portid=0,Id=0,Protocol=c021,EventType=0,fAuth=0
[164] 02-11 19:55:20:031: InsertInTimerQ called portid=0,Id=0,Protocol=0,EventType=3,fAuth=0
[1916] 02-11 19:55:20:453: Packet received (38 bytes) for hPort 12
[1916] 02-11 19:55:20:453: Packet received (9 bytes) for hPort 12
[164] 02-11 19:55:20:453: >PPP packet received at 02/12/2005 02:55:20:453
[164] 02-11 19:55:20:453: >Protocol = LCP, Type = Configure-Req, Length = 0x26, Id = 0x1, Port = 12
[164] 19:55:20:453: >C0 21 01 01 00 24 01 04 05 F4 02 06 00 0A 00 00 |.!...$..........|
[164] 19:55:20:453: >03 05 C2 23 05 07 02 08 02 13 09 03 00 D0 52 01 |...#.........R.|
[164] 19:55:20:453: >43 E6 1B 04 02 02 00 00 00 00 00 00 00 00 00 00 |C...............|
[164] 02-11 19:55:20:453:
[164] 02-11 19:55:20:453: <PPP packet sent at 02/12/2005 02:55:20:453
[164] 02-11 19:55:20:453: <Protocol = LCP, Type = Configure-Reject, Length = 0x13, Id = 0x1, Port = 12
[164] 19:55:20:453: <C0 21 04 01 00 11 13 09 03 00 D0 52 01 43 E6 1B |.!.........R.C..|
[164] 19:55:20:453: <04 02 02 00 00 00 00 00 00 00 00 00 00 00 00 00 |................|
[164] 02-11 19:55:20:453:
[164] 02-11 19:55:20:453: >PPP packet received at 02/12/2005 02:55:20:453
[164] 02-11 19:55:20:453: >Protocol = LCP, Type = Configure-Reject, Length = 0x9, Id = 0x0, Port = 12
[164] 19:55:20:453: >C0 21 04 00 00 07 0D 03 06 00 00 00 00 00 00 00 |.!..............|
[164] 02-11 19:55:20:453:
[164] 02-11 19:55:20:453: RemoveFromTimerQ called portid=0,Id=0,Protocol=c021,EventType=0,fAuth=0
[164] 02-11 19:55:20:453: <PPP packet sent at 02/12/2005 02:55:20:453
[164] 02-11 19:55:20:453: <Protocol = LCP, Type = Configure-Req, Length = 0x16, Id = 0x1, Port = 12
[164] 19:55:20:453: <C0 21 01 01 00 14 02 06 00 00 00 00 05 06 70 4C |.!............pL|
[164] 19:55:20:453: <1B 85 07 02 08 02 00 00 00 00 00 00 00 00 00 00 |................|
[164] 02-11 19:55:20:453:
[164] 02-11 19:55:20:453: InsertInTimerQ called portid=0,Id=1,Protocol=c021,EventType=0,fAuth=0
[1916] 02-11 19:55:20:593: Packet received (25 bytes) for hPort 12
[164] 02-11 19:55:20:593: >PPP packet received at 02/12/2005 02:55:20:593
[164] 02-11 19:55:20:593: >Protocol = LCP, Type = Configure-Req, Length = 0x19, Id = 0x2, Port = 12
[164] 19:55:20:593: >C0 21 01 02 00 17 01 04 05 F4 02 06 00 0A 00 00 |.!..............|
[164] 19:55:20:593: >03 05 C2 23 05 07 02 08 02 00 00 00 00 00 00 00 |...#............|
[164] 02-11 19:55:20:593:
[164] 02-11 19:55:20:593: <PPP packet sent at 02/12/2005 02:55:20:593
[164] 02-11 19:55:20:593: <Protocol = LCP, Type = Configure-Ack, Length = 0x19, Id = 0x2, Port = 12
[164] 19:55:20:593: <C0 21 02 02 00 17 01 04 05 F4 02 06 00 0A 00 00 |.!..............|
[164] 19:55:20:593: <03 05 C2 23 05 07 02 08 02 00 00 00 00 00 00 00 |...#............|
Start | FullShot 99 | D:\WINDOWS\system32 | Search Results | PPP.LOG - Notepad | 9:06 PM
```

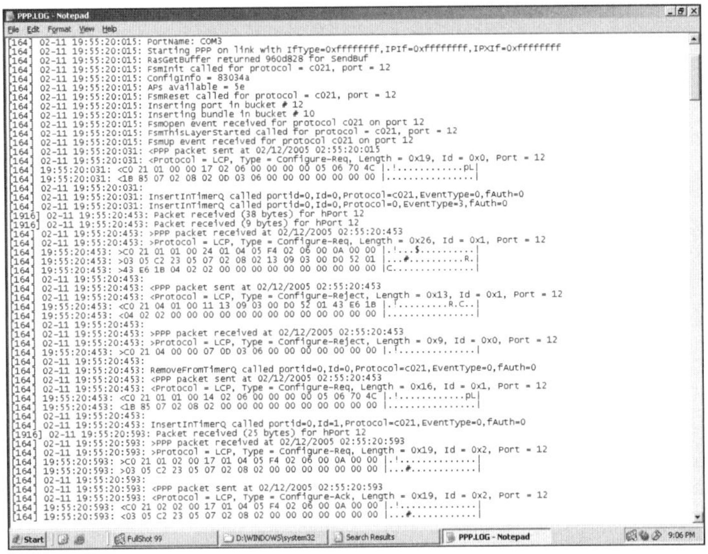

Figure 12-12 PPP log

A Routing and Remote Access service has an extensive tracing capability that you can use for troubleshooting when network problems become complex. You can enable the components in Windows Server 2003 to log tracing information to files. The tracing information is complex and very detailed. You can enable tracing by changing settings in the registry under: HKEY_LOCAL_MACHINE\SOFTWARE\Microsoft\Tracing. To enable tracing for each routing protocol, you can configure the following registry entry for each protocol key by entering: EnableFileTracing REG_DWORD 1. You can change the default location of the tracing files by setting FileDirectory to the path you want and changing the size of the log file by setting different values for MaxFileSize. The default value is 10000 (64K).

CAUTION

Tracing consumes system resources and should be used sparingly only to help identify network problems. Once the trace is captured or the problem is identified, immediately disable tracing. Do not leave tracing enabled on multiprocessor computers.

Tracing is most often used by Microsoft Product Support Services engineers or network administrators who are very experienced with Routing and Remote Access.

Activity 12-6: Enable RAS Accounting and Logging

Time Required: 10 minutes

Objective: Use the Routing and Remote Access console to enable accounting and logging.

Description: In this exercise, you will discover how to use the Routing and Remote Access console to enable accounting and logging.

1. Log on to your Windows Server 2003 computer with your **AdminXX** account, where *XX* is your assigned student number.

2. Click **Start**, **Administrative Tools**, **Routing and Remote Access**.

3. Expand your server. Select the **Remote Access Logging** folder.

4. On the right side of the screen, right-click the **Local File** and select **Properties**.

5. On the Settings tab, select the **Accounting requests** and **Authentication requests** boxes, if necessary.

6. On the Log File tab, select the **Weekly** radio button. Click **Apply**. Click **OK**.

7. In the left pane, expand **IP Routing**, then right-click the **General** interface, click **Properties**, and select the **Log the maximum amount of information** radio button. Click **Apply**. Click **OK**.

8. Choose **File**, **Exit** to close the console.

Network Monitor

Network Monitor is another troubleshooting tool that you should already be familiar with. It is a protocol analyzer used to capture network traffic and generate statistics for creating reports. Network Monitor can capture the network traffic between a dial-up networking client and the remote access server. By analyzing remote access traffic, you can find answers to remote access problems and possible solutions or workarounds. Network Monitor can be used to capture traffic sent during the PPP connection process and during data transfer. Remember that this is an advanced troubleshooting tool, and the proper interpretation of remote access traffic using Network Monitor requires an in-depth understanding of PPP and other protocols. Figure 12-13 shows a Network Monitor capture screen from a captured event. Notice all the detailed information provided.

Connection Manager Administration Kit

As you learned in Chapter 10, the Connection Manager Administration Kit (CMAK) allows the administrator to create and configure the service profile by creating a small, self-installing package. This is useful when you deploy a large number of remote access clients.

12

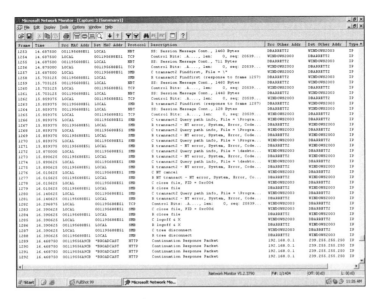

Figure 12-13 Network Monitor capture

Under normal conditions, only the credentials of the user are verified, and a user with the correct credentials can connect even if the user's configurations do not comply with corporate network policy. For example, a remote access user with valid credentials can connect to a network with a computer that does not have required antivirus or spyware detection software installed on it. **Network Access Quarantine Control**, a new feature of Windows Server 2003, delays normal remote access to a private network until the configuration of the remote access computer has been examined and validated by an administrator-provided script. A Network Access Quarantine Control script can be implemented by using a Connection Manager profile. Because Network Access Quarantine Control introduces a delay in obtaining normal remote access, if you are running applications immediately after the connection is complete, you might encounter problems. To minimize the delay, separate your script into two scripts. Configure one to run as a preconnect action and the other one to run as a postconnect action.

For security reasons, custom actions cannot be run when users log on to the network using dial-up networking unless certain registry keys have been set.

NOTE

When building a service profile, the security settings allow you to select the authentication method for VPN or dial-up users and the VPN strategy for VPN clients. You can choose to use basic or advanced security settings for all computers or use a combination of these. If you choose a combination of both basic and advanced security settings, Connection Manager uses the advanced security settings for clients running on the operating systems that support them and the basic security settings for clients running on operating systems that do not support advanced security settings.

If you configured the security settings of the VPN entries in the CMAK Wizard to use L2TP/IPSec, you might need to distribute certificates to your users. Because the profiles are mainly used on computers outside the administrator's control, when service profiles are distributed, the users should be informed of their responsibilities in protecting the organization's resources. Table 12-3 lists some of the issues associated with using CMAK and their resolutions.

Table 12-3   Troubleshooting CMAK

Problem	Resolution
Users can connect to the server when using the service profile, but authentication fails.	Verify connectivity between the server running Routing and Remote Access and the authentication server. Verify that the authentication server specified in the service profile is correct. Check the user account and make sure that dial-up access has been enabled and check for rules that might restrict access by time or date.
VPN service profile takes too long to connect	Delays often indicate a failure in the L2TP/IPSec protocol negotiation. Make sure that all service profile users have the newest certificates installed on their computers. Make sure that each VPN server is configured to accept the profile and that each server is responding.
The connection failed to complete after the user was authenticated.	Check the Connect Actions section in the service profile's .cms files for proper behavior on target platforms.
Clients cannot connect.	Check to be sure that a VPN connection can be established to the company's VPN remote access server. Confirm that the phone books are being updated from the update URL provided by reviewing the Connection Manager log file. When using a double-dial connection to several phone numbers provided by the ISP, check the Connection Manager log file to confirm that the phone books are being updated from the update URL provided by ISP.

12

TROUBLESHOOTING WIRELESS ACCESS

Because the business benefits of using wireless technology include improving worker productivity and enabling business processes to happen more quickly and more efficiently, the implementation of wireless technology is increasing at a fast pace. Keeping pace with the widespread use of wireless devices also creates issues with security and keeping all devices in communication. There are various tools that can be used to troubleshoot a wireless network. When using 802.1X authentication, the particular areas that are involved in the troubleshooting process include the Windows XP wireless client, a wireless access point

(WAP), and the Internet Authentication Service (IAS). In addition, it may be necessary to troubleshoot IAS authentication and authorization, certificate properties, and the process of certificate validation for both the wireless client certificates and IAS server certificates. This section looks at those areas, beginning with the client side because this is likely where you will find the most issues.

Windows XP Troubleshooting Tools

The two basic tools used for troubleshooting wireless connections in Windows XP are the Network Connections folder and tracing. The Network Connections folder and the Windows XP notification icons provide information about the state of the authentication. The client side of wireless authentication has help for the user. For example, if an authentication requires additional information from the user, a text balloon appears instructing the user. Windows XP Service Pack 2 (SP2) has enhanced troubleshooting capabilities by providing more information about the authentication process. These improvements give the user and the network troubleshooter more information about how the wireless connection is progressing, from the initial association to the allocation of a valid IP address. The Repair capability has also been enhanced for wireless connections. When you repair a wireless connection, it is disabled and reenabled, which clears many error conditions on wireless network adapters. If the wireless connection obtains an Automatic Private Internet Protocol Addressing (APIPA) address, Windows XP with SP2 warns the user that the connection has limited or no connectivity. Additionally, when you obtain status on the connection, you can view the signal strength on the General tab and the IP address configuration on the Support tab. Figure 12-14 shows the signal strength on the General tab.

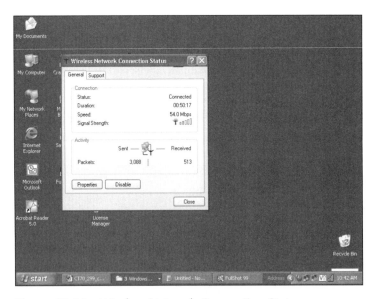

Figure 12-14   Wireless Network Connection Status

To obtain detailed information about the Wireless Zero Configuration service for Windows XP SP2 and the EAP authentication process, you must enable tracing by using the netsh command. Once tracing is enabled, you can obtain detailed information from the Wireless Zero Configuration service by viewing the Wzcdlg.log and Wzctrace.log files in the %SYSTEMROOT%\Tracing folder, and detailed information about the EAP authentication process can be found in the Eapol.log and Rastls.log files in the %SYSTEMROOT%\Tracing folder. Figure 12-15 shows the information from a Eapol.log file.

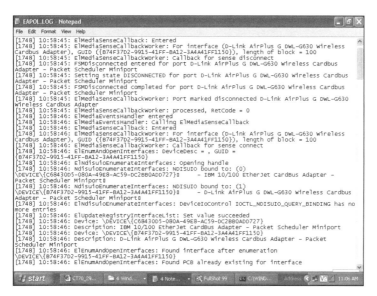

Figure 12-15   Client Eapol.log file

When troubleshooting authentication issues for Windows XP with no service packs installed and Windows 2000, the names of the servers must match the names of the authenticating servers or authentication will fail. If the wireless client is validating the server certificate and the Connect if the server name ends with string is not correct, authentication will fail. Verify that this string is correct from the properties of the Smart Card and Other Certificate EAP type on the Authentication tab from the properties of the wireless connection that corresponds to the wireless LAN network adapter.

Wireless AP Troubleshooting Tools

Because each manufacturer has different tools for troubleshooting a wireless AP, the options available depend on the tool set and management software provided with the WAP. The following is a list of some of the tools you may find:

- A ping interface for testing packets and blocking WAN pings
- A firmware upgrade utility
- A time synchronization utility
- Performance settings

Figure 12-16 shows the interface of the management software for a wireless AP. The Advanced and Tools tabs can be used for troubleshooting connectivity issues.

Figure 12-16   Access point tools

In this section, we use a D-Link WAP, but each WAP will be somewhat different in the tools available and configuration options. In addition to using troubleshooting tools provided by the AP vendor, here are some points to keep in mind:

- Locate the APs close enough together to provide ample wireless coverage but far enough apart to not interfere with each other and increase the error rate.
- Maintain the best average ratio of wireless clients to APs. The greater the number of wireless clients that are associated with the AP, the lower the effective data transmission rate.
- Create a map of the building, with one drawing per floor displaying the location, name, IP address, and channel information for each AP.

- Note any device that operates on the same frequencies as your wireless devices such as Bluetooth-enabled devices, microwave ovens, or medical equipment.

- Indicate any building construction materials used that may interfere with wireless signals.

- To reduce interference between wireless APs, ensure that wireless APs with overlapping signals use unique channel frequencies.

- Use a spectrum analyzer to determine the location and strength of interfering signals as you move from one signal area to another.

Finally, don't forget about using the **Wireless Monitor MMC Snap-in**, included with Windows Server 2003, to gather and view statistical and configuration information for wireless APs and the Windows Server 2003 wireless clients.

ACTIVITY

Activity 12-7: Use MMC to View the Activity of Wireless Access Points and Clients

Time Required: 15 minutes

Objective: Learn how to use the Wireless Monitor MMC Snap-in to view the activity of wireless devices.

Description: In this exercise, you will learn how to use the Wireless Monitor MMC Snap-in to view the activity of wireless devices.

1. Log on with your **AdminXX** account, where *XX* is your assigned student number.

2. Click **Start**, **Run**. In the Open box, type **mmc**. Click **OK**.

3. On the Console Root panel, choose **File, Add/Remove Snap-in**. On the Stand-alone tab, click **Add** and highlight the **Wireless Monitor** Snap-in. Click **Add**.

4. Click **Close** on the Add Standalone Snap-in screen. Click **OK** on the Add/Remove Snap-in screen.

5. In the console tree, expand the Wireless Monitor, expand your server, double-click the **Wireless Client Information** folder. Click on one of the errors listed. Your screen should look similar to Figure 12-17.

6. Scroll through and look at the errors and warnings. When finished click **File**, **Exit** to close the console. When asked to save the console settings, click **No**.

IAS Troubleshooting Tools

As you learned in Chapter 10, servers running the Internet Authentication Service (IAS) component of Windows Server 2003 perform centralized authentication, authorization, auditing, and accounting for many types of network access. This includes wireless and 802.1X authenticating switch access. It also provides enhanced EAP configuration for

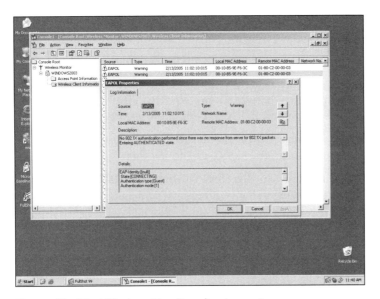

Figure 12-17   Wireless Monitor client warning message

remote access policies. This flexibility allows you to select multiple EAP types for wireless connections in situations where some wireless clients use EAP-TLS authentication and some of them use PEAP with MS-CHAPv2. PEAP fast reconnect allows wireless clients to move between wireless access points without repeated requests for authentication. If wireless access points are placed on the same subnet where an IP address range is specified, all of the RADIUS clients in the range must use the same configuration and shared secret. As you can see, with all this flexibility comes more detailed troubleshooting. The following tools are used to troubleshoot IAS:

- *IAS event logging and Event Viewer*—Ensure that event logging is enabled for all types of IAS events

- *Network Monitor*—Includes a RADIUS parser, which you can use to view the attributes of a RADIUS message and troubleshoot connection issues

- *Tracing*—Look through the log files that begin with IAS and the Rastls.log file

- *SNMP service*—Monitor status information for your IAS server

- *System Monitor counters*—Monitor IAS-related performance objects

ACTIVITY

Activity 12-8: Use System Monitor Counters to Monitor IAS Performance Objects

Time Required: 10 minutes

Objective: Use the System Monitor to enable counters to monitor IAS performance objects.

Description: In this exercise, you use the System Monitor to enable counters to monitor IAS performance objects.

1. Log on to your Windows Server 2003 computer with your **AdminXX** account, where *XX* is your assigned student number.

2. Click **Start**, **Administrative Tools**, **Performance**. Expand **Performance Logs and Alerts**.

3. Right-click **Counter Logs**. Select **New Log Settings**. In the New Log Settings Name box, type **IAS**. Click **OK**.

4. On the **General** tab, click **Add Objects**. In the Performance objects box, select **IAS Accounting Proxy**, **IAS Accounting Server**, **IAS Authentication Proxy**, **IAS Authentication Server**, **IAS Remote Accounting Servers**, and **IAS Remote Authentication Servers**. Click **Add**, and then click **Close**.

5. Click **Apply**. If a dialog box appears to create a folder, click **Yes**. Click **OK**.

6. Choose **File**, **Exit** to close the console.

Troubleshooting IAS Authentication and Authorization

Although IAS provides enhanced security for wireless access, changes in the number of access clients, changes in WAN technology, and other factors can reduce the performance of IAS. For example, certificate-based authentication can generate a large volume of authentication traffic that is transmitted every time a client logs on to the network. Wireless deployments should use PEAP with fast reconnect. Cached authentication is necessary for wireless deployments because wireless clients authenticate each time they move to and connect with a new access point. PEAP fast reconnect significantly reduces the latency of authentication and the public key operation overhead on both the client and the RADIUS server. Remember that the computer certificate must meet the certificate requirements for PEAP authentication. When troubleshooting the most common issues with IAS authentication and authorization, it may help to verify the following:

- The wireless AP can reach the IAS servers by using ping and checking the IPSec policies.

- Each IAS server and wireless AP pair is configured with a common shared secret.

- When using a third-party certification authority, verify that the IAS server can reach the Internet to verify the CRL.

12

- The IAS servers can reach a global catalog server and an Active Directory domain controller.

- The computer accounts of the IAS servers are members of the RAS and IAS Servers group.

- The user or computer account is not locked out and the time corresponds to the permitted logon hours.

- The connection is authorized by the remote access policy.

- The IAS server can validate the certificate of the wireless client.

- The certificate has a valid digital signature.

- The wireless client certificate has the Client Authentication certificate purpose.

- The IAS server has the root CA certificate of the issuing CA of the wireless client certificate installed in its Trusted Root Certification Authorities store.

- The wireless client has the root CA certificate of the issuing CA of the IAS server certificate installed in its Trusted Root Certification Authorities store.

CHAPTER SUMMARY

❑ Groups and Group Policy are common areas where you will regularly have to troubleshoot. The Effective Permissions tab is a new advanced option in Windows Server 2003. It lets you see all of the permissions that apply to a security principal for a given object, including the permissions resulting from memberships in security groups.

❑ Inheritance allows administrators to easily assign and manage permissions. This feature automatically causes objects within a container to inherit all the inheritable permissions of that container. Dsrevoke is meant to complement the functionality provided by Delegation of Control Wizard by providing the ability to revoke delegated administrative authority.

❑ Remember that there is a difference between NTFS permissions and share permissions. Shared resources are resources available to users and groups other than the resource's owner. With NTFS permissions, you also have the choice of assigning special permissions to groups or users.

❑ Kerberos is the default authentication protocol, so any issue related to authentication such as console logon, network logon, access to network resources, or remote access might indicate some sort of Kerberos error.

❑ Authentication issues may also arise that are associated with SSL certificates. To troubleshoot these issues, first confirm whether you can telnet to port 443 on the IP addresses of the client and server computers.

❑ Certutil is a tool for troubleshooting problems associated with certification authorities. It is a command-line program that is installed as part of Certificate Services used to export and display CA configuration information, configure Certificate Services, back up and restore CA components, and verify certificates, key pairs, and certificate chains.

❑ Authentication and accounting logging is particularly useful for troubleshooting remote access policy issues. A VPN server running Windows Server 2003 with Windows accounting enabled supports the logging of information for remote access and site-to-site VPN connections in local logging files. Authentication and accounting logging information is used to track remote access usage and authentication attempts.

❑ The Routing and Remote Access service has an extensive tracing capability that you can use for troubleshooting when network problems become complex. You can enable the components in Windows Server 2003 to log tracing information to files.

❑ A fast and simple method to troubleshoot unsuccessful L2TP/IPSec connections is to use the Audit Logging feature to monitor IPSec-related events. PPP logging is used to troubleshoot PPP functions and PPP control messages during a connection. This log is a valuable source of information when you are trying to understand why a PPP connection failed.

❑ Network Access Quarantine Control, a new feature of Windows Server 2003, delays normal remote access to a private network until the configuration of the remote access computer has been examined and validated by an administrator-provided script. A Network Access Quarantine Control script can be implemented by using a Connection Manager profile.

❑ Because each manufacturer has different tools for troubleshooting a WAP, the options available depend on the tool set and management software provided with the WAP. The two basic tools used for troubleshooting wireless connections in Windows XP are the Network Connections folder and tracing.

❑ The tools used to troubleshoot IAS are IAS event logging and Event Viewer, Network Monitor, tracing, the SNMP service, and System Monitor counters.

12

KEY TERMS

autoenrollment —The ability to automatically enroll users and computers for certificates, retrieve existing certificates, and renew expired certificates without user interaction.

Authority Information Access (AIA) — The AIA extension specifies where to find up-to-date certificates for the CA.

Certutil — A command-line utility included with Windows Server 2003 Certificate Services that performs a large number of certificate management tasks.

Dsrevoke — A command-line tool used to view and remove all permissions specified for a particular user or group.

DSStore — A command-line tool used to manually pulse the autoenrollment event on the domain controller.

Effective Permissions — A new advanced option in Windows Server 2003. It lets you see all of the permissions that apply to a security principal for a given object, including the permissions resulting from memberships in security groups.

event logging — Records remote access server errors, warnings, and other detailed information in the system event log.

inheritance — Allows administrators to easily assign and manage permissions. This feature automatically causes objects within a container to inherit all the inheritable permissions of that container.

key recovery agent (KRA) — A method used to recover a key should it be lost by accidental deletion, corruption, or other means.

Key Recovery Tool (KRT) — A GUI tool that enables a key recovery agent (KRA) with appropriate permissions to recover private keys from a Windows Server 2003 CA.

Network Access Quarantine Control — A new feature of Windows Server 2003 that delays normal remote access to a private network until the configuration of the remote access computer has been examined and validated by an administrator-provided script.

Network Monitor — A protocol analyzer used to capture network traffic and generate statistics for creating reports.

NTFS permissions — File system permissions that allow you the choice of assigning special permissions to groups or users. Special permissions are permissions on a more detailed level than share permissions.

Oakley logging — Logging that is used exclusively with L2TP/IPSec data transmission. The Oakley log is not enabled by default.

Perms — A command-line tool that displays user access permissions for a file or directory on an NTFS file system volume by querying the permissions.

PPP logging — Logging used to troubleshoot the functions and PPP control messages during a connection. This log is a valuable source of information when you are trying to understand why a PPP connection failed.

share permissions — Permissions that are set in much the same way file and folder permissions are set in NTFS.

tracing — Logging information that is complex and very detailed. You can enable tracing on the Logging tab on the properties of a remote access server or by changing settings in the registry.

Wireless Monitor MMC Snap-in — A snap-in included with Windows Server 2003 to gather and view statistical and configuration information for WAPs and the Windows Server 2003 wireless clients.

REVIEW QUESTIONS

1. Which of the following tabs lets you see all of the permissions that apply to a security principal for a given object, including the permissions resulting from memberships in security groups?

   a. Inheritance

   b. Advanced

   c. Effective Permissions

   d. Options

2. Which of the following can be used on domain controllers that are running Windows Server 2003 or Windows 2000 Server to view and remove permissions specified for a particular user or group?

   a. Perms

   b. DSStore

   c. Certutil

   d. Dsrevoke

3. Which of the following is a command-line tool that displays user access permissions for a file or directory on an NTFS file system volume by querying the permissions?

   a. Perms

   b. DSStore

   c. Certutil

   d. Dsrevoke

4. Full group nesting is permitted for which of the following groups? (Choose all that apply.)

   a. Windows NT

   b. Windows 2000 Native

   c. Windows Server 2003

   d. Windows 2000 mixed mode

5. When troubleshooting Kerberos authentication, if you use a firewall, which of the following ports must be open because they are used by the Kerberos ticket-granting service? (Choose all that apply.)

   a. TCP port 8108

   b. TCP port 88

   c. UDP port 8108

   d. UDP port 88

12

6. Which of the following tools can be used to troubleshoot Kerberos authentication? (Choose all that apply.)

   a. Klist

   b. Kerbtray

   c. Setspn

   d. DSStore

7. Which of the following is a command-line program for troubleshooting problems associated with certification authorities?

   a. Perms

   b. DSStore

   c. Certutil

   d. Dsrevoke

8. Which of the following tools can be used with Certificate Services to recover the key should it be lost by accidental deletion, corruption, or other means?

   a. DSStore

   b. Key Recovery tool

   c. Tracing

   d. Dsrevoke

9. Several users in the research.test.com domain attempt to enroll for a user certificate but receive a message that the template was not found. What should you do?

   a. Include a group containing the required users in the access control list (ACL) for the User Certificate template.

   b. Create a duplicate of the User Certificate template and specify the autoenroll permission for the Authenticated Users group.

   c. Configure the Web enrollment pages to use basic authentication.

   d. Configure the automatic certificate request policy in a GPO linked to the research. quepublishing.com domain.

10. Which of the following permissions are required to enable the autoenrollment of users for certificates? (Choose all that apply.)

   a. Read

   b. Enroll

   c. Modify

   d. Autoenroll

11. Which of the following tools can be used to manually pulse the autoenrollment event on the domain controller?

    a. DSStore

    b. Key Recovery tool

    c. Tracing

    d. Certutil

12. You are deploying a remote access connection strategy and will be issuing IPSec certificates to secure the connection between remote client computers and network servers. Which of the following must be true so that connections will successfully take place?

    a. Each client computer must have a computer certificate, and each server must have a user certificate.

    b. Both client and server computers require a certificate from the same CA.

    c. Client computers need certificates from enterprise CAs located in the internal network, while servers need certificates from a public CA.

    d. Client computers need certificates from standalone CAs located in the internal network, while servers need certificates from a public CA.

13. To configure authentication and accounting logging, you must first enable either Windows Authentication or Windows Accounting. The log files are stored in which of the following folders?

    a. %SYSTEMROOT%\System32\Oakley

    b. %SYSTEMROOT%\Tracing

    c. %SYSTEMROOT%\System32\LogFiles

    d. %SYSTEMROOT%\

14. The Oakley log tracks events related to IKE negotiations and is recorded in which of the following files?

    a. %SYSTEMROOT%\Oaklcy.log

    b. %SYSTEMROOT%\Debug\Oakley.log

    c. %SYSTEMROOT%\Log Files\Oakley.log

    d. %SYSTEMROOT%\Log Files\Debug\Oakley.log

15. Which if the following is used to troubleshoot the PPP functions and PPP control messages during a connection?

    a. Wzcdlg logging

    b. PPP logging

    c. Oakley logging

    d. Network logging

12

16. Which of the following is an extensive capability of the Routing and Remote Access service that you can use for troubleshooting when network problems become complex?

    a. Oakley logging

    b. PPP logging

    c. Tracing

    d. IAS logging

17. Which of the following is a troubleshooting tool that is a protocol analyzer used to capture network traffic and generate statistics for creating reports?

    a. IAS logging

    b. Performance Monitor

    c. Event Viewer

    d. Network Monitor

18. Which of the following is a new feature of Windows Server 2003 that delays normal remote access to a private network until the configuration of the remote access computer has been examined and validated by an administrator-provided script?

    a. Network Access Quarantine Control

    b. Network Monitor

    c. Connection Manager Administration Kit

    d. Wireless Zero Configuration

19. Once tracing is enabled, you can obtain detailed information from the Wireless Zero Configuration service by viewing which of the following log files? (Choose all that apply.)

    a. ppp.log

    b. Wzcdlg.log

    c. Rastls.log

    d. Wzctrace.log

20. After revoking the certificate of a user, audit information indicated that the user had logged on, using his certificate, and deleted some files. Which of the following is the most likely reason that the user was able to log on and delete files?

    a. The user imported a copy of his private certificate to the computer that he used to log on.

    b. The CRL had not yet been replicated to the server at which the user logged on successfully.

    c. The server at which the user logged on was unable to locate a copy of the most recent CRL and delta CRL.

    d. The purpose of the certificate was not specified.

21. Once tracing is enabled, you can obtain detailed information about the EAP authentication process in which of the following log files? (Choose all that apply.)

    a. ppp.log

    b. Eapol.log

    c. Rastls.log

    d. Wzctrace.log

22. Which of the following tools can be used to troubleshoot IAS? (Choose all that apply.)

    a. Network Monitor

    b. SNMP Service

    c. System Monitor

    d. IAS MMC snap-in

23. Which of the following is a tool included with Windows Server 2003 to gather and view statistical and configuration information for WAPs and the Windows Server 2003 wireless clients?

    a. Wireless Access Policy

    b. Routing and Remote Access MMC Snap-in

    c. IAS MMC Snap-in

    d. Wireless Monitor MMC Snap-in

24. Remote Access diagnostic functions used to collect detailed logs and information about a remote access connection can be set in which of the following ways? (Choose all that appply.)

    a. Diagnostics can be set from the Diagnostics tab of the properties of the connection in the Network Connection folder.

    b. Run specific diagnostics by typing the diag.exe diagnostics command at the command line.

    c. Run specific diagnostics by typing the netsh ras diagnostics command at the command line.

    d. Diagnostics can be set from the Settings tab of the properties of the connection in the Network Connection folder.

25. When troubleshooting CMAK, if the users can connect to the server when using the service profile but authentication fails, which of the following actions should you take? (Choose all that apply.)

    a. Verify connectivity between the server running Routing and Remote Access and the authentication server.

    b. Make sure that each VPN server is configured to accept the profile and that each server is responding with it.

    c. Check the user account and make sure that dial-up access has been enabled, then check for rules that might restrict access by time or date.

    d. Verify that the authentication server specified in the service profile is correct.

12

CASE PROJECTS

Case Project 12-1

Evergrow is currently running Windows XP on all client computers. The client computers have Service Pack 2 installed. The clients are having issues with their wireless connections. Management has asked you to figure out exactly what the problem is and want you to solve the issue as soon as possible. Explain what steps you will take to determine what the issue is and how you would troubleshoot wireless clients.

Case Project 12-2

You are the network administrator at Evergrow. You have a forest and several domains. You have a VPN server running Windows Server 2003 that the users are having problems making connections with. Management has asked you to solve this problem by enabling authentication and accounting logging. Explain why this is or is not a viable solution and prepare a report outlining the steps you would take to implement this solution.

Case Project 12-3

You are the network administrator at Evergrow. You have a forest and several domains. You have a VPN server running Windows Server 2003 that the users are having problems making connections with. Management has asked you to solve this problem by enabling Oakley logging. Explain why or this is or is not a viable solution and prepare a report outlining the steps you would take to implement this solution.

Case Project 12-4

You are the network administrator at Evergrow. Your company has just merged with another company, and you have a forest and several domains. The servers are using Windows Server 2003 and Windows 2000 Server. The users are experiencing some authentication issues in accessing Web pages, applications, and sites. Management has asked you to figure out exactly what the problem is, and they want you to resolve this issue as soon as possible. Explain what steps you will take to determine what the issue is and how you would troubleshoot authentication issues for Web clients.

Case Project 12-5

Evergrow is currently running Windows XP on all client computers. The clients are having issues obtaining certificates. Management has asked you to figure out exactly what the problem is, and they want you to resolve the issue as soon as possible. You have narrowed the problem down to either an autoenrollment issue or a problem with the publication of the CRL. Explain what steps you will take to determine what the issue really is and how you would troubleshoot both autoenrollment and CRL issues.

Case Project 12-6

Evergrow is currently running Windows XP on all client computers. The client computers
have Service Pack 2 installed. The clients are having issues with their wireless connections.
The problem has been traced to a dozen new WAPs that were recently installed. Management
has asked you to figure out exactly what the problem is, and they want you to resolve
the issue as soon as possible. Explain what steps you will take to determine what the issue is
and how you would troubleshoot WAPs.

12

13

ADVANCED PROBLEM RESOLUTION

After reading this chapter, you will be able to:

♦ Plan and configure auditing

♦ Plan and configure logging

♦ Use tools for troubleshooting

In the last chapter, you learned about troubleshooting techniques that used auditing and logging. Auditing and logging are an important part of protecting your network. The general goal of monitoring is to detect malfunctions and suspicious behavior by external users or employees. How much you should audit and log depends on how much information you want or are required to store. You can audit as much or as little as you want, but if you don't read the log files, they are not serving the purpose they were intended for. Auditing and logging use system resources and space. If you aren't careful, you can fill an entire disk in a relatively short period of time.

More complex network environments mean that the potential for connectivity and performance problems in networks may be high, and the source of these problems is often hard to pin down. So, where do you go when you don't know how to solve a problem? In actuality, you don't need to know all the answers; you just need to know where to find them. There are plenty of additional tools and resources that can help in your quest to solve that ever-elusive problem.

This chapter will guide you through properly planning and configuring auditing and logging. In addition, it will provide you with troubleshooting resource information and discuss some of the most common troubleshooting tools available.

PLANNING AND CONFIGURING AUDITING

You can use several tools to track what is happening on the network. These include Windows events, log files, and audit files. **Auditing** is the process of tracking users and their actions on the network. Some of activities that can be audited include reading, modifying, or deleting files, logging on or off the network, using services such as remote access or Terminal Services, and using devices such as printers. Auditing should be built around security goals and policies. Do not monitor everything; instead, monitor what's really essential. It is also important to set the proper size of the security log based on the number of audit events that you generate.

Computer Roles

The roles of the computers will determine how you audit and log. For example, auditing a developer's computer might include auditing process tracking, whereas auditing a desktop computer might include the auditing of access to the server's directory services. To audit objects on a member server or a workstation, turn on the audit object access. To audit objects on a domain controller, turn on the audit directory service access. Chapter 3 described the various settings and their purpose. Table 13-1 lists some of the best practices for auditing events as recommended by Microsoft, the reason why you would audit them, and additional information on auditing the event.

Table 13-1 Best Practices for Auditing

Event to Audit	Reason	Additional Information
Audit success and failure events in the system events category.	Unusual activity may indicate that an intruder is attempting to gain access to the computer or network.	The number of audits that are generated when this setting is enabled is relatively low, and information gained tends to be relatively high.
Audit success events in the policy change event category on domain controllers.	A logged event indicates someone has changed the Local Security Authority (LSA).	Auditing failed events increases resource use, which usually outweighs the benefits.
Audit success events in the account management event category.	Used to verify changes that are made to account properties and group properties.	Auditing failed events increases resource use, which usually outweighs the benefits.
Audit success events in the logon event category.	Records when each user logs on to or off a computer.	The possibility of a denial-of-service attack increases with the auditing of failure events in this category.

Table 13-1 Best Practices for Auditing (continued)

Event to Audit	Reason	Additional Information
Audit success events in the account logon event category on domain controllers.	Used to verify when users log on to or off the domain.	Auditing failed events increases resource use, which usually outweighs the benefits.

Do not audit the use of user rights unless this is strictly necessary for your environment. If you must audit the use of user rights, it is advisable to purchase or write an event-analysis tool that can filter on only the user rights of interest to you. The following user rights are never audited:

- Bypass Traverse Checking
- Generate Security Audits
- Create A Token Object
- Debug Programs
- Replace A Process Level Token

In addition to auditing events on domain controllers and user computers, servers that perform specific roles such as a DHCP, SQL, or Exchange Servers should have certain events audited. For example, you should enable audit logging for DHCP servers on your network and check the log files for an unusually high number of lease requests from clients. DHCP servers running Windows Server 2003 include several logging features and server parameters that provide enhanced auditing capabilities such as specifying the following:

- The directory path in which the DHCP server stores audit log files. By default the DHCP audit logs are located in the %windir%\System32\Dhcp directory.
- A minimum and maximum size for the total amount of disk space that is available for audit log files created by the DHCP service.
- A disk-checking interval that determines how many times the DHCP server writes audit log events to the log file before checking for available disk space on the server.

Microsoft Windows Server 2003 supports only SQL Server 2000 with Service Pack 3 (SP3) or later. SQL Server 2000 provides auditing as a way to trace and record activity that has happened on each instance of SQL Server such as successful and failed logins. SQL Server 2000 also provides an interface called SQL Profiler, for managing audit records. Auditing can be enabled or modified only by members of the sysadmin fixed security role, and every modification of an audit is an auditable event. There are two types of auditing, regular auditing and C2 auditing, which require that you follow very specific security policies.

 CAUTION If all audit counters are turned on for all objects, there could be a significant performance impact on the server.

An audit failure produces an entry in the Microsoft Windows event log and the SQL Server error log. It is strongly recommended that during SQL Server setup you create a new directory to contain your audit files. \mssql\audit is the suggested path. If you are running SQL Server on a named instance, the suggested path is MSSQL$Instance\audit.

When troubleshooting the performance of a server that is running Microsoft Exchange Server 2003, there are tools that come with the Microsoft Windows operating system or are available on the Internet that can be of help, such as the Best Practices Analyzer tool. When configuring Exchange auditing, at a minimum, you should configure the following:

- Shut Down Your System Immediately if Unable to Log Security Audits - Disabled
- Account Logon Event Auditing - Failure
- Logon Event Auditing - Failure

Microsoft's Windows Server 2003 security guide has additional information on the auditing of specific server roles such as IIS, IAS, bastion, and print servers. This guide can be found on the Microsoft Security Guidance Kit CD-ROM that you used in the exercises in the first couple of chapters of this book.

ACTIVITY

Activity 13-1: Configure Audit Policies

Time Required : 10 minutes

Objective: Configure audit policies based on Microsoft-recommended best policies for auditing.

Description: In this exercise, you will learn to configure audit policies based on Microsoft-recommended best policies for auditing.

1. Log on to your Windows Server 2003 computer with your **AdminXX** account, where *XX* is your assigned student number.

2. Click **Start, Administrative Tools, Active Directory Users and Computers**.

3. In the console tree, click **Domain Controllers**.

4. Click **Action**, and then click **Properties**.

5. On the Group Policy tab, click **Open**. Select the **Default Domain Controllers Policy**. Click **Edit**. Expand Computer Configuration, expand the **Windows Settings** folder, expand **Security Settings**, and select **Audit Policy**.

6. Right-click the **Audit system events** category, and then click **Properties**.

7. In the Audit system events Properties dialog box, check the **Failure** box.

8. Click **Apply** and click **OK**. Be sure that the rest of the audit policies are in line with the best practices from Table 13-1. The policies should look like those configured in Figure 13-1. Click **OK** to close the Domain Controllers Properties dialog box.

9. Choose **File, Exit** to close the console.

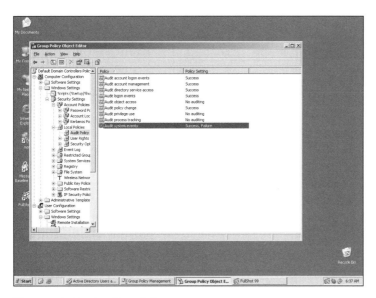

Figure 13-1 Audit policies

You can also audit successful and failed attempts of the types of file and directory access listed in Table 13-2.

Table 13-2 File and Directory Access Types

File Access Type	Directory Access Type
Views of the file data	Views of the filenames in the directory
Views of the file attributes	Views of the directory attributes
Views of the file permissions and owner	Views of the directory's owner and permissions
Changes to the file	Changes to the directory permissions
Changes to the file attributes	Changes to the directory attributes
Changes to the file's permissions	Creation of subdirectories and files
File deletion	Directory deletion
File execution	Accesses of the directory's subdirectories
Changing the file's ownership	Changing directory ownership

To set auditing on a file or folder, use Group Policy to enable auditing, and then use Windows Explorer to specify which files to audit and which type of file access events to audit. When you audit a file or folder, an entry is written to the Event Viewer security log whenever the file or folder is accessed in a certain way. You specify which files and folders to audit, whose actions to audit, and what types of actions are audited.

Windows Events

The event viewer records events in the system event log. **Event Viewer** allows you to view certain events that occur on the system. Event Viewer maintains three log files: one for system processes, one for security information, and one for applications. The security log records security events and is available for view only to administrators. For security events to be monitored, auditing must be enabled. The application and system logs are available to all users to view. The application log can be used to tell how well an application is running. The system log shows events that occur on the individual system. Settings such as the size of the file and the filtering of events can also be configured. You will find two other logs, the directory service log and file replication log, when the server is configured as a domain controller. In addition, there will be a DNS server log if the server is also a DNS server. Event logging is used for troubleshooting or for notifying administrators of unusual circumstances. It is important to be sure that you have the log file size set properly, that the size is monitored, and that the logs are periodically archived and cleared. Consider carefully where you store them to make sure that hackers don't have access to the log file so that they can cover their tracks. Table 13-3 lists the fields and definitions of windows events.

Table 13-3   Event Viewer Fields and Descriptions

Field Name	Field Description
Type	The type of the event, such as Error, Warning, or Information
Date	The date of the local computer on which the event occurred
Time	The time of the local computer at which the event occurred
Source	The application that logged the event, such as MSSQL Server
Category	The type of event that generated the event, such as a Windows event log
Event	The Windows event number
User	The account under which the event occurred
Computer	The computer on which the event occurred

Of these fields, it is important to note the event ID and the description text. The event ID is the easiest way to research the event in the **Microsoft Knowledge Base**, and the description text usually describes what happened in simple language. The Microsoft Knowledge Base is a searchable database to find answers to your issues.

Also, the description field often contains unique information about a specific event, especially security events. Table 13-4 is a sample of Event ID codes and explanations that are found in the security log.

Table 13-4   Event ID Codes and Explanations

Event ID Code	Explanation
512	Windows is starting up.
513	Windows is shutting down.

Table 13-4   Event ID Codes and Explanations (continued)

Event ID Code	Explanation
514	An authentication package was loaded by the Local Security Authority.
515	A trusted logon process has registered with the Local Security Authority.
516	Internal resources allocated for the queuing of security event messages have been exhausted, leading to the loss of some security event messages.
517	The audit log was cleared.
518	A notification package was loaded by the Security Accounts Manager.
519	A process is using an invalid local procedure call (LPC) port in an attempt to impersonate a client and reply or read from or write to a client address space.
520	The system time was changed.

Windows Server 2003 Events and Errors on the TechNet Web site can be used to find any Event ID code. You simply put in the source and ID. The link is *www.microsoft.com/technet/support/eventserrors.mspx*.

 CrashOnAuditFail is a system-wide setting that will cause the system to halt if the security log fills up. In most cases, CrashOnAuditFail is an undesirable setting.

NOTE

13

ACTIVITY

Activity 13-2: Add Another View of an Event Log

Time Required : 20 minutes

Objective: Use the Event Viewer to customize how Event Viewer displays the information of an existing log and then apply a new name to the new log view, while keeping the defaults or the options you set for the original log intact.

Description: In this exercise, you will learn to customize how Event Viewer displays the information of an existing log and then apply a new name to the new log view, while keeping the defaults or the options you set for the original log intact.

1. Log on to your Windows Server 2003 computer with your **AdminXX** account, where *XX* is your assigned student number.

2. Click **Start**, **Administrative Tools**, **Event Viewer**.

3. In the console tree, select the **Security node**.

4. On the Action menu, click **New Log View**. A copy of the log appears in the console tree with a default name of Security (2). Right-click this log and select **Rename**. Type **Custom Security**, and then press **Enter**.

5. Right-click the **Custom Security** log and choose **Properties**.

6. Select the **Filter** tab, and uncheck the **Information** and **Warning** boxes. In the Event source, using the drop-down box, select the **SC Manager** event. Click **OK**.

7. Right-click the **Custom Security log**, and choose **View**, **Add/Remove Columns**.

8. Remove **Category**, **Computer**, **Source**, and **User**. Click **OK**.

9. The view should now look like Figure 13-2.

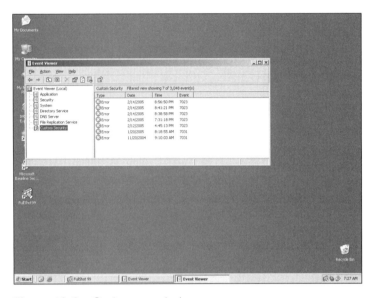

Figure 13-2   Custom event view

10. Choose **Action**, **Export List**. In the Save in box, select **Desktop**. In the File name box, type **custom**. Click **Save**.

11. Choose **File**, **Exit** to close the console.

12. Open the **Custom.txt** file on the desktop to be sure the file content contains the information that was in the original view. When finished, close the file.

PLANNING AND CONFIGURING LOGGING

Before you can configure logging, it is essential to identify what is typical behavior for your network. If you don't know what normal behavior is, you will have a time identifying what is abnormal behavior. For example, UDP ports 137 and 138 and TCP port 139 are used for NetBIOS activity. If you don't know that this is a normal part of the way a Microsoft operating system works, you may think that someone is trying to attack your network.

This measure of normal activity is known as a **baseline**. This gives you a point of reference when something on the network goes awry. Without a baseline, it is harder to see what is wrong because you don't know what is normal. Baselines must be updated on a regular basis and certainly when the network has changed or new technology has been deployed. Baselining should be done for both network and application processes so that you can tell whether you have a hardware or software issue. Once you have a baseline of activity, then you can configure logging.

Internet Information Services

Internet Information Services (IIS) logs information specific to the events and processes of the service. The IIS logs may include information about site visitors and their viewing habits. They can be used to assess content, identify bottlenecks, or to investigate attacks. Plan the selection of the fields that will be logged carefully to limit the size of the logs. To improve server performance, logs should be stored on a nonsystem striped or striped/mirrored disk volume. Besides logging the IIS service, you can enable logging for individual Web and FTP sites. After you enable logging on a Web or FTP site, all traffic to the site, including virtual directories, is written to the corresponding file for each site. Should you choose, you can disable logging for specific virtual directories.

ACTIVITY

Activity 13-3: Enable ODBC Logging on a Web Site

13

Time Required : 10 minutes

Objective: Use the IIS manager to enable ODBC logging on a Web site.

Description: In this exercise, you will use the IIS manager to enable ODBC logging on a Web site.

1. Log on to your Windows Server 2003 computer with your **AdminXX** account, where *XX* is your assigned student number.

2. Click **Start**, **Administrative Tools**, **Internet Information Services (IIS) Manager**.

3. Expand the local computer, expand the Web Sites folder, right-click the default Web site, and click **Properties**.

4. On the Web Site tab, if it is not already done, check the **Enable Logging check box**.

5. In the Active log format list box, select **ODBC Logging**. Click **Properties** and type **IISODBCLOG** in the ODBC Data Source Name (DSN) box. Click **OK**.

6. Click **Apply**, and then click **OK**. Close the Internet Information Services Manager.

Log Manager and Trace Report are reporting tools supplied with Windows Server 2003. Log Manager creates trace data, which is then processed by the Windows Trace Report utility. The Trace Report utility creates a detailed, formatted report that can be used to assess IIS-related activity in the operating system. Log Manager can be used in either Application mode or Dedicated mode.

Activity 13-4: Perform a Capacity-Planning Trace

Time Required : 10 minutes

Objective: Use batch files to perform a capacity-planning trace.

Description: In this exercise, you will use batch files to perform a capacity-planning trace. Note: In making the .guid and .bat files, do not leave any blank lines in the file, and type the list in rows as shown in Figure 13-3. You will also have to be sure that IIS is running on the machine.

1. Log on to your Windows Server 2003 computer with your **AdminXX** account, where *XX* is your assigned student number.

2. Click **Start**, **All Programs**, **Accessories**, **Notepad**.

3. Create a plaintext file containing the following list of Log Manager Query Providers: **1fbecc45-c060-4e7c-8a0e-0dbd6116181b} 0 5 IIS: SSL Filter {3a2a4e84-4c21-4981-ae10-3fda0d9b0f83} 0 5 IIS: WWW Server {06b94d9a-b15e-456e-a4ef-37c984a2cb4b} 0 5 IIS: Active Server Pages (ASP) {dd5ef90a-6398-47a4-ad34-4dcecdef795f} 0 5 Universal Listener Trace {a1c2040e-8840-4c31-ba11-9871031a19ea} 0 5 IIS: WWW ISAPI Extension** as shown in Figure 13-3.

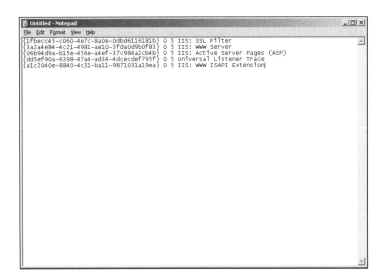

Figure 13-3   Creating a trace

4. Click **Save As**, and navigate to the %SYSTEMROOT%\System32 directory. Type **iistrace.guid** in file name box. Change the file type to **All Files**. Click **Save**.

5. Click **Start**, **All Programs**, **Accessories**, **Notepad**. Create a text file containing the following: **logman start "NT Kernel Logger" -p "Windows Kernel Trace" (process, thread,disk) -ct perf -o krnl.etl -ets logman start "IIS Trace2" -pf iistrace.guid -ct perf -o iis.etl -ets**.

6. Click **Save As**, navigate to the %SYSTEMROOT%\System32 directory. Type **startlogiis.bat** in File name box. Change the file type to **All Files**. Click **Save**.

7. Click **Start**, **All Programs**, **Accessories**, **Notepad**. Create a text file containing the following: **logman stop "IIS Trace2" -ets logman stop "NT Kernel Logger" -ets**.

8. Click **Save As**, and navigate to the %SYSTEMROOT%\System32 directory. Type **stoplogiis.bat** in File name box. Change the file type to **All Files**. Click **Save**.

9. Open a command prompt window and use the CD command to switch to the **%SYSTEMROOT%\System32** directory. At the command prompt, type **startlogiis** and press **Enter**.

10. Wait for a little while for the trace data to be collected. While you are waiting, go to **Start**, **Administrative Tools**, **Internet Information Services (IIS) Manager**, expand your server, and access your Default Web Site to be sure it is running.

11. At the command prompt, type **stoplogiis** and press **Enter**.

12. At the command prompt, type **tracerpt iis.etl krnl.etl -o -report -summary** and press **Enter**. The Trace Report tool analyzes the log files and creates three formatted reports: workload.txt, summary.txt, and dumpfile.csv. All are located in the %SYSTEMROOT%\System32 directory.

13. Examine the workload.txt and summary.txt files by typing **edit workload.txt** and **edit summary.txt** at the command prompt. Press **Ctrl+F** to close the files. When finished, type **Exit** at the command prompt to close the window.

Custom error messages do not return specific error message content, including the **substatus code**, to remote client computers. This is to reduce the attack surface of IIS. If a custom error message contains an explanation of why a particular request failed to execute or too much information about the core Web server, malicious individuals could use the information to attack the Web server. Therefore, substatus error codes can only be logged using W3C Extended logging.

Activity 13-5: Log Substatus Error Codes

Time Required: 10 minutes

Objective: Use the Internet Information Services (IIS) Manager to log substatus error codes.

Description: In this exercise, you will learn how to use the IIS Manager to log substatus error codes.

1. Log on to your Windows Server 2003 computer with your **AdminXX** account, where *XX* is your assigned student number.

2. Click **Start**, **Administrative Tools**, **Internet Information Services (IIS) Manager**.

3. Expand the local computer, expand the **Web Sites** folder, right-click the **Default Web Site**, and click **Properties**.

4. On the Web Site tab, if not already done, check the **Enable logging** check box.

5. In the Active log format list box, select **W3C Extended Log File Format**. Click **Properties**.

6. Click the **Advanced** tab. Under Extended properties, select the **Protocol Substatus** check box if necessary, as shown in Figure 13-4.

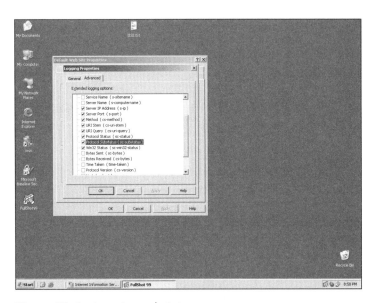

Figure 13-4 Logging substatus errors

7. Click **OK** twice. Click **File, Exit** to close the window.

If you are using the W3C Extended log file format for a Web or FTP site, you can customize the data by selecting the properties you want to log. You can also limit unnecessary data and reduce the size of the log file by omitting unneeded properties. This is done on the Advanced tab that you just selected in the prior exercise.

Remote logging enables you to set up centralized log file storage and backup. Although this is convenient, it is highly recommended that you enable Internet Protocol security (IPSec) between your Web server running IIS and the remote server before configuring remote logging. If IPSec is not enabled, data packets containing log data are potentially at risk of being intercepted by malicious individuals or wire-sniffing devices while the data packet travels across the network.

In addition to using the log files and windows events, the following tools are useful for troubleshooting problems that occur with IIS 6.0:

- *WFetch (WFetch.exe)*—Allows you to generate customized HTTP requests and view request and response data.

- *File Monitor (FileMon.exe)*—Allows you to view and capture real-time file system activity.

- *Registry Monitor (RegMon.exe)*—allows you to view and capture real-time system registry activity.

- *IIS Enterprise Tracing for Windows*—Allows you to enable tracing for various providers. IIS Enterprise Tracing for Windows is new in Windows Server 2003. Logman.exe and Tracerpt.exe are the tools used to enable IIS ETW tracing.

Firewall Log Files

Firewall logs contain entries about the packets that have been handled by the packet filter. All manufacturers have some type of logging capability. The following are some events you want to take a closer look at:

- *Repeated traffic to particular ports*—This can indicate a denial-of-service (DoS) or distributed DoS (DDoS) attack.

- *Blocked attempts*—A large number of blocked attempts can indicate an intrusion attempt.

- *Suspicious signatures*—These can indicate activity by worms or malicious code.

If you are simply using a router and depending on an Microsoft Internet Security and Acceleration (ISA) server for filtering activity, by default, only dropped packets are logged. If you want to log all of the packets that are dropped and enabled by the firewall, the option is available in the IP packet filters. However, if you enable this option, the packet filter logs can become quite large, depending upon the amount of traffic that the server handles. In ISA Server, when you configure firewall logging or Web proxy logging to use the MSDE database format or the SQL database format, fields that you do not configure to appear may appear in the log file. You can define filter criteria to query log files to display specific data that may help troubleshoot common Web connectivity issues. ISA Server contains an HTTP filter, which is an application-layer filter that examines HTTP commands and data. The HTTP filter screens all HTTP traffic that passes through the ISA Server computer and allows only compliant requests to pass through. This significantly improves the security of your Web servers, by helping ensure that they respond only to valid requests. It also enables you to control the specifics of ISA Server client Internet access.

13

Netlogon.dll

If you are using older operating systems such as Windows NT with Windows 98 clients, account lockouts can be very difficult to track. One reason for this is that the bad password attempts are recorded only on the domain controller that processed the logon attempt. A relatively easy way to track bad password attempts in a domain is to install the checked build of Netlogon.dll on the primary domain controller (PDC). This creates a text file on the PDC that can be examined to determine which clients are generating the bad password attempts, for both Windows NT-based and Windows 95-based clients. In the event that you are having issues with accounts being locked out such as in a brute force attack, you should install the Netlogon.dll and then examine the Netlogon.log files. The most common errors are:

- 0xC0000234 User logon with Account Locked
- 0xC000006A User logon with Misspelled or bad Password
- 0xC0000072 User logon to account disabled by Administrator
- 0xC0000193 User logon with Expired Account
- 0xC0000070 User logon from unauthorized workstation
- 0xC000006F User logon Outside authorized hours
- 0xC0000224 User logon with "Change Password at Next Logon" flagged
- 0xC0000071 User logon with Expired Password
- 0xC0000064 User logon with Misspelled or Bad User Account

Remote Access Service Log Files

In the previous chapter, you learned about the various logging capabilities of Routing and Remote Access. Remember that RRAS supports the following types of logging:

- Event logging
- Local authentication and accounting logging
- RADIUS-based authentication and accounting logging
- Netsh command-line utility

Because we went into the logging and troubleshooting of remote access quite extensively in the last chapter, this section will focus on some of the common the issues you may encounter with dial-up connections or VPN connections. Remote access VPN problems typically fall into the following general categories:

- Demand dial
- Router to router
- Client remote access

Some common issues and their solutions are listed in Table 13-5.

Table 13-5 Common VPN Issues and Resolutions

Issue	Solution
Connection attempt is rejected when it should be accepted	Use the ping command to verify that the host name is being resolved to its correct IP address. Verify that the VPN client's credentials are correct and can be validated by the VPN server and that the user account has not been locked out. Verify that RRAS is running on the VPN server and that the VPN server supports the tunneling protocol of the VPN client.
L2TP/IPSec authentication issues	Check the Local Computer certificate stores of both the remote access client and remote access server. Be sure that computer certificates are installed on the VPN client and the VPN server and that the certificates are valid. Check for NAT servers and firewalls.
EAP-TLS authentication issues	Verify that the current date is within the validity dates of the certificate and that the certificate has not been revoked. Check that the certificate has a valid digital signature and the VPN client certificate has the Client Authentication certificate purpose.
Unable to establish tunnel	Confirm that packet filtering on a router interface between the VPN client and the VPN server is not preventing the forwarding of tunneling protocol traffic. Make sure that the Winsock Proxy client is not currently running on the VPN client.
Connection attempt is accepted when it should be rejected	Verify that the remote access permission on the user account is set to either Deny access or Control access through Remote Access Policy and that the policy conditions, remote access permission, and profile settings are correctly set.
Unable to reach locations beyond the VPN server	Check that the protocol is enabled for routing and that dial-up clients are allowed to access the entire network, and verify the IP address pools of the VPN server. Verify that there are no packet filters on the profile properties of the Remote Access Policy corresponding to VPN connections.

13

TOOLS FOR TROUBLESHOOTING

Unfortunately, all problems won't be easy to fix, and for those that are not you will have to do additional research and testing. There are myriad resources you can use while troubleshooting network issues. They may include online services, Web sites, subscription services, books, and magazines. One of the best places for troubleshooting a problem is the manufacturer's Web site. This applies not only to operating systems but also to hardware and other software support. For example, if you are having a problem with a video card not working properly in a specific type of computer, a good place to start is the Web site of the video card manufacturer or the computer manufacturer. Most sites provide troubleshooting information, suggest steps to resolve common problems, offer the latest updated drivers, and list phone numbers for technical support.

You can use Microsoft Management Console (MMC) consoles to group the tools you use most often so that you can view and modify your client, server, and network components and services from a single location. Perhaps you like using the command line better than the GUI. Using command-line tools allows for easier automation of a variety of management tasks. When customizing a task, the number of parameters might be greater with the command-line tool. By using scripts or script-based tools, you can customize a task or set of tasks down to fine detail, and a script can be run from either a GUI-based or command-line tool.

The next sections offer some insight into where you can find additional information that may help resolve your issue. Remember, you don't need to have all the answers; you have to know where to look for them.

Help and Support Center

The Microsoft Knowledge Base, located on Microsoft's Web site, is a search engine that offers support for Microsoft products. To look up an issue you are having, click the Search the Knowledge Base option. But even closer to your fingertips is the Help and Support Center. Figure 13-5 shows the Error and Event Log Message area of the Help and Support Center. This is quite convenient because you don't have to go to Microsoft's site; you can simply click in the troubleshooting area you desire and search for a solution.

Figure 13-5   Help and Support Center error and event log

In addition to the Help and Support Center, you can use the **TechNet** subscription service. TechNet is used for supporting all aspects of networking, with an emphasis on Microsoft products. It is updated via monthly CD-ROMs, and also is available online. TechNet includes a searchable database of Microsoft articles and documentation on nearly all of the products, updated drivers, the most recent service packs, and beta copies of new releases and tutorials. There is a really good chance that someone else has actually already had the same problem that you are having, and TechNet is likely to contain some documentation about how that person solved the problem.

TechNet is also a good resource for information on updates and service packs. Recently, Windows 2003 Server SP1 was released. Included are the following enhancements:

- Windows Firewall, which is the successor to the Internet Connection Firewall.

- Post-Setup Security Updates (PSSU), which uses the Windows Firewall to block all inbound connections to the server after initial installation until the latest security updates are applied.

- Security Configuration Wizard, which configures server security based upon existing server roles.

ACTIVITY

Activity 13-6: Use TechNet to Explore Windows Server 2003 SP1

Time Required: 15 minutes

Objective: Use TechNet to Explore Windows Server 2003 SP1.

Description: In this exercise, you use TechNet to Explore Windows Server 2003 SP1.

1. Log on to your Windows Server 2003 computer with your **AdminXX** account, where *XX* is your assigned student number.

2. Click **Internet Explorer** and go to *www.microsoft.com*.

3. Click on **Site Map** and choose **Knowledge Base**.

4. In the Search For box, type **Windows 2003 Server SP1**. Choose **How to obtain the latest service pack for Windows 2003**. Click the link under **MORE INFORMATION**. Choose the link for 32-bit version under **To obtain from the Microsoft download center**.

5. On the right side of the screen, select the **Windows Server 2003 SP1 Technical Information** link. Under Evaluate and Plan, choose **Technical Overview**.

6. When the page comes up, select **Technical Overview**. Read the section up until the **Summary**.

7. Close your browser when finished.

13

Operating System and Driver Tools

Resource kits are another excellent source of information about your operating system. Resource kits often contain additional documentation on your operating system that may have been too comprehensive to cover in the standard documentation. Often they contain tools that will make your life as a network administrator easier. Microsoft has a Tools and Settings Collection page located at: *www.microsoft.com/resources/documentation/WindowsServ/ 2003/all/techref/en-us/Default.asp?url=/Resources/Documentation/windowsserv/2003/all/ techref/en-us/W2K3TR_tool_ref.asp*, which has the following options available:

- Command-Line References
- Event and Error Messages
- Group Policy Settings Reference
- Registry Reference
- Resource Kit Tools Help
- Resource Kit Tool Updates
- Support Tools Help

Vendor-provided CDs should be one of the first places you go to look for information. The vendor-provided CDs may also contain a technical information base, with a number of known issues and their resolutions or workarounds. Many technicians overlook these CDs and spend countless hours troubleshooting on their own. You should at least look at the readme.txt file even before the product is installed, because usually the CD provides preinstallation tips and warnings that are critical for a smooth installation.

As with many new operating systems, it takes awhile for the manufacturers to get drivers updated to work properly with the operating system. Windows XP Service Pack 2 is no exception. The Driver Protection List for Windows XP SP1 and Windows Server 2003 can be found at: *www.microsoft.com/whdc/driver/security/drv_protect.mspx#ECAA*. The Driver Protection List for Windows XP SP2 is found at: *www.microsoft.com/whdc/driver/security/drv_ protect.mspx#EBAA*. With Windows XP Service Pack 2, Driver Protection messages are displayed using a local help file. The messages are not hosted on the Internet, so the best source of reference is the local help file.

Networking Tools

Internet Control Message Protocol (ICMP) is a protocol meant to be used as an aid for other protocols, as well as system administrators, to test for connectivity and search for configuration errors in a network. **Ping** uses the ICMP echo function and is the lowest-level test of whether a remote host is alive. A small packet containing an ICMP echo message is sent through the network to a particular IP address. The computer that sent the packet then waits for a return packet. If the connections are good and the target computer is up, the echo message return packet will be received. It is one of the most useful network tools available because it tests the most basic function of an IP network. It also shows the time to live (TTL) value and the amount of time it takes for a packet to make the complete trip, also known as round trip time (RTT), in milliseconds (ms). Figure 13-6 shows an example of how ping is used.

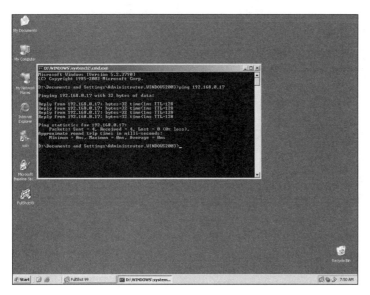

Figure 13-6 The ping utility

Traceroute is used to track the path a packet takes to get to its destination. In other words, it measures how long it takes to travel through each hop to get to its target. Traceroute uses an ICMP echo request packet to find the path. It sends an echo reply with the TTL value set to 1. When the first router sees the packet with TTL 1, it decreases it by one to zero and discards the packet. As a result, it sends an ICMP time exceeded message back to the source address. The source address of the ICMP error message is the first router address. Now the source knows the address of the first router. Generally, three packets are sent at each TTL and the RTT is measured for each one. Most implementations of traceroute keep working until they have gone 30 hops, but this can be extended over up to 254 routers. In Figure 13-7, you can see that the packet traveled 15 hops to get to its final destination. Looking closer, you can follow the path that it traveled through routers before getting to its destination.

Pathping is a route-tracing tool that combines features of the ping and tracert commands along with additional information. The pathping command uses traceroute to identify which routers are on the path. Once the traceroute is complete, pathping then sends pings periodically to all of the routers over a given time period and computes statistics based on the number packets returned from each hop. By default, pathping pings each router 100 times, with a single ping every 0.25 seconds. Consequently, a default query requires 25 seconds per router hop. Notice in Figure 13-8 that pathping shows the degree of packet loss at any given router or link. This is especially helpful in identifying routers that cause delays or other latency problems on a connection between two IP hosts.

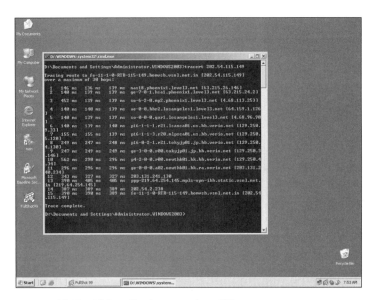

Figure 13-7 Using the traceroute utility

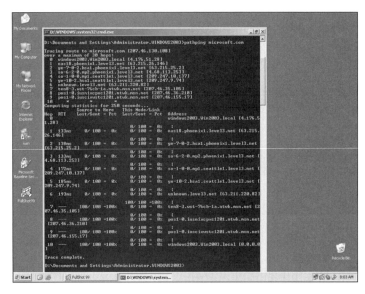

Figure 13-8 Using the pathping utility

Some other useful network tools include:

- Netstat, which displays the status of active network connections, such as active TCP connections, ports on which the computer is listening and Ethernet statistics

- Nbtstat, which displays NetBIOS over TCP/IP statistics, NetBIOS name tables, and the NetBIOS name cache

- RoutePRINT, which displays the IP routing table to show the most efficient route for printing

- Nslookup, which can be used to troubleshoot DNS and name resolution issues

ACTIVITY

Activity 13-7: Use PING, Traceroute, and Pathping

Time Required: 15 minutes

Objective: Use ping, traceroute, and pathping to determine network connectivity.

Description: In this exercise, you use ping, traceroute, and pathping to determine network connectivity.

1. Log on to your Windows Server 2003 computer with your **AdminXX** account, where *XX* is your assigned student number.

2. Click **Start**, click **Run**, type **cmd** in the Open text box, and click **OK**.

3. At the command prompt, type **ipconfig /all** and press **Enter**. Record your IP address, subnet mask, and default gateway or the DNS server address.

4. At the command prompt, type **ping with address of the default gateway** and press **Enter**.

5. At the command prompt, type **ping www.yahoo.com** and press **Enter**.

6. When the ping has finished and the command prompt is back on the screen, type **tracert www.yahoo.com** and press **Enter**.

7. When the traceroute has finished and the command prompt is back on the screen, type **pathping www.yahoo.com** and press **Enter**.

8. After you have examined the results, type **Exit** to close the command prompt.

Remote Management Tools

Local administration is the most secure way to manage the computers in a networked environment. In many organizations, the cost, staffing, and system availability requirements make this nearly impossible, especially in medium to large organizations. With Windows Server 2003, you can choose to remotely perform server and client management tasks that previously could be done only locally. The remote management tools that are provided by Microsoft include:

- Remote Assistance, which enables another individual to assist someone with a computer problem. The assistant can view the screen of the user requesting assistance and offer advice. With the permission of the user, the assistant can even take control of the user's computer and perform tasks remotely.

- Remote Administration, which allows the remote administration of a server running Windows Server 2003. This is done by using Remote Desktop for Administration rather than Terminal Server. Remote Desktop for Administration allows you to administer your server from any computer on your network running the Windows 2000 or higher operating systems.

13

- Web Interface for Remote Administration allows you to manage your application server by using a Web browser on a remote computer.

- Emergency Management Services is a new feature that is included with Windows Server 2003 used to perform remote-management tasks when the server is unavailable through standard remote-administration tools and mechanisms. These types of tool are sometimes referred to as **out-of-band** tools because they use a connection that does not depend on network drivers.

CHAPTER SUMMARY

- Auditing is the process of tracking users and their actions on the network. Auditing should be built around security goals and policies. Do not monitor everything; instead, monitor what's really essential. It is also important to set the proper size of the security log based on the number of audit events that you generate.

- The roles of the computers will determine how you audit and log. To audit objects on a member server or a workstation, turn on the audit object access. To audit objects on a domain controller, turn on the audit directory service access.

- Microsoft's Windows Server 2003 security guide has additional information on the auditing of specific server roles such as IIS, IAS, bastion, and print servers. This guide can be found on the Microsoft Security Guidance Kit CD-ROM that you used in the exercises in the first couple of chapters of this book.

- Event logging is used for troubleshooting or for notifying administrators of unusual circumstances. It is important to be sure that you have the log file size set properly, that the size is monitored, and that the logs are periodically archived and cleared. Consider carefully where you store the logs and make sure that hackers don't have access to the log file so that they can cover their tracks.

- The measure of normal activity is known as a baseline. This gives you a point of reference when something on the network goes awry. Without a baseline, it is harder to see what is wrong because you don't know what is normal. Baselines must be updated on a regular basis and certainly when the network has changed or new technology has been deployed.

- TechNet is used for supporting all aspects of networking, with an emphasis on Microsoft products. It is updated via monthly CD-ROMs. Resource kits are another excellent source of information about your operating system. Resource kits often contain additional documentation on your operating system that may have been too comprehensive to cover in the standard documentation.

- Remote logging enables you to set up centralized log file storage and backup. Although this is convenient, it is highly recommended that you enable IPSec between your Web server running IIS and the remote server before configuring remote logging. Plan the selection of the fields that will be logged carefully to limit the size of the logs.

❑ ICMP is a protocol meant to be used as an aid for other protocols, as well as system administrators, to test for connectivity and search for configuration errors in a network. This protocol is used by utilities such as ping, tracert, and pathping.

❑ Emergency Management Services is a new feature that is included with Windows Server 2003 used to perform remote-management tasks when the server is unavailable through standard remote-administration tools and mechanisms.

KEY TERMS

auditing — The process of tracking users and their actions on the network.

baseline — A measure of normal activity that gives you a point of reference when something on the network goes awry.

Event Viewer — Allows you to view certain events that occur on the system. Event Viewer maintains three log files: one for system processes, one for security information, and one for applications.

Internet Control Message Protocol (ICMP) — A protocol meant to be used as an aid for other protocols, as well as system administrators, to test for connectivity and search for configuration errors in a network.

Microsoft Knowledge Base — A searchable database located on Microsoft's Web site used to find answers to technical problems.

out-of-band tool — A tool that uses a connection that does not depend on network drivers or is unavailable through standard remote-administration tools and mechanisms.

pathping — A route-tracing tool that combines features of the ping and tracert commands, along with additional information.

ping — A network utility that uses the ICMP echo function and is the lowest-level test of whether a remote host is alive.

Resource kits — Additional documentation on your operating system that may have been too comprehensive to cover in the standard documentation.

substatus code — Custom error messages that contain specific error message content.

TechNet — A monthly subscription service used for supporting all aspects of networking, with an emphasis on Microsoft products. It is updated via monthly CD-ROMs.

traceroute — A utility used to track the path a packet takes to get to its destination. In other words, it measures how long it takes to travel through each hop to get to its target.

13

REVIEW QUESTIONS

1. The measure of normal activity that gives you a point of reference when something on the network goes awry is known as which of the following?

   a. Performance Monitor
   b. Baseline
   c. Network Monitor
   d. Event

2. Some of activities that can be audited include which of the following? (Choose all that apply.)

   a. Reading, modifying, or deleting files

   b. Bypass traverse checking

   c. Logging on or off the network

   d. Using devices such as printers

3. When configuring Exchange auditing, at a minimum, you should configure which of the following? (Choose all that apply.)

   a. Shut Down Your System Immediately If Unable To Log Security Audits - Disabled

   b. Account Logon Event Auditing - Failure

   c. Logon Event Auditing - Failure

   d. Account Logon Event Auditing - Success

4. Which of the following event logs is available for view only to administrators?

   a. Application

   b. Security

   c. DNS server

   d. System

5. When monitoring the event logs, which of the following event log fields are the most important to note? (Choose all that apply.)

   a. Event ID

   b. Source

   c. Provider Type

   d. Description text

6. Which of the following is a system-wide setting that will cause the system to halt if the security log fills?

   a. CrashOnAuditFail

   b. Do not allow anonymous enumeration of SAM accounts

   c. Clear virtual memory page file

   d. CrashOnAuditSuccess

7. Which of the following is a route-tracing tool that combines features of the ping and tracert commands along with additional information?

   a. Netstat

   b. Pathping

   c. Nbtstat

   d. Nslookup

8. Which of the following types of logging is supported by RRAS? (Choose all that apply.)
   a. Event logging
   b. Circular logging
   c. RADIUS-based authentication and accounting logging
   d. Local authentication and accounting logging

9. Which of the following categories will you find on Microsoft's Tools and Settings Collection page? (Choose all that apply.)
   a. Service Packs
   b. Resource Kit Tool Updates
   c. Event and Error Messages
   d. Command-Line References

10. Which of the following is used to track the path a packet takes to get to its destination?
    a. Ping
    b. Pathping
    c. Tracert
    d. Nslookup

11. Substatus error codes can only be logged using which of the following log formats?
    a. IIS
    b. W3C Extended logging
    c. ODBC
    d. NCSA

12. Which of the following user rights assignments are never audited? (Choose all that apply.)
    a. Add Workstations to the Domain
    b. Bypass Traverse Checking
    c. Generate Security Audits
    d. Create a Token Object

13. Which of the following are reporting tools supplied with Windows Server 2003 for use with IIS to create trace data, which is then processed by a reporting utility?
    a. Log Manager
    b. Event Viewer
    c. Trace Report
    d. Performance Monitor

13

14. Firewall logs contain entries about the packets that have been handled by the packet filter. All manufacturers have some type of logging capability. Which of the following are some events you want to take a closer look at? (Choose all that apply.)

    a. Repeated traffic to particular ports

    b. Blocked attempts

    c. UDP port 137 traffic

    d. Suspicious signatures

15. Which of the following is a small packet containing an ICMP echo message that is sent through the network to a particular IP address and is the lowest-level test of whether a remote host is alive?

    a. Netstat

    b. Pathping

    c. Nslookup

    d. Ping

16. Which of the following are tools that are useful for troubleshooting problems that occur with IIS 6.0?

    a. WFetch

    b. File Monitor

    c. Registry Monitor

    d. All of the above

17. The Event Viewer security log file shows error 514. Which of the following resources would you use to find out what this error means and how to resolve it?

    a. The ODBC log

    b. Microsoft Security Guidance Kit

    c. Microsoft Knowledge Base

    d. The trace log

18. Why is it is highly recommended that you enable Internet Protocol Security (IPSec) between your Web server running IIS and the remote server before configuring remote logging? (Choose all that apply.)

    a. Because all users have full control over the log files.

    b. Data packets containing log data are potentially at risk of being intercepted by malicious individuals.

    c. There is no danger because remote logs are encrypted by default.

    d. Wire-sniffing devices can intercept the data packet as it travels across the network.

19. Which of the following are areas of remote access where you will have to do troubleshooting? (Choose all that apply.)

a. Demand dial

b. Client to client

c. Router to router

d. Client remote access

20. Which of the following enhancements are contained in Windows Server 2003 SP1? (Choose all that apply.)

a. Security Configuration Wizard

b. Post-Setup Security Updates (PSSU)

c. Addprep

d. Windows Firewall

CASE PROJECTS

Case Project 13-1

Evergrow is currently running Windows XP on all client computers. The client computers have Service Pack 2 installed. The clients are having issues with some drivers not working properly. Management has asked you to figure out exactly what the problem is and want you to resolve the issue as soon as possible. Explain what steps you will take to determine what the issue is and where you would find information on this issue.

Case Project 13-2

You are the network administrator at Evergrow. You have a forest and several domains. You have a VPN server running Windows Server 2003 that the users are having problems making connections with. Management has asked you to solve this problem. Prepare a report outlining the steps you will take to troubleshoot this issue.

Case Project 13-3

You are the network administrator at Evergrow. You have a forest and several domains. You have a VPN server running Windows Server 2003 that the users are having problems making connections with. Management has asked you to solve this problem. You have tried everything you can think of. Make a list, in order, of where you would go to try to resolve this issue as quickly as possible.

Case Project 13-4

You are the network administrator at Evergrow. Your company has just merged with another company and has a forest and several domains. The servers are using Windows Server 2003 and Windows 2000. The users are experiencing some issues accessing Web pages on the extranet. Management has asked you to figure out exactly what the problem is, and they want you to resolve this issue as soon as possible. Explain what steps you will take to determine what the issue is and how you would troubleshoot IIS issues for clients.

Case Project 13-5

Evergrow is currently running Windows XP on all client computers. You have an office that has added eight new workstations. When the workstations were set up, you were part of the process and verified that they all were set up correctly for network and Internet connectivity. Several weeks have passed since the workstations were added, and the owner calls to inform you that the network has become very slow. It is taking a long time to open some applications, and network access to the Internet has become extremely slow. You make an appointment to look at the problem the next day. Besides, the information that the owner gave you, you know that the company uses several Web-based applications. When you get to the work site, what steps should you take to troubleshoot the issue?

Case Project 13-6

Evergrow is currently running Windows Server 2003 on all server computers. Management recently read some information about the Security Configuration Wizard that comes with SP1 and wants to have it installed. Go to Microsoft's Web site and read information on this tool. Then download and install it to a test machine. Afterward, prepare a report on why this tool should or should not be implemented.

A

EXAM OBJECTIVES FOR MCSE CERTIFICATION

EXAM #70-299: IMPLEMENTING AND ADMINISTERING SECURITY IN A MICROSOFT WINDOWS SERVER 2003 NETWORK

Implementing, Managing, and Troubleshooting Security Policies

Objective	Chapter: Section	Activity
Plan security templates based on computer role. Computer roles include SQL Server computer, Microsoft Exchange Server computer, domain controller, Internet Authentication Service (IAS) server, and Internet Information Services (IIS) server.	Chapter 1: Introduction to Windows 2003 Security; Chapter 2: Defining Computer Roles; Chapter 2: Creating Baseline Servers Based on Roles; Chapter 5: Deployment Considerations for Various Machines	Activity 2-2 Activity 2-3 Activity 2-4 Activity 2-5 Activity 2-6
Configure security templates. • Configure registry and file system permissions. • Configure account policies. • Configure .pol files. • Configure audit policies. • Configure user rights assignment. • Configure security options. • Configure system services. • Configure restricted groups. • Configure event logs.	Chapter 3: Working with Security Templates; Chapter 11 : Planning Groups and Group Policy for Wireless Access; Chapter 11: Planning Wireless Access Policies; Chapter 13: Planning and Configuring Auditing	Activity 3-4 Activity 3-5 Activity 3-6 Activity 11-2 Activity 11-3 Activity 13-1 Activity 13-2
Deploy security templates. • Plan the deployment of security templates. • Deploy security templates by using Active Directory–based Group Policy objects (GPOs). • Deploy security templates by using command-line tools and scripting.	Chapter 3: Working with Security Templates; Chapter 3: Deploying Security Templates; Chapter 11: Planning and Configuring Security for Wireless Networks	Activity 3-5 Activity 3-6 Activity 11-2 Activity 11-3
Troubleshoot security template problems. • Troubleshoot security templates in a mixed operating system environment. • Troubleshoot security policy inheritance. • Troubleshoot removal of security template settings.	Chapter 4: Troubleshooting Security Policies	Activity 4-1 Activity 4-2 Activity 4-3 Activity 4-4 Activity 4-5 Activity 4-6 Activity 4-7 Activity 4-8

Objective	Chapter: Section	Activity
Configure additional security based on computer roles. Server computer roles include SQL Server computer, Exchange Server computer, domain controller, Internet Authentication Service (IAS) server, and Internet Information Services (IIS) server. Client computer roles include desktop, portable, and kiosk. • Plan and configure security settings. • Plan network zones for computer roles. • Plan and configure software restriction policies. • Plan security for infrastructure services. Services include DHCP and DNS. • Plan and configure auditing and logging for a computer role. Considerations include Windows Events, Internet Information Services (IIS), firewall log files, Netlog, and RAS log files. • Analyze security configuration. Tools include Microsoft Baseline Security Analyzer (MBSA), the MBSA command-line tool, and Security Configuration and Analysis.	Chapter 2: Defining Computer Roles; Chapter 2: Creating Baseline Servers Based on Roles; Chapter 2: Planning Security Based on Client Roles; Chapter 3: Analyzing Current Security Configuration; Chapter 12: Authentication and Accounting Logging; Chapter 13: Planning and Configuring Logging	Activity 2-1 Activity 2-2 Activity 2-3 Activity 2-4 Activity 2-5 Activity 2-6 Activity 2-7 Activity 2-8 Activity 2-9 Activity 2-10 Activity 2-11 Activity 2-12 Activity 3-1 Activity 3-2 Activity 3-3 Activity 12-6 Activity 12-8 Activity 13-3 Activity 13-4 Activity 13-5

A

Implementing, Managing, and Troubleshooting Patch Management Infrastructure

Objective	Chapter: Section	Activity
Plan the deployment of service packs and hotfixes. • Evaluate the applicability of service packs and hotfixes. • Test the compatibility of service packs and hotfixes for existing applications. • Plan patch deployment environments for both the pilot and production phases. • Plan the batch deployment of multiple hotfixes. • Plan rollback strategy.	Chapter 5: Planning the Deployment of Service Packs and Hotfixes; Chapter 5: Evaluating the Applicability of Service Packs and Hotfixes; Chapter 5: Testing the Compatibility of Service Packs and Hotfixes for Existing Applications; Chapter 5: Implementing Microsoft Software Update Services (SUS) Architecture; Chapter 5: Planning a Rollback Strategy	Activity 5-1 Activity 5-2 Activity 5-3 Activity 5-4 Activity 5-5 Activity 5-6 Activity 13-6
Assess the current status of service packs and hotfixes. Tools include MBSA and the MBSA command-line tool. • Assess current patch levels by using the MBSA GUI tool. • Assess current patch levels by using the MBSA command-line tool with scripted solutions.	Chapter 6: Automated Processes to Verify Software Updates; Chapter 6: Using MBSA to Assess the Current Status of Service Packs and Hotfixes; Chapter 6: Providing a Critical Patching Process	Activity 6-1 Activity 6-2 Activity 6-3 Activity 6-4 Activity 6-5 Activity 6-6 Activity 6-7
Deploy service packs and hotfixes. • Deploy service packs and hotfixes on new servers and client computers. Considerations include slipstreaming, custom scripts, and isolated installation or test networks. • Deploy service packs and hotfixes on existing servers and client computers.	Chapter 5: Planning the Batch Deployment of Multiple Hotfixes; Chapter 5: Deployment Considerations for Various Machines; Chapter 5: Post Deployment Review	Activity 5-1 Activity 5-2 Activity 5-3 Activity 5-4 Activity 5-5 Activity 5-6

Implementing, Managing, and Troubleshooting Security for Network Communications

Objective	Chapter: Section	Activity
Plan IPSec deployment. • Decide which IPSec mode to use. • Plan authentication methods for IPSec. • Test the functionality of existing applications and services.	Chapter 7: IPSec Concepts; Chapter 7: Weighing IPSec Tradeoffs	Activity 7-1

A

Objective	Chapter: Section	Activity
Configure IPSec policies to secure communication between networks and hosts. Hosts include domain controllers, Internet Web servers, databases, e-mail servers, and client computers. • Configure IPSec authentication. • Configure appropriate encryption levels. Considerations include the selection of perfect forward secrecy (PFS) and key lifetimes. • Configure the appropriate IPSec protocol. Protocols include Authentication Header (AH) and Encapsulating Security Payload (ESP). • Configure IPSec inbound and outbound filters and filter actions.	Chapter 7: Planning an IPSec Deployment; Chapter 7: Understanding Default IPSec Policies; Chapter 7: Configuring IPSec Policies between Networks and Hosts	Activity 7-1 Activity 7-2 Activity 7-3 Activity 7-4 Activity 7-5
Deploy and manage IPSec policies. • Deploy IPSec policies by using Local policy objects or Group Policy objects (GPOs). • Deploy IPSec policies by using commands and scripts. Tools include IPSecPol and NetSh. • Deploy IPSec certificates. Considerations include deployment of certificates and renewing certificates on managed and unmanaged client computers.	Chapter 7: Deploying IPSec Policies; Chapter 7: Deploying IPSec Certificates	Activity 7-2 Activity 7-3 Activity 7-4 Activity 7-5 Activity 7-6
Troubleshoot IPSec. • Monitor IPSec policies by using IP Security Monitor. • Configure IPSec logging. Considerations include Oakley logs and IPSec driver logging. • Troubleshoot IPSec across networks. Considerations include network address translation, port filters, protocol filters, firewalls, and routers. • Troubleshoot IPSec certificates. Considerations include enterprise trust policies and certificate revocation list (CRL) checking.	Chapter 8: Troubleshooting IPSec Policies; Chapter 12: Troubleshooting CRLs	Activity 8-1 Activity 8-2 Activity 8-3 Activity 8-4 Activity 8-5 Activity 8-6 Activity 8-7 Activity 12-4 Activity 12-5

Objective	Chapter: Section	Activity
Plan and implement security for wireless networks. • Plan the authentication methods for a wireless network. • Plan the encryption methods for a wireless network. • Plan wireless access policies. • Configure wireless encryption. • Install and configure wireless support for client computers.	Chapter 11: Planning and Configuring Security for Wireless Networks; Chapter 12: Troubleshooting Wireless Access	Activity 11-1 Activity 11-2 Activity 11-3 Activity 11-4 Activity 11-5 Activity 11-6 Activity 12-3 Activity 12-7
Deploy, manage, and configure SSL certificates, including uses for HTTPS, LDAPS, and wireless networks. Considerations include renewing certificates and obtaining self-issued certificates instead of publicly issued certificates. • Obtain self-issued certificates and publicly issued certificates. • Install certificates for SSL. • Renew certificates. • Configure SSL to secure communication channels. Communication channels include client computer to Web server, Web server to SQL Server computer, client computer to Active Directory domain controller, and e-mail server to client computer.	Chapter 10: Deploying and Managing SSL Certificates; Chapter 10: Configuration of the Web Server for SSL Certificates; Chapter 10: Configuration of the Client for SSL Certificates; Chapter 11: Using SSL Certificates with Wireless Networks	Activity 10-1 Activity 10-2 Activity 10-3
Configure security for remote access users. • Configure authentication for secure remote access. Authentication types include PAP, CHAP, MS-CHAP, MS-CHAP v2, EAP-MD5, EAP-TLS, and multifactor authentication that combines smart cards and EAP. • Configure and troubleshoot virtual private network (VPN) protocols. Considerations include Internet service provider (ISP), client operating system, network address translation devices, Routing and Remote Access servers, and firewall servers. • Manage client configuration for remote access security. Tools include remote access policy and the Connection Manager Administration Kit.	Chapter 10: Configuring Security for Remote Access Users; Chapter 10: Providing Remote Access over a VPN; Chapter 10: Managing Client Configuration for Remote Access Security; Chapter 12 : Troubleshooting; Chapter 13: Remote Access Tools for Troubleshooting	Activity 10-4 Activity 10-5 Activity 10-6 Activity 10-7 Activity 12-1 Activity 12-2 Activity 12-3 Activity 12-4 Activity 12-5 Activity 12-6 Activity 12-7 Activity 12-8 Activity 13-7

A

Planning, Configuring, and Troubleshooting Authentication, Authorization, and PKI

Objective	Chapter: Section	Activity
Plan and configure authentication. • Plan, configure, and troubleshoot trust relationships. • Plan and configure authentication protocols. • Plan and configure multifactor authentication. • Plan and configure authentication for Web users. • Plan and configure delegated authentication.	Chapter 4: Troubleshooting Security in a Mixed Operating System Environment; Chapter 4: Troubleshooting Security in a Mixed Domain Level Environment; Chapter 9: Planning Authentication	Activity 4-2 Activity 4-3 Activity 4-4 Activity 9-1 Activity 9-2 Activity 9-3
Plan group structure. • Decide which types of groups to use. • Plan security group scope. • Plan nested group structure.	Chapter 9: Planning PKI Group Structure	Activity 9-1 Activity 9-2 Activity 9-3
Plan and configure authorization. • Configure access control lists (ACLs). • Plan and troubleshoot the assignment of user rights. • Plan requirements for digital signatures.	Chapter 9: Planning Authorization; Chapter 12: Troubleshooting PKI, Remote Access, and Wireless Policies	Activity 9-1 Activity 9-2 Activity 9-3 Activity 12-1 Activity 12-2
Install, manage, and configure Certificate services. • Install and configure root, intermediate, and issuing certification authorities (CAs). Considerations include renewals and roles. • Configure certificate templates. • Configure, manage, and troubleshoot the publication of certificate revocation lists (CRLs). • Configure archival and recovery of keys. • Deploy and revoke certificates to users, computers, and CAs. • Backup and restore the CA.	Chapter 9: Installing Certification Authority Roles; Chapter 9: Selecting a Certificate Enrollment and Renewal Method; Chapter 9: Configuring and Deploying Certificate Authorities; Chapter 9: Backing Up and Restoring the Certificate Authority; Chapter 12: Troubleshooting PKI	Activity 9-4 Activity 9-5 Activity 9-6 Activity 9-7 Activity 12-1 Activity 12-2 Activity 12-3 Activity 12-4 Activity 12-5 Activity 12-6 Activity 12-7 Activity 12-8

Glossary

802.1x — A standard developed by IEEE for wireless local area networks. It employs port-based network access control.

802.1x authentication standard — An authentication standard that relies on the Extensible Authentication Protocol for its authentication needs.

access point (AP) — A device that functions as a transparent bridge between the wireless clients and the existing wired network.

account lockout policy — The account lockout policy can be used to secure the system against attacks by disabling the account after a certain number of attempts, for a certain period of time.

account policies — Account policies are policies defined on computers that affect how user accounts can interact with the computer or domain.

administrative boundaries — Boundaries dividing the administrative control of services and data within the current Active Directory design.

administrative templates — Templates that define how the policy settings appear. You can set restrictions either on a per-computer basis to apply to any user on the computer or on a per-user basis.

approval log — A log file that tracks the content that has been approved or not approved on a SUS server.

assurance level — The security of a certificate. It measures the strength that binds the subject of the certificate to the certificate itself.

audit policy — A policy that determines the security events to be reported to the network administrator.

auditing — The process of tracking users and their actions on the network.

authentication — The process of verifying that an individual or object is who or what it claims to be.

Authentication Header (AH) — AH provides an authenticity guarantee for packets, by attaching a strong crypto checksum to packets.

Authority Information Access (AIA) — An extension that specifies where to find up-to-date certificates for the CA.

authorization — The process of verifying that an authenticated party has the permission to access a particular resource.

autoenrollment — The ability to automatically enroll users and computers for certificates, retrieve existing certificates, and renew expired certificates without user interaction.

back door — A program that allows access to a system without using security checks. Usually programmers put back doors in programs so they can debug and change code during test deployments of software.

base CRLs — A complete list of revoked certificates.

baseline — A measure of normal activity that gives you a point of reference when something on the network goes awry.

bastion host — A publicly accessible computer located on a perimeter network. You may also hear this referred to as the DMZ (demilitarized zone), or screened subnet.

Block Inheritance — The setting that allows an OU administrator to stop the flow of Group Policies from affecting his or her OU, provided that the policy does not have No Override or Enforce assigned by a higher-level administrator.

Block Policy — Block Policy inheritance blocks all Group Policy settings that would filter down to the site, domain, or OU from a parent, no matter from which GPO those settings originate.

brute force — A term used to describe a way of cracking a cryptographic key or password. It involves systematically trying every conceivable combination until a password is found or until all possible combinations have been exhausted.

buffer overflow — An attack in which more data is sent to a computer's memory buffer than it is able to handle, causing it to overflow. Usually, the overflow crashes the system and leaves it in a state in which arbitrary code can be executed or an intruder can function as an administrator.

CERT Coordination Center — A center for Internet security expertise that was established in 1988. CERT maintains a Web site that has the latest news about security vulnerabilities and attacks.

certificate — A method of granting access to users based on their unique identification and the fact that they possess the algorithms to access the appropriate information.

Certificate Revocation List — A component in a Public Key Infrastructure (PKI) that is used to inform the network that a certificate is no longer considered valid. This list can be automatically published whenever changes are made.

Certificate Services — A service that allows the use of IPSec to restrict network access to a server by publishing the computer certificate as an attribute of a domain computer account.

certificate stores — A protected area of the registry where certificates are stored.

certificate templates — Predefined models that ease the management of multiple certificate types especially across multiple CAs.

Certutil — A command-line utility included with Windows Server 2003 Certificate Services that performs a large number of certificate management tasks.

chain building — The building of a trust chain, or certification path, from the end certificate to a root CA that is trusted by the security principal.

Challenge Handshake Authentication Protocol (CHAP) — An authentication protocol that can be used to provide on-demand authentication within an ongoing data transmission. CHAP uses a one-way hashing function that first involves a service requesting a CHAP response from the client.

client certificates — Electronic documents that contain certificate information about clients. These certificates contain not only certificate information but also public encryption keys that form part of the SSL security feature of IIS.

common language runtime — A framework that simplifies the development environment itself so that programmers can write less code and reuse more code.

Connection Manager — A component of Windows 2003 used to provide customized remote access to your network through a dial-up or a virtual private network (VPN) connection.

Connection Manager Administration Kit (CMAK) — A part of Connection Manager managed by a wizard that guides you through the process of building profiles customized for your business. You can use CMAK to fully customize a connection and provide additional functionality for a user.

content distribution point — A place that will host the content that you want your SUS servers to offer.

critical patching process — A strategy that is specific to an organization and ensures that the most critical security patches are installed properly on the appropriate computers in a timely manner.

CRL distribution point (CDP) extension — An extension that specifies where to find up-to-date CRLs that are signed by the CA.

cross-certification model — A model in which all CAs are self-signed and trust relationships between CAs are based on cross-certificates.

Data encryption standard (DES) — The lowest encryption strength of the Diffie-Hellman algorithms. It produces only a 56-bit key and is not for use in a high-security environment.

delegated authentication — Delegation that occurs when a network service accepts a request from a user, then assumes that user's identity in order to initiate a new connection to a second network service.

delta CRL — A list that includes all revoked certificates since the previous full CRL was published. This is similar in theory to differential backups.

demilitarized zone (DMZ) — Also called a perimeter network, the DMZ is the last of your networks that traffic will traverse on the way to the Internet or the first of your networks that traffic will traverse on the way into your internal network. A DMZ can be viewed as a layer of privacy between corporate infrastructure and the Internet, exposing only those systems that have to be known to the public.

denial of service and distributed denial of service attacks (DoS/DDoS) — Attacks that are focused on disrupting the resources or services that a user would expect to have access to. These types of attacks are executed by manipulating protocols and can happen without the need for the manipulated packets to be validated by the network.

Diffie-Hellman (DH) algorithm — An encryption algorithm used for public key encryption.

digital signature — A digital signature acts as an electronic signature that is used to authenticate the identity of the sender, as well as ensure that the original content sent has not been changed.

distribution groups — Groups that are used for membership purposes only. These are actually an extension of Microsoft Exchange distribution lists.

domain — An administrative unit that groups together various capabilities for management convenience.

domain controller — A computer that stores directory data for Active Directory and manages communication between users and domains. This includes functions such as user logon processes, authentication, and directory searches.

domain functional level — A setting that can be configured in Active Directory Users and Computers or Active Directory Domains and Trusts, which determines the functionality of a domain, what types of domain controllers it can have, and the security features that the domain can use.

domain local groups — Combinations of members in Active Directory that are used to manage access to a resource. Can contain users, global groups, universal groups, or other domain local groups.

Domain Name System (DNS) — A hierarchical database that contains mappings of domain names to IP addresses.

Domain Name System (DNS) servers — Network servers that resolve IP addresses to domain names so that names can be used to locate resources instead of having to know the IP addresses.

Dsrevoke — A command-line tool used to view and remove from all permissions specified for a particular user or group.

DSStore — A command-line tool used to manually pulse the autoenrollment event on the domain controller.

Dynamic Host Control Protocol (DHCP) — A service that offers dynamic configuration of IP addresses and related information to clients.

EAP-Microsoft Challenge Handshake Authentication Protocol version 2 (EAP-MSCHAPv2) — A protocol that provides mutual authentication using password-based user and computer authentication. Both server and client must prove knowledge of the user's password for successful authentication.

EAP-Transport Layer Security (EAP-TLS) — A security approach that uses certificate-based mutual authentication, negotiation of the encryption method, and encrypted key determination between the client and the authenticating server.

Effective Permissions — A new advanced option in Windows Server 2003. It lets you see all of the permissions that apply to a security principal for a given object, including the permissions resulting from memberships in security groups.

Encapsulating Security Payload (ESP) — ESP provides a confidentiality guarantee for packets, by encrypting packets with encryption algorithms.

encapsulation — The process of adding a security header to every packet to protect the packet.

Encrypted File System (EFS) — A method whereby users can encrypt files and folders on an NTFS volume disk to keep them safe from access by intruders.

encryption — A method whereby a plaintext message is converted to a ciphertext message so that only the recipient with the proper key can decrypt the message.

Enhanced Key Usage (EKU) — The certificate extension that lists the purpose of the certificate.

enterprise CA — A certificate authority that is integrated with Active Directory.

Enterprise Client — Template settings that are designed to work in an Active Directory domain with member servers and domain controllers running Windows Server 2003 and clients running Windows 2000.

Enterprise trust policies — A tool used for creating trust lists that establish your company's trust of root CAs from other organizations.

event logging — A process that records server errors, warnings, and other detailed information in the event log.

Event Logs — The Event Logs define characteristics that are related to the application, security, and system logs.

Event Viewer — Allows you to view certain events that occur on the system. Event Viewer maintains three log files: one for system processes, one for security information, and one for applications.

Extensible Authentication Protocol (EAP) — An extension of Point-to-Point Protocol (PPP). It is an arbitrary authentication mechanism that authenticates a remote access connection.

Extensible Authentication Protocol-Transport Layer Security (EAP-TLS) — An authentication protocol that is designed for use with a certificate infrastructure and either certificates or smart cards.

fast reconnect — A cached credentials strategy allowing for subsequent logon until the cache expires, which is set to 8 hours by default.

file server — A server that provides the most essential services for the network; therefore, they can be a challenge to secure. They often provide services for applications that require protocols such as NetBIOS, SMB (Server Message Block), and CIFS (Common Internet File System).

File Transfer Protocol (FTP) servers — Servers that are used for posting files. They do not have Web pages, only a place to post and take files.

filter action — A setting for each type of traffic as identified by a filter list.

Firewalls — Protects your network by filtering incoming and outgoing traffic. They examine each packet to determine what type of packet it is and then make a decision whether to forward the packet or discard it. How you configure firewall filters and the filters on the VPN router depends on the position of the VPN router relative to the firewall.

Forest — One or more Active Directory domains that share a schema and global catalog.

global groups — Combinations of users and other global groups in Active Directory that are used to manage security. All members must come from the same domain.

gpresult — A tool that can be used to query computers running Windows 2000, Windows XP Professional, and Windows Server 2003 to determine the effect of the Group Policies on the local computer with the user currently logged on.

Gpupdate — This is a command-line utility that can be used if the policy needs to be refreshed immediately.

Group Policy — A feature of Active Directory that allows administrators granular control of users and computers in sites, domains, and OUs. You can use Group Policy to control the Automatic Updates settings of hundreds or even thousands of computers.

Group Policy Management Console (GPMC) — A new tool for Group Policy management. It aids administrators in managing their enterprise more cost-effectively by providing a single place for managing core aspects of Group Policy.

Group Policy Objects (GPOs) — A collection of Group Policy settings, stored at the domain level, that affects users and computers contained in sites, domains, and organizational units.

group scope — The scope of a group determines the level to which the group is applied within a domain or forest.

group type — The group type determines whether a group can be used to assign permissions from a shared resource for security groups or if a group can be used for e-mail distribution lists only for distribution groups.

hierarchical database — A database that has multiple levels of authority and control such that one object is considered to be within another object.

High Security — Template settings that are designed to work in the same environment as the enterprise client settings; however, the High Security settings are extremely restrictive and many applications may not function.

IIS lockdown tool — The IIS Lockdown tool turns off unnecessary features to better protect the server from attackers.

IIS metabase — A repository for most IIS configuration values.

IKE negotiation — The communication between two computers that includes the exchange of keys and the negotiation in regard to how communication can take place.

inheritance — Allows administrators to easily assign and manage permissions. This feature automatically causes objects within a container to inherit all the inheritable permissions of that container.

intermediate CA — A CA subordinate to a root CA, but that also serves as a higher certifying authority to one or more subordinate CAs.

Internet Authentication Service (IAS) — Microsoft's implementation of a RADIUS server and proxy. IAS performs authentication, authorization, and accounting of various types of network connections.

Internet Connection Firewall (ICF) — Firewall software that is used to set restrictions on what information is communicated between your home or small office network and the Internet.

Internet Control Message Protocol (ICMP) — A protocol meant to be used as an aid for other protocols, as well as system administrators, to test for connectivity and search for configuration errors in a network.

Internet Key Exchange (IKE) — IKE is the protocol used for exchanging encryption keys.

Internet Protocol Security (IPSec) — A set of protocols developed by the Internet Engineering Task Force (IETF) to ensure private, secure communications over Internet Protocol (IP) networks by using cryptographic security services.

Internet Security Association Key Management Protocol (ISAKMP) — A protocol that allows the receiver to obtain a public key and authenticate the sender using digital certificates.

Internet zone — This zone allows access to sites that are not included in other zones By default, it is set to the medium security level.

IP Compression (IPComp) — IPComp is IP compression used to compress raw IP data.

IP Security Monitor — An MMC snap-in used to monitor IPSec policies.

IP Security Policy Management console — An MMC snap-in used to create, modify, and deploy IPSec policies.

IPSec certificate-to-account mapping — An administrative tool for controlling which computers are authorized to use IPSec by configuring Group Policy security settings and assigning them to individual or multiple computers, as needed.

IPSec driver startup mode — The "master switch" for the IPSec driver that is located in the Services console. This can be used to control the startup of IPSec and to troubleshoot IPSec-related problems.

IPSec filter — A specification in the IPSec rule that is used to match IP packets to filter actions such as permit, block, or negotiate security.

IPSec filter list — The part of a rule that contains one or multiple filters and can be shared among different IPSec policies.

IPSec logging — The detailed recording of IPSec-related events for the purpose of troubleshooting IPSec.

IPSec NAT Traversal (NAT-T) — A process that works by providing UDP encapsulation of IPSec packets to enable Internet Key Exchange (IKE) and Encapsulating Security Payload (ESP)–protected traffic to pass through the NAT.

IPSec offload network adapter — An adapter that processes IPSec functions at a high rate of speed so that there is minimal performance degradation.

issuing CA — The CA that issues certificates to users and computers.

Kerberos policy settings — The Kerberos policy settings are used for authentication services. In most environments, the default settings should be sufficient.

Kerberos V5 — The default authentication method for Windows 2000 Server and Windows Server 2003.

key recovery agent — A method used to recover a key should it be lost by accidental deletion, corruption, or other means.

Key Recovery Tool — A GUI tool that enables a key recovery agent (KRA) with appropriate permissions to recover private keys from a Windows Server 2003 CA.

key regeneration — The process of generating new keys at specified intervals.

Key usage — A restriction method that determines what a certificate can be used for. This allows the administrator to issue certificates that can be used for only specific tasks or for a broad range of functions.

kiosk — A publicly accessible computer used for e-mail or other Internet access. Because of the nature of this type of computer, it should be tightly configured and have no direct connections to internal networks.

L2TP/IPSec — L2TP/IPSec uses PPP user authentication methods and IPSec encryption to encrypt IP traffic. It combines certificate-based computer authentication with PPP-based user authentication.

Layer Two Tunneling Protocol (L2TP) — An extension of the PPP protocol created by combining the best qualities of PPTP and Layer 2 Forwarding (L2F). L2TP is a datalink extension of PPP that sets up a single point-to-point connection between two computers.

Legacy Client — Template settings that are designed to work with member servers and domain controllers running Windows Server 2003, and clients running Microsoft Windows 98, Windows NT 4.0, and later.

Lifetime settings — Settings that determine when a new key is generated.

Light EAP (LEAP) — A protocol that combines centralized two-way authentication with dynamically generated Wireless Equivalent Privacy keys, or WEP keys. LEAP was developed by Cisco for use on WLANs that use Cisco 802.11 wireless devices.

Lightweight Directory Access Protocol (LDAP) — The primary access protocol for Active Directory.

local Intranet zone — This zone consists of sites with a firewall or those specified to bypass the proxy server. By default, it is set to the medium security level.

Loopback policy — A special policy used to override user-based Group Policy with computer-based Group Policy Network.

man-in-the-middle attack — An attack that takes place when an attacker intercepts traffic and then tricks the parties at both ends into believing that they are communicating with each other.

master key perfect forward secrecy (PFS) — A key generation setting that sets the session key limit to 1, forcing key regeneration each time.

mbsacli.exe command — MBSA command-line interface can perform two types of scans: MBSA scans and HFNetChk scans. The MBSA scan can be run from the command line to run the same commands as the GUI.

member server — A server that does not contain a configuration file. One or more servers can operate as member servers.

Message Digest-5 Challenge — MD5 can be used to authenticate the credentials of remote access clients by using username and password–based security systems. It can also authenticate the integrity of the message. MD-5 Challenge uses the same challenge handshake protocol as CHAP.

metadata cache — An in-memory database that SUS uses to manage updates.

Microsoft Baseline Security Analyzer (MBSA) — A tool that you cAN use to scan a Windows 2000, Windows XP, or Windows Server 2003 computer for security vulnerablilities.

Microsoft Challenge Handshake Authentication Protocol (MS-CHAP) — A protocol that uses the same type of challenge/response mechanism as CHAP but it uses a nonreversible encrypted password. MPPE uses this encryption key as a basis for encrypting all PPTP data sent over the VPN connection.

Microsoft Challenge Handshake Authentication Protocol version 2 (MS-CHAP v2) — A protocol that uses a challenge/response mechanism but is much more sophisticated than MS-CHAP. With MS-CHAP v2, the server must first prove to the client that it knows the correct password that the client should send.

Microsoft Knowledge Base — A searchable database located on Microsoft's Web site used to find answers to technical problems.

Multifactor authentication—The combining of two or even three of these factors for proof of identification.

Mutual authentication — An authentication method in which the client must prove its identity to the server and the server must also prove its identity to the client.

NAT Traversal (NAT-T) — A new feature of Windows Server 2003 and allows IPSec and NAT to work together.

nested groups — Group nesting occurs when one security group is made a member of another security group.

nesting — The act of placing one group into another group; usually used to simplify permissions.

netsh ipsec command — A command-line scripting tool to configure IPSec configuration. It also provides some advanced fine-tuning for management and security that is not available in the GUI mode.

Network Access Quarantine Control — A new feature of Windows Server 2003 delays normal remote access to a private network until the configuration of the remote access computer has been examined and validated by an administrator-provided script.

Network Address Translation (NAT) — A widely used technology that allows more than one computer to share a single IP address or simply translates addresses from one network to another.

network infrastructure services — These services connect production applications to the actual network and store information about network components such as user access privileges and applications on the network. Services such as DNS, RADIUS, LDAP, DHCP, and PKI are known as network infrastructure services.

Network Monitor — A protocol analyzer included in Windows Server 2003 that allows you to "sniff" the network and view the contents of packets flowing into and out of a computer.

Network News Transfer Protocol (NNTP) servers — Servers that are used for newsgroup postings.

network security zones — A flexible way to enforce your organization's Internet security policies and Web content.

No Override or Enforced — The setting on a Group Policy that specifies that lower-level administrators cannot block the inheritance of the security settings in the policy. This is generally used by a domain administrator to ensure that policies are applied to all OUs in the domain, regardless of settings applied by OU administrators.

NT LAN Manager — This is an authentication protocol used by Windows operating systems.

NTFS permissions — File system permissions that allow you the choice of assigning special permissions to groups or users. Special permissions are permissions on a more detailed level than share permissions.

Oakley logging — Logging that is used exclusively with L2TP/IPSec data transmission. The Oakley log is not enabled by default.

Oakley logs — Detailed tracing logs that can be used to troubleshoot IKE interoperability under controlled circumstances. Interpreting these logs requires an expert knowledge of ISAKMP and standards and policies.

open authentication — An authentication method that allows access to anyone providing the correct service set identifier (SSID) or Wired Equivalent Privacy (WEP) key for the access point.

Organizational unit — Active Directory containers where you can place users, groups, computers, and other organizational units.

out-of-band tool — A tool that uses a connection that does not depend on network drivers or is unavailable through standard remote-administration tools and mechanisms.

Password Authentication Protocol (PAP) — An older, simple remote access authentication protocol. PAP uses a two-way handshake to provide for user authentication in which the server asks for the credentials and the user supplies them.

password policies — Password policies control the complexity and lifetime settings for passwords so that they become more complex and secure.

patch management — A term used to describe the methods for keeping computers current with new software updates that are developed after a software product is installed

pathping — A route-tracing tool that combines features of the ping and tracert commands, along with additional information.

Perms — A command-line tool that displays user access permissions for a file or directory on an NTFS file system volume by querying the permissions

ping — A network utility that uses the ICMP echo function and is the lowest-level test of whether a remote host is alive.

Point-to-Point Protocol (PPP) — The protocol in traditional dial-up connections that is responsible for compressing data before it gets encrypted.

Point-to-Point Tunneling Protocol (PPTP) — A protocol that allows tunneling at Layer 2 of the OSI model and enables a single point-to-point connection.

policy application order — The order in which Group Policies are applied to an object when the object has multiple Group Policies applied to it. The order is typically site, domain, and then OU; however, some exceptions do apply.

PPP logging — Logging used to troubleshoot the functions and PPP control messages during a connection. This log is a valuable source of information when you are trying to understand why a PPP connection failed.

predefined security templates — The predefined security templates are provided as a starting point for creating custom security policies to meet the diverse requirements of organizations.

preshared key — A symmetric key: a shared secret key that is agreed upon by administrators who wish to secure the computer's communications by using IPSec.

print server — A computer that is dedicated to managing the printers on a network. The print server can be any computer on the network.

Protected EAP (PEAP) — A protocol that provides several additional benefits within TLS including an encrypted authentication channel, dynamic keying material from TLS, fast reconnect using cached session keys, and server authentication that protects against the setup of unauthorized access points.

Public Key Infrastructure (PKI) — A technology that includes a series of features relating to authentication and encryption. PKI is based on a system of certificates, which are digitally signed statements that contain a public key and the name of the subject.

QChain.exe — A command-line tool that allows updates to be chained together so that they install without restarting the computer between each installation.

Qfecheck.exe — A tool that you can use to determine which patches are properly installed on a computer. It enumerates all of the installed patches by their associated Microsoft Knowledge Base article.

remote access policy — A collection of conditions and settings that define authorization and access privileges for connection attempts. Remote access policies consist of three components that work together to allow or deny a connection.

Remote Authentication Dial-In User Services (RADIUS) — A dial-up authentication protocol designed to bridge the gap between network access servers and an internal network infrastructure.

Remote Installation Services — A service used to automatically install client operating systems on new machines by connecting to the network via booting, obtaining a DHCP address, and then obtaining the proper image for the machine.

Resource kits — Additional documentation on your operating system that may have been too comprehensive to cover in the standard documentation.

Restricted Groups policy — This security setting allows an administrator to define two properties for security groups: Members and Member Of.

Restricted zone — This zone is allowed to perform only minimal, safe operations because the content is questionable.

Resultant Set of Policy (RSoP) — A tool that queries computers running Windows XP Professional or Windows Server 2003 and provides details about all policy settings that are configured for existing policies based on site, domain, domain controller, and OU.

Rights Management Services (RMS) — A rights management technology that helps to protect data.

root CA — A final authority that certifies other certification authorities to publish and manage certificates within the organization.

rooted trust model — A model in which the root CA has a self-signed certificate, and the CA issues a certificate to all direct subordinate CAs.

rsop.msc — A command used for starting the RSoP console from the Run line.

Secedit.exe — The command-line tool Secedit.exe can be used in a batch file or script to configure security on multiple computers and do so at scheduled times.

Secure Hash Algorithm (SHA) — A very-high-security method that uses a 160-bit encryption key. It is used as part of the Federal Information Processing Standard (FIPS).

Secure Sockets Layer (SSL) — A protocol that can be used with IIS 6.0. SSL is a public key–based security protocol that is used by Internet services and clients for authentication, message integrity, and confidentiality.

security association (SA) — The combination of a negotiated key, a security protocol, and the security parameters index (SPI) used to determine the level of IPSec security.

security boundaries — Boundaries that define the independence or separation of different groups within an organization.

Security Configuration and Analysis (SCA) — An MMC snap-in tool that can be used to configure security settings onto a computer, a group of computers, or an entire domain. This tool can also be used to analyze the settings in a database against the current settings on a computer and indicate the differences.

security groups — Objects that are used to simplify permissions by combining users that share the same role in an organization and therefore need the same access to specified resources. Access to a resource can be granted by group membership rather than by assigning permission directly to a user account. Security group scopes include global, domain local, and universal.

security inheritance — The concept of the hierarchical model of Active Directory and the fact that permissions are often assigned higher in the hierarchy and inherited by the objects that are lower in the hierarchy.

Security Options — Security Options, which are the last of the local policies, enable or disable security settings for the computer. You use these policies to enhance security.

security patch management — A term used to describe patch management with a concentration on reducing security vulnerabilities.

security settings — These settings enable administrators to configure the behavior and appearance of the desktop, including the operating system, components, and applications. They can be used with administrative templates in Group Policy to restrict the settings users can change.

security template — A security template is a text file that represents a security configuration.

Security Templates snap-in — A method by which you can create a security policy for your network or computer by using security templates.

service set identifier (SSID) — The name designated for a specific wireless local area network.

session hijacking — A term given to an attack that takes control of a session between the server and a client.

share permissions — Permissions that are set in much the same way file and folder permissions are set in NTFS.

shared key authentication — An authentication method similar to a challenge-response authentication process.

Simple Mail Transport Protocol (SMTP) servers — Servers that are used to store and forward electronic mail.

slipstreaming — A method used to simultaneously install service packs with an operating system.

smart card — A physical card inserted as a means to initiate a logon. The user is then prompted for the smart card PIN code, which controls access by using the private key stored on the smart card.

social engineering — An attack targeted by exploiting human nature and human behavior.

software exploitation — A method of searching for specific problems, weaknesses, or security holes in software code.

Software restriction policies — A method whereby you can control which programs run on your computer, permitting users to run only specific files on multiple-user computers, and can prevent any files from running on your local computer, your organizational unit, your site, or your domain should you get a virus infection.

Software Update Services (SUS) — A service that allows you to configure a server that contains content from a live site in your own environment to update internal servers and clients.

spoofing — Making data appear to come from somewhere other than where it really originated. This is accomplished by modifying the source address of traffic or source of information.

standalone CA — A certificate authority that is not integrated with Active Directory.

substatus code — Custom error messages that contain specific error message content.

symmetric key — A shared key method whereby the same key that is used to encrypt can also be used to decrypt.

synchronization log — A log maintained on each SUS server to keep track of the content synchronizations it has performed.

System Services policies — The System Services policies allow an administrator to determine how services will start and who has access permissions.

Systems Management Server (SMS) — A Microsoft program that is designed for hardware and software inventory contol, asset management, and software distribution in large enterprise networks. You can use SMS as part of your patch management process.

TechNet — A monthly subscription service used for supporting all aspects of networking, with an emphasis on Microsoft products. It is updated via monthly CD-ROMs.

traceroute — A utility used to track the path a packet takes to get to its destination. In other words, it measures how long it takes to travel through each hop to get to its target.

tracing — Logging information that is complex and very detailed. You can enable tracing on the Logging tab on the properties of a remote access server or by changing settings in the registry.

transitive trust — A trust relationship that passes throughout a group of domains, forming a relationship between one domain and all other domains that trust that domain.

Transport Layer Security (TLS) protocol — A protocol based on Secure Sockets Layer (SSL).

transport mode — A mode used to secure communications between two computers on the same network.

Triple DES — A stronger Diffie-Hellman algorithm that produces a 168-bit key. It is recommended for use in medium- and high-security networks.

Trojan horses — Programs disguised as useful applications. Trojan horses do not replicate themselves like viruses, but they can be just as destructive.

trust — An authentication medium that allow users in one domain to access resources in another domain.

Trusted zone — This zone is intended for sites that can be trusted to never cause harm, such as those of business partners.

Trustworthy Computing — Microsoft's objective of safe computing using the following three dimensions to describe perspectives on trust: goals, means, and execution.

tunnel mode — A mode used to secure communications between two networks.

two-way trust — A trust relationship between two domains in which both domains trust each other.

universal groups — Combinations of users in Active Directory that are used to control permissions of users in multiple domains to objects that are also in multiple domains.

update — A file or a collection of files that can be applied to the Windows Server 2003 family of servers to correct a specific problem.

URLScan — A tool that screens incoming requests to an IIS Web server against a ruleset.

user rights assignment — The use of the user rights assignment is twofold: It can grant specific privileges, and it can grant logon rights to users and groups in your computing environment.

version 1 templates — Read-only certificate templates used for backward compatibility.

version 2 templates — An editable template for configuring certificates.

virtual private network (VPN) — An extension of a private network that allows for traffic to be encapsulated, encrypted, and authenticated across public networks such as the Internet.

virus — A program or piece of code that is loaded onto your computer without your knowledge and is designed to attach itself to other code and replicate.

warchalking — A method used to mark buildings, curbs, and other landmarks indicating the presence of an available access point and its connection.

wardriving — The process of driving around with a laptop system configured to listen for open wireless access points.

Wi-Fi Protected Access (WPA) — Authorizes and identifies users based on a secret key that changes automatically at a regular interval.

Windows Management Instrumentation Command-Line (WMIC) — A scripting tool that can be used to deploy security templates.

Windows Management Instrumentation (WMI) — A management infrastructure in Windows that supports monitoring and controlling system resources through a common set of interfaces and provides a logically organized, consistent model of Windows operation, configuration, and status.

Windows Update — A feature that is included in Windows 2000 SP3, Windows XP, and Windows Server 2003 computer operating systems that facilitates automatic updates from Microsoft's Windows Update Web site.

Wired Equivalent Privacy (WEP) — The most basic form of encryption that can be used on 802.11-based wireless networks to provide privacy of data sent between a wireless client and its access point.

Wireless Monitor MMC snap-in — A snap-in included with Windows Server 2003, to gather and view statistical and configuration information for WAPs and the Windows Server 2003 wireless clients.

Wireless Zero Configuration — Configuration option which enables computers to automatically connect to available wireless networks.

worms — A worm is built to take advantage of a security hole in an existing application or operating system, find other systems running the same software, and automatically replicate itself to the new host.

Index